Scandinavia and Europe 800–1350

Contact, Conflict, and Coexistence

MEDIEVAL TEXTS AND CULTURES OF NORTHERN EUROPE

4

SCANDINAVIA AND EUROPE 800–1350

Contact, Conflict, and Coexistence

Edited by

Jonathan Adams

and

Katherine Holman

BREPOLS

British Library Cataloguing in Publication Data

Scandinavia and Europe 800-1350 : contact, conflict and coexistence.
(Medieval texts and cultures of Northern Europe ; 4)
1. Vikings – History – Congresses
2. Civilization, Viking – Congresses
3. Vikings – Great Britain – History – Congresses
4. Literature, Medieval – History and criticism – Congresses
5. Vikings in literature – Congresses
6. Europe – Civilization – Scandinavian influences – Congresses
7. Scandinavia – Civilization – Foreign influences – Congresses
8. Great Britain – History – Anglo-Saxon period, 449-1066 – Congresses
9. Scandinavia – History – To 1397 – Congresses
10. Scandinavia – Church history – Congresses
I. Adams, Jonathan II.Holman, Katherine
948'.02

ISBN 250351085X

© 2004, Brepols Publishers n.v., Turnhout, Belgium

D/2004/0095/25
ISBN: 2-503-51085-X

Contents

Historical and Archaeological Evidence for Contact with the British Isles

Evidence for the Linguistic Impact of Scandinavian Settlement

Evidence for the Impact of Christianity on Scandinavia

Textual Evidence for Contact, Conflict, and Coexistence

Contributors

Jonathan Adams is Lecturer in Danish, University of Hull, and is currently writing his doctoral thesis at University College London on a fifteenth-century Birgittine manuscript. Publications include 'An Introduction to the Danish Translations of St Birgitta's *Revelations*', in *The Vernacular Translations of St Birgitta of Sweden* (1999), and 'Three Newly "Discovered" Danish Sermons in the Austrian National Library', *International Medieval Sermons Studies* (2002). His translation of the Faroese poet Tóroddur Poulsen's *Villvísi* was published in 2001. Jon has been awarded several scholarships enabling study and research in manuscript libraries in Denmark. His main areas of interest are language contact and mixture in Scandinavia during the Middle Ages and the development of the Scandinavian languages up to *c.* 1550.

Sverre Bagge is Professor of Medieval History at the University of Bergen. His books include *The Political Thought of 'The King's Mirror'* (1987), *Society and Politics in Snorri Sturluson's 'Heimskringla'* (1991), *From Gang Leader to the Lord's Anointed: Kingship in 'Sverris Saga' and 'Hákonar Saga'* (1996), *Da boken kom til Norge: Norsk idéhistorie*, vol. 1 (2001), *Kings, Politics, and the Right Order of the World in German Historiography c. 950–1150* (2002). Current interests include medieval historiography and comparative studies of centre and periphery in medieval Europe.

Michael P. Barnes is Professor of Scandinavian Studies in the Department of Scandinavian Studies, University College London. He has written widely on the Scandinavian languages, from both a historical and a synchronic perspective. His major areas of interest are in runology, Faroese, Norn, and the development of the Scandinavian languages in the period *c.* 200–1300. Recent publications include *The Runic Inscriptions of Maeshowe, Orkney* (1994), *The Norn Language of Orkney and Shetland* (1998), *A New Introduction to Old Norse*, vol. 1, *Grammar* (1999), *Faroese Language Studies* (2001), and, co-authored with Jan Ragnar Hagland and R. I. Page, *The Runic Inscriptions of Viking Age Dublin* (1997). Together with R. I. Page he is currently compiling a scholarly edition of the Scandinavian runic inscriptions of Britain.

Axel Bolvig is Professor in the Department of History, University of Copenhagen. His major publications include *Kirkekunstens storhedstid: Om kirker og kunst i Danmark i romansk tid* (1992), *Bondens billeder: Om kirker og kunst i dansk senmiddelalder* (1994), *Reformationens rindalister: Om kunst og arkitektur i 1500-tallets Danmark* (1996), *Altertavlen i Roskilde domkirke: Et ualmindeligt kunstværk* (1997), *Kalkmalerier i danske kirker på internettet* (1997), *Kalkmalerier i Danmark* (1999), *Kalkmalerier omkring Øresund* (2000), and *Politikens bog om kalkmalerier* (2002). He has written numerous articles on wall paintings, art, and images from the Middle Ages. Axel produced a CD-ROM *Wall Paintings in Danish Medieval Churches* (2000) and is the director of two image databases: www.kalkmalerier.dk (Danish wall paintings) and www.medieval-image.org (joint Nordic database).

Stefan Brink, Associate Professor in Scandinavian Philology at Uppsala University, has the positions of Researcher in Landscape and Settlement History at the Swedish Research Council and Director of the Seminar for the Study of Early Scandinavian Society and Culture at Uppsala University.

David H. Caldwell is Keeper of History and Applied Art in the National Museums of Scotland and Director of the Finlaggan Archaeological Project. He is an archaeologist by training and has directed excavations and fieldwork on medieval and postmedieval sites in Scotland, including the *trace italienne* fort at Eyemouth, the seventeenth- and eighteenth-century pottery kilns at Throsk, and the castle at Auldhill, Portencross. He has published three books on Scottish weapons and warfare and, recently, *Islay, Jura and Colonsay: A Historical Guide* (2001).

Chris Callow is currently Lecturer in Archaeology in the Department of Ancient History and Archaeology at the University of Birmingham. He completed a PhD at the same institution on 'Landscape, Tradition and Power in a Region of Medieval Iceland: Dalir *c.* 900–*c.* 1262' (2001). He is co-editor of a forthcoming volume, *New Perspectives on Medieval Iceland*. His main area of research is the social, economic, and environmental history of pre-industrial Iceland.

Randi Eldevik, a native of Minnesota, received her PhD in Comparative Literature from Harvard University in 1987. In the same year she joined the faculty of Oklahoma State University, where she is now an Associate Professor of English. Her most recently published article in *Spenser Studies*, 12, concerns *The Faerie Queene*. Her English translation of Torfi Tulinius's book *The Matter of the North: The Rise of Literary Fiction in Thirteenth-Century Iceland* has just been published by Odense University Press. Randi Eldevik's newest project is an investigation of the portrayal of Hercules in seventeenth-century Scandinavian literature, drama, and art. As a scholar she is chiefly concerned with the reception of the classical tradition in the Middle Ages and after.

Gillian Fellows-Jensen, PhD, dr. phil. was formerly Reader in Name Studies at the Institute of Name Research, University of Copenhagen. She is a member of the

Arnamagnæan Commission, the governing body of the Icelandic manuscript collection at the same university. Major publications are an edition of *Hemings þáttr Áslákssonar* (1962), *Scandinavian Personal Names in Lincolnshire and Yorkshire* (1968), *Scandinavian Settlement Names in Yorkshire* (1972), *Scandinavian Settlement Names in the East Midlands* (1978), *Scandinavian Settlement Names in the North-West* (1985), and *The Vikings and their Victims: The Verdict of their Names*, (1995).

Peder Gammeltoft is Associate Professor at the Institute of Name Research, University of Copenhagen. His publications include *The Place-Name Element 'bólstaðr' in the North Atlantic Area* (2001). His research interests are place-names of Scandinavian origin in Scotland, onomastic theory, and historical linguistics.

Derek Gore is a part-time Lecturer in the Departments of Archaeology and Lifelong Learning at the University of Exeter. He specializes in early medieval Europe and the Viking Age. Derek contributed to *Sources for York History to AD 1100* (1998) and has published *The Vikings and Devon* (2001) in the series Concise Histories of Devon. He is currently working on aspects of the post-Roman period in the West Country.

Jan Ragnar Hagland, Dr. Philos., has been Professor of Old Norse Philology since 1986 at the Norwegian University of Science and Technology (NTNU), Trondheim. He has also been visiting professor at the University of Chicago, University College London, University of Iceland, and L'École Pratique des Hautes Études, Paris. Jan Ragnar has published widely on Old Norse philology, language history, and runology, including *Riksstyring og språknorm: Spørsmålet om kongskanselliets rolle i norsk språkhistorie på 12- og første halvdel av 1300-talet* (1986), *The Runic Inscriptions of Viking Age Dublin* (together with Michael P. Barnes and R. I. Page, 1997). Jan Ragnar has also translated several Icelandic sagas into modern Norwegian.

Katherine Holman is Lecturer in Scandinavian Studies at the University of Hull. She obtained her PhD, 'Scandinavian Runic Inscriptions in the British Isles: Their Historical Context', from the University of Nottingham in 1996. Katherine's research interests are in the nature and extent of Scandinavian settlement in the various regions of the British Isles, post-Conquest links between Scandinavia and England, and the historical and cultural evidence that medieval epigraphy, particularly runic inscriptions, provides about Viking Age and medieval Britain and Scandinavia. She is currently working on *A Historical Dictionary of the Vikings*.

Andrew Jennings is currently an independent researcher, focusing on the Vikings in the Hebrides and their contact with the native Gaelic population. He is the owner of an antiquarian bookshop in Bridge of Allan, which stocks predominantly Scottish books, particularly history. He attended the 14th Viking Congress in 2001 and will have a paper written together with Arne Kruse published in the proceedings.

Janus Møller Jensen is a PhD student at the University of Southern Denmark working on a thesis entitled 'Crusade during the Renaissance, the Reformation, and the Early Modern State, 1450–1650'. He has written 'Danmark og den hellige krig:

En undersøgelse af korstogsbevægelsens indflydelse på Danmark ca. 1070–1169', *Historisk Tidsskrift*, 100 (2000); and has two forthcoming articles on crusading in *Medieval History Writing and Crusading Ideology* and the journal *Crusades*. His main research interests are Denmark and the Crusades, the origin and early development of the idea of crusade, the historiography of the Crusades, and post-Reformation crusading ideology.

Judith Jesch is Professor of Viking Studies at the University of Nottingham and Joint Honorary Secretary of the Viking Society for Northern Research. Her major publications include, as author, *Women in the Viking Age* (1991) and *Ships and Men in the Late Viking Age* (2001) and, as editor, *Scandinavians from the Vendel Period to the Tenth Century* (2002). She is also author of numerous articles on Old Icelandic prose, skaldic verse, and runic inscriptions. Her current research interests are in skaldic poetry of the eleventh and twelfth centuries, *Orkneyinga saga*, and the vocabulary of the Viking Age and medieval runic inscriptions.

Arne Kruse is Senior Lecturer in Scandinavian Studies, School of Literatures, Languages, and Cultures, University of Edinburgh. He has a Cand. philol. degree from the University of Trondheim (1983). Arne has worked at the University of Lund, University of Wisconsin, Volda College, and, since 1989, at Edinburgh. His book *Mål og med: Målføre og mednamn frå Smøla* was published in 2000. Arne has published articles on Norwegian language and place-names in Norway and America.

Brian J. Levy, MA, PhD (Edinburgh), É.dipl.É.H.É. (Paris) is Reader in French, University of Hull. He has published widely in the fields of medieval French and Anglo-Norman culture and society (comic and moralizing texts, epic and lyric poetry, historiography). Major publications (individual and joint) include *Nine Verse Sermons by Nicholas Bozon* (1981), *The Old French Epic* (1983), *The Anglo-Norman Lyric* (1990), *The Comic Text: Patterns and Images in the Old French Fabliaux* (2000), and *An Old French – English Dictionary* (2000). An edited bilingual volume on the Bayeux Tapestry is in press (Caen/CNRS). Brian is currently completing a bibliography of the works of the thirteenth-century French satirical and religious poet Rutebeuf, on whom he is also preparing a monograph.

Christopher D. Morris is a graduate of Durham University, specializing in Anglo-Saxon and Viking history and archaeology. He began his career as Assistant Lecturer in History and Archaeology at Hockerill College of Education in 1968. He was appointed to a Lectureship in Archaeology at Durham University in 1972 and was promoted to Senior Lecturer in 1981. In 1990 he left Durham for the Appointed Chair of Archaeology at Glasgow University. His archaeological fieldwork has been undertaken in northern England, the Isle of Man, Cornwall, Caithness, Sutherland, Orkney, and Shetland. He founded the Viking and Early Settlement Archaeological Research Project (VESARP) in the 1970s. VESARP publications include three monographs on the surveys and excavations at Birsay Bay in Orkney and Freswick Links in Caithness, as well as two edited volumes on Viking and Late Norse archaeology in northern Scotland and the North Atlantic region. The most recent work of this group has been at Tintagel Castle in Cornwall for English Heritage, in multiperiod coastal surveys and rescue excavations in north Sutherland for Historic Scotland, on the survey of pre-Reformation chapel-sites in Shetland, the re-examination of St Ninian's Isle, and the investigation of Brei Holm, a stack-site off Papa Stour.

Alan V. Murray is Editor of the *International Medieval Bibliography* and teaches history and medieval studies at the University of Leeds. His research interests include the crusader states, Germany, and the Baltic in the later Middle Ages and the medieval chronicle. His recent publications include *The Crusader Kingdom of Jerusalem: A Dynastic History, 1099–1225* (2000) and the edited volume *Crusade and Conversion on the Baltic Frontier, 1150–1500* (2001).

Tore Nyberg studied in Uppsala and later in Lund, where he did his fil. dr. in 1965 by thesis on Birgittine medieval monastic foundations. After research in Munich and other European archives and libraries and publishing an edition of Birgittine documents, he was appointed in 1970 as lecturer in medieval history at Odense University, Denmark, the present-day University of Southern Denmark. Among his publications are studies on St Birgitta and her Order, the Christianization of Scandinavia, military Orders, and, in 2000, *Monasticism in North-Western Europe, 800–1200*. He retired in 2001.

Olwyn Owen is a Principal Inspector of Ancient Monuments with Historic Scotland. Olwyn is also area inspector for Scotland's cities (Aberdeen, Dundee, Edinburgh, and Glasgow), for field monuments in Lothian, and for properties in care in Dundee and Holyrood Park. A graduate of Durham University, Olwyn was awarded scholarships to Sweden and then Norway where she lived and worked for several years and pursued her specialist interest in the Viking Age. She completed her MA thesis on late Viking art in 1979. Olwyn excavated widely over many years and has directed archaeological projects in Orkney, Shetland, Borders, Norway, and elsewhere. She joined the Scottish Central Excavation Unit in 1986 and became an Inspector in 1992. She has published widely on Viking Age archaeology and other topics, including several major excavation reports (for example, Kebister, Shetland; Scar, Orkney; and Eildon Hill North, Borders). She has a broad interest in medieval archaeology, especially the archaeology of towns, and specializes in Viking-period archaeology and artefacts. She is currently working on a Historic Scotland/Tempus book on the archaeology of Scotland's towns.

Anne Pedersen was awarded a PhD in prehistoric and early medieval archaeology from Aarhus University for her thesis 'Viking-Age Burials with Weapons and Horse Gear in the Old Danish Area: Contents and Date, Ideology and Purpose'. She is currently a curator in the Medieval and Renaissance Section of the National Museum of Denmark and is responsible for, among other things, metal-detector finds of medieval and renaissance date. Anne is the author of articles on Viking and early medieval subjects, such as burial customs of the Viking Age, as well as artefact studies including personal ornaments from the time of religious transition, weaponry, and horse trappings. She is the editor and co-author of the CD-ROM *Looking for the Vikings* (1998).

Elisabeth Ridel is a researcher in medieval studies at the Comité National de Recherches Scientifiques in Paris. She is currently writing her PhD on Scandinavian toponymy and loan-words in Normandy. Her other research interests include French maritime vocabulary and the iconography of medieval ships in western Europe. Elisabeth is the author of numerous articles about Viking influence in Normandy and France and is editor of a new collection of articles entitled *L'Héritage maritime des Vikings en Europe de l'Ouest* (2002).

Terje Spurkland is Associate Professor at the Centre for Viking and Medieval Studies, University of Oslo. He was awarded his Doctor Philosophiae in Runology and Old Norse Philology, and his doctoral thesis, *En fonografematisk analyse av runematerialet fra Bryggen i Bergen*, was published in 1991. He is the author of *Innføring i norrønt språk* (1989) and *I begynnelsen var fuþark: Norske runer og runeinnskrifter* (2001), as well as many articles on runes, runic inscriptions, and medieval literacy. He has a special interest in Scandinavian medieval literacy in a European context.

Úlfar Bragason is Director of the Sigurður Nordal Institute. Having studied in Reykjavik and Oslo, Úlfar wrote his PhD thesis on 'The Poetics of *Sturlunga*' (1986) at University of California, Berkeley. He has published widely on Icelandic literature. Recent publications include 'Laxness's Wives Tell their Stories', in *Folia Scandinavica Posnaniensia* (1996), 'In the Scriptorium of Sturlunga's Compiler', in *International Scandinavian and Medieval Studies in Memory of Gerd Wolfgang Weber* (2000), and '*Fóstbræðra saga*: The Flateyarbók Version', in *Studien zur Isländersaga* (2000). Úlfar's research interests are in medieval Icelandic literature and the Icelandic emigration to America.

Introduction

JONATHAN ADAMS AND KATHERINE HOLMAN

W hat impact did the Scandinavians make on European politics, cultures, and societies, both during and after the Viking Age, and vice versa: what impact did Europeans make on Scandinavia during the same period?

The front cover of this volume shows a fifteenth-century wall painting of Edmund, the last English king of East Anglia (r. 855–69), which can be found in the church of St Peter and St Paul, Pickering, North Yorkshire. The painting depicts the martyrdom of Edmund at the hand of some decidedly medieval-looking Vikings, armed with longbows and arrows. According to the *Anglo-Saxon Chronicle*, Edmund was killed in battle by the 'Great Army' in 869 or 870, and the F recension of the *Anglo-Saxon Chronicle* adds that the leaders of the men who killed Edmund were called Ivar (*Ingware*) and Ubba. In the 930s, Edmund's armour-bearer is said to have related the story of his death to the English king, Athelstan; the audience at Athelstan's court included St Dunstan, who in turn told the story to the Frankish scholar and cleric Abbo of Fleury. At the end of the tenth century, Abbo of Fleury wrote his *Passio Sancti Eadmundi*, and it was later translated into English by Ælfric and incorporated into his *Lives of Saints*. Abbo of Fleury claims that Edmund was captured, not killed, in battle near present-day Hoxne in Suffolk, and that he was then martyred for refusing to deny his Christian faith or to rule East Anglia as Ivar's puppet. The wall painting at Pickering thus reflects Abbo's version of events.

The subsequent development of Edmund's cult is remarkable, particularly as it seems to have been promoted by the Danish settlers of East Anglia at a very early date. Already by the end of the ninth century, they were issuing a St Edmund memorial coinage, inscribed with the Latin legend SC EADMUND REX ('St Edmund, King'), and the cult of Edmund was also later promoted by the Danish king of England, Cnut the Great. Edmund's remains were translated to the monastery at *Bedricesweord*, now known as Bury St Edmunds, Suffolk, in the tenth century. The cult of St Edmund became popular in Ireland, on the European continent, and in Scandinavia. For example, Ari Þorgilsson, writing in twelfth-century Iceland, used the martyrdom of Edmund as one of the key dates in his chronological framework for the *Book of the Icelanders* (*Íslendingabók*).

The death and subsequent elevation of Edmund to sainthood seems to unite various aspects of the relationship between Scandinavia and Christian Europe that this volume deals with: the starting point was clearly conflict, but the Scandinavian colonization of parts of England led, very rapidly, to conversion to Christianity and the adoption of English customs, such as the issuing of a coinage with a Latin inscription in roman letters. The cult of Edmund then spread from England to Scandinavia, presumably through the missionary church. The life and cult of Edmund therefore provides a link between the Viking and medieval periods, as well as demonstrating the reciprocal nature of the contact between Scandinavia and Europe during this period.

This collection gives readers a unique perspective on relations between Scandinavia and Europe from the beginning of the ninth century to the middle of the fourteenth century. In particular, it transcends conventional historical boundaries in bringing together work on both the Viking and the medieval periods. English-language histories of medieval Scandinavia generally end around 1050/1100, giving the impression that the vibrant political, cultural, and religious contact between Scandinavia and Europe suddenly stopped. The broader timespan of this work (800–1350) clearly demonstrates that the links between Scandinavia and Europe which were established during the Viking Age continued to be important; it also allows one to follow developments from their beginning in the Viking Age into the later medieval period. Indeed, a wider perspective illustrates the changing nature of contact and the gradual integration of Scandinavia into European society: by 1350 Scandinavia was no longer a heathen outpost on the periphery of the known world; it was an integral part of Western Christendom.

Furthermore, this volume examines the ways in which Europe itself influenced Scandinavia. Traditionally, English-language accounts of medieval Scandinavia focus on the Viking impact on Europe. However, Scandinavians were influenced by European ideas of kingship, law, and social organization, and their literature demonstrates knowledge of classical and continental writing. The cultural impact of Europe on Scandinavia, frequently mediated through religious channels, although less dramatic, arguably had a more significant long-term impact than the Viking raids had on Europe. Certainly, the current volume reflects the fact that a majority of scholars currently working on aspects of the relationship between Scandinavia and Europe are working on forms of contact that go beyond the traditional image of conflict. Two main strands of research emerge from this collection: the integration of Scandinavians in a colonial setting, as settlers in England, Scotland, the Northern and Western Isles, and Normandy; and the reception and adaptation of European customs and ideologies in Scandinavia. Nevertheless, these papers also demonstrate that conflict remained and indeed was revived in new forms, rooted in European models, as crusades against their pagan countrymen and neighbours, as internal civil wars, and as battles for a wider political dominance within the Scandinavian world.

Acknowledgements

This collection of articles started life as a two-day conference on the theme 'Scandinavians and Europe 800–1350: Contact, Conflict, and Coexistence', held on 22–23 May 1999 at the University of Hull. Neither the conference nor this volume would have been possible without the support of large numbers of people and organizations. In particular, we would like to thank the following for financial assistance: Det Danske Undervisningsministerium (especially Dinah Bechshøft); the Faculty of Arts Research Executive, the Centre for Medieval Studies, and the Department of Scandinavian Studies, all at the University of Hull; and Brepols, Turnhout, Belgium. Thanks are also due to the Heritage House Group Ltd for their generous permission to use the photograph of the Edmund wall painting on our front cover, and to Rev. Canon Francis Hewitt of Pickering for his kind assistance in this matter. We would also like to thank the following individuals: Wendy Scase who, as then Director of the Centre for Medieval Studies (Hull), encouraged us to organize the conference in the first instance and provided practical advice and guidance throughout the project; colleagues in the Department of Scandinavian Studies; Alan Deighton, Simon Forde, Judith Jesch, Brian Levy, Bridget Morris, and Veronica O'Mara, who negotiated us through the minefield that is conference organization and the intricacies of the editing process; and all those who participated in the conference and made it such an interesting and enjoyable occasion. Finally, we would like to thank all the contributors to this volume for their hard work and patience with the editors.

A Note on Spelling and Referencing

For the sake of consistency and coherence, we have endeavoured to standardize spellings and referencing across the volume. However, one particular problem with editing a book of this nature is that there are many different spellings of personal names. For example, the King of Denmark between *c*. 987 and 1014 is variously referred to as Sveinn, Svein, Sven, Svend, Swein, Swegn, Swegen, and Sweyn. As well as differences between various parts of the Scandinavian world, the long timespan of the volume means that linguistic changes altered the sound and consequently the spelling of many names between 800 and 1350. The use of standardized Old (West) Norse forms, found in many volumes, would, for example, be inappropriate when referring to people living in fourteenth-century Denmark. If there is a widely recognized anglicized form found in academic publications, we have used it — so we have the form Cnut, rather than Old Norse Knútr, modern Danish Knud, or the old-fashioned English Canute, to refer to the King of England, Denmark, and Norway in the early eleventh century. However, with other medieval Scandinavian people of this name, who are not widely referred to in English-language scholarship, we have used what seems to us to be a sensible, standardized form of the name — Knut. We have been guided by the same principle in our treatment of other personal names. Place-names are given in their native form, except when there is a familiar and current English form — for example, we use Jutland rather than Danish Jylland.

Abbreviations

MGH	Monumenta Germaniae Historica
SS	Scriptores
SS rer. Ger.	Scriptores rerum Germanicarum in usum scholarum separatim editi

Historical and Archaeological Evidence
for Contact with the British Isles

The Scar Boat Burial — and the Missing Decades of the Early Viking Age in Orkney and Shetland[*]

OLWYN OWEN

Introduction

The 'devastation of all the islands of Britain by heathens'[1] during the 790s, so eloquently chronicled by its monastic victims, traditionally marks the start of the Viking Age. Recent debates have challenged the popular caricature of the Viking Age as an era of sudden onslaught by ferocious northern foreigners and have attempted to place the raids more firmly in the context of the time.[2] Whatever their

[*] The rescue of the Scar Viking boat burial would not have been possible without the enthusiastic cooperation of Mrs Caroline Deerness and her family. Scar was excavated under the expert direction of Magnar Dalland, without whose efforts very little of this research would have been possible; and the success of the project relied on the hard work and skills of many people, excavators, colleagues and specialists, to all of whom I extend my thanks. I am grateful to the many scholars, too many to mention, both in Scotland and Scandinavia, who have so generously offered advice and information on comparanda for the Scar artefacts. A full account of the Scar boat burial was published in 1999. The site archive has been deposited in the National Monuments Record of Scotland, Edinburgh, and the artefacts are on display in Tankerness House Museum, Kirkwall. The project was funded by Historic Scotland.

Fig. 1 was drawn by Christina Unwin and the Scar artefacts were photographed by Michael Brooks of Historic Scotland. I am grateful to the following individuals and organizations for permission to reproduce illustrations: David Simon (fig. 8); Mick Aston (fig. 9); and the Trustees of the National Museums of Scotland (fig. 10). All other illustrations are © Crown Copyright: Historic Scotland.

[1] *The Annals of Ulster*, ed. by Seán Mac Airt and Gearóid Mac Niocaill (Dublin: Institute for Advanced Studies, 1983), s.a. 794.

[2] Peter Sawyer is an influential advocate of this new perspective; see, for example, P. H. Sawyer, *The Age of the Vikings*, 2nd edn (London: Edward Arnold, 1971); P. H. Sawyer,

initial impact, scholarly reinterpretation of the evidence, bolstered by modern archaeological enquiry, has demonstrated that piracy soon evolved into subtly complex
and differing forms of interaction and political arrangement between the various
native groupings and Scandinavian incomers across the British Isles.[3] Arguably, at
least in part, the fascination of the Vikings today lies in what the age has to teach us
about what happens when shifting but established groupings are suddenly (at least in
historical terms) faced with an alien force. Over the course of two or three centuries,
the arrival of the Vikings onto the European stage proved to be a catalyst for the
transmogrification of a range of identities, cultures, and political and religious
ideologies, out of which recognizable nation states would begin to emerge.

   In the Northern Isles of Scotland, however, the evidence appears more starkly
black and white (fig. 1). Here, Scandinavians seem to have made such an impact that
the native islanders vanished from the record in a remarkably short space of time. In
Wainwright's evocative phrase, they were 'overwhelmed — politically, linguistically, culturally and socially',[4] so much so that it is hard to resist the contemporary
parallel of ethnic cleansing. The overwhelming dominance of Scandinavian culture
is necessarily a retrospective view, but it is a view that is hard to avoid. The strongly
Scandinavian cultural roots of the islands are plain to see. Today, some 95% of the
place-names of Orkney and Shetland are Norse in origin, a permanent testimonial to
the men and women who travelled the sea road and made the Northern Isles their
home.[5] The great twelfth-century monuments of St Magnus Cathedral and the
Bishops' Palace in Kirkwall, St Magnus's Church on Egilsay, Kolbein Hruga's
Castle on Wyre, and Orphir round church, and the plethora of runic inscriptions in
the Neolithic tomb Maes Howe, amongst many others, all bear witness to the
vibrancy of Scandinavian culture in medieval Orkney and its relevance on the
European stage.[6]

   Examples of the Viking legacy abound in Orkney and Shetland. The islands
remained Scandinavian in language and customs for centuries after the Viking Age;
the Norn language, descended from Old Norse, was still being spoken in the

Kings and Vikings: Scandinavia and Europe AD 700–1100 (London: Methuen, 1982); P. H.
Sawyer, 'The Causes of the Viking Age', in *The Vikings*, ed. by Robert T. Farrell (London:
Phillimore, 1982), pp. 1–7.

   [3] Most recently summarized by Julian D. Richards, 'The Scandinavian Presence', in *The
Archaeology of Britain*, ed. by John Hunter and Ian Ralston (London: Routledge, 1999), pp.
194–209.

   [4] Frederick T. Wainwright, 'The Scandinavian Settlement', in *The Northern Isles*, ed. by
Frederick T. Wainwright (Edinburgh: Nelson, 1962), pp. 117–62 (pp. 125–26).

   [5] Hugh Marwick, *Orkney Farm-Names* (Kirkwall: Mackintosh, 1952).

   [6] Royal Commission on the Ancient and Historical Monuments of Scotland (RCAHMS),
Inventory of the Ancient Monuments of Orkney and Shetland, 3 vols (Edinburgh: HMSO,
1946), II, nos 399, 402, 611, 618–19, 483, 886.

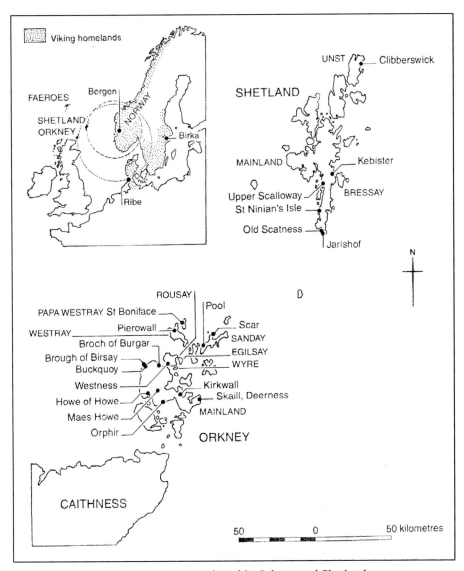

Figure 1. Places mentioned in Orkney and Shetland.

eighteenth century and is evident in Shetland dialect today.[7] Traditional implements found in crofthouses, on farms, and on boats are hard to distinguish from their Norwegian counterparts, as are often their local names.[8] The Norse ancestry of the Ness yole, a traditional Shetland small boat, is apparent in its every line;[9] and the same type of Norse horizontal mill as discovered at Orphir continued in use into the twentieth century.[10] Today's visitor is immediately aware that the cultural heritage of these islands is different from that of the rest of Scotland, and today's Orcadians and Shetlanders celebrate their Scandinavian inheritance in customs, traditions, festivals, and cultural links, and in continuing close relations with Norway and the other Scandinavian countries.

By the twelfth and thirteenth centuries then, it is certainly true that Scandinavians had made an overwhelming and indelible impression on the landscape and culture of the Northern Isles, the effect of which was, as Wainwright implied, obliteration of most traces of their predecessors. Pondering the fate of the Picts in the Northern Isles has been a favourite pastime of Scottish archaeologists for many a long year and shows little sign of abating.[11] The purpose of this brief foray into muddy waters, however, is to turn the question around and place the spotlight on the early Vikings — for it is not only Picts but also Vikings who are surprisingly difficult to find in early-ninth-century Orkney and Shetland.

[7] Michael P. Barnes, *The Norn Language of Orkney and Shetland* (Lerwick: Shetland Times, 1998), pp. 28–30.

[8] Alexander Fenton, *The Northern Isles: Orkney and Shetland* (Edinburgh: John Donald, 1978), e.g. p. 619.

[9] Thomas Henderson, 'Shetland Boats and their Origins', and Ian Morrison, 'Aspects of Viking Small Craft in the Light of Shetland Practice', in *Scandinavian Shetland*, ed. by John Baldwin (Edinburgh: Scottish Society for Northern Studies, 1978), pp. 49–55 and 57–75 respectively.

[10] Colleen E. Batey and Christopher D. Morris, 'Earl's Bu, Orphir, Orkney: Excavation of a Norse Horizontal Mill', in *Norse and Later Settlement and Subsistence in the North Atlantic*, ed. by Christopher D. Morris and D. James Rackham (Glasgow: Department of Archaeology, University of Glasgow, 1992), pp. 33–41.

[11] Examples from the 1970s to 1990s include Isabel Henderson, 'The Problem of the Picts', in *Who Are the Scots?*, ed. by Gordon Menzies (London: British Broadcasting Corporation, 1971), pp. 51–65; *Pictish Studies: Settlement, Burial and Art in Dark Age Northern Britain*, ed. by J. G. P. Friell and W. G. Watson, British Archaeological Reports, 125 (Oxford: B.A.R., 1984); Raymond G. Lamb, 'Papil, Picts and Papar', in *Northern Isles Connections: Essays from Orkney and Shetland Presented to Per Sveaas Andersen*, ed. by Barbara E. Crawford (Kirkwall: The Orkney Press, 1995), pp. 9–27; John R. Hunter, *A Persona for the Northern Picts* (Inverness: Groam House Museum, 1997).

The Pagan Viking Graves

Probably the most tangible reminder of the impact and alienness of the Scandinavian invaders is the pagan Viking graves, which emphatically demonstrate the arrival in the islands of a foreign people with a wholly different culture and set of beliefs. According to several generations of scholars, these ought to represent the first generation of Norse settlers: 'They are primarily the graves of the first generation, the heathen emigrants from Norway, people who stuck to the burial customs of their ancestors [. . .] it is more than likely that the persons buried in the heathen graves were actually born and bred in Norway and came over as adults';[12] 'burials accompanied by weaponry and jewellery in Scandinavian forms probably represent a first generation of pagan settlers'.[13] Close examination of the graves and their contexts, however, does not seem to support this neat chronology.

It was in 1991 that a now-famous Viking boat burial was discovered eroding from the low cliff at Scar, Sanday, in Orkney,[14] and rescued from the teeth of the winter storms in a great drama that even hit the pages of *The Sun*. This exceptional pagan burial contained the bodies of not one, but three people (fig. 2), and at first we assumed — almost certainly completely wrongly — that it was a family group, perhaps a husband, wife, and child, probably newly arrived in Orkney from Norway. When the human remains were examined, however, it became clear that although the man was in his late twenties or thirties when he died, and the child was about ten, the woman was surprisingly old by the standards of the time, perhaps in her seventies — hardly a marriage made in Valhalla.

There are many fascinating aspects to this wealthy grave: it is at once both a classic of its type and yet distinctly odd. The fact that it contains three bodies is in itself highly unusual. The vast majority of Viking graves contain only one body, some contain two, and very few three or more.[15] The burial chamber was constructed by the simple expedient of inserting a single makeshift wall across the width of the

---

[12] Kristján Eldjárn, 'Graves and Grave Goods: Survey and Evaluation', in *The Northern and Western Isles in the Viking World: Survival, Continuity and Change*, ed. by Alexander Fenton and Hermann Pálsson (Edinburgh: John Donald, 1984), pp. 2–11 (p. 7).

[13] Richards, 'The Scandinavian Presence', p. 195.

[14] A full account of the Scar boat burial, including specialist reports on all the excavated materials, can be found in Olwyn Owen and Magnar Dalland, *Scar: A Viking Boat Burial on Sanday, Orkney* (Edinburgh: Tuckwell Press, 1999).

[15] The recently published report on excavations in the gravefields at Kaupang, Norway, suggests that here, too, there were instances of several burials being found within one boat. It should be noted, however, that these excavations were carried out nearly fifty years ago and some of the details are imprecise. See Charlotte Blindheim and Birgit Heyerdahl-Larsen, *Kaupang-funnene*, vol. II, *Gravplassene i Bikjholbergene/Lamøya Undersøkelsene 1950–1957* (Oslo: Institutt for Arkeologi, Kunsthistorie og Numismatikk Oldsaksamlingen, 1995), p. 138 (English summary).

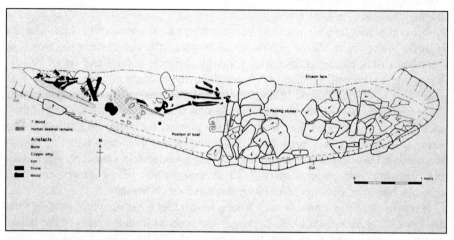

Figure 2a. A plan of the Scar boat burial and its precious cargo.
Almost half the boat had already been lost to the sea,
and the skeletons were all damaged and incomplete.

Figure 2b. The Scar boat, emptied of its cargo.
The wood had rotted away in the ground leaving a ghost impression in the sand.
The markers show the location of the boat rivets.

boat. Normally, a Viking burial chamber would be a discrete entity, perhaps formed by two walls across the boat, as in one of the boat graves in the cemetery at Westness, Rousay.[16] In the great Oseberg ship burial in Norway, the burial chamber was a separate wooden structure erected behind the mast.[17] The presence of even this makeshift chamber at Scar demonstrates that the boat was not just a convenient container, but an important symbolic component of the burial.

Once this wall was in place, only some two-thirds of the boat's total length was available to hold the three bodies, which was barely sufficient. This could imply that the family or community responsible for the burial had not intended to bury three people when the grave was first planned. The elderly woman and child seem to have occupied pride of place, as they were laid out next to each other, both fully extended on their backs, in the centre of the boat. It may be that the grave was originally meant only to take the woman and child and that, had the man not been buried with them, a corresponding chamber wall might have been inserted at their head end to match that at their feet. On a somewhat macabre note, the man's lower leg had been twisted round into an unnatural position and his foot was actually broken off, with all the bones still articulated. This may have occurred when he was forced into the space left in the stern of the boat, which suggests that rigor mortis had set in by the time he was buried. It follows that he may have lain unburied for some time after his death, but this begs the question of why he was evidently buried last. Did the whole grave lay open for some time after the woman and child were placed in it, perhaps as part of an extended ceremony; or was there perhaps a lengthy dispute about whether to bury the man with the woman and child, which delayed completion of the burial?

There is no evidence at all that the grave was reopened once it had been sealed, or that the three bodies were interred at different times, which would in any case be highly unusual for a Viking grave. These three people, therefore, almost certainly died at around the same time. It is rare to be able to discover the cause of death from analysis of archaeological skeletons, and Scar is no exception. All that is left is surmise and speculation. Did they die together, through some dreadful accident such as drowning; or within a few days of each other from an infectious disease; or, more unpalatably, might the man and child have been sacrificed to accompany the woman to the afterworld when she died of natural causes in old age? There are some precedents for human sacrifice in Viking times,[18] but, on the whole, this seems

---

[16] Sigrid H. H. Kaland, 'The Settlement of Westness, Rousay', in *The Viking Age in Caithness, Orkney and the North Atlantic*, ed. by Colleen E. Batey, Judith Jesch, and Christopher D. Morris (Edinburgh: Edinburgh University Press, 1993), pp. 308–17 (pp. 314–16, fig. 17.7).

[17] Arne Emil Christensen, Anne Stine Ingstad, and Bjørn Myhre, *Osebergdronningens grav: Vår arkeologiske nasjonalskatt i nytt lys* (Oslo: Schibstedt, 1992), p. 81.

[18] At Ballateare on the Isle of Man, for example, when a young man was buried with all the symbols of his power and wealth, the body of a slave-girl with her arms raised upwards was placed over the top of the grave. Her skull has a large hole in it, made by the slashing blow of

unlikely at Scar. The man was clearly no thrall; on the contrary, the man and woman would seem to have had equal status to judge from the rich panoply of grave goods. A boat burial would have been especially appropriate for the man: analysis of the skeleton showed that he was about 1.76 m (5' 10") tall with a well-developed physique, honed quite probably by years of rowing. It is not known whether the child's burial was accompanied by grave goods because the sea had washed away most of that part of the boat in which the body was lying. Not only is there a question mark over the child's status, it is also unknown whether this was a boy or girl because of the incompleteness of the skeleton. Indeed, almost half of the boat had already been lost to the sea before excavation, together, almost certainly, with some of the grave goods. Any objects placed along the man's left side, for instance, on or near the upper part of his body and head, or in the east end of the boat had probably been washed away already.

Turning to the surviving artefacts (fig. 3), at first sight Scar seems to have all the typical components of a wealthy Viking grave: a mixture of everyday implements, weapons for the man, and personal items for both the man and woman; and yet a second look also gives pause for thought. Despite the incompleteness of the assemblage, the man was still richly equipped with a magnificent sword in its scabbard, a quiver of eight arrows, a fine bone comb, a set of twenty-two whalebone gaming pieces, originally in some kind of container, possibly two lead bullion weights, and, tentatively, a shield. This was no slave and, on the surviving evidence anyway, no simple farmer either, for he had none of the common domestic and agricultural tools.

The man's sword was broken before burial. The ritual 'killing' of weapons is well attested in the archaeological record, with many examples elsewhere for the symbolic breaking of weapons before their burial in Viking graves. At Hesket-in-the-Forest, Cumbria, for instance, the weapons had all been deliberately damaged: the sword and spears were bent and the shield was broken in two.[19] At Scar, however, the broken sword blade had been placed, very carefully, in a flimsy scabbard made of two laths of wood, bound together by textile and lined with a layer of fleece. This would not have been a usable scabbard and can only have been for storage and holding the broken sword together, which seems to imply that the break in the sword was not publicly displayed; on the contrary, it may have been deliberately hidden. The sword could have become broken accidentally, perhaps even in combat, but it certainly seems to have been old and well worn at the time of burial; it may even have been a family heirloom.

---

a heavy implement. See Gerhard Bersu and David M. Wilson, *Three Viking Graves in the Isle of Man*, Society for Medieval Archaeology, Monograph Series, 1 (London: Society for Medieval Archaeology, 1966), pp. 45-62.

[19] B. J. N. Edwards, 'The Vikings in North-West England: The Archaeological Evidence', in *Viking Treasure from the North West: The Cuerdale Hoard in its Context*, ed. by James Graham-Campbell, National Museums and Galleries on Merseyside, Occasional Papers, 5 (Liverpool: National Museums and Galleries on Merseyside, 1992), pp. 43–62 (pp. 45–46, fig. 5.2).

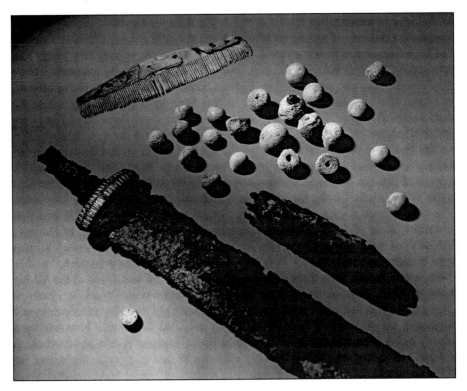

Figure 3. A selection of the artefacts accompanying the male burial at Scar.

The woman's grave assemblage had survived more completely than the other two, although this burial, too, had been disturbed, this time by otters intruding into the sealed grave. The woman was accompanied by a magnificent carved whalebone plaque, a gilded bronze equal-armed brooch, a comb, a pair of shears, a needle tidy containing two iron needles, an iron weaving batten, a small sickle, a small maple-wood box with iron fittings, and two spindle whorls, one of steatite and the other of sandstone.

One of the surprising things about the woman was her age at death. In her seventies, she must have been revered by her community, in an age when living to fifty was quite a feat. This probably accounts, at least in part, for the respect accorded to her in death, although how she herself viewed or used her biological rarity in her later years we shall never know. It seems a little unlikely that this elderly woman had newly arrived in Orkney to start a new life, and yet there is little sign among her plentiful grave goods of any assimilation of native culture. Of what survived, with the sole exception of a spindle whorl made probably of Orkney sandstone, every item in the Scar grave was almost certainly made in Scandinavia. Even the boat was an import; sand grains trapped in the caulking between the planks contained an

exotic suite of minerals not known in the British Isles, and almost certainly Scandinavian. We can only speculate on what she was doing in Orkney and how long she
had been there: a few weeks, a year, a decade, twenty, thirty, or even fifty years? The
relationship between the woman, man, and child remains equally enigmatic. Were
they mother, son, and grandchild; or mistress, warrior kinsman, and young servant,
or some other unfathomable combination? The Scar grave is a salutary lesson for
archaeological science, for there are no answers to these questions. All we have are
the twin temptations of hypothesis and speculation, which are strong indeed.

The two most diagnostic artefacts — the whalebone plaque and the equal-armed
brooch — seemed both, at first glance, to be north Norwegian objects, which
suggested that the origins of the people probably lay in northern Norway, perhaps
north of the Arctic Circle; but even this initial conjecture proved to be premature.
The Scar brooch is of a type known as 'Troms type', because when it was first
identified, most of the then-known examples came from the far north of Norway,
half of them from Troms district (fig. 4).[20] However, five other fragmentary Troms-
type brooches are now known from sites in central and southern Sweden,[21] and in
1993, a clay mould for a Troms-type equal-armed brooch was found at the Viking
town of Birka, Sweden, in the later levels of a bronze-casting workshop perhaps
dating to the first half of the ninth century.[22] At least eight Troms-type brooch mould
fragments are now known from Birka. These so-called Troms-type brooches were
clearly being manufactured in workshops at Birka, together with oval brooches, in
the early ninth century. This is the only evidence to date of a production centre for
these brooches.

The richly ornate Scar brooch is one of the finest pieces of Scandinavian metalwork to have been found in a Scottish grave (fig. 5a). It is a highly unusual type of
Viking brooch to find in Britain, and fairly rare in Scandinavia. One of the many
puzzling things about the Scar female burial is the apparent absence of oval
brooches, those ubiquitous dress fasteners across the Viking world. The Scar equal-
armed brooch should have been the 'third' brooch, worn singly to fasten a shawl or
cloak over the woman's dress. The brooch was worn by the woman when she was
buried, but may no longer have been capable of being properly secured, and some of
the gilding had also worn off in antiquity. In short, it was probably old and no longer
very useful when buried. It is tempting to deduce that the brooch might have been in

---

[20] Jan Petersen, *Vikingetidens smykker i Norge* (Stavanger: Stavanger Museum, 1928), pp.
81–82.

[21] Three from Småland (Norrgården, Hamneda; Trotteslöv, Berga; and one from another
grave in Småland (Björn Ambrosiani, personal communication)), two from Uppland (Fornsig-
tuna, Håtuna; and Nyby, Old Uppsala). See Owen and Dalland, *Scar: A Viking Boat Burial*,
p. 69, fig. 48b.

[22] Björn Ambrosiani, personal communication.

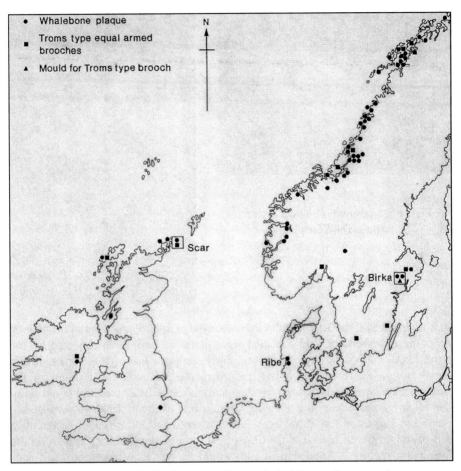

Figure 4. Distribution map of carved whalebone plaques and
Troms-type brooches in Scandinavia and the British Isles.

the Scar woman's possession through much of her long life; indeed, its very opulence and rarity may indicate that it was already an heirloom when she acquired it.

On close examination, there is an unnerving impression that many of the items in the Scar grave may have been of limited use by the time they were buried. The sword was broken; the lead weights may have had no place in the economy of Viking Age Orkney; the sickle was small; the weaving batten was short and broken; the gaming pieces were probably an incomplete set; even the whalebone plaque had been rarely used and may have been out of fashion.

There are caveats to all these observations and it might be misleading to take this argument much further; but the impression is that the assemblage overall reflects the *floruit* of paganism in Viking Orkney, whilst not being actually contemporary with

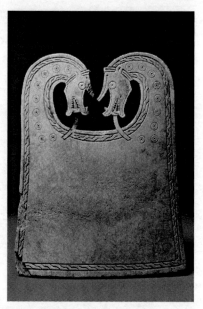

Figure 5. a (above): The Scar brooch;
b (right): The Scar plaque.

it. It is almost as if the Scar burial reflects the type of accompanied burial the woman might have wished for, had she died when it might have been expected by the standards of the Viking Age — twenty, thirty, forty, or more years earlier. If this burial can be interpreted as a late gesture to the old gods and customs of the Scandinavian homeland, perhaps because the woman still adhered to the old faith, this might go some way to explaining why aspects of the assemblage seem 'odd'. Lamb has suggested that extravagant Norse funerals in Orkney might represent 'a self-conscious pagan revival at the time of the establishment of the earldom' in the later ninth century.[23] Another possibility could be that they represent a self-conscious flourishing of pagan belief and ritual in the face of encroaching acceptance of Christianity in the tenth century — and what better way to symbolize the vitality of pagan beliefs than by an elaborate boat burial?

The beautiful carved whalebone plaque (fig. 5b) was originally placed in the grave in a prominent position, propped up against the upright slab marking the east end of the chamber, with its decorated side facing the elderly woman. It was evidently a highly valued and probably symbolic artefact. About sixty-five carved whalebone plaques are known from the Viking world, the vast majority from coastal areas in the northern half of Norway, especially Nord-Trøndelag, Nordland, and Troms (fig. 4). Perhaps the finest known example, prior to that discovered at Scar,

---

[23] Raymond G. Lamb, 'Carolingian Orkney and its transformation', in *The Viking Age in Caithness, Orkney and the North Atlantic*, ed. by Batey, Jesch, and Morris, pp. 260–71 (p. 269).

comes from Grytøy, Troms,[24] but very few of these similarly ornamented plaques were executed to such a high standard. This suggests that plaques were being carved and copied by more than one craftsman, probably in several, perhaps many, locations along the long north Norwegian coastline. A small and elegant plaque, found in 1970 at Kvæfjord, Troms, is perhaps the closest parallel for that from Scar, but is also a less accomplished piece.[25] The two plaques may derive from a common prototype, but are most unlikely to be by the same hand. Nonetheless, the Scar plaque probably came from the far north of Norway, in the Troms area.

At the prosaic level, the plaque functioned as a smoothing board for small linen garments. As late as the nineteenth century, women in Scandinavia and Scotland were using similar objects for ironing linen caps, with stone or glass smoothers.[26] Glass linen smoothers also occur frequently in wealthy female Viking graves, but only one glass linen smoother has actually been found in the same grave as a carved plaque, in Grave 854, Birka, and even here the two items were not placed together.[27] If the plaques functioned primarily as smoothing boards, then the apparent separation in death of the board from the smoother, two apparently complementary pieces of equipment, is difficult to explain.

Recent research on the Viking fertility goddess, Freya, may have supplied part of the answer.[28] It seems likely that carved plaques like that from Scar had a religious significance and were used primarily on ceremonial occasions. This recent work has highlighted the symbolic value of flax — a connection which may also link the carved plaques to Freya. Indeed, one of the names given to Freya derives from the Old Norse word for flax, which was 'surrounded by many magical perceptions'.[29] It protected against evil and gave fertility to humankind. Flax was connected with women; it was even called the 'seed of woman' and had to be sown on a Friday (Freya's day) by women dressed in their best clothes. The spinning of flax was also connected with Freya, and the product, linen, was highly prized by well-placed

---

[24] Jan Petersen, *Vikingetidens redskaper*, Skrifter utgitt av Det Norske Videnskaps-Akademi i Oslo, II. Historisk-filosofisk Klasse, 4 (Oslo: Det Norske Videnskaps-Akademi, 1951), pp. 334–35; Owen and Dalland, *Scar: A Viking Boat Burial*, pp. 82–84, fig. 53a.

[25] Owen and Dalland, *Scar: A Viking Boat Burial*, pp. 82, 85, fig. 53b.

[26] Joseph Anderson, 'Notes on the Contents of Two Viking Graves in Islay, Discovered by William Campbell, Esq., of Ballinaby; with notices of the burial customs of the Norse sea-kings, as recorded in the sagas and illustrated by their grave-mounds in Norway and in Scotland', *Proceedings of the Society of Antiquaries of Scotland*, 14 (1880), 63–64.

[27] Holger Arbman, *Birka I: Die Gräber*, 2 vols (Stockholm: Kungl. Vitterhets Historie och Antikvitets Akademien, Almqvist & Wiksell, 1940–43), I (1940), 329, fig. 275, 8, 14; Owen and Dalland, *Scar: A Viking Boat Burial*, pp. 78–79, fig. 52a; p. 144, fig. 98.

[28] Britt-Mari Näsström, *Freyja: The Great Goddess of the North*, Lund Studies in History of Religions, 5 (Lund: University of Lund, 1995).

[29] Näsström, *Freyja*, pp. 85–86.

Viking women and an important part of bridal dress. It is a reasonable supposition, then, that the finest carved whalebone plaques were used for pressing precious linens for ceremonial occasions, perhaps especially the linen elements of the 'best clothes' worn to sow the flax seed or get married in. This might well explain why highly carved plaques were valued as grave goods by wealthy women, and, because they were primarily symbolic artefacts, why they are so rarely found with smoothers — without which they would have been, quite literally, of no earthly use at all.

In a recent reanalysis of the Scandinavian custom of boat burials, Crumlin-Pedersen has argued persuasively that a boat was present in a grave as an attribute of one of the heathen gods.[30] Since only a small fraction of the population received a boat burial, he suggests that 'the best explanation for this fact is to consider those buried with boats as persons involved directly in the fertility cult as priests or their helpers and therefore so closely connected to the god — or even to be looked on as part of the family of the gods — that they are "authorised" to be marked out with the attribute as an offering in their graves'.[31] If so, might not this be the real significance of the plaque, displayed so prominently within the Scar boat grave? Could it be that the plaque marked out the Scar woman not only as a worshipper of Freya, but as one of Freya's servants in the Viking world? This is highly speculative of course, and casts no light on the roles of the man and child, but it might help to explain some of the stranger aspects of this burial.

The dating of Scar, and indeed most Viking burials in Scotland, is fraught with difficulties. There is 'inevitable haziness of the chronological distinctions':[32] a grave assemblage can only provide a terminus post quem for the date of the burial itself; and dating graves in the Viking colonies is even more difficult than usual, based on artefacts found in contexts distant from their source and which may already have been of some antiquity when they were buried. At Scar, the scientific and artefactual dating do not agree. On the basis of the most diagnostic artefacts, namely the brooch, the plaque, and the two combs (which 'ought to mirror that person's generation'[33]), the assemblage as a whole appears to date from sometime during the ninth century. The three radiocarbon dates, however, one for each skeleton, combine to produce a

---

[30] Ole Crumlin-Pedersen, 'Boat-Burials at Slusegaard and the Interpretation of the Boat-Grave Custom', in *The Ship as Symbol in Prehistoric and Medieval Scandinavia*, ed. by O. Crumlin-Pedersen and B. M. Thye (Copenhagen: National Museum of Denmark, 1995), pp. 86–99 (p. 94).

[31] Crumlin-Pedersen, 'Boat-Burials at Slusegaard', p. 94.

[32] Christopher D. Morris, 'Viking Orkney: A Survey', in *The Prehistory of Orkney BC 4000–1000 AD*, ed. by Colin Renfrew (Edinburgh: Edinburgh University Press, 1985), pp. 210–42 (p. 211).

[33] Kristina Ambrosiani, *Viking Age Combs, Comb Making and Comb Makers in the Light of Finds from Birka and Ribe*, Acta Universitatis Stockholmiensis, Stockholm Studies in Archaeology, 2 (Stockholm: Stockholm University, 1981), p. 15.

calibrated date for the boat burial of 965–1025 (at 1 sigma), and 895–1030 (2 sigma). Statistical analysis of the dates shows that it is 65% probable that the burial dates to the tenth century, 32% probable that it is later than 1000, and only 3% probable that it is earlier than 900. On the basis of all strands of evidence from the excavated assemblage, the excavators concluded that the grave most probably dates to sometime between the end of the ninth century and the first half of the tenth century (*c.* 875 to 950), but more likely the later end of this date range.

This raises the vexed question as to whether there are any graves from the first half of the ninth century, as would be expected if the raids were shortly followed by colonization and the establishment of settlements. Unfortunately, our understanding of the early Viking period in Scotland is bedevilled by the lack of modern excavated, scientifically examined, and published pagan graves. Indeed, one (hopefully temporary) reason why the Scar burial is so important — despite its ambiguous dating evidence — is precisely because it is one of only a handful of modern, published excavations of Viking graves in Scotland. Wainwright expressed a common frustration when he referred to the 'inextricably muddled' reports and the 'chaos' between reports and surviving finds which befuddle attempts to classify, quantify, and assess the significance of the graves in the Northern Isles.[34] The Links of Pierowall, Westray, Orkney, where Viking finds and graves were discovered through sand-blowing and piecemeal diggings between 1839 and 1863, with a minimum of twenty graves represented, including possibly two boat burials, is a case in point.[35] Nevertheless, James Graham-Campbell's and Caroline Paterson's detailed study of the artefacts in pagan Viking graves in Scotland and the evidence for their find circumstances (shortly to be published by the National Museums of Scotland) seems to suggest that there are no graves from the early ninth century. Instead, it seems likely that all the pagan Viking graves can be dated to between about 850 and 950 — in short, the same general dating bracket as Scar.

The 'benchmark' for Viking burials in the Northern Isles, and indeed Scotland, is the cemetery at Westness, on Rousay, Orkney, where approximately forty graves have so far been examined.[36] Two of them were boat burials, each containing the body of a single man, richly accompanied by weapons and tools, in a central stone-built burial chamber (fig. 6). There was also a fairly massive, boat-shaped stone setting, which may have been a cenotaph since no burial was found within it. The cemetery was discovered in 1963 when a farm worker burying a dead cow chanced upon the grave of a Viking woman and her newborn baby, buried in a slab-lined pit. The woman was richly accompanied by grave goods, including the famous Westness

---

[34] Wainwright, 'The Scandinavian Settlement', p. 149

[35] Arne Thorsteinsson, 'The Viking Burial Place at Pierowall, Westray, Orkney', in *The Fifth Viking Congress, Tórshavn, July 1965*, ed. by Bjarni Niclasen (Torshavn: Føroya Landsstýri, Tórshavnar Býrað, Føroya Fróðskaparfelag & Føroya Fornminnissavn, 1968), pp. 151–63.

[36] Kaland, 'The Settlement of Westness, Rousay', pp. 312–17.

Figure 6. One of the boat burials from the Pictish and Viking cemetery at
Westness, Rousay. This burial contained a male warrior.

brooch. This is an Irish type which Stevenson suggests was made in about 725–50,[37] and which, like the discovery of insular material in Norwegian Viking graves,[38] clearly shows that the settlers valued and had access to precious objects of Celtic manufacture.

A fascinating new report on the analysis of most of the human skeletal assemblage has revealed that the whole population is represented in the Westness cemetery: men, women, and children, from infants to relatively elderly people.[39] Of particular interest from the point of view of Scar is that the women tended to live longer than men: the average age at death was forty-one for men and forty-five for women; but four women were aged about fifty to seventy, and one sixty to eighty at death, in other words comparable in age to the woman at Scar.

It is not generally well known that only eight of the forty graves in the Westness cemetery actually contained Norse grave goods, which raises fascinating questions about the religion and ethnicity of the individuals buried there. A series of radiocarbon dates shows that this cemetery was in use from Pictish times through to the later Viking period, with several graves clearly spanning the Pictish-Viking overlap, though with the usual tantalizing lack of dating precision.[40] The skeletal evidence shows that the Picts were far from being pygmies, as was suggested in the twelfth-century *Historia Norwegiae*, but were well within the range of statures in north-west Europe. Nonetheless, differences between the Picts and the Vikings were detectable in the assemblage; for example, a particular Pictish family had a congenital anomaly of eleven pairs of ribs and at least six members of the Pictish population had extreme overbites; some members of the Pictish community also suffered from tuberculosis.

Despite the variety of grave types — rectangular cists, stone-lined oval pits, boat-shaped graves and boat burials, shallow pits, graves with and without goods — all the Westness burials, Pictish and Viking, were inhumations, and, like Scar, they were all flat graves, apparently not marked on the ground surface by mounds or

---

[37] Robert B. K. Stevenson, 'The Celtic Brooch from Westness, Orkney, and Hinged-Pins', *Proceedings of the Society of Antiquaries of Scotland*, 119 (1989), 239–70 (p. 239).

[38] Egil Bakka, 'Some Decorated Anglo-Saxon and Irish Metalwork Found in Norwegian Viking Graves', in *The Fourth Viking Congress, York, August 1961*, ed. by Alan Small, Aberdeen University Studies, 149 (Edinburgh: Aberdeen University Press, 1965), pp. 32–40; Egon Wamers, 'Some Ecclesiastical and Secular Insular Metalwork Found in Norwegian Viking Graves', *Peritia*, 2 (1983), 277–306; Egon Wamers, *Insularer Metallschmuck in wikingerzeitlichen Gräbern Nordeuropas: Untersuchungen zur skandinavischen Westexpansion* (Neumünster: Wachholtz & Offa-Bücher, 1985); Egon Wamers, 'Insular Finds in Viking Age Scandinavia and the State Formation of Norway', in *Ireland and Scandinavia in the Early Viking Age*, ed. by Howard B. Clarke, Máire Ní Mhaonaigh, and Raghnall Ó Floinn (Dublin: Four Courts, 1998), pp. 37–72.

[39] Berit J. Sellevold, *Picts and Vikings at Westness: Anthropological Investigations of the Skeletal Material from the Cemetery at Westness, Rousay, Orkney Islands*, Norsk Institutt for Kulturminneforskning (NIKU), Scientific Report, 10 (Oslo: NIKU, 1999).

[40] Sellevold, *Picts and Vikings at Westness*, p. 7, table 1.

cairns. Nonetheless, there are strong indications that when the cemetery was in use, the graves must have been marked in some way. In one or two cases, grave markers can be deduced; for example, in an oval stone-lined pit containing the body of a young man accompanied by grave goods, the stone setting, whose shape perhaps symbolized a boat, had a higher 'prow' stone which may have stood proud of the ground surface. In the case of the boat burials, at Westness and Scar, the boat sterns may have stood proud of the graves. Other graves may have had wooden markers which have since rotted away.

It is important to note that not a single burial at Westness cut through or impinged on earlier pre-Viking or Viking graves, which clearly indicates that, throughout the several centuries that the cemetery was in use, gravediggers of whatever ethnic background were aware of the locations of earlier graves. It also clearly implies that the pagan Viking gravediggers respected earlier Christian graves. It seems clear that the Norse settlers either continued to use or reused an earlier Christian Pictish burial ground. Neither is it completely impossible that natives and incomers were both being buried at Westness at around the same time. It is also possible that some of the unaccompanied burials are Viking Age Christian burials. Others may have been unaccompanied by goods for reasons not decipherable through the archaeological record, ranging from poverty or lack of status through to a lack of regard for the dead person or simple meanness.

It is increasingly accepted that the traditional date of 995 is probably too late for the date of conversion of Viking Orkney to Christianity. As well as such clues as the early presence of cross-inscribed stones in the Northern Isles[41] and the discovery of a pagan axe in a Shetland churchyard,[42] the continued use of Celtic religious sites in the islands, such as Westness, points to an earlier and less disruptive process of conversion of the Viking settlers in the Orkney earldom. In truth, such conjectures are never clear-cut. It is perfectly possible, for instance, that later waves of Viking settlers, born and bred in Norway, might have been arriving as pagans in the Northern Isles in the tenth century, at a time when people of Scandinavian origin in the islands had already begun to adopt Christian burial practices.

The possibility of Christian Viking burials at Westness, and of Viking burials unaccompanied for other reasons, raises a familiar conundrum for scholars of the Viking period: the difficulties of identifying the graves of ethnic Scandinavians which are unaccompanied by grave goods. The traditional argument would be that

---

[41] Robert B. K. Stevenson, 'Christian Sculpture in Norse Shetland', *Fjölnupur i ä, 20/21* (1981), pp. 283–92; Barbara E. Crawford, *Scandinavian Scotland*, Scotland in the Early Middle Ages, 2 (Leicester: Leicester University Press, 1987), pp. 169–71; Olwyn Owen and Christopher Lowe, *Kebister: The Four-Thousand-Year-Old Story of One Shetland Township*, Society of Antiquaries of Scotland, Monograph Series, 14 (Edinburgh: Society of Antiquaries of Scotland, 1999), pp. 220–22.

[42] *Viking Antiquities in Great Britain and Ireland*, ed. by Haakon Shetelig, 6 vols (Oslo: Aschehoug, 1940–54), VI (1954), p. 69; Crawford, *Scandinavian Scotland*, pp. 163–64.

since pagan Viking graves are accompanied by grave goods, then unaccompanied
graves cannot be Viking; but the fallibility of this premise is obvious. It is highly
probable that some or many unaccompanied graves in Scotland, either at known
Viking burial locations or elsewhere in known areas of Viking settlement, are
actually the graves of Viking settlers. This conundrum is amply demonstrated in the
cemetery at Kneep, Valtos, Lewis, in the Western Isles, where, of seven graves so far
examined (excluding an early discovery of a wealthy female burial 'from Valtos'[43]),
only four are demonstrably Viking.[44] The others are similar in type and were found
in the immediate vicinity, but there are no clear indications as to whether these
unaccompanied graves are those of Vikings or not. Again, as at Westness, Viking
period radiocarbon dates do not solve the problem for, as the excavators of Kneep
point out, it is possible that some of the burials are those of members of a native
Celtic population, which certainly survived in the Western Isles.

Other Viking graves in the Northern Isles appear relatively few and far between,
although a concentration of excavation efforts in the Birsay area over the last twenty-
five years has seen a concomitant rise in the number of known Viking Age burials;
for example, a pagan Viking grave from Buckquoy, Birsay, dated to the tenth century
on coin evidence,[45] and probably Viking Age cist burials found overlying Pictish
burial cairns along the Brough Road, Birsay.[46] The Westness cemetery also lies close
to a recently excavated Viking settlement, and it is highly likely that modern excavations in prime areas of Viking settlement in Orkney will continue routinely to reveal
a few or many associated Viking Age graves — pagan and/or Christian. Conversely,
the discovery of a Viking grave or graves is quite likely to indicate the presence of
Viking settlement in the vicinity, as must be likely at both Scar and Pierowall.

In Shetland, pagan Viking graves are so far conspicuous by their absence,
although two are known from Unst;[47] but perhaps this should be seen in the context
of growing signs of the persistence of Christianity in the Northern Isles through the
early Viking Age. Stevenson's dating for Christian sculpture such as the Papil cross-

[43] D. J. MacLeod and others, 'An Account of a Find of Ornaments of the Viking Time
from Valtos, Uig, in the Island of Lewis', *Proceedings of the Society of Antiquaries of
Scotland*, 50 (1916), 181–89.

[44] Andrew J. Dunwell and others, 'A Viking Age Cemetery at Cnip, Uig, Isle of Lewis',
Proceedings of the Society of Antiquaries of Scotland, 125 (1995), 719–52.

[45] Anna Ritchie, 'Excavation of Pictish and Viking-Age Farmsteads at Buckquoy, Orkney',
Proceedings of the Society of Antiquaries of Scotland, 108 (1976–77), 174–227.

[46] Christopher D. Morris, *The Birsay Bay Project*, vol. I, *Coastal Sites beside the Brough
Road, Birsay, Orkney: Excavations 1976–1982*, University of Durham, Monograph Series, 1
(Durham: Department of Archaeology, University of Durham, 1989), pp. 109–27.

[47] Sigurd Grieg, *Viking Antiquities in Scotland*, vol. II of *Viking Antiquities in Great Britain
and Ireland*, ed. by Shetelig (1940), pp. 103–05; James Graham-Campbell, *The Viking-Age
Gold and Silver of Scotland AD 850–1100* (Edinburgh: National Museums of Scotland, 1995),
p. 154, plate 71b.

slab puts it squarely into the ninth century, with the Bressay cross-slab perhaps as late as about 900;[48] and we see clearly Christian burials only a little later at such unlikely sites as Kebister, Shetland.[49] Here, slight indications of a Christian Norse presence have been inferred from the discovery of two east-to-west aligned wooden coffins (fig. 7), located just beyond the east end of a putative wooden chapel, with one of the pine coffins radiocarbon-dated to around the tenth century; and yet there is no persuasive evidence of a Norse settlement, Christian or otherwise, at Kebister until the twelfth century or later. Could it be that these were the burials of native, tenth-century Christians? And if so, what might this imply about the so-called 'overwhelming' nature of the Viking takeover in the north?

The Evidence for the Viking Takeover in the North

In the north then, at least on the evidence of the graves, not only do we seem to be lacking Vikings in the very early Viking Age, but we may also be seeing evidence for the survival of native traditions in the persistence of Christian burial customs well into the ninth and even the tenth century. This fact alone suggests that the story of the early ninth century was not a simple case of native peoples being over-whelmed by incomers. The next question of course must be whether there is any evidence for early Viking settlement in the decades between about 800 and 850. With evidence emerging in places in the Scandinavian homelands for Viking material culture from as early as the mid-eighth century (which has led to a heated debate about the date of the beginning of the Viking Age),[50] and given the clear documentary evidence for significant Viking forays westwards before the end of the eighth century, some evidence for early Viking settlement in the Northern Isles would surely be expected.

A working model of the process of the Viking takeover in the north has been neatly summarized into three broad stages:[51]

1. a 'pioneer stage' of contact, raiding, and trade, with perhaps some raiding or establishment of winter bases, but still in a land otherwise Pictish;

---

[48] Stevenson, 'Christian Sculpture', pp. 284–85.

[49] Owen and Lowe, *Kebister*, pp. 290–93.

[50] See, for example, Helen Clarke and Björn Ambrosiani, *Towns in the Viking Age* (Leicester: Leicester University Press, 1991), pp. 46–89; Stig Jensen, *The Vikings of Ribe* (Ribe: Den Antikvariske Samling, 1991); Bjørn Myhre, 'The Archaeology of the Early Viking Age in Norway', in *Ireland and Scandinavia*, ed. by Clarke, Ní Mhaonaigh, and Ó Floinn, pp. 3–36.

[51] This fairly common settlement model was summarized by Simon Buteux in *Settlements at Skaill, Deerness, Orkney: Excavations by Peter Gelling of the Prehistoric, Pictish, Viking and Later Periods, 1963–81*, British Archaeological Reports, 260 (Oxford: Archaeopress, 1997), p. 262.

Figure 7. a (right): One of two tenth-century coffins excavated at Kebister, Shetland, with b (below), a detail of the Scots pine coffin after conservation.

2. a 'consolidation stage' where more permanent settlements become established but much in the way of Pictish institutions and culture survived;
3. and finally, an 'establishment stage' during which virtually all Pictish culture and institutions are swept away and replaced by those of wholly Norse character.

The only incontrovertible evidence for the pioneer stage is the contemporary accounts of the chroniclers, although, unfortunately, not chroniclers in Orkney or the north. We have nonetheless taken them at face value and extrapolated a truism: the Vikings were lords of all the seas around Britain. There can be little doubt that Viking raids intensified in the last decade of the eighth century. The *Annals of Ulster* report that in 794 there was 'devastation of all the islands of Britain by heathens',[52] although whether this included the Northern Isles is not specified. It is clear that all the Scottish islands, including Orkney and Shetland, came under Norse control within a century or so; but the more specific early references always have a western Scottish bent. The entry for 795 is very clear: the raiders attacked Skye, Iona, and several islands around Ireland; in 798 they wrought 'great devastation between Ireland and Scotland'; and they attacked Iona again and again.[53] It is interesting,

---

[52] *The Annals of Ulster*, ed. by Mac Airt and Mac Niocaill, s.a. 794.

[53] *The Annals of Ulster*, ed. by Mac Airt and Mac Niocaill, s.a. 795; 798; 802, 806, and 825.

though, that never do the *Annals* say the Vikings attacked Orkney, not even wealthy Pictish Birsay,[54] nor St Boniface, on Papa Westray, which Lamb has argued was the base of a powerful Roman Church in Pictish Orkney in the mid-eighth century,[55] nor anywhere else.

Perhaps the most likely explanation for the vacuum of information about the north is simply due to the accident of survival of the written records. Alternatively, perhaps it is because the chroniclers were from other parts of the British Isles and neither knew nor cared about raids in the far north. On the whole this seems unlikely given that the chroniclers seem to have been well informed about the Scandinavians' activities over a wide geographical area, and that depicting the atrocious behaviour of the heathens was useful for both political and evangelizing reasons. Even the Venerable Bede knew of Orkney, which was an important part of the Christian Pictish kingdom; had there been serious raids or atrocities in the north, it is unlikely that the chroniclers would not have known about them. Neither is there any reason to believe that Christian sites in Orkney were any less rich than sites to the south and west and in Ireland. On the contrary, the great silver treasure buried in about 800 beneath the floor of the church on St Ninian's Isle, Shetland,[56] testifies to the wealth present in the islands, as does a lost Pictish treasure from the Broch of Burgar.[57]

The key to this conundrum, as to so many intriguing facets of the Viking Age, may lie in geography. It is almost inconceivable that maritime contact between Norway and the Northern Isles began only in the Viking Age proper. Shetland is no further from Bergen than is Trondheim; Orkney is no further from Stavanger than is southern Denmark. In Scandinavia, technological developments in boat-building and the adoption of the sail went back at least decades, if not centuries. This must raise the possibility that the Vikings may not have raided in Orkney and Shetland — at least not in the same way or to the same degree as they did in the west — because they were already involved in some level of interaction, albeit superficial, with the inhabitants of these islands. When ferocious Vikings were bursting onto the scene for the first time at Lindisfarne and Iona, perhaps they were already a familiar sight in northern waters, and not seen primarily as aggressors. The Venerable Bede described Orkney as being at the back (*a tergo*) of Britain, 'where it lies open to the

---

[54] Cecil L. Curle, *Pictish and Norse Finds from the Brough of Birsay 1934–74*, Society of Antiquaries of Scotland, Monograph Series, 1 (Edinburgh: Society of Antiquaries of Scotland, 1982).

[55] Lamb, 'Carolingian Orkney', pp. 262–66.

[56] David M. Wilson, 'The Treasure', in *St Ninian's Isle and its Treasure*, ed. by Alan Small, Charles Thomas, and David M. Wilson, Aberdeen University Studies, 152, 2 vols (London: Oxford University Press, 1973), I, 45–148 (with plates in vol. II).

[57] James Graham-Campbell, 'A Lost Pictish Treasure (and Two Viking-Age Gold Arm-Rings) from the Broch of Burgar, Orkney', *Proceedings of the Society of Antiquaries of Scotland*, 115 (1985), 241–61.

Figure 8. Reconstruction painting of the probable Viking beach market
at Pierowall, Westray. © David Simon

endless ocean',[58] implying both its physical vulnerability and distance from the
Anglo-Saxon kingdom and its susceptibility to outside influences. He was probably
right. It seems likely that there was already contact between western Norway and
Pictish Orkney and Shetland when the Viking raids began; and, for a while at least,
Picts and Vikings may have had an understanding, formal or informal, or at the very
least a mutually convenient neutrality, based perhaps on many decades of contact
and trade (fig. 8).

Norway and Orkney have always had much to trade, Norway's timber for Orkney's grain being the most obvious example. This trade in timber for grain persisted
long after the Viking Age, but might it not also have been taking place before it? The
Pictish aristocracy was overwhelmingly land-bound,[59] and no conceivable threat to

---

[58] F. Donald Logan, *The Vikings in History* (London: Hutchinson, 1983), p. 41.

[59] There are frequent depictions of naturalistic hunting and horse-riding scenes in Pictish
sculpture, but in the whole corpus there is only one representation of a boat (on a stone from
Cossins, Forfarshire: see John Romilly Allen, *The Early Christian Monuments of Scotland*,
introd. by Joseph Anderson, 2 vols (Edinburgh: Society of Antiquaries of Scotland, 1903));
see also Leslie Alcock, 'Image and Icon in Pictish Sculpture', in *The Age of Migrating Ideas*,
ed. by R. Michael Spearman and John Higgitt (Edinburgh: National Museums of Scotland,
1993), pp. 230–36; and Lamb, 'Carolingian Orkney', pp. 267–68. This contrasts starkly with
the roughly contemporary picture stones from Gotland, Sweden, where depictions of boats

the Vikings with their mastery of the seas. The Scandinavians, moreover, with their nautical superiority, must have had the whip hand in initiating and sustaining any seaborne contact and trade, with the Picts in an increasingly subordinate role.

It may also be that the islands were more valuable to the Vikings as an unharried stopover than as a quarry for treasure. The Northern Isles might already have been seen by the individual boatloads of Vikings which embarked on the sea road west- wards as a convenient harbourage, a familiar stopping-off point for taking on water and general provisions, and a ready source of shelter and labour on an irregular basis. It must at least be possible that Viking ships were leaving Norway in the late eighth and early ninth centuries loaded with timber and furs, exchanging them for foodstuffs and other provisions in fertile Orkney, raiding and harrying in the west and Ireland, and returning to Norway, via the Northern Isles, with a booty of mainly Irish treasure and Orkney grain. If so, in the late eighth and early ninth centuries, even as the Pictish aristocracy remained intact and the Scandinavians made little impact on the structure of Pictish society, unconsciously the Northern Isles were already being absorbed into the Scandinavian sphere of influence.

The evidence for early trade is understandably sparse, since, by the very nature of the contact, much of it must have been in perishables. At Skaill, Deerness, only steatite and possibly reindeer antler provide evidence of exotic exports into eighth- century Orkney.[60] The identification of reindeer antler needs to be treated with the utmost caution; but it is true that steatite was becoming available — in quantities not seen since the Bronze Age — to the Late Iron Age inhabitants of Skaill; and the same phenomenon is seen in the contemporary levels of other multi-period sites, such as Howe of Howe, Orkney Mainland.[61]

At Pool, Sanday, steatite artefacts obligingly make their earliest appearance in the primary phase of Scandinavian presence.[62] At Upper Scalloway, Shetland, however, a steatite bar mould and steatite vessels which would normally have been ascribed to the Viking period were found in contexts securely dated to the fifth or sixth cen- turies.[63] Whether this means that steatite is not as reliable a chronological indicator as has previously been thought and that in Shetland, where it was available locally, it

---

and ships abound: see Erik Nylén and Jan Peder Lamm, *Stones, Ships and Symbols*, 2nd edn (Stockholm: Gidlunds, 1987).

[60] Buteux, *Settlements at Skaill, Deerness, Orkney*, p. 262.

[61] Beverley Ballin Smith and others, *Howe: Four Millennia of Orkney Prehistory*, Society of Antiquaries of Scotland, Monograph Series, 9 (Edinburgh: Society of Antiquaries of Scotland, 1994), p. 186, table 52.

[62] John R. Hunter, Julie M. Bond, and Andrea N. Smith, 'Some Aspects of Early Viking Settlement in Orkney', in *The Viking Age in Caithness, Orkney, and the North Atlantic*, ed. by Batey, Jesch, and Morris, pp. 272–84.

[63] Niall Sharples, *Scalloway: A Broch, Late Iron Age Settlement and Medieval Cemetery in Shetland* (Oxford: Oxbow Books, 1998), pp. 161–62, fig. 103.8.

Figure 9. Small offshore islands and headlands such as this one
on Sanday are often thought to have been used as raiding bases
by the earliest Viking visitors. © Mick Aston

was being used in the centuries before the Viking Age, or whether it points to contacts between Norway and the Northern Isles from a very early date, is not known.

Many scholars have surmised that the Northern Isles were raiding bases for the
early Viking visitors, with headlands and small offshore islands being taken
specifically for the purpose (fig. 9).[64] There is an obvious military and naval logic to
this assertion, and yet no raiding base has yet been positively identified. If, on the
other hand, the Scandinavians were tolerated, even accommodated, within Pictish
Orkney, then they may have had little need of fortified headlands or special raiding
bases. Instead, undefended encampments close to wherever the boats were drawn up
might have been all that was necessary, and the Pictish population may sensibly have
concluded that it was preferable not to quarrel with the Vikings wherever they
decided to camp. This might partly account for the apparent insouciance of the Norse
settlers in the Orkney earldom a little later, when their hegemony was so absolute
that they had no need of defences whatsoever. Even the Brough of Birsay, a centre of
Pictish Orkney and, later, the political centre of the earldom, was completely without
defences. It was not until well into the twelfth century that the Norse began to build
fortified residences in Orkney and Shetland.

---

[64] For example, Crawford, *Scandinavian Scotland*, pp. 46–47.

Figure 10. Part of the St Ninian's Isle silver treasure.
© Trustees of the National Museums of Scotland

Another commonly cited sign of trouble on the horizon for the Picts is the deposi-
tion of silver hoards, traditionally an indication of times of stress. Early historic
Scotland, however, was not a peaceful place, and the Vikings were 'simply another
warring band in a time of warring bands'.[65] Against this background, the burial of
precious metals and other valuables for safekeeping was a sensible precaution. It
may be no coincidence that the St Ninian's Isle silver (fig. 10) was buried beneath
the floor of the church, where it was still convenient and easy to access. Its burial
some distance away, at an anonymous spot in the surrounding landscape, might have
suggested a more serious attempt at concealment and, perhaps, a greater threat. No
doubt the clerics thought it a good idea to keep the church silver out of sight of both
native inhabitants and Vikings. The St Ninian's Isle hoard has little to tell us about
the relationship between Picts and Vikings.

---

[65] Christopher D. Morris, 'Raiders, Traders and Settlers: The Early Viking Age in
Scotland', in *Ireland and Scandinavia*, ed. by Clarke, Ní Mhaonaigh, and Ó Floinn, pp. 73–
103 (p. 75).

The wealth of insular metalwork in Norwegian Viking graves has more to say, and testifies especially to the success of the Viking raids on Irish monasteries. Some of the items, however, must be Pictish; examples include a penannular brooch from Bergøy[66] and a group of Pictish reliquaries.[67] Raiding in the Northern Isles is undeniably a potential source of this material, but so is gift exchange and trade, as Morris has pointed out.[68] Equally, it is most unlikely that Vikings and Picts had an identical relationship across the whole Pictish kingdom. Viking raids in eastern and north-eastern Scotland continued intermittently through the ninth century; for example, in 866, the *Annals of Ulster* report that the Norsemen Óláfr and Auisle 'plundered the entire Pictish country and took away hostages',[69] probably from bases in Ireland and the west. It is also worth remarking that the Westness brooch is another example of insular Irish metalwork finding its way into a pagan Viking grave, but this time in Orkney.

It is very important to remember that the pioneer stage in the north was not an organized enterprise, but dominated by freelancers. It is also important to recognize the highly structured nature of the society that these Viking visitors encountered. *Historia Norwegiae* names two classes of inhabitant before the Norse in Orkney, the Picts and the *Papar*. Lamb has argued persuasively that the *Papar* were the pastoral hierarchy of the Roman Church and that their acquisition of estates was part of a planned process by which the Pictish kings consolidated their power in Orkney and extended it towards Shetland.[70] By the mid-eighth century, he suggests, about one-third of the best land in Orkney may have been in the hands of the Church.

It is possible, then, that the ever pragmatic late-eighth-century Viking freelancers found some kind of modus vivendi with this highly structured, land-based Pictish society, and that there was contact of one sort or another, probably not exactly peaceful, but sometimes more constructive than we might have expected. If so, it may be that the resulting, albeit superficial, ebb and flow of interaction which marks the so-called

---

[66] David M. Wilson, 'The Exhibition of Viking Age Art', in *ROSC '71 The Poetry of Vision: An International Exhibition of Modern Art from Outside Ireland and Viking Age Art Held at the Royal Dublin Society from October 24 to December 29 1971*, ed. by A. Crookshank and David M. Wilson (Dublin: Committee of the RoSC '71 Exhibition, 1973), pp. 136–37.

[67] See, for example, Martin Blindheim, 'A House-Shaped Irish-Scots Reliquary in Bologna, and its Place Among the Other Reliquaries', *Acta Archaeologica*, 55 (1984), pp. 1–53; Martin Blindheim, 'The Ranuaik Reliquary in Copenhagen: A Short Study', in *Proceedings of the Tenth Viking Congress; Larkollen, Norway, 1985*, ed. by James E. Knirk, Universitetets Oldsaksamlings Skrifter, Ny Rekke, 9 (Oslo: Universitetets Oldsaksamling, 1987), pp. 203–18; *The Work of Angels: Masterpieces of Celtic Metalwork, 6th–9th Centuries AD*, ed. by Susan Youngs (London: British Museum, 1989), pp. 134–40.

[68] Morris, 'Raiders, Traders and Settlers', p. 82.

[69] *The Annals of Ulster*, ed. by Mac Airt and Mac Niocaill, s.a. 866.

[70] Lamb, 'Papil, Picts and Papar', pp. 18–20.

pioneer stage of the takeover may have lasted for decades, including all through the 'missing decades' of Orkney's early Viking Age, well into the ninth century.

In a few places, recent excavations at settlement sites in Orkney and now in Shetland are beginning to produce evidence of a Pictish-Norse interface, and specifically the mixing of cultural material. It is important, however, even in the light of this new evidence, to guard against a natural tendency to see the imposition of Norse culture in the Northern Isles at too early a stage. As Hunter has said of Pool, 'the Viking/ Norse phase is best viewed as part of a process of continuity'.[71]

It is remarkable that almost all identified Viking period settlements in the Northern Isles are found on top of, or close to, sites occupied in the preceding Pictish period, and normally on Pictish settlements which had been of some size and importance; Birsay, Skaill, and Pool in Orkney all fit this pattern, as do Jarlshof and Old Scatness in Shetland.[72] This is not necessarily the result of a straightforward political conquest, however, nor of the slighting of Pictish settlements and their symbolic replacement by Norse buildings on the same sites. It bears repeating here: there is no evidence whatsoever of a Pictish-Viking conflict in the Northern Isles, let alone of wholesale slaughter. Instead, the changes in culture and economy are altogether much subtler and more gradual than Wainwright would have expected, and do seem to be evolutionary. What we seem to be witnessing is the mutation of long-lived settlements towards the adoption of Norse culture and architecture, not necessarily all at the same pace or in precisely the same way.

An important site for advancing our understanding of this period is Pool, Sanday, now approaching publication.[73] Here, there was a clearly identifiable period of overlap between the two cultural groups. The Pictish buildings were adapted and reused by inhabitants who had access to typically Norse material, notably steatite, at a time when the cultivation of flax was also introduced (fig. 11). Yet major elements of the economic and cultural basis remained unchanged; for example, aspects of animal husbandry. Furthermore, steatite was used as an alternative to pottery, not a replacement, throughout the interface. Native wares not only persisted in use, but continued to evolve in both typology and fabric; and this picture is now being replicated at Old Scatness in Shetland. This does not smack of the obliteration of native culture in the missing decades of the Viking Age in the north.

---

[71] Hunter, Bond, and Smith, 'Some Aspects of Early Viking Settlement', p. 275.

[72] James R. C. Hamilton, *Excavations at Jarlshof Shetland* (Edinburgh: HMSO, 1956), *Old Scatness Broch: Retrospect and Prospect*, ed. by Rebecca A. Nicholson and Steven J. Dockrill, Bradford Archaeological Sciences Research, 5 / North Atlantic Biocultural Organisation Monograph, 2 (Bradford: University of Bradford, Shetland Amenity Trust, and North Atlantic Biocultural Organisation, 1998).

[73] John R. Hunter and others, *Archaeological Investigations on Sanday, Orkney*, Society of Antiquaries of Scotland, Monograph Series (Edinburgh: Society of Antiquaries of Scotland, forthcoming).

Figure 11. This Late Iron Age roundhouse at Pool, Sanday, contained Norse cultural material in its latest phase and may have been reused by the Vikings.

If this was the consolidation stage of Norse settlement, then, like the pioneer stage, it seems to have been neither planned nor particularly forceful. Scandinavian settlers in the ninth century must still have been far outnumbered by native Picts, as would be expected; but then this was no organized takeover. If it is accepted that the arrival of Scandinavians was taking place against a background of decades of increasing contact, then perhaps we can begin to see how some Scandinavian freelancers might have stayed, might have coexisted with native inhabitants, and begin to understand how Scandinavian cultural material and new technologies began to make an appearance on native occupied sites in the eighth and early ninth centuries.

This does not entirely answer the question of what happened to the Picts, because in the final analysis, of course, Wainwright was right. By about 900, the Picts had been, if not overwhelmed, then certainly eclipsed — politically, linguistically, culturally, and socially. Lamb's perceptive analysis of Pictish society must provide at least part of the answer here.[74] Lamb suggests that the Pictish aristocracy was only gradually displaced by Viking war-leaders. Although the Vikings always had superior military and nautical capability, in the early days there were probably concessions to Pictish authority; perhaps an estate was granted here or there, in return for some level of allegiance and a promise to expel other raiders. This could also explain

[74] Lamb, 'Carolingian Orkney', pp. 267–69.

why the early Norse land division seems to have been based so completely on its Pictish precursor. As the Norse leaders grew in number and status, and began to exercise authority on their own behalf, at first they did it through the existing Pictish power structures, including that of the Church.

In the end, it may not have been the Vikings who finally 'did for' the Picts in the Northern Isles, but events taking place further south. Kenneth MacAlpin's (Cínaed mac Alpín) overthrow of the Pictish kingdom in the heartlands of eastern Scotland in 843 possibly heralded a dismantling of Pictish culture and institutions, including the special relationship between the Roman Church and the Pictish dynasty (fig. 12). MacAlpin was in no position, and made no attempt, to secure Orkney as part of his kingdom, but the effects on the Orcadian ecclesiastical and secular elite were as devastating as if he had: they must have been left high and dry, cut off from their parent institutions.

And so it was that Pictish Orkney withered on the vine, just as the emerging kingdom of Norway in the shape of Harald Fine-Hair was forced to take an interest in the Northern Isles: 'One summer Harald Fine-Hair sailed west over the North Sea in order to teach a lesson to certain Vikings whose plunderings he could no longer tolerate. These Vikings used to raid in Norway over summer and had Shetland and Orkney as their winter base.'[75] What clearer picture could there be of the Northern Isles under no central or political control, an amalgam of dissident land-holding Scandinavians and native inhabitants with no recourse to the Pictish heartlands who had already coexisted for decades? The establishment of the Orkney earldom in the late ninth century was no coincidence. The establishment phase filled a vacuum and probably marks the beginning of large-scale colonization by newcomers from Norway — and the extraordinary, albeit short-lived era of pagan Viking burials like Scar.

The Viking Age was an era of high mobility and of a high level of interaction between peoples. The extraordinary boat burial from Scar, Orkney, with its wealthy cargo of three pagan individuals, found far from their origins in Scandinavia, is at once a potent emblem of the Viking Age and a salutary reminder of how difficult it is really to penetrate the complexities of human relations and interactions — especially at a distance of over 1000 years.

---

[75] *Orkneyinga Saga: The History of the Earls of Orkney*, trans. by Hermann Pálsson and Paul Edwards (London: Penguin, 1978), p. 26.

Figure 12. The reconstructed Pictish symbol stone on the Brough of
Birsay, Orkney, which was an important centre in both Pictish and
Viking times, shows three aristocratic warriors.

Britons, Saxons, and Vikings in the South-West*

DEREK GORE

An attack by a Viking army on Carhampton in Somerset, a royal estate left by Alfred to his son and successor Edward, was reported in the *Anglo-Saxon Chronicle* for 836 and heralded a pattern of intermittent Viking activity in and around the south-west peninsula for the next two hundred years. Carhampton is close to the Bristol Channel coast and the attack may have been part of Norse activities in the Irish Sea area generally. The event at Carhampton also fits into a pattern of attacks on royal centres in the south-west and was one of a number of landings by Scandinavians on the north Devon and north Somerset coasts.

Two years later at 'Hengestes dune', almost certainly Hingston Down near Callington in east Cornwall, a Viking army joined with the Cornish against Egbert of Wessex, who defeated them and put them to flight.[1] Was this an early example of Scandinavian leaders exploiting a local political situation? Egbert had recently campaigned in a hostile Cornwall. He was reported raiding from east to west in the territory in 815, and ten years later his army engaged the Britons at 'Gafulford' — probably Galford in west Devon.[2] The Cornish were apparently trying to preserve their independence by whatever means available.

Putting these events in context briefly it should be appreciated that, in common with much of western Britain in the post-Roman era, the south-west, comprising at least the later medieval shires of Cornwall, Devon, and Somerset, appears to have been organized into a kingdom or kingdoms. Gildas referred to it as 'Dumnonia',[3]

---

* I am grateful to my colleagues Henrietta Quinnell and Robert Higham for reading and commenting upon earlier drafts of this paper. Any errors remaining are my own.

[1] *The Anglo-Saxon Chronicle*, ed. and trans. by Michael Swanton (London: Dent, 1996), E, s.a. 835.

[2] *The Anglo-Saxon Chronicle*, ed. and trans. by Swanton, A, E, s.a. 813, 823.

[3] Gildas, *The Ruin of Britain and Other Works*, ed. and trans. by Michael Winterbottom (Chichester: Phillimore, 1978), 28.1, p. 29.

and there are several references to British territory and kings in the south-west in later Anglo-Saxon sources.[4] We cannot, however, be at all certain either of the geographical extent of the kingdom or whether the scanty evidence is showing us a single kingdom right through this period — that is, from the fifth to the eighth centuries.

The extent of the putative kingdom is even more obscure — Britons appear to have maintained their cultural independence from the Germanic peoples for a time as far east as Wareham[5] and as far north as Bath and Cirencester,[6] although it would be too much to claim that all these areas were within a single kingdom of Dumnonia. However, the distribution of Anglo-Saxon pagan cemeteries certainly suggests that much of Somerset and western Dorset were free of Anglo-Saxon interference in the fifth and sixth centuries.[7] So we can reconstruct a large area which remained under forms of British control for at least two hundred years after the end of Roman Britain, but whether it was ruled by one king or by a high king with subordinate rulers or whether it consisted of a series of independent territories is impossible to reconstruct from the evidence.

In 658 the *Anglo-Saxon Chronicle* records that 'Cenwalh fought at "Peonnum" against the Welsh and put them in flight as far as the Parrett'.[8] 'Peonnum' is most plausibly located in the area of Penselwood close to the boundaries of Somerset, Wiltshire, and Dorset. While it could hardly be claimed that an English forest could act as a physical barrier between two peoples, Penselwood may have acted at some stage as an agreed boundary between the Britons to the west and the English to the east. Once it was pierced it allowed Anglo-Saxon control of Somerset to be established over the next two to three generations. Surviving charters suggest that the kings of the Gewisse/Wessex were granting land to Glastonbury Abbey, Somerset at least from the reign of Centwine, 676–85.[9] The *Chronicle* implies that both Taunton in Somerset and Axminster in east Devon were in Anglo-Saxon hands by 722 and 755 respectively.[10]

---

[4] For example, *The Anglo-Saxon Chronicle*, ed. and trans. by Swanton, A, E, s.a. 710, and Aldhelm's letter to Gerontius of Domnonia in Aldhelm, *Aldhelm: The Prose Works*, trans. by Michael Lapidge and Michael Herren (Cambridge: Brewer, 1979), pp. 155–60.

[5] David Hinton, 'The Inscribed Stones in Lady St Mary Church, Wareham', *Proceedings of the Dorset Natural History and Archaeological Society*, 114 (1993), p. 260.

[6] *The Anglo-Saxon Chronicle*, ed. and trans. by Swanton, A, E, s.a. 577.

[7] See the map in Barbara Yorke, *Wessex in the Early Middle Ages* (London: Leicester University Press, 1995), p. 13.

[8] *The Anglo-Saxon Chronicle*, ed. and trans. by Swanton, A, E, s.a. 658 (see also p. 32, n. 1).

[9] P. H. Sawyer, *Anglo-Saxon Charters: An Annotated List and Bibliography* (London: Royal Historical Society, 1968), pp. 130–31.

[10] *The Anglo-Saxon Chronicle*, ed. and trans. by Swanton, A, E, s.a. 722: 'Here Queen Æthelburh threw down Taunton, which Ine built earlier' (see also p. 43, n. 12); A, E, s.a. 755 mentions the burial of the ætheling Cyneheard at Axminster.

So most likely Devon passed under Anglo-Saxon control during the eighth century and not earlier, as has been argued.[11]

By the time of the events of the 830s, part of the south-west had thus only recently come under Wessex control. Were Scandinavian attacks in the ninth century instrumental in preventing Wessex from fully absorbing the whole peninsula? Did Scandinavian leaders deliberately exploit potential opposition to Wessex rule in the area?

Further attacks on Devon and Somerset were reported in Æthelwulf's reign,[12] and in the winter of 877/8, when Guthrum and a Viking force seized Chippenham, a force from Dyfed besieged the ealdorman of Devon in a fortification on the north Devon coast at 'Cynuit', probably Wint Hill, Countisbury above Lynmouth.[13] These events suggest that the two Viking armies were working in concert, one using the south-west peninsula, with which the Vikings were now familiar. If this was the plan then of course it failed, since both armies were eventually defeated.

Other Viking activity in Cornwall at about this time, unrecorded in the written sources, may be suggested by the find in 1774 of a hoard of precious objects and coins at Trewhiddle close to St Austell in south Cornwall.[14] The objects included ecclesiastical items such as a scourge and chalice. More significant for our purposes perhaps is that a degree of Cornish independence may be suggested by the record in the Welsh Annals under 875 of the death by drowning of 'Durngarth, king of "Cernyw", that is of the Cornish'.[15] This may be the Doniert whose memorial stone, asking us to pray for him, is still visible on a ridge west of Bodmin Moor at Redgate.[16] Was he, as Todd suggests,[17] a dependent king ruling as a vassal of Alfred in a conquered land, or did the Britons beyond the Tamar enjoy a greater degree of independence — an independence gained for them in part by the increased activities of Scandinavians in southern England which diverted the attention of Egbert's successors in Wessex?

In his will Alfred left lands in Cornwall to his two sons, but these were concentrated in the eastern part of the province. He left Stratton in Triggshire in the extreme north-eastern corner to Edward, and lands belonging to the estate at Lifton in west

---

[11] For example, William G. Hoskins, *The Westward Expansion of Wessex* (Leicester: Leicester University Press, 1960), pp. 17–18.

[12] *The Anglo-Saxon Chronicle*, ed. and trans. by Swanton, A, E, s.a. 840, 845, and 851.

[13] *The Anglo-Saxon Chronicle*, ed. and trans. by Swanton, A, E, s.a. 878; Asser, *Alfred the Great: Asser's Life of King Alfred and Other Contemporary Sources*, trans. by Simon Keynes and Michael Lapidge (Harmondsworth: Penguin, 1983), p. 54.

[14] D. M. Wilson and C. E. Blunt, 'The Trewhiddle Hoard', *Archaeologia*, 98 (1961), 75–122.

[15] *Nennius' British History and the Welsh Annals*, ed. and trans. by John Morris (Chichester: Phillimore, 1980), p. 48.

[16] Elizabeth Okasha, *Corpus of Early Christian Inscribed Stones of South-West Britain* (London: Leicester University Press, 1993), pp. 213–17.

[17] Malcolm Todd, *The South-West to A.D. 1000* (London: Longman, 1987), p. 273.

Devon, and therefore most likely in the east of that territory, to his second son
Æthelweard.[18] Asser's strange account of Alfred hunting in Cornwall before he
became king appears to be localized in the same area.[19] The *Burghal Hidage* names
four *burhs* in Devon but none in Cornwall, and one possible interpretation of the
construction of the *burh* at Lydford to the west of Dartmoor is that it was meant to
afford protection against the Cornish,[20] although the protection of tin and silver
deposits nearby is perhaps another factor in its siting.

Edward the Elder's reported protection of the north coast against Viking attack in
915 or 918, from Cornwall in the west, eastwards as far as Avonmouth, need not
necessarily imply more than from the Cornish border or perhaps defence of his own
lands in north-east Cornwall.[21] A case can be made then, that much of Cornwall
remained substantially independent of the Wessex kings as late as the end of the
ninth century and perhaps well into the tenth century, as I shall argue later, and that
Scandinavian leaders were able to take advantage of this.

The Scandinavians remained active in the Bristol Channel in the tenth century.
The *Anglo-Saxon Chronicle* reported in 915 or 918 the arrival of a Viking fleet from
Brittany in the Severn causing Edward the Elder to protect the north coast. This did
not, however, prevent the Vikings landing near Watchet and at Porlock on the north
Somerset coast, or from using the islands in the Severn as bases. Eventually they
departed to Dyfed and finally joined other Scandinavian forces gathering in Ireland.

Again a pattern emerges. Watchet was targeted presumably because it was a shel-
tered landing place and a market centre and port serving the important royal estate at
Williton.[22] Other attacks on it were recorded in 988 and 997 although the south coast
was also attacked — Tavistock Abbey in 997, the royal centre at Teignton in 1001,
and the Exeter *burh* in 1001 and 1003.[23] Metcalf suggests that in about 980 'there
was a sea-change in the monetary economy of the Irish Sea province'.[24] There was a
marked decline in the volume of coins minted at Chester and a parallel decline in its
connections with Dublin. This was replaced by much closer connections between

---

[18] Asser, *Alfred the Great*, p. 175.

[19] Asser, *Alfred the Great*, p. 175, n. 17; p. 89; pp. 254–55, n. 142.

[20] Alfred P. Smyth, *King Alfred the Great* (Oxford: Oxford University Press, 1995), p. 212.

[21] *The Anglo-Saxon Chronicle*, ed. and trans. by Swanton, D, s.a. 915; A, s.a. 918.

[22] Michael Aston, 'The Towns of Somerset', in *Anglo-Saxon Towns in Southern England*,
ed. by Jeremy Haslam (Chichester: Phillimore, 1984), pp. 167–201 (p. 193).

[23] *The Anglo-Saxon Chronicle*, ed. and trans. by Swanton, C, E, s.a. 988; E, s.a. 997; A, E,
s.a. 1001 and 1003.

[24] D. M. Metcalf, 'The Monetary Economy of the Irish Sea Province', in *Viking Treasure
from the North West: The Cuerdale Hoard in its Context*, ed. by James Graham-Campbell,
National Museums and Galleries on Merseyside, Occasional Papers, 5 (Liverpool: National
Museums and Galleries on Merseyside, 1992), pp. 89–106 (p. 102).

Dublin and the West Country.[25] Coins from the Barnstaple and Exeter mints began
to appear in Dublin. Trading links between Exeter and Ireland may have been established about this time and continued to at least the early thirteenth century with tin
perhaps one of the commodities exported.[26] Watchet was the site of a mint from
about 980. In the late 990s minting began in Dublin in part using a reverse die from
Watchet.[27] Was this obtained through raiding or trading?

Nor were these the last of the Irish Viking connections with the south-west. After
Harold Godwinson's defeat and death at Hastings in October 1066, his sons fled to
Ireland from where, with the assistance of Diarmait mac Maíl na mBó, king of
Leinster, and Hiberno-Norse fleets, they attacked the Somerset and Devon coasts in
1068 and 1069, raiding into the estuaries of the rivers Avon and Taw.[28] The family,
part Scandinavian, had considerable landholdings in the West Country before the
defeat at Hastings. A note in the margin of the Exeter Domesday Book records nine
manors laid waste by the Irish between the river Erme and the Kingsbridge estuary
in south Devon.[29] This devastation was perhaps caused during the 1069 expedition,
or it may have occurred earlier in the eleventh century. Of possible significance may
be the find of an armlet of twisted gold wires with a facetted rectangular knob on
Goodrington beach, south Devon, in 1978. The closest parallels are from Scandinavia, especially from a mixed hoard from Gotland of mid-eleventh-century date.[30]
Was this a relic of the same raids?

Scandinavian raiding in the south-west does not appear to have given way to settlement as it did, for example, in other Irish Sea provinces. The distribution of Scandinavian place-name elements along the coast of south Wales, suggesting at least
limited settlement, finds no parallel on the south side of the Bristol Channel,
although several of the island names in the Channel, including Lundy, are Scandinavian.[31] They were most likely used as bases and/or as navigational points. The
authors of *The Place-Names of Devon* found little Scandinavian influence on the

---

[25] Metcalf, 'Monetary Economy', pp. 102–03.

[26] John R. Maddicott, 'Trade, Industry and the Wealth of King Alfred', *Past and Present*,
123 (1989), 3–51 (pp. 26, 42).

[27] Metcalf, 'Monetary Economy', pp. 102–03; Mark A. S. Blackburn, 'The Mint of
Watchet', *The British Numismatic Journal*, 44 (1974), 13–38 (pp. 18–19).

[28] *The Anglo-Saxon Chronicle*, ed. and trans. by Swanton, D, s.a. 1067 and 1068. See also
Dáibhí Ó Cróinín, *Early Medieval Ireland 400–1200* (London: Longman, 1995), p. 277.

[29] John Alexander, 'An Irish Invasion of Devon', *Transactions of the Devonshire Association*, 55 (1923), 125–30.

[30] Henry Sykes-Balls, 'Viking Treasure', *Transactions and Proceedings of the Torquay
Natural History Society*, 18 (1980), 10–13.

[31] For example, Flatholm and Steepholm; see Henry Loyn, *The Vikings in Wales*, The
Dorothea Coke Memorial Lecture in Northern Studies Delivered 2 March 1976 at University
College London (London: University College London, 1976), map 2.

county's names,[32] and Wakelin's more recent research into Cornish place-names produced a similar result.[33] Scandinavian influence can be seen on some of the stone sculptures in Cornwall, notably the hogback at Lanivet[34] and three other possible derivatives spread across the county,[35] and the cross at Cardinham, east Cornwall, has ring-chain ornament.[36] These traces may suggest settlement, although general influences are probably more likely. However, they do fit into a pattern of Viking activities in and around the peninsula. Significantly, surviving stone sculpture of this period from Devon shows no Scandinavian influence.

One major theme of this essay has been the degree of independence which the Britons of the south-west peninsula retained in the face of the developing power of the West Saxons to the east. Egbert's difficulties in the region illustrate this, and these were compounded once the Scandinavians arrived in the south-west. After Egbert's death in 839, Wessex's problems with the Vikings increased and neither Æthelwulf, his son and successor, nor Alfred, his grandson, were able to exercise firm control over Cornwall. Not perhaps until the reign of Alfred's grandson, Athelstan, in the tenth century was such control established and even then it was Athelstan's assertion of power over Exeter and Devon and the fixing of the Tamar boundary which was emphasized by William of Malmesbury, not conquest.[37]

In about 930 Athelstan did establish or re-establish a bishop's see in Cornwall at St Germans, just west of the Tamar boundary,[38] although the Celtic name of the bishop, Conan, hints that local feelings were perhaps taken into account. At about the same time he appears to have confirmed grants of land to the church at St Buryan in Penwith,[39] and later Edgar confirmed a similar grant to St Kew.[40] Was the Church being used to further the political interests of the English kings in Cornwall, a policy reminiscent of Centwine's interest in Glastonbury and Somerset earlier?

Scandinavian leaders perhaps saw the south-west peninsula as the Achilles heel through which Wessex and later England could be effectively attacked. Political

[32] J. E. B. Gover, A. Mawer, and F. M. Stenton, *The Place-Names of Devon*, English Place-Name Society, 8–9 (Cambridge: English Place-Name Society, 1931–32), VIII.1 (1931), p. xxvi.

[33] Martyn F. Wakelin, 'Norse Influence in Cornwall: A Survey of the Evidence', *Journal of the Institute of Cornish Studies*, 4/5 (1976), 41–49.

[34] J. T. Lang, 'The Hogback: A Viking Colonial Monument', *Anglo-Saxon Studies in Archaeology and History*, 3 (1984), 85–176 (p. 144).

[35] St Tudy, St Buryan, and Phillack.

[36] Arthur G. Langdon, *Old Cornish Crosses* (Truro: Pollard, 1896), pp. 354–57.

[37] *English Historical Documents*, vol. I, c. 500–1042, ed. by Dorothy Whitelock (London: Eyre Spottiswode, 1955), p. 281.

[38] Della Hooke, *Pre-Conquest Charter-Bounds of Devon and Cornwall* (Woodbridge: Boydell & Brewer, 1994), p. 18.

[39] Hooke, *Pre-Conquest Charter-Bounds*, pp. 22–25.

[40] Hooke, *Pre-Conquest Charter-Bounds*, pp. 33–37.

considerations rather than wealth were more likely to have attracted the interest of Scandinavian leaders in the peninsula, although commerce is a possibility from the late tenth century. Its geographical position and the topography of the area encouraged contacts particularly with the Vikings of the Irish Sea area, and these appear to have increased through the period. The evidence does not, however, support Viking settlement even on the scale suggested for Wales.

Anglo-Danish Contact across the North Sea in the Eleventh Century: A Survey of the Danish Archaeological Evidence

ANNE PEDERSEN

Research into the presence of Danes in England may draw upon a large body of very different sources ranging from written accounts describing Viking raids, settlement, and conquest to place-names and a steadily increasing number of objects of Scandinavian origin, as well as objects reflecting influence from Scandinavian art styles and craftsmanship. For Denmark, the opposite is the case. For instance, there is nothing equivalent to the letters of Alcuin of York which so vividly describe his reaction to the attack on Lindisfarne in 793. We have no records of what the attacking forces thought nor any idea of how, for instance, the progress of the 'Great Army' (*micel here*) in England between 865 and 879 or the success of the Danish settlers in the next decades was followed at home. Only a few rune-stones tell of men who died in England. One from Valleberga in Skåne reads, 'Sven and Thorgot made this monument in memory of Manne and Svenne. God help their souls well. And they lie in London'.[1] Another fragmentary stone from Schleswig was raised in memory of a man buried at *Skia*, an unknown site in England.[2]

Specific events or general conditions in Denmark are only rarely recorded in foreign sources. As to the social or political consequences of the activities in England, we find next to no evidence, although it is likely that the events — or at least the proceeds of the attacks and trading ventures as well as the interchange between individuals across the North Sea — had an impact at home.

Written sources or linguistic evidence in Denmark of contact with England before the attacks and great campaigns around 1000 are almost totally lacking. As Olaf

---

[1] Erik Moltke, *Runes and their Origin: Denmark and Elsewhere* (Copenhagen: National Museum of Denmark, 1985), p. 238.

[2] Moltke, *Runes and their Origin*, p. 243.

Olsen stated in the catalogue for the 1981/82 exhibition *Vikingerne i England og hjemme i Danmark*, the archaeological evidence seemed so limited that doubts could be raised about the ability of archaeology to cast light on the historical events.[3] The prospects no longer appear quite so bleak, and the aim of this essay is to present a survey of old and new finds from Denmark that reflect contact with England, especially objects dated to the late Viking Age and the early Middle Ages beginning with the reign of Svein Forkbeard (Sveinn tjúguskegg Haraldsson, *c.* 985/86–1014), as this period has witnessed the most marked increase in finds. However, the archaeological picture of the preceding centuries is also improving.

Ninth- and Tenth-Century Finds

The first record in England of a payment to ward off Vikings (later known as Danegeld) is from the *Anglo-Saxon Chronicle* s.a. 865, but apart from a few single coins there is very little archaeological evidence of minted silver returning to Denmark from England. Hardly any treasure hoards contain Anglo-Saxon coins from the ninth and tenth centuries.[4] However, it is possible that much of the silver in the early hoards came from western Europe where the chroniclers recorded large sums of tribute and plunder taken by the Vikings. Gold and silver could be melted down and reused in objects of traditional Scandinavian type. An alternative explanation for the scarcity of western European coins in Denmark is that the newly won wealth was spent or reinvested abroad by Danes who chose not to return home.[5] Not until the late tenth century does this picture change, and the number of hoards containing Anglo-Saxon coins and the number of Anglo-Saxon coins in these hoards greatly increase.[6]

Apart from precious metals, one would expect to find complete or broken and re-used objects such as decorated metal mounts, but they are few in number. Denmark thus contrasts with Norway where pieces of jewellery and reused insular ornaments, as well as liturgical vessels and reliquaries, have been found.[7] One reason for the

---

[3] Olaf Olsen, 'The English in Denmark', in *The Vikings in England*, ed. by Else Roesdahl and others (London: Anglo-Danish Viking Project, 1981), pp. 171–75 (p. 171). For a survey of the linguistic evidence, see also Gillian Fellows-Jensen, 'From Scandinavia to the British Isles and Back Again: Linguistic Give-and-Take in the Viking Period', in *The Twelfth Viking Congress: Developments Around the Baltic and the North Sea in the Viking Age*, ed. by Björn Ambrosiani and Helen Clarke, Birka Studies, 3 (Stockholm: The Birka Project at Riksantik-varieämbetet and Statens Historiska Museer, 1994), pp. 253–68.

[4] See Roar Skovmand, 'De danske Skattefund fra Vikingetiden og den ældste Middelalder indtil omkring 1150', *Aarbøger for nordisk Oldkyndighed og Historie*, 1942, 1–275 (pp. 19–20, table 5).

[5] P. H. Sawyer, *The Age of the Vikings*, 2nd edn (London: Edward Arnold, 1971), pp. 99–101.

[6] Skovmand, 'De danske Skattefund fra Vikingetiden', pp. 17–21.

[7] See Egon Wamers, *Insularer Metallschmuck in wikingerzeitlichen Gräbern Nordeuropas: Untersuchungen zur skandinavischen Westexpansion* (Neumünster: Wachholtz & Offa-

lack of Anglo-Saxon or insular objects generally in Denmark probably lies in the burial customs of the Viking Age. Most of the known graves from the ninth century are simply furnished, unlike many graves in Sweden and Norway. In Denmark, richly furnished burial is a custom mainly linked with the tenth century, but even in this context the number of imports other than, for instance, whetstones of foreign slate is not overwhelming. There is no complete survey of all foreign objects in Danish burials, but an impression of the finds may be gained from surveys of inhumation and cremation graves as well as publications of individual cemeteries excavated in this century.[8]

Among the objects originating in the British Isles are the remains of a decorated copper-alloy cauldron from a tenth-century male burial uncovered in 1926 at Nørre Longelse on the island of Langeland. The weapons and riding equipment in the grave suggest a man of wealth and high standing in society, a man who would probably also appreciate fine tableware from foreign countries. Only fragments remain of the cauldron but much of the cast enamelled rim-mount can be pieced together. The ornament, consisting of scrolls and stylized rhombic vegetable elements, suggests that the bowl was made in northern England at the beginning of the tenth century, some time before it was placed in the grave.[9]

Another example of an insular vessel is a silver hanging bowl with gold mounts dated to the eighth century. It was found at Lejre on Sjælland in 1850 as part of a drinking set deposited together with beads and other objects in the tenth century.[10] Apart from the bowl, the drinking set contained a second silver bowl, a small decorated globular cup, and four small shallow silver cups, probably all of local or Danish manufacture.

A damaged sword from Støvringgård in northern Jutland, dated to *c.* 900 or the tenth century, may have been a valued possession brought home from England. The broken remains of the hilt point to an Anglo-Saxon origin, and the sword shows signs of repair next to the guard.[11] Two similar swords with curved guards have been

---

Bücher, 1985), p. 51, map 4; and Egon Wamers, 'Insular Finds in Viking Age Scandinavia and the State Formation of Norway', in *Ireland and Scandinavia in the Early Viking Age*, ed. by Howard B. Clarke, Máire Ní Mhaonaigh, and Raghnall Ó Floinn (Dublin: Four Courts, 1998), pp. 37–72.

[8] See, for instance, Johannes Brøndsted, 'Danish Inhumation Graves of the Viking Age', *Acta Archaeologica*, 7 (1936), 81–228; Thorkild Ramskou, 'Viking Age Cremation Graves in Denmark: A Survey', *Acta Archaeologica*, 21 (1950 (1951)), 137–82; Else Roesdahl, *Danmarks Vikingetid* (Copenhagen: Gyldendal, 1980), pp. 247–48, n. 77 and n. 80; and *The Vikings in England*, ed. by Roesdahl and others.

[9] Brøndsted, 'Danish Inhumation Graves', pp. 173–76, plate X.

[10] Skovmand, 'De danske Skattefund fra Vikingetiden', pp. 115–17; and David Wilson, 'Irsk-britisk import i Lejre', *Nationalmuseets Arbejdsmark*, 1960, 36–37.

[11] Jan Petersen, *De norske vikingesverd: En typologisk-kronologisk studie over vikinge-tidens våben*, Videnskapsselskapets Skrifter, II. Historisk-Filosofisk Klasse, 1 (Christiania

recovered from the harbour of the trading settlement of Hedeby (Haithabu), and an Anglo-Saxon or Scandinavian origin has been suggested.[12]

Dress fittings such as a tenth-century strap-end found during excavations at Aggersborg in 1946–52 along with inter alia an Irish or Scottish enamelled button are also recorded in Denmark.[13] The strap-end is Anglo-Saxon in shape and size, and it may be compared with one from York, but the ornament is of Scandinavian inspiration. Another small item is a hooked-tag of silver alloy with a decorated circular attachment plate found in 1989 in a pithouse excavated at Endebjerg on Samsø.[14] A close parallel is known from Grave 348 at Birka in Sweden,[15] but both artefacts probably came from England where hooked-tags are most common. Similar versions made of silver with niello inlay from inter alia Norfolk and Kent are dated to the ninth century.[16]

Stray finds from the last decade or two include reused mounts for Anglo-Saxon books or fittings for Irish crosses and reliquaries uncovered on so-called metal detector sites or in excavated settlements, among them the wealthy settlement areas west of Lake Tissø and at Toftegård on Stevns, both on Sjælland.[17] Although still limited in number when compared with the insular metalwork in Norway, these recent additions indicate that the overall distribution pattern for insular imports in the early

---

[Oslo]: A. W. Brøggers, 1919), p. 115; *The Vikings in England*, ed. by Roesdahl and others, p. 177, no. K1.

[12] Alfred Geibig, 'Die Schwerter aus dem Hafen von Haithabu', *Berichte über die Ausgrabungen in Haithabu*, 33 (1999), 9–91 (p. 53).

[13] Else Roesdahl, 'Vikingernes Aggersborg', in *Aggersborg gennem 1000 år: Fra vikingeborg til slægtsgård*, ed. by F. Nørgård, E. Roesdahl, and R. Skovmand (Herning: Poul Kristensen, 1986), pp. 53–93 (p. 72, fig. 23).

[14] Christian Adamsen, 'Stavns Fjord i jernalder og vikingetid', in *Stavns Fjord: Et natur- og kuturhistorisk forskningsområde på Samsø*, ed. by Hanne H. Hansen and Bent Aaby (Copenhagen: Nationalmuseet, 1995), pp. 68–96 (p. 84, fig. 15).

[15] Holger Arbman, *Birka I: Die Gräber*, 2 vols (Stockholm: Almqvist & Wiksell/Kung. Vitterhets Historie och Antikvitets Akademien, 1940–43), I, 99.

[16] James Graham-Campbell, 'Some New and Neglected Finds of Ninth-Century Anglo-Saxon Ornamental Metalwork', *Medieval Archaeology*, 26 (1982), 144–51; and Leslie Webster, 'No. 196: Hooked-tag', 'No. 197: Three Hooked-tags', 'No. 198: Hooked-tag', 'No. 199: Hooked-tag', in *The Making of England: Anglo-Saxon Art and Culture AD 600–900* (London: British Museum, 1991), pp. 235–36.

[17] Lars Jørgensen and Lisbeth Pedersen, 'Vikinger ved Tissø: Gamle og nye fund fra et handels- og håndværkscenter', *Nationalmuseets Arbejdsmark*, 1996, 22–36; Svend Åge Tornbjerg, 'Toftegård: En fundrig gård fra sen middelalder og vikingetid', in *Centrala platser – centrala frågor: Samhällsstrukturen under järnåldern. En vänbok till Berta Stjernquist*, ed. by Lars Larsson and Birgitta Hårdh, Acta Archaeologica Lundensia Series in 8°, 28 (Stockholm: Almqvist & Wiksell, 1998), pp. 217–32; and Wamers, 'Insular Finds', pp. 48–51, distribution map, fig. 2.3 and n. 31.

centuries of the Viking Age in Denmark may yet change, particularly in light of the increased use of metal detectors.

Archaeological Evidence from the Eleventh Century

The archaeological evidence from the late Viking Age differs in quantity as well as in the range of artefact types from that of the earlier centuries. An increasing number of finds dated to the eleventh and early twelfth centuries may now be added to the information coming from stylistic analyses, numismatic research, and historical studies of, for instance, the Anglo-Saxon influence on the early Christian church in Denmark.[18] Some of the finds came to light more than a century ago, but most have appeared within the last decades mainly as a result of metal detecting.

Among the well-known, older finds are swords and riding equipment. An iron sword with silver inlay (fig. 1), dated to *c.* 1000, is kept at Forhistorisk Museum Moesgård. It formed part of the early collections of the museum established in Århus in 1861, and the provenance is unknown. However, the sword may well have been found in Denmark. The curved guards are English in type but the decoration is in the Ringerike style, and the sword is interpreted as an Anglo-Scandinavian weapon made either in Scandinavia under English influence or, as suggested by Signe Horn Fuglesang, in England under Scandinavian influence.[19]

Two other swords of approximately the same date come from Skåne, now in Sweden but once part of Denmark. They are related to Petersen's 'Scandinavian type Z' but appear far more elaborately decorated than most of the swords of this type.[20] One is the magnificent iron sword from Dybäck, Östra Vemmenhög parish in southern Skåne.[21] The grip was bound with gold wire which still survives but without the

---

[18] See, for instance, David Wilson, *Anglo-Saxon Art from the Seventh Century to the Norman Conquest* (London: Thames & Hudson, 1984); Signe Horn Fuglesang, 'The Relationship between Scandinavian and English Art from the Late Eighth to the Mid-Twelfth Century', in *Sources of Anglo-Saxon Culture*, ed. by Paul E. Szarmach and Virginia Darrow Oggins (Kalamazoo: Medieval Institute Publications, 1986), pp. 203–41; and Ellen Jørgensen, *Fremmed Indflydelse under den danske Kirkes tidligste Udvikling*, Det Kongelige Danske Videnskabernes Selskabs skrifter, 7. Række, Historisk og Filosofisk Afdeling, 1: 2 (Copenhagen: Bianco Luno, 1908).

[19] Signe Horn Fuglesang, *Some Aspects of the Ringerike Style: A Phase of 11th Century Scandinavian Art*, Medieval Scandinavia Supplements, 1 (Odense: Odense University Press, 1980), p. 42.

[20] Petersen, *De norske vikingesverd*, pp. 175–77.

[21] Monica Rydbeck, 'Skånska praktsvärd från vikingatiden', *Meddelanden från Lunds Universitets Historiska Museum*, 1932, pp. 38–47; and Märta Strömberg, *Untersuchungen zur jüngeren Eisenzeit in Schonen*, Acta Archaeologica Lundensia, Series in 4°, 4, 2 vols (Bonn: Rudolf Habelt, 1961), II, 66–67.

Figure 1. Iron sword with silver inlay, unknown provenance probably Denmark. Forhistorisk Museum Moesgård, old inv. no. 224, no scale. Photo: Forhistorisk Museum Moesgård.

inner support, and the silver-gilt guards are decorated with birds and snakes in high relief (fig. 2). The style of the decoration is mainly Anglo-Saxon in character with close parallels within the Winchester style, whereas the cast silver scabbard mount is a foreign element which is Scandinavian in origin. A similar mount of copper alloy thought to be of local origin was found in the stream bed running through Hedeby around 1936.[22]

The second sword, of which only a silver-gilt sword pommel and upper guard decorated with niello survive, comes from Vrångabäck, Sövde parish.[23] The composition of the ornament as well as the birds and snakes on the pommel are almost identical to those on the upper guard of the Dybäck sword. The fragments were uncovered in 1879 at the edge of a burial mound and may represent an accidental loss or a small hoard, possibly even the remains of a burial.

As with the silver-inlaid sword above, it has not been determined whether the two valuable swords from Skåne were made in southern Scandinavia under strong English influence, perhaps by a craftsman trained in England, or in England and brought to Scandinavia.[24] However, they leave no doubt that Anglo-Saxon artistic trends were present in Scandinavia, and the Dybäck sword shows that elements of different origin could be combined.

A pair of heavy stirrups and an ornate set of gilt copper-alloy strap-plates and bridle mounts

---

[22] Alfred Geibig, 'Zur Formenvielfalt der Schwerter und Schwertfragmente von Haitabu', *Offa*, 46 (1989 (1990)), 223–67 (p. 250).

[23] Strömberg, *Untersuchungen zur jüngeren Eisenzeit in Schonen*, II, 21–22, table 65.1.

[24] See Strömberg, *Untersuchungen zur jüngeren Eisenzeit in Schonen*, I, 138–40; James Graham-Campbell, *Viking Artefacts: A Select Catalogue* (London: British Museum, 1980), pp. 70–71, no. 250; and Leslie Webster, 'No. 96 Sword', in *The Golden Age of Anglo-Saxon Art 966–1066*, ed. by Janet Backhouse, D. H. Turner, and Leslie Webster (London: British Museum, 1984), pp. 103–04.

dated to the early eleventh century are another example of this complex interaction (fig. 3). The stirrups and fittings were recovered in 1851 along with a horse-bit and an axehead of iron (now lost) from a burial mound at Velds in northern Jutland.[25] The fronts of the two strap-plates depict incised bird and floral ornaments, and the bridle mounts are decorated with linear patterns and animal heads in a style pointing to southern England.

The whole set of riding gear from Velds has been regarded as an import from England, the basic argument being that it differs from most of the equipment in the Danish equestrian burials.[26] However, there are a few related finds from Scandinavia which support another interpretation. Stirrup-plates of this type do not seem to occur in England despite the many examples of decorated Late Saxon strap-mounts made of cast copper alloy.[27] However, a few Swedish finds contain large rectangular strap-plates although these are made of iron and not copper alloy. A pair of iron plates ending in a cruciform top ornament were found in a cremation burial uncovered at Raglunda in Västmanland, Sweden.[28] The fronts of the two plates appear to have been decorated with interlace, and the associated bridle mounts show definite traces of thin silver sheet with a stamped interlace pattern similar to that on other Scandinavian harness sets. Another example is a short stirrup with an iron plate from a cremation burial excavated at Åsta, Björskog parish, also in

Figure 2. Sword with silver-gilt guards and pommel, Dybäck in Skåne, Sweden. Statens historiska Museum Stockholm inv. no. 4515, no scale. Photo: Antikvarisk-Topografiska Arkivet, Stockholm.

---

[25] Brøndsted, 'Danish Inhumation Graves', pp. 102–04.

[26] See Holger Arbman, 'Vikingatidsgravar vid Ulunda vad', *Upplands Fornminnesförenings Tidskrift*, 45 (1935–37 (1937)), 261–75 (pp. 268–80).

[27] David Williams, *Late Saxon Stirrup-Strap Mounts: A Classification and Catalogue*, CBA Research Report, 111 (York: Council for British Archaeology, 1997).

[28] Gunnar Westin, 'En västmanländsk ryttargrav', *Fornvännen*, 36 (1941), 84–101; see also Brøndsted, 'Danish Inhumation Graves', pp. 162–64, figs 71–73.

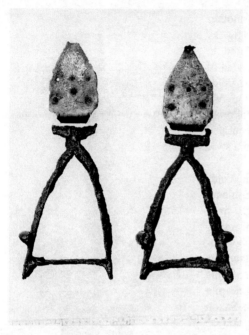

Figure 3. Stirrups and strap-mounts, Velds, Denmark. National Museum of Denmark inv. no. 11519, no scale. Photo: National Museum, Copenhagen.

Västmanland.[29] The objects from Raglunda indicate a date between the second half of the tenth century and the first half of the eleventh century, whereas the Åsta burial is from the early eleventh century.

The stirrup-irons from Velds appear Scandinavian rather than Anglo-Saxon in type.[30] Not only the shape of the stirrup-irons, but also the ornamental details such as the lead-alloy bosses decorated with gilt copper alloy next to the tread-plates, may be found on other Scandinavian stirrups, among them a pair from Loose in Schleswig, Germany, fitted with lead-alloy bosses decorated with silver.[31]

Leslie Webster has described the ornament on the strap-plates from Velds as an amalgam of Late Saxon acanthus and bird decoration and Scandinavian Ringerike tendrils, probably made in an Anglo-Scandinavian milieu.[32] She suggests that the strap-plates may have been made in southern England for a Scandinavian follower of King Cnut, or that a set of Anglo-Saxon motifs were adapted by a Danish craftsman for the Scandinavian-type stirrups. In either case, the stirrups and strap-mounts testify to the close contacts between England and Scandinavia in the early

[29] Henry Simonsson, 'Ett senvikingatida gravfält från Västmanland', *Fornvännen*, 64 (1964), 69–89.

[30] Anne Pedersen, 'Weapons and Riding Gear in Burials: Evidence of Military and Social Rank in Tenth Century Denmark', in *Military Aspects of Scandinavian Society in a European Perspective, AD 1–1300: Papers from an International Research Seminar at the Danish National Museum, Copenhagen, 2–4 May 1996*, ed. by Anne Nørgård Jørensen and Birthe L. Clausen (Copenhagen: National Museum, 1997), pp. 123–35; and Anne Pedersen, 'Riding Gear from Late Viking-Age Denmark', *Journal of Danish Archaeology*, 13 (1996–97 (1999)), 133–60.

[31] Michael Müller-Wille, 'Krieger und Reiter im Spiegel früh- und hochmittelalterlicher Funde Schleswig-Holsteins', *Offa*, 34 (1977), 40–74 (p. 70, Abbildung 8.6–7).

[32] Leslie Webster, 'No. 98. Stirrup Plates', in *The Golden Age of Anglo-Saxon Art*, ed. by Backhouse, Turner, and Webster, p. 104.

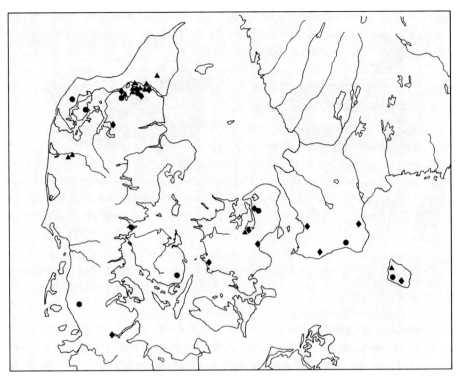

Figure 4. Distribution of copper-alloy cheekpieces (dots),
stirrup strap-mounts (diamonds), and stirrup terminals (triangles)
in late Viking Age/early medieval Denmark. Map: A. Pedersen.

eleventh century and not least the possibility of cultural influence as reflected in ornaments and objects passing both ways across the North Sea.

Recent finds of copper-alloy fittings for horse harnesses strengthen this view (fig. 4). Complete iron horse-bits fitted with copper-alloy cheekpieces in the Ringer-ike style are known from Swedish and Norwegian burials, and broken examples of the decorative cheekpieces have come to light in Scandinavia as well as in England (fig. 5).[33] Related to these cheekpieces are copper-alloy strap-links with characteristic

---

[33] See James Graham-Campbell, 'Anglo-Scandinavian Equestrian Equipment in Eleventh-Century England', *Anglo-Norman Studies*, 14 (1992), 77–89; and Pedersen 'Riding Gear from Late Viking-Age Denmark'.

Copper-alloy cheekpieces in Denmark, Schleswig, and Skåne (Status 1999, cf. fig. 4): Unknown provenance, Denmark (The National Museum of Denmark inv. no. D46); Græse, Sjælland (Museet Færgegaarden inv. no. 41/91); Store Myregård, Nylarsker, Bornholm (Bornholms Museum inv. no. 1478x7); Uhrenholtgård, Gudme, Fyn (Odense Bys Museer inv. no. 7529x15); Tinggård, Sjørring, Jutland (Museet for Thy og Vester Hanherred inv. no. 3471x746);

Figure 5. Cheekpieces of copper alloy from Dueholm Mark, Mors (left), and
Bøgeskov Strand, eastern Jutland (right). National Museum of Denmark inv. nos
C23648 and D473/1994; scale 1:2. Photos: National Museum, Copenhagen.

rhombic eyes for the harness straps. Most are fairly simple versions with two or four
eyes, but exceptions do occur. One such link decorated with an animal figure was
excavated in Lund in a context dated to the first half of the eleventh century, and an
almost identical mount with a slightly more elaborate mane was recently found at
Saxilby in Lincolnshire (fig. 6).[34]

Roughly contemporary are cast copper-alloy stirrups with fixed decorative strap-
plates and Late Saxon stirrup-strap mounts of which more than five hundred from
England belonging to different types have recently been published by David
Williams.[35] Stirrup-strap mounts were not a recognized type in Denmark, but now at
least fourteen have been recorded from Danish sites including sites in Skåne and
Schleswig (fig. 7).[36] Not all of the types distinguished by David Williams are

Dueholm Mark, Nykøbing, Mors (The National Museum of Denmark inv. no. C23648);
Nørholm, Jutland (The National Museum of Denmark inv. no. C32941); Sønderholm, Jutland
(The National Museum of Denmark inv. no. D418/1990); Sebbersund, Sebber, Jutland (The
National Museum of Denmark inv. no. C31559); Bøgeskov Strand, Vejlby, Jutland (The National Museum of Denmark inv. no. D473/1994); Leck, Schleswig (Archäologisches Landesmuseum der Christian-Albrechts-Universität Schleswig inv. no. K.S. 14658 a–c); Gärarp
church ruin, Tosterup, Skåne (Lunds Universitets Historiska Museum inv. no. 28674).

[34] Find presented at the conference 'Scandinavians and Europe 800–1350: Contact, Conflict and Coexistence', The University of Hull, 1999, and shown here with the kind permission
of Kevin Leahy, Keeper of Archaeology, North Lincolnshire Museum, Scunthorpe.

[35] Williams, *Late Saxon Stirrup-Strap Mounts*.

[36] Stirrup strap-mounts in Denmark, Schleswig, and Skåne (Status 1999, cf. fig. 4): Græse,
Sjælland (The National Museum of Denmark inv. no. C32653); Ellehalen/Gl. Køgegård,
Køge, Sjælland (The National Museum of Denmark inv. no. D348/1994); Flengemarken, Ros-
kilde, Sjælland (The National Museum of Denmark inv. no. C30902); Langetofte, Boeslunde,
Sjælland (The National Museum of Denmark inv. no. C32676); Hjulmagergård, Åker,

present, but his main types have been identified as well as one that at present appears
to be a special Danish type. This latter
mount, recorded in three almost identical
examples from Hedeby in Schleswig,
Gedsted in Jutland, and Lund in Skåne
(fig. 7d), depicts a four-legged animal with
a raised front paw and a curved tail. The
jaws are open and the head seen in profile
is dominated by a large round eye. Stylistically these animal mounts belong to the
Ringerike style, and the one found in Lund
comes from a pit excavated in cultural deposits with dendrochronological dates of
1060–70.[37] This date is supported by the
mount from Västra Klagstorp in Skåne
(fig. 7a) which resembles the fixed strap-
plates of the typologically late copper-alloy
stirrups with semicircular hoops that are
dated to the eleventh century. The few
English mounts associated with datable
material also point to a date after *c.* 1000.[38]

Figure 6. Strap-links from Lund in
Skåne, Sweden (above), and Saxilby in
Lincolnshire, England (below). Kulturen
Lund inv. no. 66166:711; scale 1:2.
Photos: Lunds Universitets Historiska
Museum, North Lincolnshire Museum.

Yet another group of stirrup mounts has recently been identified in England; they
are small copper-alloy terminals shaped as animal heads in the Ringerike/Urnes style
and thus linked to the eleventh and possibly early twelfth centuries. Their hollow
backs often contain traces of the lead solder that secured the terminals at the bottom
of the two sides of an iron stirrup. This interpretation is supported by a triangular
stirrup with mounts still in place found at Chalgrove in Oxfordshire as well as by a
few stirrups showing curved sides with attached stylized animal heads next to the

---

Bornholm (The National Museum of Denmark inv. no. D119/1997); Postgården, Sønder-
Tranders, Jutland (The National Museum of Denmark inv. no. C33414); Bejsebakken, Hasseris, Jutland (Ålborg historiske Museum 961); Sønderholm, Jutland (The National Museum
of Denmark inv. no. D4929); Sebbersund, Sebber, Jutland (Ålborg historiske Museum
2863x4210); Gedsted, Jutland (The National Museum of Denmark inv. no. 7032); Haithabu,
Schleswig (Archäologisches Landesmuseum der Christian-Albrechts-Universität Schleswig
inv. no. LMS Hb 1931); Hjälmaröd 9:30, Vitaby, Skåne (Statens Historiska Museum Stockholm); Västra Klagstorp 7, Skåne (Private ownership); Lund, Skåne (Kulturen Lund inv. no.
71.075:689). See also Pedersen 'Riding Gear from Late Viking-Age Denmark'.

[37] Anders W. Mårtensson, 'Några söljor och beslag i Lund från sen vikingatid', *Kulturen*,
1982, 160–68.

[38] Williams, *Late Saxon Stirrup-Strap Mounts*, p. 8.

Figure 7. Danish stirrup-strap mounts from a. Västra Klagstorp, Skåne (above left; Privately owned); b. Ellehalen/Gl. Køgegård, Sjælland (above right; National Museum of Denmark inv. no. D348/1994); c. Flengemarken near Roskilde, Sjælland (below left; National Museum of Denmark inv. no. C30902); d. Lund, Skåne (below right; Kulturen Lund inv. no. 71.075:689); scale 1:1. Photos: National Museum, Copenhagen, and Lunds Universitets Historiska Museum.

Figure 8. Stirrup terminals from a. Skelagervej (left), and b–c. Nørholm, northern Jutland (center and right). National Museum of Denmark inv. nos D37/1987, D48/1998, D282/1998; side view, scale 1:1. Photos: National Museum, Copenhagen.

tread-plate.[39] A few years ago it became evident that identical terminals were present in Denmark (fig. 8), and to date fourteen have been recorded.[40] Like the other groups of copper-alloy fittings most of the stirrup terminals have been found in northern Jutland, a distribution that may, however, in part reflect the intensive use of metal detectors in this area.

The copper-alloy strap mounts and terminals are only few in number when compared with the English finds. On the other hand only one related copper-alloy stirrup is known from England against six from the medieval Danish kingdom and a further three finds from Sweden (including one matched pair) and three from Iceland.[41] The finds taken as a whole suggest the possibility of these horse trappings being manufactured on both sides of the North Sea.

[39] David Williams, *Stirrup Terminals*, Finds Research Group 700–1700, Datasheet, 24 (Stoke-on-Trent: The Finds Research Group, 1998); Strömberg, *Untersuchungen zur jüngeren Eisenzeit in Schonen*, I, 145, fig. 18; and Strömberg, *Untersuchungen zur jüngeren Eisenzeit in Schonen*, II, plate 67.1.

[40] Stirrup terminals in Denmark (Status 1999, cf. fig. 4): Flengemarken, Roskilde, Sjælland (The National Museum of Denmark inv. no. C30904); Baggård, Klemensker, Bornholm (The National Museum of Denmark inv. no. C31786); Stentinget, Hellevad, Jutland (The National Museum of Denmark inv. no. C31438 STT91); Gjøl mark, Jutland (The National Museum of Denmark inv. no. D321/1993); Skelagervej, Hasseris, Jutland (The National Museum of Denmark inv. no. D37/1987); Nørholm, Jutland (The National Museum of Denmark inv. nos D514/1993, D48/1998, D282/1998); North of Lindholm Høje, Nørresundby, Jutland (The National Museum of Denmark inv. no. D298/1989); Sebbersund, Sebber, Jutland (Ålborg historiske Museum 2863x01712); Nørregård, Nørre Felding, Jutland (The National Museum of Denmark inv. no. D1179/1995); Nørre Felding kirke, Jutland (The National Museum of Denmark inv. no. D53/1997). See also Pedersen 'Riding Gear from Late Viking-Age Denmark'.

[41] Pedersen 'Riding Gear from Late Viking-Age Denmark', with references.

Figure 9. Two types of cloisonné enamel brooches from a. Toftegård Sydøst on Fyn (left), and b. Bejsebakken near Ålborg in northern Jutland (right). National Museum of Denmark inv. nos D19/1999 and C30557; scale 2:1. Photos: National Museum, Copenhagen.

If we turn to personal ornaments, a group of small circular enamel brooches may be mentioned. They consist of a cloisonné enamel centrepiece fastened to a base-plate of copper (fig. 9). The face, edges, and back of the brooches are often gilded, and the use of translucent enamel together with copper is a characteristic feature. Translucent enamel depends on the effect of light reflecting through it. It is commonly used on a gold or silver base, but not on copper as an oxide layer tends to form at the interface between the glass and the copper enamel base, thus spoiling the effect. The designs include flower, star, and cross motifs in different colours set against an often translucent dark blue background.[42]

These brooches are known from East Anglia and south-eastern England, and about twenty have been recorded from Denmark and Skåne as well as two from the island of Öland. However, in spite of the relation of the ornament to Ottonian brooch types, none has as yet been recorded in the Ottonian area, for which reason they have been termed *angelsächsisch-südskandinavische Zellenemailfibeln* by Hans-Jörg Frick.[43]

---

[42] David Buckton, 'Late 10th- and 11th-Century *cloisonné* Brooches', *Medieval Archaeology*, 30 (1986), 8–18. My thanks are due to Fritze Lindahl, former curator at the National Museum of Denmark, who has kindly supplied information from her research on the cloisonné brooches.

[43] Hans-Jörg Frick, 'Karolingisch-ottonische Scheibenfibeln des nördlichen Formen-kreises', *Offa*, 49/50 (1992–93 (1993)), 243–463. Cloisonné enamel brooches in Denmark and Skåne (Status 1999, cf. fig. 4): Jutland (The National Museum of Denmark inv. no. D1502); Veddelev, Himmelev, Sjælland (The National Museum of Denmark inv. no. D159/1982); Roskilde, Sjælland (Roskilde Museum inv. no. 1351x4001); Stenagergård, Solrød, Sjælland (The National Museum of Denmark inv. no. C32305); Vindinge, Sjælland (The National Museum of Denmark inv. no. D141/1994); Skibelund, Hoby, Lolland (The National Museum of Denmark inv. no. D147/1999); Viby, Fyn (The National Museum of Denmark inv. no. D1216/1983); Odense, Fyn (Odense Bys Museer inv. no. 1305-1970); Toftegård Sydøst, Fyn

All of the Danish brooches are single finds, coming mainly from settlements, for instance Roskilde and sites close to the town of Odense, and the wealthy sites of Sebbersund and Bejsebakken on the Limfjord in northern Jutland (fig. 10).

Just as was the case with the copper-alloy harness fittings, the enamel brooches have rarely been found in datable contexts. A probable background for the brooches may be sought in Byzantine and Ottonian jewellery and enamels of the last third of the tenth century and the first half of the eleventh century, and the limited archaeological evidence points to an approximate dating in the eleventh and early twelfth centuries.[44] A date around 1100 has been suggested for the Swedish finds, and one brooch from Löddeköpinge in Skåne was found in cultural deposits dated to *c.* 1100 or the early twelfth century. Another brooch came to light at the bottom of a well during excavations in Skomagerstræde in Odense in 1971. Dendrochronological analysis indicates that the well had been in use for a few years around 1120; the second brooch, from north-eastern Fyn, is of approximately the same date. Finally, a brooch from Billingsgate in London is from a site with no documented activity until the second half of the tenth century. The few dates emphasize one of the basic problems connected with many of the finds recorded in the last ten to fifteen years. Metal detecting has lead to a great increase in the number of artefacts and has often revealed new types, but without well-dated parallels or secured archaeological contexts the dating of single objects is often difficult.

Enamel work and gilding require specialist knowledge. The brooches from Sebbersund were recovered in an area with extensive evidence of metalworking, but there were no clear signs of work involving enamel, and it is uncertain whether glassworking in Denmark included enamel. Attempts at enamel work may have been made, for instance, at Lund,[45] but the early cloisonné brooches are generally all

---

(The National Museum of Denmark inv. no. D19/1999); Sønder Tranders, Jutland (The National Museum of Denmark inv. no. D291/1989); Bejsebakken, Jutland (The National Museum of Denmark inv. no. C30557); Nibe, Jutland (The National Museum of Denmark inv. no. D230/1991); Nørholm, Jutland (The National Museum of Denmark inv. no. D184/1999); Sebbersund, Jutland (Ålborg historiske Museum inv. no. 2863x120 and The National Museum of Denmark inv. no. D31390); Glemminge, Skåne (Statens Historiska Museum inv. no. 2109); Håslöv, Skåne (Statens Historiska Museum inv. no. 3217:C.5); Helsingborg, Skåne (Statens Historiska Museum inv. no. 14214); Löddeköpinge, Skåne (Lunds Universitets Historiska Museum); Lund, Skåne (Lunds Universitets Historiska Museum inv. no. 12814); Trelleborg, Skåne (Lunds Universitets Historiska Museum inv. no. 3798). The list is based on Frick and research by Fritze Lindahl with the later additions. After completion of the manuscript a similar brooch from Flessenow in Germany was published; see, *Europas Mitte um 1000*, ed. by Alfried Wieczorek and Hans-Martin Hinz (Stuttgart: Theiss, 2000), p. 171.

[44] Buckton, 'Late 10th- and 11th-Century *cloisonné* Brooches', pp. 15–16 with references; David Buckton, 'Further Examples of Late 10th- and 11th-Century *cloisonné* Enamel Brooches', *Medieval Archaeology*, 33 (1989), 153–55 (p. 154).

[45] Maria Cinthio, 'Guldsmed i Lund', in *Beretning fra attende tværfaglige Vikingesymposium*, ed. by Gillian Fellows-Jensen and Niels Lund (Højbjerg: Hikuin, 1999), pp. 35–52 (pp. 42–43).

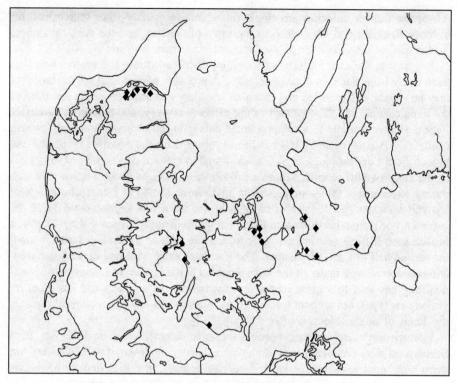

Figure 10. Distribution of cloisonné enamel brooches
in late Viking Age/early medieval Denmark. Map: A. Pedersen.

considered to be imported, like the roughly contemporary small *Grubenemail*
brooches which originated in Germany.

Hooked-tags of copper alloy represent a much simpler type of functional dress
ornament, but again one with links to England. The copper-alloy tags dated to the
eleventh century are fairly simple when compared with the silver versions mentioned
above. They were made of sheet metal cut into a circular plate with a triangular point
that was bent over into a hook. The plate usually has holes for fastening and a
decoration of dot-circle ornaments. These hooked-tags are known from, for instance,
Thetford and Norwich in East Anglia and now also from early medieval Denmark.
Excavations at Lund in Skåne and at Lejre on Sjælland have revealed almost identical tags, and it is worth noting that the finds from Lund include sheet metal as well
as cut, but unfinished, tags (fig. 11) which appear to be concentrated on a single site
in the town. This indicates the presence of a workshop or a single craftsman possibly
working for a limited group of customers used to wearing hooked-tags.[46]

---

[46] Information from Maria Cinthio, Lund, who is currently working on material from the
Lund excavations. See Cinthio, 'Guldsmed i Lund', p. 43.

A pen-case lid made of maplewood, an oft-cited find from the area of Färgaren 22 in Lund, bears witness to contact of a different kind in the form of a personal name (fig. 12). The curved lid is elaborately carved, and at one end it terminates in a lion's head gripping an un-identified animal in its jaws. Stylistically the ornament is related to the Winchester style and may have been made in south-eastern England. The flat underside of the lid has a recessed area to hold a layer of wax and a damaged in-

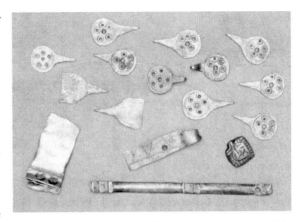

Figure 11. Hooked-tags and other objects produced in the same workshop in Lund, Skåne. Kulturen Lund inv. no. 70.361:1248 and others; no scale. Photo: L. Westrup, Kulturen Lund.

scription reading LEOFWINE MY...ER... It is interpreted as 'Leofwine moneyer', and the lid has been associated with a moneyer named Leofwin who worked first in Lincoln then in Lund during the reign of Cnut the Great and Svein Estridsson.[47] More cautious interpretations suggest it to be linked with one of the English church-men coming to Scandinavia or see it as a souvenir brought back from England.[48]

Two bone combs supply evidence of a similar nature, one from Lund bearing the name Eadrinc **(iatrink)** and one from Århus with the name Hægwin **(hik:uin)** (fig. 13).[49] The latter comb was saved from fire in a pithouse by some pieces of cloth, and the finely incised runes reading from the end towards the middle of the comb indicate a date not much later than *c.* 1000. The Lund comb is dated to the first half of the eleventh century at the latest. Both combs could have been made in Denmark, and the names may suggest English people living in Denmark or possibly English influence on Danish name giving.

---

[47] Maria Cinthio, 'Myntverk och myntare i Lund', in *Kulturen 1990: Lund 1000 års krönika*, 1990, 48–53 (p. 49).

[48] Ragnar Blomqvist and Anders W. Mårtensson, *Thulegrävningen 1961: En berättelse om vad grävningarna för Thulehuset i Lund avslöjade*, Archaeologica Lundensia Investigationes de Antiqvitatibus Urbis Lundae, 2 (Lund: Kulturhistoriska Museet), pp. 213–16; and Graham-Campbell, *Viking Artefacts*, p. 91, no. 317.

[49] H. Hellmuth Andersen, P. J. Crabb, and H. J. Madsen, *Århus Søndervold: En byarkæolo-gisk undersøgelse*, Jysk Arkæologisk Selskabs Skrifter, 9 (Copenhagen: Jysk Arkæologisk Selskab, 1971), p. 150; Moltke, *Runes and their Origin*, pp. 359, 361, 373, 461, 466.

Figure 12. Decorated pen-case lid from Lund, Skåne. Kulturen Lund inv. no.
53.436:1125; length 33 cm. Photo: B. Centervall, Lund.

Another example of bone working, although without a name, is a triangular carved
object found in 1998 at Gasværksgrunden in Odense on Fyn (fig. 14).[50] The function
of the carving is uncertain, but it may be the top of an ornamental pin or writing implement, the stem of which has broken off. The dragon-like animal and the plaited
decoration suggest a date in the early twelfth century, and although the origin of the
carving has not been determined, parallels to both elements in the decoration exist in
carvings from the British Isles.[51] Odense is first mentioned as the seat of a bishop
under the archbishopric of Hamburg-Bremen in a charter issued in 988 by Emperor
Otto III, but evidence of important contacts with England may be found in ecclesiastical history of the late eleventh century. King Knut II (1080–86, son of Svein
Estridsson), who made a final attempt to win back the rule of England, was killed in
1086 in St Alban's Church in Odense, probably a royal church with relics of the English saints Alban and Oswald. The first monastery in Odense dedicated to St Knut
was established in the late eleventh century by monks sent out from the Benedictine
monastery at Evesham.[52] The bone carving may belong in this context, but along
with the enamel brooch from Odense it may also reflect contact at a secular level.

---

[50] Anne Pedersen, 'Danefæ: Middelalder og Renæssance', *Arkæologiske Udgravninger i
Danmark*, 1998 (1999), 270–83 (pp. 272–78).

[51] See, for instance, *English Romanesque Art 1066–1200*, ed. by George Zarnecki, Janet
Holt, and Tristram Holland (London: Weidenfeld & Nicolson, 1984), p. 166, no. 124.

[52] Per Kristian Madsen, 'De gejstlige institutioner i og ved Odense', in *Middelalderbyen
Odense*, ed. by A. S. Christensen, Projekt Middelalderbyen, 5 (Viby: Centrum, 1988), pp. 97–
118, with references; see also Anne Riising and Birgitte Bøggild Johannsen, 'S. Knuds Kirke.
Odense Domkirke: Træk af domkirkens historie', in *S. Knuds Kirke Odense Domkirke*, ed. by
Birgitte Bøggild Johannsen and Hugo Johannsen, vol. I.1, Danmarks Kirker, 9 (Herning: Poul
Kristensen, 1990), pp. 75–86 (pp. 75–77); and Birgitte Bøggild Johannsen and Hugo
Johannsen, *Odense Domkirke. S. Knud. Inventar*, vol. II.5–7, Danmarks Kirker, 9 (Herning:
Poul Kristensen, 1995), p. 426.

Figure 13 (above). Runic inscription on the bone comb from Århus Søndervold, Jylland. Forhistorisk Museum Moesgård inv. no. 1393/EQN; no scale. Photo: Forhistorisk Museum Moesgård.

Figure 14 (right). Bone object of uncertain function, Gasværksgrunden in Odense, Fyn. National Museum of Denmark inv. no. D73/1998; length 9.5 cm. Photo: National Museum, Copenhagen.

Apart from the weapons and ornaments the archaeological evidence from Denmark for contact with England in the eleventh century includes pottery. Four shards of non-local unglazed pottery from the earliest phase of settlement (the eleventh century) at Viborg Søndersø in Jutland have been determined as probable Torksey-ware, thus indicating contact between the east coast of England and northern Jutland,[53] and shards of early lead-glazed pottery from the late tenth or early eleventh century have been found at Lund in Skåne and at Lejre on Sjælland.[54]

In Lund the lead-glazed pottery is tied to the earliest occupation phases of the town. The first few shards were excavated in 1961 on the Thule site, where they caused some surprise as no early medieval glazed pottery had previously been found in Lund or in

---

[53] Jesper Hjermind, 'Keramik', in *Viborg Søndersø 1000–1300: Byarkæologiske undersøgelser 1981 og 1984–85*, ed. by J. Hjermind, M. Iversen, and H. Krongaard Kristensen, Jysk Arkæologisk Selskabs Skrifter, 34 (Århus: Aarhus Universitetsforlag, 1998), pp. 93–121 (pp. 113–14).

[54] Anders W. Mårtensson, 'Tidigmedeltida glaserad keramik', in *Uppgrävt förflutet för PK-banken i Lund: En investering i arkeologi*, ed. by Anders W. Mårtensson, Archaeologica Lundensia investigationes de Antiqvitatibus Urbis Lundae, 7 (Lund: Kulturhistoriska Museet i Lund, 1976), pp. 266–68; and Tom Christensen and others, 'Early Glazed Ware from Medieval Denmark', *Medieval Ceramics*, 18 (1994), 67–76.

fact anywhere else in Scandinavia. Further finds appeared, and during the large-scale excavations in 1974 to 1975 on the so-called PK-Bank site a large number of glazed shards were recovered from cultural deposits sealed by a large landslide and dated by dendrochronology to before 1050.[55] The early glazed shards from Lund appear oxidized with a thin external lead glaze ranging from yellowish brown to dark green in colour (fig. 15), and two main types were identified: a handled and spouted pitcher and a stratigraphically slightly later small bowl type. Due to the small quantities and the quality of these early medieval glazed wares compared to the local earthenware it was assumed that they were imported, most likely from England.[56]

More shards were found in Lund in 1980 and again in 1992–93 in the western part of the town, and in 1992 the first finds of glazed pottery very similar to those from Lund were excavated at Lejre on Sjælland. About thirty shards were found in two pits, a sunken-floored building (*grubehus XIV*), and an occupation layer, all within a limited area and in well-stratified contexts associated with archaeological material dated to the beginning of the eleventh century.[57]

Recent petrological analysis of a sample of the shards from Lejre and Lund indicates that the origin of the pottery (the clay) should be sought in the Baltic rather than in western Europe. However, the shards are wheel-thrown and glazed, thus showing a marked technical difference from the local handmade, black-fired earthenware, and a comparison of the technical features and the vessel types with western European wares suggests that the early glazed pottery was produced by an immigrant potter from England, most probably from Stamford where a similar range of vessel forms is present.[58]

A final group of objects that deserve mention here are the Danish coins of the eleventh century. Before the reign of Cnut the Great minting in Denmark was limited. It is possible, though much debated, that the first coins (*sceattas*) were minted in Ribe in the eighth century, and coins based on Carolingian prototypes were issued in the ninth and tenth centuries but apparently not on a continuous basis or on a very extensive scale.[59] Instead, coins from many different areas were in use. Towards the end of the tenth century this picture was beginning to change, and contact with England played a significant role in the early phases of minting in Lund and at other Danish sites.

---

[55] Mårtensson, 'Tidigmedeltida glaserad keramik'; and Claes Wahlöö, 'Lager bild och fasindelning', in *Uppgrävt förflutet för PK-banken i Lund*, ed. by Mårtensson, pp. 15–20.

[56] Mårtensson, 'Tidigmedeltida glaserad keramik', p. 268.

[57] Christensen and others, 'Early Glazed Ware from Medieval Denmark', p. 67.

[58] Christensen and others, 'Early Glazed Ware from Medieval Denmark', p. 75.

[59] See, for instance, Brita Malmer, *Nordiska mynt före år 1000*, Acta Archaeologica Lundensia, Series in 80, 4 (Bonn: Rudolf Habelt, 1966); and D. M. Metcalf, 'Viking Numismatics 2: Coinage in the Northern Lands in Merovingian and Carolingian Times', *The Numismatic Chronicle*, 156 (1996), 399–428.

Figure 15. Early lead-glazed pottery, mainly from the PK-Bank site, Lund. Kulturen Lund inv. no. 66.166 and others; no scale. Photo: L. Westrup, Kulturen Lund.

Many of the early coins were copies of foreign issues, and copies of English prototypes are sometimes found in late Viking Age hoards. Analysis of die-linked coins has demonstrated that not only were copies made but original English dies were taken to Denmark to be used for striking coins and as patterns for local copies.[60] Many of these dies were used in the period *c.* 991 to 1003, and the transfer of dies apparently took place a decade before the conquest of England by Svein Forkbeard in 1013. English dies were occasionally transferred to Denmark in the following decades but not in the same numbers as in this early period.

Svein Forkbeard was the first Danish king to issue coins in his own name *c.* 995, possibly in Lund.[61] The coins bear a portrait and the inscription ZAEN REX AD DENER on the obverse and a cross on the reverse surrounded by the name of the moneyer Godwine, a name common in England but also occurring on contemporary Norwegian and Swedish coins. The coin type is rare and the inscription not always legible on all variants; however, the coins are clearly based on the CRUX type of King Æthelred II of England.

During the reign of Cnut the Great (1018–35) minting spread throughout the country with many mints employing English moneyers, and influence from contemporary English coinage is evident in the coins struck for the king in Denmark.[62] Inscriptions referring to the moneyer are one of the common features, and many Anglo-Saxon names occur on Cnut's Danish coins. Some of the names may derive from reused Anglo-Saxon dies or represent copied inscriptions of Anglo-Saxon coins. Others, however, appear to be the names of Anglo-Saxon moneyers employed in Denmark. Lund was the most important mint in the early eleventh century, and more than twenty moneyers, many of whom had apparently also struck coins in England for Cnut or his predecessor Æthelred II, are known to have worked here during the king's reign or after his death. An Old English origin can be determined for some moneyers' names, and although others are Scandinavian they may represent descendents of Scandinavians returning to Denmark rather than native-born Danes. Fewer English names are known from other Danish mints but they are present, for instance, at Roskilde.

The Anglo-Saxon element in the Danish coinage is especially clear in the early part of the eleventh century, when almost half of the moneyers striking coins for King Cnut appear to have been English. Many of them continued under his successors, but after a time their number declined. The coinage issued during the reign of Svein Estridsson (1047–74) shows increasing Byzantine influence, not only in stylistic elements but also in the form of imitations of Byzantine coins, and a certain independence is seen in coins with runic inscriptions.

---

[60] *Tusindtallets danske mønter fra Den kongelige Mønt- og Medaillesamling: Danish Coins from the 11th Century in the Royal Collection of Coins and Medals*, ed. by Jørgen Steen Jensen (Copenhagen: Nationalmuseet, 1995), p. 26.

[61] *Tusindtallets danske mønter*, ed. by Jensen, pp. 22–24.

[62] Cinthio, 'Myntverk och myntare i Lund'; and *Tusindtallets danske mønter*, ed. by Jensen, pp. 28–30.

Conclusion

During the past centuries there has been extensive research into the activities and presence of Scandinavians in England. This research was based on a wide range of sources among which archaeological finds, such as single artefacts, burials, and settlements, show definite links back to the homelands. Turning to Scandinavia, the evidence of activity abroad is of a different nature and the distribution of sources is often very uneven. Thus, there is very little in Denmark to illustrate the first centuries of Danish activity in England. The picture changes towards the late tenth and early eleventh centuries during the reign of Svein Forkbeard and his son Cnut the Great, and English influence in Scandinavian art styles, early Danish coinage, and the development of the Church have been studied for many years. An increasing body of archaeological material may now be added to this evidence, giving research an extra dimension. The geographical distribution of the finds from the eleventh century (see figs 4 and 10) indicates that the ties across the North Sea were strongest in northern and eastern Denmark, that is, the area from the Limfjord, past Fyn and Sjælland, towards Skåne and the entrance to the Baltic. Although the distribution patterns should be treated with some caution due to inter alia the varying intensity in the use of metal detectors, it is not improbable that Germany played a greater role in southern Denmark, and extensive contact with the Baltic area is evident in eastern Denmark.

The present survey includes objects of Anglo-Saxon origin, objects showing Anglo-Saxon influence in style but of Scandinavian form and type, and finally objects produced in Scandinavia as well as in Anglo-Saxon England. They range from single, impressive luxury items to humble everyday ornaments and fittings. Whereas the former have been known for some time, it is only recently that the smaller and simpler objects are beginning to appear, the first examples coming from excavations in, for instance, the early medieval town of Lund, but the most recent finds turning up on a wider scale in excavated settlements and among the objects recovered with metal detectors. Considering the different types of objects and their find locations, it is unlikely that their presence in Denmark is due to any single factor.

Foreign luxury items in a Danish context may have been stolen, but it is also possible that they were purchased or acquired as gifts. Objects such as the two decorated swords from Skåne and the riding equipment from Velds in Jutland dated to *c.* 1000 may be associated with warfare and the social elite. The combination of Scandinavian types and Anglo-Saxon ornamental design suggests that they were made to order in a milieu which would accept this mixture of elements. The owners may have arranged the design with the craftsmen themselves. An alternative interpretation is that they received the swords and riding equipment possibly even with a horse as a valuable gift from their lord. The presenting of gifts as a reward for service and loyalty or at specific events is well known from written sources, and this practice is supported by, for instance, the quality of individual objects and the similarity between some of the sets of riding equipment in Danish equestrian burials of the tenth century.[63]

Copper-alloy bridle mounts, stirrups, and strap mounts are also associated with horsemanship, but do not appear to have been quite so valuable. The latest increase in the number of recorded single mounts and fittings suggests that they were more widely used and not tied specifically to an elite milieu, although this may have been the case in some areas where a few complete sets have been found in burials.[64] The decoration on stirrup strap-plates, mounts, and cheekpieces is related to the Scandinavian Ringerike and Urnes styles, but the technique and use of copper alloy have been seen as foreign elements. However, a few Danish finds of types that do not seem common in England as well as the typological development of horse equipment in Scandinavia in general support the possibility of an independent production of copper-alloy horse trappings in Scandinavia. James Graham-Campbell has stressed the importance of influence from Denmark in the innovation and improvement of Anglo-Saxon riding equipment in the tenth and eleventh centuries,[65] and the recent finds reveal that this was not a one-sided transfer of knowledge or equipment. The copper-alloy fittings in Denmark may represent imports, but workshops producing horse equipment within an Anglo-Scandinavian milieu building on common traditions is a probable alternative for the almost identical types that are now coming to light in England as well as in Denmark.

Some of the personal ornaments found in Denmark such as the cloisonné enamel brooches were probably brought back from England, but the production of hooked-tags in Lund as well as English-type pottery suggests that English moneyers were not the only craftsmen from England employed in the town and that not necessarily all worked in a royal context. Whether these craftsmen worked for the local market in general or for a group of English customers is uncertain. The petrological analysis of the pottery from Lund and Lejre indicates that the early glazed wares were made by the same potters, apparently only over a fairly short period of time. The Lund finds seem to have a wide distribution throughout the area belonging to the earliest phase of the town, and it has been suggested that the use of glazed pottery was not limited to the upper levels of society.[66] On the other hand, the Lejre finds point to an elite context for the specialist wares, and it is possible that the main customers in Lund should be sought among wealthy households and property owners.

Archaeological excavations in Lund have revealed further support for the presence of an English community in the town. Around 1020–30, a wooden church

---

[63] On an earlier example of possible gift exchange, the Hedeby boat-chamber grave dated to the ninth century, see for instance, Egon Wamers, 'König im Grenzland: Neue Analyse des Bootkammergrabes von Haithabu', *Acta Archaeologica*, 65 (1994), 1–56.

[64] Pedersen, 'Riding Gear from Late Viking-Age Denmark'.

[65] Graham-Campbell, 'Anglo-Scandinavian Equestrian Equipment'.

[66] Christensen and others, 'Early Glazed Ware from Medieval Denmark', p. 72.

built during the reign of Svein Forkbeard, *c.* 990, was replaced by a stone-built church dedicated to the Saviour and the Trinity. The stone church was apparently planned with a western extension of several storeys. The size and proportions of the building were similar to those of other churches laid out in accordance with a set of rules from a *concilium* held in Winchester *c.* 973, and the Old Minster in Winchester may have been a model for it.[67] Associated with yet another wooden church immediately south of this stone church were burials containing charcoal. In England, similar burials have been found inter alia at Winchester. By contrast other Lund burials contain hazel sticks, a custom widespread in northern Europe. Thus, the church south of Trinitatis may have been built for or by Englishmen in Lund. Englishmen or returning descendants of Danes who had settled in England may also have been involved with a church built around the middle of the eleventh century and dedicated to Saint Botulf, a mainly local saint in eastern England.[68]

Taken as a whole the Danish Viking Age finds seem to reflect the changing conditions and consequences of contact across the North Sea. The periods of intense raiding and settlement in England in the early centuries and the later attacks and conquest under Svein Forkbeard and Cnut the Great resulted in different archaeological patterns that may be sketched as follows:

1. Early raids and attacks: The attained wealth was probably reinvested abroad or at home, but there appears to have been limited direct return and reuse of objects.
2. Viking settlement in England: Evidence of Scandinavian influence and artefacts of Scandinavian type are found in the new area, but the interaction and changing customs here are not necessarily reflected back in Denmark.
3. Renewed campaigns and joint reign: The extensive contact formed the basis for the exchange of objects, travelling craftsmen, and artisans.

The variety of objects reflecting contact with England in eleventh-century Denmark suggests traffic and exchange during the period of joint reign leading to adoption and in some cases manufacture of similar objects on both sides of the North Sea. Artefacts such as the cloisonné enamel brooches and some of the pottery provide evidence of continued contact between England and Denmark beyond the breakdown of the North Sea empire in 1042, a process already underway after the death of King Cnut in 1035, and we may imagine that family ties and relations, the potential for trade, as well as the ecclesiastical organization contributed to keeping the contacts alive in spite of the political divide.

---

[67] Maria Cinthio, 'Trinitatiskyrkan i Lund: Med engelsk prägel', *Hikuin*, 24 (1997), 113–34 (pp. 113–22).

[68] Cinthio, 'Trinitatiskyrkan i Lund', pp. 130–31.

The Scandinavian Heritage
of the Lordship of the Isles

DAVID H. CALDWELL

In the fourteenth century the MacDonald Lords of the Isles rose to power as great Highland magnates. By the fifteenth century they controlled the Western Isles, large portions of the western seaboard, and the vast Earldom of Ross (fig. 1). They were leaders and patrons of Gaelic culture and society, often at odds with the Stewart Kings of Scotland whose power base was in the Scots-speaking Lowlands. They presided over a lordship which was culturally distinct from the rest of the country.[1]

One of the main reasons the cultural achievement of this lordship is of significance to us now is because it, rather than the dominant culture of the Lowlands, is what underlies the present-day image of Scottishness. Its Scandinavian heritage, however, has largely been forgotten, if not deliberately suppressed during the medieval period. It is the purpose of this essay to consider the extent to which the medieval West Highlands were shaped by their Scandinavian past.

Viking raids on the Western Isles of Scotland are first recorded in 794. These pagan pirates from Scandinavia were to return year after year on looting and pillaging missions. By the mid-ninth century many of them had settled in the Western Isles and had married into the local population, creating a hybrid Norse/Gaelic (*Gall-Gaedhil*) society owing no allegiance to the kings of the Scots. Lip service, at least, was paid to the ultimate authority of the Kings of Norway, but more local leadership was provided by strong-men, like Ketil Flat-Nose (Ketill flatnefr) in the ninth century, and the Earls of Orkney from the late tenth century.[2]

---

[1] Important source material and discussion on the lords and their lordship is contained in K. A. Steer and J. W. M. Bannerman, *Late Medieval Monumental Sculpture in the West Highlands* (Edinburgh: Royal Commission on the Ancient and Historical Monuments of Scotland, 1977), and *Acts of the Lords of the Isles* [hereafter *ALI*], ed. by J. Munro and R. W. Munro (Edinburgh: Scottish History Society, 1986).

[2] For the Viking contribution to Scotland in general, see Barbara E. Crawford, *Scandinavian Scotland: Scotland in the Early Middle Ages* (Leicester: Leicester University Press, 1987).

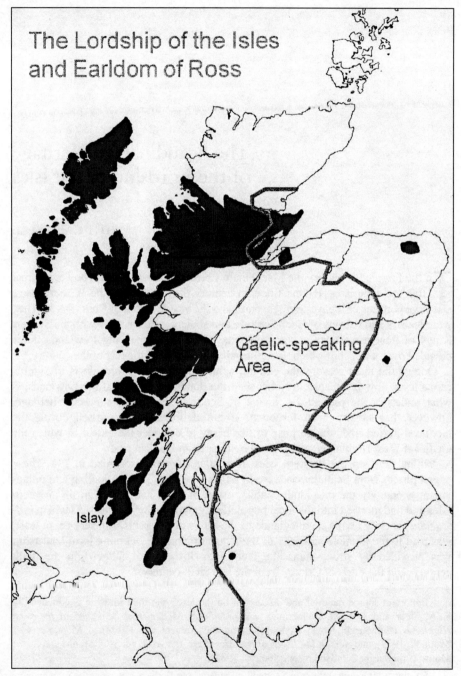

Figure 1. Map showing the fullest extent of MacDonald power
in the fifteenth century. Map: D. Caldwell.

In 1079 Godred Crovan (Guðrøðr *crobh-bhán?), who had been one of the commanders of the Norwegian army defeated by King Harold of England at Stamford
Bridge in 1066, took the Isle of Man, thus founding a dynasty of Norse kings ruling
that island and the other Western Isles of Scotland. Godred died on Islay in 1095.
Three years later, the King of Norway, Magnus Bare-Foot (Magnús berfœttr), subjected the Isles to a devastating raid and collected tribute. The Manx kings were now
clearly subservient to the Norwegian monarchy. Then in 1156 this Kingdom of the
Isles received a further set-back when the Southern Hebrides — those to the south of
the Ardnamurchan peninsula, including Islay and Mull, and probably also Arran and
Bute — were annexed by Somerled, who founded a rival kingdom and dynasty of
the Isles.[3]

Somerled (Sumarliði), described in early sources as ruler of Argyll and with a
genealogy extending back to Ireland, has been portrayed in later clan histories as the
spearhead of Gaelic resistance against Norse domination. His name, however, is
Norse, and he was married to the sister of King Godfrey of Man. The partition of the
Isles between Somerled and Godfrey followed a sea battle fought and won by the
former. Two years later Somerled again defeated Godfrey, this time on the Isle of
Man, and took over all the Isles and Man. Godfrey only managed to re-establish
himself in Man and the Northern Hebrides after Somerled's death.[4]

Somerled met his death in battle at Renfrew in 1164. He clearly felt under considerable threat from the new Anglo-Norman lords in Scotland, especially the
Steward, intent on expanding westwards. Somerled's lands were split between his
sons Dougal, Ranald, and Angus. Three major West Highland clans trace their origins to the first two sons, the MacDougalls being descended from Dougal, and the
MacDonalds and MacRuairis from two sons of Ranald.

Some of Somerled's descendants, collectively known as the MacSorleys, were
recognized as kings of the Isles, but it should be understood that this kingship did not
pass automatically from father to son. Ranald, son of Somerled, took the title but there
is no evidence that either of his sons Donald and Ruairi claimed it. It was held by some
of Ruairi's descendants and at least two descendants of Ranald's brother Dougal.

In 1266, by the Treaty of Perth, Norway ceded the Western Isles to Alexander III,
king of Scots. This effectively meant a demotion in status for the MacSorley kings.
There could only be one king in the kingdom of Scotland and kingship was by then
firmly established in the house of Canmore with succession determined by strict
principles of primogeniture. The MacSorley chiefs were now merely barons of the
realm, and it is as such that Angus, son of Donald, and Alexander (MacDougall) of

---

[3] The history of the Western Isles in the period preceding the Lordship of the Isles, from *c.*
1100 to *c.* 1336, is dealt with by R. Andrew McDonald, *The Kingdom of the Isles: Scotland's
Western Seaboard c. 1100–c. 1336* (East Linton: Tuckwell Press, 1997).

[4] Somerled's ancestry is dealt with by W. D. H. Sellar, 'The Origins and Ancestry of
Somerled', *Scottish Historical Review*, 45 (1966), 123–42. For a useful survey of his career
see also McDonald, *Kingdom of the Isles*, pp. 39–67.

Argyll appear in the Scottish Parliament in 1284.[5] Their lands also now became subject to feudal principles of tenure, and several royal grants survive from the fourteenth and fifteenth centuries demonstrating the superiority and authority, at least in theory, of the Kings of Scotland over West Highland chiefs and their lands.[6]

The Kings of Scotland may have viewed them as barons of the realm, but in Gaelic society they could still aspire to be Kings of the Isles. Irish sources recognized Ruairi MacRuairi as King of the Isles when he died at Dundalk in 1318, fighting for Edward Bruce.[7] This title in Gaelic is *Ri Innse Gall*. The word for king, *ri*, could also be used for rulers of less status than is implied by the English word king. A more appropriate translation of *Ri Innse Gall* in 1318, reflecting the status of its holder, might thus be Lord of the Isles.

By the 1330s the most powerful of the MacSorley kindreds were the MacDonalds. They had benefited from supporting Robert Bruce in his struggle for the Scottish throne, whereas the MacDougalls had lost most of what they had, as supporters of the English, and the MacRuairi inheritance was soon to fall to the MacDonalds through marriage with the heiress. The way was clear for the new leader of the MacDonalds, John, to claim the title *Ri Innse Gall*, and we thus find him calling himself *Dominus Insularum* in a letter to King Edward III of England in 1336.[8] It may be of significance that he omitted this title in a letter written the same day, on the same subject, to King Edward (Balliol) of Scotland,[9] and whereas he and his successors came to use the title regularly, the earliest evidence surviving that it was recognized by a Scottish government is in 1431 when some charters issued by Donald, Lord of the Isles were confirmed under the Great Seal.[10]

In 1476, after John II, Lord of the Isles was forfeited for treason, the title Lord of the Isles was granted to him by King James III as a parliamentary lordship,[11] the first time the dignity had been recognized as a Scottish peerage. However, this could hardly have been considered as anything but a demotion, given the pedigree of the title and the extent of the lands held. John was again forfeited in 1493, and the title was never restored to any MacDonald claimants. It is now one of the dignities of the heir to the throne.

---

[5] *The Acts of the Parliaments of Scotland* [hereafter *APS*], ed. by T. Thomson and C. Innes (Edinburgh: printed by command of [HM Queen Victoria/George III etc.] in pursuance of an address of the House of Commons of Great Britain, 1814–75), I (1844), 424.

[6] They are listed in appendix A of *ALI*, pp. 207–23.

[7] *The Annals of Loch Cé*, ed. by William M. Hennessy, Rolls Series, 54, 2 vols (London: HMSO, 1871), I, 595.

[8] *ALI*, pp. 3–4, no. 3.

[9] *ALI*, pp. 2–3, no. 2.

[10] *ALI*, p. 210, no. A11.

[11] *APS*, II (1814), 113.

Much Norse blood flowed in the veins of the MacDonalds and other leading West Highland families. Traditional pedigrees claim that the MacLeods are descended from a younger son of the thirteenth-century Manx king, Óláfr the Black, and the MacNicols from the kings of Norway.[12] Certainly several important West Highland families have Norse named eponyms, Áskell, Óláfr, Ljótr, and Sveinn for, respectively, the MacAskills, MacAulays, MacLeods, and MacSweens. When *Orkneyinga Saga* described Ranald, son of Somerled, as 'the greatest warrior then in the western lands',[13] it is clear from the context that he would be considered by the Scandinavian audience of the saga as one of them. The reason for his greatness is one dear to a Viking's heart. Three winters he had been out in warships 'without coming under a sooty rafter',[14] and it was a war-ship that he chose as the device for the back of his seal. Ranald was most likely bilingual in Norse and Gaelic, the former tongue probably surviving in use in the Isles into the mid-thirteenth century.[15]

Angus Mor of Islay, son of Donald and grandson of Ranald, with other Isles chiefs joined King Hákon of Norway's invasion fleet in 1263, taking their ships up Loch Long and then carrying them across into Loch Lomond to harry the Lennox.[16] A contemporary Irish praise poem to Angus says that 'the Irish strand is rare from which his graceful long ships have not taken cattle',[17] and his seal also has a ship on it. The poem really portrays Angus as a latter-day Viking.

Ranald's seal is only known from a description in a notarial instrument of 1426 where it is described as a ship (*navis*) full of men-at-arms.[18] It may have been like the ship represented on the seal of King Harald of Man, of the rival Isles dynasty, dating to 1246 but now only known from a drawing of 1641.[19] It is clearly a longship of

---

[12] I. F. Grant, *The MacLeods: The History of a Clan 1200–1956* (London: Faber & Faber, 1959), pp. 24–25; W. D. H. Sellar and A. MacLean, *The Highland Clan MacNeacail* (Waternish: MacLean, 1999), p. 5.

[13] *The Orkneyinga Saga*, ed. by Joseph Anderson (Edinburgh: Edmonston & Douglas, 1873), p. 195.

[14] *Orkneyinga Saga*, ed. by Anderson, p. 195. The identification of this warrior as Ranald, son of Somerled, rather than his cousin Ranald, son of Godred of Man, has recently been made by W. D. H. Sellar in 'Hebridean Sea Kings: The Successes of Somerled, 1164–1316', in *Alba Celtic Scotland in the Medieval Era*, ed. by E. J. Cowan and R. Andrew McDonald (East Linton: Tuckwell Press, 2000), pp. 187–218 (pp. 196–97).

[15] Crawford, *Scandinavian Scotland*, p. 92.

[16] *Early Sources of Scottish History A.D. 500–1286*, ed. by Alan Orr Anderson, 2 vols (Edinburgh: Oliver & Boyd, 1922; repr. Stamford: Paul Watkins, 1990), II, 625.

[17] Osborn Bergin, 'An Address to Aonghus of Islay', *Scottish Gaelic Studies*, 4 (1934–35), 57–69 (p. 65).

[18] *Registrum Monasterii de Passelet* (Edinburgh: Maitland Club, 1832), p. 149.

[19] Basil Megaw, 'Norseman and Native in the Kingdom of the Isles', in *Man and Environment in the Isle of Man*, ed. by Peter Davey, 2 vols, British Archaeological Reports, British Series, 54 (Oxford: British Archaeological Association, 1978), II, 265–314 (p. 291).

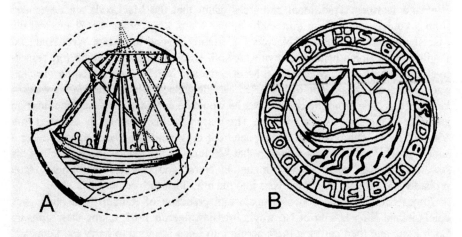

Figure 2. Seals. A: Harald, King of Man, 1246 (after Basil Megaw),
and B: Angus Mor of Islay, from the late thirteenth century
(after a cast in the National Museums of Scotland). Drawing: D. Caldwell.

traditional Viking type, whereas the ship on Angus's seal, possibly dating to fairly late
in the thirteenth century, is clearly recognizable as a West Highland galley (fig. 2).

This is the earliest evidence for these ships, best known from their representations
on fourteenth- to sixteenth-century West Highland sculpture. They are clinker-built
craft with a single mast for a rectangular sail. Where the carved detail is good, as on
the cross-shaft at Iona Abbey, dated 1489, commemorating Lachlan MacKinnon and
his son John, abbot of Iona, oar ports can be seen (fig. 3). These ships have the same
high stem and stern posts as Viking ships, some carved with figureheads. Indeed the
main difference between them and their Viking predecessors appears to be the
provision of a stern rudder and the more upright form of the stern and stem. The term
galley is used here to cover ships which were distinguished in earlier documents as
lymphads, birlinns, and (Highland) galleys in ascending order of size. A document
prepared for the Privy Council in 1615 states that birlinns had twelve to eighteen
oars (a side?) and galleys eighteen to twenty-four, with three men to each oar.[20]

In the Lordship of the Isles some lands were specifically held in return for ship
service, for instance Lossit in Islay for a boat of fourteen.[21] In 1304 Lachlan

---

[20] *The Register of the Privy Council of Scotland*, ed. by David Masson, 14 vols (Edinburgh:
H. M. General Register House, 1877–98), X (1891), 347.

[21] First recorded in a charter of 1617, printed in *The Book of Islay*, ed. by G. Gregory Smith
(privately printed: 1895), p. 356.

MacRuairi, lord of Garmoran, ordered that each *davoch* of land should
provide a galley of twenty oars.[22] The
lands of Garmoran, including the
Uists, Barra, the small isles, and the
west coast of the mainland shire of
Inverness, were soon afterwards incorporated into the Lordship of the
Isles. The 1498 royal charter to Alexander MacLeod of Dunvegan of lands
in Harris and Skye previously held of
the Lords of the Isles requires him to
maintain a galley (*navis*) of twenty-
six oars and two of sixteen, for the
service of the king in peace and
war.[23] The concept of ship service
dates back to the days of the Scottish
kingdom of Dal Riata in Argyll and is
described in the *Senchus Fer nAlban*
(*History of the Men of Scotland*),

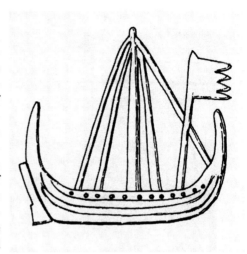

Figure 3. A *birlinn*, as represented
on the MacKinnon cross-shaft of 1489
at Iona Abbey. Drawing: D. Caldwell.

originally composed in the seventh century.[24] Ship service was also well understood
in Norway which had the *leiðang* system for the provision of ships for war.[25]
However much the instances of ship service cited above owe to old Dal Riata, it was
thanks to Scandinavian settlement and technology that they survived. That clinker-
built vessels were constructed in the Western Isles in the Viking period is clearly
demonstrated by the recovery of two unfinished end-posts from a ship estimated to
have been around 10.4 m by 2.05 m in size, from peat on the island of Eigg. One has
been radiocarbon dated to 885–1035.[26]

Much else besides ships gave the medieval Lordship a Viking flavour, not least the
typical military kit employed as late as the sixteenth century and represented on many
grave slabs and commemorative crosses. The body was protected by a long padded
or quilted coat, known as an *aketon*, sometimes with a mail coif (hood) or *pisane*
(collar), or even a habergeon (mail-coat) worn over it for additional protection.

---

[22] A *davoch* was equivalent to four ploughgates, that is four times the amount of land that a
team of oxen could deal with.

[23] *ALI*, pp. 227–28, no. A51.

[24] For a translation and discussion of this document, see J. Bannerman, *Studies in the
History of Dalriada* (Edinburgh: Scottish Academic Press, 1974).

[25] Crawford, *Scandinavian Scotland*, p. 86.

[26] Information supplied by Dr Alison Sheridan of the Department of Archaeology, National
Museums of Scotland.

Figure 4 (left). A fourteenth-century effigy of a warrior at Iona Abbey, as drawn by James Drummond.

Figure 5 (above). Two walrus ivory chessmen of the late twelfth century, from the hoard discovered at Uig on Lewis. They are both in the National Museums of Scotland, Edinburgh. Drawing: D. Caldwell.

On the head was a pointed iron helmet known as a basinet and the earlier warriors carry a shield (fig. 4). There was little difference in reality between this armour of the medieval Highlanders and their Scandinavian forebears, as represented on the warriors in the late-twelfth- or early-thirteenth-century cache of chessmen recovered from Uig on Lewis, and now split between the British Museum in London and the National Museums of Scotland in Edinburgh. Their helmets mostly do not cover their ears but are otherwise similar in shape, and their shields are of larger size. Although their coats are not represented as quilted they are long and have the same front opening as the later *aketons* (fig. 5). The coats of two are cross-hatched, apparently to indicate mail.

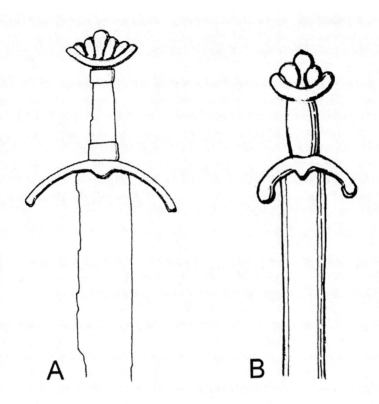

Figure 6. Swords. A: early-twelfth-century sword from Korsødegården in Norway, and B: represented on a fourteenth- or fifteenth-century grave slab at Finlaggan, Islay. Drawing: D. Caldwell.

The main weapons of the fourteenth and fifteenth centuries obviously had a similar pedigree. The swords with lobated pommels and down-turned quillons, known only from representations on sculpture, are clearly derived from weapons like the early-twelfth-century sword from Korsødegården in Norway (fig. 6).[27] Broad/ Danish/type M battleaxes were a favourite throughout the period of the Lordship.[28]

At Finlaggan, excavations directed by this writer have demonstrated that building types associated with the Norse continued to be erected throughout the medieval

---

[27] *From Viking to Crusader: The Scandinavians and Europe 800–1200*, ed. by Else Roesdahl and David M. Wilson (Copenhagen: Nordic Council of Ministers and The Council of Europe, 1992), p. 374, no. 557.

[28] David H. Caldwell, 'Some Notes on Scottish Axes and Long Shafted Weapons', in *Scottish Weapons and Fortifications 1100–1800*, ed. by David H. Caldwell (Edinburgh: John Donald, 1981), pp. 262–76.

period, including houses with sub-basements and barrel- or boat-shaped houses. The site at Finlaggan consists of two islands, *Eilean Mor* (large island) and the smaller *Eilean na Comhairle* (Council Isle), in a freshwater loch on the island of Islay. Finlaggan has been identified as the centre of the Lordship of the Isles.[29]

Building 12.2 on *Eilean Mor*, supposed to be of fifteenth-century date, is a relatively small house, about 8 m long with a maximum width of 3.6 m, represented by stone packing for a timber superstructure, set in the crest of low banks representing the remains of earlier houses (fig. 7). At the external corners are stone pads interpreted as the bases for roof couples. The entrance is in the middle of one side. The earlier houses underlying building 12.2 had central hearths set in earth floors, but there was no obvious floor to go with 12.2, leading to the cautious suggestion that it had had a sprung timber floor. It is unlikely, however, that timber floors could have been typical of small medieval houses in Scotland. A functional explanation for building 12.2 might be that it was a food store, in which case a wooden floor might have been a considerable advantage for keeping food dry.

Houses with a barrel- or boat-shaped plan are not difficult to find in the Viking world, and there is no evidence for them in Scotland from pre-Viking times. Close parallels to house 12.2 have, however, still to be found and excavated.

Another type of house at Finlaggan is represented by structure V (fig. 8). It had an overall size of about 11 m by 8 m, apparently with its entrance (unexcavated) in one of its short walls. The evidence for the walls consists of beam slots and corner pads for roof couples, set on substantially surviving earth banks. These were revetted in the interior by dry-stone walling to a height of 0.7 m, but there was no associated floor at their base. The excavators concluded that the floor must have been of sprung timber at the crest of the banks. It is probable that other excavated houses at Finlaggan were similar, but none were nearly as well preserved.

Houses with sprung timber floors can also be found in the Viking world. This house at Finlaggan is reminiscent of ones excavated at Waterford in Ireland.[30] Here the excavators postulated that the space beneath the floorboards could be used as a sub-basement for storage. The Waterford houses date to the eleventh century. Structure V at Finlaggan, on the basis of coin evidence, was occupied in the fifteenth century.

Finally in this essay attention is drawn to the Scandinavian administrative contribution to the Lordship of the Isles. According to the dean of the Isles, Donald

---

[29] For a general account of Finlaggan and an early report on the excavations, see D. H. Caldwell and G. Ewart, 'Finlaggan and the Lordship of the Isles: An Archaeological Approach', *Scottish Historical Review*, 72 (1993), 146–66.

[30] There is a reconstruction of the most completely surviving Waterford house in Maurice Hurley, 'Waterford in the Late Viking Age', in *The Illustrated Archaeology of Ireland*, ed. by Michael Ryan (Dublin: Country House, 1991), pp. 160–63 (p. 162). Cf. the reconstruction drawing of the same house in Maurice F. Hurley and Orla M. B. Scully, *Late Viking Age and Medieval Waterford Excavations 1986–1992* (Waterford: Waterford Corporation, 1997), p. 48, fig. 6:2.

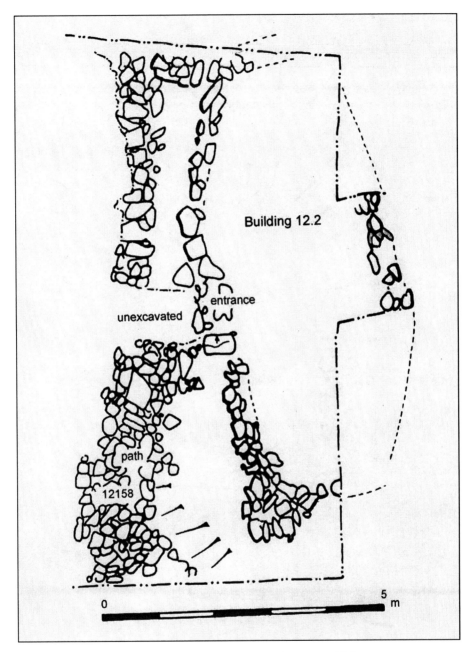

Figure 7. Plan of building 12.2 on *Eilean Mor*, Finlaggan,
dated to the fifteenth century. Drawing: D. Caldwell.

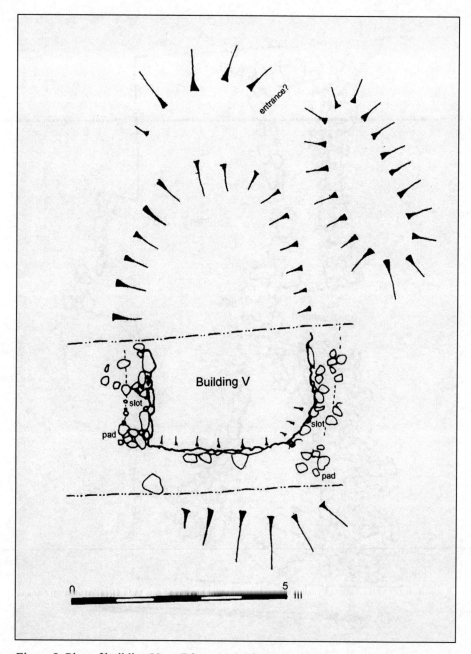

Figure 8. Plan of building V on *Eilean Mor*, Finlaggan, dated to the fifteenth century.
Drawing: D. Caldwell.

Monro, writing in 1549, the Lords of the Isles had a council composed of fourteen of the great men of the Lordship, including Leaders of Clan Donald and other important families, the Bishop of the Isles, and the Abbot of Iona. They are said to have met at Finlaggan in a council chamber erected on the Council Isle, *Eilean na Comhairle*.

Kings and great lords in medieval Europe surrounded themselves with professionals, friends, and relatives to give them advice on day-to-day business, and often these groups were formally constituted as councils. In Scotland, it is known that several of the magnates had councils, including the Dukes of Albany, the Earls of Douglas, and the Earls of Mar.[31] That the Lords of the Isles should have had such a council is not surprising.

When we read of the Council of the Isles in surviving acts by the Lords of the Isles, it is clear that it might be convened anywhere the lord happened to be, to offer advice. The witness lists of charters suggest that the council was often in attendance on the lord as he travelled around his lordship. Eleven surviving charters dating to the years from 1444 to 1492 state that they were issued with the consent of the Council of the Isles; six of them are dated at Dingwall, one at Inverness, and only three within the Lordship, at Aros on Mull, Colonsay, and Oronsay.[32] The meetings of the council at Finlaggan, however, seem to have been something worthy of particular attention, perhaps because they took place as part of a larger event with a fixed place in the calendar, and because they were of a different nature.

The meetings of the Council of the Isles at Finlaggan, if we follow Monro, appear to have had the same dignity and remit as royal parliaments elsewhere. The clue to this is his statement that the council 'gave suits furth upon all debaitable matters'.[33] The Council was here not acting as a mere barony court but as the ultimate source of law in a lordship with its own regional judges, one in every island according to the seventeenth-century Skye *Seanachie*.[34] Martin, writing in the late seventeenth century, described it as the 'High Court of Judicature, consisting of fourteen [...] and there was an appeal to them from all the Courts in the isles'.[35]

Unfortunately, when the supposed council chamber was excavated in 1994, it was found to have suffered from earlier, unrecorded excavations, and little more could be

---

[31] R. W. Munro, *Monro's Western Isles of Scotland and Genealogies of the Clans 1549* (Edinburgh: Oliver & Boyd, 1961), pp. 56–57.

[32] *ALI*, nos 42 (pp. 63–65), 76 (pp. 117–19), 78 (pp. 121–24), 80 (pp. 126–29), 82 (pp. 130–32), 90 (pp. 143–46), 91 (pp. 146–48), 96 (pp. 152–56), 119 (pp. 187–89), 122 (pp. 194–95), 123 (pp. 195–97).

[33] Munro, *Monro's Western Isles*, p. 57.

[34] *Highland Papers*, ed. by J. R. N. Macphail, 4 vols (Edinburgh: Scottish History Society, 1914–34), I (1914), 25.

[35] Martin Martin, *A Description of the Western Islands of Scotland circa 1695* (London, printed for Andrew Bell, at the Cross-Keys and Bible, in Cornhill, near Stocks-Market, 1703; repr. Edinburgh: Birlinn, 1994), p. 273.

said about it than that it was a rectangular building about 4.8 m by 7.5 m with walls about 1 m thick. That the Council of the Isles should have had its own chamber is remarkable and marks out its meetings at Finlaggan as of more significance or status than just the meetings of lordly advisors.

There is also a tradition that inaugurations of Lords of the Isles took place at Finlaggan. The earliest source for this is a seventeenth-century MacDonald history which describes them as taking place in the presence of clerics and the chieftains of all the principal families. The ceremony involved the new lord putting his foot in a footprint carved in the rock while he received the symbols of his authority: a sword, a rod, and a cloak.[36]

When the sources on Finlaggan speak of council meetings and inauguration ceremonies they should not be thought of as totally separate, but as events which took place in the context of annual assemblies. It is not unlikely that they were scheduled for midsummer. The surviving acts of the Lords demonstrate they were present at Finlaggan or 'our place of Islay' on 23 June 1427, 14 June 1456, and 10 July 1486, and none of the other 126 documents are dated in late June or early July at other places with the exception of two notarial instruments of 18 and 19 June 1456, done at Cara, a short sail from Islay.[37]

An understanding that there was more to events at Finlaggan than attendance at council meetings is contained in Dean Monro's aside that they carried on 'albeit thair Lord were at his hunting or at ony uther games'.[38] In the nineteenth century 'a circular green' was pointed out on *Eilean Mor* 'where the most agile of the people were wont to exhibit their gracefulness in the "mazy dance", in which exercise it is reasonably presumed, the magnates also joined'.[39] It might also be observed that one of the farms which borders Loch Finlaggan is called Keppols — certainly a Norse name and possibly meaning 'the farm of the assemblies'.[40]

The interpretation advanced here is that Finlaggan was the setting for annual assemblies during which council meetings were held, inauguration ceremonies took place, and games were played. These were evidently equivalent to the Irish *óenaige*, the periodic, usually annual, assemblies of a king's subjects, a similar combination of political assembly, market-fair, and games.[41] More specifically, there are many parallels between the Finlaggan inauguration ceremonies and those for Irish kings,

---

[36] *Highland Papers*, ed. by Macphail, I, 24.

[37] *ALI*, pp. 34, 90, 92, 94, 189.

[38] Munro, *Monro's Western Isles*, p. 57.

[39] W. MacDonald, *Descriptive and Historical Sketches of Islay* (Glasgow: George Gallie, 1850), p. 19.

[40] D. Mac Eacharna, *The Lands of the Lordship* (Port Charlotte: Argyll Reproductions, 1976), p. 86.

[41] N. B. Aitchison, *Armagh and the Royal Centres in Early Medieval Ireland* (Woodbridge: Cruithne Press/Boydell & Brewer, 1994), pp. 61–66.

and indeed for the early kings of the Scots, and there is no doubting that they fit firmly in an Irish tradition. But these Finlaggan events did not emanate directly from an Irish tradition, but via the Norse kingdom of Man.

On the Isle of Man there has been a long tradition of midsummer assemblies at the Tynwald Hill. It is thought that these were the meetings at which the Kings of Man were inaugurated and heirs apparent recognized.[42] They were not just gatherings of the great and the good, but of all and sundry. They were fairs at which people traded and participated in games. These assemblies obviously reflect the Isle of Man's close links with Ireland and the considerable Gaelic element in its population.

The specifically Scandinavian element of the Tynwald proceedings was the meeting of the Manx parliament. Other Norse parliaments are known to have been established elsewhere, in Iceland and the Faroes, as early as the tenth century, and it is possible that the Manx parliament is also that early. It consisted of thirty-two members, half from Man and half from the Western Isles. It is reasonable to conclude that the Council of the Isles only came into being after Somerled annexed the Isles and that its earliest councillors were the representatives who had previously gone to Man.

All societies inherit much of their culture and many of their administrative practices from their predecessors or forebears. It is therefore not unexpected that Scandinavian elements can be traced in the medieval West Highlands. It is surprising, however, just how long they lingered. West Highland society was very conservative and well adapted to the environmental constraints of its island world. It is difficult to untangle the unambiguously Norse from the Irish or Gaelic in the Lordship of the Isles, and there appears to have been little consciousness of it. There is little sense in surviving documents that after 1266 Scandinavia or its culture was looked to for inspiration or guidance. The leaders of medieval West Highland society were more concerned with their relationship to the rest of Scotland, in particular, whether to integrate culturally and politically with their countrymen or pursue their own way, as independently as circumstances allowed. For most of the time the latter course was chosen, leading to conflict with the Stewart kings and the final forfeiture of the Lordship in 1493.

---

[42] Megaw, 'Norseman and Native in the Kingdom of the Isles', p. 287.

Evidence for the Linguistic Impact
of Scandinavian Settlement

Contact or Conflict? What Can We Learn from the Island-Names of the Northern Isles?

PEDER GAMMELTOFT

aving worked with the place-names of the Northern Isles for the last few years, I have noticed some peculiarities in the place-name material which I feel say something about the relationship between the Scandinavian settlers and the indigenous population in the early phase of the Viking Age (*c.* 800). The Northern Isles completely lack contemporary accounts of the settlements, and the North Atlantic area in general is only extremely rarely mentioned in written sources during this period. It is for this reason that place-names are very important. Apart from archaeological finds, place-names are the only source of information about this significant historical era. Place-names can be described as small fragments of text, fragments that may, if carefully treated, reveal information about times and conditions which it would otherwise be impossible to obtain. For this article, I have chosen to concentrate on the names of islands, partly to limit my subject, and partly because the names of islands generally belong among the oldest place-name material.

The Northern Isles comprise two archipelagos, Orkney and Shetland. Orkney is situated just off the north-eastern tip of Scotland (fig. 1). A further 100 km or so north-north-east of Orkney lies Shetland. To the east of the Northern Isles lies Norway. It is estimated that the journey from western Norway to the Northern Isles in the Viking Age took little more than a couple of days' sailing with a favourable wind. Owing to the relative proximity of the Northern Isles to Norway, they were probably among the first places in the British Isles to have encountered a Scandinavian influx.

It has long been generally accepted that the element *Pap-* in island-names like *Papa Stour* in Shetland (fig. 2) or *Papa Westray* in Orkney (fig. 3) refer to an ethnic and religious group called *papar* by the Scandinavians.[1] The designation *papar* is

---

[1] Apart from the two examples stated above, there are an additional three place-names of this type in the Northern Isles, namely *Papa Little* and *Papa* in Shetland (fig. 2) and *Papa Stronsay* in Orkney (fig. 3).

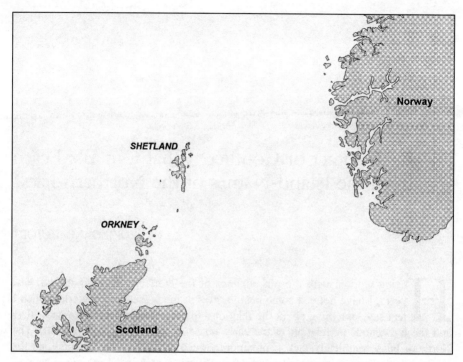

Figure 1. A map of the Northern Isles of Scotland. Map: P. Gammeltoft.

ultimately related to the same word as *pope* and appears to refer to Christian — probably Irish — monks who created retreats for themselves in the area in the centuries immediately preceding the Viking Age.[2] Island-names of the **Papaey*-type are actually fairly common. Throughout the North Atlantic, there are at least ten place-names of this type, half of which are situated in the Northern Isles.[3] Many of the island-names of this type are directly associated with chapel or graveyard sites, so it is likely that the majority of them refer to monks living or having lived at the locality at the time of naming.

I mentioned above that the *papar* had themselves migrated to the area just prior to the Scandinavian invasion. In other words, the *papar* did not constitute an

---

[2] See Aidan D. S. MacDonald, 'Old Norse "papar" Names in N. and W. Scotland: A Summary', in *Studies in Celtic Survival*, ed. by Lloyd R. Laing, British Archaeological Reports, British Series, 37 (Oxford: BAR, 1977), pp. 107–11 (p. 109).

[3] Gillian Fellows-Jensen, 'Language Contact in Iceland: The Evidence of Names', in *Language Contact Across the North Atlantic: Proceedings of the Working Groups held at University College, Galway (Ireland), August 29 – September 3, 1992 and the University of Göteborg (Sweden), August 16–21, 1993*, ed. by P. Sture Ureland and Iain Clarkson (Tübingen: Max Niemeyer, 1996), pp. 115–24 (pp. 116–17).

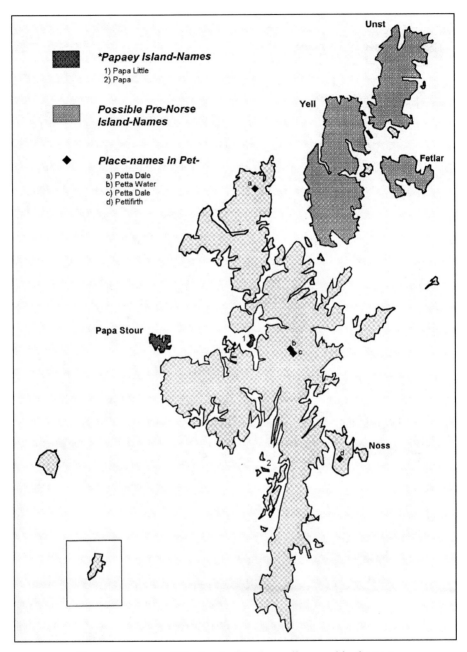

Figure 2. A map of Shetland with places discussed in the text.
Map: P. Gammeltoft.

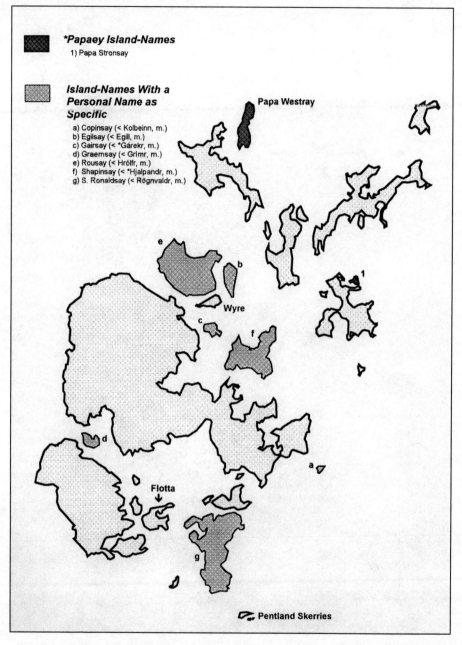

Figure 3. A map of Orkney with places discussed in the text. Map: P. Gammeltoft.

indigenous population. The indigenous population of Shetland and Orkney was probably Pictish. Later Scandinavian references certainly suggest that Picts lived in these islands before the arrival of the Scandinavians.[4] The Picts were usually termed *pettar* by the Scandinavians, and this designation is found forming part of the Old Norse name for the *Pentland Skerries* (fig. 3), which is recorded as *Petlandz skær* in 1329.[5] *Petland* is a Scandinavianized form of the name Pictland, the skerry being situated halfway between Orkney and the Scottish mainland. It would, therefore, not seem unreasonable that the tribal designation *pettar* should form the specifying part of place-names in the Northern Isles. Reality, however, is different. Not a single island-name contains a reference to the Picts by their tribal designation, and this is a general feature of the place-name material in the Northern Isles. There are only four place-names in total in Shetland which contain *pettar*, and none in Orkney. The four primary place-name formations in *Pet-* in Shetland are *Petta Dale* (2), *Petta Water*, and *Pettifirth* (fig. 2).[6] Whether these place-names actually refer to the presence of Picts at or near these localities is not known. It is problematic that the age of the above-mentioned place-names is difficult to establish. *Pettifirth* is the only place-name of the four that seems to have been recorded prior to the seventeenth century; the rest were not recorded until much later.[7] Therefore, the possibility remains that some of the names may be late, in which case they would most likely not refer to actual Picts, but rather to mythical beings. If this is the case, place-names in *Pet-* cannot be used as evidence of a Pictish presence.

To me, it seems significant that there are surprisingly few Norse island-names which relate to the previous inhabitants. Each place-name signifies a relevance on its own, and any element forming part of a place-name gives a picture of what was known and of importance to the namer. When an element occurs as a constituent of a place-name, such as *papar* or *pettar*, it is because it is significant within its context.

---

[4] A curious and fanciful entry in the *Historia Norwegiae* describes the original inhabitants of Orkney in the following way: 'These islands were first inhabited by the Picts and Papae. Of these, the one race, the Picts, little exceeded pigmies in stature; they did marvels, in the morning and in the evening, in building [walled] towns, but at mid-day they entirely lost all their strength, and lurked, through fear, in little underground houses' (*Early Sources of Scottish History, A.D. 500–1286*, ed. and trans. by Alan Orr Anderson, 2 vols (Edinburgh: Oliver & Boyd, 1922; repr. Stamford: Paul Watkins, 1990), I, 330–31).

[5] *Diplomatarium Norvegicum: Oldbreve til kundskap om Norges indre og ytre forhold, sprog, slegter, seder, lovgivning og rettergang i middelalderen*, ed. by C. C. A. Lange and others, I–XXII (Christiania [Oslo]: P. T. Malling/Det Mallingske Bogtrykkeri/Kommisjonen for Diplomatarium Norvegicum, 1849–1992), II (1852), no. 170. This series will hereafter be referred to as *DN*.

[6] Additionally, there are a number of place-names whose specifying element is derived from one of the above mentioned *Pet-* place-names. These have not been included, as they only reflect a relation to a place-name in *Pet-*.

[7] John Stewart, *Shetland Place-Names* (Lerwick: The Shetland Times, 1987), p. 284.

On these grounds, it would be tempting to argue that the monks, the *papar*, were of relevance and well known to the Scandinavian settlers. Conversely, it may be argued that the Picts did not constitute a relevant, or even identifiable, ethnic grouping. If we take this one step further, it may be argued that the Northern Isles were uninhabited, bar a few Christian monks, at the time of the arrival of the Scandinavians. This supposition is, however, impossible to support, as non-reference does not equal non-relevance. The appearance or non-appearance of a certain linguistic element in place-names may result from several factors, not least chance.

That the above supposition is untrue can be seen from the fact that the indigenous Picts or *pettar* appear to have left traces of a different kind in the island-name material. The names of three of the northernmost islands in Shetland are the most distinctive examples. The names Unst, Yell, and Fetlar (fig. 2) do not comply with the typical structure of Norse island-names in the Northern Isles, which is *specifying element* + *ey*, f., 'an island' / *holmr*, m., 'an islet'. An example of this would be *Flotta* (fig. 3) in Orkney, which is a compound of Old Norse *flatr*, adj., 'flat' + *ey*, f., 'an island'.[8] Not all Norse island-names in Orkney and Shetland conform to this structure, however. Some belong to the category of *comparative names*, which are place-names which describe the appearance of the locality by a term to which it is comparable. Important examples are: *Noss*, Bressay, Shetland (fig. 2), and *Wyre*, Orkney (fig. 3). *Noss* derives from Old Norse *nǫs*, f., 'a nose, nostril', whereas *Wyre* originates from Old Norse *vigr*, m., 'a javelin, spearhead'.[9]

From their modern appearance alone, it is immediately clear that *Unst*, *Yell*, and *Fetlar* do not fall under the typical compound island-name structure. If anything, they appear to correspond better with the group of *comparative names*. But in order to be a genuine *comparative name*, it is necessary that the linguistic entity of which the place-name is made up relates to something with which the island may be compared. This proves to be a problem in the case of *Unst*, *Yell*, and *Fetlar*. For instance, the earliest recording of *Unst* is *Aumstr* (*c*. 1387–95).[10] On the basis of this form, the

---

[8] The origin of *Flotta* is clearly visible in its earliest recorded form: *Flatey c.* 1350 (*c*. 1640), in *Diplomatarium Islandicum: Íslenzkt fornbréfasafn, sem hefir inni að halda bréf og gjörnínga, dóma og máldaga, og aðrar skrár, er snerta Ísland eða íslenzka menn*, ed. by Jón Sigurðsson and others, 16 vols (Copenhagen/Reykjavik: Hið Íslenzka Bókmenntafélagi, 1857–1972), III (1896), 51 n. This series will hereafter be referred to as *DI*.

[9] *Noss* is first recorded as *Nws*, 1490 in *DN*, VIII, no. 426, and *Noss*, 1582 in *Shetland Documents, 1580–1611*, ed. by John H. Ballantyne and Brian Smith (Lerwick: Shetland Islands Council & The Shetland Times, 1994), no. 41 (this publication will hereafter be referred to as *SheDoc*). *Wyre* is recorded as *Vigur, c.* 1350 (*c*. 1640) in *DI*, III, 50 n, and *Vigr, c.* 1387–95 in *Orkneyinga saga*, ed. by Sigurður Nordal, Samfund til udgivelse af gammel nordisk litteratur, 40 (Reykjavik: S. L. Møllers Bogtrykkeri, 1913–16), p. 214. (This saga will hereafter be referred to as *Orkn*.)

[10] *Orkn*, p. 137, n.

origin might be Old Norse *ǫmstr*, m., 'a stack, heap'.[11] However, this etymology can hardly be correct, as, phonologically, Old Norse [ǫ] did not develop into Shetlandic [ʌ] under normal circumstances. What the true etymology of this name is it is impossible to say. But it does not appear to be Scandinavian in origin, as no Old Norse linguistic material fits this name.

The same problem is found with the place-name *Fetlar*. Judging from the earliest references, *Føtalare* (1490)[12] and *Fetlair* (1587),[13] the origin might be *fetlar*, the plural of Old Norse *fetill*, m., 'a carrying-strap'.[14] Although this is a possibility, to name an island from a carrying-strap is unprecedented, and I would say that this derivation can hardly be correct. Again this leaves us with no clear explanation of this name.

The name of *Yell* might derive from *ála*, genitive plural of Old Norse *áll*, m., 'a deep furrow in a stream or sound', on the basis of the form *Alasund* (*c*. 1300) which is the earliest reference to *Yell Sound*.[15] From a topographical point of view, this might seem a viable interpretation, *Yell* being surrounded by several narrow straits, such as *Yell Sound*, *Bluemull Sound*, and *Colgrave Sound*. Later independent recordings of the name Yell are *Iala* (1405),[16] *Iaale*, and *Zaill* (1485).[17] These make an origin in *ála* very problematic, since all show forms in initial [j-]. This initial [j-] cannot reflect a breaking of [a:], as this sound change does not occur with long vowels in Old Norse. Instead, the form *Ála-* probably represents an attempt at re-etymologizing the name to make it fit into a Norse framework.

What is common for *Unst*, *Fetlar*, and *Yell* is the fact that they appear to be pre-Norse in origin but have been given a thin layer of Scandinavian 'varnish'. This layer of 'varnish' has not been applied in order to conceal the fact that they are not Scandinavian — after all, a place-name only needs to function, not to mean anything — but rather to make them palatable to the Scandinavian tongue and morphology. That place-names of pre-Norse origin may exist in Shetland is extremely interesting and important. The transfer of place-names from one language into another relies on a prolonged period of contact of a peaceful character.

We have now established that the pre-Norse inhabitants of the Northern Isles, the *Picts* and the *Papae*, are reflected in the local island-name material in vastly different ways. The traces of the indigenous population, the Picts or *pettar*, in island-names centre on names which appear to be of pre-Norse origin, whereas the clerical

---

[11] Stewart, *Shetland Place-Names*, p. 1.

[12] *DN*, VIII, no. 426.

[13] *SheDoc*, no. 102.

[14] Stewart, *Shetland Place-Names*, p. 5.

[15] *Orkn*, p. 159.

[16] *DN*, I, no. 606.

[17] *Records of the Earldom of Orkney, 1299–1614*, ed. by J. Storer Clouston (Edinburgh: Scottish History Society, 1914), p. 72.

minority, the *papar*, are referred to in island-names of Norse origin by their group designation. I find that these differences contain some important clues to the contact and interaction of these peoples and the incoming Scandinavians.

The simple fact that place-names of a seemingly pre-Norse origin exist in the Northern Isles shows that some minimal amount of contact between this population, the Picts, and the Scandinavians existed. Unfortunately, place-names cannot reveal the nature and extent of the interaction which furthered the transfer of *Unst, Yell,* and *Fetlar* into Old Norse, except to suggest that it was at least peaceful. It is remarkable that there are no place-names of apparent pre-Norse origin in Orkney; the pre-Norse element is confined to three island-names in the extreme northeast of Shetland, the area closest to Norway. It is, therefore, reasonable to assume that the earliest phase of interaction may have been that of a mercantile and exploratory nature on the fringes of the Pictish world. Only under these circumstances, it seems, would it make sense to transfer place-names of a Pictish origin into Old Norse. When the Scandinavian settlement of the Northern Isles began, the Scandinavians assumed a much more active naming role and named places exclusively in Old Norse. Therefore, the low number of Pictish-related place-names in the Northern Isles suggests to me that the Picts ceased to be an ethnic group of relevance at a very early stage. Exactly what happened to them is unknown, but judging from their apparently sudden disappearance, it is very likely that they were obliterated by the incoming Scandinavians, either by warfare, slave trade, or disease — or a combination of these.

The *papar*, on the other hand, have not left traces in the island-name material of the same nature as the *pettar*. Instead, they are referred to by their group designation as the specific in purely Norse place-name constructions. It has been argued that the **Papaey*-type island-names may originally have been given to islands abandoned by monks.[18] I find this supposition somewhat unlikely, however. Why should it be more relevant to name abandoned *papar* sites than abandoned *pettar* sites, the latter often being more distinctive with their broch structures? Instead, I think we should consider that the *papar* lived alongside the Scandinavians in the Northern Isles for a prolonged period. This fits well with the fact that a large number of *papar* sites are associated with post–Viking Age chapels or graveyards, which presupposes a prolonged period of Christian worship at these sites. Whether this means a continuous clerical presence from pre–Viking Age times or not is uncertain. However, if this is the case, then the presence of the Christian *papar* might well represent attempts at converting the heathen Scandinavians. Judging from the many Christian Scandinavians from Scotland, who, according to *Landnámabók,* settled in Iceland only a couple of generations after the settlement of the Northern and the Western Isles of Scotland,[19] they seem to have been fairly successful.

---

[18] Fellows-Jensen, 'Language Contact in Iceland', p. 116.

[19] See, for example, 'Landnámabók', in *Early Sources of Scottish History A.D. 500–1286,* ed. and trans. by Anderson, I, 342–43.

Although the evidence for the scenario that I have pictured here is not conclusive, I feel that the place-name evidence points in the direction of the Scandinavians' treating the Picts and the *Papae* differently. The Picts, although probably good trading partners, did not fit into the settlement equation and were thus expendable. The *Papae*, on the other hand, do not appear to have threatened the expansion process, and they were allowed to live alongside the Scandinavians. If the stories in *Landnámabók* of the converted Scandinavians from the Scottish Isles are to be trusted, the Scandinavians and the monks must have enjoyed a close and lengthy relationship.

Norse Topographical Settlement Names on the Western Littoral of Scotland

ARNE KRUSE

To be an immigrant with an interest in onomastics in Scotland is a sobering experience. While in Norway there is a single Germanic onomasticon (with Sámi and Finnish strata in certain areas), Scotland — with a topography quite similar to Norway — shows a multitude of ethnic strata that is both exciting and a bit off-putting in all its complexity. Aware of my own linguistic limitations, I will in this essay try to steer clear of detailed etymological analyses. Instead my intention here is, as a foreigner dealing with a research tradition that is not his own, to share some thoughts of a more general nature. I intend to discuss some aspects of the most central work in Scottish onomastics, W. F. H. Nicolaisen's *Scottish Place-Names*,[1] and in particular the chapter on Scandinavian names, which is, of course, the most interesting chapter for a Scandinavian reader.

Years after it was first published, *Scottish Place-Names* is still referred to, quite justifiably, as *the* authority on the interpretation of individual Scottish names, as well as on onomastic theory. In a book with so many new observations, overviews, and ideas, it is hardly surprising that there are aspects of it which one finds rather unexpected or with which one even disagrees. I would like to discuss the slight surprise I had whilst reading the chapter on Scandinavian names, focusing on an attitude towards settlements bearing topographical names that I find rather unfamiliar.

Here is a central quotation from the chapter on Scandinavian names, where Nicolaisen comments on the distribution map of names containing the generic *dalr*:

> There is no reason to think that it has ever meant anything but what it still means in Norwegian today, i.e. 'a valley'. [. . .] It must be remembered that *dalr* primarily refers to natural features, although the name of a valley was quite often, at a later date, transferred to a settlement situated in it. A distribution map of *dalr*-names is therefore

[1] W. F. H. Nicolaisen, *Scottish Place-Names* (London: B. T. Batsford, 1976).

not a map of permanent Norse settlement but rather of the sphere of Norse influence. It includes those areas adjacent to permanent settlements in which seasonal exploits such as hunting and fishing and summer grazing were carried out, and probably the odd military raid or friendly visit. In most of those undertakings Norsemen must have been accompanied by Gaelic-speakers as otherwise the names concerned would not have come down to us because of a break in communication. [. . .] the distribution of *dalr* (Map 8) serves as a reminder that 'settlement area' and 'sphere of influence' are not the same and that the Norsemen must have known the western coastal districts of the mainland from Cape Wrath to the Mull of Kintyre extremely well even if they never (or hardly ever) had any permanent farms or other settlements there. It would be risky to read any more out of, or into, these maps. [2]

In the quotation it seems to be taken for granted that the Norse arriving on the west coast littoral would have ignored the arable and cultivated land in the area. This is certainly not obvious, as this was a most valuable resource to an agrarian-based people. Let us, however, for the time being, follow the assumption that the Norse were only seasonal visitors to the mainland and that they, in contact with the local population, left behind their own names for the area. The first part of this essay will be a discussion of this hypothesis in the light of onomastic theory.

Traditional onomastics has been dominated by etymology. Aspects such as the relationship between the place-name and the user-group(s) of the name, and the function of the name as a means of communication, have only more recently appeared on the agenda of place-name researchers. However, an early pioneer in the discussion of such aspects was the Norwegian Magnus Olsen.[3] He stressed that we, as individuals, all have a certain inventory of names stored in our memory. Certain people will know certain names within an area, according to the need which the individual has for the names. Olsen divided the place-names of an area into three types, depending on the creator and/or the user of the names. First, there are names connected with the farm; second, names that are used within the village; and third, names used by people travelling through the area. A farmer knows the detailed land-scape within his farm and will need to use names in this microsphere to refer to the landscape within the farm when communicating with others living on the farm. Farmers are not likely to know the names of all the locations on a neighbour's farm. However, within the wider neighbourhood, farmers will together be able to refer to locations by names within the village or the local community. These might include local roads, important natural features, shared areas of utilization, such as common grazing in the hills, and other farms within the community. Finally, according to Magnus Olsen, merchants, fishermen, pilgrims, and other kinds of travellers, for example, along a coast, will be unfamiliar with the names of all the farms in a par-ticular region, but they will know names of importance to them along a wider area of

---

[2] Nicolaisen, *Scottish Place-Names*, pp. 94, 96.

[3] Magnus Olsen, *Hvad våre stedsnavn lærer oss* (Oslo: Stenersen, 1934).

travel routes.[4] Names known by people travelling, Olsen says, are names of larger areas and points of orientation, that is, easily recognizable topographical features, such as islands, larger fjords, and headlands.

A weak point in Olsen's theory is that he does not clearly distinguish between the creator of a name and the user of a name, but it seems that he has in mind the actual creators of the various name types.[5] In a recent article, Ola Stemshaug questions the very existence of names created by travellers.[6] He argues that travelling will often be the *reason* for giving a location a certain name, but the actual creators of the names will be locals. Seafarers may have their own names for locations along a coast, but these names will only exceptionally become widely accepted denotations of the locations. In other words, travellers as a user-group of names may have a different onomasticon than locals, but their name inventory will normally not become generally accepted.

A very clear example which illustrates this is the Swedish names of the rapids along the Dniepr, recorded in *c.* 950 in the writings of the Byzantine Emperor Constantine Porphyrogenitus.[7] These are obviously names coined by Swedes struggling with their boats past the difficult rapids of the river. Importantly, the Swedish names have not survived outside this account. They were frozen in time, being recorded from the onomasticon of a very limited user-group who only had the need for the names as long as their travels took them along the Dniepr. As they were only used by people passing by, the Swedish names had no chance of survival in competition with local names which could be passed on through many generations. There was no reason for the locals to accept new, foreign names from visitors for a topography that they already had names for in their own language.[8]

---

[4] Olsen, *Hvad våre stedsnavn*, pp. 10–12.

[5] See, for example, Magnus Olsen, *Ættegård og helligdom: Norske stedsnavn sosialt og religionshistorisk belyst*, Instituttet for sammenlignende kulturforskning, Serie A: Forelesninger, 9a (Oslo: Aschehoug, 1926), p. 18. This book has also been published in English as *Farms and Fanes of Ancient Norway: The Place-Names of a Country Discussed in their Bearings on Social and Religious History*, trans. by Th. Gleditsch (Cambridge, MA: Harvard University Press, 1928).

[6] Ola Stemshaug, 'Vegens namn – kva er det?', in *Ortnamn i språk och samhälle. Hyllningsskrift till Lars Hellberg*, ed. by Svante Strandberg, Nomina Germanica, 22 (Uppsala: Uppsala Universitet, 1997), pp. 253–65.

[7] Constantine Porphyrogenitus, *De Administrando Imperio*, ed. by Gyula Moravcsik and trans. by Romilly J. H. Jenkins, Corpus Fontium Historiae Byzantinae, 1, rev. edn (Washington: Dumbarton Oaks, 1967).

[8] For a discussion on these names, see Knut-Olof Flak, *Dneprforsarnas namn i Kejsar Konstantin VII Porfyrogennetos' 'De administrando imperio'*, Lunds universitets årsskrift, N. F. Avd. 1, Bd. 46, Nr 4, Slaviska institutet vid Lunds universitet, Slaviska och baltiska studier, 1 (Lund: Gleerup, 1951).

There are some names coined by travellers which are now widely used, for example, *Norway* ('the northern way'), *Strait of Magellan*, and *Easter Island*. These are names obviously not coined by locals. However, the latter two are typical examples of the type of names which a dominant, map-making culture has given to the world. The point is that such names normally denote large areas or distinct features along major travel routes, and they are not likely to be frequent. It is highly unlikely that any farm names or names of valleys and bays will be coined by non-residents or by people that are not neighbours of the farms or topographical features.

The names with the generic *dalr* that Nicolaisen refers to denote either modern farms or relatively small valleys — both categories of names which typically belong to the nomenclature of the local community. This is the group of people who have the greatest need for such names as a means of reference, and this is the group of people who will have preserved the names through time, preventing them from falling into oblivion.

It is time to mention that Nicolaisen's own view has mellowed somewhat over the years.[9] However, in a comparatively recent article on the place-names of Arran, Nicolaisen reintroduces old thoughts.[10] He sees Arran as part of the Norse 'sphere of influence', along with the mainland littoral. About the Norse place-names on the island, he has this to say:

> [It is] not the nomenclature of a settled people but of occasional, albeit fairly regular but not always welcome, visitors. It is a nomenclature that experiences the island from the sea, not only visually but also while exploring and utilising it. It is a sailor's toponymic vocabulary and that of the fisherman and the hunter and the herdsman involved in transhumance.[11]

And in characteristic style he gives the underlying semantics of the names:

> [. . .] they are the names of seasonal intruders depleting the rivers and grazing their heifers and their yearlings on shielings on the best grassland easily accessible from the shore. These names are more like onomastic graffiti: 'Skorri was here' proclaims *Scorradel*, 'Skapto rules O.K.' announces *Skaftigill*.[12]

This seems insupportable to me. Although it is more than likely that if the Norse were non-residents in the area, they would have had their own names for the

---

[9] See, for example, W. F. H. Nicolaisen, 'Place-Name Maps – How Reliable Are They?', in *Studia Onomastica: Festskrift till Thorsten Andersson*, ed. by Lena Peterson and S. Strandberg (Stockholm: Almqvist & Wiksell, 1989), pp. 262–68 (p. 265), where he hints that the absence of primary settlement names may even reflect 'less permanence of occupation, or at least a very different attitude towards the land'.

[10] W. F. H. Nicolaisen, 'Arran Place-Names: A Fresh Look', *Northern Studies*, 28 (1992), 1–13.

[11] Nicolaisen, 'Arran Place-Names', p. 8.

[12] Nicolaisen, 'Arran Place-Names', pp. 8–9.

landscape they utilized as fishermen, hunters, and herders, it is unlikely that such names would enter the onomasticon of the locals resident in the area. I have researched such an in-group's onomasticon, viz. how fishermen in Norway use their own names on land-kennings, that is, mountains or other topographical features they need in order to navigate.[13] I found that names used by fishermen whilst fishing typically never leave the narrow context within which they exist. They only exist as long as there is a professional need for them, and they hardly ever influence the names that people living next to the mountains have for the mountains. Consequently, they will, as a rule, never appear on a map.

While this is the case within a stable monolingual and monoethnic society like the west coast of Norway, the additional problem of an ethnic and linguistic barrier would have had to be crossed in Scotland. How and why would Norse names have won general acceptance within a Gaelic-speaking community to the degree that they were passed on to future Gaelic-speaking generations? In the first quotation, Nicolaisen suggests a solution to this problem by saying that the Norse would have had local Gaels who came with them on their expeditions to the mainland coast and that these Gaels picked up the Norse names and passed them on to future Gaelic generations. However, in a situation like this, the opposite to the suggested scenario is more likely to have happened. We know from history that in similar situations, where newcomers have made use of natives as scouts and interpreters, the normal way of communicating place-names is that the locals pass on their own native names to the newcomers. The maps of Africa, America, and Australia are scattered with names that have been handed down to us from locals informing Europeans of the onomasticon of the area. All in all, it is difficult to see why and how the local, resident Scots, inspired by those of their own who were in Norse service, would have suppressed central names in their name inventory in place of names coined in a totally different language to their own.

The word order and the specifics in the compound names show that there is no question of any borrowing of Norse appellatives into Gaelic at the time. The names in question are clearly coined by speakers of Norse. Therefore, could it be that the resident Scots actually adopted the language of the Norse visitors? Even if this were the case, it still would not be the answer to the very high frequency of Norse names on the west coast littoral. Place-names usually survive a language shift, because names, contrary to words, need not carry meaning. As long as there is population continuity within a given area, the fundamental onomasticon of the population is likely to survive, even if the population happens to switch language. For example, the names of major settlements and large natural features are still Gaelic in areas of Scotland where the Gaelic language itself has succumbed to English. Therefore, a language shift in itself cannot explain why so many important place-names on the Scottish west coast are of Norse origin.

---

[13] Arne Kruse, 'Sjønamn på médfjella', *Namn og Nemne*, 15 (1998), 21–31.

The most reasonable explanation for the many Norse names in this area is an ethnic shift; an ethnic (and with it a linguistic) discontinuity which would have seen the Norse taking over substantial parts of the mainland west coast in the form of settlements. Only an ethnically Norse community explains the pattern and frequency of the Norse names that have survived to the present. Furthermore, both the distribution and the sheer number of names of Norse origin indicate a continuum of settlements where Norse was once spoken along the western littoral.

If the Norse were able to leave names for locations they explored and used as visitors, we would expect to have found Norse names spread over a much wider area than we actually do. It is surely not out of the question that the Norse would have explored and also have made certain use of the more inland areas of Scotland, at least as far in as the sea lochs penetrate the Highlands. However, Norse names are not found very far inland. There are many Norse names along the outer coast of the mainland but hardly any single, isolated names at any significant distance from other Norse names. Either an area has several Norse names or none at all. Such a distribution pattern indicates a Norse continuum along significant parts of the mainland coast. Here a fairly unbroken chain of Norse settlers would have meant that most farmers had Norse neighbours not very far away in both directions along the coast.

To illustrate what a Norse speech continuum might have looked like, we can briefly focus on two areas on the west coast, one up towards the north and one in the south. Ian Fraser has analysed the names along the coast of Wester Ross, from Loch Broom to Loch Carron.[14] He lists forty Norse names (including one single habitative name, *Ullapool*) from this section of the coastline and twelve Gaelic names, most of which he regards as post-medieval.[15] Implicitly, Fraser clearly regards the names as denotations of settlements.

On the east coast of Kintyre (see figs 1 and 3 in the article by Jennings in this volume), from Tarbert to Campbeltown, we see the same pattern again. The modern settlement names are mostly of Norse origin (again with one habitative name, *Smerby*, probably from **Smjörbýr*), and at least some of the relatively few purely Gaelic names are of a secondary type, for example, *Dippen* 'dark half-penny-land' and names with *achadh* 'field'. It is very difficult to see such stretches of Norse names as anything but products of Norse-speaking neighbourhoods.

Nicolaisen's hypothesis that it was Norse visitors and not settlers who left their onomastic imprint on the coast of the mainland is closely linked to the idea that the Norse topographical names are not settlement names — so closely linked that the argument sometimes feels circular. Nicolaisen starts his discussion on the distribution of *dalr*-names by stating, 'There is no reason to think that it [i.e. *dalr*] has ever

[14] Ian A. Fraser, 'Norse Settlement on the North-West Seaboard', in *Scandinavian Settlement in Northern Britain*, ed. by Barbara E. Crawford (London: Leicester University Press, 1995), pp. 92–105 (p. 98, fig. 21).

[15] Fraser, 'Norse Settlement', p. 97.

meant anything but what it still means in Norwegian today, i.e. "a valley".[16] He argues that in spite of the fact that many such names now denote farms, they would initially have denoted a topographical feature and only become attached to a settlement at a later stage. A name like *Crossaig* in Kintyre would then have been used by Norse visitors to designate the bay itself, and likewise *Carradale* and *Torrisdale* to denote the respective glens; only at a later stage were the names used to denote the settlements in the said locations.

One must admit that it is true that *dal* in modern Norwegian means nothing but 'valley'. However, one is discussing *names*, not appellatives, and the semantics of the name *Dal* in modern Norwegian is not so clear-cut. In Norway today, simplex primary topographical names without the definite article like *Dal*, *Nes*, and *Vik* designate settlements. Many of these simplex topographical farm names are likely to have come about during the transition to permanent settlement, around the time of the birth of Christ.[17] The earliest farms were 'super-farms' which actually occupied whole valleys or whole headlands. One can easily understand why neighbours within an area could best refer to these early settlements by indicating their location, and that with names like *Dal* and *Nes* the descriptive appellative side to the name and the address location of the settlement were semantically inseparable. In modern usage, such names are clearly dominated by the settlement itself and not so much by the topographical location of the settlement. From my own area in Nordmøre, Norway, 'nedi Dala' first and foremost designate the houses and/or the people living there. I believe this is a very early development. If there is a settlement within the area of, for example, a valley or bay, a topographical name — if it still makes sense to the users — will have dual *designata*; it will refer both to the topographical feature and the settlement itself, and the latter will probably be the most important.

Nicolaisen has coined the term *instant names* for 'ready-made' names that the colonists brought with them, like *Breiðvík* and *Sandvík*. We could also claim that the Norse brought with them a set of *instant name connotations*, where, among other things, certain types of names carried more prestige than others. The most prestigious of all would certainly be the topographical names for settlements. As a rule, even today in Norway, the early type of topographical names designate the largest farms, positioned on the best and most central land within an area. It is likely that the Norse settlers in the Viking Age would have chosen to use such prestigious names for the very first names of new settlements.

The importance of social ranking in place-names is seen when nineteenth-century Norwegian immigrants to America were told to choose a family name — patronymics were still the norm in Norway at that time. Very many chose to use a place-name as their family name, but rather than the name of the poor cottar's farm they

---

[16] Nicolaisen, *Scottish Place-Names*, p. 94.

[17] See, for example, Ola Stemshaug, *Namn i Noreg: Ei innføring i norsk stadnamngransking*, 2nd edn (Oslo: Det Norske Samlaget, 1976), p. 91.

had left behind, many of them chose the name of the main farm on which their cottar's farm was situated or simply the biggest farm in the area they had left. As a result, there are a disproportionate number of family names such as Lee (from Li) and Dahl (from Dal) among Norwegian-Americans today.

The increased frequency of compound topographical names used during the Viking period could be explained by the need for specifics to single out *designata* in more densely populated areas than were previously known. Also, the development of the ship and the resulting migration had vastly increased the geographical radius in which individuals needed names as address tags. In order to distinguish between the farms situated in the many valleys of Iceland, they were mostly given compound names. Even Ingólfr, the first Norse settler in Iceland, established himself at *Reykjavík* ('The Smoky Bay'), and when Erik the Red (Eiríkr hinn Rauði) founded his farm in Greenland, the simplex **Hlíð* ('Slope') was not found to be precise enough and a specific was added, giving *Brattahlíð* ('Steep Slope').

Between the first establishment of farms in Scandinavia and the Viking exodus, society organized around the extended family unit disintegrated. There was a gradual move towards a social organization where the individual played a more important role. We can observe this in the names of the many farms established during the Viking Age, when the person who cleared the land or took up residence on the farm starts to be remembered in the name of the farm. We see it in habitative names all over *Terra Scandinavica*, for example, *Grimshader* and *Swanibost*; and we can probably see the same process taking place in the many farms that carry a personal name compounded with a topographical generic, for example, *Torrisdale* and *Skorridale*.

By the Viking Age, there were certainly some very fashionable generics used for new settlements, for example, *staðir*, *setr*, and *bólstaðr*. However, we can observe that new settlements established during this period — in Scandinavia as well as in its colonies — were certainly also given topographical names. In Finnur Jónsson's register of over 7100 Icelandic farm names, around half are topographical names.[18] Furthermore, and perhaps of more relevance to the initial settlement, the nine most used generics indicating topography are found in approximately 35% of all the farm names of *Landnámabók*, while the eleven most used habitative generics make up approximately 33%.[19]

On the Faroe Islands we see a similar frequent usage of topographical names for settlements. Of the *bygdir* 'small villages' and *býlingar* 'farms' which are recorded by the end of the sixteenth century, 68% of the *bygd*-names and 53% of the *býlingur*-

---

[18] Finn[ur] Jónsson, 'Bæjanöfn á Íslandi', and Jóhann Kristjansson, 'Skrá við Bæjanöfn á Íslandi', in *Safn til sögu Íslands og íslenzkra bókmenta að fornu og nýju*, vol. IV (Copenhagen: Hið íslenzka bókmentafélag, 1907), pp. 412–584 and 917–37 respectively.

[19] Oskar Bandle, 'Die Ortsnamen der *Landnámabók*', in *Sjötíu ritgerðir helgaðar Jakobi Benediktssyni 20. júlí 1977*, ed. by Einar G. Pétursson and Jónas Kristjánsson (Reykjavik: Stofnun Árna Magnússon, 1977), pp. 47–68.

names have topographical generics, while the figures for habitative generics in *bygd*-names and for *býlingur*-names are 15% and 26% respectively.[20]

In the name material from the Faroes there is a striking absence of the habitative elements *staðir* and *setr/sætr*, which distinguishes the nomenclature of these islands from that of Shetland and Iceland. Lindsay MacGregor has made a convincing analysis of the similarities and differences between the Faroes and Shetland.[21] She points to the many primary farms on Shetland with topographical names and the relative secondary nature of the farms with habitative generics, and she attributes the lack of habitative generics on the Faroes to the settlement pattern on the islands. The habitative naming elements are not present because the type of settlement that they indicate is not found:

> In Shetland, *staðir*-names were applied to secondary but favourable sites, separate from primary farms; *bólstaðr*-names were given to large farms established on existing cultivated fields or to divisions of existing farms; and *sætr*-names were given to marginal settlements on hill-grazing land. All these types of settlements are absent from Faroe, precluded by the constraints of the landscape.[22]

Parts of what MacGregor says about the Faroes are applicable to the west coast of mainland Scotland, although the explanation for the lack of habitative elements is likely to be different. What is relevant is the strong argument for the primary character of farms carrying topographical names and the importance of considering the particular topography and settlement type in connection with place-name chronology.

MacGregor claims that when you take into consideration topographical and land assessment evidence, primary farms are easily distinguished from secondary farms, and that this is also reflected in the generics of secondary inland farms with topographical names.[23] The primary sites are named after the most prominent, mostly coastal, topographical features in the locality, such as *eið* 'isthmus', *strönd* 'strand'/'shore', *vágr* 'bay'/'creek', and *dalr* 'valley'. In both Shetland and the Faroes, the majority of sites with topographical names of a more secondary character relate to inland features, such as *á* 'river', *haugr* 'mound', *hamarr* 'crag'/'precipice', *brekka* 'slope', and *fjall* 'mountain'.

The Norse topographical generics used on the Scottish west coast are much more one-dimensional than those found in Shetland and the Faroes. They are basically *dalr* 'valley' and *vík* 'inlet'/'small bay', while the topographical generics of a more secondary character are, to a great extent, absent. This, along with the absence of

---

[20] Arne Thorsteinsson, 'Færøske bebyggelsesnavne med –bø', in *Den ellevte nordiske navneforskerkongressen, Sundvollen 19.-23. juni 1994*, ed. by Kristoffer Kruken, NORNA-Rapporter, 60 (Uppsala: Swedish Science Press, 1996), pp. 183–96.

[21] Lindsay J. MacGregor, 'Norse Naming Elements in Shetland and Faroe: A Comparative Study', *Northern Studies*, 23 (1986), 84–101.

[22] MacGregor, 'Norse Naming Elements', p. 99.

[23] MacGregor, 'Norse Naming Elements', p. 87.

habitative place-names, surely points to a scenario whereby a Norse population established itself along the coast. They used prominent topographical features to name their primary settlement sites, and when the time came for further expansion and division of farms, this did not happen within the medium of the Norse language.

There seems to be a growing agreement among scholars that nature-names have been used in the Scandinavian colonies to designate settlements and, more particularly, very early settlements. This is more or less explicitly expressed in works by scholars such as Ian Fraser and, not least, Barbara E. Crawford who has expressed strong reservations towards the elimination of topographical names from any settlement chronology.[24] Still, Nicolaisen's main idea has not been directly contradicted, neither by himself nor by others, and his interpretation of the distribution of the Norse settlement is still often referred to.

Hugh Marwick, the first scholar to establish a chronology of Norse settlement names in Orkney, did indeed recognize the importance of settlements with topographical names, which, he says, 'have undoubtedly to be classed among the very earliest settlements'.[25] Marwick, and later Nicolaisen, still chose to leave out such names from their chronologies, as the age of topographical names is difficult to establish. Not much has been done to correct this obvious error in the chronological schemes. It would, for example, be possible to examine the correlation between name-types and primary farms, using archaeological, geographical, and fiscal methods, as shown by MacGregor and Fraser.[26] Also, a closer study of the fringes of Norse settlement in Scotland may reveal information about chronology, and it is in this context that the west coast of the mainland is interesting.

This essay is written with the conviction that the discrepancy between habitative names and topographical names, which Nicolaisen observed, is significant, and that it might even say something important about the sequence of events during the Norse period. The usual explanation of the discrepancy, however, is not acceptable, mainly because it would assume that the Norse on the west coast of Scotland established naming patterns that were significantly different to those they used elsewhere.

What the disparity may rather indicate is an intense but short-lived Norse period on the mainland. In such a scenario the newcomers established a Norse-speaking continuum of settlements where they made use of the most prestigious naming

---

[24] Fraser, 'Norse Settlement'; Barbara E. Crawford, *Scandinavian Scotland*, Scotland in the Early Middle Ages, 2 (Leicester: Leicester University Press, 1987), p. 111; Barbara E. Crawford, 'Introduction: The Study of Place-Names', in *Scandinavian Settlement in Northern Britain*, ed. by Crawford, pp. 1–16 (pp. 10–13).

[25] Hugh Marwick, *Orkney Farm-Names* (Kirkwall: Mackintosh, 1952), p. 248.

[26] MacGregor, 'Norse Naming Elements'; Ian A. Fraser, 'What Is a *vík*? An Investigation into an Old Norse Coastal Typonym', in *Peoples and Settlement in North-West Ross*, ed. by J. R. Baldwin (Edinburgh: The Scottish Society for Northern Studies, 1994), pp. 69–78. This method has more recently, and more thoroughly, been used by Peder Gammeltoft in *The Place-Name Element bólstaðr in the North Atlantic Area* (Copenhagen: Reitzels, 2001).

elements that they knew from home in order to name farms in a rugged landscape that invited and reinforced the use of topographical naming elements. The lifespan of this Norse-speaking community seems to have been short, as there is hardly any use of topographical generics of a secondary character nor of traditional habitative elements to indicate the division of farms or the clearing of new land. By the time this was necessary, it seems that Gaelic naming elements were being used.[27] As this only points to a language shift, not an ethnic shift, this Gaelic-speaking community continued to use the Norse names that were by then well established.

---

[27] See more on this in Andrew Jennings's article in this volume.

The Norse Place-Names of Kintyre

ANDREW JENNINGS

Kintyre is the most south-westerly peninsula of the western Highlands lying between Ireland and Arran. It stretches 64 km from Tarbert to the Mull and averages 13 km in width. The landscape with its green fringe of rolling farmland and backbone of low, rounded hills in the middle, reaching only 450 m on Beinn an Tuirc, can claim pre-eminent place as the most fertile part of the Highlands. The east coast is hillier than the west with a series of wooded valleys and, with the heathery Mull, is really the only part of the peninsula which merits the description highland. The peninsula has a mild climate with a comparatively low annual rainfall of between 113 cm and 138 cm and so, given its manifest attractions, agriculture is advanced and productive with sheep, beef cattle, and dairy farming all being practised. The landscape of Kintyre is densely crowded with cairns, *duns*, and forts, clear testimony that its agricultural attractions have been known for millennia.[1]

The toponymy of Kintyre is predominantly Gaelic. This was the dominant language for about 1400 years, from the fifth century, when the *Dal Riata*, attracted by Kintyre's fertility, sailed across from Antrim in Northern Ireland, until about 1900, after which it suffered a catastrophic decline at the hands of the English. It is one of the frustrations of Gaelic onomastics that Gaelic place-names can be very difficult to date, unless early written evidence exists, because many of the generics are as intelligible today as they were a thousand years ago or more. However, some early names can be teased out. For example, two entries in the *Annals of Ulster* under 712 appear to refer to places in Kintyre, namely 'the siege of *Aberte*', which should probably be identified with modern Dunaverty, a Dark Age fort and medieval castle on the southern tip of the peninsula, and the 'burning of *Tairpert-boitter*', probably modern Tarbert, the isthmus between Kintyre and Knapdale.[2] The farm name Tirfergus, 'Land of

---

[1] See *The Archaeology of Argyll*, ed. by G. Ritchie (Edinburgh: Edinburgh University Press, 1997) for a recent overview of Kintyre's archaeological record.

[2] *The Annals of Ulster*, ed. by Seán Mac Airt and Gearóid Mac Niocaill (Dublin: Institute for Advanced Studies, 1983), s.a. 712.

Fergus', is also likely to be old, as *tír* 'land' is not a common farm name, although it is common in Irish place-names, and its combination with a male personal name brings to mind Dark Age Irish names like Tyrone (*Tír Eoghainn* 'Land of Eoghan'). Similarly, as a class of names, those in *dún* 'fort', such as Dunskeig and High and Low Dunashry in eastern Kintyre and Dunglass and the aforementioned Dunaverty in southern Kintyre, are also likely to be early, as they refer to Iron or Dark Age defended settlements.[3] Therefore, at least six of the Gaelic place-names of Kintyre are probably of Dark Age date, and many more are likely to lie, as yet, unidentified.

Into this overwhelmingly Gaelic milieu, two strata of Germanic place-names have been added: most recently, a thin patina of English names such as Stewarton, Mill Park, and Bridgend; and, at some point in the early Middle Ages, a much more important feature for the purposes of this essay, a layer of Norse names. The most recent Ordnance Survey Landranger 68 map shows that at least thirty-six settlements have Norse names.[4] These are plotted on figure 1. This number includes settlements which are now of very different sizes, ranging from the tourist town of Carradale, at the larger end of the scale, to High Cattadale and Amod, both small farms. The range of generics is similar to that found along other parts of the West Highland littoral. There are nineteen names in *dalr* 'dale' — for example, the aforementioned Carradale and High Cattadale, as well as Saddell, Muasdale, and Torrisdale; four names incorporating *á* 'river' — Lussa, Langa, Amod, and Aros; one each in *bakki* 'hill', *tangi* 'small point of land projecting onto the sea', and *völlr* 'field' — Backs, Tangy, and Lagalgarve; two in *erg* 'shieling' — Ormsary and Mingary; and about six in *gil* 'ravine' — Arnicle (*Arnegyil* 1505), Glenramskill, Dalsmirren (*Dal Smerill* 1505), Glen Remuil (*Glenmurgill* 1507), Trodigal (*Troddigil* 1793), and Uigle (*Wegill* 1505).[5]

The Norse place-names are clearly an important element within the onomasticon of Kintyre and, although they are predominantly topographical generics, they are attached to present-day settlements. There are very few habitative generics. There is one in *býr* (Smerby) and two in *ból* (Calliburn (*Kellepol* 1505) and Glenskible (*Glenskipboll* Roy 1755)). Kintyre's relative wealth of topographical generics but dearth of habitative ones places the peninsula in that region of Scotland which has been regarded, following Nicolaisen, as an area over which the Norse wielded influence but did not settle, at least not to any great degree.[6] Nicolaisen believes that this region was exploited seasonally by Norsemen, from their adjacent colonies in

---

[3] Place-names such as Dunottar, Dunollie, and Dunadd are all recorded in the Dark Ages.

[4] South Kintyre and Campbelltown, *Landranger*, 68 (Southampton: Ordnance Survey, 2001).

[5] *Gil* seems to have had a somewhat different meaning in Kintyre than in the Scandinavian homeland; there are no ravines as such in Kintyre. The name seems to be applied to small valleys or corries, in opposition to *dalr* which refers to larger valleys. This, in addition to the presence of names in *-erg*, gives the Norse toponomy of Kintyre a similarity to that of the north of England.

[6] W. F. H. Nicolaisen, *Scottish Place-Names* (London: B. T. Batsford, 1976), pp. 95–96.

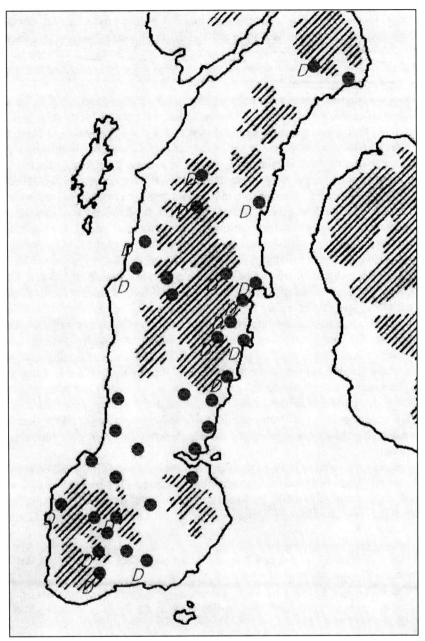

Figure 1. Norse place-names in Kintyre; Dalr marked by D. Map: A. Jennings.

the Hebrides. He reached this conclusion when he compared the relative distribution of the generic *dalr* with the habitative generics *bólstaðr*, *staðir*, and *setr* and showed that there was a definite division in western Scotland, between the western littoral and the Hebrides.[7] There is no doubt that the division exists; however, this essay will offer a different explanation.

Does the onomastic evidence really suggest that Kintyre was only within the area of Norse influence, rather than the Norse settlement area proper? It has already been pointed out that Kintyre is good farming land and a priori it is surely unlikely that the Norse, if they wielded power and influence in the western Highlands, would avoid settling in the best farming land, merely exploiting it seasonally for transhumance and hunting. If the Norse were dominant in the region, apparently dominant enough to influence the onomasticon, they would surely have taken at least some of the farming land for themselves. After all, the desire for farmland was surely one of the motivating forces behind their emigration from Norway. Indeed, Kintyre's agricultural potential was well known to them and highly regarded. According to *Heimskringla*, 'Saltíri er mikit land ok betra en in bezta ey í Suðreyjum nema Mön.'[8]

In addition to the unlikelihood of acquisitive Norsemen avoiding the best farmland, how can the survival of Norse generics as the names of modern Kintyre settlements, farms, and estates, rather than landscape features, be explained if the Norse did not settle? It is not that topographical generics make poor names for farms. Quite the reverse. The Norse very often gave their first settlements, in any given area, topographical names.[9] Topographical generics often have dual *designata*: they designate a landscape feature and the settlement thereon.[10] But in Kintyre the fact that they now designate modern settlements surely implies that ultimately the most important aspect of the name was to designate a farm. How did this come about? Is it likely that a Gaelic population, if strong enough to deter Norse settlement on the best land in western Scotland, would adopt Norse place-names for their own settlements? Surely not.

Thankfully, a solution to these problems has presented itself. The whole premise of an area of Norse onomastic influence without settlement has been seriously undermined, on theoretical grounds, by Kruse in this volume. In his discussion of user-group theory, he shows the unlikelihood of a resident farming population adopting

---

[7] However, his maps are not definitive and he did not include the two *ból*- generics of Kintyre; see Nicolaisen, *Scottish Place-Names*, p. 96.

[8] Snorri Sturluson, *Heimskringla*, ed. by Finnur Jónsson (Copenhagen: Gad, 1911), p. 524. 'Kintyre is a great land, and better than the best island in the Hebrides, excepting Man', in *Early Sources of Scottish History A.D. 500–1286*, ed. and trans. by Allan Orr Anderson, 2 vols (Edinburgh: Oliver & Boyd, 1922; repr. Stamford: Paul Watkins, 1990), II, 113.

[9] Barbara E. Crawford, *Scandinavian Scotland*, Scotland in the Early Middle Ages, 2 (Leicester: Leicester University Press, 1987), p. 104.

[10] See Arne Kruse's essay in this volume.

place-names from an itinerant one, whether they be fishermen, traders, or Vikings with a Gaelic-speaking crew (in the latter case, he points out that the Norse were more likely to have borrowed names than vice versa). He argues that if one applies user-group theory to western Scotland, one has to accept that the only explanation for Norse place-names in any given area is a resident Norse community. Without a continuum of actual Norse settlement there would be no Norse names preserved. So, even if one accepted that the Norse topographical names in Kintyre did not designate settlements, the Gaels themselves would not have borrowed them, leaving us with the problem of having to posit a Norse community because we have the names, but not being able to identify any of their settlements.

All things being considered, it is logical to propose that a modern settlement with a Norse name in Kintyre can be traced back to a Norse settlement. This also removes the inconsistency whereby modern farms and villages with Norse topographical names in Lewis are regarded as bona fide Norse settlements, but those in Kintyre are not.

Despite the lack of a *Landnámabók* for Kintyre, stating categorically that a particular settler established a particular farm, giving it a particular topographical name, some very useful later historical sources provide reasonable corroboration for the position that the Norse names have always primarily designated farming settlements. As can be seen, the distribution of Norse names is also highly suggestive of the type of linguistic/ethnic continuum Kruse postulates for the creation of the names.[11] There is a dearth of names on the west coast, but on the east coast there are many, and most of the major settlements there bear Norse names.

Kintyre is fortunate in having an extensive series of sixteenth-century rentals. These Crown Rentals of 1505 and 1506 were drawn up in the aftermath of the demise of the Lordship of the Isles, there being a desire on the behalf of the crown to see the value of their new territory. Norse names are an important feature of the estates recorded: 136 names or 79% are definitely Gaelic, as would be expected, but thirty names or about 17% are Norse (most of them are still in existence today). These names clearly refer to estates and farms, each owing certain rents, both monetary and in kind, to the Crown. For example, *Mongastill* and *Ballach* (a combined estate worth 8 *merks*)[12] owed 8 *merks* in money, eight great stones weight of cheese with *cain* (an old Gaelic tax), and a pig. *Rynnadil*, on the other hand, owed 4 *merks* in money, four weights of cheese with *cain*, and a sheep. This is the same range of dues as those owed by the Gaelic-named estates. When a comparison is made, it is clear that Norse-named farms and estates are as valuable, on average, as those with Gaelic names.

There are some problems in making the comparison. For example, some of the names are grouped together in multiple entries, when more than one estate was held by one person. *Katadill, Gartmayn, Kapergan, Brokland,* and *Gartloskin* were held by the poet (originally the *fili*) of the Lord of the Isles and altogether they make up

---

[11] See Arne Kruse's essay in this volume.

[12] A *merk* was worth two-thirds of a Scottish pound.

8 *merks* of land. Of these only *Katadill* is clearly a Norse name (*Brokland* is possibly Norse), and its value is unclear. However, there are a sufficient number of free-standing estates to make a comparison. The average value of estates in -*dalr* is 3.25 *merks*, which compares with the average of 3.42 *merks* for all the Gaelic-named estates. Further, if one leaves out the anomalous *Kyllewnane*, which, at the huge value of 17 *merks*, is worth much more than any other estate, the average value of the Gaelic-named estates falls to 3.16 *merks*, which is exactly the same as the average of all the Norse-named estates. Clearly, there is nothing odd about the Norse-named estates which would lead one to suspect their origin was different from those with a Gaelic pedigree. One appears to be dealing with a pattern of old, established estates, some of which happen to have Norse names. These thirty Norse-named estates may represent pre-existing estates given Norse names by new Norse owners. At the very least, in 1505 the Norse topographical generics are functioning as the names of estates in the same way as their Gaelic-named neighbours. Surely, there is no reason to suppose that the situation was different in the Norse period.

Clearly, the weight of argument and onomastic evidence suggests that the Norse did settle in Kintyre and that the topographical generics represent their farms and estates. However, to return to the problem of the missing habitative generics, why did the Norse not establish farms with habitative generics in Kintyre? The answer may lie in the relative date at which topographical and habitative names were laid down. Nicolaisen may have isolated chronological strata in the development of Norse settlement, but not the ones he initially believed.

The distributions of the habitative generics *staðir* and *bólstaðr* suggested to Nicolaisen that one could map the gradual spread of Norse settlement down the western seaboard, from the north to the south. To Nicolaisen, *staðir* represented the initial area of Norse settlement, whilst *bólstaðr*, with the wider distribution, represented the greatest area of settlement.[13] This hypothesis has met with criticism, primarily because it ignores the topographical generics.[14] Throughout the Norse world, habitative settlement names tend to be secondary to those bearing topographical names. The need to call one's farm '. . . farm' becomes paramount when the local landscape has already been used to designate a settlement. For example, the most widespread Norse habitative generic *bólstaðr* (often perhaps just -*ból*) used by Nicolaisen to define the area of Norse settlement proper, is likely to represent the division of an older, bigger farm, which probably had a topographical name.[15] MacGregor defines the *bólstaðr* farms

---

[13] Nicolaisen, *Scottish Place-Names*, pp. 90–91.

[14] See Crawford, *Scandinavian Scotland*, p. 111, and Gillian Fellows-Jensen 'Viking Settlement in the Northern and Western Isles: The Place-Name Evidence as Seen from Denmark and the Danelaw', in *The Northern and Western Isles in the Viking World: Survival, Continuity and Change*, ed. by Alexander Fenton and Hermann Pálsson (Edinburgh: John Donald, 1984), pp. 148–68 (p. 154).

[15] Crawford, *Scandinavian Scotland*, p. 110.

as those established on existing cultivated fields or on divisions of existing farms,[16] whilst Thomson suggests *bólstaðr* names were generated by splitting townships.[17]

If *bólstaðr* does signify secondary settlement, the map of its distribution, as the widest occurring habitative generic, represents the widest possible area where secondary Norse settlement took place, not the complete area of Norse settlement in Scotland. The difference between the distributions of *bólstaðr* and *dalr* would then show that primary and secondary Norse settlement was not completely coterminous. The area with topographical elements but no *bólstaðr*-names is not an area of Norse influence (which, as already mentioned, is a questionable concept), but an area of restricted Norse settlement, where for some reason secondary settlement did not take place to any great extent.

Kintyre falls within this area of restricted secondary Norse settlement. Here, for some reason, the Norse user-group which created Norse topographical names was unable or unwilling to create secondary, habitative farm-names. Why?

On the Faroe Islands, essentially uninhabited before the arrival of the Norse, secondary settlement was restricted by geographical considerations.[18] However, in Kintyre, and by extension elsewhere along the western littoral, the answer is more likely to lie in the interaction between the Norse and the native population. This native population could have hindered the development of further Norse settlement. One can posit a swift absorption of the Norse settlers into the Gaelic-speaking milieu. If so, the settlers would no longer have coined Norse place-names as further settlements developed; rather they would now use Gaelic elements. There is nothing to suggest that a Gaelic-speaking community did not coexist with the Norse settlers in Kintyre, and indeed the distribution of Norse place-names, when compared to the distribution of the *duns* (see fig. 2), strongly suggests that the Norse settlement avoided the area of densest native settlement.[19]

There is also evidence for settlements with Gaelic names being secondary to those with Norse names, which would fit the hypothesis. If one looks at figure 3, there is clearly a continuum of Norse settlement in the Carradale area. The major settlements bear *dalr* names, but there are no secondary Norse habitative names. However, there appear to be secondary Gaelic elements, in *achadh* 'field' (Auchnasavil, secondary to Rhonadale) and *peighinn* 'pennyland' (Dippen, secondary to Carradale; Lephin-corrach, secondary to Torrisdale; and Lephinmore, secondary to Saddell).

---

[16] L. J. MacGregor, 'Norse Naming Elements in Shetland and Faroe: A Comparative Study', *Northern Studies*, 23 (1986), 84–101 (p. 99).

[17] W. P. L. Thomson, 'Orkney Farm-Names: A Re-Assessment of Their Chronology', in *Scandinavian Settlement in Northern Britain*, ed. by Barbara E. Crawford (London: Leicester University Press, 1995), pp. 42–63 (p. 58).

[18] MacGregor, 'Norse Naming Elements', p. 14.

[19] Although the *duns* are difficult to date, they are indicative of the area most densely settled during the Iron and Dark Ages.

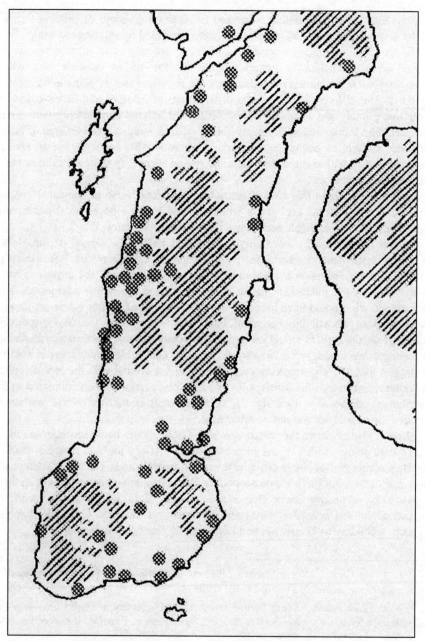

Figure 2. Distribution of Duns in Kintyre. Map: A. Jennings.

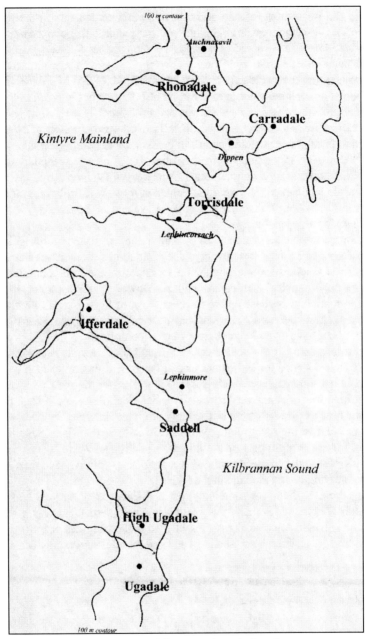

Figure 3. Carradale area. Map: A. Jennings.

Achadh can be seen to refer to secondary farming settlements in the rentals. In these, the Gaelic-named estates fall into a clear pattern: the two names in *baile* 'farming settlement' are valued at 4 *merks* (*Ballegrogane, Ballemaenach*[20]), while the three names in *achadh* 'field' are all worth 2 *merks* (*Achtydow, Achynriche, Achinnasawle*). In other words, an *achadh* is valued at half that of a *baile*, indicating the division of an earlier *baile* estate. There are also four names in *ceathramh* 'fourth', presumably 'fourth of a *baile*' which are worth 1 *merk* (*Kerre Maenach, Kerref Nacreg, Kerref Nasee, Kerref Callyn*). This is good corroboration of Nicolaisen's position that throughout Scotland names in *achadh* are generally secondary to those in *baile*.[21] However, in the Saddell area, Auchnasavil is clearly secondary to Rhonadale. In the rentals, as already mentioned, Auchnasavil (*Achinnasawle*) is valued at 2 *merks*, while Rhonadale (*Rynnadill*) is valued at 4 *merks*. Similarly, in the case of Dippen and Carradale, the former (*Dwpeyn*) is valued at 3 *merks* while the latter (*Ardcardale*) is valued at 4 *merks*.[22]

In summary, the Norse place-names of Kintyre appear to tell an intriguing story. The Norse came to an inhabited territory. They settled in sufficient numbers amongst the indigenous Gaelic-speaking population to establish a Norse community which coined the topographical settlement names. However, they cannot have been completely dominant, because unlike in other areas of Scandinavian Scotland, they had become naturalized before any significant secondary settlement took place. This process need not have taken longer than a generation or two.

The absolute date for the settlement is difficult to ascertain, because as yet no archaeological evidence for settlement has surfaced, and theoretically it could have happened at any time during which Norse was spoken in the west of Scotland. So any suggestion must remain very speculative. For example, it could have happened at the same time as the settlement of the Inner or Outer Hebrides, in the first flush of Norse expansion in the early ninth century. However, at that time, Kintyre was an important, indeed central, part of the kingdom of the *Dal Riata*, which was sufficiently powerful under the leadership of Kenneth MacAlpin (Cínaed mac Alpín) to undertake the conquest of Pictland in the 840s.[23]

Perhaps the *Dal Riata*, for some now lost political reason, allowed Norse settlement within Kintyre, or perhaps this particular Norse settlement was a secondary wave from the Norse colonies already established in the Hebrides or Ireland. It could be argued that the generics *-erg* 'shieling' and *-gil* 'ravine' suggest the latter.[24] *Erg* is

---

[20] This estate is divided into two parts of 2 *merks* apiece.

[21] Nicolaisen, *Scottish Place-Names*, p. 141.

[22] The form *Ardcardale* 'High Carradale', from Gaelic *ard* 'high', suggests a division of the original Carradale estate, again within a Gaelic-speaking milieu.

[23] For an account of this period, see A. P. Smyth, *Warlords and Holy Men: Scotland AD 80–1000* (Edinburgh: Edinburgh University Press, 1984).

[24] The place-names bearing these generics are given at the beginning of this essay.

a borrowing from Old Gaelic *airge* and it occurs frequently in the Faroe Islands, Man, and northern England.[25] One must allow some time for the borrowing to have taken place, and, unless Kintyre is seen as the area of its genesis, it would appear to be a good marker for a secondary wave. Similarly, one must allow time for a semantic shift in the meaning of *gil*, which has changed from its original Norse meaning of 'ravine' to 'small valley'.

Taking these factors into account, the second half of the ninth century might be the most likely period for the setting down of Norse names in Kintyre, perhaps in response to a power vacuum caused by Kenneth MacAlpin's conquest of Pictland.

---

[25] E. Megaw, 'The Manx "Eary" and its Significance', in *Man and Environment in the Isle of Man*, ed. by Peter Davey, British Archaeological Reports, British Series, 54, 2 vols (Oxford: British Archaeological Association, 1978) I, 327–45.

The Scandinavian Languages in the British Isles: The Runic Evidence

MICHAEL P. BARNES

Efforts have been made previously to squeeze linguistic information out of the Scandinavian runic inscriptions found in the British Isles. These have almost all concerned limited geographical areas. As part of an attempt to assess how long the Scandinavian language survived in England, Ekwall pondered the Pennington (E 9) and Carlisle (E 3) inscriptions.[1] Other parts of the corpus he dismissed as uninterpretable or having nothing to do with 'the Scandinavians who settled in England in the 9th century'.[2] Returning to the theme some forty years later, Page offered a more thorough survey of the epigraphical material, examining all the then-known Scandinavian runic inscriptions from England, as well as a number in Anglo-Saxon runes and the roman alphabet recording Anglo-Saxon language.[3] In later articles Page has considered the intermixture of Celtic and Norse on the Manx rune-stones.[4] I have

---

[1] Eilert Ekwall, 'How Long Did the Scandinavian Language Survive in England?', in *A Grammatical Miscellany Offered to Otto Jespersen on his Seventieth Birthday*, ed. by N. Bøgholm, Aage Brusendorff, and C. A. Bodelsen (Copenhagen: Levin & Munksgaard; London: Allen & Unwin, 1930), pp. 17–30. The numbers in brackets refer to the system of classification I have devised for Scandinavian runic inscriptions found in the British Isles. A complete list of inscriptions, ordered by this system, is found in the appendix to this article; the letter refers to the region where the inscription was found (e.g. E for England; OR for Orkney) and the number to the date of discovery, with 1 representing the first inscription discovered in that particular region.

[2] Ekwall, 'How Long Did the Scandinavian Language Survive in England?', p. 25.

[3] R. I. Page, 'How Long Did the Scandinavian Language Survive in England? The Epigraphical Evidence', in *England before the Conquest: Studies in Primary Sources Presented to Dorothy Whitelock*, ed. by Peter Clemoes and Kathleen Hughes (Cambridge: Cambridge University Press, 1971), pp. 165–81.

[4] R. I. Page, 'The Manx Rune-Stones', in *The Viking Age in the Isle of Man*, ed. by Christine Fell and others (London: Viking Society for Northern Research, 1983), pp. 133–46.

myself contributed a little to the field. A 1991 article[5] (revised in 1994)[6] discussed in detail the language of the Maeshowe inscriptions from Orkney, while the linguistic status of other Orcadian inscriptions, as well as the few from Shetland, was treated briefly in a 1998 booklet on Norn.[7] Sporadic comments on language can be found in my 1992 survey of the Scandinavian runic material from the Northern Isles, Scotland, England, and Ireland,[8] and in a 1993 revaluation of the evidence for the occurrence of Norse in the British Isles I drew in part on runic sources.[9] Finally, the edition Hagland, Page, and I compiled of the runic inscriptions of Ireland includes a section on language.[10]

The aim of the present essay is to pull some of these scattered threads together: to provide a language-orientated overview of the relevant runic material and to consider the contribution the corpus as a whole can make to our knowledge of Scandinavian speech in the British Isles.

Altogether there are about 140 complete or fragmentary inscriptions in Britain and Ireland that employ Scandinavian runes. The language of most is Scandinavian of one type or another, but some are so fragmentary as to make linguistic identification impossible. A number do not, or do not seem, to record language at all. One of the inscriptions from England is in Middle English,[11] and another in an idiom that has been said to incorporate features from both Scandinavian and English.[12]

Where no linguistic message is discernible, the occurrence of Scandinavian runes offers evidence of Scandinavian background or influence, but little more. Sometimes rune forms may suggest the tradition of one part of Scandinavia more than another.

Raymond I. Page, 'Celtic and Norse on the Manx Rune-Stones', in *Medialität und mittelalterliche insulare Literatur*, ed. by Hildegard L. C. Tristram (Tübingen: Gunter Narr, 1992), pp. 131–47.

[5] Michael P. Barnes, 'Norwegian, Norn, Icelandic or West Norse? The Language of the Maeshowe Inscriptions', in *Festskrift til Ottar Grønvik på 75-årsdagen den 21. oktober 1991*, ed. by John Ole Askedal, Harald Bjorvand, and Eyvind Fjeld Halvorsen (Oslo: Universitetsforlaget, 1991), pp. 70–87.

[6] Michael P. Barnes, *The Runic Inscriptions of Maeshowe, Orkney* (Uppsala: Institutionen för nordiska språk, Uppsala universitet, 1994), pp. 44–60.

[7] Michael P. Barnes, *The Norn Language of Orkney and Shetland* (Lerwick: Shetland Times, 1998), pp. 10–11.

[8] Michael P. Barnes, 'Towards an Edition of the Scandinavian Runic Inscriptions of the British Isles: Some Thoughts', *Northern Studies*, 29 (1992), 32–42.

[9] Michael P. Barnes, 'Norse in the British Isles', in *Viking Revaluations*, ed. by Anthony Faulkes and Richard Perkins (London: Viking Society for Northern Research, 1993), pp. 65–84.

[10] Michael P. Barnes, Jan Ragnar Hagland, and R. I. Page, *The Runic Inscriptions of Viking Age Dublin* (Dublin: Royal Irish Academy, 1997), pp. 13–15.

[11] Bridekirk, Cumbria (E 1); see appendix.

[12] Pennington, Cumbria (E 9); see appendix.

We should remember in this connection, however, that agreement has not yet been reached on whether variation in runic usage in the northern homelands — at least during the Viking Age — was determined primarily by geography or function.

Other uncertainties beset attempts to use the Scandinavian inscriptions of the British Isles as evidence for the language or languages the Norse immigrants brought with them. Ekwall rejected the testimony of some of the inscriptions found in England on the grounds that they were not made by descendants of ninth-century settlers. He was referring here in particular to the St Paul's stone (E 2) and the Lincoln comb case (E 4), the former because he thought it likely to commemorate 'some Dane who came over with Cnut', the latter because there was 'nothing to prove that the comb was made in England'.[13] To the extent Ekwall's objections are accepted, their implications invalidate as linguistic evidence a great many more than the two inscriptions concerned. Recent English discoveries, for example, include the Winchester rune-stone fragment (E 12), also likely to be connected with Cnut's campaign and rule during the early eleventh century, and the ninth- or tenth-century Penrith penannular brooch (E 15), part of a Celtic hoard, whose runes were probably inscribed far from the spot where it was found. Eight of the fifteen Scottish inscriptions occur in a rock overhang on Holy Island, off Arran. Scottish though these may be in terms of location, there is every reason to believe they were carved not by natives of the islands but by visitors from Norway anchored up for a few days in Lamlash Bay, the stretch of water dividing Holy Island from Arran. An even more striking example of a group of inscriptions left by visitors is the Maeshowe collection from Orkney. It is likely that most, if not all, of these were carved by Norwegians who joined Earl Rǫgnvaldr Kali for his crusade to the Holy Land 1151–53.[14] If this was not the group responsible, it was surely some other party or succession of Norwegians. The runic versatility exhibited in Maeshowe has no counterpart elsewhere in Orkney, or indeed anywhere else in the British Isles with the possible exception of the Isle of Man, and there is little in the language or runic usage of the inscriptions incompatible with an assumption of Norwegian authorship.

The Penrith brooch excepted, these are relatively clear-cut examples of runic inscriptions made by visitors from Scandinavia, or at least by people newly arrived from the North. About the authorship of certain others one cannot be anything like as sure. The twelve found in Dublin during excavations of the 1970s and '80s are all carved on portable objects. Since, however, these are mostly objects of little value — bits of wood and bone — it is probable they were acquired in Dublin and the runes scratched on them there. But this need not have been done by long-standing or even recent residents; it could as easily be the work of people passing through — merchants, soldiers, or other visitors.

There is a further general problem to be considered before drawing conclusions from runic evidence about language in the Viking Age or its aftermath. This concerns

---

[13] Ekwall, 'How Long Did the Scandinavian Language Survive in England?', p. 25.

[14] Barnes, *The Runic Inscriptions of Maeshowe, Orkney*, pp. 37–43.

the status of the inscriptions on which the conclusions are based. Many more inscribed objects found in the British Isles than the ones I list or mention in the appendix at the end of this essay have at one time or another been declared runic. Some, for example Harrogate and Knockando (Speyside), have been shown to bear only 'rune-like' characters, and thus to hold no linguistic message — none that can be recovered, at least.[15] Others, for example Barnspike (Cumbria), are fakes — modern inscriptions carved with intent to deceive.[16] Yet others are modern inscriptions carved for fun. Orkney in particular is well endowed with the efforts of the fun-loving rune-carver. The ready availability in the islands of a postcard featuring prominently the name **ingibiorh** from Maeshowe inscription no. 9 has inspired copies in Cuween Hill Cairn and at the Ring of Brogar, while implausible and incomprehensible sequences of runes or rune-like symbols adorn stones in Unstan Cairn and at the Broch of Borwick. These and similar carvings elsewhere in Orkney so obviously announce themselves as modern that there is no danger of confusing them with the real thing. Not all of the Orcadian runic material can be so easily pronounced modern or old, however. In a recent article,[17] I attempted to show that doubt attaches to about half the accepted corpus outside Maeshowe, in particular the twig-rune inscriptions,[18] most of which have no clear provenance or context and none of which makes any sense. In as far as they do not appear to record language, Orkney's twig-runes are of course of little interest in the present connection, but they warn us against believing inscriptions to be old simply because they were held to be so by earlier scholars.

Bearing the foregoing reservations very much in mind, I will now consider what can be learnt from the Scandinavian runic inscriptions of the British Isles about the fate of Scandinavian speech in the areas of Viking settlement.

The seven inscriptions from Shetland so far accepted as runic are all fragmentary. Four, possibly five, of these pieces seem to belong to Viking Age commemorative

---

[15] Page, 'How Long Did the Scandinavian Language Survive in England?', pp. 169–70; Aslak Liestøl, 'Runes', in *The Northern and Western Isles in the Viking World: Survival, Continuity and Change*, ed. by Alexander Fenton and Hermann Pálsson (Edinburgh: John Donald, 1984), pp. 224–38 (p. 225).

[16] W. G. Collingwood, 'Remains of the Pre-Norman Period', in *The Victoria History of the Counties of England: A History of Cumberland*, ed. by James Wilson (London: Archibald Constable, 1901), I, 253–93 (pp. 279–80).

[17] Michael P. Barnes, 'Runic Tradition in Orkney: From Orphir to the Belsair Guest House', in *International Scandinavian and Medieval Studies in Memory of Gerd Wolfgang Weber*, ed. by Michael Dallapiazza and others (Trieste: Edizioni Parnaso, 2000), pp. 43–54.

[18] Twig-runes are one of several related manifestations of a runic cipher based on a division of the *fuþark* into three groups. In Viking Age and medieval Scandinavian tradition, where the *fuþark* consists of sixteen characters, the division is normally 6:5:5, that is, **f u þ ã/o r k : h n i a s : t b m l y/R**. Twig-runes are composed by arranging branches on either side of a vertical, the number on one side denoting the group and on the other position within the group. Thus **Y**, for example, will normally stand for group 2, rune 1, that is, **h**. To add to the puzzle, the groups are numbered in reverse order, **t b m l y/R** counting as 1, **f u þ ã/o r k** as 3.

stones (SH 1–5). The rune forms used are similar to those found in tenth-century western Norway and Man: fundamentally short-twig, but probably — dependent on the reading of two damaged characters — incorporating long-branch Ψ (**m**) and ⴕ (**h**);[19] the single example of **b** appears to have the rare form ⴕ, found once or twice in the North Atlantic colonies. In addition to these five stone fragments there is what appears to be part of a graffito of indeterminate age (SH 7),[20] and a badly worn medieval grave slab (SH 6).[21] Little can be concluded from the rune forms on either of these. The two diagnostic characters of the graffito, ⴕ and ⅂, can tell us nothing without some indication of the inscription's age, and the twenty or so runes still legible on the grave slab are compatible with medieval usage anywhere in Scandinavia.

In terms of their phonology, morphology, syntax, and vocabulary the Shetland inscriptions contain nothing that is not also found in Norway. The *u*-mutated form **foþur** (SH 3) typifies West Scandinavian usage as does the preserved diphthong in **ra(i)s(ti)** (SH 4) and **staïn** (SH 6).

Not surprisingly, the meagre runic evidence only confirms what we already knew: Shetland in the Viking Age and early medieval period was an integral part of a West Scandinavian world that had spread from Norway across the North Atlantic. Throughout the period there was lively contact with the motherland, and to that extent we cannot be sure whether the preserved inscriptions were carved by descendants of the early settlers, later settlers, or kinsfolk from Norway. The Eshaness grave slab seems very likely to have been the product of imported skill — if not itself imported. One cannot but be struck by the lack of analogues — indeed, the absence of any evidence of a runic tradition in the islands stretching into the Middle Ages. Who on the north-west mainland of Shetland in the thirteenth or fourteenth century, one wonders, would have had the knowledge and skill to fashion such an object?

Though the Orkney runic corpus holds considerable general interest, it tells us little more about the use of Scandinavian in the British Isles than its Shetland counterpart. As already indicated, most, if not all, of the Maeshowe inscriptions seem to have been the work of Norwegian visitors to the islands. Orthographic idiosyncrasies appear here and there in the collection, but they are difficult to localize. Two phonological features of Maeshowe, apparent confusion of historical /au/ and /ɔ/ and the loss of initial /h-/, might, but need not, reflect early Orcadian dialect.[22]

Relevant information is equally hard to extract from the rest of the Orkney material. As already indicated, its ubiquitous twig-runes shed no light on linguistic

---

[19] See Aslak Liestøl, 'Runer', in *Kulturhistorisk leksikon for nordisk middelalder*, 22 vols (Copenhagen: Rosenkilde & Bagger, 1956–78), XIV (1969), cols 471–78 (cols 472–73).

[20] See Michael P. Barnes and R. I. Page, 'Two Runic Inscriptions from the Northern Isles', *Nytt om runer*, 10 (1995 (1996)), 12–13.

[21] See Michael P. Barnes, 'The Runic Stone at Cross Kirk, Eshaness, Shetland', *Nytt om runer*, 8 (1993), 12–14.

[22] Barnes, *The Runic Inscriptions of Maeshowe, Orkney*, pp. 58–59.

matters and may in any case be recent products. Of three inscriptions containing both plain and twig-runes, Unstan (OR 2) is certainly modern; Stackrue (OR 1) and Skara Brae (OR 13) look suspicious, but could be old. Including Stackrue and Skara Brae, there are sixteen inscriptions that might in theory yield information about language in Viking Age and medieval Orkney. This can readily be reduced to thirteen, however. Since so little is visible on Birsay II, III, and V (OR 8–9, 16), it is unsafe to conclude anything other than that we have here the remains of runes.

None of the thirteen is easy to date. As probable fragments of raised commemorative inscriptions, Isegarth (OR 17) and Skaill (OR 18) are likely to be from the Viking Age, and so, with the phonological form **uas** 'was' (later Scandinavian *var*), is the apparent graffito, Orphir II (OR 15). Taken together, the runes of these three inscriptions, with certain ᚼ (**n**), ᛅ (**a**), ᛁ and ᚼ (**s**), and ᛒ (**b**), are typologically closest to the mix of short-twig and long-branch forms that came to be common in Norway around the beginning of the eleventh century and are often called the 'Norwegian mixed' alphabet.[23] Birsay I (OR 6), also apparently a graffito, exhibits the same inventory, provided one accepts ᛏ as a bind (runic ligature) of ᛅ and ᚼ. The dotted ï[24] of Orkney (OR 3) and the dotted k̈s of Orphir I (OR 10) point to the eleventh century or later, dotting apparently making its first appearance in Denmark towards the end of the tenth century. With a *terminus post quem* of *c*. 1000, the runes of these inscriptions could perhaps be classed as 'expanded Norwegian mixed', but they might equally well be medieval, which would make them more difficult to place in terms of geographical origin. Tuquoy (OR 14) has rune forms compatible with those in Maeshowe, making, for example, a graphemic distinction between ᛅ (**a**) and ᛏ (**æ**). There are not enough diagnostic forms, however, for us to pronounce it typologically identical with the Maeshowe corpus and thus early medieval Norwegian; like OR 3 and 10, it could equally well be plain medieval. Birsay IV (OR 11), the beginning of a *fuþark*, contains ᚠ (**ã/o**). This form of the fourth rune with branches pointing right is found in Norway almost exclusively in short-twig inscriptions, probably from the middle or later part of the Viking Age. In East Scandinavia, on the other hand, it continues to be used, though with decreasing frequency, until 1200 or so. With Orkney so firmly within the West Scandinavian ambit, it is likely that Birsay IV's ᚠ represents early Norwegian usage, but with a portable object of this kind one cannot be entirely sure. The five remaining inscriptions, OR 1, 12–13, 19, and Belsair, have either no diagnostic forms at all or so few they cannot be used to assign the runes to a particular type or period. Archaeological context is too uncertain to narrow this range of possibilities. It does not conflict with a Viking Age date for Orphir II, but that is about the extent of the help it can offer.

Little in the way of phonological, grammatical, or lexical information is to be had from the Orkney inscriptions outside Maeshowe. Only some twenty words are

---

[23] Liestøl, 'Runer', col. 475.

[24] On the reasons for the use of diacritic ¨ in transliteration, see Barnes, Hagland, and Page, *The Runic Inscriptions of Viking Age Dublin*, p. 10.

recorded more or less in their entirety, and even with considerable good will fewer than six sentences can be recognized. As examples of Viking Age or medieval Scandinavian, these bits and pieces are indistinguishable from contemporary Norwegian. We see indications of phonological change (older **uas** 'was' *v.* younger **ir** 'is'), which, like runic dotting, could reflect contact with linguistic development in Norway, or even the wider Scandinavian world. If **koþ** in Orphir I (OR 10) is the dative of Old Norse *goð/guð* 'God', it has an older West Scandinavian form with the root vowel /o/ — not entirely surprisingly (possibly also documented in OR 1) — and lacks the appropriate -*i* ending. The non-marking of grammatical endings is sometimes taken as a sign of break-down in the inflectional system resulting from intimate contact with a foreign tongue,[25] but that is hardly likely in Norse Orkney. It is in any case not certain Orphir's **koþ** has anything to do with 'God'.[26]

Like Shetland, Orkney was an integral part of the West Scandinavian world. To that extent there must be the same uncertainty whether runic inscriptions found there — even if it is likely they were made in the islands — are the work of native Orcadians and thus indicative of local usage. The Maeshowe carvings stand as a warning against such a facile assumption.

This warning, it turns out, applies with equal force to Scotland. As noted above, eight of the fifteen inscriptions that make up the Scottish corpus appear, like those in Maeshowe, to have been carved by Norwegians. These casual graffiti (SC 3–7, 9, 12–13), probably to be associated in their entirety with the abortive Scottish campaign of King Hákon Hákonarson in 1263, reveal a number of things about runic usage and language, but not the runic usage and language of the Scottish islands.

Of the seven remaining Scottish inscriptions two are from Caithness (SC 11, 15), three from the Hebrides (SC 8, 10, 14), one from Strathclyde (SC 2), and one from Angus (SC 1). All but the two last are on stone — raised crosses or grave slabs, or (as far as can be determined) fragments thereof, and thus likely to have been made close to the place where they were found. The Strathclyde and Angus inscriptions are on portable objects and their places of origin impossible to determine.

Thurso I and II (SC 11, 15), the former a grave slab of uncertain date in the form of a cross, the latter no more than a fragment, are from an area as firmly integrated into the West Scandinavian world in its time as the Northern Isles. Runic usage and language by and large reflect this. The rune forms are compatible with the Norwegian mixed alphabet, except for a possible ᚾ (**n**) on Thurso II, which may be an overcut ᚽ, and the unique ᛁ on Thurso I, almost certainly a form of short-twig **s**, with full-length vertical and point at the top. As quite often in the British Isles, but only sporadically in Norway, **b** denotes [β] as well as [b] (Thurso I: **ubirlak, ikulb** for

---

[25] See Barnes, Hagland, and Page, *The Runic Inscriptions of Viking Age Dublin*, p. 15.

[26] For an alternative interpretation, see Jan Ragnar Hagland, 'Two Runic Inscriptions from Orphir, Orkney', in *The Viking Age in Caithness, Orkney and the North Atlantic*, ed. by Colleen E. Batey, Judith Jesch, and Christopher D. Morris (Edinburgh: Edinburgh University Press, 1993), pp. 370–74.

yfirlag, Ingólf). Of linguistic forms, West Scandinavian **foþur** with *u*-mutation may be noted (Thurso I), and the hapax legomenon **ubirlak**, derived from the verb phrase *leggja yfir* 'place over'. Whether this latter is a purely local word or existed more widely without otherwise being recorded cannot be determined.

As distinct from Orkney and Shetland, it is just possible we see here signs of local usage: the 'upside-down' **s**, the use of **b** for [β], and the word *yfirlag* — though the first may be a plain error, the second is occasionally found in Norway and elsewhere in Scandinavia, and the third may have been a more common word than appears from the existing sources.

The three Hebridean inscriptions, Kilbar, Inchmarnock, and Iona (SC 8, 10, 14), are geographically quite widely separated and would seem to have little in common. None can easily be dated. Kilbar is a raised stone of some size, decorated by a cross in low relief on the face opposite the inscription. Inchmarnock is a fragment of a stone that may have been raised or laid, sculptured into the shape of a cross. Iona is the remains — about half — of a smallish grave slab; the slab sports an elaborate incised cross within a double border, the border providing framing lines for the runes, which are not necessarily contemporaneous with the decoration.

The Kilbar runes are much worn. The diagnostic forms clearly visible are compatible with either the short-twig or the Norwegian mixed alphabet. The same might be said of Inchmarnock but for the presence of ï (concerning dotting, see the description of OR 3 and OR 10's runes above). The runes on the Iona slab look to be of short-twig type, though both ᚤ and ᚠ occur for **a**, and three important diagnostic forms, those of **h**, **m**, and **R**, are missing. As in the case of Thurso I, Iona uses **b** (in the rare form ᛔ, compare Shetland above) for [β]. Unusually, it represents the initial vowel in the name *Ǫlvir/Ølvir* by the digraph **ou**; digraphic spelling of /ɔ/ is common enough in both Scandinavia and the British Isles, but the rune preceding **u** is then normally **a**.

In terms of language and content these three inscriptions exhibit a high number of unusual forms and constructions. Kilbar has accusative **þur(:)kirþu** with final **-u** for normal *Þorgerði* with *-i* ending; **s(t)i∗ar**, supposedly for *Steinar(s)*, and **ristr** for *reistr*, with monographic spelling of /ei/; and **kurs** for *kross* with apparent metathesis. Inchmarnock contains demonstrative **þinï** (acc. m.) with what seems to be a reduced final vowel (normally *þenna*), and preposition **til** for expected *aft/eftir* following **krus:þinï**. Iona has **laþi** for *lagði* with missing velar spirant, **stan** for *stein* with a monographic spelling of /ei/ different from the one on Kilbar, and demonstrative **þinsi** (acc. m.), rare in Norway, but common in Denmark and Sweden. Kilbar, furthermore, does not appear to record the name of the person who commissioned the monument. As commonly interpreted it says: 'In memory of Þorgerðr Steinarsdóttir is this cross raised' — wording reminiscent of that on a few early Viking Age stones from Scandinavia, which state, 'In memory of X stands this stone/stand these runes', rather than the usual, 'X raised this stone in memory of Y'.

The question is: what is to be made of these various aberrations? No clear pattern emerges and some of the word forms, for example **laþi**, **stan**, have been dismissed as carving errors. Such forms are, however, attested in Scandinavia — whatever the reason for them.[27] Another possible error is **kurs**, occasioned perhaps by the similarity of **u** and **r**, though metathesis of a vowel and /r/ is a common enough phenomenon in Norwegian,[28] and *kors* is the usual form of the word in Danish and Swedish. Not uncommon in Norway either is the monographic spelling of /ei/ with **i**.[29]

Possibly indicative of local usage is the *u*-ending in Kilbar's **þur(:)kirþu**, the final -**ï** in Inchmarnock's **þinï**, and the use of the preposition **til** for expected *aft/eftir* in the same inscription. The last can only feature as demotic Norse if we are certain **til:kuþ∗(ï)∗∗** is a preposition phrase intended to mean 'in memory of Guð . . .'. Alternative interpretations are possible, though none is wholly convincing. Regarding **þur(:)kirþu** Magnus Olsen hypothesized that it might reflect confusion of accusative and dative 'there in the Hebrides, where Norsemen and Celts had early come into contact with each other'[30] — conceivable but unverifiable.

The demonstrative form **þinï** reminds one of **sinï** 'his' (acc. f. sg.?) on the Manx Kirk Michael III stone.[31] This is not least of interest because of the association by some of both Kilbar and Iona — though not Inchmarnock — with Manx runic tradition.[32] It is not impossible that Man and the Hebrides may have formed some kind of extended runic province, though in terms of hard evidence there is little to go on. The notion rests chiefly on the conviction that the Bjǫrn **fra(:)kuli** mentioned on the Manx stone Andreas I was from the island of Coll,[33] situated between Barra and Iona and not too far distant from either. What evidence there is, however, suggests clear divergences between Hebridean and Manx tradition. Iona's ᚽ contrasts with Man's ᛏ as the realization of **b**; the Kilbar commemorative formula is strikingly different from the general Manx 'X raised this cross in memory of Y', and rune-inscribed grave slabs are unattested in Man. Inchmarnock's **þinï** and Kirk Michael III's **sinï** may indicate a weakening of unstressed end vowels in Man and the Isles, but there is little evidence of it outside these two forms. What the two **ï**s — together with occasional

---

[27] *Norges Innskrifter med de yngre Runer*, ed. by Magnus Olsen, Aslak Liestøl, and James E. Knirk, 6 vols (Oslo: Norsk Historisk Kjeldeskrift-Institutt, 1941–), III (1954), 145; Lena Peterson, *Svenskt runordsregister*, 2nd edn (Uppsala: Institutionen för nordiska språk, Uppsala universitet, 1994), pp. 33, 62–66.

[28] Didrik Arup Seip, *Norsk språkhistorie til omkring 1370*, 2nd edn (Oslo: Aschehoug, 1955), pp. 181, 295.

[29] See, for example, *Norges Innskrifter med de yngre Runer*, ed. by Olsen, Liestøl, and Knirk, I (1941), 235; III, 216, 219.

[30] Magnus Olsen, 'Runic Inscriptions in Great Britain, Ireland and the Isle of Man', in *Viking Antiquities in Great Britain and Ireland*, vol. VI, ed. by Haakon Shetelig (Oslo: Aschehoug, 1954), pp. 151–233 (p. 177).

[31] See Page, 'The Manx Rune-Stones', p. 140.

[32] See, for example, Aslak Liestøl, 'An Iona Rune Stone and the World of Man and the Isles', in *The Viking Age in the Isle of Man*, ed. by Fell and others, pp. 85–93.

[33] See Page, 'The Manx Rune-Stones', pp. 136, 145, n. 18.

further occurrences of this character in Man — do imply is a modicum of contact with runic writing practices elsewhere, at least until the early part of the eleventh century. As we have seen, the earliest examples of dotting do not antedate the eleventh century by many years and the practice must have spread westwards from Scandinavia long after the Viking settlement in Man and the Isles and some time after the establishment of a runic tradition or traditions there. All in all it cannot be said that these three Hebridean inscriptions offer more than tantalizing glimpses of Scandinavian speech in the islands.

Even less informative are the two final items in the Scottish corpus, Laws (SC 1) and Hunterston (SC 2). Of Laws all we have today is a drawing.[34] Eight runes are shown incised into a fragment of what is described as a bronze plate, decorated with Celtic motifs. The Hunterston inscription is found on a silver penannular brooch, whose artwork is likewise Celtic. Both objects seem likely to have been inscribed with runes after manufacture, presumably at a time when they were in the possession of a Scandinavian speaker.

Three of the Laws runes are diagnostic, but since one is ᛐ, long-branch **a** or medieval **æ**, and the other two are short-twig **t** and long-branch **m**, no sensible conclusions about provenance or date can be drawn from them. Hunterston seems to be written in short-twig runes; the diagnostic forms are ᛆ (**a**), ᛁ (**s**), ᛐ (**t**), ᛓ (**b**), ᛘ (**m**).

Laws may contain part of the name *Grímketill*, as surmised by many, but what the following þa could be, unless the past tense of *þiggja* 'get, receive', I do not know. Clearly, it can offer little in the way of linguistic evidence. Hunterston seems to contain the Gaelic name, *Maelbrigte* or *Maelbrighde*, found on the Manx Kirk Michael II cross in the form **mail:brikti**,[35] and in *Orkneyinga saga* as *Melbrigda* (nom. and gen. or dat. — presumably with 'd' for [ð] as usual in fourteenth-century Icelandic manuscripts) and *Melbrigþason* (gen.).[36] In the Norse context it appears to be a male name, whatever the form. The remaining runes have been assumed to give *á stilk* 'owns [the] stem', where 'stem' is taken to be synonymous with *nál* 'needle' and, like it, to refer to the brooch as a whole. Providing this is the correct interpretation, we have here evidence, as in Man, of an intermingling of cultures: a man with a Gaelic name writing in Scandinavian. The use of *stilk* in the sense *nál*, and thus 'brooch', is unparalleled and could be a local development. Since we have no idea where the runes were carved, however, we cannot name the locality.

As noted at the outset, the language of the Scandinavian runic inscriptions of Man, England, and Ireland has already been carefully analysed by modern scholars

---

[34] See, for example, J. Romilly Allen, *The Early Christian Monuments of Scotland*, introd. by Joseph Anderson, vol. I (Edinburgh: Society of Antiquaries of Scotland, 1903), p. lxxxv.

[35] See Page, 'The Manx Rune-Stones', p. 140.

[36] *Orkneyinga saga*, ed. by Sigurður Nordal, Samfund til udgivelse af gammel nordisk litteratur, 40 (Copenhagen: Samfund til udgivelse af gammel nordisk litteratur, 1913–16), pp. 6–8, 161, 169.

of repute. Though one might quibble about the odd detail, there seems no reason to disagree with the principal conclusions reached. For present purposes, then, it will be enough to restate these conclusions, modified and supplemented where necessary by my own views.

The Manx inscriptions exhibit a largely West Scandinavian type of language. This was used to commemorate people with both Norse and Gaelic names, whereas Gaelic, on the evidence of what has survived, was never so used. It is thus reasonable to conclude that at the time the runic crosses were raised, Scandinavian of a western type was the prestige language in the island. Uncertainty about inflections in several inscriptions, particularly Kirk Michael III, suggests that during the tenth century the Scandinavian of Man, prestigious or not, was affected by contact with Gaelic and began as a result to take on a local flavour. There is evidence in the form of occasional innovations of contact with runic traditions elsewhere, but this ceases about 1050, if not before. The implications of Maughold I and II, inscriptions that seem to have been carved by a man 'not well acquainted with runes, and perhaps not even with the Norse language',[37] are that at the time they were made — possibly the late twelfth century — runes were no longer in common use in Man, and Scandinavian speech had either died out or become heavily influenced by Gaelic.

Unlike Man, England shows no homogeneous tradition of writing in Scandinavian runes. In the south-east there is evidence of people fresh from East Scandinavia making monumental and casual inscriptions in the style of their homelands. There is also an indication of the mingling of Scandinavian and Anglo-Saxon, both runic script and language, in the **wufr(ik)** of St Alban's II (E 14), where an un-Scandinavian initial [w-] is represented by Þ, lost from the runic alphabets of the North by about 700. Unlike the other inscriptions from the south-east of England, this suggests a user of Scandinavian runes thoroughly integrated into local society.

Local talent seems also to have been behind at least some of the Scandinavian inscriptions of northern England. Three, Bridekirk (E 1), Skelton (E 8), and Pennington (E 9), are texts on public monuments, and so presumably tell us something about speech and writing traditions in the districts where they were made. The language of Bridekirk is Middle English and its runes, which include the medieval form Ͱ for **e** (suggesting contact with runic tradition elsewhere), are augmented by four bookhand characters. The Skelton runes probably record some form of Scandinavian; they stand side-by-side with a fragmentary inscription in roman letters, in which several apparently Scandinavian words can be made out. Pennington — the part of it that is legible — is entirely in Scandinavian runes, but the language is far removed from classical Old Norse and shows signs of interference from English. The picture of an intermingling of languages and cultures that emerges from these three monumental inscriptions is reinforced by the graffito in Carlisle Cathedral (E 3), in Scandinavian runes but ungrammatical Old Norse. Two other graffiti from nearby using Scandinavian runes, Dearham (E 6) and Conishead (E 11), give no clues about language, but

---

[37] Page, 'Celtic and Norse on the Manx Rune-Stones', p. 136.

with its unusual and late dotted Ť, Conishead (like Bridekirk) suggests awareness of runic innovations in Scandinavia. There is of course no compelling reason to believe casual scratchings like these reflect local speech and writing traditions. Though all three are on substantial blocks of stone, and thus almost certain to have been made at or close to the place where they were found, they could as easily be the work of someone passing through as of a local resident.

The general conclusion to be drawn from the evidence of these six inscriptions is that some form or forms of Scandinavian were in use in northern England as late as the twelfth century — the time most of them seem to have been made. Whether they represent a continuous tradition of Scandinavian speech and writing in the north or a reintroduction from elsewhere is unclear. Page suggests 'an influx of Scandinavian speakers from areas such as Man',[38] but on the evidence of Maughold I and II (see above) this is perhaps unlikely.

The four remaining inscriptions from England can tell us little about the position of Scandinavian in that country. Settle (E 5) seems to be modern,[39] the Penrith short-twig *fuþark* (E 15), as noted earlier, was probably carved far from its find spot, while Lincoln I (E 4), as Ekwall and others have argued, could well be a Danish import. Lincoln II (E 16) is slightly more informative.[40] Being inscribed on a piece of bone, it is likely to be of local origin. Its runes seem to be Norwegian mixed; they could also be medieval, but the archaeological context for the find suggests a date in the late Viking Age. If the runes are Norwegian, we appear to have monographic spelling of /ei/ in **hitir** '?heats' and certainly in **stin** — as on Kilbar (above). Norwegian runes might not be what one would immediately expect in Lincoln, but being a trading centre it is likely to have attracted people from all over the North Sea and North Atlantic area.

The Irish inscriptions are probably all to be dated within the period 950–1125. Only two, Killaloe (IR 2) and — less certainly — Beginish (IR 3) suggest settled rune-using communities. Both of these look to have Norwegian runes — mixed Norwegian, augmented by ľ in the case of Killaloe — but diagnostic forms are few. The presence of a dotted rune suggests continuing contact with Scandinavian tradition. Monographic spelling of /ei/ (if not monophthongization) is also a feature of both inscriptions. Like several of the Manx stones, Killaloe exhibits an *r*-less nominative, possibly a sign of a weakened inflectional system following prolonged contact with Gaelic. Equally, however, there are indications on the stone of a clear distinction being made between Scandinavian and Irish. Its runic inscription is wholly in Scandinavian, but it also has one in ogam, and this, as befits the script, is

---

[38] Page, 'How Long Did the Scandinavian Language Survive in England?', p. 174.

[39] Michael P. Barnes, 'The Strange Case of the Settle Stone', *NOWELE*, 28/29 (1996), 297–313.

[40] John McKinnell, 'A Runic Fragment from Lincoln', *Nytt om runer*, 10 (1995 (1996)), 10–11.

in Irish, even though the TOROQR[IM] it commemorates was probably the same person as the (þ)urk̃ri∗ who raised the monument.

The remainder of the Irish corpus consists entirely of loose objects, mostly from Dublin. As argued above, the Dublin inscriptions are as likely to have been carved by people passing through as locals, while the two remaining loose objects, Greenmount (IR 1) and Roosky (IR 15), might even be imports, although the name **tomnal** on the former suggests a Gaelic connection, at least. While they can thus tell us something about the language and runic practices of people present in Ireland, these inscriptions do not necessarily record the speech and writing traditions of Scandinavian speakers who lived there permanently. They hint at a range of Scandinavian traditions. Some have runes of Norwegian, some of Danish — or at least East Scandinavian — type, while others are typologically mixed. Linguistically there is evidence of input from different parts of Scandinavia too. Eastern **nubR** (IR 8) and **hiartaR** (IR 12), for example, ending in 'palatal' *r*, vie with western **soþr** (IR 6), which, if correctly interpreted, has /θr/ for earlier /nθR/ (rather than eastern /n:R/ or /ndr/), and **soïrþïta** (IR 1), which exhibits the word order head + modifier — in the medieval period increasingly a West Scandinavian marker. Possible evidence of Gaelic influence is the missing nominative *-r* in **kirlak** (IR 4) and dative *-i* in **üs** (IR 12), if the latter does indeed represent the dative singular of *óss* 'river mouth'. It has also been argued that the spelling **tomnal** (IR 1) for assumed [doṽnəl:] indicates familiarity with Irish orthography, but this need not be so.[41] To the extent Gaelic influence really is at work here, it leads to the assumption that of the loose objects, IR 1, 4, and 12, at least, had their runes carved by locals — or residents of the Gaelic-speaking parts of the British Isles — rather than by visitors from Scandinavia.

Beyond this it is not easy to draw conclusions about Scandinavian speech in Ireland from its runic inscriptions. The most characteristic feature of the Dublin pieces is their opacity.

All in all, the inscriptions discussed provide only sporadic and weak pointers to the type, position, and ultimate fate of Scandinavian speech in the British Isles. They do nothing to undermine the view of the Northern Isles and north-eastern Caithness as wholly within the West Scandinavian sphere of influence. They give evidence of both East and West Scandinavian involvement in England and Ireland. They suggest the development of demotic forms of Norse in Man and north-west England, and perhaps in the Hebrides and Ireland, but offer scant guidance about the shapes they took. Most interesting, perhaps, is the indication that in Man Scandinavian had become extinct by 1200, or was at least on the way out. If this is so, it has strong implications for the fate of the language in most other parts of the British Isles. Man must have been a relatively compact linguistic community, and it was one in which Scandinavian seems to have been the dominant language in the tenth century. If it could not survive there more than a couple of hundred years, it is unlikely to have lasted beyond the second or third generation anywhere the Norse settlers were more thinly spread.

---

[41] Barnes, Hagland, and Page, *The Runic Inscriptions of Viking Age Dublin*, pp. 51–52.

APPENDIX

The Inscriptions in Transliteration

(excluding Maeshowe and Man for which see Barnes, *The Runic Inscriptions of Maeshowe, Orkney*, and Page, 'The Manx Rune-Stones')

SH 1, Cunnlngsburgh I	](krlmr)+[
SH 2, Cunningsburgh II	](þa)+(a)∗[
SH 3, Cunningsburgh III	]þi∗∗∗∗(+)∗ftir+foþur(·)sinþurbio(r)[f
SH 4, Papil	]r⋮ra(i)s(ti)⋮s[
SH 5, Eshaness I	]∗∗(·hk)ku∗[
SH 6, Eshaness II	þïnnastaïn∗(a)...(n)∗(ni)o(n)...k...f...k
SH 7, Gungstie	]∗(uko͡k)tu
OR 1, Stackrue	r ǀ k(oþ) ǀ 3/1 a ǀ (o͡ln)
OR 2, Unstan	(n ukf) (1/4 p)i∗ii
OR 3, Orkney	∗∗ka∗∗∗r(r)ïs∗run∗∗
OR 4, Brogar I	2/2 r 4/3 3/2 2/2
OR 5, Brogar II	3/4
OR 6, Birsay I	rune-like symbols, then: filibusra͡nru
OR 7, Brogar farm	2/3 1/3 (1/3)
OR 8, Birsay II	lower half of fragment (illegible)
OR 9, Birsay III	bottom part of fragment (illegible)
OR 10, Orphir I	ikirk͡irkiakoþ(li)ufs∗[
OR 11, Birsay IV	∗uþork∗
OR 12, Westness	aaa
OR 13, Skara Brae	2/3 1/2 2/4 r∗r
OR 14, Tuquoy	þorst∗∗n∗inarssunr:ræist:runarþ∗sar
OR 15, Orphir II	]∗(t)a·bain:uas·i∗(u)∗∗[
OR 16, Birsay V	?bottom part of fragment (illegible)
OR 17, Isegarth	]nxin:osk(a)∗∗(:)r
OR 18, Skaill	þurfinr:r∗∗∗∗∗∗∗∗∗:∗∗n∗:∗∗... 16–18 verticals, one or two (k)s and (r)s
OR 19, Orphir III	∗∗∗∗(ss)r, (o) or (f), and a few individual verticals
[Loch of Stenness	(5/2 5/7)
Cuween Hill	3/1 (3/1 1/4 3/1)
Belsair	(∗∗um∗)]

SC 1, Laws	**mkitil:þa**
SC 2, Hunterston	**malbriþaastilk** followed by some 25 rune-like symbols among which the occasional runic form can be found
SC 3, Holy Island I	**(+n)[ik]ul[os]*[ahænï]+ræist**
SC 4, Holy Island II	**suæin**
SC 5, Holy Island III	**ono(n)tr:r(a)*st:ru**
SC 6, Holy Island IV	**(a)mu̇ẗar**
SC 7, Holy Island VIII	**uik̈læikr s*alla͡rïræiss(t)**
SC 8, Kilbar	**]*ir'þur(:)kirþu:s(t)i*ar** **]*r(·)is(:)kurs(:)s**·**ristr** **]*(·)**
SC 9, Holy Island VI	**ioan**
SC 10, Inchmarnock	**]krus:þinï:til:kuþ*(ï)**[**
SC 11, Thurso I	**]*þi:ubirlakþita:aft:ikulb:foþur(s)in**
SC 12, Holy Island V	**ola(b)r**
SC 13, Holy Island VII	**(m)**
SC 14, Iona	**ₓkaliₓouluisₓsunrₓlaþiₓstanₓþinsiₓubirₓfuklₓbruþur[**
SC 15, Thurso II	**]*unil*i*u(n)usin[**
E 1, Bridekirk	**+rikarþ:he:me͡:iwr*ktï͡:7:to:þis:me:rᴅ:3er:**:me͡:brokt͡ï**
E 2, St Paul's	**:k*na:lït:lïkia:st** **in:þïnsi:auk:tuki:**
E 3, Carlisle	**tolfinuraitþisarunraþisastain** **aif**
E 4, Lincoln I	**kamb:koþan:kiari:þorfastr**
E 5, Settle	**o͡framr**
E 6, Dearham	**hnirm**
E 7, Rochester	**[]*(ki):*[]**
E 8, Skelton	**]**[** **]***ïbïl·ok·[**
E 9, Pennington	**]kml:lï(ta):þïna:kirk:(h)ub*rt:masu(n):***:...**
E 10, Canterbury	**(anu)***
E 11, Conishead	**[töotbrt]**
E 12, Winchester	**](ʀ:)auk(o)l(:)*[** **]*usk**[**
E 13, St Albans I	**](þ):þü:uur:uur** **risti** **run(a)ʀ:tr**
E 14, St Albans II	**wufr(ik)**

E 15, Penrith	**fuþorkhniastbmm**
	fu
E 16, Lincoln II	**b...lxhitirxstinx[**
IR 1, Greenmount	**tomnalsïlshofoþasoïrþïta**
IR 2, Killaloe	**](þ)urk̈ri∗(⊕)risli+**
	][k]rusþina
IR 3, Beginish	**∗(i)r(·)r(is)ti(·)st(i)∗(·)∗∗n∗∗mu∗u∗∗∗risti...**
IR 4, Dublin CP I	**kirlak∗**
IR 5, Dublin CP II	**onaa∗su∗∗**
IR 6, Dublin CP III	**so[þ]rmiþ[f]ris[**
	]um∗oþ·sis:is∗∗∗∗[
IR 7, Dublin CP IV	**[stixl(in)r∗]**
	[stili(n)r∗ ka...]
IR 8, Dublin FS I	**nubRnubþi∗**
IR 9, Dublin CP V	**tïli ∗∗**
	sua:sua
	i∗∗ir ïhhï tal
IR 10, Dublin FS II	**sa∗ ritisanat∗aolua͡mn∗[**
	a(i)kuaitu
IR 11, Dublin FS III	**fuþorkxhniastbmlR**
	fuþorkhniastbmlR
IR 12, Dublin FS IV	**hurn:hiartaR·la:aüsaR**
IR 13, Dublin FS V	**(nrþ)∗∗**
IR 14, Dublin Castle	**fuþor∗**
IR 15, Roosky	**r∗**
IR 16, Dublin FS VI	**∗sb∗∗∗**

CP = Christchurch Place; FS = Fishamble Street.

Scandinavian Settlement in the British Isles and Normandy: What the Place-Names Reveal

GILLIAN FELLOWS-JENSEN

The most convenient sailing routes between Scandinavia and the British Isles and Normandy go a long way towards explaining the distribution of the areas of Scandinavian settlement and the predominant nationality of the Vikings in the individual areas. Setting out from the west coast of Norway, the Norwegians would have come first to Shetland and Orkney and proceeded on from there along the northern and western coast of mainland Scotland to the Hebrides. This explains the presence of the first two of the four zones of Scandinavian settlement in Scotland identified by Barbara Crawford.[1] Zone 1 is made up of Shetland, Orkney, and northeast Caithness. Viking settlement was so dense in the Northern Isles that no recognizable traces of pre-Scandinavian place-names have been found there and, although Shetland and Orkney did come under Scottish rule in 1472, Gaelic place-names made no inroads there. To this very day the place-names are still overwhelmingly recognizably Scandinavian and typically West Scandinavian.[2] There are topographical names such as *Birsay* (**byrgis-ey* 'island with a fortified building') and *Twatt* (**þveit*, f., 'clearing in woodland') in Orkney, as well as names of temporary and permanent habitations, such as *Skaill* in Orkney (**skáli*, m., 'hut, shed, shieling', possibly with a secondary meaning 'hall'), and *Wethersta* (**Viðars-staðir*), *Gunnister* (**Gunna-setr*), and *Fladdabister* (**flat-bólstaðr*) in Shetland, containing the typically Norwegian habitative generics *staðir* m. pl., *setr* n., and *bólstaðr* m. There are

---

[1] Barbara E. Crawford, *Scandinavian Scotland*, Scotland in the Early Middle Ages, 2 (Leicester: Leicester University Press, 1987), pp. 92–94.

[2] See Gillian Fellows-Jensen, 'Viking Settlement in the Northern and Western Isles: The Place-Name Evidence as Seen from Denmark and the Danelaw', in *The Northern and Western Isles in the Viking World: Survival, Continuity and Change*, ed. by Alexander Fenton and Hermann Pálsson (Edinburgh: John Donald, 1984), pp. 148–68.

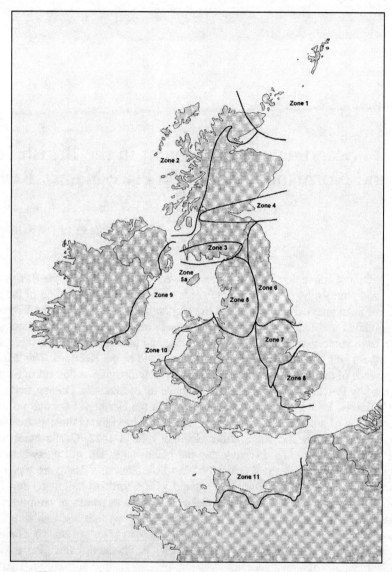

Figure 1. The zones of Scandinavian settlement in the British Isles and Normandy. Map: G. Fellows-Jensen and P. Gammeltoft. Zone 1: Shetland, Orkney, and north-east Caithness. Zone 2: Hebrides, Sutherland, Easter Ross, northern and western seaboards of Scotland. Zone 3: Dumfriesshire and Galloway. Zone 4: Central Lowlands of Scotland. Zone 5: North-west England. Zone 5a: Isle of Man. Zone 6: North-east England. Zone 7: East Midland. Zone 8: East Anglia. Zone 9: Eastern seaboard of Ireland. Zone 10: Northern and southern seaboards of Wales. Zone 11: Northern Normandy.

also *Tingwall*s in both Orkney and Shetland, the names of the island-sites on which justice was dispensed, close parallels to *Þingvellir* in Iceland.[3]

From Shetland and Orkney we can follow the Norwegians to zone 2, Sutherland, Easter Ross, the Hebrides, and the northern and western seaboard of Scotland, where the onomastic situation has been greatly complicated both by the possible survival of some pre-Viking names and by the resurgence of the Gaelic language.[4] Account has consequently to be taken of Gaelic influence on the development of the names. It can be very difficult for a non-Gaelic scholar to be able to recognize a name as being of Scandinavian origin, let alone to draw the necessary distinction between Norse names borrowed into Gaelic as names, for example *Laimeseadar* (**lamba-sætr* 'lambs' shieling'), Norse names borrowed into Gaelic as names but only surviving as the specific of a younger Gaelic name, for example *Loch Lacsabhat* (Gaelic *loch* + **laxa-vatn* 'salmon lake'), and Scandinavian loanwords in Gaelic functioning as place-names or place-name elements, for example *sgeir*, f. (< *sker*, n., 'rocky islet').[5] It can often be very difficult to recognize that a Hebridean place-name is of Scandinavian origin. It is far from obvious, for example, that *Tiongal* in Lewis is a reflex of the assembly-place name *Tingwall*.

When we move south to zone 3, Galloway and Dumfriesshire, it is less difficult to recognize the West Scandinavian names but they are of comparatively rare occurrence in the most gaelicized part of the zone, that is west of the Nith. There are a number of topographical names along the coast of Galloway, for example *Kirkdale* (**kirkja-dalr* 'church valley') and *Gategill* (**geit-gil* 'she-goat ravine'), but there is not a single certain occurrence of the habitative generics *-staðir*, *-setr*, or *bólstaðr*, which occur so frequently in the Northern and Western Isles, nor of the Gaelic loanword in Scandinavian *-ærgi* 'shieling' functioning as a place-name generic, even though this element is assumed to have been carried by the Scandinavians from zone 2 to zones 5 and 6 in England, where it does occur in place-names.[6] The only name in zone 3 which points definitely in the direction of zones 1 or 2 is *Tinwald* in Dumfriesshire,

---

[3] Gillian Fellows-Jensen, 'Tingwall: The Significance of the Name', in *Shetland's Northern Links: Language and History*, ed. by Doreen J. Waugh (Edinburgh: Scottish Society for Northern Studies, 1996), pp. 16–29.

[4] See Richard A. V. Cox, 'Allt Loch Dhaile Beaga: Place-Name Study in the West of Scotland', *Nomina*, 14 (1990–91), 83–96; and Ian A. Fraser, 'Norse Settlement on the North-West Seaboard', in *Scandinavian Settlement in Northern Britain*, ed. by Barbara E. Crawford (London: Leicester University Press, 1995), pp. 92–105.

[5] Richard A. V. Cox, 'Questioning the Value and Validity of the Term "Hybrid" in Hebridean Place-Name Study', *Nomina*, 12 (1988–89), 1–9.

[6] Gillian Fellows-Jensen, 'Scandinavians in Dumfriesshire and Galloway: The Place-Name Evidence', in *Galloway: Land and Lordship*, ed. by Richard D. Oram and Geoffrey P. Stell (Edinburgh: Scottish Society for Northern Studies, 1991), pp. 77–95; and Richard D. Oram, 'Scandinavian Settlement in South-West Scotland with a Special Study of Bysbie', in *Scandinavian Settlement in Northern Britain*, ed. by Crawford, pp. 127–40.

yet another example of the recurrent name for an assembly-place. I shall return to the two most commonly occurring Scandinavian generics in eastern Dumfriesshire, -bý and -þveit, in connection with my discussion of place-names in the Danelaw.

Zone 3 adjoins, and is closely related in some respects to, zone 5, north-west England, but zone 5 displays considerably more Scandinavian place-names, for example in Cumberland the topographical names *Thackthwaite* (*þak-þveit 'thatch clearing'), *Dockray* (Old English *docce, f., 'dock-plant' + Scandinavian vrá 'nook, corner'), *Matterdale* (*maðra-dalr 'madder valley'), and *Skelgill* (*skáli-geil 'narrow valley with a hut').[7] *Portinscale* in Cumberland probably originated as a Scandinavian name for a seasonal habitation. It is borne by a settlement at the head of Derwentwater on the opposite side of the Derwent from the town of Keswick, whose English name (*cēse-wīc 'cheese farm') was scandinavianized by the Vikings, who found difficulty in pronouncing the English sound /tʃ/ and substituted /k/. The generic of Portinscale is the same word, *skáli* 'hut', as the specific of Skelgill. I would explain its specific as the Scandinavian word *portkona*, f., 'prostitute', literally 'woman of the town'. In a recent paper entitled 'The Ladies of Portinscale', however, Carole Hough pointed out that the Old English word corresponding to *portkona*, that is *portcwēn(e)*, denotes a woman of rather higher standing.[8] Since there is no doubt that the Scandinavian word is a derogatory term and the generic is a Scandinavian word for a very humble structure, I refuse to believe that Portinscale was the meeting-place of the Viking Age townswomen's guild, although doubts have been thrown on the willingness of the men of Keswick to walk all the way to Portinscale and back in pursuit of sexual satisfaction. Shieling-names are of frequent occurrence in zone 5, not only names in -*skáli*, but also names in the Gaelic loanword -*ærgi* 'shieling', as for example *Grimsargh* in Lancashire, containing the personal name *Grímr*, and in -*sætr*, as for example *Ambleside* in Westmorland, containing as its specific a Scandinavian place-name *á-melr 'river sand-bank'.[9] The element -*sætr* tends to denote a more well-established shieling in less mountainous areas than does *skáli*. As in zone 3, there are numerous names in -bý in zone 5. To these I shall return later.

I have treated the Isle of Man as a kind of appendix to zone 5 and called it zone 5a. It shares, however, several types of names with zones 1 and 2, particularly names in -*staðir*, for example *Grest* (*grjót-staðir 'stony farm'), and one doubtful instance of -*bólstaðr*, *Bravost* (*breiða-+bólstaðr).[10] As in zone 2 the Scandinavian names

[7] Gillian Fellows-Jensen, *Scandinavian Settlement Names in the North-West*, Navnestudier, 25 (Copenhagen: Reitzel, 1985), pp. 60, 152, 160, 210.

[8] Carole Hough, 'The Ladies of Portinscale', *Journal of the English Place-Name Society*, 29 (1997), 71–78.

[9] Fellows-Jensen, *Scandinavian Settlement Names in the North-West*, pp. 49–51, 60, 64.

[10] Gillian Fellows-Jensen, 'Scandinavian Settlement in the Isle of Man and Northwest England: The Place-Name Evidence', in *The Viking Age in the Isle of Man*, ed. by Christine Fell and others (London: Viking Society for Northern Research, 1983), pp. 37–52.

often appear in gaelicized form, for example *Agneash* (**egg-nes* 'edge ness'), while other names remain more or less transparent, for example *Ramsey* (**hramsa-á* 'wild-garlic river') and *Tynwald*, the recurrent assembly-place name, which is still borne by the site of the annual assembly at which the Manx laws are read aloud. In common with zones 3 and 5, zone 5a has numerous Scandinavian names in -*bý*, to which I shall return.

The only settlement names in zone 9, the eastern seaboard of Ireland, which would seem to have been coined by the Vikings are the names of coastal strongholds. *Wexford, Waterford, Carlingford,* and *Strangford,* for example, would all seem to be names containing the Scandinavian generic -*fjörðr* 'fiord or inlet'.[11] There are a few scattered settlement names in other parts of Ireland that reflect Scandinavian influence. The Irish name of *Limerick*, for example, was and is *Luimneach* 'barren spot of land'. This was scandinavianized by the Vikings to *Hlymrekr* and it was this form that was borrowed into English as Limerick.[12] Viking influence is also evident in connection with the Irish name *Dublin* (**dubh-linn* 'black pool'). This originally denoted the place where the Vikings anchored their ships. The Irish, however, referred to the town as *Áth Cliath* 'the ford of the wattles', a name which denoted the strategically important ford upstream from the black pool. The onomastic contribution of the Vikings to the name of the chief city of Ireland is thus to have ensured that it was the name of the black pool that passed into the English language and became the internationally accepted name of the capital. Other Scandinavian names in Ireland may perhaps have been lost. The Vikings would certainly seem to have exerted influence over the hinterland of Dublin and more names might have been expected to occur here.[13] The western edge of this territory is marked by one of the rare surviving Scandinavian names, *Leixlip* (**lax-hleypa* 'salmon leap').[14]

The southern limit of Scandinavian settlements on the western side of the British Isles is marked by zone 10, the northern and southern seaboard of Wales. As in Ireland the Scandinavian names in Wales are borne by settlements or topographical features around the coast. The Vikings would not seem to have established fortified centres here but *Milford Haven* (**melr-fjörðr* 'sand-bank fiord') and *Swansea*

---

[11] Magne Oftedal, 'Scandinavian Place-Names in Ireland', in *Proceedings of the Seventh Viking Congress, Dublin, 15–21 August 1973*, ed. by Bo Almqvist and David Greene (Dublin: Royal Irish Academy, 1976), pp. 125–33.

[12] David Greene, 'The Evidence of Language and Place-Names in Ireland', in *The Vikings*, ed. by Thorsten Andersson and Karl Inge Sandred (Stockholm: Almqvist & Wiksell, 1978), pp. 119–23.

[13] John Bradley, 'The Interpretation of Scandinavian Settlement in Ireland', in *Settlement and Society in Medieval Ireland*, ed. by John Bradley (Kilkenny: Boethius Press, 1988), pp. 49–78 (pp. 51–62).

[14] Donnchadh Ó Corráin, *Ireland Before the Normans*, The Gill History of Ireland, 2 (Dublin: Gill and Macmillan, 1972), p. 104.

(*Sveins-sær or -ey 'Svein's lake or island') would seem to have developed as commercial centres in the Viking period[15] and therefore received Scandinavian names in
addition to their older Welsh ones, *Aberdaugleddyf* 'mouths of the rivers Cleddyf'
and *Abertawe* 'mouth of the river Tawe' respectively.[16] Many of the Scandinavian
names in Wales would seem to have been given by seafarers to landmarks and they
bear no relationship to the Welsh names of these features. It is noticeable that they are
of particularly frequent occurrence along the south coast and in the Bristol Channel,
reflecting the great importance of this sailing-route between Dublin and Bristol in
the medieval period.[17] The four names in *-bý* in Wales I shall return to later.

At this point, however, I shall transfer my attention to the Danish Vikings, most
of whom would presumably have set out from the west coast of Jutland and sailed
south along the coast of Frisia before heading out across the North Sea to England.
Zone 6, north-east England, appears very large on the map but it is only in the three
ridings of Yorkshire and the southernmost part of County Durham that Scandinavian
place-names survive in any numbers. Although there is evidence in written sources
that a number of settlements in the eastern part of the county of Durham were in
Danish ownership at different periods in the early tenth century,[18] there is hardly any
trace of Danish influence on the place-names borne by the vills in question, presumably because they came under English control again fairly quickly so that there was
little opportunity for the Danish settlers to establish their rights over units of land by
giving these new names.

This, however is exactly what would seem to have been done in Yorkshire. In the
North and East Ridings well over 40% of the place-names are either of Scandinavian
origin or show traces of Scandinavian influence.[19] The most frequently occurring
Scandinavian generic here is *bý* 'settlement'. Sometimes the specific is a common
noun, for example *dalr* 'valley' in *Dalby* or *kirkja* 'church' in *Kirkby Moorside*. It is
my impression that this kind of name was often given to English settlements that
were taken over as going concerns by the Vikings, perhaps soon after the partitions

[15] Wendy Davies, *Wales in the Early Middle Ages*, Studies in the Early History of Britain
(Leicester: Leicester University Press, 1982), p. 117.

[16] B. G. Charles, *Non-Celtic Place-Names in Wales* (London: University College London,
1938), pp. 69, 130–31.

[17] Henry Loyn, *The Vikings in Wales*, The Dorothea Coke Memorial Lecture in Northern
Studies Delivered 2 March 1976 at University College London (London: University College
London, 1976), pp. 18–20.

[18] Christopher D. Morris, 'Viking and Native in Northern England: A Case-Study', in
Proceedings of the Eighth Viking Congress: Århus 24–31 August 1977, ed. by Hans Bekker-
Nielsen, Peter Foote, and Olaf Olsen, Mediaeval Scandinavia Supplements, 2 (Odense:
Odense University Press, 1981), pp. 223–44.

[19] Gillian Fellows Jensen, *Scandinavian Settlement Names in Yorkshire*, Navnestudier, 11
(Copenhagen: Reitzel, 1972), p. 169.

of land that took place in 876 in Yorkshire, in 877 in the East Midlands, and in 880 in East Anglia. A name such as Kirkby would have been given to a settlement which already had a church when the Danes arrived. To settlers who were unaccustomed to seeing stone buildings, the Anglo-Saxon churches must have appeared very impressive. The names in -*bý* whose specific is a Scandinavian personal name, however, for example the original by-name *Slengr* 'idler' in *Slingsby*, are more likely to have been given to smaller units of settlement early in the tenth century, when the Danish leaders no longer had full command over their soldiers and the large English estates were being split up into smaller units which were given to individual Danes as reward for their service or bought by them with silver they had received as payment.[20] The name *Normanby* apparently refers to an isolated settlement of Norwegians in an area where most of the inhabitants were of other nationalities. Most of the Normanbys are found in eastern England, where the Scandinavian settlers were predominantly Danish.

The Scandinavian generic that appears next most frequently after -*bý* in Yorkshire is -*þorp* 'dependent, secondary settlement'. It is usually borne by settlements established on the outfields of older settlements. *Copmanthorpe* (**kaupmanna-þorp*) in the West Riding is not far from York and it seems likely that it was originally a place where merchants camped when visiting the trading centre in that city. That York developed as an important commercial centre in the Viking period is shown by the numerous Scandinavian street-names there, particularly names in -*gata* 'street', for example *Coppergate* (**koppari* 'cup-maker'), *Skeldergate* (**skjaldari* 'shield-maker'), but also names in –*geil*, f., 'alley', for example *Fothlausgayl* 1218x1220 (**fótlauss* 'foot- or legless, that is a cripple'), now Museum Street.[21] None of the names in -*geil* survives to the present day but many of the names in -*gata* do.

In addition to the numerous names in -*bý* and -*þorp* in Yorkshire, there are many names in –*þveit*, f., 'clearing in woodland', for example *Husthwaite* (**hús-þveit* 'clearing with a house'). Names in -*þveit* probably provide the best indication of areas of land brought under cultivation for the first time by the Danes. There are also hybrid names in Old English -*tūn*, for example *Oulston*, in which the specific is the Scandinavian personal name *Ulfr*, possibly the name of a man who took over an English settlement at the time of the partition of land between the Danes but possibly that of a Dane who was first granted the land in the eleventh century or who had bought it for himself with the reward he had received for his services.

There is a similar mixture of names in zone 7, the East Midlands, although no names in -*þveit* are found here, perhaps because there was little woodland left in the zone to be cleared by the Vikings. We find names in -*bý* such as *Asterby* (*eystri*

---

[20] Gillian Fellows-Jensen, *The Vikings and their Victims: The Verdict of the Names*, The Dorothea Coke Memorial Lecture in Northern Studies Delivered 21 February 1994 at University College London (London: University College London, 1995; repr. 1998).

[21] A. H. Smith, *The Place-Names of the East Riding of Yorkshire and York*, English Place-Name Society, 14 (Cambridge: Cambridge University Press, 1937), pp. 285, 287, 297.

'eastern'), *Scamblesby* (the personal name *Skamlauss*), *Goulceby* (a personal name *Kolkr*), and *Ranby* (Danish *rand*, f., 'ridge') in Lincolnshire; *Saxelby* (the personal name *Saksulfr*), *Asfordby* (the personal name *Ásfrøðr*), *Frisby* (the genitive plural *Frísa* 'of the Frisians'), and *Hoby* (Old English *hōh*, m., 'promontory') in Leicestershire; names in *-þorp* such as *Authorpe* (the personal name *Agi*) and *Cawthorpe* (the personal name *Kali*) in Lincolnshire; and *Gunthorpe* (probably the feminine personal name *Gunnhildr*) in Nottinghamshire; and hybrid names in *-tūn* such as *Thurgarton* (the personal name *Þorgeirr* in anglicized form *Thurgār*) in Nottinghamshire.[22] In the city of Lincoln, as in York, there are many street-names in Scandinavian *-gata*, for example *Hungate* (genitive plural *hunda* 'of the dogs').[23]

The final zone of Scandinavian settlement in England is East Anglia. The same types of names are found here as in zones 6 and 7 but there are far fewer place-names in *-bý*.[24] It is only in the island of Flegg, where it seems likely that an enclave of Danish settlers remained behind after the English had regained control of most of zone 8, that names in *-bý* lie thick on the ground, for example *Filby*, which probably contains *fíli*, n., 'planks', perhaps referring to a wooden causeway, *Mautby*, probably containing *malt*, n., 'malt', and *Hemsby*, probably containing a personal name *Heimir*. Of more general distribution in East Anglia are the names in *-þorp*, for example the originally simplex formation *Thorpe Abbots* and *Ingoldisthorpe*, originally containing *Ingulfr*, which was later replaced by another Scandinavian personal name *Ingjaldr*, both in Norfolk. An interesting feature about the Scandinavian place-names in East Anglia is that they sometimes contain Scandinavian personal names in an anglicized form characteristic of the early period of settlement, for example *Kettlebaston* (*Cytelbeornes-tūn*).

In zone 11, Normandy, the most frequently occurring type of name revealing Scandinavian influence is the compound of a Scandinavian personal name with the Romance generic *-ville* < Latin *villa*, for example *Quetiéville* containing *Ketill*.[25] There are also many originally topographical names borne by settlements in Normandy, for example *Houlgate* (*hol-gata* 'hollow road') and *Etalondes* (Old English *stān* 'stone' + Scandinavian *lundr*, m., 'grove'). The interesting feature about this name is that the specific either is originally English or has been anglicized. That there was English influence on the place-names of Upper Normandy is also illustrated by the occurrence of English agricultural terms such as *hēafodland* 'headland' and *furlang*

---

[22] Gillian Fellows Jensen, *Scandinavian Settlement Names in the East Midlands*, Navnestudier, 16 (Copenhagen: Reitzel, 1978), pp. 31–32, 46, 49, 53, 63, 66, 102, 106, 111, 196.

[23] Gillian Fellows Jensen, 'Hungate: Some Observations on a Common Street-Name', *Ortnamnssällskapets i Uppsala årsskrift*, 1979, 44–51.

[24] Gillian Fellows-Jensen, 'Scandinavian Settlement Names in East Anglia: Some Problems', *Nomina*, 22 (1999), 45–60.

[25] Gillian Fellows-Jensen, 'Les Noms de lieux d'origine scandinave et la colonisation viking en Normandie: Examen critique de la question', *Proxima Thulé*, 1 (1994), 63–103.

'furlong' in the microtoponymy. In spite of this evidence for contact between England and Normandy in the Viking period, however, and the possibility that some of the Scandinavian names there may have been coined by settlers from the Danelaw, there is not a single certain example of a name in -*bý* and the general word employed by the Vikings when coining a name for a settlement would seem to have been -*toft* 'building plot', possibly because there had been much destruction in Normandy and the word *toft* could be used of a derelict structure. There are, however, a few names in -*þorp* in Normandy and several in -*þveit*. Many of these latter names are Romance formations that must have been coined by French-speakers after the Scandinavian word had been borrowed into French in the form *tuit*.[26]

Having now completed a breakneck tour of the eleven zones of Scandinavian settlement, I should like to return to the Danelaw and the names in -*bý* which are so common there. I have earlier argued that these names were coined at two different periods, with *bý*s with personal names as specifics probably being younger that those whose specifics are appellatives.[27] At a somewhat later date, the settlers in the Danelaw began to move out in search of more territory, taking with them the practice of forming place-names by compounding personal names with -*bý*. Most marked was their penetration into north-west England via the Pennine valleys, particularly along the Eden valley and down to the Carlisle plain. Here there are numerous names in -*bý* containing personal names of Norman or Flemish origin, for example *Allonby* in Cumberland, containing the Breton name *Alein*. This type of hybrid compound is considered by John Insley[28] and Brian K. Roberts[29] to show that the name-type remained current even after the Norman Conquest, but I would prefer to see the names in question as the result of the substitution of a Norman personal name for an earlier specific to mark a change of ownership at the time when the Norman kings for strategic reasons planted their supporters in these settlements so close to the Scottish border. From Cumberland the name-type was carried into Dumfriesshire, where there are many examples in the Annan valley, for example *Lochard* in *Locherbie*.[30] Another element that was probably carried from the Danelaw to

---

[26] François de Beaurepaire, *Les Noms des communes et anciennes paroisses de l'Eure* (Paris: A. et J. Picard, 1981), p. 197; Åse Kari Hansen, 'Noms de lieu Normands d'origine Scandinave: Quelles dimensions et perspectives offre l'étude des noms de lieu dans le domaine plurilinguistique?', in *Scope, Perspectives and Methods of Onomastics: Proceedings of the XIXth International Congress of Onomastic Sciences, Aberdeen, August 4–11, 1996*, ed. by W. F. H. Nicolaisen, 3 vols (Aberdeen: Department of English, 1998), II, 163–68.

[27] See, for example, Gillian Fellows-Jensen, 'Anthroponymical Specifics in Place-Names in -*bý* in the British Isles', *Studia anthroponymica Scandinavica*, 1 (1983), 45–60.

[28] John Insley, 'Topography and Settlement in the North-West', *Nomina*, 10 (1986), 169–76.

[29] Brian K. Roberts, 'Late -*bý*-Names in the Eden valley, Cumberland', *Nomina*, 13 (1989–90), 25–40.

[30] Gillian Fellows-Jensen, 'Scandinavians in Southern Scotland?', *Nomina*, 13 (1989–90), 41–60.

Dumfriesshire and Galloway via Cumberland is -*þveit*. There is only one name in -*þveit* in mainland Scotland outside zone 3 and this is *Moorfoot* (**mōr-þveit*) in Midlothian, which was probably named on analogy with *Moorthwaite*s in England by settlers moving from England to Scotland.

I would also argue that such settlers carried the place-name-forming generic -*bý* with them into the Central Lowlands of Scotland. I originally thought that these settlers from England probably came to Scotland in separate waves, with the first one perhaps dating to as early as the late ninth or early tenth century and consisting of men sent to guard the important transport route between the Clyde and the Forth.[31] I am now more inclined to think, however, that many of the *bý*-names in the Central Lowlands were coined on analogy with names in the Danelaw by settlers arriving in Scotland at later dates, probably in part the settlers who also brought with them the fashion for hogback tombstones.[32] This fashion in funeral monuments would seem to have developed in northern Yorkshire, perhaps at Brompton, where there is a particularly fine collection, and moved on via Cumberland to the Central Lowlands, where there is also an impressive collection at Govan.[33] There is a marked similarity of style between the hogbacks in Cumberland and those in Scotland.

Many of the place-names in -*bý* in the Central Lowlands have parallels in the Danelaw or north-west England, for example the two *Busby*s and two *Busbie*s containing *buski*, n., 'shrubbery', which can be compared with *Busby* near Brompton in Yorkshire, the four *Humbie*s containing *hundr*, m., 'hound, dog', which can be compared with *Hanby* in Lincolnshire, and the two *Crosby*s, two *Crosbie*s, and *Corsbie* containing the Gaelic loanword in Scandinavian *kross* 'cross as a religious symbol', which can be compared with six *Crosby*s in north-west England.

After I had become convinced that most of the *bý*-names in the Central Lowlands of Scotland were analogical formations, I realized that the same must apply to the four *bý*-names in Wales. *Colby* containing the personal name *Koli*, *Homri* containing the topographical term *horn*, n., 'promontory', and *Womanby* containing the occupational term *hundamaðr*, m., 'houndsman' all have counterparts in England, although *Lamby* (**lamb*, n., 'lamb') does not.

I also realized that many of the *bý*-names in the Isle of Man must be analogical formations and that some of these may post-date the Viking period.[34] No fewer than

---

[31] G. W. S. Barrow, *The Anglo-Norman Era in Scottish History* (Oxford: Clarendon Press, 1980), pp. 40, n. 37, and pp. 47–48. Fellows-Jensen, 'Scandinavians in Southern Scotland', p. 54.

[32] Barbara E. Crawford's suggestion in *Scandinavian Scotland*, p. 100.

[33] J. T. Lang, 'Hogback Monuments in Scotland', *Proceedings of the Society of Antiquaries of Scotland*, 105 (1972–74), 206–35; J. T. Lang, 'The Hogback: A Viking Colonial Monument', *Anglo-Saxon Studies in Archaeology and History*, 3 (1984), 85–176; J. T. Lang, 'The Govan Hogbacks: A Re-appraisal', in *Govan and its Early Medieval Sculpture*, ed. by Anna Ritchie (Stroud: Alan Sutton, 1994), pp. 123–32.

[34] Gillian Fellows-Jensen, 'The Place-Name Evidence', in *A New History of Man*, vol. III, ed. by Seán Duffy (Liverpool: Centre for Manx Studies, forthcoming).

fifteen of the twenty-eight relevant names in Man have exact parallels in England. In some cases the names were coined so early that they have undergone Manx linguistic developments so that the modern forms differ from their English counterparts, for example *Jurby* (**djúra-bý*), which is identical in origin with English *Derby*, *Sulby* containing *súla*, f., 'cleft, fork', which is identical in origin with two English *Soulby*s, and *Regaby* containing *hryggr*, m., 'ridge', which is identical in origin with English *Ribby*. Other Manx names in -*bý*, however, still resemble their English parallels exactly, for example *Dalby* containing *dalr*, m., 'valley', and the possibility must be borne in mind that the English administrators who arrived in Man after its cession to the English Crown, many of them coming from Lancashire, can have had a great influence on the form in which the Manx names of Scandinavian origin survived. Names whose similarity to names in England was recognized can have been adjusted to fall into line with these.

I shall therefore close my essay with the warning words that while the distribution pattern of place-names of Scandinavian origin provides us with the best general indication of the areas where Norwegians and Danes chose to settle, many of the names can have been bestowed upon the settlements that now bear them long after the Viking Age by people who no longer spoke, or even understood, a Scandinavian language. The picture is more complicated than has sometimes been thought.

The Linguistic Heritage of the Scandinavians in Normandy

If the Scandinavians who established themselves on Frankish soil during the ninth and tenth centuries have apparently left few convincing archaeological traces of their presence, they have bequeathed an important linguistic heritage, particularly on the level of toponymy. The aim of this essay is to take a closer look at the Scandinavian words which have been assimilated into langue d'oïl (northern French) and to propose the establishment of a glossary of certain specific words.

Before actually presenting the aims of any such project,[1] which raises several methodological questions, it is important to outline the Scandinavian linguistic material present in Normandy, to sum up those sources in which these words appear, and to itemize the different lexical fields.

Description of the Linguistic Material

The Scandinavians' influence in what was Carolingian Neustria amounts essentially to the contribution of new words. Indeed, it seems that as far as grammar is concerned, there was no Old Norse influence. Phonology was the most affected area, but without its having been changed drastically. Old Norse was able to reinforce, indeed even develop, certain dialectal features laid down during the earliest Germanic invasions by the Saxons and the Franks.[2] The linguistic material of Scandinavian

---

[1] This project is now the subject of my doctoral thesis, 'Des Vikings et des mots: L'apport des Vikings au lexique de la langue d'oïl' (University of Caen).

[2] These features include the development of Latin /k/ and /g/ before /a/ (Latin *cattu*, Norman *cat*; but French *chat* /ʃ-/), the development of Germanic /w/ (Old Norse *vík*, Norman *viquet*; but French *guichet*), and initial expiration: 'Les mots d'origine germanique ou

origin in Normandy mainly comprises three types of words: anthroponyms, toponyms (including microtoponyms), and common names. It is the common names that
best allow us to appreciate the degree of Scandinavian influence on langue d'oïl.[3]
Indeed, they represent a fresh contribution to the lexis of the Norman dialect, as
distinct from other dialects of Northern France. These words reflect a coexistence
and a cultural exchange between two populations speaking two different languages.

Several studies over many years have highlighted this particular vocabulary, but
none has properly collated all attested words of Scandinavian origin in Normandy
either comprehensively, that is, from the eleventh century to the present day, or
objectively. Firstly, one should mention Charles Joret, a pioneer in the field, who at
the end of the nineteenth and the beginning of the twentieth century had found a
certain number of these words both in twelfth-century Old French texts written in
Normandy as well as in dialectal vocabulary.[4] This research is now rather outdated;
several proposed etymologies need to be completely revised. For example, he proposes a Scandinavian origin for the words *hourdel*, from the Old French *hourdeis*
'fence'/'pallisade' (Old Norse *hurð* 'door') and *cotin* 'hut' (Old Norse *kot* 'hut'), but
a continental Germanic origin (Frankish) is certainly more likely. Another more significant example: he proposes for the Modern French *écraser* 'to crush', the Old
Norse *krasa*, but the word came from Middle English *crasen* during the Hundred
Years' War.[5] We also find scattered words in some dictionaries of patois, which
contain some details of local Norman dialects, and of course in French etymological
dictionaries.[6] Secondly, although the following authors look particularly closely at

---

scandinave dont l'initiale était jadis /h/ ont conservé localement cette marque' (Words of Germanic or Scandinavian origin whose initial sound was formerly /h/ have preserved this feature
locally). For this quotation and details about these linguistic phonemes, see René Lepelley, *La
Normandie dialectale* (Caen: Presses Universitaires de Caen, 1999), pp. 58–59, 61, and 71.

[3] Langue d'oïl is far from being uniform — it is made up of various dialects from the north
of former Gaul. These dialects are descended from Vulgar Latin (or Gallo-Romance) which
was spoken in the north of Gaul during the first centuries AD — a time which was strongly
influenced by the Germanic invasions of the fifth and sixth centuries. For an introduction to
dialect, patois, langue d'oïl, and French, see Lepelley, *La Normandie dialectale*.

[4] Charles Joret, *Des Caractères et de l'extention du patois normand* (Paris: Vieweg, 1883);
Charles Joret, 'Les Noms de lieux d'origine non romane et la colonisation germanique et
scandinave en Normandie', in *Congrès du Millénaire de la Normandie (911–1911): Comte
rendu des travaux*, ed. by Georges Monflier, 2 vols (Rouen: Léon Gy, 1912), II, 97–160.

[5] For *hourdel* and *cotin*, see Algirdas Julien Grimas, *Dictionnaire de l'ancien français*
(Paris: Larousse, 1992). For *écraser*, see *Le Nouveau Petit Robert: Dictionnaire alphabétique
et analogique de la langue française*, ed. by Josette Rey-Debove and Alain Rey (Paris: Le
Robert, 1993).

[6] O. Bloch and W. von Wartburg, *Dictionnaire étymologique de la langue française*, 5th
edn (Paris: Presses Universitaires de France, 1964); A. Dauzat, J. Dubois, and H. Mitterand,
Dictionnaire étymologique et historique du français (Paris: Larousse, 1964); *Dictionnaire
historique de la langue française*, ed. by Alain Rey, 2 vols (Paris: Le Robert, 1992).

these words, they disagree as to their number. In his *Französisches etymologisches Wörterbuch*, Walter von Wartburg proposes 178 Scandinavian etyma, whilst Ralph Paul de Gorog's *The Scandinavian Elements in French and Norman* has about 260.[7] The latter author has been sharply criticized in an article by Professor Lucien Musset because he missed out Scandinavian words attested from the eleventh century, while mentioning words that are attested toponymically but which were never used by speakers of langue d'oïl.[8] As for the *Französisches etymologisches Wörterbuch*, which offers a more realistic number, it would nevertheless benefit from a reconsideration of the Scandinavian origin of some Norman words and even from a check on the validity of certain Scandinavian etyma.[9]

To conclude this first section one observation is essential: we still do not know how many words the Scandinavians have bequeathed to Normandy.

Summary of the Sources

In order to find out how many words there are of Scandinavian origin, it is essential to know where to find them. The different studies and etymological dictionaries quoted above allow us to itemize and briefly describe the sources in which these words are attested. There could have been a late Scandinavian influence on French during the thirteenth century or during more recent times through commercial contact — an influence that has nothing to do with the Vikings. This is why it is necessary to make sure that the sources are Norman.

Latin Sources (Eleventh and Twelfth Centuries)

Lucien Musset used the term 'Old Norman' to describe the corpus of words of Scandinavian origin that appear in Latin texts of the eleventh century. By far the majority of these texts are charters or to be precise the decrees of the Dukes of Normandy. In them

---

[7] *Französisches etymologisches Wörterbuch*, ed. by Walter von Wartburg, 25 vols to date + index (Bonn: Klopp, 1928–); Ralph Paul de Gorog, *The Scandinavian Element in French and Norman* (New York: Bookman, 1958).

[8] Lucien Musset, 'Bibliographie critique', *Etudes germaniques*, 18 (1963), 365–67.

[9] Criticisms set out by Jean-Paul Chauveau, 'Influences normandes sur les parlers de l'Ouest', in *Mélanges René Lepelley*, ed. by Catherine Bougy, Pierre Boissel, and Bernard Garnier, Cahier des Annales de Normandie, 25 (Caen: Musée de Normandie, 1995), pp. 137– 46 (pp. 139 and 140). The same criticisms could be made of the vocabulary list of nautical terms supplied by Jean Renaud in his work *Les Vikings et la Normandie* (Rennes: Ouest-France, 1989), pp. 147–49. The Scandinavian origin of some words is doubtful insofar as it seems more likely that the proposed etyma are Dutch, or even English.

we can find some dozen attested words from *c*. 1030 to 1060.[10] Lucien Musset noticed the major importance of this 'Old Norman' because, according to him, 'il permet de jalonner le passage d'un dialect nordique à un dialecte roman'.[11] Perhaps this assertion begs to be qualified but it is undeniable that these words are precious linguistic clues. In fact, they still appear to be phonetically little affected by Romance. Moreover the wording of deeds and decrees sometimes gives us information about the way these words were used. The clerics who drew up charters adapted these words to fit Latin declensions, which strongly suggests that such terms were part of their everyday vocabulary. Take, for example, *fisigardum* which represents the Latin masculine accusative form of the word *fisigard* which is derived from Old Norse **fiskigarðr* 'a fishery' (cf. *Fishguard* in Wales, and *Fistard* on the Isle of Man). Or indeed they make it plain that they belong to the vernacular (as opposed to Latin) by mentioning *vulgo* or *lingua barbara*. This is the case with the word *isnechia*, derived from *snekkja* 'a warship'.[12] Pierre Bouet's computerized concordances of the main Norman historians in Latin (viz. Dudo of Saint-Quentin, William of Jumièges, William of Poitiers, and Guy of Amiens) are extremely useful for this sort of research.[13]

Sources in Old French (Twelfth and Thirteenth Centuries)

Latin was a hindrance to the written expression of langue d'oïl, which is why it is normal to find a greater number of attested words of Scandinavian origin in Old French texts, in particular those of the twelfth century. These texts are of a literary nature and were composed by Norman and Anglo-Norman historiographers.[14] For the twelfth century we need to consult about twenty texts to establish a corpus of Scandinavian words. The most linguistically regional author is Wace, in whose works the largest number of words of Scandinavian origin are to be found, principally in his two great verse histories: the *Roman de Brut* dated to 1155 and the *Roman de Rou* completed around 1170. One passage in the *Roman de Brut* is particularly remarkable as it contains about ten words of Scandinavian origin in just

---

[10] *Recueil des actes des ducs de Normandie (911–1066)*, ed. by Marie Fauroux, Mémoire de la Société des Antiquaires de Normandie, 61 (Caen: Caron et Compagnie, 1961).

[11] Musset, 'Bibliographie critique', p. 366 ('It allows us to trace the route from a Norse dialect to a Romance dialect').

[12] For the word *fisigardum* and a detailed explanation of the word *isnechia*, see Elisabeth Ridel, 'Viking Maritime Heritage in Normandy from a British Isles Perspective', *Northern Studies*, 35 (2000), 79–93.

[13] Unfortunately, these concordances are not available to the public.

[14] The Anglo-Norman period did not really enrich Norman vocabulary with English words; on the whole words were rather borrowed from Norman into English. There can be common words on both sides of the Channel because they have the same Germanic origin.

twenty-seven lines. But it must be said that all these words belong to nautical vocabulary and that nowhere else is such a concentration to be found. Another author, William of Berneville, also makes use of this same basic nautical vocabulary. It is interesting to note that these two authors were not at all conscious that they were using a vocabulary specific to Normandy.[15] Two words indicating items specific to Viking ships are particularly worth mentioning here: *betas*, from *beitáss* 'sail-yard, yard-arm'; and *brant*, from *brandr*, referring to the 'sword-shaped' timbers curving up to the ship's prow, and by extension to the prow itself.[16]

Norman Texts from the Fourteenth, Fifteenth, and Sixteenth Centuries

A smaller number of attested words can be found in the fourteenth, fifteenth, and sixteenth centuries, in specific texts written in Normandy. The most representative for our purposes is a nautical text written in Rouen in 1382, *Le Compte du Clos des Galées de Rouen*.[17] It contains several attestations of technical nautical words that have passed into Modern French, such as *bitte* from *biti* 'a cross beam on a ship', or *quille* from *kjölr* 'ship's keel'.

Present-Day Oral Sources

Present-day dialects offer several words of Scandinavian origin, although it is difficult to give an exact number. In his *Dictionnaire du français régional de Normandie*, René Lepelley has collected about sixty words of Scandinavian origin that are still used — or at least known — in Normandy.[18] There must be still more words in the local patois, since Lepelley's list only draws from the wider domain of regional French. For example, some specific words of nautical vocabulary which were in use at the beginning of this century have disappeared with modern developments in shipbuilding, which is probably true for other skill-related vocabularies. Given that all these words belong to an oral culture, the absence of an older form should lead one to treat them with the greatest caution. However, some words are so phonetically and semantically close to their original etymon that there is no room for doubt. For

---

[15] Wace, *Le Roman de Brut* [1155], ed. by Ivor Arnold, 2 vols (Paris: Société des Anciens Textes Français, 1938–40); Wace, *Le Roman de Rou* [c. 1170], ed. by A. J. Holden, 3 vols (Paris: Société des Anciens Textes Français, 1970–73); Guillaume de Berneville, *La Vie de Saint Gilles* [c. 1170], ed. by G. Paris (Paris: Société des Anciens Textes Français, 1881).

[16] The word *brandr* means both a 'ship's beak' (like a *svíri*) and a 'blade of a sword'.

[17] *Le Compte du Clos des Galées de Rouen* [1382–84], ed. by Charles Breart (Rouen: Cagniard, 1893).

[18] René Lepelley, *Dictionnaire du français régional de Normandie* (Paris: Bonneton, 1993).

example, the word *ha* is still found along the Norman coast, to refer to the 'dogfish' (*galeorhinus canis*), a fish of the small shark species, and derives from the Old Norse *hár* 'small shark, dogfish'.

Toponymy

Toponyms that are preceded by the definite article are evidence that at a certain period they were appellatives in current usage. They then became fossilized in the toponymic landscape and no longer appear except on geographical or survey maps. This, for example, is the case with *Le Tot* (derived from *topt* 'homestead'), *Le Torp* (from *þorp* 'secondary homestead'), or *Le Vicq* (from *vík* 'bay'). As Lucien Musset has pointed out, we should also add an entire rural vocabulary borrowed from Old English, brought by the Anglo-Saxons who arrived with those Scandinavians who had settled in the British Isles.[19] Examples here include the following names for portions of ground: *forlenc* derived from Old English *furlang* (furlong), *veindinc* derived from *wending* (the place where the plough was turned), and *hovelland* from *heafodland* (the highest part of a piece of ground).

Lexical Fields

Determining the lexical registers of words that are already known enables us to deepen our research and to focus it more effectively. It is possible to find four main lexical fields: maritime vocabulary, vocabulary to do with land, domestic vocabulary, and legal vocabulary. In the following lists, those examples with an asterisk indicate that the word is only found toponymically.

Maritime Vocabulary

The originality of maritime vocabulary is due to its variety and its cohesiveness. This vocabulary effectively covers all aspects of maritime life and spans the centuries from the eleventh to the present day. At the moment I have counted about one hundred words relating to maritime vocabulary: about fifty concern boats, twenty-five fishing, and twenty-five navigation. This maritime heritage is hardly surprising given the maritime nature of the Vikings.

---

[19] Lucien Musset, 'Les Apports anglais en Normandie de Rollon à Guillaume le Conquérant (911–1066)', in his *Nordica et Normannica: Recueil d'études sur la Scandinavie ancienne et médiévale, les expéditions des Vikings et la fondation de la Normandie*, Studia nordica, 1 (Paris: Société des études nordiques, 1997), pp. 447–66 (pp. 456–60, 'le domaine rural').

a) Nautical vocabulary
- Names of boats of Viking design
  - *isnechia* and *esneque* (eleventh and twelfth centuries) / *snekkja* 'small warship'
  - *eschei* (twelfth century) / *skeið* 'war-ship, galley'
  - *kenar* (twelfth century) / *knörr* 'merchant-ship'
- Ship-building terms
  - *callengue* (fourteenth century) / *kerling* 'keelson'
  - *rem* (dialectal vocabulary) / *rúm* 'room for a pair of rowers'
- Rigging vocabulary
  - *sigle* (eleventh century) / *segl* 'sail'
  - *raque* (fourteenth century) / *rakki* 'parrel'
  - *feste* (fifteenth century) / *festr* 'mooring rope'
- Crew and life aboard
  - *eschipre* (twelfth century) / *skipari* 'skipper'
  - *esturman* (twelfth century) / *stýrimaðr* 'skipper, captain, steersman'
  - *tialz* (twelfth century) / *tjald* 'tent'

b) Fishing vocabulary
- Marine fauna (fish, crustaceans, and marine mammals)
  - *célan* (dialectal vocabulary) / *sild* 'herring'
  - *flondre* (fourteenth century) / *flyðra* 'flounder'[20]
- Marine flora (seaweed)
  - *tangue* (twelfth century) / *þang* 'seaweed'
  - *milgreu* (dialectal vocabulary) / *melr* + *gras* 'lyme-grass'
- Fishing gear and vocabulary (nets, fishing grounds)
  - *havenet* (dialectal vocabulary) / *hafnet* 'net'

c) Navigation
- Names of rocks and islets
  - **etaque* / *stakkr* 'high rock in the sea'
  - **equet* / *sker* 'skerry'
  - *boe* (dialectal vocabulary) / *boði* 'sunken rock'
  - *grunne* (dialectal vocabulary) / *grunnr* 'bottom (of the sea)'
- Names of bays
  - *ho* / *hóp* 'small inlet'
  - **vicq* / *vík* 'bay'
  - *crique* (Modern French) / *kriki* 'creek'
- Shape of the landscape (capes and headlands)
  - **nez* / *nes* 'headland'
- Water vocabulary (currents)
  - *raz* / *rás* 'course, channel'
  - *run* / *run* 'current'

---

[20] See s.v. 'flounder *n.*' in *The Oxford English Dictionary*, ed. by J. A. Simpson and E. S. C. Weiner, 2nd edn (Oxford: Clarendon Press, 1989).

Land Vocabulary

The study of this vocabulary is closely linked to that of toponyms and microtoponyms. Given that the study of Scandinavian toponymy in Normandy is far from exhaustive, it is not possible to exclude the discovery of any new terms.

a) Description of the landscape
- landscape features
  - *dalle* / *dalr* 'dale, valley'
  - *hougue* / *haugr* 'hill'
  - *torve* (dialectal vocabulary) / *torf* 'turf'
- Plants and vegetation
  - *lunda* (eleventh-century Latin form, fem. acc.) and **Londe* / *lundr* 'grove'
  - *gade* '(red/black) currant' / *gaddr* 'spike, prickle'
  - *génotte* / *jörð* + *hnot* 'peanut'
- Animals
  - *crax* 'stonechat' / *krákr* 'crow, raven'
b) Naming of dwellings
   This vocabulary is mainly attested in toponymy
  - **tot* / *topt* 'homestead'
  - **torp* / *þorp* 'secondary homestead'
c) Agricultural vocabulary
- Naming of plots of land
  - *delle* (dialectal vocabulary) / *deild* 'portion of land'
  - **thuit* / *þveit* 'clearing'
- Farming vocabulary[21]
  - *bequerel* (fourteenth century) / *bekri* 'ram'
  - *harousse* (dialectal vocabulary) 'old horse' / *hárr* + *hross* 'grey horse'

Domestic Vocabulary

No study has been undertaken to measure the extent of Old Norse influence in this field.

a) Personal vocabulary
  - *gabber* (twelfth century) / *gabba* 'to mock'
  - *muler* (dialectal vocabulary) 'to sulk' / *múli* 'snout'

---

[21] Some words of Scandinavian origin concerning rural life have been collected by René Lepelley in *Le Parler normand du Val de Saire (Manche)*, Cahiers des Annales de Normandie, 7 (Caen: Musée de Normandie, 1974).

b) Clothing
- *sairch* (fourteenth century) / *serkr* 'shirt'

c) Food
- *flique* (twelfth century) / *flikki* 'flitch of bacon'

d) Tools and utensils
- *heitier* (dialectal vocabulary) 'stove' / *heitr* 'burning, hot'
- *tro* (dialectal vocabulary, Jersey) / *trog* 'kneading-trough'
- *tille* (twelfth century) 'axe of a carpenter' / *telgja* 'to cut'

Legal Vocabulary

This vocabulary does not contain a great number of words, but it is remarkable in as far as they appear in the oldest texts concerning Normandy, that is, from the eleventh century. These words have been studied by Lucien Musset in an article on the subject of the Scandinavian influence on Norman law.[22]

a) Maritime law
- Law concerning wreckage
  - *varech* (eleventh century) / *reki* 'something drifted ashore'
- Whalers
  - *waumannus* (twelfth century) / *hvalr* + *maðr* 'whaler'

b) Domestic law
- Law concerning breaking and entering
  - *hamfara* (eleventh century) / *heimfǫr* 'attack on one's home'

c) Personal law
- Law concerning exile
  - *ullac* (eleventh century) / *útlagi* 'outlaw'

Conclusion

The drawing-up of a glossary of Scandinavian words in Normandy must meet two main objectives:

1. A complete note of each word
   - by clarifying the different attestations of the word (sources)
   - by explaining the linguistic development of the word: both phonetically and semantically
   - by trying to clarify the localization of the word in Normandy

---

[22] Lucien Musset, 'Les Apports scandinaves dans le plus ancien droit normand', in his *Nordica et Normannica*, pp. 245–61.

- by comparing the word to other terms derived from different languages:
  — Nordic languages: Norwegian, Danish, Swedish, Icelandic, Faroese, and the now dead languages of Orkney and the Shetland Islands (Norn).
  — languages which have been in contact with Old Norse: Old English, Old Irish, and Old Gaelic.

2. The establishment of the number of words
- Count all the words, while indicating the number of words derived from the same etymon; although a single Scandinavian etymon has, in general, resulted in a single Norman word, it often happens that this word has itself led to further derived terms.
- Clarify if there is another possible Germanic etymon: Old Saxon, Dutch, or Continental Germanic.
- Carry out a diachronic study: the number of words that have disappeared over the centuries; the number of words used solely in Normandy or on the borders of Normandy.

The completion of this project will better enable us generally to measure the influence of the Vikings in Normandy and thus to offer a more precise picture of their settlement.

SYNOPTIC TABLE

MARITIME VOCABULARY		
nautical vocabulary	fishing	navigation
• texts from 12th century • text from 14th century • dialectal vocabulary	• Latin charter, 11th century • dialectal vocabulary	• maritime toponyms and microtoponyms
LAND VOCABULARY		
agricultural vocabulary	dwellings	landscape
• Latin charters, 11th century • Anglo-Scandinavian vocabulary • dialectal vocabulary	• words attested in toponymy	• Latin charters, 11th century • words attested in toponymy • dialectal vocabulary

DOMESTIC VOCABULARY			
personal	clothing	food	tools and utensils
• dialectal vocabulary	• texts from 14th century	• texts from 12th century	• texts from 12th century • dialectal vocabulary

LEGAL VOCABULARY		
maritime	domestic	personal
• Latin charters, 11th and 12th centuries	• Latin charter, 11th century	• Latin charter, 11th century

Evidence for the Impact
of Christianity on Scandinavia

New Perspectives on the Christianization of Scandinavia and the Organization of the Early Church

STEFAN BRINK

To discuss the conversion of Scandinavia may seem to be a rather adventurous and even fruitless task. In the first place, there are practically no contemporary written sources that can throw some light upon the process. Secondly, several continental travellers have during the last few centuries seriously doubted that Christianity ever reached these northern countries, on account of the inhabitants' ungodly way of life. However, I shall here challenge these doubtful voyagers and state that Scandinavia did become Christian, though much later than the continent and the British Isles and perhaps not so deeply. This idea has in itself crossed the minds of most of the scholars who have discussed the subject, but my statement rests in particular upon some profound research that recently has been undertaken by the interdisciplinary project, *Sveriges kristnande* ('The Christianization of Sweden').[1]

To start from the end, two of the main conclusions that we have reached during the last few years are (1) that there were regional differences in Scandinavia in several respects, and (2) that the period of Christianization was much longer than was previously thought. The conversion was certainly not a single event; it was a protracted process lasting well over a couple of centuries. We also have a new view of how the Christian religion was introduced to these northern parts, a view that conflicts with the earlier one. I will try to elaborate these themes in this essay. In particular, I hope to shed some light on the new evidence that we have gained from archaeological excavations in recent years. I will focus on Scandinavia and will exclude Iceland and its Christianization, which is a very interesting problem in its own right, though it is also linked particularly with Norway.

---

[1] *Kristnandet i Sverige: Gamla källor och nya perspektiv*, ed. by Bertil Nilsson, Projektet Sveriges Kristnande Publikationer, 5 (Uppsala: Lunne Böcker, 1996).

For my doctoral thesis, on the formation of the Scandinavian parish, published in 1990, I found myself compelled to write an introductory *Stand der Forschung* chapter on the conversion of the Scandinavians.[2] I spent most of the late 1980s reading a lot of what had been written — up till then — on this theme. It was clear that there had been a shift in the view of the conversion during the previous three decades. The old view of the introduction of Christianity pictured bold and godly missionaries wandering around northern Europe, preaching, baptizing, and winning disciples for the new faith, very much mirroring the life and adventures of Jesus in Palestine as described in the New Testament, and finally being killed by some pagan villains and then declared saints. However, the new picture sees the Christian religion as being first introduced to the upper strata of society, before trickling down to the lower social classes.[3] Christianization is thus, in its primary phase, now regarded as having been a matter for kings and chieftains. The older view that the conversion was a single event — for Sweden, when the Christians tore down the famous pagan temple in Uppsala around 1080; for Denmark, when King Harald Blue-Tooth 'made the Danes Christian' in the 960s; and for Iceland, when the Icelanders took the famous decision to convert to Christianity at the Althing in the year 1000 (or 999) — has therefore been replaced by a new view that the Christianization of Scandinavia should rather be looked upon as a lengthy process.[4]

This process made way for a gradual change in the mentality of the Scandinavians during the Viking Age and early Middle Ages:[5] from an agriculture-centred world-view to an individual-centred, intellectual faith; from a crowd of gods, goddesses, and other beings to one god, and that god a man, something attested by the rune-stone from Galteland, Norway, which has the line 'God is one'.[6] The ideological side

---

[2] Stefan Brink, *Sockenbildning och sockennamn: Studier i äldre territoriell indelning i Norden*, Acta academiae regiae Gustavi Adolphi, 57 (Stockholm: Almqvist & Wiksell, 1990).

[3] See, for example, P. H. Sawyer, *Kings and Vikings: Scandinavia and Europe AD 700– 1100* (London: Methuen, 1982), p. 139.

[4] For another recent discussion of the present state of research, see Birgit Sawyer and Peter Sawyer, *Medieval Scandinavia: From Conversion to Reformation circa 800–1500* (Minneapolis: University of Minnesota Press, 1993), pp. 100–28.

[5] See, for example, Gro Steinsland, 'Religionsskiftet i Norden og *Völuspá* 65', in *Nordisk hedendom: Et symposium*, ed. by Gro Steinsland and others (Odense: Odense Universitetsforlag, 1991), pp. 335–48; Gro Steinsland, 'Hvordan ble hedendommen utfordret og påvirket av kristendommen?' in *Møtet mellom hedendom og kristendom i Norge*, ed. by Hans-Emil Lidén (Oslo: Universitetsforlaget, 1995), pp. 9–27; and Anders Hultgård, 'Religiös förändring, kontinuitet och ackulturation/synkretism i vikingatidens och medeltidens skandinaviska religioner', in *Kontinuitet i kult och tro från vikingatid till medeltid*, ed. by Bertil Nilsson (Uppsala: Lunne Böcker, 1992), pp. 49–103.

[6] See James E. Knirk, '"Tolv vintrer hadde kristendommen vært i Norge": Norske runesteiner forteller om kristningen', in *Fra hedendom til kristendom: Perspektiver på religionsskiftet i Norge*, ed. by Magnus Rindal (Oslo: Gyldendal, 1996), pp. 43–53.

of the transformation was much more of an 'event': the building of churches, the passing of new Christian laws, and the political acceptance of the new faith as a kind of 'state religion' among the upper social strata. The passing of laws must not be neglected, because early Scandinavian society was a markedly legal society, with *thing* assemblies at many different levels, ranging from the local to the pan-regional. The new rules for a correct life in the Christian faith and under the supervision of the Church were adopted at these *thing* assemblies, and the punishments for breaking the rules were severe. When one is writing history, it is natural to focus upon this ideological dimension rather than upon changes in mentality. Our history books detail decisive events and persons, in order to provide a historical framework that is easily comprehensible. When talking about religion, it is practically impossible to write about the more fundamental history of changes in mentality.[7] The reason why the conversion was so radical in Scandinavia was this dual change in society, in *mentality* and in *ideology*, the latter manifested by new laws and new cultic buildings, the churches.

All that has been written on the conversion of Scandinavia naturally relies upon written records, especially the *Vita Anskarii* and Adam of Bremen's *Gesta Hammaburgensis ecclesiae pontificum*.[8] These sources state that the Swedes were converted somewhat later than their neighbours in Denmark and Norway. However, although the written records actually state this, I seriously doubt it. Instead, I believe that what we today call Sweden was in line with Denmark and Norway in every respect regarding the conversion. However, as I have said above, there were obviously regional differences.

Although my aim here is to give an updated picture of the state of research regarding the new knowledge and the new approaches that have been discovered in the field of the Christianization of Scandinavia during the last couple of years or so — a field that, alas, more or less lacks any contemporary sources throwing light upon the process — I shall, as my starting point for the discussion, focus on three of these contemporary written sources, namely three historically important rune-stones dating from the tenth and eleventh centuries.

---

[7] See Håkan Möller, 'Mentalitet och kristnande: Reflexioner kring ett tvärvetenskapligt studium – exemplet Jämtland', in *Jämtlands kristnande*, ed. by Stefan Brink, Projektet Sveriges Kristnande Publikationer, 4 (Uppsala: Lunne Böcker, 1996), pp. 189–99.

[8] Rimbert, *Vita Anskarii*, ed. by Georg Waitz, MGH, SS rer. Ger., 55 (Hanover: Hahn, 1884); Rimbert, *Boken om Ansgar: Ansgars liv*, trans. by Eva Odelman (Stockholm: Proprius, 1986); Adam von Bremen, *Magistri Adami Bremensis Gesta Hammaburgensis ecclesiae pontificium*, ed. by B. Schmeidler, MGH SS rer. Ger., 2, 3rd edn (Hanover: Hahn, 1917); Adam av Bremen, *Historien om Hamburgstiftet och dess biskopar*, trans. by Emanuel Svenberg (Stockholm: Proprius, 1984).

The Jelling Rune-Stone — Denmark

Beside the church at Jelling in Jutland stand two famous Viking Age rune-stones. On one of them, we can read that 'King Harald had this monument made in memory of Gorm, his father, and Thorvi, his mother. That was the Harald who won all of Denmark for himself, and Norway, and made the Danes Christian' (**haraltr : kunukʀ : baþ : kaurua | kubl : þausi : aft : kurmfaþursin | aukaft : þaurui : muþur : sina : sa | haraltr : ias : saʀ : uan : tanmaurk | : ala : auknuruiak | : aukt(a)ni(karþi)kristną**). This rune-stone dates from *c*. 960. Thus, it seems that the question of when Denmark became Christian is easy to answer. According to King Harald Blue-Tooth, he made the Danes Christians *c*. 960.[9]

We do not know what Harald's word is worth, that is, what role he actually played in the Christianization of Denmark. It is obvious that Christian infiltration was in several respects much earlier than this, probably one or more centuries earlier, but from the ideological point of view, Harald may well have been a central figure in the process of conversion.

Harald's reign also coincides with the period when Denmark saw a change in burial customs, from pagan to Christian, a change which, according to recent archaeological evidence, took place in the middle and the second half of the tenth century.[10] Perhaps the most sensational of this new archaeological evidence comes from Sebbersund by Limfjord in Jutland. Here a Viking Age port and trading place has been found, with more than 150 pit houses and a hall some 50 m in length. One has thus the impression of a royal port or proto-town. To the south there is a churchyard, measuring 40 m by 40 m and surrounded by a ditch. Approximately one thousand burials have been found there. The graveyard is typically divided into male and female graves and no grave-goods have been found. In the middle of the churchyard there is an empty space with no graves, but with several post holes. Obviously a small church, measuring some 13 m by 6 m, stood here. The church was erected around the year 1000 and stood for about a century, until the trading place was abandoned. One grave has been found within the area of this church. At Sebbersund, then, we have an early church and Christian graveyard, probably built by the king on his port and trading place.[11]

Harald's rune-stone, the larger of the two Jelling stones, is an impressive and important monument. It appears to have rapidly become famous in Scandinavia, and

---

[9] See *Danmarks runeindskrifter*, ed. by Lis Jacobsen and Erik Moltke, 3 vols (Copenhagen: Ejnar Munksgaard, 1941–42), I (1941), no. 42; Erik Moltke, *Runes and their Origin: Denmark and Elsewhere* (Copenhagen: National Museum of Denmark, 1985), pp. 202–20.

[10] Leif Chr. Nielsen, 'Hedenskab og kristendom: Religionsskiftet afspejlet i vikingetidens grave', in *Fra stamme til stat i Danmark*, ed. by Peder Mortensen and Birgit M. Rasmussen, 2 vols (Århus: Aarhus Universitetsforlag, 1988–91), II: *Høvdingesamfund og Kongemagt* (1991), 245–67.

[11] Peter Birkedahl Christensen and Erik Johansen, 'En handelsplads fra yngre jernalder og vikingetid ved Sebbersund', *Aarbøger for nordisk Oldkyndighed og Historie*, 1991 (1992), 199–229; Peter Birkedahl and Erik Johansen, 'Nikolajbjerget', *Skalk*, 1993, no. 1, 3–8.

soon led to a new vogue, that of erecting rune-stones to commemorate one's relations, to declare one's faith, or just to brag, all of which purposes are to be found on the Jelling stone.[12] In central Sweden, this vogue led some decades later to a veritable explosion in the number of rune-stones being raised. Here, hundreds of rune-stones were erected in only a couple of decades, rune-stones very much linked with the introduction of the new Christian faith.

The Kuli Rune-Stone — Norway

In the vicinity of the farm of Kuli on the island of Smøla in the province of Nord-møre, Norway, there earlier stood a modest but remarkable rune-stone. The runic text ends by saying that 'twelve winters had Christendom been in Norway' (**tualf : uintr : hafþi : kristin : tumr : uirit : i : nuriki**).[13] This statement has been con-nected with a famous 'national' *thing* assembly that King Olaf Haraldsson and his bishop, Grímkell, held on the island of Moster in 1022 or 1023, at which the first Christian law was accepted, something that has been interpreted as the point at which western Norway, at least, formally adopted the Christian faith.[14] This dating of the rune-stone has gained support from the dendrochronological dating of a bridge, situated where the stone once stood, to 1034.[15]

The Kuli stone probably throws light upon a memorable political event. Most certainly this event was not when Christianity was first introduced to Norway. During the last decade, archaeological research in particular has moved forward the position in this field considerably. On the farm of Hernes on the famous peninsula of Frosta, where the *thing* assembly met in *Frostuþingslög*, that is the district where the law of the *thing* at Frosta was valid, several skeletons have been found. The graves were orientated east–west and the burials lacked artefacts. Hence, the burials were classified as Christian. Radiocarbon dating has revealed that some of these burials date from the eleventh century.[16]

---

[12] Knirk, '"Tolv vintrer"', pp. 43–44.

[13] Aslak Liestøl, 'Kuli', in *Norges Innskrifter med de yngre Runer*, ed. by Magnus Olsen, Aslak Liestøl, and James E. Knirk, 6 vols (Oslo: Norsk historisk kjeldeskrift-institutt, 1941–), IV (1957), no. 449, pp. 280–86.

[14] Nils Hallan, 'Kulisteinen og kristenrettsvedtaket på Mostertinget', *Du mitt Nordmøre*, 1966, 21–28; Magnus Rindal, 'Frå heidendom til kristendom', in *Fra hedendom til kristendom*, ed. by Rindal, pp. 9–19 (p. 11).

[15] Jan Ragnar Hagland, 'Kulisteinen: Endå ein gong', in *Heidersskrift til Nils Hallan på 65-årsdagen 13. desember 1991*, ed. by Gulbrand Alhaug, Kristoffer Kruken, and Helge Salvesen (Oslo: Novus, 1991), pp. 157–65.

[16] Oddmund Farbregd, 'Kongsmakt, kristning og Frostatinget', *Spor*, 1986, no. 2, 38–41; Merete Røskaft, 'Religionsskiftet og lokale maktforhold i Trøndelag', in *Kultursamanhengar i Midt-Norden*, ed. by Steinar Supphellen (Trondheim: Tapir, 1997), pp. 101–12.

An even more interesting site is an early Christian graveyard on the small island of Veøy in the province of Romsdal.[17] This island has been totally deserted since the late nineteenth century, and hence the possibilities for intensive investigations are excellent. The name of the island is itself very interesting. It is a compound of *øy* 'island' and the Old West Norse word *vé*, here most probably to be understood as an old adjective *vé* (< Proto-Germanic **wiha-*) 'holy'.[18] Most probably, this small island was called the 'Holy Island' in pagan times, but one cannot exclude the possibility that the first element had Christian connotations. There is nothing in the word *vé* that suggests a pagan content in the meaning of 'holy'. Beside the stone church, two small graveyards have been located, both surrounded by an enclosure, a stone wall. Several radiocarbon datings have been taken from these burials, the earliest of which were in the tenth century. The excavator, Brit Solli, suggests that we probably have here, on Veøy, a rare example of an early Christian graveyard, in use from *c.* 950.

On the basis of her finds at Høre in Valdres, southern Norway, the archaeologist Inger Helene Vibe Müller has put forward a perhaps controversial hypothesis that the early Christians in Scandinavia at first continued to use the pagan graveyards for their Christian burials, and that the churches belong to a somewhat later phase, namely the middle of the eleventh century onwards.[19] This hypothesis has to be tested by future research.

The Norwegian counterpart to our research project is called *Religionsskiftet i Norden* ('The Change of Religion in Scandinavia') and has produced several illuminating and interesting articles and books.[20] However, the person who has most recently contributed new ideas to the discussion of the Christianization of Norway is the archaeologist Dagfinn Skre.[21] He has found that Christian burial practices started

---

[17] See Britt Solli, 'Narratives of Encountering Religions: On the Christianization of the Norse around AD 900–1000', *Norwegian Archaeological Review*, 29 (1996), 89–114.

[18] See Walter Baetke, *Das Heilige im Germanischen* (Tübingen: Mohr, 1942), p. 196; Stefan Brink, 'Har vi haft ett kultiskt **al* i Norden?', in *Sakrale navne*, ed. by Gillian Fellows-Jensen and Bente Holmberg, NORNA-rapporter, 48 (Uppsala: NORNA, 1992), pp. 107–21 (p. 116).

[19] Inger Helene Vibe Müller, 'Fra ættefellesskap til sognefellesskap: Om overgangen fra hedensk til kristen gravskikk', in *Nordisk hedendom*, ed. by Steinsland and others, pp. 359–72; Inger Helene Vibe Müller, 'Fra gravplass til kirkegård: Om ættens, kongens og kirkens rolle ved etablering av kirkesteder', in *En norrlandsbygd möter yttervärlden*, ed. by Leif Grundberg and Pia Nykvist, Styresholmsprojektets skrifter, 3 (Härnösand: Länsmuseet i Västernorrland, 1994), pp. 35–38.

[20] For example, *Three Studies on Vikings and Christianization*, ed. by Magnus Rindal (Oslo: The Research Council of Norway, 1994); *Fra hedendom til kristendom*, ed. by Rindal; *Studier i kilder til vikingtid og nordisk middelalder*, ed. by Magnus Rindal (Oslo: Norges forskningsråd, 1996); Gunn Cathrine Varder Løwe, *Religionsskiftet i samspill med de politiske maktforholdene i Norge: En historiografisk undersøkelse*, KULTs skriftserie, 72 (Oslo: Norges forskningsråd, 1997).

[21] See, for example, Dagfinn Skre, 'Kirken før sognet: Den tidligste kirkeordningen i Norge', in *Møtet mellom hedendom og kristendom i Norge*, ed. by Lidén, pp. 170–233.

to be used in southern Norway in the middle of the tenth century, and in the south-west the change in burial practices may have taken place as early as the beginning of the century. Many of Skre's analyses relate to the early organization of the Church, a subject that I shall comment upon shortly.

The Frösö Rune-Stone — Sweden

On the centrally located island of Frösö in the province of Jämtland in northern Sweden, we find the northernmost rune-stone in Sweden and also the only rune-stone in this province. It may be dated to the second half of the eleventh century. The runic text has historical implications in several respects. As far as we are concerned, the most important part of the inscription is: 'Östman Gudfast's son [...] made the bridge and he Christianized Jämtland' (**austmoþ(r)kuþfastaʀsun : lit [...] kiruabruþisauk h(onli)t kristnoeotalont**.[22] The Frösö stone is hence a kind of counterpart to the Jelling stone. Someone is stating that he has in some way Christianized somewhere: on the Jelling stone, it was King Harald; on the Frösö stone it is Östman Gudfast's son. The latter must have been some kind of leader in the province, a 'king-like' person, perhaps a chieftain or the lawman. Anyway, he dares to state that he has Christianized the province of Jämtland. However, in the same way as we saw with Harald and the Jelling stone above, Östman cannot have Christianized the province. Maybe this statement on the rune-stone reflects a situation in which the assembly of Jämtland had taken a decision that the Christian religion was to be the 'official' religion of the province, thus in line with what had happened some decades earlier in Iceland.

In our research project on the Christianization of Sweden, we have used the province of Jämtland as a case study for an intensive investigation of all the possible sources that may throw some light upon the conversion.[23] The Frösö rune-stone was, of course, the natural and obvious starting-point for this discussion. As well as the inscription, the ornamentation on the stone is of interest. This is a typical, central-Swedish rune-stone dating from the eleventh century. This is to be contrasted with the fact that, during the Middle Ages, Jämtland was politically a part of Norway. However, the province belonged ecclesiastically to the archbishopric of Uppsala, Sweden. Thus, we have here in Jämtland a rather strange situation, with different political and ecclesiastical connections. The picture that finally emerged from our analyses was that the province had more or less Christianized itself, although obviously with contacts and influences from both east and west. The fact that Jämtland came under the see of Uppsala is probably a reflection of the old and intimate contacts between Jämtland and the Mälar valley region in central Sweden.

---

[22] See Henrik Williams, 'Runjämtskan på Frösöstenen och Östmans bro', in *Jämtlands kristnande*, ed. by Brink, pp. 45–63.

[23] *Jämtlands kristnande*, ed. by Brink.

From the eleventh century onwards, the cult of St Olaf played a very important role in the introduction and establishment of the new religion, especially in a province like Jämtland. The cult of this early saint became the most important one in medieval Scandinavia, and this is especially true of Norrland, the northern part of Sweden. Although under the Swedish archbishop of Uppsala, the inhabitants of Norrland voluntarily paid a kind of tax to the Norwegian archbishop in Niðaróss (present-day Trondheim), the so-called *Sankt Olafs hœtsla* or *Votum Beati Olavi*, during the early Middle Ages.[24]

After focusing on the province of Jämtland, it is appropriate to turn to the neighbouring provinces to the east, Ångermanland and Medelpad. Here, the archaeologist Leif Grundberg has conducted several important excavations that have thrown new light upon the conversion in northern Sweden.[25] In the hamlet of Björned in the parish of Torsåker, the very centre of the province of Ångermanland, Grundberg has excavated a prehistoric settlement and a graveyard. The settlement seems to have been established *c.* 300–500 and continued to be occupied in the Viking Age and the Middle Ages. In the immediate vicinity of this settlement was also an obviously Christian graveyard measuring approximately 25 m by 12 m and containing about thirty burials, a site never mentioned in written sources. The skeletons have been radiocarbon-dated to the Viking Age and early Middle Ages (from the tenth to the thirteenth century). Osteological analyses have revealed that the people buried in this graveyard were related. No remnants of any building (such as an early church) have been found. However, it is possible that a small church stood in the centre of the churchyard. If so, a burial was placed in the middle of the presumed church, which may be understood as a founder's or a patron's grave. The Björned site is probably a rare, early-Christian burial ground, possibly with a small wooden church, for a family or a farm dating from the tenth century onwards. A probable hypothesis is that, when later parishes were formed in the province, the church and the graveyard at Björned became obsolete, and the inhabitants of Björned had to bury their dead in the graveyard at the parish church in Torsåker some kilometres away. This excavation

---

[24] See, for example, Nils Ahnlund, *Från medeltid och Vasatid: Historia och kulturhistoria* (Stockholm: Hugo Gebers, 1933); Nils Ahnlund, *Jämtland och Härjedalens historia: Intill 1537* (Stockholm: Norstedt, 1948), pp. 61–82; Carl F. Hallencreutz, 'Hellig Olav i ett internationellt perspektiv', in *Før og etter Stiklestad 1030: Religionsskifte, kulturforhold, politisk makt*, ed. by Øystein Walberg (Verdal: Stiklestad nasjonale kultursenter, 1996), pp. 69–78; Carl F. Hallencreutz, 'Jämtland i ett europeiskt perspektiv', in *Jämtlands kristnande*, ed. by Brink, pp. 9–20; Stefan Brink, 'Land, makt och tro: Något om de norrländska landskapssamhällena och centralmakten under medeltid, jämte S:t Olofskultens betydelse för Norrland', in *Før og etter Stiklestad 1030*, ed. by Walberg, pp. 109–27; *Helgonet i Nidaros: Olavskult och kristnande i Norden*, ed. by Lars Rumar, Skrifter utgivna av Riksarkivet, 3 (Stockholm: Riksarkivet, 1997).

[25] Leif Grundberg, 'Gravar, kyrkor och människor – aspekter på religionsskiftet i Mittnorden: Några exempel från pågående undersökningar i Ångermanland och Medelpad', in *Kultursamanhengar i Midt-Norden*, ed. by Supphellen, pp. 29–53.

in Ångermanland may point to a vital factor in early Christian society in Scandinavia, namely that there were small wooden churches with small graveyards on farms and in hamlets, used only by one family or the people of the hamlet.[26] The reason why we have not found these kinds of remains before is probably because this phase is so early, presumably the ninth to the twelfth century. Therefore there are no written records describing this phenomenon, and parish formation during the twelfth and thirteenth centuries has made the older structure completely obsolete and obscure.

New archaeological excavations in other places in Sweden, on the islands of Öland and Gotland and in the provinces of Dalarna, Uppland, and Skåne, have also yielded interesting information.[27] We have early, clearly Christian, burials, from the tenth century and onwards, normally with an east–west orientation, but with several pagan traits, such as furnished burials with clothing, grave-goods, or food. Obviously there were regional and chronological differences in burial customs: typically Christian burials are found in Skåne in the late tenth century, while pagan burials can be found in northern Uppland in the late twelfth century.

This is, from a Baltic perspective, not surprising. Estonia was forced by the Germans and the Danes to become Christian in the early thirteenth century; Latvia was Christianized in the late twelfth and thirteenth century; while in Lithuania the Christian religion was accepted in 1386. Typical for the Baltic countries was the parallel existence of churchyards and local burial grounds, and furnished burials; in other words, a similar situation to what has been found in Scandinavia for the preceding centuries.[28]

---

[26] This is something that has earlier been discussed for Gudbrandsdalen in Norway by Dagfinn Skre, 'Gård og kirke, bygd og sogn: Organiseringsmodeller og organiseringsenheter i middelalderens kirkebygging i Sør-Gudbrandsdalen' (unpublished master's dissertation, University of Oslo, 1984).

[27] *Tusen år på Kyrkudden: Leksands kyrka, arkeologi och byggnadshistoria*, ed. by Birgitta Dandanell, Dalarnas fornminnes- och hembygdsförbunds skrifter, 25 (Falun: Leksands församling, 1982); Lars Ersgård, *Det starka landskapet: En arkeologisk studie av Leksandsbygden i Dalarna från yngre järnålder till nyare tid*, Riksantikvarieämbetet Arkeologiska Undersökningar, Skrifter, 21 (Stockholm: Riksantikvarieämbetet, 1997); Mats Anglert, *Kyrkor och herravälde: Från kristnande till sockenbildning i Skåne*, Lund Studies in Medieval Archaeology, 16 (Stockholm: Almqvist & Wiksell, 1995); Anders Broberg, *Bönder och samhälle i statsbildningstid: En bebyggelsearkeologisk studie av agrarsamhället i Norra Roden 700–1350*, Upplands fornminnesförenings tidskrift, 52 (Uppsala: Almqvist & Wiksell, 1990); Dan Carlsson, *Gård, hamn och kyrka: En vikingatida kyrkogård i Fröjel*, CCC papers, 4 (Visby: Centrum för Östersjöstudier, Högskolan på Gotland, 1999).

[28] See, for example, Heiki Valk, 'Reflections of Folk-Religion and Beliefs in Estonian Burial Customs of the 13th–19th Centuries: Archaeology, Folklore and Written Data', in *Archaeology East and West of the Baltic: Papers from the Second Estonian-Swedish Archaeological Symposium, Sigtuna, May 1991*, ed. by Ingmar Jansson, Theses and Papers in Archaeology, n.s., 7 (Stockholm: Department of Archaeology, University of Stockholm, 1995), pp. 131–53; Heiki Valk, 'About the Transitional Period in the Burial Customs in the Region of the Baltic

We have now reached the time when the Christian religion had become more established in Scandinavia and we are entering the period of ecclesiastical or parochial organization of the Church.

The Organization of the Early Church

The earliest church we have evidence for is at Birka in central Sweden, mentioned in the *Vita Anskarii* and therefore presumably dating from the beginning of the ninth century.[29] The oldest archaeologically dated churches in Scandinavia are from the late tenth and the eleventh centuries, for example, the church in Jelling, Jutland, from *c*. 980 or a little later;[30] the predecessor to the Holy Trinity Church in Lund, from *c*. 990;[31] the church of St Clement in Oslo, from *c*. 1000;[32] the church of St Clement in Helsingborg, from the first half of the eleventh century;[33] and St Stephen's wooden church in the town of Lund, from the middle of the eleventh century, also mentioned on a rune-stone from that century found in Lund.[34] We also have a church mentioned on an eleventh-century rune-stone from Oddernes in southern Norway. The inscription says that 'Eyvind, St Olaf's godson, made this church on his family (*óðal*) farm'.[35]

The great period for the building of churches in Scandinavia was during the twelfth and thirteenth centuries, coinciding with the period of parish formation. Several hundred stone churches were erected during the latter part of the twelfth and thirteenth centuries. This phase was preceded by the building of 'private' churches, especially in the southern parts of Scandinavia. How many of these churches, often made of wood, were built, we do not know.

I have myself studied the organization of the early Church in Scandinavia and have found a rather heterogeneous picture.[36] In southern Scandinavia, there were

Sea', in *Culture Clash or Compromise?*, ed. by Nils Blomkvist, Acta Visbyensia, 11 (Visby: Gotland Centre for Baltic Studies, 1998), pp. 237–50.

[29] *Boken om Ansgar*, chs 11 and 28.

[30] Knud J. Krogh, 'The Royal Viking-Age Monuments at Jelling in the Light of Recent Archaeological Excavations', *Acta Archaeologica*, 53 (1982), 183–216.

[31] Anders Andrén, *Den urbana scenen: Städer och samhälle i det medeltida Danmark*, Acta Archaeologica Lundensia, Series in 8°, 13 (Malmö: Liber; Bonn: Habelt, 1985), p. 208.

[32] Rindal, 'Frå heidendom til kristendom', p. 14; For the cult of St Clement, see Barbara E. Crawford, 'The Dedication to St Clement, Rodil, Harris', in *Church, Chronicle and Learning in Medieval and Early Renaissance Scotland*, ed. by Barbara E. Crawford (Edinburgh: Mercat, 1999), pp. 24–32.

[33] Andrén, *Den urbana scenen*, p. 200.

[34] Andrén, *Den urbana scenen*, p. 209, and Anglert, *Kyrkor och herravälde*, pp. 137–38.

[35] Knirk, '"Tolv vintrer hadde kristendommen vært i Norge"', p. 46.

[36] Brink, *Sockenbildning och sockennamn*; Stefan Brink, 'Sockenbildningen i Sverige', in *Kyrka och socken i medeltidens Sverige*, ed. by Olle Ferm (Stockholm: Riksantikvarieämbetet,

clearly many private churches, especially those erected on the farms belonging to the early aristocracy.[37] Today we know of several Viking Age 'manors' with an early church in southern Scandinavia, such as Bjäresjö in Skåne and Lisbjerg in Jutland.[38] This picture of the building of churches is, thus, congruent with what we find on the continent and on the British Isles. Other early actors in the building of churches were the kings in all three Scandinavian countries. During the twelfth century in particular, it seems that kings erected many stone churches on their royal estates and in trading places across Scandinavia. A third church-building phase started with the introduction of tithes, during the mid-twelfth century. In the thirteenth century, especially in northern Scandinavia, many churches were built and parishes formed. During this process, several churches, especially in southern Scandinavia, were abandoned, churches that had no role in the new parochial system.[39]

1991), pp. 113–42; Stefan Brink, 'Tidig kyrklig organisation i Norden – aktörerna i socken-bildningen', in *Kristnandet i Sverige*, ed. by Nilsson, pp. 269–90; Stefan Brink, 'The Formation of the Scandinavian Parish, with Some Remarks Regarding the English Impact on the Process', in *The Community, the Family and the Saint: Patterns of Power in Early Medieval Europe*, ed. by Joyce Hill and Mary Swan, International Medieval Research, 4 (Turnhout: Brepols, 1998), pp. 19–44.

[37] See Jes Wienberg, *Den gotiske labyrint: Middelalderen og kirkerne i Danmark*, Lund Studies in Medieval Archaeology, 11 (Stockholm: Almqvist & Wiksell, 1993), and Anglert, *Kyrkor och herravälde*.

[38] For *Bjäresjö*, see Sten Skansjö, Mats Riddersporre, and Anders Reisnert, 'Huvudgårdarna i källmaterialet', in *By, huvudgård och kyrka: Studier i Ystadsområdets medeltid*, ed. by Hans Andersson and Mats Anglert, Lund Studies in Medieval Archaeology, 5 (Stockholm: Almqvist & Wiksell, 1989), pp. 97–102. For *Lisbjerg*, see Jens Jeppesen and Hans Jørgen Madsen, 'Stormandsgård og kirke i Lisbjerg', *Kuml*, 1988–89 (1990), 289–310; Jens Jeppesen and Hans Jørgen Madsen, 'Storgård og kirke i Lisbjerg', in *Høvdingesamfund og kongemagt*, ed. by Mortensen and Rasmussen, pp. 269–75; Jens Jeppesen and Hans Jørgen Madsen, 'Trækirke og stormandshal i Lisbjerg', *Kuml*, 1995–96, 149–71. For other interesting examples and discussion, see Ebbe Nyborg, 'Enkeltmænd og fællesskaber i organiseringen af det romanske sognekirkebyggeri', in *Strejflys over Danmarks bygningskultur: Festskrift til Harald Langberg*, ed. by Robert Egevang (Copenhagen: Nationalmuseet, 1979), pp. 37–64; Hans Stiesdal, 'Gård og kirke: Sønder Jernløse-fundet belyst ved andre sjællandske eksempler', *Aarbøger for nordisk Oldkyndighed og Historie*, 1980, 166–70; Lilli M. Ingvaldsen, 'Storgård og kirkested', *Arkeo*, 1977, no. 1, 26–31; *Tamdrup: kirke og gård*, ed. by Ole Schiørring (Horsens: Skippershoved, 1991); Brink, 'Tidig kyrklig organisation i Norden'; Dagfinn Skre, 'Kirken før sognet: Den tidligste kirkeordningen i Norge', in *Møtet mellom hedendom og kristendom i Norge*, ed. by Lidén, pp. 170–233; Dagfinn Skre, *Herredømmet: Bosetning og besittelse på Romerike 200–1350 e. Kr.*, Acta Humaniora, 32 (Oslo: Universitetsforlaget, 1998); Dagfinn Skre, 'Misjonsvirksomhet i praksis – organisasjon og mål', in *Kultursamanhengar i Midt-Norden*, ed. by Supphellen, pp. 55–68.

[39] See Brink, 'Tidig kyrklig organisation i Norden'.

174 STEFAN BRINK

In the province of Trøndelag in Norway, Jan Brendalsmo is undertaking analyses of the early churches.[40] He has been able to show that these early churches were erected by kings on their royal estates or by chieftains on their farms. Several of the farms with churches had obviously been confiscated by the Crown from local chieftains. The conclusion is obvious — the early churches, at least in Trøndelag, were built by kings or chieftains. Again, this testifies to the new view of the way in which Christianity came to Scandinavia, trickling down from the uppermost stratum of society to the lower levels.

As noted above, Dagfinn Skre has made many new and interesting observations and has put forward several new ideas regarding the early Church in Norway.[41] His interpretations are very much in line with the new views mentioned earlier, namely that the early Church in Scandinavia addressed itself to society's upper classes. He argues for a model, previously suggested by several scholars,[42] in which the early Norwegian Church was very much a copy of the Anglo-Saxon minster *parochia*, with its bishop and colleges of priests working in the field. Skre reconstructs an early, very loose 'organization' in Norway during the tenth and eleventh centuries, with no fixed sees. In the first phase, the churchmen were under the direct protection of the king in the provinces, actually travelling with the king's entourage as his counsellors. During the eleventh century, when the Church became more established, the bishop had a retinue of his own for his protection. In the province of Romerike in southern Norway, Skre has demonstrated the possible existence of an early 'grand *parochia*'. During the Middle Ages, Romerike had thirty-seven parishes. However, four of the churches differed from the others and are obviously what the early provincial laws in Norway call *hovudkirker* 'main churches'. Three of these may be interpreted as the 'main churches' of the three medieval districts (*þriðjungar*) known from Romerike. The fourth 'main church', at Eid, is probably to be linked with the *thing* assembly, *Eiðsifaþing*, for the whole province. There is also strong evidence for the assumption that this church at Eid was built by the king on his land. Dagfinn Skre believes that this structure, with three or four main churches, represents an early phase in the organization of the Church and its work in the Christianization of the Norwegians. In the same way as at an English minster, several priests were stationed at the main church, serving the surrounding settlements in religious matters. At the end of the eleventh century and particularly in the twelfth century, small churches were built on many farms and were served by priests, and therefore the older organization became more and more unnecessary. In a later stage, many of these new churches were elevated to the status of parish churches, while others were abandoned.

---

[40] Jan Brendalsmo, 'Kristning og politisk makt. Høvdingemakt og kirkebygging i middelalderen: Hvordan gjøre seg synlig i det politiske landskapet', in *Kultursamanhengar i Midt-Norden*, ed. by Supphellen, pp. 69–99.

[41] Skre, 'Kirken før sognet'; Skre, *Herredømmet*; Skre, 'Misjonsvirksomhet i praksis'.

[42] See Brink, 'The Formation of the Scandinavian Parish', pp. 26–28, for references.

The New Stand der Forschung

To sum up, recent archaeological excavations have detected a change from pagan to Christian burial customs in the tenth century in the Scandinavian countries of Denmark, Norway, and Sweden.[43] This change, however, was obviously not universal. In certain regions, the change to Christian burial practice obviously took place much later than in other areas. For example, in the northern part of the province of Uppland in central Sweden, the change can be dated to the latter part of the twelfth century.[44] There were obviously also regional differences regarding burial practices, from typical 'continental' burials with shrouded corpses without any grave-goods, as at Sebbersund in Denmark, to more pagan customs with clothing, grave-goods, and food, as on Bornholm and Gotland. The building of churches and the formation of parishes also show regional differences. In the southern parts of Scandinavia, there were early private churches, whereas the northern parts had a different church pattern, with probably small churches on farms (as at Björned), early churches on royal farms, and a major period of church building during the process of parish formation. In the southern and central agrarian regions in Scandinavia, parishes were formed around existing churches; in the northern and peripheral parts, many churches were built at the same time as parishes were being formed. These regional differences regarding the Christianization of Scandinavia and the organization of the early Church should probably partly be seen in the light of economic and social differences in Viking and medieval Scandinavian society, a theme worthy of another essay of its own.

---

[43] For some general views of the problem of the change in burial customs, see Anne-Sofie Gräslund, 'Den tidiga missionen i arkeologisk belysning – problem och synpunkter', *Tor*, 20 (1985), 291–313.

[44] Anders Broberg, 'Religionsskifte och sockenbildning i Norduppland', in *Kyrka och socken i medeltidens Sverige*, ed. by Ferm, pp. 49–79 (p. 62).

From Birsay to Brattahlíð: Recent Perspectives on Norse Christianity in Orkney, Shetland, and the North Atlantic Region[*]

CHRISTOPHER D. MORRIS

Introduction: Traditions of the Norse Adoption of Christianity in the North Atlantic

Within the history of the Norse expansion and settlement in the North Atlantic region, Birsay, at the eastern end, and Brattahlíð, at the western end, are places of fundamental importance. The importance of these places is underlined by various episodes recorded in *Orkneyinga saga*, *Erik the Red's Saga* (*Eiríks saga rauða*), and the *Saga of the Greenlanders* (*Grænlendinga saga*). Birsay was clearly a place of 'permanent residence' for the Norse earls of Orkney-Shetland-Caithness,[1] and Brattahlíð was the home of Erik the Red, the founder and leader of the Norse community in the so-called 'Eastern Settlement' of Greenland.[2]

Not the least important by any means are the accounts in the sagas of the adoption of Christianity in the two areas. In Orkney, Olaf Tryggvason (king of Norway) appears to have had a key role *c.* 995 in persuading Earl Sigurðr (under pain of death)

---

[*] I wish to thank Kevin Brady for his help, not only with the work on the Shetland Chapel-Sites Project, but also particularly with checking both the texts and references for this paper. I should also thank Úlfar Bragason, Director of the Sigurður Nordal Institute in Reykjavik, who invited me to deliver the same paper at a conference on 'The North Atlantic Saga', later in 1999, and readily accepted that the paper had been promised to this publication.

[1] *Orkneyinga Saga: The History of the Earls of Orkney* (hereafter *OS*), trans. by Hermann Pálsson and Paul Edwards (London: Penguin, 1978), ch. 31, p. 71.

[2] 'Eirik the Red's Saga' (hereafter *ESR*), trans. by Gwyn Jones in *The Norse Atlantic Saga*, 2nd edn (Oxford: Oxford University Press, 1986), chs 2 and 3, pp. 209 and 217.

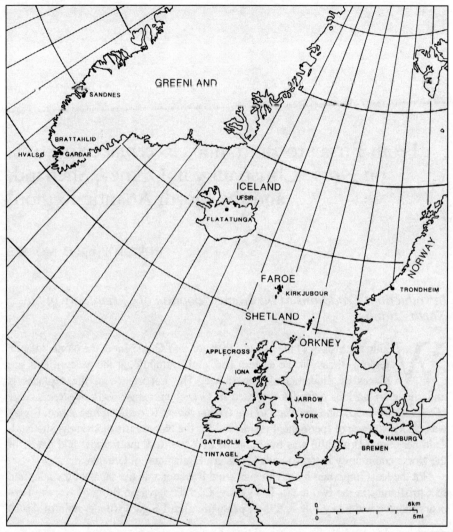

Figure 1. Places mentioned in the text: the wider setting. Map: N. Emery.

to accept Christianity,[3] and in Greenland, Erik's son, Leif, was charged with acting in effect as a Christian emissary (along with a priest or 'shyster' as his father unkindly described him)[4] shortly after that — almost certainly at the time of the traditional

---

[3] *OS*, ch. 12, p. 39; Gwyn Jones discusses the general context for this in *A History of the Vikings*, 2nd edn (Oxford: Oxford University Press, 1984), pp. 133–35.

[4] 'The Greenlanders' Saga' (hereafter *GS*), trans. by Gwyn Jones in *The Norse Atlantic Saga*, ch. 1a, p. 188; *ESR*, ch. 4, p. 217.

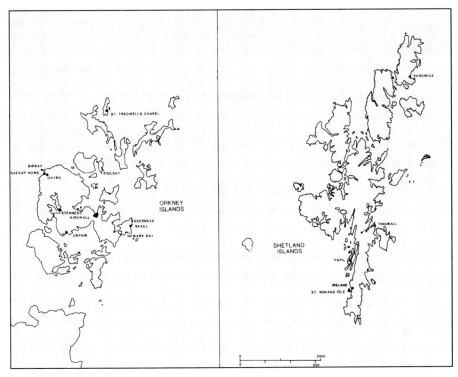

Figure 2. Places mentioned in the text: Orkney and Shetland. Map: N. Emery.

adoption of Christianity by the Althing of Iceland in *c.* 1000.[5] Priests were also left in Orkney by Olaf who were to 'instruct the people and to teach them holy lore'.[6] Within fifty years, Christ Church, Birsay was built by Earl Thorfinn as 'a fine minster, the seat of the first bishop of Orkney',[7] and Adam of Bremen averred that 'it

---

[5] 'The Book of the Icelanders' (*Íslendingabók*; hereafter *Íbk*), in Gwyn Jones, *The Norse Atlantic Saga*, ch. 7, pp. 148–51; Dag Strömbäck, *The Conversion of Iceland: A Survey* (London: Viking Society for Northern Research, 1975); 'Olaf Tryggvason's Saga', in Snorri Sturluson, *Heimskringla: The Olaf Sagas*, trans. by Samuel Laing and Jacqueline Simpson, rev. edn, 2 vols (London: Everyman, J. M. Dent, 1964), I, 29–84; Jones, *A History of the Vikings*, pp. 132–35.

[6] See 'Flatey-book Version of Olaf's Saga.c.187', trans. by Alan Orr Anderson in *Early Sources of Scottish History A.D. 500–1286*, 2 vols (Edinburgh: Oliver & Boyd, 1922; repr. Stamford: Paul Watkins, 1990), I, 509–10 (p. 509); see also Christopher E. Lowe, 'Early Ecclesiastical Sites in the Northern Isles and Isle of Man: An Archaeological Field Survey' (unpublished doctoral thesis, University of Durham, 1988), pp. 26–27; Barbara E. Crawford, *Scandinavian Scotland*, Scotland in the Early Middle Ages, 2 (Leicester: Leicester University Press, 1987), p. 70.

[7] *OS*, chs 31 and 32, p. 71; see also Alexander B. Taylor, *The Orkneyinga Saga: A New Translation with Introduction and Notes* (Edinburgh: Oliver & Boyd, 1938), pp. 188–89, and 368, n. 3.

was Thorfinn's permanent achievement that Orkney became fully accepted in the Christian world of European Christendom'.[8] Similarly, albeit over a longer period, Greenland, too, developed a Christian infrastructure with bishop and cathedral. It is by no means improbable that this was initially based at Brattahlíð, even though later the bishop's seat was established at a new site, with monumental structures, at Garðar[9] — just as, in Orkney, the bishopric was moved to Kirkwall and a major Romanesque cathedral built there in the twelfth century.[10]

Whilst, in political terms, the Earldom of Orkney and the Eastern Settlement of Greenland were quite distinct and unconnected, it is manifestly the case that in religious terms they both became part of a wider European Christian community across the North Atlantic region, in which the emphasis would have been upon uniformity of ideology and practice, and within which architectural and artistic, as well as spiritual, influences went from east to west. Hvalsey Church in Greenland, in which marriage banns were read in September 1408,[11] could as easily be seen as Norwegian or Shetlandic in building style, for instance.[12]

Greenland may have been at 'the world's end' and often an unpopular ecclesiastical posting and elevation to the episcopate for a cleric,[13] but it was most definitely a

---

[8] *OS*, chs 31 and 32, p. 71; Adam of Bremen, *History of the Archbishops of Hamburg-Bremen*, trans. by Francis Joseph Tschan, Records of Civilisation Sources and Studies, 53 (New York: Columbia University Press, 1959), Book 3, 62, pp. 179–81. See also Barbara E. Crawford, 'Birsay and the Early Earls and Bishops of Orkney', *Orkney Heritage*, 2 (1983), 97–118 (pp. 101–05).

[9] Finn Gad, *The History of Greenland*, 3 vols (Montreal: McGill-Queen's University Press, 1971–83), I, 57–63, 111–14, 128–30; Poul Nørlund and Aage Roussell, 'Norse Ruins at Garðar, the Episcopal Seat of Mediaeval Greenland', *Meddelelser om Grønland*, 76 (1930), 1–170.

[10] *OS*, chs 52, 56, and 57, pp. 88–89 and 94–99; *St Magnus Cathedral and Orkney's Twelfth Century Renaissance*, ed. by Barbara E. Crawford (Aberdeen: Aberdeen University Press, 1988), provides a comprehensive study of the historical context in Gordon Donaldson's introductory essay on 'The Contemporary Scene', pp. 1–10, and in the articles by C. A. Ralegh Radford, 'St Magnus Cathedral, Kirkwall, and the Development of the Cathedral in North-West Europe', pp. 14–24; D. E. R. Watt, 'The Church in Scotland in 1137', pp. 25–35; Peter Sawyer, 'Dioceses and Parishes in Twelfth-Century Scandinavia', pp. 36–45; Knut Helle, 'The Organisation of the Twelfth-Century Church in Norway', pp. 46–55; and Per Sveaas Andersen, 'The Orkney Church of the Twelfth and Thirteenth Centuries: A Stepdaughter of the Norwegian Church?', pp. 56–68.

[11] Gad, *History of Greenland*, I, 148–49.

[12] Aage Roussell, 'Farms and Churches in the Mediaeval Norse Settlements of Greenland', *Meddelelser om Grønland*, 89 (1941), 120–25; Gad, *History of Greenland*, I, 133–35; Joel Berglund, *Hvalsø: The Church and the Magnate's Farm* (Reykjavik: Reykjavik Culture House, 1982), pp. 21–23.

[13] Pope Alexander VI (1492) cited in Jones, *The Norse Atlantic Saga*, p. 87; and in F. Donald Logan, *The Vikings in History* (London: Hutchinson, 1983), p. 79; see also Gad, *History of Greenland*, I, 120–22, 135–36, 148, 157, 179–81.

part of the mainstream medieval Christian European community which embraced the North Atlantic islands from Shetland in the east to Greenland in the west.

The Vikings and the Church

It is arguable that this was simply a re-establishment of an older Christian order in part, at least, of the North Atlantic region. Various sources indicate the presence of what have usually been taken to be monks in Iceland, Faroe, Shetland, and Orkney in the immediate pre-Viking period.[14] Monks such as Cormac (who was associated with Columba of Iona) sought 'a desert place in the ocean' in the sixth century, and *papa-* place-names in these areas have been seen as an extension of the movement of hermits seeking a 'desert place apart'.[15] Aidan MacDonald originally interpreted the British examples of *papa-* place-names in such eremitic terms, emphasizing their location on 'small islands and extreme marginal areas',[16] and he drew a parallel with

---

[14] Book VII, chapters 14 and 15 in Dicuil, *Liber de mensura orbis terrae*, ed. by J. Joseph Tierney, Scriptores Latini Hiberniae, 6 (Dublin: Dublin Institute of Advanced Studies, 1967), pp. 75–77; Jones, *The Norse Atlantic Saga*, pp. 33–37; *Íbk*, ch. 1, pp. 143–44; 'The Book of Settlements' (*Landnámabók*; hereafter *Lbk*) in Jones, *The Norse Atlantic Saga*, pp. 156–85 (ch. 1, p. 156); Raymond G. Lamb, 'Papil, Picts and Papar', in *Northern Isles Connections: Essays from Orkney and Shetland Presented to Per Sveaas Andersen*, ed. by Barbara E. Crawford (Kirkwall: The Orkney Press, 1995), pp. 9–27 (pp. 12–14).

[15] Adomnan, *Adomnan's Life of Columba*, ed. and trans. by Alan Orr Anderson and Marjorie O. Anderson (London: Nelson, 1962), Bk II, 42, pp. 440–47; 'Rule of S. Columba', in *Councils and Ecclesiastical Documents Relating to Great Britain and Ireland*, trans. by Arthur West Haddan and William Stubbs (Oxford: Clarendon Press, 1873), II, 119–21 (p. 119); *Vita Sanctorum Hiberniae*, ed. by Charles Plummer (Oxford: Clarendon Press, 1910), p. 61; Dicuil, *Liber de mensura orbis terrae*, p. 115; Aidan D. S. MacDonald, 'Two Major Early Monasteries of Scottish Dalriata: Lismore and Eigg', *Scottish Archaeological Forum*, 5 (1973), 58–60; C. A. Ralegh Radford, 'Birsay and the Spread of Christianity to the North', *Orkney Heritage*, 2 (1983), 13–35 (p. 14); W. P. L. Thomson, *History of Orkney* (Edinburgh: The Mercat Press, 1987), pp. 8–9; Lowe, 'Early Ecclesiastical Sites in the Northern Isles and Isle of Man: An Archaeological Field Survey', pp. 13, 347–51 (Appendix 3). This tradition may itself go back to a pre-Christian period, see Andrew Robert Burn, 'Holy Men on Islands in Pre-Christian Britain', *Glasgow Archaeological Journal*, 1 (1969), 2–6.

[16] Aidan D. S. MacDonald, 'Old Norse "papar" Names in N. and W. Scotland: A Summary', in *Studies in Celtic Survival*, ed. by Lloyd R. Laing, British Archaeological Reports, British Series, 37 (Oxford: BAR, 1977), pp. 107–11 (p. 109) (also printed in *Northern Studies*, 9 (1977), pp. 25–30 (pp. 25–26)); Crawford, *Scandinavian Scotland*, p. 165; Thomson, *History of Orkney*, p. 40; but see Anton Wilhelm Brøgger, *Ancient Emigrants: A History of the Norse Settlements of Scotland* (Oxford: Clarendon Press, 1929), pp. 60–61.

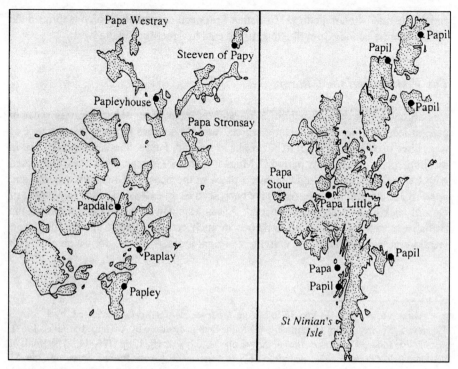

Figure 3. Location of *papa-* names in Orkney and Shetland. Map: R. G. Lamb.

both the *papar* mentioned in Dicuil and the *Book of Settlements* and similar place-name evidence from Iceland (for example, Papey).[17]

However, it is perhaps worth also making the point here that a later source, the *Historia Norwegiae* (arguably written in Orkney *c.* 1200), speaks of the presence of both *peti* ('Picts') and *papae* ('Fathers' or 'Priests') at the time of the Norse incursion there.[18] This indicates that the Scandinavians were acquainted with clerics as some of the inhabitants of the islands at the time of their settlement, and the origin of the *papa-* place-names (i.e. as names given by the Norse) would appear to reinforce this. Although the general view has been that the *papar* should be seen as hermits,[19]

---

[17] Kristján Eldjárn, 'Papey: Fornleifarannsóknir 1967–1981', *Árbók hins íslenzka fornleifa-félags*, ed. by Guðrún Sveinbjarnardóttir (Reykjavik: Hið Íslenzka Fornleifafélag, 1988), pp. 35–188 (pp. 69–78 and 185).

[18] Crawford, *Scandinavian Scotland*, p. 3; Frederick T. Wainwright, 'Picts and Scots', in *The Northern Isles*, ed. by Frederick T. Wainwright (Edinburgh: Nelson, 1962), pp. 91–116 (p. 99).

[19] Emrys George Bowen, *Britain and the Western Seaways* (London: Thames & Hudson, 1972), pp. 87–91; Emrys George Bowen, *Saints, Seaways and Settlements in the Celtic Lands*, 2nd edn (Cardiff: University of Wales Press, 1977), pp. 73–79; Geoffrey Jules Marcus, *The*

both William Thomson and Raymond Lamb have asserted that there are good reasons for now considering them in a missionary, rather than a monastic, context. Described by the author of the *Historia Norwegiae* as having white robes and books, they may well have been the successors of the priests who are implied by the St Boniface legend of 150 churches being built in Pictland, and dedicated to St Peter in the eighth century, rather than being hermits.[20] Certainly, the *Historia* states that 'all clerics are called *Papae* in the Norse tongue'.[21] In this context, an unusual Pictish sculpture from Papil, Burra, Shetland, is perhaps of some interest, as it appears to depict clerics with hoods, long robes, and crosiers — presumably the *papae* themselves — from a site with a name meaning 'buildings [or farm] of the Papar'.[22] A second, upright slab from Papil also depicts similar figures, and this, in turn, appears to have been copied for the design of a stone from Bressay.[23]

While not wishing as yet to suggest that the *papar* of *The Book of Settlements* and Dicuil's *De mensura orbis terrae* were not necessarily monks, it is worth pointing out that we need no longer go along with Aidan MacDonald's interpretation of the place-names named after the *papar* as being on 'small islands and extreme marginal areas', which would fit an eremitical model. Both Thomson and Lamb have challenged this for the Orcadian and Shetlandic evidence. In considering the significant cluster of *papa-* place-names in Orkney and Shetland, and their location, they do not conform to the pattern of alleged remoteness, but would seem to be as much in fertile locations on major islands, as on small ones.[24] As Christopher Lowe and others have shown, the Orcadian evidence is more credibly explained in terms of missionary activity and might be interpreted as implying the survival of more than just the occasional religious centre into the Norse period.[25] Indeed, Lamb has argued recently for them as indicating the former presence of estates of the Pictish Church in Orkney, which he has asserted was in the mainstream of Roman Christian traditions in the eighth century.[26]

Conquest of the North Atlantic (Woodbridge: Boydell Press, 1980), pp. 16–32; Lowe, 'Early Ecclesiastical Sites in the Northern Isles and Isle of Man', pp. 347–51 (Appendix 3).

[20] Thomson, *History of Orkney*, pp. 9–10.

[21] Wainwright, 'Picts and Scots', p. 99, n. 3.

[22] Lamb, 'Papil, Picts and Papar', pp. 11–12 and 15.

[23] Joanna Close-Brooks and Robert B. K. Stevenson, *Dark Age Sculpture* (Edinburgh: National Museum of Antiquities/HMSO, 1982), pp. 34–35; Lamb, 'Papil, Picts and Papar', pp. 15–17.

[24] Thomson, *History of Orkney*, p. 40; Lamb, 'Papil, Picts and Papar', pp. 15–17.

[25] Lowe, 'Early Ecclesiastical Sites in the Northern Isles and Isle of Man', pp. 347–51 (Appendix 3).

[26] Raymond G. Lamb, 'Carolingian Orkney and its Transformation', in *The Viking Age in Caithness, Orkney and the North Atlantic*, ed. by Colleen E. Batey, Judith Jesch, and Christopher D. Morris (Edinburgh: Edinburgh University Press, 1993), pp. 260–71.

In this context, the further tradition in an account of the life of an Irish saint, St Findan, apparently written in the late ninth century, is especially interesting. This Irish saint, originating in Leinster, was carried off from Ireland by Norsemen and was taken to the Orkney Islands, by then clearly under Norse, not Pictish, control. Here, he managed to escape to a bishop's seat or *civitas* on a neighbouring island.[27] Thomson has speculated that the incident might be located in and around Papa Westray, with a bishop's seat on that island. The tradition does seem here to indicate a church organization, and the presence of a bishop, apparently coexisting with the Vikings. As William Thomson has said:

> The presence of a bishop [. . .] a generation or more after the first arrival of the Norse hardly squares with the traditional image of bloodthirsty raiders who obliterated all traces of Christianity. It suggests conquest and settlement by Norwegians in circum-stances which permitted the survival of Pictish institutions.[28]

The fieldwork of both Lamb and Lowe has further emphasized the relationship of chapel-sites to pre-existing Iron Age settlement sites of some significance (especially broch-sites) in both Orkney and Shetland. In Orkney, Lowe claims that as many as perhaps 25% of the chapel-sites are 'spatially coincident with sites for which an Iron Age label could be given'.[29] Although this was a hypothesis based upon survey work, recent excavation work by him at St Boniface Chapel, Papa Westray, has now confirmed the likelihood of this hypothesis as having some reality.[30] Lamb has fur-ther suggested that the Peterkirk dedications (together with one to Boniface) have a significant location in relation to Iron Age broch sites, abandoned by the Pictish period and conceivably thus available for reuse in a religious context.[31] On this basis, then, as Lamb suggests, the *papar* represent an apparatus of power (related to the ruler) and 'a power to be reckoned with' by the incoming Scandinavians, and there is certainly a case for survival into the Viking period.[32]

---

[27] 'St Findan and the Pictish-Norse Transition' (comprising William P. L. Thomson, 'Introductory Note', and Christine J. Omand, 'The Life of Findan Translated from the Latin'), in *The People of Orkney*, ed. by R. J. (Sam) Berry and Howie Firth (Kirkwall: The Orkney Press, 1986), pp. 279–87.

[28] Thomson, 'Introductory Note', p. 280.

[29] Christopher E. Lowe, 'The Early Historic Church Sites of the Northern Isles and Isle of Man: Problems of Identification, Chronology and Interpretation' (paper given at Shetland Settlement Conference, Lerwick, 1998, publication forthcoming).

[30] Christopher E. Lowe, 'Preliminary Results of the Excavation Assessment at Munker-hoose Cliff-Section and Farm Mound, St Boniface Church, Papa Westray, Orkney', *Northern Studies*, 30 (1993), 19–33; Christopher E. Lowe, *St Boniface Church, Orkney: Coastal Erosion and Archaeological Assessment* (Stroud: Sutton Publishing/Historic Scotland, 1998).

[31] Lamb, 'Carolingian Orkney', pp. 262–64; Lamb, 'Papil, Picts and Papar', pp. 18–20; Thomson, *History of Orkney*, p. 10.

[32] Lamb, 'Carolingian Orkney', pp. 266–68; Lamb, 'Papil, Picts and Papar', pp. 22–26; Thomson, *History of Orkney*, pp. 39–40; Crawford, 'Scandinavian Scotland', pp. 165–67.

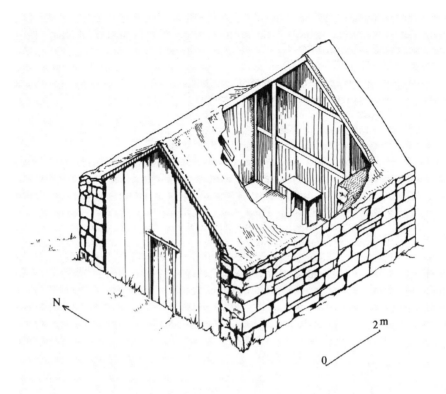

Figure 4. The Brough of Deerness, Orkney: timber phase chapel reconstruction.
Drawing: N. Emery.

Pagan Viking Graves and their Implications

Another group of evidence, the presence of ninth- and tenth-century pagan Viking graves, has been seen as another aspect of the cultural dominance of the native culture by the incoming Vikings.[33] However, such graves are not found in

---

[33] Brøgger, 'Ancient Emigrants', pp. 95–134; Anton Wilhelm Brøgger, *Den norske boset-ningen på Shetland-Orknøyene: Studier og resultater*, II. Historisk-filosofisk Klasse (Oslo: Jacob Dybwad, 1930), pp. 157–247; Sigurd Grieg, *Viking Antiquities in Scotland*, vol. II of *Viking Antiquities in Great Britain and Ireland*, ed. by Haakon Shetelig (Oslo: Aschehoug, 1940), pp. 11–105; Haakon Shetelig, 'The Viking Graves in Great Britain and Ireland', *Acta Archaeologica*, 16 (1945), 1–55 (reprinted in Alexander O. Curle, Magnus Olsen, and Haakon Shetelig, *Civilisation of the Viking Settlers in Relation to their Old and New Countries*, vol. VI of *Viking Antiquities in Great Britain and Ireland*, ed. by Haakon Shetelig (Oslo: Aschehoug, 1954), pp. 65–111); Frederick T. Wainwright, 'The Scandinavian Settlement', in *The*

overwhelming numbers (if occasionally, as with the recent find from Scar, Sanday, Orkney, of a spectacular nature).[34] Increasingly, it would seem that most graves (and especially those most recently excavated, as at Scar and Westness, Rousay)[35] relate to earlier in this period, rather than later. Indeed, Olwyn Owen, in discussing Scar and other graves, has recently questioned whether we can really see any significant number of pagan graves at all in the tenth century.[36] This returns to the position put forward by Frederick T. Wainwright, when he concluded that the evidence for a pagan period in the Northern Isles was minimal and put forward the argument that this was evidence that Christianity was adopted by 900.[37]

What I believe should now be questioned is whether this material really can sustain such an interpretation. Indeed, do we have to assume that paganism was exclusive in the Norse areas of northern and western Scotland? Is there not now a case to be made for some degree of religious coexistence and toleration? What evidence do we have anywhere for an aggressive and exclusive pagan Norse religion? Is it not rather the case that, in general, by its nature it was the Christian religion at this time which tended towards exclusivity? An interesting archaeological reflection of pagan acceptance of Christian features may well be at Kiloran Bay, Colonsay (in the Inner Hebrides), where in addition to a form of grave structure which is reminiscent of pre-Norse Pictish burial cairns and enclosures, two of the corner posts had crosses on them, while enclosing a pagan Viking burial.[38] Certainly, I myself wonder if we can now question whether we need to assume that Christianity in the *Norðreyjar* and *Suðreyjar* only became acceptable to the Scandinavians after 1000 (the traditional date in *OS*).

Northern Isles, ed. by Wainwright, pp. 117–62 (pp. 147–50); Kristján Eldjárn, 'Graves and Grave Goods: Survey and Evaluation', in *The Northern and Western Isles in the Viking World: Survival, Continuity and Change*, ed. by Alexander Fenton and Hermann Pálsson (Edinburgh: John Donald, 1984), pp. 2–11; Crawford, *Scandinavian Scotland*, pp. 116–27 and 159–64; Colleen E. Batey, 'Viking and Late Norse Graves of Caithness and Sutherland', in *The Viking Age in Caithness, Orkney and the North Atlantic*, ed. by Batey, Jesch, and Morris, pp. 148–64; Anna Ritchie, *Viking Scotland* (London: Batsford/Historic Scotland, 1993), pp. 37–39 and passim; James Graham-Campbell and Colleen E. Batey, *Vikings in Scotland: An Archaeological Survey* (Edinburgh: Edinburgh University Press, 1998), pp. 113–54.

[34] Olwyn Owen and Magnar Dalland, 'Scar, Sanday: A Viking Boat-Burial from Orkney: An Interim Report', in *The Twelfth Viking Congress: Developments Around the Baltic and the North Sea in the Viking Age*, ed. by Björn Ambrosiani and Helen Clarke, Birka Studies, 3 (Stockholm: The Birka Project at Riksantikvarieämbetet and Statens Historiska Museer, 1994), pp. 159–72; Olwyn Owen and Magnar Dalland, *Scar: A Viking Boat Burial on Sanday, Orkney* (Edinburgh: Tuckwell Press, 1999); see also Olwyn Owen, this volume.

[35] Sigrid H. H. Kaland, 'The Settlement of Westness, Rousay', in *The Viking Age in Caithness, Orkney and the North Atlantic*, ed. by Batey, Jesch, and Morris, pp. 308–17.

[36] Olwyn Owen, this volume.

[37] Wainwright, 'The Scandinavian Settlement', pp. 160–61.

[38] Crawford, *Scandinavian Scotland*, pp. 161–63.

Stone Sculpture

Further, Robert Stevenson some time ago asserted that a group of sculptures from Bressay, Papil, and Whiteness in Shetland indicated the continued production of Christian sculpture well into the Viking period. Stevenson noted that these 'Christian stones were being sculptured in the middle of Shetland's Norse pagan period',[39] and at the least this implies tolerance to, and recognition of, the native religious susceptibilities (if not organization) by the incoming Norse. We do well to remember that, unlike Christianity, Norse pagan religion was not necessarily exclusive and, conversely, concepts of syncretism were not unknown in the early medieval period. Indeed, it could be argued that much of the large corpus of northern English Anglo-Scandinavian sculpture of the ninth and tenth centuries is precisely focused upon a rapprochement between the native Christian and incoming Scandinavian religions and outlook, ethos and symbolism,[40] and there is no reason to suppose it need be very different in northern Britain at the same time. Against this background, perhaps it is not so surprising that Stevenson asserted that there were 'active Christians erecting sculptured monuments in the tenth century, and most probably about the middle and end of the ninth century as well'.[41]

Archaeological Sites

I have elsewhere (and at considerable length) attempted an initial reassessment of the evidence for Norse Christianity in the Northern Isles of Orkney and Shetland.[42] In the process, I hope I have demonstrated that previous associations of a number of well-known chapel-sites with the so-called Celtic Monastery are no longer apposite, and instead I have proposed reinterpretation of them as Norse Christian chapels.[43]

The key site here is the Brough of Deerness in Orkney, traditionally seen as an early Christian monastic site on a promontory, which my excavations showed had two major building phases, which could both be from the period of Scandinavian

[39] Robert B. K. Stevenson, 'Christian Sculpture in Norse Shetland', *Fróðskaparrit*, 28–29 (1981), 283–92 (p. 287).

[40] Richard N. Bailey, *Viking Age Sculpture in Northern England* (London: Collins, 1980), gives the best overview of this subject.

[41] Stevenson, 'Christian Sculpture in Norse Shetland', p. 289.

[42] Christopher D. Morris, *Church and Monastery in the Far North: An Archaeological Evaluation*, Jarrow Lecture, 1989 (Jarrow: Rector and Parish of St Paul's, 1990), pp. 17–28.

[43] C. A. Ralegh Radford, 'The Celtic Monastery in Britain', *Archaeologia Cambrensis*, 111 (1962), 1–24; Christopher D. Morris, 'From Birsay to Tintagel: A Personal View', in *Scotland in Dark Age Britain*, ed. by Barbara E. Crawford, St John's House Papers, 6 (Aberdeen: Scottish Cultural Press, 1996), pp. 59–65.

control.[44] This then raises questions about other well-known alleged pre-Norse chapel-sites such as the Brough of Birsay and St Ninian's Isle. I have now compared them with examples in the North Atlantic region from Faroe, Iceland, and Greenland and from the period of Norse control there.[45]

It would be straightforward enough to suggest that these relate to a post-1000 chronology, to fit in with our written accounts from the sagas and other sources of the adoption of Christianity across the region. However, just as we have, in my opinion, been too obsessed with the recorded dates of formal recognition of the Scandinavian organization of political control in the North Atlantic islands, so too I consider it to be likely that we have been obsessed with the year 1000 date for the Scandinavian organization of religious control. I have argued elsewhere for an informal period of settlement in the Northern Isles preceding the formal recognition in the written sources.[46] I would now like to propose that it is the same with the religious organization. We can, in my opinion, expect Christian chapels well before 1000, especially in the context of the Norse equivalents of *Eigenkirchen* or private chapels of chieftains, adjacent to their halls. The formal adoption in 1000 need, then, be no more than the official de jure recognition of a de facto situation with existing groups of Christians, rather than the act of a missionary church in a hostile religious environment — and may then be marked by further chapel building (or rebuilding).

New Work on Chapel-Sites in Shetland

This is a hypothesis that can now be explored, and the Viking and Early Settlement Archaeological Research Project (VESARP) under my direction intends in the next

---

[44] Christopher D. Morris, 'The Brough of Deerness, Orkney: A New Survey', *Archaeologia Atlantica*, 2 (1977), 65–79; Christopher D. Morris with Norman Emery, 'The Setting for the Brough of Deerness, Orkney', *Northern Studies*, 23 (1986), 1–30; Christopher D. Morris with Norman Emery, 'The Chapel and Enclosure on the Brough of Deerness, Orkney: Survey and Excavations, 1975–1977', *Proceedings of the Society of Antiquaries of Scotland*, 116 (1986), 301–74, and microfiche 2–4.

[45] Morris, *Church and Monastery*, pp. 28–29; Knud J. Krogh, *Qallunaatsiaaqarfik Grønland / Erik den Rødes Grønland* (Copenhagen: National Museum of Denmark, 1982), pp. 35–47 and 123 (for an earlier edition in English, see Knud J. Krogh, *Viking Greenland* (Copenhagen: National Museum of Denmark, 1967), pp. 19–28 and 94–95); Kristján Eldjárn, 'Carved Panels from Flatatunga, Iceland' *Acta Archaeologica*, 24 (1953), 81–101, Þór Magnússon, *A Showcase of Icelandic National Treasures* (Reykjavik: Iceland Review, 1987), pp. 15–16, 51 (fig. 46) and 77 (fig. 81); Knud J. Krogh, 'Seks kirkjur heima á Sandi', *Mondul*, 2 (1975), 21–54; Arne Thorsteinsson, 'The Testimony of Ancient Architecture', *Faroe Isles Review*, 1 (1976), 11–19; Sverri Dahl, 'Timber Churches of the Faroes', *Faroe Isles Review*, 1 (1976), 24–31.

[46] Christopher D. Morris, 'Viking Orkney: A Survey', in *The Prehistory of Orkney BC 4000–1000 AD*, ed. by Colin Renfrew (Edinburgh: Edinburgh University Press, 1985), pp. 210–42 (pp. 210–13).

phase of research to examine Norse Christianity in the eastern North Atlantic region, initially through a programme of fieldwork, followed by selective excavation. Some of the foundations have already been laid, for instance by Lamb's work on some of the stack-sites of the North of Britain[47] and Lowe's field surveys in Unst and Papa Westray.[48] However, in some areas of Northern Britain, practically nothing has been undertaken on chapel-sites and buildings since the pioneering work of Henry Dryden in the 1860s and 1870s,[49] and that of the other contributors to the overall survey of ecclesiastical sites in the 1890s by MacGibbon and Ross.[50]

So, in Shetland, for instance, there is a good basis for further work in the Island of Unst, where we have started follow-up survey work on twenty-five known sites,[51] but in the adjacent islands of Fetlar and Yell we are having to undertake very basic documentary research to identify potential sites before even venturing out onto the ground. In Fetlar, Kevin Brady identified from various sources nineteen sites, which were investigated in the summer of 1999.[52] As well as identifying these on the ground, we are following up some of the implications of the previous work undertaken by

---

[47] Raymond G. Lamb, 'Coastal Settlements of the North', *Scottish Archaeological Forum*, 5 (1973), 88–93; Raymond G. Lamb, 'The Burri Stacks of Culswick, Shetland, and Other Paired Stack-Settlements', *Proceedings of the Society of Antiquaries of Scotland*, 107 (1975–76), 144–54.

[48] Lowe, 'Early Ecclesiastical Sites in the Northern Isles and Isle of Man'.

[49] Sir Henry E. L. Dryden, *Ruined Churches in Orkney and Shetland* [papers from *The Orcadian*] (Kirkwall: privately produced, hand-paginated copy in The Orkney Library, 1870).

[50] David MacGibbon and Thomas Ross, *The Ecclesiastical Architecture of Scotland from the Earliest Christian Times to the Seventeenth Century*, 3 vols (Edinburgh: David Douglas, 1896–97).

[51] Christopher D. Morris and Kevin J. Brady, *Unst Chapel Survey 1997*, GUARD Report, 515 (Glasgow: Glasgow University Archaeological Research Division, 1998); Kevin J. Brady and Paul G. Johnson, *Unst Chapel Survey 1998. Phase I: Report 1*, GUARD Report, 515.3 (Glasgow: Glasgow University Archaeological Research Division, 1998); Kevin J. Brady and Paul G. Johnson, *Unst Chapel-Sites Survey 1999*, GUARD Report, 515.4 (Glasgow: Glasgow University Archaeological Research Division, 2000); Christopher D. Morris and Kevin J. Brady with Paul G. Johnson, 'The Shetland Chapel-Sites Project: 1997–98', *Church Archaeology*, 2 (1999), 25–33; Christopher D. Morris, 'Norse Settlement in Shetland: The Shetland Chapel-Sites Project', in *Denmark and Scotland: The Cultural and Environmental Resources of Small Nations*, ed. by Gillian Fellows-Jensen, Historisk-filosofiske Meddelelser, 82 (Copenhagen: Royal Danish Academy of Sciences and Letters, 2001), pp. 58–78.

[52] Kevin J. Brady, *Fetlar Chapel Survey: Desk-top Assessment 1998*, GUARD Report, 636 (Glasgow: Glasgow University Archaeological Research Division, 1998); Kevin J. Brady and Christopher D. Morris, *Fetlar Chapel-Sites Survey*, GUARD Report, 636.2 (Glasgow: Glasgow University Archaeological Research Division, 2000). Also, see now Kevin J. Brady, *Yell Chapel-Sites Survey: Desk-top Assessment 1999*, GUARD Report, 733 (Glasgow: Glasgow University Archaeological Research Division, 2000); Kevin J. Brady, *Yell Chapel-Sites Survey 1999–2000* (Glasgow: Glasgow University Archaeological Research Division, 2000).

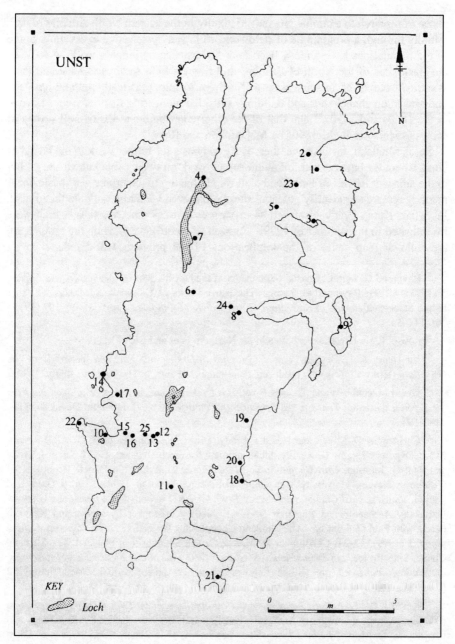

Figure 5. Unst, Shetland: map of chapel-sites. Map: C. Evans.

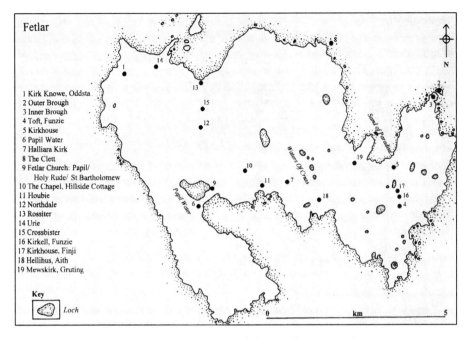

Figure 6. Fetlar, Shetland: map of chapel-sites. Map: D. Swan.

historians such as Ronald Cant, Brian Smith, and William Thomson on issues such as the relationship of these sites to land units known as 'scattalds' in these islands.[53]

Also, it has to be added that in such areas as these islands, there are very strong folk-traditions, which are of considerable assistance here. On Unst, for instance, Lowe was able to follow up the work of Jessie Saxby from the early twentieth century

[53] Ronald G. Cant, 'The Church in Orkney and Shetland and its relations with Norway and Scotland in the Middle Ages', *Northern Scotland*, 1 (1972–73), 1–18; Ronald G. Cant, *The Medieval Churches and Chapels of Shetland* (Lerwick: Shetland Archaeological and Historical Society, 1975); Ronald G. Cant, 'Settlement, Society and Church Organisation in the Northern Isles', in *The Northern and Western Isles in the Viking World*, ed. by Fenton and Pálsson, pp. 169–79; Ronald G. Cant, 'The Medieval Church in Shetland: Organisation and Buildings', in *Shetland's Northern Links: Language and History*, ed. by Doreen J. Waugh (Edinburgh: Scottish Society for Northern Studies, 1996), pp. 159–73; William P. L. Thomson, 'Funzie, Fetlar: A Shetland Runrig Township in the 19th Century', *Scottish Geographical Magazine*, 86 (1970), 170–85; William P. L. Thomson, 'Township, "House" and Tenant-Holding: The Structure of Run-Rig Agriculture in Shetland', in *The Shaping of Shetland: Developments in Shetland Landscape Archaeology*, ed. by Val Turner (Lerwick: Shetland Times, 1998), pp. 107–27; Brian Smith, 'What Is a Scattald? Rural Communities in Shetland, 1400–1900', in *Essays in Shetland History: Heiðursrit to T. M. Y. Manson*, ed. by Barbara E. Crawford (Lerwick: Shetland Times, 1984), pp. 99–124.

identifying traditional sites of old chapels, and Margaret MacKay has shown that there is an interesting relationship between the scattalds in Fetlar and social obligations in relation to burials.[54] Further, Doreen Waugh is investigating the place-name heritage of these areas, following earlier work by John Stewart.[55] Already, in addition to the obvious *kirkja* names, she has identified in the documents a 'Binnas' on Unst — presumably a reference to a 'prayer-house', or *bænhús*, a term which is known elsewhere and which has been identified archaeologically in the North Atlantic (for example, in Leirvík, Faroe).[56] Such evidence can give pointers to the earlier existence of an archaeological site. The known presence of a 'Papil' name on each of the three northerly Shetlandic islands is itself of considerable interest, as a linguistic relic of the ecclesiastical structure which the Scandinavians encountered on their arrival there.[57]

Further, these chapels and associated churchyards would have associated church furniture, fittings, and burial monuments. As Stevenson has emphasized, we do not have to see these as necessarily pre-Viking (i.e. notionally pre-800),[58] and I would now suggest that they no longer have to be alternatively post–Olaf Tryggvason (d. 1000). We may perhaps now begin to see a Viking Age context as a possibility

---

[54] Jessie M. E. Saxby, 'Sacred Sites in a Shetland Isle', *The Antiquary*, 41 (1905), 133–38 (also published in *Saga Book of the Viking Club*, 4 (1904–05), 24–35); Margaret A. MacKay, 'The Sib and the Fremd': Community Life in the Dictionaries', in *The Nuttis Schell: Essays on the Scots Language*, ed. by Caroline Macafee and Iseabail Macleod (Aberdeen: Aberdeen University Press, 1987), pp. 211–18.

[55] John Stewart, 'Shetland Farm Names', in *The Fourth Viking Congress, York, August 1961*, ed. by Alan Small, Aberdeen University Studies, 149 (Edinburgh: Oliver & Boyd, 1965), pp. 247–66; John Stewart, 'The Place-Names of Fetlar', in *The Fifth Viking Congress, Tórshavn, July 1965*, ed. by Bjarni Niclasen (Torshavn: Føroya Landsstýri, Tórshavnar Býráð, Føroya Fróðskaparfelag & Føroya Fornminnissavn, 1968), pp. 174–85; Steffen S. Hansen and Doreen J. Waugh, 'Scandinavian Settlement in Unst, Shetland: Archaeology and Place-Names', in *The Use of Place-Names*, ed. by Simon Taylor, St John's House Papers, 7 (Edinburgh: Scottish Cultural Press, 1998), pp. 120–46; Doreen Waugh. '"Fae da nort tae da suddart": Norse Settlement in Shetland with Special Reference to Unst and Old Scatness', in *Denmark and Scotland*, ed. by Fellows-Jensen, pp. 47–57.

[56] Gillian Fellows-Jensen, 'The Vikings' Relationship with Christianity in the British Isles: The Evidence of Place-Names Containing the Element *kirkja*', in *Proceedings of the Tenth Viking Congress; Larkollen, Norway, 1985*, ed. by James E. Knirk, Universitetets Oldsaksamlings Skrifter, Ny Rekke, 9 (Oslo: Universitets Oldsaksamling, 1987), pp. 295–307 (pp. 299–300); Lindsay J. MacGregor, 'Sources for a Study of Norse Settlement in Shetland and Faroe', in *Essays in Shetland History*, ed. by Crawford, pp. 1–17 (pp. 9–10); Arne Thorsteinsson, 'On the Development of Faroese Settlements', in *Proceedings of the Eighth Viking Congress. Århus 24–31 August 1977*, ed. by Hans Bekker-Nielsen, Peter Foote, and Olaf Olsen, Mediaeval Scandinavia Supplements, 2 (Odense: Odense University Press, 1981), pp. 189–202.

[57] Lamb, 'Papil, Picts and Papar', p. 15.

[58] Stevenson, 'Christian Sculpture in Norse Shetland', p. 287.

Figure 7. Norse grave markers from Lundawick, Unst, Shetland.
Photo: C. D. Morris.

for the whole group of monuments from Papil and Bressay.[59] This is, of course, in addition to the interesting and distinctive group of grave markers to be associated with the Late Norse church in these islands, such as those from Norwick, Framgord, and Lundawick on Unst.[60] Ian Fisher of the Royal Commission on Ancient and Historical Monuments in Scotland (RCAHMS) has kindly agreed to assist VESARP in their work on this aspect of the surveys.

Finally, in 1999 and 2000, VESARP (under Rachel Harry) re-excavated St Ninian's Isle,[61] and I hope perhaps we will have an opportunity in due course to examine any surviving evidence for the earlier church (and other features) below the Late Norse standing building. And if we accept the possibility of an earlier Norse (rather than pre-Norse) chapel at St Ninian's Isle below the existing building,[62] then it is not impossible even for the remains of a remarkable stone shrine to be Viking Age in date — indeed Stevenson suggested it was 'no earlier than mid-ninth century, rather than before 800'.[63]

Conclusion: The Wider Perspective

Of course, this work needs to be put in a broader context, and we intend to extend our survey project to the mainland of Scotland (in Caithness and Sutherland), as well as to the *Suðreyjar* or Hebrides (perhaps a project in Lewis/Harris). But it also needs to be seen in the broader North Atlantic context, and it will be vital to link this with

---

[59] Close-Brooks and Stevenson, *Dark Age Sculpture*, pp. 34–35; Stevenson, 'Christian Sculpture in Norse Shetland', passim.

[60] Morris and Brady, *Unst Chapel Survey 1997*.

[61] Rachel Harry with Paul G. Johnson, *St Ninian's Isle Survey and Excavation 1999*, GUARD Report, 689 (Glasgow: Glasgow University Archaeological Research Division, 2000); Rachel Barrowman with Alan J. Hall, *St Ninian's Isle, Shetland: Excavations in July 2000* (Glasgow: Glasgow University Archaeological Research Division, 2000).

[62] *St Ninian's Isle Treasure*, ed. by A. C. O'Dell, Aberdeen University Studies, 141 (Edinburgh: Oliver & Boyd, 1960), pp. 4–5; Charles Thomas, *The Early Christian Archaeology of North Britain*, The Hunter Marshall Lectures, 1968, University of Glasgow (London: Oxford University Press, 1971), pp. 14–15; Alan Small, 'The Site: Its History and Excavation', in *St Ninian's Isle and its Treasure*, ed. by Alan Small, Charles Thomas, and David M. Wilson, 2 vols, Aberdeen University Studies, 152 (London: Oxford University Press, 1973), I, 1–7 (pp. 5–7); Charles Thomas, 'Sculptured Stones and Crosses from St Ninian's Isle and Papil', in *St Ninian's Isle and its Treasure*, ed. by Small, Thomas, and Wilson, I, pp. 8–44 (pp. 11–13); Charles Thomas, 'The Double Shrine "A" from St Ninian's Isle, Shetland', in *From the Stone Age to the 'Forty-Five: Studies to R. B. K. Stevenson*, ed. by Anne O'Connor and David V. Clarke (Edinburgh: John Donald, 1983), pp. 285–92; Morris, *Church and Monastery in the Far North*, pp. 10–11.

[63] Stevenson, 'Christian Sculpture in Norse Shetland', p. 291.

similar evidence in other areas of the North Atlantic (i.e. Faroe, Iceland, and Greenland) and to exchange information with, if not collaborate with, colleagues in these other islands. This would be a project hopefully both in the spirit of and under the aegis of the North Atlantic Biocultural Organisation (NABO).

Finally, as a postscript, it is worth adding that, quite independently, very similar ideas are being brought forward now in Scandinavia by Stefan Brink, emphasizing the presence of early, small churches on farms in the tenth century, perhaps particularly associated with estates in the southern part of Scandinavia.[64] Clearly both Brink and I, in our separate areas, are bringing forward perhaps heretical ideas in seeing the gradual adoption during the 'pagan' Viking Age of Christianity at the local private landowner level reflected in small chapels at a date significantly earlier than that indicated by the written sources for the adoption of Christianity at the higher political level. But at least I can now take comfort from the fact that if, as an archaeologist, I am uttering a historical heresy, then at least I shall have company when I am metaphorically roasted alive or burnt at the stake.

---

[64] Stefan Brink, this volume.

Early Monasticism in Scandinavia[*]

TORE NYBERG

I

Monasticism in Scandinavia's first Christian centuries, the period from *c.* 830 to 1080, first brings to mind a small number of missionaries with a monastic education. The Corvey monk St Ansgar is the best known among the monastic missionaries. He died as Archbishop of Hamburg-Bremen in 865 after having been sent on several journeys to Denmark and Sweden by Archbishop Ebo of Reims. He has been duly treated in Alf Härdelin's commentary, which accompanies the most recent Swedish translation of Ansgar's *vita*.[1] Then there is a gap during the Viking Age, until we reach some of the Anglo-Saxon missionaries to Norway, Denmark, and Sweden in the eleventh century. Some of these missionaries, who were normally made bishops before they left England, may have been monks or at least educated in an early cathedral community of priests. This is the case for the assistants of the missionary Bishop Sigfrid, who was an Englishman and seems to have ended his days in Växjö, where he also was buried. His three followers, said to have been Cluniac monks, were killed while the bishop was away on a journey, and their reputation as saints, according to Sigfrid's *vita*, depended entirely upon the bishop's identification of their cut-off heads floating on the water and calling loudly upon his attention.[2] Another missionary, St David, who worked in a place called Munktorp north of Lake Mälaren, is called 'abbot' in liturgical sources, without any

---

[*] Printed here with kind permission of Ashgate Publishers. For full references see my book, *Monasticism in North-Western Europe, 800–1200* (London: Ashgate, 2000).

[1] Alf Härdelin, 'Ansgar som munk', in Rimbert, *Boken om Ansgar. Rimbert: Ansgars liv*, trans. by Eva Odelman (Stockholm: Proprius, 1986), pp. 147–61.

[2] Tore Nyberg, 'Hunaman, Vinaman et Sunaman', *Dictionnaire d'histoire et de géographie ecclésiastiques*, 25 (1998), 397–99.

further mention of where he came from or if there was a small community of monks around him. Even if both these pieces of evidence open the possibility of a monastic tradition at work during the first wave of missionary efforts in the eleventh century, there is no conclusive evidence for monastic institutions in Scandinavia prior to *c.* 1060. The idea that monasticism was introduced in Denmark by Cnut the Great, king of England and Denmark 1019–35, cannot be upheld. Cnut brought three English bishops with him to Denmark, probably upon his first return *c.* 1018/20, and he placed them as supervisors of the mission on Fyn, Sjælland and in Skåne.[3] There is, however, no indication that they had a monastic background — such a background would probably have left some traces in the sources. Jutland had three dioceses: Schleswig (Slesvig), Ribe, and Århus, but it is unlikely that there were ever six bishops working in Denmark at any one time in a coordinated way. Adam of Bremen tells us that only the old Bishop Wal administered Christian life in all Jutland in the first years of Svein Estridsson's reign (1047–74/76).[4]

II

Around 1060, after this diocesan structure in the Danish lands had apparently caused a setback in the missionary work inaugurated by the baptism of King Harald a hundred years earlier, Denmark got its definitive system of medieval dioceses. It was Svein Estridsson, Cnut the Great's nephew and king of Denmark, who negotiated the final diocesan organization for Denmark *c.* 1060 and who obtained approval for it from Archbishop Adalbert of Hamburg-Bremen.[5]

Through his church policy, King Svein, who is highly praised in the writings of Adam of Bremen (from the 1070s), provided a real basis for monasticism in Denmark along English and continental European patterns. The new bishops whom the Archbishop of Bremen now ordained for the new or vacant Danish bishoprics certainly did not attain office without the approbation of King Svein. This increased the importance of bishops and made them more stable figures in church life.

During the last decades of the eleventh century, resources were set aside by some of these new bishops in order to secure monastic life in Scandinavia. The earliest monasteries in Denmark came into being as fruits of this diocesan reorganization, and in many foundations episcopal initiative was no doubt involved. One of these

---

[3] Adam von Bremen, *Magistri Adami Bremensis Gesta Hammaburgensis ecclesiae pontificium*, ed. by Bernhard Schmeidler, MGH SS rer. Ger., 2, 3rd edn (Hanover: Hahn, 1917), Book II, chapter 55. An English version is also available: Adam of Bremen, *History of the Archbishops of Hamburg-Bremen*, trans. by Francis Joseph Tschan, Records of Civilisation Sources and Studies, 53 (New York: Columbia University Press, 1959).

[4] Adam of Bremen, Book IV, ch. 2.

[5] Adam of Bremen, Book III, ch. 25.

could have been the small St Michael's Abbey outside Schleswig with its remarkable circular church, which is, however, not an example of proper monastic architecture. The theory that this abbey dates from *c.* 1010 is no longer supported by scholars who have worked on the local history of Schleswig, such as Christian Radtke.[6]

The Roskilde Chronicle from *c.* 1137 says that Bishop Svein the Norwegian (d. 1088), founded religious communities in Roskilde, Ringsted, and Slagelse. However, scholars have not normally trusted the Chronicle on this point, except as regards the nuns of Roskilde, where the Church of Our Lady points to a construction period prior to *c.* 1100. Of the two other religious communities allegedly founded by Bishop Svein, doubts concerning Ringsted have arisen because of the much later royal donation to the Abbey of Our Lady in Ringsted in 1135, which scholars have normally looked upon as the very beginning of its history. And since no later sources mention a monastery in Slagelse, the traces of an early wooden church under the floor of its St Michael's Church are considered as the remains of an early missionary centre.

One might have expected some of the great donations of King Svein's son and second successor, King Knut II (1080–86), to have resulted in a proper monastic foundation, but this was not to be the outcome of his royal generosity. King Knut II's great donation to the cathedral in Lund in 1085[7] laid the foundation for a community of canons there, who used the Rule of St Augustine as their guide, but who by *c.* 1110 finally decided to drop St Augustine and remain secular. According to the first *Passio* of King Knut II, composed *c.* 1095,[8] not only the church in Lund but also those in both Dalby and Roskilde had received gifts and donations from the Martyr King. The diocese of Dalby, which probably covered north-eastern Skåne, was one of those created *c.* 1060, but it had been absorbed by Lund prior to 1070. With its crypt from *c.* 1060, from the same decades as that of the oldest Cathedral of Our Lady in Århus, Dalby became the site of a community of Austin regular canons which was firmly established by *c.* 1100 at the latest. Knut II gave gifts to Roskilde during the time Bishop Svein the Norwegian was active there. As a result of all three great gifts said to have been made to the church by King Knut II, communities of secular or regular canons were created but none for monks. As for the daily life of clerics or canons in western Denmark we do not know the degree of King Knut II's intervention, or if there was any at all. The centre for Austin canonical life in Jutland became the Austin cathedral chapter of Viberg (Viborg) established *c.* 1100.

---

[6] Christian Radtke, 'Die Entwicklung der Stadt Schleswig: Funktionen, Strukturen und die Anfänge der Gemeindebildung', in *Die Stadt im westlichen Ostseeraum*, ed. by Erich Hoffmann and Frank Lubowitz, Kieler Werkstücke A:14, 1 (Frankfurt: Peter Lang, 1995), pp. 47–91.

[7] *Diplomatarium Danicum*, ed. by C. A. Christensen and others, Series 1, 7 vols (Copenhagen: Det Danske Sprog- og Litteraturselskab, 1957–90), II (1963), no. 21.

[8] *Vitae Sanctorum Danorum*, ed. by M. Cl. Gertz (Copenhagen: Gad, 1908–12), pp. 62–71.

III

Proper Benedictine monastic traditions must have been brought to Scandinavia in two main streams: by Anglo-Saxon monks — some presumably emigrating from England after 1066 — and by monks belonging to the monastic reform movement in Saxony and Lotharingia.

The Anglo-Saxon impulses left early traces which predate 1100 on islands off the coast of Norway. Solid evidence is provided by the excavations on the island of Nidarholm (present-day Munkholm) opposite Trondheim and on the island of Selja midway between Trondheim and Bergen, with its monastic church dedicated to St Alban and its possible prehistory of Irish hermits. The *Passio* of King Knut II composed *c.* 1095 and Ælnoth's *Gesta Swenomagni Regis et filiorum eius* from *c.* 1122 testify to the arrival of monks from Evesham on the Danish island of Fyn *c.* 1095 during the reign of King Erik I Ejegod (1095–1103).[9] These monks made it their task to uphold the cult of King Knut II as a holy martyr and the royal patron saint of Denmark — he was elevated in Odense with papal approval on 19 April 1100. The main church in Odense had relics of St Alban which the Martyr King probably had brought there from England before he was elected king. At Veng Abbey in the Gudenå river basin, architecture points to Anglo-Saxon impulses, whilst slightly more recent written sources suggest a royal initiative; if we can trust these sources, the most reasonable guess would be that Veng was founded by King Erik I Ejegod or by King Niels (1103–34) at the beginning of his reign.

Then there is the Benedictine tradition in the diocese of Lund. All Saints' Abbey outside Lund, which took on a leading position among the Danish Benedictines, may go back to German impulses under Bishop Rikwal (1072/74–89), who came from Paderborn.[10] Episcopal initiative is also recorded for St Peter's nunnery in Lund. Also in western Denmark, monastic impulses from the Saxon empire may have been at work. If this is so, the foundation of the double monastery of Seem outside Ribe might be attributed to Bishop Gerald of Ribe (*c.* 1095–*c.* 1125), a former chaplain of King Knut II. Unfortunately, no foundation date is recorded for Seem.

Finally, the beginnings of monasticism in Sweden also belong to the years around 1100. Nils Ahnlund has proved beyond doubt that King Inge of Sweden and his wife, Helena, founded a monastery in Vreta, Östergötland, *c.* 1100,[11] so they must have had clerics or missionaries at court who induced them to live up to international standards of royal behaviour towards the Church. What type of religious life was lived in Vreta, whether it was for men or women, is unknown, since evidence is lacking until its transformation into a Cistercian nunnery in 1161.

---

[9] *Vitae Sanctorum Danorum*, ed. by Gertz, pp. 77–136.

[10] Erik Cinthio, 'Benediktiner, augustiner och korherrar', in *Skånska kloster*, ed. by Erik Cinthio, Skånes Hembygdsförbund, Årsbok 1987/88 (Kristianstad : Skånes hembygdsförbund, 1989), pp. 19–45 (pp. 31–36).

[11] Nils Ahnlund, 'Vreta klosters äldsta donatorer', *Historisk Tidskrift*, 65 (1979), 301–51.

Recently, Henrik Janson has interpreted Adam of Bremen's account of the adversaries of the Bremen mission in Uppsala in the 1070s as Gregorian reformists, the enemies in the Investiture Contest of the Imperial German mission.[12] Janson sees traces of Lotharingian monastic reform as having been transmitted via Poland to the Swedish royal court. There it gave birth to a monastic community under royal protection as early as in the 1070s. These ideas, of course, will have to be more closely scrutinized.

Even in the first decades of the twelfth century, evidence for the spread of monasticism in Scandinavia is scarce. The Evesham monks in Odense received royal favours from Erik I Ejegod, who died in 1103, and from his brother and successor, King Niels. The institution's status as a Benedictine cathedral chapter was formally settled in 1117, and we know the text of the papal approval of this arrangement of 1117 from an authentic copy.[13] There can be no doubt that English models were at work in this construction. Veng Abbey's monastic church with its elaborate Anglo-Saxon style must already have been under construction. But, as recent research has shown, stylistic details do not necessarily prove that the monks or the architect came from England.[14]

Monks must also have settled in the Danish town of Randers during these decades; around the mid-twelfth century these monks handed over the site to nuns of their order and withdrew to Essenbæk further east. The Roskilde Chronicle tells us that there was an abortive initiative in 1124 to settle a community of Benedictine monks on Sjælland at the church of St Clement near the harbourside in Roskilde. In Norway, the Benedictine abbey of Munkeliv outside the growing west-coast town of Bergen came into being as a royal foundation. Some of the Benedictine nunneries we know of later in Denmark and Norway, possibly also Gudhem in western Sweden, may have originated in these first decades of the twelfth century. The spread of the Austin canons in Jutland from their nuclear community, the Augustinian cathedral chapter of Viberg-Viborg, probably meant that even by the early decades of the twelfth century they had reached the northernmost insular diocese of Børglum. We find them later in Vestervig, the burial place of the holy priest St Thøger (Theodgarus), a former chaplain of the king, St Olaf (Óláfr Haraldsson) of Norway, whose cult flourished here from the second half of the eleventh century.

---

[12] Henrik Janson, *Templum nobilissimum: Adam av Bremen, Uppsalatemplet och konflikt-linjerna i Europa kring år 1075* (Gothenburg: Göteborgs Universitet, Historiska institutionen, 1998).

[13] *Diplomatarium Danicum*, ed. by Christensen and others, II, no. 42.

[14] *Danmarks Kirker* (Copenhagen: Nationalmuseet, 1933–), XVI.6: *Aarhus Amt* (1988–89), 3190–3214.

IV

In 1135, two great Benedictine donations on the island of Sjælland changed the monastic map of all Scandinavia. The usurper king, Erik II Emune (1134–37), having got revenge and killed King Niels's son Magnus, who in turn had murdered his brother Knut Lavard (1131), declared that he had made a huge donation to the *congregationem fratrum regulariter viventium*,[15] in Ringsted, where Knut Lavard was buried, in order to secure the prayers of the monks for him. According to Niels Skyum-Nielsen in the *Diplomatarium Danicum*, Erik's charter used another donation charter as its model: that of a gift given by King Niels to the monks in Odense prior to their final papal approbation of 1117.[16] This makes it plausible that the situation in Ringsted, at the time of King Erik's donation, was analogous and that the king made his donation to an already existing monastery, not as the foundation of a new one. The community which received the donation might have been the one founded there by Bishop Svein the Norwegian before 1088 or a follower of the abortive Roskilde effort of 1124.

King Erik's donation to Ringsted gives only the year 1135 but no day or month. The high-ranking Peder Bodilsen, who had witnessed the king's donation to Ringsted, on behalf of his mother and his brothers and with the approval of Bishop Eskil of Roskilde, later Archbishop of Lund, on 29 November 1135,[17] gave his family fortune for the foundation of a Benedictine abbey in Næstved, where monks were given the pre-existing Church of St Peter. Unlike the King's gift to Ringsted, Peder Bodilsen provided all charters necessary for a new monastic foundation, for which there was no predecessor in Næstved.

The two gifts in the same year for two Benedictine communities on Sjælland may be interpreted as an indication of tensions in a society recently torn apart by civil war which was to last for another two decades. There is some evidence that Eskil, who became archbishop in 1137, tried by all means to stop the diffusion of Knut Lavard's reputation as a saint in Ringsted. I think there can be little doubt that Peder Bodilsen's foundation of a monastery at St Peter's in Næstved resulted from the split between Bishop Eskil's party and that of King Erik II Emune.

This interpretation of the support for two monastic communities on Sjælland as the expression of a tension between two different parties is supported by the fact that, a few years later, we witness a similar pattern at work in the next important stage of monastic life in Scandinavia, namely the two first Cistercian foundations in Sweden, Alvastra and Nydala, in 1143. Usually this event has simply been understood as the beginning of the history of the Cistercian Order in Scandinavia.[18] But if we forget for

[15] That is the 'community of brothers who live a regular life'.

[16] *Diplomatarium Danicum*, ed. by Christensen and others, II, no. 65.

[17] *Diplomatarium Danicum*, ed. by Christensen and others, II, no. 64.

[18] Brian P. McGuire, *The Cistercians in Denmark: Their Attitudes, Roles, and Functions in Medieval Society*, Cistercian Studies Series, 35 (Kalamazoo: Cistercian Publications, 1982).

a moment the difference in monastic observance between the monastic events on Sjælland in 1135 and those in Sweden in 1143, then we see a new type of similarity in the two events. In 1143, King Sverker and his wife founded Alvastra near the shore of Lake Vättern, on the king's estate, in a highly cultivated and settled area, certainly no desert. However, in the same year, Bishop Gisle of Linköping, the diocese in which Alvastra was also situated, made a foundation for monks in Nydala, deep in the forest inland and in the southern part of the diocese. That was to a much higher degree a place in the 'desert', although it was situated at the crossing of some important inland roads. In both cases, the monks came from Clairvaux. In both cases, the monks arrived in a place which had no pre-existing form of monastic life. And in both cases, the two new foundations were situated in one and the same diocese. King Sverker had good relations with some of the parties in the Danish civil war; however, not with Eskil, who in the meantime had become Archbishop of Lund and who therefore was now the metropolitan of all Scandinavia. As far as we can tell, Bishop Gisle was one of his suffragans, as well as his confidant.

We have then two pairs of monastic foundations within just a few years of each other: Ringsted and Næstved in 1135, and Alvastra and Nydala in 1143. In my opinion, monastic expansion in Scandinavia in these decades meant something different to reformist bishops than it did to sovereign kings. I see the dividing line between the two groups and spheres of understanding as lying neither in the religious order nor in the observance chosen for the new foundations, but rather in the tension between two parties, most simply described as an episcopal faction and a royal party. This is, as far as I can see, the reason why we have to attach so much more significance to the events on Sjælland in 1135 than hitherto has been done, in order to understand the further development of monasticism in Scandinavia. Less striking is the situation in Norway where, in 1146, English Cistercians from Fountains Abbey, Yorkshire, were invited by Bishop Sivard of Bergen to settle in the valley of Lyse not far from Bergen. That was not very far from the site of the Benedictine abbey of Munkeliv, the royal foundation from *c.* 1110. Another community of Cistercian monks arrived in Norway from Kirkstall Abbey, Yorkshire, a year later and settled on an island in the Oslo fjord where a church apparently already existed.

It must have been clear to many that when donations switched from Benedictine monasteries to the Cistercians with their outspoken subordination to a foreign institution, viz. the General Chapter of Cîteaux, as yet unknown in Scandinavia, some things would have to change in monastic circles. In 1144, Archbishop Eskil settled Cîteaux monks in Herrisvad in Skåne. He went on to settle more Clairvaux monks in Esrum, Sjælland, in 1153. In 1157, after his final victory over other claimants to the throne in the civil war, King Valdemar I the Great settled Cistercians of the Clairvaux line from Sweden in Vitskøl Abbey in Jutland.[19] Undoubtedly, things had changed. Austin canons, who remained loyal to their bishops, continued their

---

[19] *Diplomatarium Danicum*, ed. by Christensen and others, II, no. 120.

expansion in Denmark in the same years, but we later find strong royal influence among some of them. These foundations need to be analysed more closely against the background of the pattern I have just outlined.

This is the situation in the middle of the twelfth century, which we normally look upon as the first great wave of foundations of Cistercian and other reformed orders in Scandinavia. The names of the earliest Cistercian sites have already been mentioned. In spite of the new waves, however, the mid-century monastic map was still dominated by Benedictine monasticism, with its independent abbeys with local variations of observance. In Jutland we have mentioned St Michael's outside Schleswig and Seem outside Ribe, furthermore Veng in the Gudenå river basin, and the Benedictine settlement in Randers, which soon split into two: the nuns in Randers and the monks in Essenbæk. The Austin canons constituted the cathedral chapter of Viberg-Viborg where the cult of their saintly prior, Kjeld (Ketillus), grew after his death in 1150.[20] Probably the daughter settlement of Austin canons in Vestervig, Thy, existed by then. This was in the northernmost diocese of Denmark, viz. Vendsyssel and Thy centred in Børglum, around the cult of St Thøger. The Bishop of Børglum, Tyge, founded a Benedictine convent at a place called *Insula Sancte Marie*, known in Danish simply as Ø kloster, north of Ålborg.[21] On the island of Fyn the Benedictine cathedral chapter of Odense was the island's only monastic community for men. The establishment of this chapter was followed by the Benedictine nuns of Nonnebakken south of the urban settlement of Odense. On Sjælland, Ringsted and Næstved became the two vital Benedictine abbeys. Nuns of the same order lived in Roskilde, and there must have been some Austin canons or hermits on the small island of Eskilsø, as can be seen by the *vita* of Abbot William of Æbelholt.[22] Skåne had its All Saints' Abbey outside Lund closely linked to the archiepiscopal see, with its nuns at St Peter's in Lund and its Austin canons in Dalby. In Vreta in Sweden, and perhaps also in Uppsala, monastic communities for women and/or for men were in existence. In Norway, Nidarholm was the northernmost monastic settlement, followed by Selja, the geographical position of which, however, was no longer so central in the communication system along the Norwegian coast. The youngest Benedictine foundation, the abbey of Munkeliv, has already been mentioned. On Iceland, the Benedictine abbey of Þingeyrar in the northern diocese of Hólar, founded 1133, was on its way to becoming a small, elite centre for the production and transmission of religious literature and poetry.

The Cistercians were still the newcomers. The community of Cîteaux monks in Herrisvad was a new feature for Skåne, the archdiocese of Lund and Denmark as a whole. In Sweden, Clairvaux monks had got a third site, a place in Västergötland. This was not actually within King Sverker's sphere of influence, so it took some

---

[20] *Vitae Sanctorum Danorum*, ed. by Gertz, pp. 251–83.

[21] *Diplomatarium Danicum*, ed. by Christensen and others, III (1976–77), no. 7.

[22] *Vitae Sanctorum Danorum*, ed. by Gertz, pp. 300–69.

time and several conflicts before they found a new site in Varnhem, where they were able to stay from the 1150s onwards. The two Cistercian abbeys in Norway were in the process of consolidation.

V

The balance between old and reformed monasticism changed in the 1150s and 1160s. Firstly, two different communities of a new reformed order of Austin canons, the Premonstratensians, who were strongly inspired by St Bernard and his monastic ideals, settled in two different areas in Denmark. In the 1140s some came, maybe directly from Prémontré, to Lund and founded an abbey at Drottens or St Saviour's Church, apparently with the support of Archbishop Eskil — at an early stage the church or its wooden predecessor might have been the cathedral of Lund. Another group from the order's reformed abbey of Steinfeld in the upper Rhineland arrived or sent representatives to Børglum where they were soon engaged by the bishop, who had not yet established a cathedral chapter there. Within a few years, the White Canons in Lund were able to settle in Tommarp in south-eastern Skåne, from where they could extend their pastoral work to the whole region. As early as 1155 they received a papal letter of protection, and within a few years they were ready to send some canons to take over the royal church of Væ in the same region. In Jutland, we do not know exactly where the White Canons first settled. The model of a Premonstratensian cathedral chapter was, however, not completely unknown to the order (we could mention Whithorn, *Candida Casa*, in Scotland and Ratzeburg in Saxony), and that was the form of service which they used for the bishopric of Børglum not long after their arrival.

The decisive blow to the balance between Benedictine and reformed observance came from the Cistercian expansion of the 1160s which could only have been made possible by the recruitment of large numbers of novices to the earliest Cistercian abbeys already mentioned: Herrisvad in Skåne, Esrum on Sjælland, Vitskøl in Jutland, and Alvastra in Östergötland. Undoubtedly such an increase in Cistercian vocations which we must suppose, considering the number of daughter foundations which now followed, damaged the number of vocations to the Benedictine communities which were probably rather small. The Cistercians offered a more intense convent discipline, their communities were larger, probably never numbering less than twelve monks in each monastery, and their resources were considerable, thanks to their privileged status and hard-working lay brothers. The recruitment to Scandinavia's only Cîteaux filiation, Herrisvad in Skåne in the archdiocese of Lund, must have been quite remarkable, since only one generation later, this abbey was able to establish no less than three daughter abbeys within a decade, from 1163 to 1172. One of these houses was the Benedictine abbey of Seem, which the new monks suppressed and transplanted to Løgum in southern Jutland; the other two were Tvis in western Jutland and Holme on Fyn. The recruitment to Esrum provided enough new

monks for the establishment of Sorø on Sjælland, where, in 1161, an incipient Benedictine foundation was taken over by the Clairvaux Cistercians. The Esrum monks
finally participated in Danish settlements in Pomerania with the foundation of Dar-
gun in 1171, later moved to Eldena. This gave rise to the city of Greifswald. Some of
the Clairvaux Cistercians from Swedish Varnhem, after having opened the royal
abbey of Vitskøl in Jutland, returned and continued their life in Sweden. Further new
recruitment to Vitskøl must be assumed to explain a second *exitus*, which led, in the
1160s, to the suppression of the Benedictine abbey of Veng and the foundation of
Øm, the *Cara Insula*, in the Gudenå river basin. In Sweden, the Alvastra Cistercians
had recruited enough novices to found Viby north of Lake Mälaren *c.* 1160, which
later moved to Julita. Meanwhile, the Nydala Cistercians were able to found a
daughter abbey on Gotland in 1164. Towards the end of the 1160s, Hospitallers of St
John came to Denmark following Archbishop Eskil's pilgrimage to Jerusalem in
1164 and his reconciliation with the king in 1167.[23]

VI

The final shift in balance in favour of the reformed orders came in 1165 with the
arrival in Denmark of the French Austin abbot William from Sainte Geneviève in
Paris. William, who died in 1203 and was canonized in 1224, was the most prominent
monastic reformer in Denmark. He began his career with the task of reforming an
existing community of Austin canons on the island of Eskilsø in the Roskilde fjord.
Abbot William was able to establish Æbelholt on Sjælland *c.* 1175, thereby creating
Denmark's most famous abbey of Austin Canons, which due to its proximity to
Esrum became one of that abbey's best partners. Abbot William worked tirelessly to
influence canonical life in northern Jutland and probably made the Austin communities there, along with the Premonstratensians, adopt a strictly reformed religious
observance. Æbelholt became famous for the many healings and the medical exper-
tise within its precinct. One of its daughter foundations was Kongehælle on Norway's border with Sweden, for which William enjoyed the support of the Norwegian
archbishop Eysteinn (1161–81).

   In spite of all the new signals from reformed monasticism, earlier monastic traditions asserted themselves to a certain degree. In the place of Veng, which was suppressed and taken over by the Cistercians, a new Benedictine abbey came into being
in the Gudenå river basin, west of the Cistercians' *Cara Insula*, the abbey of Voer.
Its Latin name, *de Oratorio*, suggests that it might have been a priory under Veng at
some earlier point in time, or it may have been a refuge for the last monks expelled

---

[23] Tore Nyberg, 'Zur Rolle der Johanniter in Skandinavien: Erstes Auftreten und Aufbau
der Institutionen', in *Die Rolle der Ritterorden in der mittelalterlichen Kultur*, ed. by Zenon
Hubert Nowak, Colloquia Torunensia Historica, 3 (Toruń: Uniwersytet Mikołaja Kopernika,
1985), pp. 129–44.

from Veng. The Randers monks moved out of the growing town and founded their new site in Essenbæk. More Austin and Benedictine convents were founded. Finally, in Sweden, one must not forget how monastic life left traces in late-twelfth-century Uppsala. Jarl Gallén has interpreted the existing evidence as an indication that a Benedictine cathedral chapter existed in Uppsala between the 1160s and *c.* 1220.[24] Perhaps this evidence uncovers earlier monastic traditions hidden behind mythical stories of fighting paganism, as recently proposed in Henrik Janson's doctoral thesis mentioned above.

VII

I will conclude this short survey with a few words on some of the forgotten evidence of early monasticism in Scandinavia. Ever since the printing of charters and chronicles of monastic history began in the late eighteenth century, scholars have used the evidence nearest at hand to its full extent. The history of monasticism was to a great extent institutional history, elucidated by foundation charters and polemical writings created to defend the positions of one party in conflict situations, like that between the Cistercians and the non-reformed Benedictines. The letter collection of Abbot William of Æbelholt belongs to this category and was therefore studied and utilized by scholars of monastic history at an early stage. Early annals of Denmark and Sweden, in combination with sources like the Cistercian filiation tree, were being used to establish a chronology. It did not take long, however, before this went as far as it could because the information was scarce and contradictory. Annals, by using the formula *conventus missus est in*, gave birth to the illusion that one could understand the spread of Cistercian monasticism only by reconstructing the chronology of foundation waves.[25] Parallel to this, sources like necrologies, lists of relics, and book catalogues were being edited and printed without always being studied in detail. This gave monastic history the character of being a collection of anecdotes, and no comprehensive history of monasticism in Scandinavia was written, as long as this dependence upon written sources alone dominated the field.

This is probably one of the reasons why archaeology has meant so much to monastic studies during the second half of the twentieth century. Excavations were felt as a liberation from so much ignorance and so many false conclusions based on the sparse fragments of written evidence left over after centuries of anti-Catholic

---

[24] Jarl Gallén, 'De engelska munkarna i Uppsala: Ett katedralkloster på 1100-talet', *Historisk Tidskrift för Finland*, 61 (1976), 1–21.

[25] The Lund Annals record the 'conversion' of St Bernard under the year 1113 and the foundation of Prémontré under 1120, then the consecutive foundations of Herrisvad 1144, Esrum 1153, Sorø 1161, and Ås 1194. In Swedish annals, Alvastra and Nydala are recorded under the year 1143, Lyse 1147, Varnhem 1150, Esrum 1153, then Vitskøl and 'Saba', which stands for Säby, the follower of Viby, finally Tvis and Øm, although not under the correct year.

feeling. Monastic sites and remaining ruins were excavated, studied, and placed in their proper frame of reference. Scholars purposely disregarded written evidence in order to reach independent conclusions from archaeological premises alone.[26]

However, in this ongoing process, which constantly brings forth new and sensational results from many monastic sites all over Scandinavia, some of the written evidence seems to have been forgotten. Although some precious manuscripts produced in early monastic scriptoria in Scandinavia have been preserved and studied for reason of their texts, their music, their illuminations, or their script tradition, there is no overall view of what was written or read in Scandinavian monasteries during their first five generations *c.* 1060–1200. Some highlights have found their way into reference works on literature. The number of specialized studies is increasing, however, so material is slowly being brought together for a fuller synthesis. One might, for instance, mention here the thousands of fragments of liturgical books preserved in the state archives of Stockholm, Copenhagen, Oslo, and Helsinki. Another neglected field is the study of the extant necrologies and obituaries from Scandinavian monasteries. Although, for example, the *Libri memoriales* from Lund were edited long ago, very few studies have dealt with efforts to reconstruct monastic populations by means of a prosopographical analysis, as practised today in several scholarly traditions. Here is certainly a field of research well suited to broadening our knowledge of what monastic life inside the walls looked like. The *Liber daticus Lundensis* was edited by C. Weeke as early as 1884–89 and reprinted in 1973.[27] Lauritz Weibull's edition of the *Necrologium Lundense* (1923) is exemplary.[28] Since the cathedral chapter of Lund upheld a prayer union with several monastic communities in Denmark, the names of the deceased members of these communities were entered into the Lund books for a period of at least two generations, which provides us with a lot of study material for this period. Another example is the complete list of all the monks of Løgum in southern Jutland since its foundation in the 1160s. It was copied in the abbey of Sorø in 1518 on the initiative of its learned abbot, and was printed more than two hundred years ago in the *Scriptores Rerum Danicarum Medii Aevi*,[29] but has not yet attracted a thorough investigation by any scholar.

There is still a long way to go before a comprehensive history of Scandinavian monasticism can be written.

---

[26] See the articles in *Hikuin*, 23 'Danske klostre: Arkæologiske undersøgelser 1972–1996' (1996).

[27] *Lunde Domkapitels Gavebøger ('Libri Datici Lundenses')*, ed. by C. Weeke (Copenhagen: Rudolph Klein, 1884–89; repr. Copenhagen: Selskabet for udgivelse af kilder til dansk historie, 1973).

[28] *Necrologium Lundense: Lunds domkyrkas nekrologium*, ed. by Lauritz Weibull (Lund: Berlingska, 1923).

[29] *Scriptores Rerum Danicarum Medii Aevi*, ed. by J. Langebek and others, 9 vols (Copenhagen: A. H. Godiche, 1772–1878; repr. Nendeln: Kraus, 1969), IV (1776), 575–87.

Norwegians and Europe: The Theme of Marriage and Consanguinity in Early Norwegian Law

JAN RAGNAR HAGLAND

C anon law constituted, needless to say, one important point of contact between Scandinavia and Europe in the later part of the period of time which forms the framework of the present volume. This applies, of course, also to Norway and Norwegians. One aspect of canon law much discussed in its varying European contexts is the canonical prohibition of endogamous marriage. The historical development of this issue within the Christian Church has been discussed at great length elsewhere and will be left at that for the time being.[1] It is only necessary here to remind ourselves that the forbidden degrees of consanguinity and affinity reached a point of culmination in Gratian of Bologna's *Decretum* (*c.* 1140) in which Gratian argues for prohibition within the seventh degree. In general the question has remained fairly open as to how widely the prohibition to the seventh degree was known, and even more so, the degree to which it was imposed. To quote Sheehan's words this is a question which 'will need much research before it will be possible to speak with authority'.[2]

I will take this opportunity to make some brief comments upon early Norwegian legislation on marriage and consanguinity as a part of the wider European context of canonical law. One good reason for doing so is the fact that although a fair amount of work has been done on these matters already, the situation in these northern church provinces has not often been included in the general discussion about

---

[1] See, for example, Christopher N. L. Brooke, *The Medieval Idea of Marriage* (Oxford: Oxford University Press, 1989), pp. 119–72; Jack Goody, *The Development of the Family and Marriage in Europe* (Cambridge: Cambridge University Press, 1983), pp. 134–46; Knut Robberstad, *Gulatingslovi*, 3rd edn (Oslo: Det Norske Samlaget, 1969), pp. 334–36; Michael M. Sheehan, *Marriage, Family and Law in Medieval Europe: Collected Studies*, ed. by James K. Farge (Cardiff: University of Wales Press, 1996), pp. 253–56.

[2] Sheehan, *Marriage, Family and Law in Medieval Europe*, p. 254.

forbidden degrees of consanguinity in the European High Middle Ages. A closer look at early Norwegian legislation may, in consequence perhaps, help to fill in at least some of the gaps in our knowledge implied by Sheehan's statement just quoted.

The legislation to be taken into consideration here are the four Norwegian provincial laws, all valid up to the 1270s when King Magnus the Lawmender (1263–80) had a new common law passed for all of Norway. The corresponding process for ecclesiastical legislation is more complicated and shall not be dealt with in any detail here. However, the ecclesiastical laws prior to the 1270s are preserved for the four legal areas, the Gulaþing, the Frostuþing, the Eiðsifaþing, and the Borgarþing (see fig. 1). All of these contain regulations concerning the limitation of marriage with regard to family relationships. Bearing the age of these laws in mind a closer look at the regulations and how they relate to the canonical prohibition of marriage within the seventh degree may, it seems to me, tell us something about the relationship between Norwegians and Europe seen from two sides: how effectively did the Church of Rome through institutions such as Gratian's *Decretum* manage to spread its laws and ideologies, for example about marriage, and how did Norwegian ecclesiastical legislation and legal usage adapt to or respond to these external claims? In order to try to answer questions such as these we need to look at the provincial laws of medieval Norway and what they actually say about forbidden marriages. The problem of dating these laws also needs consideration.

To start then with the Gulaþing Law, it is stated in paragraph 24 that 'En oss er sva lovat at taca at siauanda kne. oc siauanda lið frendkonor varar. En konor þær aðrar er frendkonor varar ero at fimta kne' ('But we are allowed to take a wife among our kinswomen in the seventh degree of kinship and in the seventh "knee", and among other women, the widows of our kinsmen, in the fifth degree and the fifth knee').[3] The penalty for breaking the law on this point is stated as follows: 'En ef maðr verðr at þui kunnr oc sannr at hann a kono nanare ser. en i logum er mælt þa scal hann bœta firi þat morcum .iij. biscope. oc lata af kononne oc ganga til scripta. oc bœta við krist' ('And if a man is accused and convicted of having a wife of nearer kinship than the law allows, he shall atone for it with a fine of three marks to the bishop and forsake the woman and go to confession and do penance').[4] The legal procedures concerning these matters stated in the law are restricted to those concerning denial of the charges of marrying too closely.

The somewhat more detailed Frostuþing Law (§ III: 1) has the following wording:

Sva er mælt at engi skal taka kono i ætt sina annars kostar en mællt er oc biscup lœyfði a mostrar þingi oc aller mænn vurðu asatter. Telia skal fra syzskinum tueim .vj. mœnn a

[3] *Norges gamle Love indtil 1387*, ed. by R. Keyser and others, 5 vols (Christiania [Oslo]: Grøndahl & Søn, 1846–95), I (1846), 15. Translation from Laurence M. Larson, *The Earliest Norwegian Laws Being the Gulathing Law and the Frostathing Law* (New York: Columbia University Press, 1935), p. 53.

[4] *Norges gamle Love indtil 1387*, ed. by Keyser and others, I, 15. Trans. by Larson, *The Earliest Norwegian Laws*, pp. 53.

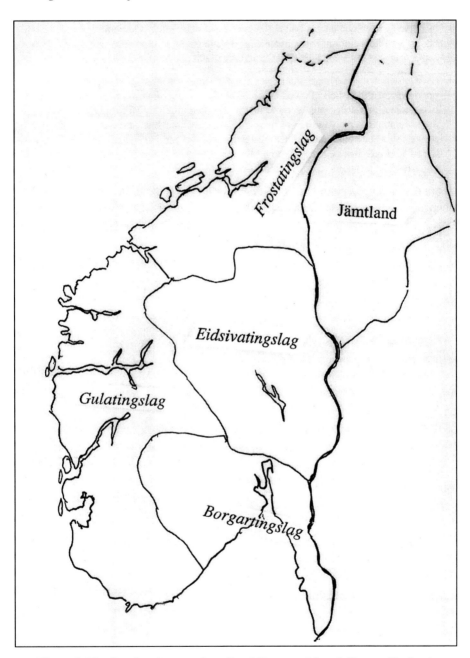

Figure 1. The four legal areas of medieval Norway. Map: J. Ragnar Hagland.

hvarntveggia vegh oc taka at hinum seaunda. En ef maðr uil taka kono þa er frende hans atte þa skal telia fiora mænn a huarntueggia vegh fra brœðrom tueim oc takazt hinum fimta. Sua skal hitt sama telia ef maðr uil taka frendkono þeirrar er hann atte aðr.

(It is enacted that no man shall take a wife within the kindred, except as the law provides and the bishop allowed at the Moster thing, to which all men agreed. From two, brother and sister, six persons shall be counted on either side and one may wed the seventh. If a man wishes to marry a woman whom his kinsman has had, four persons shall be counted on either side from two, brother and sister, and let him take the fifth. There shall be a similar count if a man wishes to marry a woman of kin to the one whom he had earlier.)[5]

There is a penalty of three marks involved for breaking the law on this point and the couple shall have to part from each other. After a detailed description of the legal procedures involved and how to free oneself from the charges of marrying too closely the ultimate penalty is stated as follows:

En ef hann lætr þa eigi af þa fare hann vtlægr en biskup hafe fe hans en hon hafe sitt fe. En ef maðr tekr brœðrungu sina eða systrungu sina þa er þar siðast .iij. marka sekt. En upp fra þui sem frendzemi oskylldizt þa skolu falla .ij. aurar af kne hueriu. þa værðr þat mork at setta kne. Samu lund er vm sifskape.

(If he still refuses to give her up, he shall go into outlawry and the bishop shall have his chattels, but the woman shall keep what is hers. If a man takes the daughter of his paternal uncle or the daughter of his maternal aunt, the penalty is still three marks; but in passing toward the point where kinship ceases (to be a hindrance) two oras[6] shall be dropped at each knee, that will make one mark at the sixth knee. Kinship through marriage (shall be dealt with) in the same way.)[7]

The Borgarþing Law (§ I: 15) quite simply states:

Nu skall ængi maðr fa frendkono sina skyldri en at .v. kne.[8] oc at fimta manne frendlæif [. . .] Þær ero .iij. guðsiviar en allar ero iamdyrar frendzeme. Su er æin at halda barne vndir brimsignan. annur at hæfia barn or hæidnum dome. þriðia at halda a barne er biscup færmir. En ef maðr fær guðciviu sinnar þa skall hava till slikar stæfnur at skilia þau sem till frenzemi byggvi.

(No man shall marry his kinswoman more closely related than to the fifth 'knee' and his kinswoman's widow to the fifth 'man' [. . .]. There are three god-relatives who are all equal to kinship. One is she who holds the child at the *prima signatio*, the second is she who lifts the child out of heathendom, and the third she who holds the child when

---

[5] *Norges gamle Love indtil 1387*, ed. by Keyser and others, I, 147. Trans. by Larson, *The Earliest Norwegian Laws*, pp. 245.

[6] one ora = one eighth of a mark.

[7] *Norges gamle Love indtil 1387*, ed. by Keyser and others, I, 149. Trans. by Larson, *The Earliest Norwegian Laws*, pp. 246.

[8] Variants: § II: 6 and § III: 6 *at .vij. kne.*

the bishop confirms it. And if a man marries his female gossip the same measures shall be taken to separate them as is the case with forbidden kinship.)[9]

As in the Gulaþing and the Frostuþing laws the penalty for breaking the law is a fine of three marks which will rise to nine if the charge is rejected and ignored after three successive writs of summons. The legal procedures involved resemble those of the Frostuþing Law even if details, which do not concern us here, may differ.

The Eiðsifaþing Law (§ I: 30) has the following wording:

> Þat er oc firiboðet at nockor maðr skal fa frenkono sinnar ser til kono eða frenndlæiuar sinnar. ne guðciuia sin. [. . .] Nu skal tælia frensemi þæirra i .vta.[10] kne oc take at .vijda. En at frennlæif. tæli .iij. kne[11] oc take at .vta. En ef maðr tæckr ner mæir. þa ma æi æiga at lagum.

> (It is forbidden for any man to marry his kinswoman or his kinsman's widow or female gossip. [. . .] Now the kinship shall be counted to the fifth degree [var. 'from the sixth'] and marry at the seventh. And when a kinsman's widow is concerned three degrees [var. 'four'] be counted and marriage is allowed at the fifth. If a man marries closer he shall not lawfully have her as wife.)[12]

The legal procedures involved in cases of conflict parallel those of the Borgarþing Law.

There is, it seems, general agreement that the regulations which have been preserved in the manuscripts are all post-1152/53 when updated canonical legislation on marriage prohibition appears to have been imposed (see below). As can be seen from the passages quoted above there is no direct textual relationship between the four variants of the text on this particular point, the closest being the texts of the Borgarþing and the Eiðsifaþing. As can also be seen the terminology for designating the prohibited degrees varies in the manuscripts containing these laws — a variation which, in my opinion, suggests some uncertainty about how to calculate degrees of relationship in order to comply with canon law. A traditional word for degree of kinship appears to have been in legal use independently of ecclesiastical law, that is, the term *kné*, n., 'knee' — a system of calculating degrees of relationship in which the sibling group, according to Hertzberg, was not counted so as to make first cousins the first 'knee', second cousins the second 'knee', and so on.[13] In Norwegian scholarly work this, to some extent at least, has been considered a terminological feature specific to Old Norse.[14] However, the terminology based on counting joints of the

---

[9] *Norges gamle Love indtil 1387*, ed. by Keyser and others, I, 350. My translation.

[10] Variant: *tælia fra .vj. kne.*

[11] Variant: *En frændlæiua skall tælia i .iiij.*

[12] *Norges gamle Love indtil 1387*, ed. by Keyser and others, I, 384. My translation.

[13] Ebbe Hertzberg, 'Glossarium', in *Norges gamle Love indtil 1387*, ed. by Keyser and others, V (1895), 57–834 (p. 349).

[14] Dag Gundersen, 'Incest', *Kulturhistorisk leksikon for nordisk middelalder*, 22 vols (Copenhagen: Rosenkilde & Bagger, 1956–78), VII (1962), cols 370–74 (col. 372).

human body seems to have been well known elsewhere in Europe and may well have been borrowed into Norse legal language (cf. Latin *geniculum*, Anglo-Saxon *cnēo*, n.). To some extent the apparently well-established term *kné* in Old Norse is mixed with the terms *liðr*, m., 'degree' and *maðr*, m., 'man' which, again, may be interpreted as uncertainty about what system of calculating to use when counting the prohibited degrees in the process of adopting ecclesiastical legislation on this particular point. In the Gulaþing Law the term *kné* seems to be used synonymously with *liðr*. The number of forbidden degrees related to both of these terms is six. At seven, marriage is permitted. Given the system of calculation described by Hertzberg this equals the canonical *ad septimam generacionem* making the terms *kné* and *liðr* in the text a tautology. A similar congruency between *kné* and *maðr* occurs in one version of the Borgarþing Law (§ I: 15), where the forbidden number of degrees is stated as five for both *kné* and *maðr*. However, in the two other versions of the Borgarþing Law,[15] the number of 'knees' equals that stated in the Gulaþing Law — that is, prohibited to the seventh *kné* for consanguinity, but to the fifth 'man' for affinity.[16] Rather than interpreting the wording in § I: 15 as reflecting an older stage of the law or as a misspelling, as Robberstad and Maurer do,[17] the phrase *.v. kne* may equally well reflect the post-1270 situation (see below) as the manuscripts containing this particular part of the text are all dated to the fourteenth century.[18]

As demonstrated by Charles-Edwards, Old English usage did distinguish between the terms corresponding to Old Norse *kné* and *maðr* for counting degrees of kinship.[19] Thus in Æthelred's law the degree of kinship of six 'men' corresponds to kinship within the fourth 'knee'.[20] This does not explain the varying use of the terms *kné* and *maðr* in the three different versions of the Borgarþing Law. But the Norse usage outlined above may well reflect some confused reception of foreign legal sources in which the terms did represent different systems of calculating (forbidden) degrees of kinship, even if a common explanation of such differences has been scribal inaccuracies when copying Roman numerals — a phenomenon well known in manuscript

---

[15] Printed in volume I of *Norges gamle Love indtil 1387*, ed. by Keyser and others, as § II: 6 and § III: 6.

[16] *.v. kne ok at fimta manne at frendlæif* as opposed to *.vij. kne ok at fimta manne at frenseme* (= § II: 6) / *frendlæif* (= § III: 6).

[17] See Knut Robberstad, 'Hadrians-løyvet i ekteskapsretten', *Historisk Tidsskrift*, 41 (1961–62), 341–44 (p. 344); Konrad Maurer, *Vorlesungen über altnordische Rechtgeschichte*, 5 vols (Leipzig: Deichetsche Verlagsbuchhandlung, 1908), II: *Über altnordische Kirchenverfassung und Eherecht*, 23.

[18] See *Norges gamle Love indtil 1387*, ed. by Keyser and others, I, 338.

[19] T. M. Charles-Edwards, 'Kinship, Status and the Origins of the Hide', *Past and Present*, 56 (1972), 3–33 (pp. 23–24).

[20] 'in VI manna sibfæce on his agenum cynne, þæt is binnan þam feorþan cneowe': Æthelred, Section VI, 12 (cf. Felix Liebermann, *Die Gesetze der Angelsachsen*, 4 vols (Halle: Max Niemeyer, 1903–16), I: *Text und Übersetzung* (1903), 250).

cultures.[21] The apparent confusion about modes of calculation displayed in these laws may in itself indicate that the canonical law of prohibition to the seventh degree was not pushed very hard in Norway.[22]

In this respect the Frostuþing Law stands by itself by consistently using the term *maðr* in the context which occupies us here even if the term *kné* is used elsewhere in the text. The text states, as we have seen, that from *syzstkinum tueim*, that is two siblings, 'six men shall be counted either way' making marriage legal at the seventh man. The text in itself does not contradict the fact that the canonical system of calculation is implied here, that is to say that the counting was meant to include the sibling group. There is, however, indirect evidence that the Frostuþing Law is in fact based upon the canonical way of calculation in these matters. It is stated in § III: 1 that 'if a man marries a first cousin on the father's side or on the mother's side then there is still (*þar siðast*) a fine of three marks. From this degree of kinship onwards until marriage is permitted, the fine is to be diminished by two *aurar* at each "knee", which amounts to one mark at the sixth "knee"'. This does not make sense mathematically, as there are eight *aurar* in a mark. Three of the manuscript variants, however, instead of *.ij. aurar* have *.ij. aurar silfrmetnir*. That is to say two *aurar* valued in silver instead of two 'counted' *aurar* which was only half the value. To get down from three to one mark (= eight *aurar*) at the sixth knee the sibling group has to be included in the calculation, that is to say the canonical system of counting prohibited degrees of kinship.[23] The expression *þar siðast* in the text underlines this in my opinion, because it means that the last degree to have this fine was the second knee, implying that the fines were not differentiated for marrying within the closest circle of kinship.[24] If this interpretation is correct, the prohibition in the Frostuþing Law was set at one degree closer than the canonical seven, which may explain some of the confusion displayed in a papal letter of 1192 discussed below.

A discrepancy between the forbidden degrees of consanguinity and affinity seems to have been present in all four of the laws under discussion. Except for one variant of the Borgarþing Law consanguinity counts to seven degrees whatever system of calculation this may reflect, whereas affinity counts to five. Robberstad explains this as an amalgam of two systems, one going back to an English system known in the laws of King Æthelred from the early eleventh century, in which marriage within the fourth 'knee' was forbidden (cf. note 11 above), the other reflecting a canonical expansion in accordance with Gratian's *Decretum*.[25] The former of these two systems,

---

[21] Robberstad, 'Hadrians-løyvet', p. 344, gives up explaining the lack of agreement between the different manuscript versions of the Borgarþing Law. The only important fact to hold on to, he states, is that § I: 15 permits marriage between cousins four times removed.

[22] See Sheehan, *The Earliest Norwegian Laws*, p. 254, for comparison with Gratian's *Decretum* on this point.

[23] I am grateful to Jørn Sandnes who pointed this out to me.

[24] See also Ebbe Hertzberg, 'Glossarium', p. 552.

[25] See Robberstad, *Gulatingslovi*, p. 335.

according to Robberstad, may represent a substratum of ecclesiastical legislation originally introduced by Bishop Grímkell and passed at the Moster assembly, probably in 1022.[26] He also suggests that the discrepancy between consanguineous and affinal kinship goes back to 1152 when the papal envoy to Niðaróss, Nicholas Breakespeare, on the occasion of the establishment of the archiepiscopal see adjusted the prohibition for consanguineous relationship to canonical standards leaving affinal kinship untouched.[27] Early Icelandic law gives further evidence to support this possibility. Prior to 1217, when prohibition was adjusted to the fourth degree (*liðr*) probably in accordance with the Fourth Lateran Council, the prohibited degree in Iceland never surpassed the fifth *liðr*.[28] This may well reflect 'the state of the art' in eleventh-century Norwegian ecclesiastical law on this point.

The evidence for attributing the introduction of the canonical rules to Nicholas Breakespeare is sought in a letter from Pope Coelestin III to Nicholas (*electus* to the bishopric of Oslo) dated to the second half of 1192.[29] In this letter, it is stated that Nicholas Breakespeare, later Pope Adrian IV (1154–59), granted the people of Norway the right to marry in *sextu gradu*. This, of course, adds to the uncertainty about the real meaning of the legal expressions discussed above, and consequently makes the question more open concerning to what degree the canonical prohibition of marriage was imposed in reality. Robberstad seems to accept a suggestion by Maurer that this again reflects terminological confusion — the sixth 'knee' having incorrectly been equalled with the sixth instead of the seventh *gradus*.[30] Convincing as this argument may appear, it should nonetheless be added that the wording *sextu gradu* in Coelestin's letter of 1192 *might* reflect the wording about affinity in the laws. The implication in either case being, as I see it, that the papal authorities were prepared to accept a less strict interpretation of the canonically prescribed seven degrees if this was considered to be in accordance with usual local practice.[31]

---

[26] For the dating of the Moster assembly see Jan Ragnar Hagland, 'Kulissteinen: Endå ein gong', in *Heidersskrift til Nils Hallan på 65-årsdagen 13. desember 1991*, ed. by Gulbrand Alhaug, Kristoffer Kruken, and Helge Salvesen (Oslo: Novus, 1991), pp. 157–65 (p. 162). In all probability Robberstad's unreserved equation of Æthelred's *þam feorþan cneowe* with Old Norse *fiorða kné* needs to be modified. As the Old Norse usage concerning the terms *maðr* and *kné* is uncertain it should be borne in mind that the principal term used in Æthelred's law (§ VI: 12) is in *VI manna sibfæce*.

[27] See Knut Robberstad, *Frå gamal og ny rett* (Oslo: Det Norske Samlaget, 1950), p. 34.

[28] See Magnús Már Lárusson, 'Frændsemis- og sifjaspell', *Skírnir*, 140 (1966), 128–42 (p. 134).

[29] See *Regesta Norvegica*, ed. by Erik Gunnes, 7 vols (Oslo: Kjeldeskriftfondet, 1978–97), I: *822–1263* (1989), no. 222.

[30] See Robberstad, 'Hadrians-løyvet', pp. 341–44.

[31] The letter referred to answers (a now lost) inquiry by Nicholas (see *Regesta Norvegica*, ed. by Gunnes, I, no. 220) concerning the question of marriage between two persons related in different degrees to a common ancestor, one in the sixth or seventh degree the other in the

There is nothing to suggest that canonical theological thought did consider consanguineous ties and affinal kinship as being incongruent phenomena as regards marriage prohibition.[32] Whatever the reason may be for the difference which we can observe in early Norwegian law, it suggests that the canonical rule of seven degrees was known well enough at the local level but not imposed with great severity.

One of Pope Alexander III's decretals (issued sometime between 1161 and 1172) makes the picture even more confusing. This decretal deals with the problems faced by the people in one particular part of the archbishopric of Niðaróss. Alexander acknowledges reports from the archbishop's (that is Eysteinn Erlendsson, 1161–88) messengers that people on an island situated twelve days' journey from Norway and who had one bishopric under the metropolitan jurisdiction of Eysteinn were experiencing difficulties in marrying legally. There is general agreement that the problems described concern Greenland.[33] The implication of this is that the initiative to refer the matter to the pope was taken by Bishop Jón Kútr, bishop of Garðar from 1150 to ?1187. Little is known about this bishop from other sources.[34] This case, however, suggests that it was considered important even for the most remote parts of the Church of Rome to pay heed to current rules and regulations. Alexander III recommended a solution which exempted the Greenlanders from the canonical rule of seven, so as to permit marriage in the fifth, sixth, and seventh degree (*ut in v° et vi et vii gradu contrahant matrimonium*).[35] These rules, as pointed out by Robberstad, correspond to a so-called *nýmæli* (or 'addition') to the Icelandic law, the *Grágás*, probably passed in 1217, which permitted marriage in the fifth, sixth, and seventh degree provided that fines were paid to the *lögrétta*, the Icelandic legislature.[36] Thus, the observance of the canonical rules contained a substantial economic potential.

---

second or third degree (*gradus*). The official answer stresses that if possible the best solution is to stick to usual local practice and avoid introducing new rules: 'Unde in hac parte consultius duximus multitudini et observate consuetudini deferendum quam aliud in dissensionem et scandalum populi statuendum, quadam adhibita novitate' (see Eirik Vandvik, *Latinske dokument til norsk historie fram til år 1204* (Oslo: Det Norske Samlaget, 1959), no. 27, p. 92).

[32] See Goody, *The Development of the Family and Marriage*, p. 59.

[33] See Vegard Skånland, 'Supplerende og kritiske bemerkninger til Eirik Vandvik: Latinske dokument til norsk historie fram til år 1204', *Historisk tidsskrift*, 41 (1961–62), 129–46 (p. 137).

[34] See *Diplomatarium Norvegicum: Oldbreve til kundskap om Norges indre og ytre forhold, sprog, slegter, seder, lovgivning og rettergang i middelalderen*, ed. by C. C. A. Lange and others, 22 vols to date (Christiania [Oslo]: P. T. Mallings Forlagshandel/Riksarkivet, 1847–), XVIIB (1913), 281; and Hallvard Magerøy, *Soga om austmenn: Nordmenn som siglde til Island og Grønland i mellomalderen*, Det Norske Videnskaps-Akademi, II. Historisk–Filosofisk Klasse, Skrifter, Ny Serie, 19 (Oslo: Det Norske Samlaget, 1993), pp. 58–60.

[35] See Vandvik, *Latinske dokument til norsk historie*, p. 64, no. 11.

[36] See Robberstad, 'Hadrians-løyvet', p. 343.

There is, however, no evidence to prove the presence of economic motives behind the paragraphs on illegal marriage in early Norwegian ecclesiastical law. But the apparent need to have exceptions imposed on canonical legislation on marriage prohibition indicated by the Greenlandic case creates the impression that the laws on marriage prohibition were expected to be adhered to.

Adjustments in accordance with the resolution of the Fourth Lateran Council in 1215 are not consistently reflected in Norwegian ecclesiastical law until after the 1270s (see above). At this point in time marriage prohibition was set to the fourth degree. In the newer Norwegian ecclesiastical law this is phrased as 'not closer than the fifth man' (*[æighi] skylldari en fimta manne*) or prohibited 'at the fourth man counted equally on each side from a brother and a sister' (*At fiorda manne fra sydzkinum iamfaret*). The fact that no binding evidence exists in the manuscripts of the early provincial laws to suggest adjustment in accordance with the resolution of the Fourth Lateran Council is, in my opinion, perhaps the strongest indication that the prohibition to the seventh degree was never really important in Norway nor pushed very hard by the Church of Rome. It was not even important enough to be revised when outdated. There is good reason to underline this, it seems, because there is a tendency to take the provincial laws on marriage prohibition at face value in recent Norwegian historiography. Criticism of this position which has recently been voiced by Jørn Sandnes thus seems well motivated.[37]

In conclusion I wish to make just a small remark on early Norwegian legislation concerning the prohibition of endogamous marriage and legislation concerning the related concept of incest as these are often treated as one in scholarly work on these matters. In the laws the two concepts are kept apart from each other. All of the provincial laws list from eleven to seventeen women (*konor*) with whom sexual contact is considered to be *frændsemisspell* (referring to kinship), *sifjaspell* (affinity), or *guðsifjaspell* (godparentship) respectively. These relationships correspond to the fifteen to seventeen cases of incest listed in the Old Testament (Leviticus 18. 6–18) and should be kept out of the discussion of canonical prohibition of marriage.

---

[37] See Jørn Sandnes, 'Claus Krag: Vikingtid og rikssamling 800–1130' [review article], *Heimen*, 33 (1996), pp. 221–26 (p. 225).

Denmark and the Holy War: A Redefinition of a Traditional Pattern of Conflict 1147–1169

JANUS MØLLER JENSEN

Paul Riant's book on Scandinavian participation in the crusading movement was translated from French into Danish in 1868.[1] The Danish foreword says that this book, which highlights the Scandinavian contribution to the Crusades, should be appreciated by every patriot. Riant has

> ved dette sit Arbeide [. . .] mægtig bidraget til at gjøre det indlysende for den hele Verden, at der under Nordens Iis altid luer en glødende Varme, rede til at flamme op for Alt hvad der er ædelt og stort, og at navnlig paa Korstogenes Tid Brødrene i Norden stadigt fulgte med levende Deeltagelse alt hvad der angik deres Troesbeslægtede i det fjerne Østerland.[2]

But because of the size of the book, certain related topics were left out, among which was the tale of the holy wars that were preached against the heathen Slavs and, not least, the influence which the expeditions against the Wends could have had on the crusades to Palestine. Even though there were plans to carry out this work, it was never done.[3] I think this a huge gap, because in Danish historiography there has for too long been a marked denial of a connection between the wars fought by the

---

[1] Paul Riant, *Skandinavernes Korstog og Andagtsreiser til Palæstina 1000–1350* (Copenhagen: Schubotes, 1868). French edition: *Expéditions et pélerinages des Scandinaves en Terre Sainte au temps des croisades* (Paris, 1865)

[2] Riant, *Skandinavernes Korstog og Andagtsreiser til Palæstina*, pp. vii–viii; 'with his work [. . .] contributed tremendously to making it apparent for the whole world, that beneath the ice of the North lurks a glowing fervour, ready to burst into flame for all that is noble and grand, and especially at the time of the Crusades the brothers in the North constantly followed with lively interest everything that happened to their fellow faithful in the faraway East' (my translation).

[3] Riant, *Skandinavernes Korstog og Andagtsreiser til Palæstina*, pp. vii–viii.

Danish royal power and Church against their heathen neighbours on the one hand, and the crusading movement on the other.[4]

In his book *The Northern Crusades*, the English historian Eric Christiansen has taken the first steps towards revising the prevailing view. He thinks that Danes, Poles, and Saxons were all well accustomed to both the crusade idea and forced conversion, the Saxons even being subjected to the latter.[5] There can be no doubt that Christiansen thinks the wars fought in the Baltic are to be seen as resulting from the crusade idea, but after the 1147 crusade the war against the heathen Slavs was fought without the normal papal apparatus, that is, without papal authorization, without preaching, and without promises of any crusade privileges. Nevertheless, 'the campaigns of Henry the Lion and Valdemar against the Wends were treated as wars carried on successfully in the shadow of the unsuccessful 1147 crusade'.[6] That is, a continuation of the 1147 crusade but without being proper crusades. I will, in the following, challenge this view. Focus here will be on the time from the Second Crusade to the conquest of Rügen in 1169. But first, I will briefly discuss Denmark's place within the crusading movement, which I think played a significant role from the very beginning here as it did everywhere else in Europe.

Denmark and the Crusading Movement

I do not think there is any need to envisage that Denmark was unfamiliar with ideas current elsewhere in Christian Europe around 1100, and the country was ready to accept the concept of freeing the Holy Sepulchre and to take on the defence of Christianity in a distant country. As early as the pontificate of Alexander II, there seems to have been close contact between King Svein Estridsson and Archdeacon Hildebrand, who later became Pope Gregory VII.[7] There was also a very close connection to the

---

[4] See, for example, Hal Koch, 'Kongemagt og kirke 1060–1241', in *Danmarks historie*, ed. by John Danstrup and others, 14 vols (Copenhagen: Politiken, 1962–66), III (1963), 339–40; Niels Skyum-Nielsen, *Kvinde og slave*, Danmarks historie uden retouche, 3 (Copenhagen: Munksgaard, 1971), p. 63.

[5] Eric Christiansen, *The Northern Crusades: The Baltic and Catholic Frontier 1100–1525* (Basingstoke: Macmillan, 1980), p. 51. Small steps have also been taken in the same direction by some Danish historians, for example, Michael Andersen, 'Ad Pommern til', *Skalk*, 1992, no. 2, 22–30; Kai Hørby, 'Danmark og korstogene: Momenter i pavernes og kongernes politik', in *Festskrift til Olaf Olsen på 60 års dagen 7. juni 1988*, ed. by Aage Andersen and others (Copenhagen: Det Kongelige Nordiske Oldskriftselskab, 1988), pp. 201–06. However, no one seems to have considered in detail the implications for the perception of the crusading movement in Danish society at large and what effect this movement might have had on the Wendish wars. Too much weight continues to be placed solely on the politics of the Crusades.

[6] Christiansen, *The Northern Crusades*, pp. 62–63.

[7] 'Cum adhoc in ordine diaconatus eramus. sêpe dilectionis tuê litteras et legatos accepimus': *Diplomatarium Danicum 1053–1169*, ed. by L. Weibull and N. Skyum-Nielsen, Series

Flemish princely house, which was to play an important role in the First Crusade.[8] We have no written evidence that the crusade was preached in Denmark. But we have evidence in written European sources that the message of Urban II reached all corners of the Christian realm, including Scandinavia and thus Denmark. The European sources are full of testimonies to Danish participation.[9] Even though during the First

---

1, 7 vols (Copenhagen: Munksgaard, 1956–90), II (1963), no. 11. This volume of *Diplomatarium Danicum* will hereafter be referred to as *DD* 1: II. See also, *DD* 1: II, nos 5, 6, and 7. These letters should be considered much more closely in connection with the political struggle for power in Europe than has hitherto been done, based on the position in the register of Gregory VII; *Das Register Gregors VII.*, ed. by Erich Caspar, 2 vols, MGH, Epistolae selectae, 2 (Hanover: Hahn, 1920–23), I (1920), nos 70–75, pp. 229–38; H. E. J. Cowdrey, *Pope Gregory VII, 1073–1085* (Oxford: Clarendon Press, 1998), pp. 423–25. See the harsh rejection of the importance of this connection in Koch, 'Kongemagt og kirke 1060–1241', pp. 51–55. During the following twenty years, where the sources do not allow us to say anything definite about the connection to the papacy, there is no need to envisage that the contact stopped. See Cowdrey, *Pope Gregory VII*, pp. 454–59; Tore Nyberg, 'König Knut der Heilige, Teuzo und der Peterspfennig aus Dänemark', *Archivum Historiae Pontificiae*, 23 (1985), 359–66.

[8] Niels Lund, *Lið, leding og landeværn: Hær og samfund i Danmark i ældre middelalder* (Roskilde: Vikingeskibshallen, 1996), pp. 130, 187–208; A. E. Christensen, 'Tiden 1042–1241', in *Danmarks historie*, ed. by A. E. Christensen and others, 10 vols (Copenhagen: Gyldendalske Boghandel/Nordisk Forlag, 1977–92), I (1977), 248; Skyum-Nielsen, *Kvinde og slave*, pp. 61–62.

[9] Albert of Aachen, in *Recueil des historiens des croisades: Historiens occidentaux* (hereafter *RHC*), ed. by Académie des Inscriptions et Belles-Lettres, 5 vols (Paris: Imprimerie Impériale, 1844–95), IV (1879), 274, 376–77. Ekkehard, *Chronicon Universale*, ed. by G. H. Pertz, MGH, SS, 6 (Hanover: Hahn, 1841), pp. 208–09. Used in *Annales Magdeburgenses*, ed. by G. H. Pertz, MGH, SS, 16 (Hanover: Hahn, 1859), p. 179; *Annales Patherbrunnenses: Eine verlorene Quellenschrift des zwölften Jahrhunderts aus Bruchstücken*, ed. by P. Scheff-Boichorst (Innsbruck: Verlag der Wagner'schen Universitäts-Buchhandlung, 1870), p. 104; *Annales Islandorum Regii*, in *Scriptores Rerum Danicarum Medii Ævi* (hereafter *SRD*), ed. by J. Langebek and others, 9 vols (Copenhagen: A. H. Godiche, 1772–1878), III (1774), 48; William of Malmsbury, *De Gestis Regum Anglorum*, 2 vols, Rolls Series, 90 (London: HMSO, 1887–89), II (1889), 399. Riant thinks this annal to be very important and reliable (Riant, *Skandinavernes Korstog og Andagtsreiser til Palæstina*, p. 179), as does Arne Bøe in 'Vestnordiske Kårstog', in *Kulturhistorisk leksikon for nordisk middelalder*, 22 vols (Copenhagen: Rosenkilde & Bagger, 1956–78), IX (1964), col. 215, who incidentally is the only Scandinavian historian to state explicitly that the 'Northerners' went on crusade for purely religious reasons. However, the annal could not have been written before 1306; see G. Storm, *Islandske Annaler indtil 1578* (Christiania [Oslo]: Grøndahl, 1888), p. xi. *Annales Colbazenses* mention that, 'hoc anno Christianorum motio fuit Ierusalem super paganos', and that the city was captured in 1099 'a Christianis', *Danmarks middelalderlige Annaler* (hereafter *DMA*), ed. by M. Cl. Gertz, M. Lorenzen, and E. Jørgensen, rev. by E. Kroman (Copenhagen: Selskabet for Udgivelse af Kilder til Danmarks Historie, 1980), p. 9. The annal for the years 1074–1255 (*Årbogen 1074–1255*) says that, 'dane fore mange thill Ierusalem att stride gen hedinge' ('many Danes went to Jerusalem to fight the heathens'): *DMA*, p. 17. *Annales*

Crusade, preaching was no precondition for participation, it seems reasonable to assume that if many Danes did participate, this crusade may well have been preached. Another piece of evidence for Danish involvement in the crusading movement which has not received any treatment in Danish historiography is the letter from Ademar of Le Puy addressed specifically to the North ('versus aquilonem in partibus septemtrionis').[10] Writing from the siege of Antioch in 1098, he urged people to go crusading and keep their vows under threat of excommunication. From the very beginning, I think these ideas came to influence the relationship between Christians and heathens in the Baltic area.[11] In fact, to deny the crusade in Denmark is to deny that Denmark

---

Lundenses also mention the expedition to Jerusalem, 'hoc anno fuit mocio euncium Ierusalem super paganos': *DMA*, p. 55. It does not seem strange that an event as significant as the crusade should have been recorded by the annalists, but why is it only *Årbogen 1074–1255* that mentions Danish participation? It is argued in Anne K. G. Kristensen, *Danmarks ældste annalistik: Studier over lundensisk annalskrivning i 12. og 13. århundrede* (Copenhagen: Gyldendal, 1969), pp. 27–30, that *Årbogen 1074–1255* is not dependent on *Annales Colbazenses* and *Annales Lundenses*, but they have used the same Anglo-Norman original independently. In *Årbogen 1074–1255*, not all international information is recorded. Maybe this accounts for the use of the word 'dane' (Danes) instead of Christians. The term Christians would not exclude Danes. The formulation could stem from *Annales Lundenses* because of partial verbal similarity in the two notices.

[10] *Epistvlæ et chatæ ad historiam primi belli sacri spectantes qvæ supersunt ævo æqvales ac genvinæ. Die Kreuzzugsbriefe aus den Jahren 1088–1100: Eine Quellensammlung zur Geschichte des ersten Kreuzzuges*, ed. by H. Hagenmeyer (Innsbruck: Verlag der Wagner'schen Universitäts-Buchhandlung, 1901), pp. 141–42; see also p. 61.

[11] Saxo Grammaticus writes that Skjalm Hvide and Erik I Ejegod went on a revenge raid against the Wends because they had caused the death of Aute, the brother of Skjalm Hvide (*Saxonis Gesta Danorum*, ed. by J. Olrik and H. Ræder (Copenhagen: Levin & Munksgaard, 1931), p. 334, line 28 – p. 335, line 16. This edition of Saxo's *Gesta Danorum* will be referred to as Saxo hereafter). This raid was just before Erik went to Rome for the first time, that is, probably 1098. See Carsten Breengaard, *Muren om Israels Hus: Regnum og sacerdotium i Danmark 1050–1170* (Copenhagen: Gad, 1982), p. 173. They succeeded in conquering Rügen which was subjected to Skjalm Hvide (Saxo, p. 337, lines 15–17). Before 1127, Rügen was made a Danish missionary field by papal decree (*DD* 1: II, no. 50). See also Robert Bartlett, 'The Conversion of a Pagan Society in the Middle Ages', *History*, 70 (1985), 185–201, where he does not mention this fact. The text of the decree itself is not known, but must have been drawn up before 1127 when Otto of Bamberg asked permission of the Danish Archbishop in Lund to mission in the area (*Danmarks Riges Breve: 789–1169*, ed. by C. A. Christensen, G. Hermansen, and H. Nielsen, Series 1, 7 vols (Copenhagen: Reitzel, 1975–90), II (1975), no. 50. This means that a possible date for the edict is the whole of the interval between the Danish subjugation of Rügen in 1098 and 1127. Maybe there is a direct connection between Erik's journey to Rome in 1098/99 and the edict. He most probably told the pope that he had conquered heathen Rügen. This placed Denmark in a strong position in political negotiations concerning secession from the archbishopric of Hamburg-Bremen, to whose missionary field Denmark had earlier belonged. Perhaps the first thoughts of crusade and war against the

was Christian, to say that Denmark stood apart from Europe. It is this perspective that has led me to re-examine the evidence from 1147 to 1169 in order to understand to what extent the crusading movement determined the relationship between Christians and non-Christians.

The Second Crusade

Paul Riant writes of the Danish participation in the Second Crusade that,

> Ingen Prædikanter havde modtaget det Hverv at henvende til disse Folk denne Kirkens Røst, som frembragte et saa stærkt Røre i Frankrig og Tydskland, kun nogle faa pavelige Breve vare henvendte til dem, og disse pavelige Skrivelser synes endogsaa at være uvidende om Skandinavernes brændende Iver efter at kjende de hellige Steder, hvorfor de indskrænke den Rolle, der overdrages de tre nordiske Riger, til nogle lidet bekjendte Tog i slavernes Skovegne.[12]

Riant makes two points here: Firstly, that the crusade was not preached in Denmark, and secondly that the Wendish crusade was inferior to the expedition to the East. However, I disagree with both these points: I believe the crusade was preached in Denmark, and the sources themselves do not give the impression that the Wendish crusade was considered less important than the Jerusalem expedition.

The Preaching of the Crusade

We are told by the sixteenth-century Danish historian Cornelius Hamsfort that a papal legate by the name of Hubaldus was in Denmark in 1146 preaching the

---

Wends occurred at this time. Nevertheless, it seems apparent that there is a connection between Erik's first visit to Rome, the mission, and the crusade. As early as 1108, a crusade against the Slavs was preached from Magdeburg, which the Danish king promised to support; see Peter Knoch, 'Kreuzzug und Siedlung: Studien zum Aufruf der Magdeburger Kirche von 1108', *Jahrbuch für die Geschichte Mittel- und Ostdeutschlands*, 23 (1974), 1–33 for a full discussion. The best edition of the sermon is printed in *Urkundenbuch des Erzstifts Magdeburg*, vol. I, *937–1192*, ed. by F. Israël and W. Möllenberg, Geschichtsquellen der Provinz Sachsen und des Freistaates Anhalt, Neue Reihe, 18 (Magdeburg: Selbstverlag der Landesgeschichtlichen Forschungsstelle, 1937), no. 193.

[12] Riant, *Skandinavernes Korstog og Andagtsreiser til Palæstina*, p. 372; 'no preacher had been given the task of conveying to the people this voice [i.e. the papal crusade encyclicals] of the Church which caused such a commotion in France and Germany, only a few papal letters were addressed to them and these papal writings also seem to be unaware of the Scandinavians' burning fervour to know the holy places, therefore they limited the role given to the three Nordic kingdoms to a few little known expeditions to the Slavic forests.'

crusade.[13] But in *Diplomatarium Danicum*, Hamsfort's date is brought into question by the fact that the only time anyone by the name of Hubaldus was absent from the Curia was from 1144 to 1145, and the legatine journey is thus dated to this period.[14] In 1929, the German historian Walter Ohnsorge found a gap in the signatures of Hubaldus of Sancti Crucis at the Curia between 6 June 1146 and December 1146.[15] This means that the now lost source of which Hamsfort knew must be taken as evidence of the actual time of the papal legation. The German historian Hans-Dietrich Kahl is therefore wrong in saying that there was a papal legate in Denmark in 1147 preaching the crusade.[16] Kahl refers to Virginia Berry who in turn refers to Riant.[17] The papal legation to Denmark should be seen in the context of the crusading bull of Eugenius III, *Quantum preadecessores*, from 1 March 1146[18] and the public preaching in Vezelay on 31 March that same year.[19]

---

[13] *Chronologia Secunda*, *SRD*, I (1772), p. 274; see also *Scriptores Minores Historiæ Danicæ Medii Ævi* (hereafter *SM*), ed. by M. Cl. Gertz, 2 vols (Copenhagen: Gad, 1917–22), I (1917), 10, n. 1. On Cornelius Hamsfort (the Younger), see *Dansk biografisk leksikon*, ed. by Sv. Cedergreen Bech, 3rd edn, 16 vols (Copenhagen: Gyldendal, 1979–84), V (1980), 535–36; *Monumenta Historiæ Danicæ*, ed. by H. Rørdam, First series, 2 vols (Copenhagen: Thieles bogtrykkeri, 1873–75), I (1873), 663–721; and Walter Ohnsorge, *Päpstliche und gegenpäpstliche Legaten in Deutschland und Skandinavien 1159–1181*, Historische Studien, 188 (Berlin: Ebering, 1929), p. 104, n. 1.

[14] *DD* 1: II, no. 86/6; P. Jaffé, *Regesta Pontificum Romanorum*, 2 vols (Graz: Akademische Druck- und Verlagsanstalt, 1956), II, 1 and 20. The Danish historian, Hans Olrik, goes as far as to say that this information is 'en vilkårlig gisning' ('an arbitrary guess'); see Hans Olrik, *Konge og Præstestand i den danske Middelalder*, 2 vols (Copenhagen: Gad, 1892–95), II (1895), 197.

[15] Ohnsorge, *Päpstliche und gegenpäpstliche Legaten*, p. 104, n. 1.

[16] H.-D. Kahl, 'Wie kam es 1147 zum "Wendenkreuzzug"?', in *Europa Slavica – Europa Orientalis: Festschrift für Herbert Ludat zum 70. Geburtstag*, ed. by K.-D. Grothusen and others (Berlin: Duncher & Humblot, 1980), pp. 286–96.

[17] V. G. Berry, 'The Second Crusade', in *A History of the Crusades*, ed. by K. M. Setton, 6 vols (Philadelphia: University of Pennsylvania Press, 1958–89), I (1958), 463–512 (p. 481); Riant, *Skandinavernes Korstog og Andagtsreiser til Palæstina*, p. 311.

[18] Erich Caspar, 'Die Kreuzzugsbulle Eugens III.', *Neues Archiv der Gesellschaft für Ältere Deutsche Geschichtskunde*, 45 (1924), 285–305. For a slightly altered version of the bull of 1 December 1145, see Jaffé, *Regesta Pontificum Romanorum*, no. 8796; *Patrologiae cursus completus, Series Latina* (hereafter *PL*), ed. by J. P. Migne, 221 vols (Paris: Garnier, 1044–65), CLXXX (1862), cols 1064–65; *Ottonis et Rahewini Gesta Friderici I. Imperatores*, ed. by G. Waitz, MGH, SS rer. Ger., 46 (Hanover: Hahn, 1978), pp. 55–57.

[19] See Giles Constable, 'The Second Crusade as Seen by Contemporaries', *Traditio*, 9 (1953), 213–79 (pp. 247–48). Hamsfort knew of some now lost collections of letters from Sorø and Odense: see Ellen Jørgensen, *Historieforskning og Historieskrivning i Danmark indtil Aar 1800* (Copenhagen: Bianco Luno, 1931), pp. 53 and 111; *Monumenta Historiæ Danicæ*, ed. by H. Rørdam, Second series, 2 vols (Copenhagen: Gad, 1884–87), II (1887), 460

The Crusade as a Designation for a Christian War on Every Front from 1147

Riant's perception of the Wendish crusade and the subsequent expeditions as playing a limited role in the crusading movement is wrong, both when viewed in the light of the war in the borderlands of Latin Christendom and when considering the contemporary view of the Second Crusade. For instance, the German chronicler Helmold writing around 1167, does not think of the Wendish crusade as being less important than those to the Holy Land. He writes that the leaders of the crusade agreed to split into three groups: one would go to the Holy Land, one to Spain, and one to Wendland, but he talks of the expedition as one undertaking.[20] In the light of the papal bull of Eugenius III, *Divini dispensatione*,[21] which authorizes this idea, and the accompanying letter from Bernard of Clairvaux,[22] it is obvious that from 1147 the crusade was considered and planned not just as a campaign against the Saracens/Muslims, but as a general Christian offensive against all non-Christians and this is the background for analysing the Wendish expeditions.[23]

---

and 517; *Repertorium diplomaticum regni Danici mediaevalis*, ed. by K. Erslev, 13 vols (Copenhagen: Gad, 1894–1939), IV (1906–12), 120–21, where the archive of the monastery of St Knud in Odense is suggested as one of Hamsfort's sources and the dating by Hamsfort is accepted without further comment by the editors. But note the inconsistency in *Repertorium diplomaticum regni Danici mediaevalis*, ed. by Erslev, I (1894–95), 3. In order to argue against Hamsfort's date, one would have to argue that he made a scribal error. Hamsfort's dating is also accepted by Walter Seegrün, *Das Papsttum und Skandinavien bis zur Vollendung der nordischen Kirchenorganisation 1164* (Neumünster: Wachholtz, 1967), p. 143.

[20] 'Visum autem fuit auctoribus expedicionis partem exercitus unam destinari in partes orientis, alteram in Hyspaniam, terciam vero ad Slavos, qui iuxta nos habitant': Helmold, *Helmoldi Presbyteri Bozoviensis Cronica Slavorum*, ed. by Bernhard Schmeidler, MGH, SS rer. Ger., 32, 3rd edn (Hanover: Hahn, 1937), p. 115. See also Constable, 'The Second Crusade as Seen by Contemporaries', p. 223 and n. 53, where this is used to counter Riant's view that Helmold 'skjelner fuldkomment mellem de tre samtidige Korstog' ('completely distinguishes between the three contemporary crusades'), in Riant, *Skandinavernes Korstog og Andagtsreiser til Palæstina*, p. 311, n. 1.

[21] *Meklenburgisches Urkundenbuch*, ed. by Dr. Wigger and others, 24 vols (Schwerin: Verein für Mecklenburgisches Geschichte und Alterthumskunde, 1863–1913), I (1863), no. 44; *PL*, CLXXX (1862), cols 1203–04; Jaffé, *Regesta Pontificum Romanorum*, no. 9017.

[22] *PL*, CLXXXII (repr. 1879), cols 651–52 (Epist. 457). As to the eschatological ideas of this letter, see H.-D. Kahl, '"... Auszujäten von der Erde die Feinde des Christennamens ...": Der Plan zum "Wendenkreuzzug" von 1147 als Umsetzung sibyllinischer Eschatologie', *Jahrbuch für die Geschichte Mittel- und Ostdeutschlands*, 39 (1990), 133–60.

[23] It seems that these letters are the basis for Saxo's description of the events of 1147: 'Singule autem Catholicorum provinciæ confinem sibi barbariem incessere iubebantur. Ne ergo Dani privatæ militiæ rebus publicæ religionis officia detrectarent, sumptis acræ peregrinationis insignibus, imperium amplectuntur', in Saxo, p. 376, lines 25–27. He places this just after

The Wendish Wars of Valdemar I the Great

In 1157, the civil war which had plagued Denmark came to an end when Valdemar
was chosen as sole king of the Danish realm. But the civil war does not seem to have
lessened enthusiasm for the religious wars against the Wends; for example, in 1136
Erik II Emune conquered Rügen and Christianized its inhabitants.[24] Despite this
raids by the Wends on Denmark had escalated during the civil war,[25] and one of Valdemar's very first moves was to try to put a stop to these. Together with Bishop
Absalon of Roskilde he started to muster his fleet to attack the inhabitants of the
southern island of Falster, just north of the area inhabited by the Wends, because he
was told that the people of Falster had betrayed him by supporting the Wends. According to Saxo, this was a grave lie, and by divine providence first Valdemar then
Absalon was struck by illness so they could not carry out this attack. This apparently
made them come to their senses and they abandoned the civil war in order to fight
with great zeal the real enemies of the realm, the pagans.[26] The second time Valdemar mustered his fleet for an expedition against the Wends, probably in 1159, was in
Lund. Initially, Archbishop Eskil was not very supportive, but according to Saxo
when he learned the true intentions of the king, he went so far as to excommunicate
everyone who would not follow Valdemar.[27]

Did Archbishop Eskil Excommunicate Those Who Would Not
Participate?

Saxo's account of events is very interesting. First, God hinders the king in fighting
an unjust war; then the archbishop excommunicates those who would not follow the

King Erik III the Lame's death and from the context it is obvious that he means the year 1147.
This is identical to the content of these letters, which were widely disseminated; see Constable, 'The Second Crusade as Seen by Contemporaries', p. 223, n. 53. There is also no doubt
that the annalist from Magdeburg had Bernard of Clairvaux's letter (Epist. 457) at his disposal. Compare: 'ut eos [paganos] aut christiane religioni subderet, aut Deo auxiliante omnino de-
leret' (*Annales Magdeburgenses*, ed. by Pertz, p. 188) with 'hostes crucis Christi [. . .] donec,
Deo auxiliante, aut ritus ipse, aut natio deleatur' (Bernard in *PL*, CLXXXII (repr. 1879), col.
652). Cf. also Kahl, 'Auszujäten von der Erde', pp. 139–40, with Friedrich Lotter, 'The Crusading Idea and the Conquest of the Region East of the Elbe', in *Medieval Frontier Societies*,
ed. by Robert Bartlett and others (Oxford: Clarendon Press, 1989), pp. 267–306 (pp. 289–92).

[24] Saxo, p. 368, line 23 – p. 369, line 6. This fits with the missionary right of Denmark as
Rügen was a fief of the Polish duke; see Skyum-Nielsen, *Kvinde og slave*, p. 151.

[25] In 1151, Sven Grathe asked the German emperor for help against the Wends: 'Et principes vestros ad Slavorum depressionem excitate. Et super hecque digna videntur rescribite'
(*DD* 1: II, no. 103).

[26] *Sakses Danesaga*, trans. by Hans Olrik, 4 vols (Copenhagen: Gad, 1906–09), IV (1909), 10.

[27] Saxo, p. 416, lines 6–8.

king, after having made certain that Valdemar had the right intentions. The Latin reads as follows: 'Escillus [. . .] non solum consilium probavit, sed etiam, qui regi comites deessent, admodum exsecratus.'[28] Hans Olrik translates this as 'Eskil [. . .] ønskede alt ondt over hver den der ej slog Følge med Kongen'.[29] I think Olrik's translation of the word *exsecratus* is far too weak. This expedition has to be a war fought under some kind of ecclesiastical jurisdiction or, at the very least, blessing. Eric Christiansen says in the notes to his translation of Saxo, that, 'if *exsecratus* means threatened with excommunication or interdiction Eskil's use of this weapon was uncanonical, since failure to accompany the king on a raid overseas could hardly be reckoned a mortal sin; it is therefore more likely that he merely cursed them'.[30] But just as with Olrik's translation, the problem only arises if you assume that the term *expeditio* means a plundering raid. Saxo's own text makes much better sense if what was at issue was a crusade. The term *expeditio* does not necessarily exclude a crusade. In the Middle Ages, the word crusade was seldom used and not until late in the period. What we today describe as a crusade the sources call *iter*, *perigrinatio*, or *expeditio*.[31] Perhaps the aforementioned letter of Ademar of Le Puy to the people of the North who allegedly would not go on crusade could present us with the solution: 'Quod vere sint excommunicati, quicumque fuerint sancta cruce signati et remanserint apostatae facti, per eandem crucem sanctam et Sepulcrum Domini monemus, obsecramus, quatenus eos omnes anathematis gladio percutiatis, nisi nos sequantur et festinent [. . .] ubi nos sumus.'[32] In my view, there can be absolutely no doubt that *exsecratus* means excommunicated, simply because Valdemar was planning to go on a crusade against the Wends.

---

[28] Saxo, p. 416, lines 6–8.

[29] *Sakses Danesaga*, trans. by Olrik, IV, 11: 'Eskil wished all evil to everyone who would not follow the king.'

[30] Saxo Grammaticus, *Danorum Regum Heroumque Historia: Books X–XVI. The Text of the First Edition with Translation and Commentary in Three Volumes*, trans. by E. Christiansen, 3 vols (Oxford: British Archaeological Reports, 1980–81), III (1981), 778.

[31] Carl Erdmann, *The Origin of the Idea of Crusade*, trans. by M. W. Baldwin and W. Goddart (Princeton: Princeton University Press, 1977), p. xv; E.-D. Hehl, 'Was ist eigentlich ein Kreuzzug?', *Historische Zeitschrift*, 259 (1994), 297–336 (p. 298); Constable, 'The Second Crusade as Seen by Contemporaries', p. 237, n. 130.

[32] *Epistvlæ et chatæ ad historiam primi belli sacri*, ed. by Hagenmeyer, p. 142; 'In this way we encourage and beg of you by the true cross and Holy Sepulchre to come to us and strike everybody with the sword of interdiction if they will not follow us and hurry to where we are, because you know well, that those truly will be excommunicated (*excommunicati sint*), who had been blessed with the Holy Cross but stays at home as deviates from the faith in their act.'

Wetheman

Before Valdemar was crowned in 1157 and Absalon began his patrols of the Danish coastlines, the idea of a coastal defence force directed against the heathen Wends had been put into practice. Saxo tells us that a guild was formed in Roskilde on the word and command of Wetheman between 1151 and 1152, as a defence against the many pirate raids.[33] We do not know who this Wetheman was, but he was most probably a layperson. The guild has therefore been seen as a purely secular institution formed for the protection of the merchants of Roskilde in particular.[34] Saxo is our only source for the statutes. But the way in which Saxo expresses himself indicates that he was writing from an original source.[35] Before the brothers of the guild went to sea, they confessed their sins to a priest, and after enduring their penance they received holy communion as if they were on the threshold of death, because they believed their undertaking would be much more successful if they had obtained the mercy of God beforehand. Even the expedition itself had a very penitential character. They carried only a little food and slept with their hands on the oars. This strategy apparently resulted in many victories almost without the loss of a single drop of blood, even against numerically superior enemies. In this confraternity everybody was equal. When dividing up the booty, the oarsman did not receive any more than the private sailor. If Christian captives were discovered on conquered ships, they were given clothes and sent to their own lands, which makes Saxo rejoice: 'so good were they towards their fellow countrymen'. Were the brothers of the confraternity lacking funds, Saxo writes, the citizens of Roskilde shared expenses in return for half the booty the confraternity won.[36] After having won a lot of supporters in Roskilde, the movement spread to the rural population and found support throughout almost all of Sjælland. All these passages are ignored by Niels Lund in his doctoral thesis on the *leding*[37] — that is, the military organization in Denmark, the Latin equivalent being *expeditio*. He only reports Saxo's statement that the confraternity had the right to take a man's ship without his approval, in return for

---

[33] The dating is established from Saxo's chronology which places it between Knud V Magnussen's defeat at the hands of Sven Grathe at Viborg in 1151, and Knud's journey to Frederick I Barbarossa in 1152. Saxo seems at this point in his story to be very well informed and have a lot of sources at his disposal. See Michael H. Gelting, 'Kansleren Radulfs to bispevielser: En undersøgelse af Saxos skildring af ærkebispe- og pavestriden 1159–1162', *Historisk Tidsskrift*, 80 (1980), 325–36 (pp. 335–36). There is then no need to date it to 1160 as Riant does (Riant, *Skandinavernes Korstog og Andagtsreiser til Palæstina*, p. 384).

[34] Christiansen, *The Northern Crusades*, p. 15; Lund, *Lið, leding og landeværn*, p. 223; Skyum-Nielsen, *Kvinde og slave*, pp. 150–51.

[35] Saxo, p. 383, lines 37–39. See also Riant, *Skandinavernes Korstog og Andagtsreiser til Palæstina*, p. 384.

[36] Saxo, p. 383, line 39 – p. 384, line 1.

[37] Lund, *Lið, leding og landeværn*.

an eighth of the booty. Lund draws two conclusions from this: 'Her ser man dels, hvorledes den menige befolkning støtter et privat initiativ til forsvar omtrent på samme måde, som man søttede konger og høvdinge, når de havde det behov og arbejdede for et formål, man fandt nyttligt, dels hvorledes det var muligt for en privatmand, Vethemans baggrund er ukendt, at rejse en militær styrke og gå i aktion med den.'[38] But no explanation is given for how Wetheman could succeed. I think the explanation not just for the possible existence of a military community under the command of a privateer, but also for its huge support among the general population, is to be found in the clearly religious nature of the confraternity. But the religious aspects have hitherto been totally overlooked in Danish historiography.[39] Wetheman also became a leading figure in the Wendish wars of Valdemar and Absalon. For instance, Valdemar makes Wetheman leader in the city of Volgast after its surrender to the king.

Belchite

Saxo is the only source that mentions the confraternity of Wetheman. But what really makes it interesting is the striking parallels to similar institutions in the borderlands of Latin Christendom. In 1122 in Saragossa a confraternity was formed for the defence of Christians, the oppression of Muslims, and the liberty of the Holy Church.[40]

---

[38] Lund, *Lið, leding og landeværn*, p. 223; 'Here you can see, partly how the population supports a private defence initiative, just as kings and chiefs were supported in times of need and when they worked for a useful purpose, and partly how it was possible for a privateer, the background of Wetheman is unknown, to raise a military force and go into action with it'.

[39] Skyum-Nielsen (*Kvinde og slave*, p. 151) questions whether all Christians were released when Wendish ships were captured. He thinks only people from Sjælland and not from other parts of the country were treated in this way. They, on the other hand, were sold as slaves and 'har hørt ind under det rov i Venderland, der skulle dække lagets udgifter, og levende arbejdskraft var så godt som rede penge' ('probably comprised part of the booty from the land of the Wends which was to cover the expenses of the guild, and living manpower was as good as ready cash'). I do not see any reason to read Saxo's text in this way. Saxo writes 'Christianos, quos expugnata classe captivos repererant, amictu donatos ad propria dimittibant' (Saxo, p. 384, lines 13–14). If they were Christians they were sent home. *Ad propria* has to relate to *christianos* and not to the people who send them away. Perhaps Skyum-Nielsen based his interpretation on the following line, which reads 'Tanta iis in conterraneos humanitas erat' (Saxo, p. 384, line 15). It is obvious that Saxo uses this phrase *conterraneos* in a more narrow regional sense, and he hereby refers to the fellow countrymen of the guild as people from Sjælland. But I think this interpretation of the text is much too harsh and does not agree with the preceding statement that all Christians will be sent home 'to their own'. See Saxo Grammaticus, *Danorum Regum Heroumque Historia*, trans. by Christiansen, III, 737–39 (p. 738).

[40] Peter Rassow, 'La Cofradía de Belchite', *Anuario del Derecho Español*, 3 (1926), 200–26 (p. 224); Elaine Lourie, 'The Confraternity of Belchite, the Ribat and the Temple', *Viator*,

The confraternity was confirmed in 1136 by King Alfonso I of Aragon in the Spanish town Belchite.[41] There had been war between Christians and Muslims on the Iberian peninsula for centuries. From the beginning of the crusading period, this fight was compared with the crusade to Jerusalem. Urban II had made the battle for the restoration of the church of Tarragona equivalent to the liberation of the Eastern Church. In this fight, it was also possible to gain salvation: 'neque enim virtutis est alibi a saracenis christianos ervere, alibi christianos Saracenorum tyrannidi oppressionique exponere'.[42] The confraternity of Belchite was open to both secular and clerical members, and its primary aim was the defence of Christendom in a very troubled region.[43] The similarities between Wetheman's guild and the confraternity of Belchite are striking. First and foremost, they were both founded as defensive pre-

---

13 (1982), 159–76; Jonathan Riley-Smith, *What Were the Crusades?* (London: Macmillan, 1977), p. 24. For the importance of the creation of military confraternities in the struggle against the Muslims in Spain and the connection to the crusading movement, see L. J. McCrank, 'The Foundation of the Confraternity of Terragona by Archbishop Oleguer Bonestruga, 1126–1129', *Viator*, 9 (1978), 157–77. Compare also the confraternity from Monreal which is known from only one diploma dated 1128 printed in *Documentos para el estudio de la reconquista y repoblación del Valle del Ebro*, ed. by José Mª. Lacarra, 2 vols, Textos Medievales, 62–63 (Zaragoza: Anubar, 1982–85), I (1982), 182–84. Cf. Marcus Bull, *Knightly Piety and the Lay Response to the First Crusade: The Limousin and Gascony, c. 970–c. 1130* (Oxford: Clarendon Press, 1993), pp. 104–05.

[41] Rassow, 'La Cofradía de Belchite', pp. 200–20; A. Urbieto Arteta, 'La Creación de la Cofradía militar de Belchite', *Estudios de Edad Media de la Corona de Aragón*, 5 (1952), 427–34.

[42] P. Kehr, *Papsturkunden in Spanien: Vorarbeiten zur Hispania Pontificia, I. Katalonien*, Abhandlungen der Gesellschaft der Wissenschaften zu Göttingen, Philologisch-Historische Klasse, Neue Folge, 18.2 (Berlin: Weidmannsche Buchhandlung, 1926), pp. 286–87, where the letter is wrongly dated to 1089–91. Erdmann, *The Origin of the Idea of Crusade*, p. 317, n. 37, corrects this to between January 1096 and 29 July 1099. It was later more precisely dated to have been sent from Nîmes or St Gilles in July 1096. See A. Becker, *Papst Urban II. (1088–1099)*, Schriften der MGH, 19, 2 vols (Stuttgart: Hiersemann, 1964–88), II (1988), 347, n. 169, and I (1964), 228–30. In a letter to the Bishop of Huesca, Urban II wrote in 1098 that: 'Nostris siquidem diebus in Asia Turcos, in Europa Mauros Christianorum viribus debellavit' (*PL*, CLI (repr. 1881), col. 504C; see also Hehl, 'Was ist eigentlich ein Kreuzzug?', pp. 303–04). This was repeated by Pope Calixtus II in two letters: U. Robert, *Bullaire du Pape Calixte II, 1119–1124*, 2 vols (Paris: Imprimerie Nationale, 1891), I, 266–67 (no. 454), 'Omnibus enim in hac expeditione [to the defence of the Church in Spain] constanter militantibus eamdem peccatorum remissionem quam orientalis Ecclesiæ defensorimus fecimus' (Jaffé, *Regesta Pontificum Romanorum*, no. 7116); and p. 261, no. 449, where the First Lateran Council equates the pilgrimage to beating the 'gentem perfidam' both in Spain and Jerusalem (Jaffé, *Regesta Pontificum Romanorum*, no. 7111).

[43] On Spanish society, see Elaine Lourie, 'A Society Organized for War: Medieval Spain', *Past and Present*, 35 (1966), 54–76.

cautions, due to the daily threat of enemy assault. In Belchite, you could, according to the privilege, win the total remission of sins after having confessed with a pure heart, in the same way as if you had entered the life of a monk or hermit. Shorter periods of service would reward you with the same indulgence as the journey to Jerusalem. There were rules concerning the spiritual reward you would get from various forms of service, whether you gave money, sent a substitute, or offered weapons to the confraternity. The headquarters of the confraternity were the castle of Belchite or any other castle found suitable for the purpose. The war fought in the service of the confraternity was a commutation of the penance placed on you after you had confessed your sins.[44] Exactly the same thing applies to Wetheman's guild. Saxo says that before they put to sea, they confessed their sins to a priest and after they had done their penance, they enjoyed communion, as if they were about to die. When Saxo says they had already won the grace of God before battle, I think it means they had confessed their sins. This means that the penance was the expedition itself.[45] This explains their ascetic behaviour during the expeditions. The crusade was indeed itself a penitential act, and 'thus to enter Belchite and earn remission of

---

[44] At the council of Clermont, Urban II exchanged the participants' penance for the *iter* to Jerusalem, which was obviously thought of and conceived as a military expedition; see Robert Somerville, *The Councils of Urban II*, Annuarium Historiae Conciliorum, Supplementum I (Amsterdam: Hableert, 1972), pp. 74, 124, with n. 14. For Urban's letter to the congregation in Vallombrosa, see W. Wiederhold, 'Papsturkunden in Florenz', *Nachrichten von der Gesellschaft der Wissenschaften zu Göttingen: Philologisch-Historische Klasse*, 1901, 306–25 (pp. 313–14); *Papsturkunden für Kirchen im Heiligen Lande*, ed. by R. Hiestand, Abhandlungen der Akademie der Wissenschaften in Göttingen. Philologisch-Historische Klasse, Dritte Folge, 136, 3 vols (Göttingen: Vandenhoeck & Ruprecht, 1972–85), III (1985), pp. 88–89, no. 2. For the letter to Bologna and Flanders, see *Epistvlæ et chatæ ad historiam primi belli sacri*, ed. by Hagenmeyer, pp. 136–37, nos 2 and 3. Around the year 1100, penitential practice was in a transitional period; see K. Müller, 'Der Umschwung in der Lehre von der Busse während des 12. Jahrhunderts', in *Theologische Abhandlungen, Carl von Weizsäcker zu seinem siebzigsten Geburtstag 11. Dezember 1892 gewidmet*, ed. by Adolf Harnack and others (Freiburg: Akademische Verlagsbuchhandlung, 1892), pp. 287–320. Therefore the indulgence theology that did not develop until the twelfth century cannot form the background to what Urban promised in 1095. The controversy in the letters to Flanders and Bologna is only apparent because a total remission of penance at that time was the same as the later plenary indulgence, that is, the total remission of the temporal punishment due to sin. For an important discussion, see H. E. J. Cowdrey, 'Bishop Ermenfrid of Sion and the Penitential Ordinance Following the Battle of Hastings', *Journal of Ecclesiastical History*, 20 (1969), 225–42 (pp. 236–40); and Bull, *Knightly Piety*, pp. 166–71, for an important discussion. It seems to me that Mayer misses this fundamental point: H. E. Mayer, *The Crusades*, trans. by J. Gillingham (Oxford: Oxford University Press, 1990), pp. 23–37 and n. 15, pp. 293–95.

[45] 'Navigationem orsuri apud sacerdotes præteritæ vitæ piacula deplorabant eorumque religiosa animadversione puniti perinde ac statim decessuri divina altaris libamenta sumebant, cuncta prosperius cessura rati, si rite Deum ante bella placassent' (Saxo, p. 384, lines 1–4).

penance was, prima facie, very similar to entering a monastery for the same purpose'.[46] This argument holds good for temporary service as well, since the same pious motivation lay behind it.[47] A similar view seems to have applied to Wetheman. In my opinion, nothing contradicts the possibility of similar arrangements concerning temporary or permanent service. Eric Christiansen says that Wetheman disappeared from the scene rather quickly, but we are told that Wetheman and Esben Snare, a Danish noble, were patrolling the seas to defend the country after 1171, that is, for more than twenty years in total.[48] It seems reasonable that Wetheman had a permanent contingent of troops around him which was supplemented by additional men during larger expeditions or crusades. The absence of later references to Wetheman may perhaps be connected with the introduction of the military orders, which could, as in the case of Belchite, have supplanted the guild.[49] The Knights of St John came to Denmark under the protection of Valdemar I c. 1160, and in the words of Skyum-Nielsen 'har vel spillet en rolle i de mange danske strids- og korstog'.[50] I think there is a very direct parallel between Wetheman and Belchite, and in my opinion there is no doubt that the crusading movement formed the background to both movements. This must also be taken as evidence of crusading fervour in the Danish populace at large.

The Use of Piratica by Saxo

One of the reasons for the obvious misinterpretation of Wetheman's guild or confraternity in Danish historiography is an erroneous translation of the guild's Latin designation piratica, which appears both as a noun and an adjective. Niels Lund

---

[46] Lourie, 'The Confraternity', p. 168.

[47] See Bull, Knightly Piety and the Lay Response to the First Crusade, pp. 115–203. He argues on page 167 that the benefaction of churches and crusades were 'intimately, even organically linked'. The same thing applies to temporary service in a religious confraternity.

[48] Saxo Grammaticus, Danorum Regum Heroumque Historia, trans. by Christiansen, II, 737; Saxo, p. 500, lines 34–36.

[49] Lourie, 'The Confraternity', pp. 172–74. See also A. J. Forey, 'The Military Orders and the Spanish Reconquest in the Twelfth and Thirteenth Centuries', Traditio, 40 (1984), 197–234. Cf. also the development of the order's activities in the Holy Land in Jonathan Riley-Smith, The Knights of St John in Jerusalem and Cyprus c. 1050–1310, A History of the Order of St. John of Jerusalem, 1 (London: Macmillan, 1967), pp. 60–84. There is evidence that the order had absorbed whole confraternities: Riley-Smith, The Knights of St John, pp. 242–46 (p. 243).

[50] Skyum-Nielsen, Kvinde og slave, pp. 128–29; 'probably played a role in the many Danish wars and crusades'. The first mention of the order in Denmark appears in a charter dated 1164–78 (DD I: 2, no. 163, pp. 308–10; see also DD I: 2, nos 147 and 162, pp. 274–75 and 305–08). For the coming of the Hospital to Denmark, see E. Reitzel-Nielsen, Johanniterordenens historie med særligt henblik på de nordiske lande, 3 vols (Copenhagen: Reitzel, 1984–91), I (1984), 142–50.

translates this as 'fribytterlag' (freebooter guild).[51] Riant translates this in roughly the same way as 'Vikingers Gilde' (Guild of Vikings).[52] Olrik also translated *piratica* with 'Viking' (Viking).[53] I think the translation 'Viking' gives a rather distorted picture of what Saxo actually meant by this phrase. 'Viking' has connotations of wild plundering raids up the Seine or the burning down of monasteries. It seems strange that this designation should be given to a religious undertaking such as Wetheman's guild, which participated in the defence of Denmark and joined Absalon and Valdemar on crusade. Absalon himself is designated as *pirata*: 'Qui mox antistes creatus non minus piratam se quam pontificem gessit.'[54] Saxo's description of Absalon is of course well known, but I would like to repeat some of it because I think it takes on an almost entirely new meaning in the light of the crusading movement. According to Saxo, Absalon often neglected the farms of the bishop's palace while fighting the Wends in the first years of his episcopate.[55] He brought peace to the country, both by patrolling the coasts and with his eloquence at political assemblies, which prevented many a violent confrontation. This is why Saxo says he was as much the father of the homeland as a bishop, and was outstanding as the glorious servant of both the military and religion.[56] Niels Lund does not think there is anything peculiar about translating *pirata* with Viking in his discussion of Saxo's use of the term, because there is nothing pejorative about it, he says. Saxo used the same word to describe many good people in his history, among others Wetheman.[57] This, I think, stems from the general idea in Danish historiography of what a crusade is and especially of what Absalon's expeditions were: 'Hvis brugen af dette ord fortæller os noget, så antyder det snarest, at man i samtiden opfattede kampen mod venderne som en fortsættelse af de gode gammeldags vikingetog, hvor man drog mod fremmede strande og hjembragte bytte i form af sølv, guld og trælle.'[58] But Saxo does not draw

---

[51] Lund, *Lið, leding og landeværn*, p. 223.

[52] Riant, *Skandinavernes Korstog og Andagtsreiser til Palæstina*, p. 384, n. 2.

[53] For example, Saxo on Wetheman during the first of Valdemar's Wendish raids in 1158 writes that he was 'piraticæ operibus clarum'. Olrik translates this as 'den navnkundige Viking' ('the renowned Viking'), in *Sakses Danesaga*, trans. by Olrik, IV, 18.

[54] Saxo, p. 413, line 25.

[55] Saxo, p. 413, lines 28–30.

[56] 'Itaque non minus patriæ parentem quam pontificem egit, militiæ et religionis sociato fulgore conspicuus' (Saxo, p. 413, lines 38–39).

[57] Lund, *Lið, leding og landeværn*, p. 226.

[58] Niels Lund, 'Absalon som kriger og politiker', in *Absalon, fædrelandets fader*, ed. by F. Birkebæk and others (Roskilde: Roskilde Museums Forlag, 1996), pp. 73–90 (p. 74); 'If the use of this word tells us anything, it most likely suggests that this age saw the expeditions against the Wends as a continuation of the good old Viking-raids on foreign shores, and the bringing back of lots of booty in the shape of gold, silver and slaves'; Lund, *Lið, ledning og landeværn*, pp. 226–27, where he builds on Skyum-Nielsen's perception of the Wendish wars as Valdemar's and Absalon's plundering raids in the south.

this picture, neither of Wetheman as I have tried to show above, nor of Absalon's raids against the Wends. At the same time as telling us of Absalon's fight for the faith at the expense of the farms of the bishop's palace, Saxo says that Absalon did not take much interest in caring for the faith at home when it was at stake abroad. He then gives an explanation of Absalon's motives which does not suggest pirate or Viking raids at all: 'Det er jo ogsaa fuld saa god en Gudsdyrkelse at slaa Troens Fjender paa Flugt som at tage Vare paa Kirketjenesten.'[59]

Piratica is used by Saxo both to designate those fighting for the faith and those fighting against it. The plundering raids of the Wends are called *piraticae* as well.[60] But, as I have shown, this latter meaning of the word cannot be used to describe, for example, Wetheman or Absalon. When Saxo mentions Wetheman's guild, it is called a *piratica*, but shortly afterwards it is the Wendish ships which are called *piraticae*, which Olrik translates as 'Vikingesnækker' (Viking ships).[61] Here we see the same word used for two very different things — Christian confraternity and its enemies.[62] Thus, the word *piratica* has no positive or negative value. It is a technical term which is used about preparing a warship and going into battle with it. It says nothing about the character of the expedition, which is determined by the intentions behind arming the ship and what was done on the raid.[63] I therefore completely agree with Niels Lund when he says there is nothing pejorative about the term, although I work from a totally different presupposition — that a translation is dependent on one's perspective. For too long, a fundamental concept in Danish historiography has been that the crusading movement was non-existent in the North — or at most, it was a

---

[59] Saxo, p. 413, lines 26–28. *Sakses Danesaga*, trans. by Olrik, IV, p. 6: 'It is every bit as good to worship by defeating the enemies of the faith, as it is to attend to the church services'.

[60] For example, Saxo, p. 384, lines 15–17.

[61] *Sakses Danesaga*, trans. by Olrik, III, 198.

[62] A striking parallel to this apparent contradiction is found in Albert of Aachen: 'Illi se christianiae professionis milites esse responderunt, a Flandria et ab Antverpia et Frisia ceterisque partibus Galliae se venisse fatentes, et pirates annis octo usque ad hanc diem se fuisse' (Albert of Aachen, *RHC*, IV, p. 348F). Here we see the *milites christianae professionis* referring to themselves as *pirates*. In J. Johrendt, '"Milites" und "Militia" im 11. Jahrhundert: Untersuchung zur Frühgeschichte des Rittertums in Frankreich und Deutschland' (unpublished doctoral thesis, University of Erlangen-Nuremberg, 1971), p. 37, the same interpretation as in Danish historiography is made, viz. as 'Seeräuber': 'Diese Ritter hatten Geschmack am Seeraub gefunden und betrieben ihn als gutgehenden Erwerb. Wenn sich nun diese Seepiraten auf den Zug gegen Jerusalem einlassen, so bestimmt nicht aus religiösen Motiven, sondern aus Abendteuer- und Beutelust' ('These knights had discovered a taste for piracy and pursued it as a thriving business. If these pirates did now get involved in the crusade against Jerusalem, then it was definitely not because of religious motives, but rather thirst for adventure and booty'). But again, I do not think this implies that they were not crusaders, at least not in their own interpretation.

[63] This is even more apparent in the above example from Albert of Aachen.

cloak for purely economic or political motives. I have shown that there is no reason to think of the wars and expeditions of Valdemar and Absalon against the Wends between 1157 and 1169 as anything other than originating in the crusading movement. This also fits much better with Saxo's description, which explicitly says that by beating the enemies of the faith, God is served just as well as during a church service.

The Slavs had not been crushed in 1147 and they continued to plunder the Danish coasts during the civil war when Sven Grathe asked the German emperor Lothar for help against the Wends. The battle continued in the light of the privileges given in 1147, at a time when the enemies of God had not been beaten. This is the background against which the expeditions against the Wends should be seen — in the light and not in the shadow of the events of 1147, as Christiansen says.[64] This is why Archbishop Eskil took such great care in ensuring that King Valdemar fought the Wends with the right intentions. Where we have written evidence of the preaching of the crusade in Denmark, it is precisely those ships which were armed for participation in the Third Crusade that are called *piraticis naves* in *De profectione Danorum in Hierosolymam*.[65] I simply cannot imagine that this expedition was conceived of as a direct continuation of the plundering raids of the Viking Age, and to translate these ships as pirate ships as Skyum-Nielsen does is plainly misleading.[66]

Conclusion

From the last quarter of the eleventh century, Denmark was part of the religious and political world of Latin Christian Europe. From the very beginning, therefore, the crusading movement influenced Danish society at large as it did everywhere else in Europe, and it came to play an integral part in the conflict with the surrounding heathen neighbours of the Danish realm. This has hitherto not been acknowledged by Danish historians. In Danish historiography, the crusading movement has been looked upon as a mere cloak for political motives. This is even more so the case in the treatment of the wars fought by the Danish Church and royal power against the heathen Wends, especially during the reign of Valdemar I the Great and Bishop Absalon. This is due to the assumption by Danish historians that the crusading movement was basically non-existent in Denmark and, at most, nothing more than foreign policy on behalf of the kingdom of Denmark. But now this picture has to be changed. It seems that the crusading movement formed the background against which the Wendish wars should be seen. An indication of the extent to which the crusading ideals had been absorbed into Danish society can be seen in the formation of a religious confraternity, Wetheman's Guild, which has some close parallels on the

---

[64] Christiansen, *The Northern Crusades*, pp. 62–63.

[65] 'Ut piraticis constructis navibus, quas "sneckas" appellamus' : *SM*, II, 468.

[66] Skyum-Nielsen, *Kvinde og slave*, p. 223.

Iberian peninsula. The institutionalization of the crusading movement followed the same pattern as in another border society of Latin Christendom, that is, Belchite. When King Valdemar died in 1182 he had a lead funeral plate buried next to his head which proclaims the greatest achievements of the king by which he wanted to be remembered and which gives a clear impression of a crusader king: 'Hic iacet Danorum Rex primus Sclanorum expugnator et dominator, patrie liberator, pacis conseruator. Qui filius sancti Kanuti Rugianos expugnauit et ad fidem Christi primus conuertit.'[67]

---

[67] *SM*, II, 87. See Kurt Villads Jensen, 'Denmark and the Second Crusade: The Formation of a Crusader state?', in *The Second Crusade: Scope and Consequences*, ed. by J. Phillips and M. Hoch (forthcoming). I would like to thank Kurt Villads Jensen for letting me see a copy of his article prior to publication.

The Adaptation of an Established European Visual Language in Denmark from the Twelfth to Fourteenth Centuries

AXEL BOLVIG

It is worth questioning the traditional historical explanation of art and culture, of artistic influence and cultural relationships. Traditional research on the subject is bound to the nineteenth century's idealistic and universalist conception of art and culture in accordance with a Kantian view of aesthetic value.[1] Historians have often applied an imperialistic way of thinking, which is expressed by the frequent use of a centre-periphery model. Finally, historical explanation implicitly accepts the concept that artistic and cultural movements go from an elitist top slowly downwards to the broad illiterate and uneducated lower classes.[2]

Nevertheless, the twentieth century witnessed a fundamental change in the conception of art and architecture. Since the Dadaist movement, art has often been declared dead which as a result entails the relegation of artistic production from its lofty peak to participate in the formation of society.[3] The decline of colonial empires has turned the centre-periphery notion upside down. We are all aware that some of the most influential cultural movements, such as movies, tango, cartoons, jazz, and rock music, have their beginnings in society's lowest classes, ultimately to be accepted by all classes, but mostly still being carried out by non-elitist classes. Being historians of this century, we have to realize that the art and architecture of the past

---

[1] Keith Moxey, *The Practice of Theory: Poststructuralism, Cultural Politics and Art History* (Ithaca: Cornell University Press, 1994), pp. 67–78.

[2] Axel Bolvig, 'Ars longa – vita brevis', *Medium Aevum Quotidianum*, 39 (1998), 9–20 (p. 12).

[3] Georges Didi-Huberman, *Devant l'image: Question posée aux fins d'une histoire de l'art* (Paris: Minuit, 1990), pp. 54–63.

might have functioned in society's discourse as influential forces that never lived a lofty life far away from people's dirty and beautiful daily life.[4]

Cultural influence has seldom been seen as an active political force in itself. Concerning the Middle Ages, it is a widespread notion among historians that cultural influence follows closely on the heels of economic and political relationships. But why has art to follow trade; why not the other way round?

It is also generally assumed that cultural and artistic influence is a matter of unproblematic acceptance by the recipients. But was import of art and architecture universally accepted in the Middle Ages? Were new ideas and forms really imported to meet a widespread need for aesthetic renovation? Is artistic migration only a matter of an unavoidable movement from the qualified to the unqualified, or is it perhaps a result of the export of ideology as part of a policy? And finally, is it reasonable to think of cultural impact only in terms of a one-way flow from so-called centres to so-called peripheries? Or do we not have to include reciprocity in cultural matters? We hear about iconoclasm, which is a reaction against the development of established art, at certain times and under certain conditions. It is impossible to think that everyone accepted without resistance an art and architecture that some groups introduced, used, and exposed.

I will try to outline new attitudes towards the interpretation and explanation of Romanesque art and architecture in Denmark during the twelfth and thirteenth centuries. Looking at Denmark's relations with the rest of medieval Europe, the view that the country belonged to the periphery of Europe has become set in stone. According to the traditional centre-periphery explanation, the Danes were the recipients of art and culture from the centres in Northern France, Germany, and England. It was a one-way communication.

Today (art) historians do not entirely accept a centre-periphery model.[5] Increased and better access to published material tends to make specific centres disappear. The establishment of databases with written and visual source material on the Internet undermines any concept of centres and dependant peripheries. We have to revise the very many traditional attempts to find connections between works of art and architecture in Denmark and in specific centres of neighbouring countries. We must look at cultural activities, first in a European, then in a local perspective, but never in a national one. The construction of the Web is in a way very similar to medieval cultural interrelationships. The roads in the Middle Ages never went directly from one place to another.

In this new light, the cultural interrelationship between Denmark and other European countries will be discussed. The Danes, or more correctly, the freeborn landowning elite in Denmark, accepted Christianity in the tenth and eleventh centuries.

---

[4] Norman Bryson, 'Semiology and visual interpretation', in *Visual Theory: Painting and Interpretation*, ed. by N. Bryson, M. A. Holly, and K. Moxey (Cambridge: Polity Press, 1989), pp. 61–73.

[5] Bolvig, 'Ars longa – vita brevis', pp. 12–14.

They used Christian art and architecture in a very self-confident way. The Romanesque art of the period fitted well with the ideology of the elitist class. Unfortunately, we do not possess written source material to tell us how other classes reacted to this new art and architecture. A likely possibility is that they were only exposed to Romanesque art at a distance. They were not meant to be the recipients of European Christian art and maybe even not to the Christian faith in its totality. Perhaps the lower classes did not care about a Christian ideology, which reflected the values of the landowning rulers.[6] It is even unthinkable to imagine that the magnates unanimously stood behind the introduction of religious institutions.[7] Later in this essay it will be shown that Romanesque art was used differently in western and eastern Denmark respectively.

Romanesque art in Denmark looked exactly like art in all other places of Europe, but we do not know if it was perceived in the same way by the newly Christianized population.[8] Did the iconographic content travel unchanged from the long-Christianized populations of Europe to the Danes, where pagan imagery was not yet entirely forgotten? It is one thing to import and use a fully developed artistic form, maybe executed by foreign artists, but how the content was perceived and understood is quite another thing. It is difficult to see whether influences during the Romanesque period went from Denmark southwards, and if so, what these influences were. Or did Danish influence simply expire with the end of the Viking Age?

In *Vita Anskarii*, we read that the Danish king allowed Ansgar to build a church in Hedeby, Schleswig. Upon hearing this news the merchants of Hamburg and Dorestad were pleased that they would now be able to visit the town without fear.[9] Without needing to trust this information, it indicates that the spread of architecture and religion might have been at the head of an economic expansion. This commercial aspect can be seen in terms of missionary work as a kind of cultural imperialism.

---

[6] Axel Bolvig, *Kirkekunstens storhedstid* (Copenhagen: Gyldendal, 1992), pp. 76–89; Axel Bolvig, *Wall Paintings in Danish Medieval Churches*, CD-ROM (Copenhagen: Department of History, University of Copenhagen, 1999).

[7] A written source reveals that at the beginning of twelfth century a rebellion headed by a magnate against priests took place. The idea behind the rebellion is unclear, and the information can only be used to indicate that the Danes did not make up a united public that unanimously accepted new cultural imprints. See 'Cronicon Roskildense', in *Scriptores Minores Historiæ Danicæ Medii Ævi*, ed. by M. Cl. Gertz, 2 vols (Copenhagen: Gad, 1917–22), I (1917), pp. 25–26.

[8] A plank from the wooden church at Hørning from about 1050 displays two kinds of decoration. The inside has a painted acanthus, a motif typical of Christian ornamentation, and the outside has a carved snake, typical of Viking ornamentation. It might indicate the presence of pre-Christian imagery outside the walls of the church at least.

[9] Rimbert, 'Vita Anskarii', in *Quellen des 9. und 11. Jahrhunderts zur Geschichte der Hamburgischen Kirche und des Reiches*, ed. by Werner Trillmich (Berlin: Rütten & Loening, 1961), pp. 3–133 (p. 24).

Figure 1. Ferslev Church, Jutland (twelfth century). Photo: A. Bolvig.

It is interesting to notice that once Christianized the elite in Denmark generally accepted and absorbed the new religious art and architecture quickly. The first churches were built in timber during the tenth and first half of the eleventh centuries. Timber represents the Nordic tradition of building in Denmark, but it may also suggest that the churches were not meant for eternity. The typical lifespan for these wooden buildings is a few decades, which is equal to the lifetime of a generation. Using wood might indicate that church building was considered a short-term investment, primarily intended to provide a burial place.[10]

In the second half of the eleventh century stone replaced wood as a building material. Stone — πέτρος — represents eternity. Maybe the change in building material was just due to the more important establishment of the religion, but it is interesting to note that to our knowledge stone was not introduced until after mankind had survived the crucial year 1000.

The typical material in western Denmark is ashlars of granite while in eastern Denmark ordinary raw stones of granite were used (figs 1 and 2). The squared cut blocks represented the ideal material for church building according to much written evidence. It is amusing to see that in eastern Denmark the raw stones were hidden behind plaster upon which lines were drawn in order to imitate a church built of ashlars.

The building material the Danes used to build their churches was stone that could be found locally, although volcanic tufa from the Rhine area was imported to the

---

[10] Bolvig, *Kirkekunstens storhedstid*, pp. 39–51

Figure 2. Slaglille Church, Sjælland (twelfth century). Photo: A. Bolvig.

south-western part of Denmark. This import is explained by the lack of appropriate building material in that part of Denmark, but it may also reflect the import of an architectural ideology. Unfortunately, we know nothing of how the Danes paid for this stone. Much money and energy was spent on the acquisition of building materials during this period.[11]

The difference in building material between eastern and western Denmark has been much debated.[12] In short, my opinion is that cutting stones was a job for freemen. The craft of masonry demanded a long apprenticeship. Law articles for stonemasons in England demanded freeborn apprentices in order to avoid a master taking his unfree servant back after having learnt the craft. And so it was probably the same in Denmark too.

The landowning elite in eastern Denmark was so small and exclusive that it could not recruit stonecutters and consequently underprivileged labourers had to collect

---

[11] Jean Gimpel, *Les Bâtisseurs de cathédrales* (Paris: Seuil, 1980), pp. 49–62 (in English as Jean Gimpel, *The Cathedral Builders*, trans. by Teresa Waugh (Salisbury: Russel, 1983)); Bolvig, *Kirkekunstens storhedstid*, pp. 52–75; Alain Erlande-Brandenburg, *Quand les cathé-drales étaient peintes* (Paris: Gallimard, 1997), pp. 104–09.

[12] See M. Mackeprang, *Vore Landsbykirker: En Oversigt*, 2nd edn (Copenhagen: Høst, 1944).

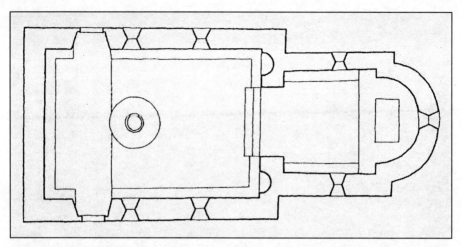

Figure 3. Groundplan of Butterup Church, Sjælland (twelfth century). *Strejflys over Danmarks bygningskultur,* ed. by Robert Egevang (Nationalmuseet, 1979), p. 74.

raw stones for building from the fields. In western Denmark, society consisted of a larger group of gentleman farmers who produced a surplus population from whom stonecutters could be recruited.

So the type of building material might indicate a differentiation in the freeborn classes. The same is the case concerning the size of the churches. This discussion demands research into the design of the buildings. A normal village church consisted of a chancel and a nave. The nave was centred around the baptismal font placed on a high podium in the middle. The west end of the nave had a special seating area for the patron of the church and his family. Along the northern and southern walls were built-in benches. These had room for fifty to sixty people and no more. Counted in very rough figures a normal parish consisted of four hundred to five hundred inhabitants of which only a few percent had a seat in the church. The arrangement of the interior thus excluded the vast majority of the population (figs 3 and 4).[13]

The elitism of the church is underlined by the special seating arrangement in the west end of some churches mainly found in eastern Denmark. The western part of the church was reserved for the church owner and his family. Architecturally this accommodation was accentuated at the expense of the rest of the nave. We find a very expressive example in Fjenneslev Church, Sjælland. Like many other eastern Danish churches it has twin towers which mark a church built by a magnate. Inside, a gallery was erected. It rests on two granite columns. Originally these columns probably came from Egypt and were used in Roman buildings before later being transported the long way from central or southern Europe to be used in the middle of the Danish island of Sjælland (fig. 5). Both the material and the arrangement are significant signs

---

[13] Bolvig, *Kirkekunstens storhedstid,* pp. 76–89.

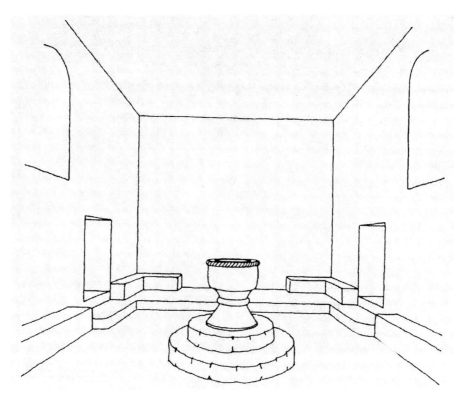

Figure 4. Schematic drawing of the nave of Blistrup Church, Sjælland
(twelfth century). Axel Bolvig, *Kirkekunstens storhedstid*
(Copenhagen: Gyldendal, 1992), p. 49.

of secular power expressed through a church building. The widespread and very old symbolism of the column as a sign of power was directly and physically imported and used by the church builder.

In the larger churches of western Denmark, we seldom find such architectural expressions. We do not have much evidence of special seating arrangements in the western part of the nave.

The interesting conclusion from an interpretation of church sizes is that the smaller ones, built from stone picked up in the fields, represent the elitist exclusive private chapels. The bigger churches, erected from impressive ashlars of granite, are the result of the joint efforts of a group of gentleman farmers who erected a building fit for housing their larger community.

All in all, the Danes adopted an established design of church building, but not the material. How the churches were to be used was also — partly for practical reasons — decided by the Danes themselves. This also goes for the arrangement of the interior, which was created with reference to the ideology of the owner or owners of the building.

Figure 5. West end of the nave of Fjenneslev Church, Sjælland (twelfth century).
Photo: A. Bolvig.

The look of the religious buildings and the arrangement of their interiors are the visible expressions of a specific ideological requirement of the powerful landowning class. The use and perception of Romanesque wall paintings must be evaluated in this perspective. The art of the period fitted perfectly into the self-understanding of a small, powerful landowning ruling class. The figures are depicted in a majestic way in static situations without violent movements. Even if they refer to biblical stories their narrative elements seem frozen or stiffened. They radiate solemnity with their frequent use of frontal depiction. There are but few analogous references to contemporary material society; on the contrary, the imagery connotes the self-understanding of the great landowners. There is a close link between style, motifs, and the person commissioning the pictures.

The wall paintings constitute the best visual material for research on cultural relationships because they were executed on the very spot where they should function. A database of Danish wall paintings and a complete index of religious iconographic subjects will be used in this survey.[14]

---

[14] The database and the index are accessible on the Internet at www.kalkmalerier.dk; see also Jesper Jerne Borrild, 'Medieval Danish Wall Paintings: An Internet Database', *Medium Aevum Quotidianum*, 39 (1998), 21–36.

Of the 1781 indexed iconographic motifs from the period 1100–1300 some of the most frequently depicted are Evangelist, *Majestas Domini*, Apostle, Angel, Mary, St Peter, St John, Founder figure, St Paul, Cain and Abel's offering to God, the Crucifixion, and Abraham's Bosom.[15] The many depictions of evangelists refer most often to the evangelist symbols surrounding the *Majestas Domini*.[16] Therefore, it can be argued that the *Majestas Domini* (God in Majesty) was the dominant motif, expressing both the idea of an almighty God and the idea of an almighty landowning magnate. This is stressed by the location of the motif. Some places in the church were of greater religious importance than other places. Contrary to the situation in the west of Denmark, the eastern Danish churches as a rule had apses that were decorated with a *Majestas Domini* motif.[17] The depiction is very similar to its European counterparts and of a high artistic standard. This image of the highest ruler is often interpreted as connoting visually the notion of secular power.[18] God surrounded by his Evangelists can and could easily be interpreted on an ideological level as the prince surrounded by his vassals. The *Majestas Domini* with its connotative world referring to an imagery of celestial and secular power was particularly prominent during the twelfth and thirteenth centuries, which were dominated by large-scale farming.[19] The subject vanishes with the collapse of this agrarian system.[20] It is interesting to note that the Passion does not appear very often with fifty-nine indexed subjects, that is, just over half the number of depictions of the Childhood. And in accordance with traditional Romanesque expression, Christ is not depicted as a dead

---

[15] Identified saints, 238 (of which St Peter, 48; St Paul, 19); unidentified saints, 181; Evangelists, 126; *Majestas*, 103; Childhood of Jesus, 90 (of which the Three Magi, 33); Apostles, 79; Angels, 77; Mary, 67; the Passion, 59 (of which the Crucifixion, 15); Saints, 54; Day of Judgement, 46; Bishops, 43; Prophets, 28; Cain and Abel's offering, 26; *Te Deum*, 25; Founder figures, 24; Genesis, 17; Bosom of Abraham, 13.

[16] Søren Kaspersen, 'Majestas Domini – Regnum et Sacerdotium: Zu Entstehung und Leben des Motifs bis zum Investiturstreit', *Hafnia: Copenhagen Papers in the History of Art*, 8 (1981), 83–146; Søren Kaspersen, 'Majestas Domini – Regnum et Sacerdotium: Das Leben des Motifs in Skandinavien während der Kirchenkämpfe unter besonderer Berücksichtigung Dänemarks im 12. Jahrhundert', *Hafnia: Copenhagen Papers in the History of Art*, 10 (1985), 24–72. See www.kalkmalerier.dk search sh/ 238, 20/ 65, 20/ 67, 21/ 163, 21/ 164, 30-2/ 77, 20/ 3.

[17] See www.kalkmalerier.dk. Out of a total of 103 indexed *Majestas* motifs, seventy-nine are located in eastern Denmark and twenty-four in western Denmark.

[18] Georges Duby, *Le Temps de cathédrales* (Paris: Gallimard, 1976), p. 64.

[19] Nils Hybel, 'The Creation of Large-Scale Production in Denmark, *c.* 1100–1300', *Scandinavian Journal of History*, 4 (1955), 259–80.

[20] There are seventy-two depictions of *Majestas* visible today. Some fifty-four belong to the eastern part of Denmark and eighteen to the western part. Out of a total of 114 registered *Majestas*-motifs, 103 belong to the period 1100–1300, whereas only eleven belong to the rest of the medieval period 1300–1550.

man on the cross.[21] This representation of the Lord is in accordance with European Romanesque art, but it also fitted perfectly with the traditional concept that power and not humiliation constituted the notion of the secular kingdom. The two most important apostles, St Peter and St Paul,[22] are depicted relatively often. They are the followers of Christ. He delegated some of his divine power to his trusted men. These two apostles connote the vassals to whom the feudal lord delegated some of his power. Abraham with souls in his bosom at the Day of Judgement belongs exclusively to the Romanesque period not only in Denmark. This subject, which disappears during the thirteenth century, can also be interpreted as a visualization of the feudal lord surrounded by and taking care of his vassals.[23]

It is also in the eastern part of Denmark that we find pictures of the Founder figures, proud men and women handing a church model to God.[24] In Jutland, where as a rule a partnership of landowners stood behind the erection and decoration of churches, this motif seems irrelevant.[25] In the same part of the church where we find images of the founders in eastern Denmark, we often find depictions of Cain and Abel's offering in western Denmark.[26] The two sons of Adam and Eve are richly dressed so they do not represent the peasant and the shepherd; on the secular level they represent the church founders' small community of landowners. In this connection it is natural that the Three Magi bringing their gifts and tribute to the new-born king constitute a third of all indexed motifs concerning the Childhood of Jesus and more than double the number of the indexed motif of the Crucifixion.[27] What is at stake is the homage of the new king.

One specific example clearly demonstrates the ideological relationship between the Three Magi and church founders. In the above-mentioned Fjenneslev Church there is a badly preserved decoration on the triumphal wall (fig. 6). In the west end of the nave there is a gallery for the benefactor. Raised high above the people down on the floor of the church, he and his nearest family could look straight at their own wall paintings. Two complementary motifs are painted here. The pictures are from the 1120s and the style is the strict, dignified Romanesque. At the top we see the Wise Men from the East (who are identical with the Three Magi) kneeling as they hand their gifts to the infant Jesus sitting on the Virgin's lap. Mother and child are sitting in an elegant building. The picture below shows the benefactor and his wife.

---

[21] www.kalkmalerier.dk search sh/ 255 (Råsted Church, Jutland, 1125–50).

[22] www.kalkmalerier.dk search 29-2/ 4 (Råsted Church).

[23] www.kalkmalerier.dk search 25/ 141 (Fraugde Church, Fyn, 1175–1200).

[24] www.kalkmalerier.dk search 15/ 114, 32-3/ 52, 25/ 61.

[25] There are twenty-one depictions of founders indexed. Some sixteen belong to the eastern and five to the western part of Denmark.

[26] www.kalkmalerier.dk search 29-3/ 73, 29-3/ 27.

[27] The Childhood has ninety examples, of which thirty-three are depictions of the Magi. The Crucifixion has just fifteen examples.

Figure 6. Wall painting of the Magi and donors in Fjenneslev Church,
Sjælland (beginning of twelfth century). Photo: A. Bolvig.

They are presumably Asser Rig and his wife, Lady Inge, who belonged to the most powerful family on Sjælland. She is standing with a gold ring and he with the model of a church, which he is holding up in the air, where God's hand is to be seen in blessing. With this image, Asser Rig and Lady Inge are demonstrating that they have built the church, which they are presenting to God, and which God accepts as their gift. By accepting a gift, you entered into an obligation with the giver. So we are witnessing a kind of contract between God and church founder. The couple are dressed in splendid clothes and, in contrast to the Three Kings, they are not kneeling, but standing upright. They show no sign of deference. They appear as God's equals. The image connotes the self-understanding of the mightiest couple on Sjælland. Both their position just beneath the image of the Three Kings presenting their gifts, and their implied equal position with God express a very arrogant appreciation of their own worth. The position of the two motifs indicates that the spectators linked the gift-giving Magi with the concept of church-building magnates.

The imagery of Romanesque art is very aristocratic so it was easily accepted by the great landowners. The expression of power in Christian imagery is more accentuated than in the ornamentation of the Viking Age. There is no indication of the organized export to Denmark of this imagery, but rather of participation within an artistic expression common to the elitist classes all over Europe. Romanesque art is very universal but also very exclusive. Maybe the dominant position of motifs that connote vassal loyalties is due to a special Danish application of Romanesque art. Only broad comparative analyses will give an answer to this.

Amongst the traditional universal religious motifs we find specific subjects that may be evaluated as specially adapted to local benefactors. In some churches in western Denmark there are Romanesque wall paintings from the twelfth and thirteenth centuries representing knights in combat. There is disagreement today as to what these scenes refer to: motifs from the Old Testament; the battle between good and evil; specific historical events? It may be that the people of that time saw all of these and more in the combat scenes. In any case, we can also see the combat scenes as expressing the attitude of the landowning classes to war and combat as part of life. It is interesting to note that these motifs are concentrated in Jutland. The battle scenes do not belong to the 'imported' imagery of European religious iconography. They are created on behalf of the landowning gentleman class of western Denmark (fig. 7).

The majority of the Danish population did not participate in communicating through Romanesque art. We do not know if they opposed it. My interpretation is that they were excluded and consequently lived in ignorance of this art. The exclusion of a massive majority from the private Romanesque stone churches is indirectly visualized in the only existing Romanesque depiction of the First Labour.[28] The twelfth-century painting in Todbjerg Church only depicts Adam and Eve (fig. 8). They have no children or clothing; there is no chair for Eve to sit on. Indeed, Eve is

---

[28] www.kalkmalerier.dk search 25/ 47 (Todbjerg Church, Jutland).

Figure 7. Wall painting of a battle scene in Ål Church, Jutland
(beginning of thirteenth century). Photo: A. Bolvig.

surprisingly sitting entirely naked on a rock. They are portrayed as miserable slaves of labour without any mitigating circumstances. The image cannot be interpreted positively contrary to late medieval depictions of the same motif.[29]

To conclude, it seems the great majority of the Danish population apparently had no interest in European Romanesque art and architecture. They were excluded from the pictures and only experienced the churches from outside. On the other hand, the freeborn landowning elite adapted the established architecture and art and transformed them in accordance with their own ideology. They adopted the aspects and the visual formulations which were useful, and they supplemented them with battle scenes, which also functioned as part of secular ideology. In order to put Danish participation in European Romanesque imagery into perspective, I will refer to the way historians and art historians have described the introduction of late medieval imagery.

During the Late Middle Ages, Denmark experienced massive influence from Lübeck and other Hanseatic towns. At times, they dominated Danish politics and the economy. The Hanseatic export of wooden sculptures and altarpieces to Denmark

---

[29] www.kalkmalerier.dk search sh/ 319 (Hyllested Church, Jutland), 29-3/ 21 (Ørum Church, Jutland), 29–1/ 1 (Lem Church, Jutland), 20/ 90 (Kävlinge Church, Skåne), 9/ 65 (Ottestrup, Sjælland), 14/ 112 (Tågerup, Lolland). Axel Bolvig, 'Images of Late Medieval "Daily Life": A History of Mentalities', *Medium Aevum Quotidianum*, 39 (1998), 94–111.

Figure 8. Wall painting of the First Labour in Todbjerg Church, Jutland
(twelfth century). Photo: A. Bolvig.

was considerable. It could be interpreted as a forerunner of the present-day American cultural influence on Europe. Were these goods considered as mere commercial products equal to salt and herring, or did they also function as an ideological means? The question needs investigating further in the future.

It is impossible for modern historians to deny the export/import of art and architecture out of and into Denmark. But their attitude towards the impact of Hanseatic art production differs from their evaluation of French and English influence. When one of the leading art historians of the twentieth century, Francis Beckett, and his fellow art historians found traces of French Gothic influence in Denmark, they used a positive and praising vocabulary. At their time, French art was the great model. As for Hanseatic influence, he and his colleagues used a vocabulary that was quite different. They talked of a 'vigorous offensive', an 'invasion', 'a fight for life', and said that 'the fight is fought on the walls of each single church'.[30] Denmark's nearest great neighbour, Germany, was a threat to which the Danes lost Southern Schleswig in the nineteenth century. Today it is a great partner. In contemporary art history we do not fight the Hanseatic Germans on the walls of the churches. We acknowledge late medieval artefacts as important products of culture.

Unlike sculpture, panel paintings, and altarpieces, wall paintings were not directly imported works of art. They were produced on the very spot where they can be seen and perceived. And looking at Danish wall paintings, we must acknowledge that they represent an imagery closely connected to the visual world of their patrons. The elitist classes of the Romanesque period easily adopted established European imagery. During the Late Middle Ages peasants took over the administration of the local churches to a considerable degree. They used a European imagery and transformed it into a visual language that represented a local culture belonging to a North European area.[31]

---

[30] Jes Wienberg, *Den gotiske labyrint: Middelalderen og kirkerne i Danmark*, Lund Studies in Medieval Archaeology, 11 (Stockholm: Almqvist & Wiksell, 1993), p. 40; Axel Bolvig, *Bondens billeder: Om kirker og kunst i dansk senmiddelalder* (Copenhagen: Gyldendal, 1994), pp. 78–81.

[31] Axel Bolvig, 'Images of Late Medieval "Daily Life"', pp. 94–111; www.kalkmalerier.dk sh/ 319, 322-3/70, 14/ 112.

Textual Evidence for Contact, Conflict, and Coexistence

Vikings on the European Continent
in the Late Viking Age

JUDITH JESCH

In their accounts of Viking activity on the European continent (south of the *Danevirke*), general surveys of the Viking Age have little to say about any such activity after the establishment of the Duchy of Normandy in the early tenth century.[1] The traditional concentration on the late eighth, the ninth, and the early tenth centuries is determined by the preservation of copious and detailed annalistic and other written sources covering these periods, such as the *Royal Frankish Annals*, the *Annals of St Bertin*, the *Annals of Fulda*, and the like.[2] Yet if Viking activity was reduced in the tenth century, it did not entirely cease. Even on the European continent, it can be said that the Viking Age lasted well into the eleventh century.[3]

The continental sources for such activity are neither as copious nor as detailed as those for the earlier period, they have rarely if ever been surveyed, and the evidence is sometimes buried in obscure local chronicles of varying date and reliability. But however imperfect this evidence, it has its own interest and is of particular value because it can, for the first time, be compared with contemporary Scandinavian texts. While Scandinavian evidence for the early Viking Age is largely archaeological, the late Viking Age provides us with two important bodies of contemporary texts from Scandinavian sources: runic inscriptions and skaldic verse. The inscriptions are certainly and the verse is arguably contemporary evidence for the late Viking Age,

---

[1] For example, Else Roesdahl, *The Vikings* (Harmondsworth: Penguin, 1998), pp. 195–209; Peter Sawyer, 'The Age of the Vikings and before', in *The Oxford Illustrated History of the Vikings*, ed. by Peter Sawyer (Oxford: Oxford University Press, 1997), pp. 1–18 (pp. 8–14).

[2] Janet L. Nelson, 'The Frankish Empire', in *The Oxford Illustrated History of the Vikings*, ed. by Sawyer, pp. 19–47.

[3] I am grateful to Lesley Abrams, Liesbeth van Houts, Michael Jones, and David N. Parsons for their help with various matters in this paper.

giving us for the first time a Scandinavian view of that period. Both types of text have their difficulties: the inscriptions are laconic, while the verse is complex and often obscure, and, as memorials, both are possibly deceitful or at best unspecific in their assertions. And both the inscriptions and the verse are extremely limited in the kinds of topics and events for which they provide information. Nevertheless, these two bodies of material provide valuable evidence for Viking activities in the late Viking Age, including the expeditions, for both raiding and trading, made by ship-borne bands of men from Scandinavia to other regions.[4]

The aim of this essay is to present this contemporary, Scandinavian evidence for 'Viking' activities on the European continent towards the end of the Viking Age. I hope also to make some links with continental sources, though it has not been possible to provide an exhaustive survey of the latter. There is certainly plenty of scope for future research elucidating the continental evidence for the activities which are sparsely, yet unmistakably, recorded in the Scandinavian sources. Here I will concentrate on drawing attention to the Scandinavian evidence and outlining its problems and possibilities. This evidence relates to Scandinavian activities in the neighbouring regions of Saxony and Frisia, in Normandy, Brittany, and regions further south in France and Spain, and in the southern part of Italy.

Saxony and Frisia

One rune-stone inscription (Sö 166) commemorates a man who had both 'divided up payment' in England and 'attacked (fortified) towns' **a sahkslanti** 'in Saxony', the area nearest to the southern border of Scandinavia.[5] This inscription has been dated to the 1020s or 1030s and is thought to commemorate Viking attacks in the Elbe region towards the end of the tenth century such as those recorded by Adam of Bremen and others, which included a battle at the 'port and garrison' (*portus et presidium*) of Stade on the Elbe in 994.[6] But such raids seem to have continued into the eleventh century: Adam refers to another attack, apparently in the 1040s, perpetrated on Lesum by a group of *Ascomanni* who had come into the mouth of the Weser.[7]

According to Adam, the attack which reached Stade also involved the devastation of Frisia, and there is a variety of evidence for Viking activity in Frisia in this period.

---

[4] These issues are discussed in ch. 1 of Judith Jesch, *Ships and Men in the Late Viking Age: The Vocabulary of Runic Inscriptions and Skaldic Verse* (Woodbridge: Boydell, 2001).

[5] *Södermanlands runinskrifter*, ed. by Erik Brate and Elias Wessén, Sveriges runinskrifter, 3 (Stockholm: Kungl. Vitterhets historie och antikvitets akademien, 1924–36), pp. 127–28.

[6] *Gesta Hammaburgensis Ecclesiae Pontificum*, II, 32, in *Quellen des 9. und 11. Jahrhunderts zur Geschichte der Hamburgischen Kirche und des Reiches*, ed. by Werner Trillmich and Rudolf Buchner, 5th edn (Darmstadt: Wissenschaftliche Buchgesellschaft, 1978), p. 266.

[7] *Gesta Hammaburgensis*, II, 77, p. 318.

The metrical text on a rune-inscribed silver neck-ring of the tenth or eleventh century (N 540) found on the island of Senja in northern Norway is often cited as a perfect expression of the warlike ethos of the Viking Age:[8]

furu* trikia frislats a uit auk uiks fotum uir skiftum

> Fórum drengja
> Fríslands á vit,
> ok vígs fǫtum
> vér skiptum.

(We went to visit the young lads of Frisia, and we it was who split the spoils of war.)

In an attempt to explore the question of how such a text came to be inscribed on such an object, I published a little kite-flying article some years ago in which I tried to show, mainly by studying the semantics of the text, that the inscription could be interpreted as arising out of trading voyages to Frisia rather than more warlike activities there, that is, that it could also be read as 'We visited our trading-partners in Frisia and bought [or "sold" or "exchanged"] war-gear'.[9]

In a response to this article, the Dutch scholar Kees Samplonius made some further valuable suggestions.[10] His interpretation takes on board one of my arguments, that the term *drengr*, previously thought to refer to Frisian opponents, has a strong first-person connotation, and so is likely to refer to a group which includes the speaker. However, Samplonius's view is still that the inscription refers to raiding rather than trading activity. He draws attention to a Frisian law (preserved in the Riustring redaction of the *Vierentwintig Landrechten* 'Twenty-Four Land Laws') which concerns a man who is kidnapped by Vikings (*Northman, witsingon*, both dative plural forms) and goes off with them to burn houses, rape women, kill men, and set fire to churches.[11] If on his return he swears an oath that he did all this under duress, then he cannot be blamed or indeed prosecuted for his deeds. This implies that there also were some Frisians who went off with Vikings of their own free will, and Samplonius concludes that the text on the Senja neck-ring was carved by a Norwegian Viking who had been on just such a joint Viking-Frisian expedition, which provided

---

[8] Transliterated and normalized text from *Norges Innskrifter med de yngre Runer*, ed. by Magnus Olsen, Aslak Liestøl, and James E. Knirk, 6 vols (Oslo: Norsk Historisk Kjeldeskrift-Institutt, 1941–), V (1960), 130–31; translation from R. I. Page, *Runes* (London: British Museum, 1987), p. 48.

[9] Judith Jesch, 'The Senja Neck-Ring and Viking Activity in the Eleventh Century', in *Blandade runstudier*, vol. II, ed. by Lennart Elmevik and Lena Peterson, Runrön, 11 (Uppsala: Institutionen för nordiska språk, Uppsala universitet, 1997), pp. 7–12.

[10] Kees Samplonius, 'Friesland en de Vikingtijd: De ring van Senja en de Vierentwintig Landrechten', *It Beaken*, 60 (1998), 89–101.

[11] *Das Rüstringer Recht*, ed. by Wybren Jan Buma and Wilhelm Ebel, Altfriesische Rechtsquellen, 1 (Göttingen: Musterschmidt, 1963), p. 54.

the booty which the verse celebrates. Samplonius's suggestion is attractive and his response has clarified some of the weaknesses of my own arguments. Although it is probably fruitless to carry on refining our interpretations of the short and laconic inscription on the Senja neck-ring, close study of its text has usefully drawn attention to Frisian evidence for Viking activity in that region in the late Viking Age.

This 'Twentieth Land Law' should also be seen in the context of a number of variants on a privilege in which the Frisians are exempted from following their rulers on expeditions because of the need to defend themselves and their homes against 'Viking' attacks.[12] Again, it is usually assumed that these provisions can be no later than from the eleventh century, when such attacks ceased, though the exact dates are problematic.[13] Like the 'Twentieth Land Law' cited above, these privileges often make use of the word *witsing* (cognate with Old Norse *víkingr*) and may represent an oblique recognition that some Frisians did go off with Vikings. The expeditions that they are free not to go on are left unspecified, and it may be that this is actually a prohibition disguised as a privilege, appealing to the Frisians' need to defend themselves to persuade them to stay at home rather than join Vikings on raiding expeditions.[14]

Further evidence for Viking raids on Frisia in the early eleventh century comes in a number of annals and chronicles attesting to such raids in its first decade.[15] The main source is a detailed and colourful, yet nearly contemporary description by Alpert of

---

[12] *The Old West Frisian Skeltana Riucht*, ed. by Sydney Fairbanks (Cambridge, MA: Harvard University Press, 1939), p. 73; *Das Rüstringer Recht*, ed. by Buma and Ebel, pp. 38, 88; *Das Fivelgoer Recht*, ed. by Wybren Jan Buma and Wilhelm Ebel, Altfriesische Rechtsquellen, 5 (Göttingen: Vandenhoeck & Ruprecht, 1962), p. 56; *Westerlauwerssches Recht: Jus Municipale Frisonum*, ed. by Wybren Jan Buma and Wilhelm Ebel, Altfriesische Rechtsquellen, 6 (Göttingen: Vandenhoeck & Ruprecht, 1977), pp. 74, 132.

[13] These laws may not be strictly contemporary sources. The earliest surviving manuscript of the Rüstringen redaction is from around 1300, though it is believed that its oldest parts originate in the eleventh century (*Das Rüstringer Recht*, ed. by Buma and Ebel, pp. 13–17). The manuscripts of the other legal compilations quoted in note 12 above are even later. However, provisions like these seem to belong to common Frisian law. Fairbanks calls such provisions 'a favorite legal doctrine of the Frisians' (*The Old West Frisian Skeltana Riucht*, ed. by Fairbanks, p. 124).

[14] The uses of the mysterious word *witsing* are of interest here. In the 'Twentieth Land Law' cited above (note 11), it is clearly used to mean 'Viking' in the sense 'Scandinavian' (cf. the synonymous use of *Northman* in the same passage). However, it is not at all clear that this sense is intended when it is used in the privileges cited above (note 12), and it may just have a more general meaning of 'pirate'; see Rolf Bremmer's communication quoted in Christine Fell, 'Old English *wicing*: A Question of Semantics', *Proceedings of the British Academy*, 72 (1986), 295–316 (p. 313).

[15] Until about 1100, 'Frisia' encompassed not only today's Friesland, but also the part of the Netherlands later known as Holland; see Dirk P. Blok, 'Holland und Westfriesland', *Frühmittelalterliche Studien*, 3 (1969), 347–61.

Metz of two raids by *Nordmanni*, one on the trading centre of Tiel and then one on Utrecht.[16] The attackers are said to have burned Tiel but, in the following year, the inhabitants of Utrecht burn their own harbour to pre-empt the incendiary activities of the raiders. Alpert does not date these raids, but similar raids are referred to, and dated, in other annals and chronicles, notably Sigebert of Gembloux, who borrows only the salient facts from Alpert ('1009 Having attacked Frisia, the Northmen burn the town of Tiel [. . .] 1010 The Northmen return to Frisia and the town of Utrecht is burned, with many killed').[17] Other annals give other dates and slightly varying information, for example, the *Annales Colonienses* ('1006 Tiel is plundered by pirates'),[18] the *Chronicon Tielense* ('1007 Tiel is burned and plundered by pirates and Danes'),[19] or the *Annales Egmondenses* ('1010 The Northmen burn Utrecht with many slain').[20]

It is not entirely clear how many such raids there were, or when and where they took place.[21] There may have been just two raids in subsequent years, which are variously given the dates of either 1006 and 1007 or 1009 and 1010, or there were two sets of two raids in these years. Or there were possibly even just two raids, not in subsequent years, in 1006/7 and 1009/10. Whatever the explanation, further consideration is needed of scholars' attempts to link these raids to the evidence of Norse sources, in particular Sighvatr Þórðarson's poem about King Olaf Haraldsson's (Óláfr Haraldsson) youthful exploits at just this period, known as the *Víkingarvísur*.[22]

---

[16] Alpertus, *De diversitate temporum*, ed. by G. H. Pertz, MGH SS, 4 (Hanover: Hahn, 1841), pp. 700–23 (pp. 704–05); *De diversitate temporum*, I, 8–10, in Alpertus van Metz, *Gebeurtenissen van deze tijd en Een fragment over bisschop Diederik I van Metz*, ed. and trans. by Hans van Rij with Anna Sapir Abulafia (Amsterdam: Verloren, 1980), pp. 18–22. Van Rij demonstrates that much of the description of the Viking attacks derives from Caesar's *Bellum Gallicum* (*Gebeurtenissen*, pp. xxxiv, 123–24).

[17] Sigebertus Gemblacensis, *Chronica*, ed. by D. L. C. Bethmann, MGH, SS, 6 (Hanover: Hahn, 1844), pp. 300–74 (p. 354): '1009 Nortmanni Fresiam infestantes, Thile oppidum incendunt [. . .] 1010 Nortmanni Fresiam repetunt, et multis cæsis, Vltraiectum opidum incensum est.' On Sigebert's dependence on Alpert, see G. H. Pertz, introduction to *Alperti Opera* in MGH SS, 4, pp. 696–97 (p. 697), and Max Manitius, *Geschichte der Lateinischen Literatur des Mittelalters* (Munich: Beck, 1931), p. 345.

[18] *Annales Colonienses*, ed. by G. H. Pertz, MGH SS, 1 (Hanover: Hahn, 1826), pp. 97–99 (p. 99): '1006 Tiela depraedata est per piratas.'

[19] *Auctoris incerti Chronicon Tielense*, ed. by Joh. Did. van Leeuwen (Utrecht: Wild & Altheer, 1789), p. 78: 'Anno Domini millesimo septimo Tyla [. . .] a piratis & Danis incensa & direpta est.'

[20] *Annales Egmundani*, ed. by G. H. Pertz, MGH, SS, 16 (Hanover: Hahn, 1859), pp. 442–79 (p. 446): '1010 Nortmanni multis interfectis Traiectum incendunt.'

[21] Jan de Vries, *De Wikingen in de lage landen bij de zee* (Haarlem: Willink & Zoon, 1923), pp. 305–10.

[22] While it is difficult to unravel the chronological detail of the 'future saint['s] [. . .] career of desultory violence and robbery round the coasts of the Baltic and the North Sea' (*Encomium*

Stanza 5 of this poem describes a battle fought by Óláfr at a place called *Kinn-limasíða:*[23]

> Víg vanntu, hlenna hneigir,
> hjǫlmum grimmt et fimmta.
> Þolðu hlýr á hári
> hríð Kinnlimasíðu,
> þar er við rausn at ræsis
> reið herr ofan skeiðum.
> Enn í gǫgn at gunni
> gekk hilmis lið rekkum.

(Suppressor of thieves, you fought the fifth battle harmful to helmets. The bows (of the ships) endured the storm at high *Kinnlimasíða* where the army rode down with pomp to the ships of the king. Still the host of the ruler went through the warriors in battle.)

The sequence of stanzas in this poem is fixed by the fact that the battles are numbered, but the identification of the places concerned is often difficult, and not helped by the fact that the prose contexts in which the stanzas of the poem are preserved do not always agree in their identifications of the locations. The only prose source to locate *Kinnlimasíða* is Snorri Sturluson's saga of St Olaf, which says it is in *Frísland.*[24] The *Legendary Saga* implies that it is in England, while *Fagrskinna* calls the place *Kinnlimafjǫrðr* but does not say where it is; neither of these two actually cites the stanza.[25] Following Snorri, then, modern scholars have located the place in the Netherlands, despite the fact that it is described as 'high': this is explained as either a misunderstanding or poetic licence by Sighvatr who, after all, was not there. They identify it with Kennemerland, a coastal district in North Holland, where there are some high sand dunes. Height is certainly relative, but it is difficult to believe that any Norwegian or Icelander would describe anything in the Netherlands as 'high'.

Emmae Reginae, ed. by Alistair Campbell with a supplementary introduction by Simon Keynes (Cambridge: Cambridge University Press, 1998), pp. 76–82 (p. 76)), it is fairly certain that it happened within the period 1007–13; see Snorri Sturluson, *Heimskringla*, vol. II, ed. by Bjarni Aðalbjarnarson, Íslenzk Fornrit, 27, 2nd edn (Reykjavik: Hið Íslenzka Fornritafélag, 1979), p. lxxxix.

[23] Text and translation of all quotations from this poem are taken from Christine Fell, '*Víkingarvísur*', in *Speculum Norroenum: Norse Studies in Memory of Gabriel Turville-Petre*, ed. by Ursula Dronke and others (Odense: Odense University Press, 1981), pp. 106–22.

[24] Snorri Sturluson, *Heimskringla*, p. 13. See also Snorri's 'separate saga', *Den store saga om Olav den hellige*, ed. by Oscar Albert Johnsen and Jón Helgason (Oslo: Dybwad, 1941), p. 41.

[25] *Olafs saga hins helga: Die 'Legendarische Saga' über Olaf den Heiligen*, ed. and trans. by Anne Heinrichs, Doris Janshen, Elke Radicke, and Hartmut Röhn (Heidelberg: Carl Winter, 1982), pp. 42–43; *Ágrip af Nóregskonunga sǫgum. Fagrskinna – Nóregs konunga tal*, ed. by Bjarni Einarsson, Íslenzk Fornrit, 29 (Reykjavik: Hið Íslenzka Fornritafélag, 1984), p. 167.

Even if we do not take everything the poet says too literally, it is possible to question the identification on philological grounds. The early forms of Kennemerland are 'in pago Kinhem', 'in Kinnin', 'in Chinheim', 'Kinhem', 'in pago Kinheim', while the form 'in Kinnemaria' (*Kinnemer-* < **Kinhemwarja-* 'dwellers in *Kinhem*') first appears in *c.* 1180.[26] The early forms clearly include the Old Dutch element *-hem*, which Old Norse speakers should have recognized as equivalent to their *-heim*, and despite the superficial similarity of the first element, it is hard to see how these would give the Norse form *Kinnlima-*, even if we accept that the descriptive suffix *-síða* 'a stretch of coast or the bank of a river' was added by the poet or other Norse speakers. Here, some diligent searching by place-name experts might well turn up some plausible alternatives. The value of this stanza as evidence for Olaf's raids on Frisia will in the end depend on a more certain identification of this place-name.

Brittany, Normandy, and Further South

The next four stanzas of *Víkingarvísur* describe battles fought in England, and these English sections of the poem have been much discussed by scholars.[27] Much less work has been done on the remaining stanzas which recount a series of battles Olaf fought on the European continent. Most of these contain troublesome place-names, and although scholars have proposed identifications, it is not always particularly clear on what grounds they have done so and the result is not always convincing.[28] Here, I will discuss just two of these stanzas in detail.

The first of these 'continental' stanzas describes an attack on a high place inhabited by 'Vikings':

> Tøgr var fullr í fǫgrum,
> folkveggs drifahreggi,
> helt, sem hilmir mælti,
> Hrings firði, lið þingat.
> Ból lét hann á Hóli
> hátt, víkingar áttu,

---

[26] R. E. Künzel, D. P. Blok, and J. M. Verhoeff, *Lexicon van nederlandse toponiemen tot 1200*, 2nd edn (Amsterdam: P. J. Meertens-Instituut, 1989), p. 204.

[27] For example, Oscar Albert Johnsen, *Olav Haraldssons ungdom indtil slaget ved Nesjar 25. mars 1016*, Videnskapsselskapets skrifter, II. Historisk-filosofisk klasse, 21 (Christiania [Oslo]: Dybwad, 1916); Margaret Ashdown, *English and Norse Documents Relating to the Reign of Ethelred the Unready* (Cambridge: Cambridge University Press, 1930), pp. 217–23; Fell, '*Víkingarvísur*'; Russell Poole, 'Skaldic Verse and Anglo-Saxon History: Some Aspects of the Period 1009–1016', *Speculum*, 62 (1987), 265–98.

[28] For identifications of the places mentioned in the poem, see Johnsen, *Olav Haraldssons ungdom*; Snorri Sturluson, *Heimskringla*, notes to pp. 7–26, passim, and index; Fell, '*Víkingarvísur*', passim.

þeir báðut sér síðan
slíks skotnaðar, brotna.

(Ten was full of the snow-storm of shields in lovely *Hringsfjǫrð*. The troops made their
way there, as the ruler said. He caused a high stronghold at *Hól* to be broken down
(which) the Vikings owned. They did not ask again for such an outcome for themselves.)

The prose sources have nothing to say about the location of this except that Snorri
specifies that Olaf went 'south across the sea' to get there from England.[29] While the
name *Hringsfjǫrðr* sounds suspiciously Scandinavian, scholars have nevertheless con-
curred that this stanza refers to an attack on Dol in Brittany. The similarity between
Hól and Dol would otherwise not be sufficient for this assumption, but here we do
have some important evidence from William of Jumièges. According to William, Duke
Richard II of Normandy called in two Scandinavian kings, whom William names as
Olaf and Lacman, to help him in a feud with Count Odo of Chartres. After a nasty trick
in which they trap the Bretons by digging disguised trenches into which their horses
fall, we are told that they 'laid siege to the town of Dol, and having captured it, they set
fire to it and burnt it after having killed all its inhabitants including Salomon, guardian
of the place'.[30] Then they go to Rouen to be fêted by Richard. According to Van
Houts, William has here confused two events, the invasion of Brittany in 1009 and
Olaf's visit to Normandy in 1013/14, on his way back to Norway.[31] The only serious,
but unconvincing, attempt to question this identification of *Hól* has been by Staffan
Hellberg, who does not see it as a place-name at all.[32] The weakness of his interpretation is that it is subordinated to his theory that the word *víkingr* in Viking Age texts
refers to an 'östlänning', a man from eastern Norway. This theory is, I think,
untenable, and I have discussed this word at length elsewhere.[33] My conclusion is
that the word *víkingr* has no national or regional implications of any sort and that, in
skaldic poetry at least, its most common use is pejorative, that is, it tends to be used
of the enemies of the king being praised in that poetry, regardless of their nationality.
Thus, there is nothing in Sighvatr's stanza to prevent the identification of *Hól* with
Dol (which is indeed a high, fortified site),[34] although the name is still a problem.

The next stanza is similarly problematic:

---

[29] Snorri Sturluson, *Heimskringla*, p. 22; *Den store saga*, p. 48.

[30] *The Gesta Normannorum Ducum of William of Jumièges, Orderic Vitalis, and Robert of
Torigni*, ed. and trans. by Elisabeth van Houts, 2 vols (Oxford: Clarendon Press, 1992–95), II
(1995), 26–27: 'Inde prolixius pagani progredientes castrum Doli obsident captumque igne
combururunt, interfectis eius incolis eam Salomone aduocato loci.'

[31] *Gesta Normannorum*, ed. and trans. by Van Houts, pp. 24–25.

[32] Staffan Hellberg, 'Vikingatidens *víkingar*', *Arkiv för nordisk filologi*, 95 (1980), 25–88
(pp. 37–38).

[33] Jesch, *Ships and Men*, pp. 44–56.

[34] It is clearly represented as such in the Bayeux Tapestry; see David M. Wilson, *The
Bayeux Tapestry* (London: Thames and Hudson, 1985), p. 215, plates 20–21.

Ǫleifr, vanntu, þar er jǫfrar,
ellifta styr, fellu,
ungr komtu af því þingi,
þollr, í Gríslupollum.
Þat frá ek víg at víttu,
Viljalms fyr bœ, hjalma,
tala minnst er þat telja,
tryggs jarls háit snarla.

(Olaf you fought the eleventh battle in *Gríslupollar*, there where princes fell; you came young from that assembly, warrior. I have heard of that battle, waged with vigour before the town of the trusty earl William, that they damaged helmets. The story is soon told.)

Scholars have identified the place-name *Gríslupollar* with Castropol on the north coast of Spain, and Fell suggests that the earl Viljalmr was invented (she does not say by whom) from the place-name Viljalmsbœr, which might be a corruption of the nearby place-name Villamea.[35] Van Houts, however, believes that this stanza reflects an attack on Aquitaine, then ruled by William V, and draws attention to an account by Adémar of Chabannes of just such an attack, although he does not name the Viking leader: 'In that time an infinite multitude of Normans [= Vikings] from Denmark and the Irish region approached the Aquitanian port with a countless fleet.'[36] Adémar goes on to say that the Vikings performed the same trick that William ascribed to them in Brittany, of digging trenches for their opponents' horses to fall into. This similarity can be interpreted in several ways. There might be a direct literary connection between Adémar (writing before 1034) and William (writing in the 1070s), or it might be a standard literary motif used independently by the two chroniclers, or it might indeed have happened twice, in both places. In the latter case, this would suggest that the same Viking troop, having tried the trick once and found it successful, used it again.[37] This may be a small additional piece of evidence to link Sighvatr's stanza with Aquitaine rather than Spain, though we are then still left with the problem of identifying *Gríslupollar*.[38]

---

[35] Fell, '*Víkingarvísur*', p. 119.

[36] Elisabeth van Houts, 'Scandinavian Influence in Norman Literature of the Eleventh Century', *Anglo-Norman Studies*, 6 (1984), 107–21 (pp. 118–19); *Ademari Cabannensis Chronicon*, ed. by P. Bourgain with R. Landes and G. Pon, Corpus Christianorum Continuatio Mediaeualis, 129 (Turnhout: Brepols, 1999), p. 172 (III, 53: 'Eo tempore infinita multitudo Nortmannorum ex Danamarcha et Iresca regione cum classe innumera appulerunt portum Aquitanicum').

[37] Such tricks were apparently common in the early Middle Ages; see Bernhard S. Bachrach, 'Toward a Reappraisal of William the Great, Duke of Aquitaine (995–1030)', *Journal of Medieval History*, 5 (1979), 11–21 (p. 14).

[38] The remaining stanzas of the poem contain several more place-names in France and Spain. Space does not permit further discussion of these here; I have some brief comments in my *Ships and Men*, pp. 84–85, but more work is needed on the identifications.

Van Houts believes that William of Jumièges, along with some other Norman writers of the period, had access to Scandinavian sources. She notes that William has Svein Forkbeard (Sveinn tjúguskegg Haraldsson) visiting Richard II in Rouen in 1003 and making a pact of mutual assistance with him.[39] William is also the only source to assert that Olaf Haraldsson was baptized in Rouen just before his return to claim the throne of Norway.[40] Finally, she draws attention to the fact that Olaf's chief poet Sighvatr visited Rouen with his friend Bergr in about 1024, concluding that 'during their visit they might possibly have told their version of the story of Olaf's Viking career, a version which might have lingered on in Normandy until the time of William of Jumièges'.[41] This is at least relatively cautious, compared for instance to the assertion of Lauren Breese that 'in 1025 a visiting skald entertained the court of Richard II with verses not likely sung in Old French'.[42] Breese has derived this from a secondary source, while the stanza in question says no such thing:[43]

> Bergr, hǫfum minnzk, hvé, margan
> morgun, Rúðuborgar
> bǫrð létk í fǫr fyrða
> fest við arm enn vestra.

(Bergr, many a morning we have remembered how in our journey I caused the ship's prow to be tied to/by the western arm of Rouen's fortifications.)

If Olaf had been entertained by Richard II in Rouen, we might very well imagine that when his skald went there on a trading journey some years later he would take a message from his king to the Norman duke, but this can be no more than a supposition, for which there is no real evidence.

However, Sighvatr's stanza is interesting for a different reason. It can be interpreted in the context of work by Bernard Gauthiez on the topography of eleventh-century Rouen.[44] In particular, it is tempting to think that Sighvatr laid up at the 'Donjon', a u-shaped structure on the river, thought to be the old ducal residence, with street-name evidence of an anchoring point along its west side,[45] west of the

---

[39] Van Houts, 'Scandinavian Influence', p. 111.

[40] *Gesta Normannorum*, ed. and trans. by Van Houts, p. 28, n.

[41] Van Houts, 'Scandinavian Influence', p. 119.

[42] Lauren Wood Breese, 'The Persistence of Scandinavian Connections in Normandy in the Tenth and Early Eleventh Centuries', *Viator*, 8 (1977), 47–61 (p. 59).

[43] Snorri Sturluson, *Heimskringla*, p. 271.

[44] Bernard Gauthiez, 'Hypothèses sur la fortification de Rouen au onzième siècle: Le Donjon, la tour de Richard II et l'enceinte de Guillaume', *Anglo-Norman Studies*, 14 (1992), 61–76.

[45] Gauthiez, 'Hypothèses sur la fortification de Rouen au onzième siècle', esp. p. 76 and fig. 3. Gauthiez argues (p. 74, see also fig. 8) that Rouen's fortifications were extended to the west between 1067 and 1087, but it is not clear whether there was a western rampart to Rouen's fortifications before this, that is, a wall at the anchorage point, which would fit the description in the stanza.

new ducal residence, the 'Tour', built *c.* 1024.[46] The date is almost too good to be true: Snorri suggests that Sighvatr composed the stanza in the year Cnut claimed Norway (*c.* 1025), while claiming that Sighvatr had been in Rouen the previous year.[47] The element *borg* in Old Norse can mean '(fortified) wall', 'fortress' or 'castle', or '(fortified) town'. The way the stanza is phrased makes it clear that Sighvatr means some kind of structure, and not just 'town' in the abstract. In particular, a structure with an 'arm' is unlikely to be circular (or rectangular), but the term would suit something u-shaped, as we see in another poem of about twenty-five years later, in which the 'arm' of the *borg* refers to the u-shaped defences of Hedeby.[48]

Snorri says that Sighvatr was in Rouen on a trading voyage (*kaupferð*) but gives no further details. There is certainly nothing in the surviving half-stanza to suggest raiding. It is almost too neat to see the end of the Viking Age, at least for this part of the continent, in this contrast between King Olaf's raiding voyages and a trading voyage by his skald a decade or so later. Certainly Musset, who notes a shift from a northern to a southern distribution of find-spots of coins minted in Rouen, saw the first three decades of the eleventh century as the period in which Normandy was detached from the 'monde nordique' and reattached to the 'monde latin'.[49] Whether or not current numismatic knowledge will support this interpretation, it is clear that there was a shift in Normandy's orientation at this time. This process is neatly illustrated in Adémar of Chabannes's chronicle, just two chapters along from the one discussed above. Adémar begins by describing an attack on Ireland by 'Nortmanni supradicti', the previously mentioned Northmen (that is, those who had attacked Aquitaine).[50] But later on in the very same chapter, the word *Nortmanni* is used of the followers of Richard II during his attack on Apulia in 1017: *Nortmanni* change from being 'Vikings' to being 'Normans' in the space of one chapter. With this, the Normans begin to engage in what David Bates called 'a substantial exodus towards

---

[46] In the absence of clear archaeological evidence, Gauthiez's interpretation is not conclusive; see for instance Dominique Léost, 'Le Château de Rouen (1204–1591)' (unpublished doctoral thesis, University of Rouen, 2001), pp. 233–47, who thinks the 'Tour' is older than 1024.

[47] Snorri Sturluson, *Heimskringla*, p. 271.

[48] Jesch, *Ships and Men*, pp. 62, 112–13.

[49] Lucien Musset, 'Les Relations extérieures de la Normandie' in his *Nordica et Normannica: Recueil d'études sur la Scandinavie ancienne et médiévale, les expéditions des Vikings et la fondation de la Normandie*, Studia nordica, 1 (Paris: Société des études nordiques, 1997), pp. 297–307 (p. 305), first published in 1954; this view has recently been reiterated by Elisabeth van Houts, *The Normans in Europe* (Manchester: Manchester University Press, 2000), p. 19.

[50] *Ademari Cabannensis Chronicon*, III, 55, ed. by Bourgain with Landes and Pon, pp. 173–74. The first part of this chapter is translated in Van Houts, *The Normans in Europe*, pp. 214–15, the second and third parts on pp. 231–32, 269–70.

southern Europe', which he saw as resulting from 'the collapse of an order which these relations with the Scandinavian world had in some part upheld'.[51]

Byzantine Italy

From the Norman point of view, this period may well be the end of the Scandinavian connection. But if we turn to southern Italy in the eleventh century, where 'Byzantium and the West touched',[52] we find Scandinavians still engaging in 'Viking' activities. This is another substantial subject which can only be sketched here, but is relevant because it links with the evidence presented above, bringing together the Normans (now no longer 'Vikings') with their distant cousins in the Varangian guard. Three or four Swedish runic inscriptions refer to the deceased having been in *Langbarðaland* 'Longobardia', the area of southern Italy controlled by the Byzantine Empire.[53] Byzantine sources record a number of campaigns in this area in which Varangian mercenaries were involved, in 1009–18, in 1032, throughout the 1040s, in 1066, until the Byzantines finally withdrew from southern Italy in 1071.[54] We also have a substantial number of skaldic stanzas referring to the youthful adventures of the Norwegian king Harald Hard-Ruler (Haraldr harðráði Sigurðarson) and his exploits in the Varangian guard: it is clear that he too was active in *Langbarðaland* and in Sicily in the late 1030s and early 1040s.[55] Harald and the other Varangians reached southern Italy by the eastern route, down through Russia to Constantinople, and Italy was the tail end of such eastern activities, or *austrvíking*. However, later Icelandic saga-writers were sometimes confused by references to *Langbarðaland* and *Frakkar* 'Franks' in these poems, taking these names in the sense which they had by then, that is 'Lombardy (in northern Italy)' and 'Frenchmen'. More recent scholars have also assumed that such references show that Harald passed through western Europe on his way to Byzantium. Thus, de Vries considers a half-stanza by Illugi bryndœlaskáld to be evidence for Harald's visit to the Netherlands in around 1035, but he is making the same mistake as the saga-authors before him.[56] As Blöndal points out,

[51] David Bates, *Normandy before 1066* (London: Longman, 1982), p. 241.

[52] Michael Angold, *The Byzantine Empire 1025–1204* (London: Longman, 1984), p. 26.

[53] Sö 65, in *Södermanlands runinskrifter*, ed. by Brate and Wessén, p. 50; U 133, U 141 in *Upplands runinskrifter*, vol. I, ed. by Elias Wessén, Sveriges runinskrifter, 6 (Stockholm: Kungliga Vitterhets historie och antikvitets akademien, 1940), pp. 198, 206; there is another possible occurrence in a fragment discovered in the 1950s, see Sven B. F. Jansson, 'Uppländska, småländska och sörmländska runstensfynd', *Fornvännen*, 49 (1954), 1–25 (p. 22).

[54] Sigfús Blöndal, *The Varangians of Byzantium*, ed. and trans. by Benedikt S. Benedikz (Cambridge: Cambridge University Press, 1978), pp. 51–111.

[55] Discussed further in my *Ships and Men*, pp. 87–88.

[56] *De Wikingen in de lage landen*, p. 312. The stanza says that Harald *gekk opt á frið Frakka fyr óttu* 'often disturbed the peace of the Franks before dawn'. Another poet says that

they did not realize that the *Langbarðaland* of the poem was the Southern Italian district which formed the Byzantine province of *Longobardia*, and that the *Frakkar* were the French Normans who were disputing this very *Langbarðaland* in *Southern* Italy. Instead they assumed that these verses meant that Harald had gone from Russia to Wendland, then on to Saxony and France, committed piracy in these countries and gone on to Lombardy in *northern* Italy, on to Rome, then southwards to Apulia, and so on to Constantinople. It is far more likely, however, that Harald went the usual Varangian way, down the Russian rivers and across the Black Sea.[57]

This is clear enough if we view Illugi's stanza in the context of the rest of his (admittedly fragmentary) poem, which refers in earlier stanzas to an 'eastern journey', to the Byzantine emperor Michael, and to the 'southern lands' in which Harald was active.

It should also be noted that, in the very late Viking Age, Scandinavians came into contact with parts of Italy other than the Byzantine part (Venice, Rome, and Bari are all mentioned in the skaldic corpus), with their increasing habit of going on pilgrimage, and probably reaching Rome by the western, rather than eastern, route.[58]

Conclusion

This essay has touched on some aspects of Viking activity on the European continent in the eleventh century, concentrating on problems in the runic and skaldic material and possible links with continental evidence. This material reveals the range and interest of the evidence for Scandinavians in Europe in the late Viking Age. This evidence has never been gathered and discussed in one study, and certainly not in one written from the Scandinavian point of view. Such a survey would of course be difficult to write, for no one can be equally expert in skaldic verse, runology, the placenames of several countries, Latin chronicles both famous and obscure, numismatics, and much else. Yet such a study is extremely important. Scandinavian contacts with the European continent do not come to an end with the end of the Viking Age (whether that was in 1000, 1042, 1066, or 1100), rather the reverse, and the foundations of later contacts of a more peaceful sort are certainly laid in the eleventh century. Just as Sighvatr traded in Rouen, so Icelandic traders could be found there in 1198, according to accounts drawn up in that city.[59] Olaf may have been baptized

---

he also campaigned *á landi Langbarða* 'in Longobardia'; for detailed references, see my *Ships and Men*, p. 87.

[57] *The Varangians of Byzantium*, p. 56.

[58] See references in my *Ships and Men*, pp. 67, 87–88.

[59] *Diplomatarium Islandicum: Íslenzkt fornbréfasafn, sem hefir inni að halda bréf og gjörninga, dóma og máldaga, og aðrar skrár, er snerta Ísland eða íslenzka menn*, ed. by Jón Sigurðsson and others, 16 vols (Reykjavik: Hið Íslenzka Bókmenntafélag, 1857–1972), I (1857), 718–19; see also *Magni Rotuli Saccarii Normanniæ sub Regibus Angliæ*, ed. by Thomas Stapleton, 2 vols (London: Society of Antiquaries, 1840–44), II (1844), pp. xxii, 306.

in Rouen, and with the conversion of Scandinavia to Christianity, connections with the continent only increased, with many Icelandic bishops trained there.[60] The full history of Scandinavian contacts with the European continent in the eleventh century still remains to be written, but I hope at least to have suggested how geographically wide ranging and various in their nature those contacts were.

---

[60] Peter Foote, 'Aachen, Lund, Hólar', in *Aurvandilstá: Norse Studies*, ed. by Michael P. Barnes and others, Viking Collection, 2 (Odense: Odense University Press, 1984), pp. 101–20 (first published in 1975).

The Image of the Viking in Anglo-Norman Literature

The word 'image' has been chosen for the title of this essay in order to suggest that term's particular medieval ambiguity. 'Image' in Old French and Anglo-Norman has indeed its modern straightforward meaning of 'depiction', but it also inherits from its Latin forebear *imago* the extra semantic charge of 'pagan idol', of the graven image.[1] The 'Norsemen' may indeed have become 'Normans' as a result of their pragmatic gift for cultural assimilation; but the original Viking incursions into Northern France led to the creation in popular consciousness (as in England) of a heathen warrior Other, sweeping down like Assyrian wolves upon the unprotected sheep. Though blurred by time, and assimilated in turn with other elements, this folk memory was to resurface from the early twelfth century, in the Old French epic genre of the *chanson de geste*. In these martial poems, the Christian hero often finds himself in mortal combat against assorted *danois* and *norrois*,[2] but in these works of legendary fiction these Danes and Norwegians find themselves in as exotic company

---

[1] The concept of 'image' has most recently, and literally, been illustrated by Michael Camille in two brilliant — and brilliantly controversial — monographs: *The Gothic Idol: Ideology and Image-Making in Medieval Art*, Cambridge New Art History and Criticism (Cambridge: Cambridge University Press, 1989); and *Images on the Edge: The Margins of Medieval Art*, Essays in Art and Culture, 6 (London: Reaktion Books, 1992).

[2] Apart from the attributive substantival adjectives *danois* or *norrois* (often found in conjunction with *gent*, 'people', 'race'), epic pagan names play onomastic variations on *Dane-* (*Danebrun, Danebur, Danebus, Danemont*, etc.), or on *No(i)r-* (*Noiron, Noradin, Norcois, Nornis, Norrein*); in this latter case, there is a fortuitous added association with 'black', or with the authentic Arabic element 'Nur-' (as in the name of the twelfth-century caliph Nur-ed-Din). See André Moisan, *Répertoire des noms propres de personnes et de lieux cités dans les Chansons de geste françaises et les œuvres étrangères dérivées*, Publications romanes et françaises, 173, 5 vols (Geneva: Droz, 1986), I, 336–39, 735–38.

as did those real Scandinavians who voyaged eastwards to Russia, Byzantium, and beyond. The *chansons de geste* are essentially feudal and crusading epics, and such nominally Viking characters as may be found in these poems are (by a nice process of historical and literary irony) fully assimilated with the new Other, the Saracens. Thus the Danes and Norwegians of the French epic find themselves fighting in the onomastic army of Islam, alongside Arabs, Turks, and Persians, and the false gods that they worship are those ascribed by twelfth-century crusaders to the Paynims: the hellish 'anti-Trinity' of *Mahom* (Mahomet), *Apollin*, and *Tervagant*. The old enemy has been completely subsumed by the new, and there is generally a world of difference between the *chanson de geste* and the much earlier, more historically inspired Old English epic of *The Battle of Maldon*. Essentially, all that remains in the *geste* of the recognizable Viking, apart from a generically ethnic name, may be two distinctive items of military equipment: the round shield, the *toenart*,[3] and above all the formidable battleaxe, the *hache daneis*, cited throughout our epic texts, but most dramatically represented in the illustrated epic of the eleventh century that is the Bayeux Tapestry (where, by a nice stroke of irony, it is wielded by the English against those Norman knights who were the true direct heirs of the Norsemen).

Two named Vikings do, however, surface in the Old French epic: one highly enigmatic, testifying in my mind to a striking degradation of the already blurred focus of the image of the Norseman; the other enabling us at least to cross the Channel and to study those insular French texts that will occupy the main body of this essay. Well after the popularity of the great warriors Roland and Guillaume d'Orange had set a benchmark for epic heroes, there appeared an avatar in the person of 'Ogier the Dane' — or rather reappeared, since *danz Ogers li daneis* ('Lord Ogier the Dane') rides valiantly into battle at Charlemagne's side towards the end of the *Song of Roland* itself,[4] and he is also mentioned, as 'Oggero spata curta', in the *Nota Emilianense*, a brief and jumbled listing (couched in bad Latin and dating possibly from the second half of the eleventh century) of a number of the heroic names of the burgeoning Old French epic cycles.[5] Although Ogier's name occurs, similarly in passing, in some twelfth-century texts, we must wait until the beginning of the thirteenth for the first surviving work devoted to him: *La Chevalerie d'Ogier de*

---

[3] The OF *toenart/tuenart* (probably deriving from ON *tœnaðr*), is clearly defined in the *chansons de geste* as a 'pagan' shield; see examples in *Altfranzösisches Wörterbuch*, ed. by Adolf Tobler and Erhard Lommatzsch, 10 vols to date (repr. Wiesbaden: Steiner 1955–) X (1976), col. 353.

[4] *La Chanson de Roland*, ed. by Alfred E. Ewert, 2nd edn (Oxford: Blackwell, 1946), line 3546. In laisses 262 and 263 of the poem, Ogier is singled out for his prowess: he exhorts Charlemagne to rally the troops, and then cuts down the Saracen Emir Baligant's own standard-bearer.

[5] Dámaso Alonzo, 'La Primitiva Épica francesa a la luz de una nota emilienense', *Revista de Filología Española*, 37 (1953), 2–94.

Danemarche, attributed to one Raimbert de Paris.[6] Around 1275, the prolific poet Adenet le Roi reworked a now-lost opening section of the hero's story, dealing with his youthful exploits: *Les Enfances Ogier*.[7] In the early fourteenth century, an anonymous continuation of the *Chevalerie*, the decasyllabic *Roman d'Ogier*, crosses over from the old epic territory into that of Romance; it was followed not long afterwards (*c.* 1335) by a new redaction, in fashionable alexandrines, with an even greater emphasis on the element of magic and enchantment.[8] Finally, the inevitable trend of the fifteenth century saw Ogier's story lose its verse form altogether and become the prose *Roman d'Ogier le Danoys*.[9]

There is an ironic paradox in Ogier's literary life. Although he was undoubtedly to enter Scandinavian popular consciousness as a national hero, thanks to the very early (*c.* 1240) reworking of his epic deeds in Branch III of the *Karlamagnús saga* (to the extent, centuries later but no less heroically, of having a Danish Second World War resistance group 'Holger Danske' named after him), in the French epic redactions he becomes something of a 'catch-all' figure. Apart from his name there is nothing really Danish about him: indeed, it has been suggested that the very name 'Ogier the Dane' may be a deformation of a Carolingian form 'Autacharius of the Ardennes' (thus coming from a quite different part of the Northern forest), and in some texts 'Dane' becomes 'Dacian'. Ogier starts his epic career as a young *preux chevalier* at Charlemagne's side; then he turns into a vengeful renegade baron (as a result of a blood feud), until reconciliation with Charlemagne brings him back into the fold of fidelity.[10] He is also a comic figure, a Samson-cum-Little John popular creation, with massive strength and a vast appetite, coarsely jesting, capable of laying about him with his

---

[6] *La Chevalerie d'Ogier de Danemarche*, ed. by Mario Eusebi (Milan-Varese: Istituto Editoriale Cisalpino, 1962).

[7] Adenet le Roi, *Les Enfances Ogier*, in *Les Œuvres d'Adenet le Roi*, ed. by Albert Henry, 6 vols (Bruges: De Tempel, 1951–71), III (1956).

[8] Neither of these two extremely long poems has been edited (the single extant manuscript of the *Roman d'Ogier en décasyllabes* (Paris, Bibliothèque nationale de France, f. fr. 1583) contains some 31,000 lines, while the *Roman d'Ogier en alexandrins* amounts to more than 29,000 lines, in its three manuscripts (Paris, Bibliothèque de l'Arsenal, 2985; London, British Library, Royal 15. E. VI; and Turin, Biblioteca Nazionale L. IV. 2).

[9] No manuscript survives, but two incunabula texts of the *Prose Ogier* were printed at the end of the fifteenth century, and there were several further editions throughout the sixteenth. See Georges Doutrepont, *Les Mises en Prose des épopées et des romans chevaleresques du XIVᵉ au XVIᵉ siècle*, Classe des Lettres et des Sciences morales et politiques, 40 (Brussels: Académie Royale de Belgique, 1939).

[10] For a chronological survey of the development of the Ogier story, see Knud Togeby, *Ogier le Danois dans les littératures européennes* (Copenhagen: Munksgaard, 1969); see also the analytical review article by Patricia Harris Stäblein, 'Patterns of Textual Shift and the Alien Hero: Ogier the Dane in the Europeanization of the Old French Epic', *Olifant*, 12 (1987), 47–61.

horse's saddle in lieu of his great sword Courtain.[11] Indeed, in the late medieval prose version, he becomes even more distinctly a figure of fun: to be laughed at and held up to some ridicule, in his new and increasingly un-epic surroundings.[12]

The second figure, much earlier in date, is also slightly more the epic Dane historically as well as in matters of presentation, although here again — as so often in our *chansons de geste* — aspects of reality seem to be tantalizingly offered, only to be whisked away again, or transformed into uncertainty or conventional stereotyping. This character is Gormont, and he appears in one of the earliest and most powerful of Old French epics, *Gormont et Isembart*.[13] Most probably of early-twelfth-century composition, the actual *chanson de geste* survives only as a 661-line fragment preserved in a thirteenth-century Anglo-Norman manuscript. What we have is part of the culminating episode of a story of which the main lines may be gleaned from other, pseudo-historiographical sources: it tells of the wronged and rebellious baron, Isembart, who quits the service of King Louis, forswears his faith, and joins forces with the pagan king, Gormont; and of the final battle with the Franks at Cayeux-sur-Mer, at which Gormont dies at Louis's hands and a mortally wounded Isembart makes due repentance of his sins before his own death on the battlefield. A vague historical connection has been noted with the Viking Guaramundus (or Geremundus) beaten by Louis III at the Battle of Saucourt in 881; and because our epic has part of its action take place in England, with specific mention of Cirencester, there is also a faint blended echo with the historical Guthrum (Guðormr) who was defeated by Alfred at Edington in 878, and who subsequently removed to Cirencester after his carefully staged baptism. An additional cross-Channel link may be provided by the presence at Fulham of another Viking force, which duly moved over to Ghent to threaten the Western Frankish kingdom in 880: an association between these groups and Guthrum's is offered by the *Life* of King Alfred, according to which they actually joined forces with Guthrum at Cirencester, before leaving for the Continent, but this statement goes against the far firmer evidence of the *Anglo-Saxon Chronicle*.[14]

---

[11] This comic dimension seems to have been established at an early date, since the twelfth-century *Pelerinage de Charlemagne* describes Ogier boasting (quasi-biblically) of his resolve to demolish the royal palace at Constantinople by bringing down its great central pillar (lines 518–25).

[12] See Emmanuelle Hoyer-Poulain, 'Ridicule d'Ogier: Vacillements du héros dans les remaniements de la chanson d'*Ogier le Danois*', and Nico Lioce, 'Burlesque et dérision dans *Ogier le Danoys* (remaniement en prose du xvᵉ siècle)', in *Burlesque et dérision dans les épopées de l'occident médiéval*, ed. by Bernard Guidot, Annales littéraires de l'Université de Besançon, 558 (Paris: Les Belles Lettres, 1995), pp. 49–57 and 281–94 respectively.

[13] *Gormont et Isembart: Fragment de Chanson de geste du XIIᵉ siècle*, ed. by Alphonse Bayot, Les Classiques français du moyen âge, 14, 3rd rev. edn (Paris: Champion, 1931).

[14] For the various attempts to solve the text's enigmatic references, and to connect epic to history, see James B. Ashford, 'État présent des recherches sur *Gormont et Isembart*', *Olifant*,

The Gormont of our fragment is, however, a very Saracen-Viking, typical of the epic image. He is described as an *Arabi* from the *Oriente*, and his troops are a motley crew of Turks, Persians, and Slavs (who were also to find themselves assimilated into the body of epic Saracens). More importantly, he is *Satenas*, the image of Antichrist, forever cursing the Christian god as one Frank after another rides desperately against him only to be slain, until King Louis himself arrives to dispatch him in epic combat.

And yet — cloaked in all the conventions of the Old French epic — there may be something legitimately, if coincidentally, Scandinavian about this massive Goliath-like figure of Gormont, holding the key point of the battlefield, joking and jeering as he invites his adversaries to come against him one at a time. There is at least the analogy with that nameless Viking giant of 1066, holding the bridge at Stamford against Harold and the English army until brought down by a well-aimed Special Operative's spear from below.[15]

With Gormont/Guthrum we have moved on to English soil, and so into English literature. Or rather into Anglo-Norman literature, that cultural vernacular given vital and prestigious impetus by the court civilization of Henry II and Eleanor of Aquitaine, and which for over two centuries flourished across a remarkably wide spread of genres. It is through a sample of these genres that we shall seek to trace the insular image of the Viking, starting logically with historiography, and with Gaimar's *L'Estoire des Engleis*, which is in fact our earliest extant historical work in the French vernacular.[16] Geffrei Gaimar composed his verse chronicle (*c.* 1135–40) for a noble patroness, the lady Constance, wife of Ralph FitzGilbert who held important lands in Lincolnshire, and also in Hampshire. Some of Gaimar's clearly localized information relating to the south and south-west and to the east coast seems to indicate that he may have started his work down south, before moving with his patroness into her husband's Lincolnshire heartland. Gaimar was a clerk, but not a religious, and had some personal knowledge of court circles. We know that he used at least two main primary sources for his *Estoire*: the *Anglo-Saxon Chronicle* (which he calls 'the

---

10 (1982–85), 188–209; and Jean Carles, 'Le *Ludwigslied* et la victoire de Louis III sur les Normands à Saucourt-en-Vimeu (881)', in *La Chanson de geste et le mythe carolingien: Mélanges René Louis, publiés par ses collègues, ses amis et ses élèves, à l'occasion de son 75ᵉ anniversaire*, ed. by Emmanuèle Baumgartner and others, 2 vols (Saint-Père-sous-Vézelay: Musée Archéologique Régional, 1982), I, 101–09. On Guthrum and the Viking Great Army at and after Edington, see Alfred P. Smyth, *King Alfred the Great* (Oxford: Oxford University Press, 1995), pp. 82–88.

[15] This detail, added by a twelfth-century scribe, can be found in *The Anglo-Saxon Chronicle*, ed. and trans. by G. N. Garmonsway (London: Everyman, 1953), p. 198.

[16] Geffrei Gaimar, *L'Estoire des Engleis*, ed. by Alexander Bell, Anglo-Norman Texts, 14–16 (Oxford: Blackwell, 1960). (Further references to this edition will be in parentheses. Here and throughout, the English translations are my own.) Anglo-Norman can in fact claim many literary 'firsts': our earliest French-language Bestiary, Lapidary, Saint's Life, Fable and Virgin Miracle collections, *Tristan* version, and short-verse narrative *lai* are all of insular origin.

Winchester Book', and which he was certainly able to read in the original), and a precious early copy of Geoffrey of Monmouth's *Historia regum Britanniae*, placed into his hands by its owner, the great Northern baron Walter Espec.[17] Gaimar's original composition included a first book delving back in time and myth to Jason and to Brutus, the eponymous and legendary founder of 'Britain'. This section has been lost to us; it was obviously superseded, submerged without trace by the subsequent popularity of the Jerseyman Wace's *Roman de Brut*, copies of which are to be found in Gaimar manuscripts, taking the place of Geffrei's own opening book. What survives of the *Estoire* is an updating (and upgrading) into recorded history, from the Saxon kingdoms to the death of William Rufus and the accession of Henry I.

It is not my intention to add to the study of Gaimar's sources or of his value and shortcomings as a historiographer; these areas have been solidly mined over the last fifty years (and there is much fascinating and enigmatic Danish material centring on Yorkshire and Lincolnshire: notably the Buern Bucecarle episodes (lines 2571–2720, 2721–2829), and the whole opening section of the *Estoire*, which retells a version of the Havelock story).[18] My brief is rather with images, and my aim is to treat the 'story' side of the *Estoire des Engleis*, to give some idea of the way in which Gaimar's narrative style deals with the Vikings. For this purpose three sets of narrative 'episodes' will be considered: the earlier Danish raids and incursions, up to Alfred's resistance and his victory over the invading Danes at Edington in 868;[19] the coming of Cnut (Knútr) to the English throne; and the events leading up to the Norman Conquest in 1066.

Geffrei Gaimar's portrayal of the Danish invasions predictably highlights his sources' fearful reporting of the *furor Normannorum*: verbs of assault, seizing, killing, and destruction multiply in their presence and in their wake. There is nevertheless here an interesting point of *translatio*. Gaimar's French narrative is coloured to a certain extent by the lexis of the epic (or rather of the conventions disseminated by the *geste*): we are dealing throughout with *fel paien* 'evil paynims' (passim), with *deffaié* 'faithless renegades' (line 3121), with *Daneis feluns* 'wicked Danes' (line 2404). In one or two places, particularly where he has more detailed local matter at his disposal,

---

[17] Gaimar mentions two other books, about which far less is known: *le bon livere de Oxeford* (line 6458), supplementing the *Historia*; and *de Wassingburc un livere engleis* 'an English book from Washingborough' (Lincolnshire) (line 6463), which may well have been a version of the Peterborough Chronicle (supplementing in turn his main *Anglo-Saxon Chronicle* source, *L'estorie de Wincestre*, line 6461).

[18] For a survey of this material, see Geffrei Gaimar, *L'Estoire des Engleis*, pp. lviii–lxiv.

[19] It is worth noting that, immediately after dealing with Alfred's victory over Guthrum, Gaimar makes passing reference to the epic Gormont story (lines 3236–76): following his stay in Cirencester, *reis Gurmund* crosses over to France and ravages Cayeux and Ponthieu before being slain in battle. There is no mention of Isembart, but Gaimar does seem to have heard a version of the *chanson de geste* (he refers significantly here, not to a *livere* or *escrit*, but to an oral source: *ço dit mis mestre*, 'my principal source told me this', line 3235).

Gaimar shows a more sustained epic feeling for violent poetic point and counterpoint. There is a good example in the Buern Bucecarle episode leading up to the death of Ælla of York, as we witness the feats and death in battle of Orin, Ælla's nephew (lines 2796–2814). Orin's first javelin transfixes a pagan through the mouth, stretching him out dead and damned, and his second pierces another foul Dane to the heart:

> Lançad le gaveloc qu'il tint,
> Un chevaler en asenad
> Si qu'en la buche li entrad,
> Deriere al col en issid fors,
> Ne pot ester en piez le cors,
> Jus chaïd mort, ne pot altre estre,
> Paiens esteit, n'ot suing de prestre.
> Orin retint un autre dart
> Qu'il lur lançat de l'autre part;
> Un fel Daneis si en ferid,
> Bien l'asenad, pas ne faillid,
> Sur la mamele lui entrad,
> Al quor lui vint, mort le getad. (lines 2790–2802)

(He threw the javelin he was holding, and struck a warrior with it: it pierced his mouth, and went right through his neck and out the other side. The man's feet gave way and, with no redress, he fell to the ground, a corpse: he was a pagan, so had no need for a priest. Meanwhile Orin took another spear and hurled it at his opponents; it flew straight and true, and struck an evil Dane, piercing his breast, lodging in his heart, and dropping him dead.)

But as Orin wheels his horse round, he is struck mortally in the throat by a Viking arrow: 'Mais al retur qu'il volt turner / Un archiers lait un dart voler; / Si l'aconsiut sur la furcele / K'al quor li vint mortel novele; / L'aneme s'en vait, li cors chaïd' ('But, just as he was about to wheel round again, an archer fired at him and struck him in the throat. This was a mortal blow to his heart: his body falls and his soul departs') (lines 2809–13). This whole scene is redolent of the battle rhythm of the *chanson de geste*, and it is interesting to note that some close poetic parallels are to be found in the *Gormont et Isembart* fragment.[20]

Similarly, in his subsequent account of St Edmund's defeat and martyrdom, Gaimar stresses the nature of the battle as a tragic epic clash between noble Christians (led by a king who is a *bon crestïen e Deu amis* 'a fine Christian and God's

---

[20] Cf., for example: 'Gormund li lança une tambre; / Par mi le cors li vait bruiante, / De l'autre part fiert en la lande; / Li cors chet jus, si s'en vait l'alme' ('Gormund hurled a spear at him, which went whistling clean through his body, and struck the ground behind him; his body falls, and his soul departs') (*Gormont et Isembart*, lines 74–77); and 'El torn qu'il prist, le fiert Gormund; / L'espié enz el cors li repont, / Qu'il le rabat sur le sablon' ('As he wheeled round, Gormund struck him, burying his spear in his body and laying him low on the sandy shore') (*Gormont et Isembart*, lines 296–98).

friend', line 2868) and evil but overwhelming pagan hordes, labels the Danish leaders Ubbi and Ivar (Ívarr) Ragnarsson as *malfed* 'demons' (line 2895), and details the torments of Edmund's death by archery.[21] Yet elsewhere, instead of a general epic lingering on battle-scenes involving the Danes, Gaimar the Anglo-Norman chronicler finds himself obliged to retain for the most part the *Anglo-Saxon Chronicle*'s sober sequences of events and clipped listings of personal and place names. In so doing, however, he adapts them ('reformatting' them, as it were) into his rhythmical octosyllabic verse, and as a result conveys a remarkable sense of sheer speed and movement. Swift sea-voyages, forced marches, place succeeding place on the route, battle succeeding battle: there is a particularly hectic quality to these Danish scenes in the *Estoire des Engleis*, which serves well to underline the character of the marauding heathen.

It is noteworthy that when he comes on to deal with events surrounding Cnut, Gaimar's whole tone and pace change, because the story's agenda has itself necessarily changed. Cnut is a Christian, with a claim to the throne that the author must needs show as valid: accordingly, the narrative slows down and contains much more positive character detail, so as to allow us to recognize in this particular Dane the image of a man of the true faith, acting wisely, dealing justly, and regularly praying or swearing solemn oaths.[22] Above all Gaimar puts into Cnut's mouth, in his meeting with Edmund Ironside, words of reconciliation that have particular resonance in mid-twelfth-century England:

> 'Jo sui Daneis e vus Engleis
> E noz peres furent dous reis.
> L'un tint la terre e l'autre l'ot,
> Chascuns en fist ço ke li plot.
> Tant cum l'orent en poësted,
> Chascuns en fist sa volented
> E bien sachiez luinteinement
> L'orent Daneis nostre parent.' (lines 4303–10)

('I am a Dane, and you are an Englishman, and both our fathers were kings. First one held this land, then the other, and each enjoyed free dominion over it. As long as both ruled the land, their writs ran in it; and remember that in times past it belonged to our own, Danish ancestors.')

---

[21] 'Tant i unt trait e tant lancet / Que son cors fud si enfichet / De darz que traistrent cil felun / Cum est la pel del heriçun / espés de puinnantes brochetes' ('They loosed so many arrows at him, and hurled so many spears, that his body positively bristled with all the darts which those criminals aimed at him, resembling a hedgehog's skin thickly covered with sharp spines') (lines 2907–11).

[22] For example, *Dunc parlat Kenut mult sagement* 'Thus spoke Cnut, very wisely' (line 4301); *Tint li reis Kenut dreite justise* 'King Cnut maintained true justice' (line 4380); and *'Tenez, ma fei jo vus afie'* '"See, I pledge my faith to you"' (line 4849).

In this speech full of literary convention,[23] there is also a clear symbolic analogy with the Anglo-Norman political situation that stressed the ideal coming-together under the Angevins of the two legitimate royal lines, and thus of the people themselves — a situation exemplified, beyond the royal family's politic marriages, by the mixed parentage of the chroniclers Henry of Huntingdon and William of Malmesbury (who most eloquently was to celebrate his own mixed blood: *utriusque gentibus sanguinem traho*[24]).

Gaimar soon goes on to underline this propaganda point with added force. Cnut will *not* in fact succeed in this essential task of uniting two peoples, because they are the wrong peoples, and he is the *wrong* king, a false Viking Messiah, no truly unifying Arthur (or for that matter William) at all. The English still suffer bitter humiliations at the hands of the colonizing Danes and rejoice when the Cnut line dies out:

> Dunc furent mort li eir Daneis,
> Grant joie en firent li Engleis
> Kar les Danois vil les teneient,
> Suventes feiz les hunisseient [. . .]
> En tel vilté erent Engleis,
> Sis laidisseient les Daneis. (lines 4759–62, 4771–72)

(And so the Danish line died out, and the English greatly rejoiced, for the Danes had held them in thrall, and had often committed shameful acts upon them [. . .] The English were in great servitude, humiliated by the Danes.)

The stage is set for the Conquest, and Gaimar's picture of the Danes reverts to its previous pattern: the accent on Viking characters moving swiftly and violently in all directions. Earl Godwin plays the not unexpected villain's role: he is an example of the *false* blending of two peoples, with his Scandinavian connections *de uxore* and his hatred of the Norman French (not to mention his complicity in the foul, Viking-like murder at Ely of Alfred Ætheling).[25] The new Viking invasions are shown to create anarchy in the North, and to threaten the land with partition, as though it were mere booty.[26] The retributive message is plain: first Tostig (Tósti Goðvinasun) and Harald Hard-Ruler (Haraldr harðráði Sigurðarson) meet well-deserved defeat and death in 1066 at Stamford Bridge; then the post-Conquest Rising of the North is put down by William with exemplary severity, meting out death and destruction to all of

---

[23] As Bell points out in Geffrei Gaimar, *L'Estoire des Engleis* (pp. lvii–lviii), Gaimar's stress on royal Anglo-Scandinavian honourable mutuality is shared by Anglo-Norman Latin chroniclers such as William of Malmesbury.

[24] William of Malmesbury, *De gestis regum Anglorum*, ed. by William Stubbs, 2 vols, Rolls Series, 90 (London: HMSO, 1887–89), II, 283.

[25] See lines 4825–36: the Ætheling is put to death in a very grim Viking way, by having his bowels extracted and wound round a stake, like an anchor-rope round a capstan.

[26] 'Ore volent primes par lur guere / Entr'els partir Engleterre' ('When they invaded they wished above all to divide England amongst themselves') (lines 5197–98).

York's Danes and Norwegians ('Kar li reis vint, la cité prist, / Daneis, Noreis tuz les ocist', 'For the king came and took the city, and slew all the Danes and Norwegians', lines 5443–44). All this is in telling contrast to Gaimar's favoured treatment of Hereward, whom he describes as an English hero, wrongfully disinherited by Normans and carrying out valiant deeds of resistance in a most epic manner. He is a *gentilz hom* 'man of noble birth' (line 5462), worthy and courteous, and a lion-hearted fighter, earning the loyalty of all his men: *de hardement semblot leupard* 'by his courage he resembled a leopard' (line 5514).[27] Gaimar's account of Hereward is the earliest we have (earlier even than the *Gesta Herewardi*), and his story (partly culled from oral tradition[28]) reveals an unaccustomed degree of enthusiasm and attention to literary effect. Beside this Anglo-Saxon heroism (worthy of celebration because it represents the innate valour of one half of the true blending of the Anglo-French peoples), the image of the Viking has been put firmly in its place, both in history and in the narrative. Gaimar is after all following a mid-twelfth-century insular agenda, and although his own *Estoire de Brut* may have been usurped by the runaway success of Wace's *Roman de Brut*, the political ambience of his *Estoire des Engleis* (celebrating the 'Englishness' of a French-speaking nobility and king) is a distinctive one, allowing us to contrast it slightly with the Channel-Islander's *Roman de Rou*, which caters for the same royal house's parallel pedigree as Dukes of Normandy, in direct line from the increasingly legendary Viking Rollo (Hrólfr Ragnvaldsson). In his account of Godwin, Wace has obviously to condemn Harold's father for his Danish wife and sympathies, but does so with rather less vigour than does Gaimar.[29]

Some thirty years after Gaimar, another Anglo-Norman cleric occupied himself with providing an image of the Vikings. He was Denis Piramus, once a court poet well-acquainted with the work of Marie de France, who became a cleric in his maturer years, probably attached to Bury St Edmund's Abbey, where he was to compose *c.* 1170 his great piece of verse hagiography, *La Vie Seint Edmund le Rei*.[30] This was, he tells us, commissioned by his superiors (most probably to celebrate the tercentenary of Edmund's martyrdom, 11 November 870), his brief being to set it into French 'from the English and the Latin', so that folk of all classes might under-

---

[27] This epic simile Hereward shares with the paladin Roland himself, who *Plus se fait fiers que leon ne leupart*, 'shows all the ferocity of a lion or a leopard' (*La Chanson de Roland*, line 1111).

[28] See Geffrei Gaimar, *L'Estoire des Engleis*, p. 269.

[29] 'Por les enfanz que jo vos di, / qui des Daneis esteient né / e de Daneis erent amé, / ama Goïne les Daneis / mult mielz qu'il ne fist les Engleis' ('On account of the children who, as I have said, were born of Danish blood and were loved by the Danes, Godwin much preferred Danes to Englishmen') (Wace, *Le Roman de Rou (c. 1170)*, ed. by A. J. Holden, 3 vols (Paris: Société des Anciens Textes Français, 1970–73), III, lines 5674–78).

[30] *La Vie de Seint Edmund le Rei: Poème anglo-normand du XIIe siècle par Denis Piramus*, ed. by Hilding Kjellman (Gothenburg: Elanders, 1935; repr. Geneva: Slatkine, 1974).

stand.[31] His new vernacular account of the life, death, and miracles of St Edmund Martyr follows two main sources, evidently placed at his disposal: the *De infantia sancti Eadmundi* of Galfridus de Fontibus, dedicated to the Abbey's Prior Ording (1148–56), and then Abbo of Fleury's classic *Passio sancti Eadmundi*, composed towards the end of the eleventh century. Denis Piramus also makes use of Geoffrey of Monmouth (in his obligatory opening review of insular chronology and genealogy), and quite probably knows Gaimar too. But he also injects into his story his own personal knowledge of East Anglia — the *Vie* is packed with local topography, from King's Lynn and Hunstanton downwards, centring on Attleborough and Caistor — and Denis seems also remarkably well aware of nautical matters, as witness his detailed account, full of mariners' terms (lines 1365–1500), of Edmund's voyage from the Frisian coast across the North Sea to the Wash.

As befits the subject, it is only to be expected that the portrait of the Viking painted by Denis Piramus should be the most unremittingly black of all the texts under consideration; and he takes full advantage of his previous secular existence as a professional poet to surpass his hagiographical source-material in descriptions of blood and cruelty. It is significant that to begin his account of the incursion leading up to the martyrdom he brings in the character of Ragnar Shaggy-Breeches (Ragnarr loðbrók): legendary in both communities, a benchmark for violent deeds (even though Ragnar was already dead when his son Ivar was historically involved in Edmund's death). We are thus from the start in the presence of utter evil:

> Meis trop esteit felun veisuns,
> Kar fel esteit vers ses procheins
> Et mut cruel vers les lonteins,
> Gopil acuz vers ses parenz
> E enemi a tutes genz.
> Lothebroc soune en engleis,
> 'Ruisel haineus' en franceis;
> Veirement haineus esteit,
> Il e ceo qui de li surdeit. (lines 1882–90)

(But he was indeed a wicked neighbour: treacherous towards those close to him, and extremely cruel towards those outside his circle. He was a cunning fox to his kinsmen, and a devilish foe to all other people. In English his name is pronounced 'Lothebroc', or 'loathsome stream' in our French tongue: he was indeed loathsome, and so was the entire line of which he was the source.)

Ragnar's three sons Ivar, Ubbi, and Björn are all equally hideous of aspect and character, but each is also described by an appropriate set of pejorative French terms evoking a particular image. For Ivar, it is of cunning treachery and criminal deceit;

---

[31] 'Qu'en franceis le poent entendre / Li grant, li maien e li mendre' ('In French, so that those of high, middling and low degree might all understand it') (lines 3269–70).

for Ubbi, it is of sorcery and diabolism; and for Björn, it is of psychotic violence.[32] Piramus then creates a family confrontation scene (vv. 1949–2002), full of the most dramatic epico-romance motifs, in which the three brothers stand before their father and proudly relate all their murderous deeds for his delectation, only to see their father burst out in teeth-grinding, eye-rolling fury: what they have done is nothing when compared with the stupendous achievements of Edmund the young Saxon, now East-Anglian monarch of all he surveys.

Thus the scene is set for Ivar's determined invasion of East Anglia, and for Edmund's torture and martyrdom, described in language that owes as much to the cumulative style of the Old French epic as to the conventions of the *Legenda Aurea*.[33] In the obligatory second part of this saint's Life, subsequent episodes have King Alfred defeating the Danes in Wessex and — back in East Anglia — Svein Forkbeard of Denmark (Sveinn tjúguskegg Haraldsson) driven away by the stout thegn, Ulfcytel, with the saint's posthumous aid (lines 3697–3864). Thus martial triumphs succeed valiant tragedy, with Svein cast in the role of another damned Gormont, fighting with berserker strength ('Se contint cume urs e leopart, / Ki se cumbat mult ferement; / Kanqu'il ateint par mi li fent', 'He performed like a bear or a leopard, fighting most fiercely: everyone he struck he cleft in twain', lines 3780–82), but ultimately worsted by the heroic English in an epic combat: out of seven thousand *feluns Daneis* ('wretched Danes'), only sixty-seven return alive to the safety of their longboats.

For a matching Anglo-Norman image of the Viking, we stay within the genre of the vernacular saint's Life, but move chronologically to the middle of the thirteenth century, and to *La Estoire de Seint Aedward le Rei*,[34] a work now recognized as attributable to Matthew Paris, the polymath monk of St Albans.[35] This poem was

---

[32] Ivar: *fel et culvert* ('perfidious swine', line 1927), *atilus* ('sly', line 1930), *fel veziez lere* ('evil cunning wretch', line 2087), *treïtour* (line 2117), *tirant* (line 2339); Ubbi: 'sorciers, si sout tut l'estre / De sorcierie, s'i fu mestre' ('A master magician, who knew all the arts of sorcery', lines 1933–34); Björn: 'si engrés, / D'ire anguisuse si irés, / L'ire de li fu si ardant, / Suz ciel nen ad homme vivant / Que il esparniast a nul foer, / Kant l'ire li munte en quoer' ('he was so cruel, so consumed by violent passion: his wrath burned so strongly that he would spare no man alive, once the fury had entered his heart', lines 1937–42).

[33] This is particularly noticeable in the culminating scene, when the Vikings pierce the saint's body with all their spears and arrows (lines 2395–2424).

[34] *La Estoire de Seint Aedward le Rei*, ed. by Kathryn Young Wallace, Anglo-Norman Texts, 41 (London: Anglo-Norman Text Society, 1983).

[35] Latin chronicler, Anglo-Norman narrative poet, calligrapher-scribe, artist, cartographer, and heraldic designer, Matthew Paris is one of thirteenth-century England's most dynamic figures. An inmate of an abbey particularly favoured by the royal family, he was well acquainted with the court politics of the reign of Henry III. The best general account of his life and work is still Richard Vaughan, *Matthew Paris* (Cambridge: Cambridge University Press, 1958), supplemented by the most recent study of his artistic achievement by Suzanne Lewis, *The Art of Matthew Paris in the 'Chronica Majora'* (Aldershot: Scholar Press, 1987).

commissioned by Queen Eleanor, Henry III's consort, probably to celebrate the 1245 restoration of Westminster Abbey church, or specifically the royal presentation in 1241 of a new shrine to receive the Confessor's body (which would not be translated there until some years later, 1268–69). Matthew Paris's direct sources are Ælred of Rievaulx's influential *Vita sancti Edwardi* (composed on the occasion of Edward's canonization in 1163) and at least one of the historiographical works available to him at St Albans (and on which he himself worked); but he also adds a number of independent and highly personal touches in his vigorous insular French verse.[36] Here in fact, is to be found a treatment of the Vikings that in its violent hostility surpasses both his Latin sources and Denis Piramus's *Life* of St Edmund. Early in the narrative, Svein Forkbeard is described as a cruel and criminal bloodsucker of a tyrant,

> Uns encresme tirant felun
> Daneis, ki Suanus out a nun.
> L'or vermeil e l'argent blanc
> Cuveite cum sansue saunc,
> Crueus, e mout sout de guere. (lines 177–81)

(Svein was his name: he was a criminal, wicked Danish tyrant, coveting bright gold and shining silver as a leech covets blood. He was cruel, and all too well-versed in the arts of war.)

Subsequently, the text is studded with hot insults: the Danes are barbarous, unnatural, alien monsters, enemies of all true Englishmen, *cuveitus feluns engrés* 'greedy criminal savages' (line 223), *nos enemis* [. . .] *estraunges e desnatureus* 'degenerate foreign foes' (lines 250, 253), *losenjurs e aliens* 'cheating foreigners' (line 916), *estranges barbarins* 'foreign barbarians' (line 4194). The poet pays particular attention to Danish atrocities in the internecine conflict during the reign of Harthacnut (Hörða-Knútr):

> Naufrent, reiment, peinent, lient,
> Femmes et enfanz ocient.
> Mettent a flaumbe e a charbun
> Nis maisuns de religiun.
> Cist ocist, cist reint, cist art,
> Cist tue enfant e cist veillard,
> E clergie e seinte iglise
> Est a duel e hunte mise. (lines 542–49)

(They damage and pillage, torture and shackle, slay women and babies, and even put to the fire the houses of God. While one kills, another loots and a third burns; one will slay a child, another an old man; and Holy Church and her clergy are grievously defiled.)

---

[36] An earlier Anglo-Norman *Life* of Edward, by an anonymous nun of Barking Abbey, is far more a literal translation of Ælred's Latin text; see *'La Vie d'Edouard le Confesseur', poème anglo-normand du XIIe siècle*, ed. by Östen Södergård (Uppsala: Almqvist & Wiksell, 1948).

Such anti-Danish sentiments are not restricted to the text of the poem. The manuscript of the *Estoire* contains eighty-three magnificent illustrations, each with its verse rubric, and is a faithful copy of Matthew Paris's own original, now lost (it may be compared with the master's fortunately surviving holograph *Vie de Seint Auban*).[37] In the compressed stanzas of the rubrics, the violent hostility is repeated and intensified. While in the text Matthew follows Ælred in his description of England laid low under Danish rule like a flock at the mercy of beasts of prey ('Engleterre est cum ouaille / As liuns e as luz livrez', 'England is like a flock given over to lions and wolves', lines 620–21), his rubric to the corresponding illustration stresses still more the horror and devastation,[38] and the Danes in his illustration itself (fol. 7^r) are depicted as ugly, wild-haired creatures of the devil. In later illustrations, similar Viking caricatures are to be found of Tostig and his Norwegians, as they invade Humberside and are defeated by Harold at Stamford Bridge (fols 57^v, 59^r).

Such virulent treatment of the Vikings, in a text of the mid-thirteenth century, is only partly to be explained by the poem's historical subject matter. There is firstly, it must be said, a degree of personal animosity at work. Throughout his writings, Matthew Paris reveals himself to be a very opinionated Englishman, with an Englishman's fine contempt for foreigners, and his patriotism often spills over into overt xenophobia. Here the Danes are the objects of his hostile attention; elsewhere, it will be the French, or the Germans, or the pope in Rome. There is also a political agenda informing this commissioned *Life* of Edward the Confessor: Matthew's own firm desire for peace in England under the continued benign and legitimate rule of Henry III, best of kings. It is this subtext, only just beneath the surface, that may be read into Edward's anguished prayer for the deliverance of his dear country and its ancient lineage,[39] into the poet's subsequent hailing of the day of liberation, when King Edward may at last ascend the English throne at the death of the Danish line:

---

[37] There is an in-facsimile edition of this manuscript (Cambridge University Library, MS Ee. iii. 59) by Montague Rhodes James (Oxford: Roxburgh Club, 1920). For Matthew Paris's *Life* of the patron of his own house, see *'La Vie de Seint Auban': An Anglo-Norman Poem of the Thirteenth Century*, ed. by A. R. Harden, Anglo-Norman Texts, 19 (Oxford: Blackwell, 1968).

[38] 'Destruite est religĭun, / N'i truvissét si dolurs nun. / Mut crest li maus par la guerre, / Maubaillie est Engleterre, / Cist reint, cist tue, cist art' ('Religion is destroyed: only sorrow is to be found. Evil profits greatly from the war, while England is cast down: here there is pillage, there murder, and there burning') (lines 4717–21).

[39] '"Suanus e Cnudz of lui Deneis / Mortz unt les gentiz Engl[eis], / Ki parenté, ki ancesur / Furent noble conquestur, / Venant en la cumpainie / Brut, a la chere hardie, / Ki s'en vint a grant navie / De la grant Troie, flur d'Asie. / Allas! Ke fras, Engleterre?"' ('"Svein and Cnut with their Danish troops have slain the gentle-born Englishmen, whose distant ancestors were noble conquerors in the company of bold-visaged Brutus, who landed here with a great fleet from mighty Troy, the flower of Asia. Alas! How will you fare now, England?"') (lines 782–90). This evocation of the Golden Age, very much in the Geoffrey of Monmouth tradition, is not found in Ælred.

Li Daneis s'en vunt confus,
N'i osent demurer plus.
Lors sunt Engleis en grant baudur
E mercient lur Creatur,
Ki, cum d'Egipte fist jadis,
Ses serfs a de servage mis. (lines 840–45)

(The Danes depart, discomforted, not daring to stay here any longer. Now the English are full of joy, and give thanks to their Creator who has led his people out of servitude, just as he did out of Egypt in olden times.)

This subtext is perhaps most evident in Matthew's fierce cry of patriotic triumph, in the accompanying illustration rubric (fol. 12^r): 'Delivré ad la terre Deus / Des sanglanz Daneis bastarz!' ('God has delivered the land from the bloody Danish bastards!') (lines 4750–51).[40]

After tracing the image of the Viking from *chanson de geste* into Anglo-Norman historiography and hagiography, we move, in the final section of this essay, into the world of narrative verse romance. Here there are two celebrated texts to consider — briefly, precisely because so much has been written about them in the general context of the medieval literatures of England — before ending with a third, far less well-known poem.

What we know as the Anglo-Norman *Romance of Horn* is a 5240-line poem composed some time around the mid-twelfth century (possibly as late as *c.* 1170, given the author's knowledge of Tristan romances), in irregular laisses of alexandrines punctuated by a strong internal caesura.[41] The author proudly names himself as *Mestre Thomas* (line 3): by all evidence a minstrel clerk with knowledge of court etiquette and entertainment, as well as of the conventions of epic and the increasingly popular romance genre. He claims his piece to be the central piece of a poetic genealogical trilogy, comprising a *Roman d'Aalof* (Horn's father), the adventure-story of *Horn* itself, and a *Roman d'Hadermod* (dealing with Horn's son and heir). His work seems partly based on a lost original vernacular poem, to which he refers variously as *ma geste* 'my copy of the story' (line 251), *la letre* 'the written text' (line 1656), and *le parchemin* 'the manuscript' (line 2933), and which may also have been the source of the evidently related, but independent thirteenth-century Middle English poem *King Horn*.

---

[40] For further details of Matthew Paris's inclusion in his work of his own opinions and prejudices, and of the dramatic, 'layered' effect of the combination of text, rubric, and illustration in his saints' lives, see Brian J. Levy, 'Autoportrait d'artiste, figure de poète: Le cas de Matthieu Paris', in *Figures de l'écrivain au moyen âge*, ed. by Danielle Buschinger, Göppinger Arbeiten zur Germanistik, 510 (Göppingen: Kümmerle, 1991), pp. 193–206.

[41] Thomas, *The Romance of Horn*, ed. by Mildred K. Pope, revised and completed by T. B. W. Reid, 2 vols, Anglo-Norman Texts, 9–10, 12–13 (Oxford: Anglo-Norman Text Society, 1955–64).

Horn has indeed many affinities with Old French epic and romance (between which genres it seems to occupy an intermediate stage);[42] Thomas clearly knows his *chansons de geste*, including those previously noted in this essay for their 'pseudo-Viking' content: he refers to Ogier the Dane's sword (*Curtein*, line 1995), and to the prowess in single combat of Louis of France (line 3466: most probably an echo of *Gormont et Isembart*), as well as to *Roullant l'enperial* 'Prince Roland' (line 1997) and (more obliquely perhaps) to the *cort nés* 'snub nose' of Guillaume d'Orange (lines 3199–3202). The story is set in a Brittany–Ireland–South Devon triangle (the latter, somewhat confusingly, called *Suddene*), and the frequent battles match the heroic Horn and his supporters against a generic pagan enemy, an invader or adversary to be fought and always defeated. This epic ethos is consistently supported by the romance's remarkably Manichaean onomastics. While Horn's line is heavily and reassuringly Germano-Saxon, the names of the evil 'Saracen' warriors with whom he and his fellow island heroes come into contact remain stubbornly Norse: Egolf (cf. Eyjólfr), Gudbrand (cf. Guðbrandr), Gudelaf (cf. Guðleifr), Gudolf (cf. Guðulfr), Herebrand (cf. Herbrandr), Hildebrand (cf. Hildibrandr), Rodlac (cf. Hróðlaugr), and Rodmund (cf. Hróðmundr). The image is clearly still that of the Viking as Other.

The *Lai d'Haveloc* was composed in the early thirteenth century (just possibly at the end of the twelfth) by an anonymous French poet, settled, like Geffrei Gaimar, in Anglo-Norman Lincolnshire.[43] The key locality is uncompromisingly Grimsby and North Lincolnshire.[44] His poem is indeed most probably dependent for material upon Gaimar, who seems to have been so taken with the Havelock story — a version of which he must himself have found in an independent local East Coast source — that he devotes to it the opening 816 lines of his *Estoire*, by way of a colourful and popular exordium; it also serves Gaimar's historico-narrative purposes of explaining the later Cnut-centred Danish claim to the English throne.

On the surface, then, in our search for Anglo-Norman images of the Viking, the *Lai d'Haveloc* seems the most clearly and authentically Scandinavian-based. The story of Havelock the Dane would undoubtedly appear to embody some incidents from the life of Anlaf Sihtricson (Óláfr Sigtryggsson), who seems very early on to have become a popular hero after the tenth-century settlement, and to whom sundry tales and adventures duly became attached. As a character, Havelock certainly seemed a very Viking hero to those early-nineteenth-century Romantics who eagerly

---

[42] For Thomas's wide-ranging debt to the matter and style of the vernacular literature of his time, see *The Romance of Horn*, II, 6–14.

[43] *'Le Lai d'Haveloc' and Gaimar's Haveloc Episode*, ed. by Alexander Bell (Manchester: Manchester University Press, 1925).

[44] The later Middle English *Havelok* is more generally knowledgeable about insular topography; the author of our Anglo-Norman *lai* betrays himself as geographically uncertain once he moves his characters further down into East Anglia (see *'Le Lai d'Haveloc'*, ed. by Bell, pp. 45–46).

seized upon, and perpetuated, the legend of a massively strong warrior wielding his great battle-axe to terrible effect.

And yet, for all its 'Danish' names and possible Danelaw source-elements, for all its initial debt to Anglo-Scandinavian legends, the *Lai d'Haveloc* shows us in effect no more than 'nominal Vikings', integrated into the commonalty of Old French or Anglo-Norman romance. The fact is that, in cultural and poetic terms, our anonymous author is less influenced by Gaimar, or by any matter of Scandinavia, than by the exciting new literary style of the octosyllabic verse 'Breton lay', as popularized in particular by Marie de France. As far as essential psychology and social preoccupations are concerned, the main characters may just as easily have been English or French; and any Scandinavian elements serve no more than to provide suitably 'exotic' touches, in lieu of other lays' more overtly Celtic matter (King Arthur himself in fact puts in an early appearance, conquering Danish territories, lines 27–40). But one important point should be noted: here at last the image of the Viking has moved away from that of the damned pagan, and we can hear of Danish victories throughout Lincolnshire with no more historical connotations of the fury of the Norsemen. By the story's end Havelock the Dane is completely, and ironically, subsumed into the poetic conventions of the lay that bears his name:

> Aveloc tint en sa baillie
> Nichole et tote Lindesie.
> Vint anz regna e si fu reis,
> Assez conquist par ses Daneis.
> [E] mult fu de lui grant parlance.
> Li ancien en remembrance
> Firent un lai de sa victoire,
> Ke tuz jorz mes seit en memoire. (lines 1105–12)

(Havelock maintained possession of Lincoln and of all Lindsey. He became king, ruling for twenty years and conquering much land, thanks to his Danish troops. His name became a household word: in his memory our ancestors composed a lay telling of his triumph, so that henceforth everyone might be reminded of it.)

This last fact, of acculturation through the diluting effect of literary convention, brings us to the *Roman de Waldef*. This is a fascinating Anglo-Norman text, very long (over 22,000 octosyllables, and still incomplete in its single extant manuscript), and only recently edited.[45] Despite earlier scholars' efforts to see in it traces of an Old English epic, or of East Anglian socio-political history from the tenth to the twelfth centuries, the fact remains from a full reading that this is a completely fictitious romance of the very early thirteenth century, showing more the influence of Wace's *Brut*, of the *Tristan* story, and of the Eustachius legend than of any actual events. The one clear historical element in the entire poem surrounds the name of the

---

[45] *Le Roman de Waldef*, ed. by A. J. Holden (Cologny-Geneva: Fondation Martin Bodmer, 1984).

hero Waldef himself: identifiable with that of the thegn Waltheof, post-Conquest
Earl of Huntingdon and Northampton, and the only rebellious English lord actually
executed by William (in May 1076) after the abortive Rising of the North with its
threat of another Viking invasion, this time against the Conqueror. Earl Waltheof
had been a great patron of Croyland Abbey in Lincolnshire, and the monks
embarked upon an assiduous, and remarkably successful, campaign of rehabilitation;
this locally disseminated propaganda may well have kept the name alive in the
popular domain, and may even explain the very high incidence of clerical characters
in the romance.[46]

Frustratingly for anyone wanting greater *historicité*, there is none. The *Roman de
Waldef* in no way deals with any aspect of the real Waltheof's life. But the truly
interesting feature for us of this text is the way in which it does blend English and
Viking elements. Set essentially in East Anglia, part of the old Danelaw, it shares
strikingly with the *Lai d'Haveloc* and with Denis Piramus's *Vie Seint Aedmund le
Rei* the same minutiae of recognizable east-coast topography: Lincoln, Grimsby, and
Lindsey; Norfolk, Caister, Thetford, and Narborough; Suffolk and Attleborough.
There is more. The romance may not reflect reality at all in any firm, detectable way;
but here at last the old sense of 'Other-ness' is lost, to be replaced by one of inter-
twined Anglo-Scandinavian identities, truly analogous with William of Malmesbury's celebration of his own mixed blood. In the *Roman de Waldef*, Saxon names
rub shoulders with Viking ones (including, for their shared heroic connotations,
'Hereward', 'Swein', and 'Cnut'). The English hero Waldef's close companion is
called Beorn, and Odo and Odard accompany his two sons. There is much sea-
voyaging off the East Anglian coast, by representatives of both peoples. Separated
from their father, Waldef's sons Guiac and Gudlac[47] travel to Scandinavia, and serve
there and subsequently in Germany; Danes come to serve King Fergus of London,
and subsequently ally themselves with the forces of Waldef. Even when a character
appears who at first seems to uphold the old epic image of the 'Saracen-Viking', like
the Swedish King Urvein, who swears by Mahomet and invades Waldef's lands, he
too is soon integrated into the romance's community. Honourably defeated by
Waldef in single combat, Urvein offers our hero eternal friendship and mutual aid:

---

[46] On this last point, see *Le Roman de Waldef*, ed. by Holden, p. 22. The 'Waltheof Affair'
is mentioned by Gaimar, with due acknowledgement of the activity of the monks of Croyland
Abbey (*Estoire*, lines 5718–28). For further details of Croyland's success, not merely in
rehabilitating their dead patron, but in actually turning him into a saintly martyr, see Brian J.
Levy, 'Waltheof *earl* de Huntingdon et de Northampton: La naissance d'un héros anglo-nor-
mand', *Cahiers de civilisation médiévale*, 18 (1975), 183–98. As an interesting by-product of
Waltheof's revolt, contemporary Scandinavians celebrated him as a heroic cousin against the
Frank: Þorkell Skallason's *Valþjófs-flokkr* sings his praises, and laments his cruel death (see
Corpus poeticum boreale, ed. by Gudbrand Vigfusson and F. York Powell, 2 vols (Oxford:
Clarendon Press, 1883; repr. New York: Russell & Russell, 1966), II, 227).

[47] The name of Waldef's son clearly echoes that of Guthlac, patron saint of Croyland Abbey.

'Vus estes mult pruz e vallant;
Trop par serroit damage grant
U de moi ore u de vus
Se il mesavenist de nus.
Ceste bataille relerrai,
La terre tute vus rendrai,
Par tel covent que des or mes
Soit entre nus amur e pes;
Que, si jo de vus ai mestier
Sucurre me vendrez e aider,
E si mestier avez de moi
Od grant esforz vendrai a toi.'
Waldef respont: 'E jo l'otroi;
Ne remeindra pas endroit moi
Que l'amur entre nus ne teingne
Et que l'un a l'altre ne viengne.'
Adunc se vunt entrebeisier
E compaingnie asseürer. (lines 5087–5104)

('You are a most valiant warrior; it would be a great pity, for you and for me, were we
to remain opposed. I shall cease fighting you, and shall return your lands, on the
understanding that there will be peace and friendship between us: if I have need of
you, you shall come to my aid, and should you need me, I shall come with a mighty
force of arms.' Waldef replies: 'So shall it be! For my part, henceforth friendship shall
bind us together, and one shall ever come to help the other.' The two now embrace and
swear an oath of comradeship.)

Urvein will keep his word. Later in the romance, he will reunite Waldef with his
wife Ernild (whom Saracen pirates have kidnapped and transported to the Swedish
king's court at Dublin) and show his English friend exemplary generosity and hospitality (lines 8645–68). Thus the Vikings in *Waldef* are seen to be just as *pruz e larges
e curtois* ('valiant, generous, and courtly') as their English counterparts. The ties that
bind them, however, go deeper still: fictional Saxon and Dane also — above all —
share a common obsession, the holding and maintaining of family lands, regularly
under threat throughout the poem. The Norfolk and Suffolk place-names are transformed in *Waldef* into so many fortresses, valiantly defended by the hero, his family,
and his allies. Here, and in Germany and Denmark, the text is punctuated with some
of the bloodiest and most desperate battle-scenes to be found anywhere in medieval
French literature, all to defend one's rightful fief or kingdom.[48] In *Waldef*, there is a
true Anglo-Danish alliance at work, cemented by a mutual feudal obsession with
safe domains and secured inheritance that was a particular feature of Anglo-Norman

---

[48] For further details of these particular features, see Brian J. Levy, '"Honor" et "honneur":
Le rôle du château-foyer dans deux romans lignagers anglo-normands', in *Château et société
castrale au moyen âge*, ed. by Jean-Marc Pastré (Rouen: Publications de l'Université de
Rouen, 1998), pp. 297–308.

society at the end of the twelfth and into the thirteenth century — and, accordingly, of the literature catering to the needs of that society.[49]

From its ominous beginnings in the medieval French epic, and from its even more uncompromisingly hostile treatment in Anglo-Norman vernacular chronicle and saint's Life, the image of the Viking finds here and there a more hospitable landfall in the newly popular romance genre. So it is that, in the *Roman de Waldef* at least, it finally comes to mirror that of a noble insular public, seeking local colour, excitement, and the wish-fulfilment of secure lands in a period of insecurity.

---

[49] See the well-documented study of this phenomenon by Susan Crane [Dannenbaum], *Insular Romance: Politics, Faith and Culture in Anglo-Norman and Middle English Literature* (Berkeley: University of California Press, 1986). In a more recent article, 'Waldef and the Matter of/with England', in *Medieval Insular Romance: Translation and Innovation*, ed. by Judith Weiss and others (Cambridge: Brewer, 2000), pp. 25–39, Rosalind Field comments tellingly on the text's 'deeply pessimistic' ending, with its bleak warnings of political disorder and injustice (which it will share with later Middle English romances).

The Danish Monarchy and the Kingdom of Germany, 1197–1319: The Evidence of Middle High German Poetry[*]

ALAN V. MURRAY

The period between the mid-eleventh and mid-twelfth centuries saw a fundamental realignment of the foreign policy aims of the Danish monarchy. The Great North Sea empire forged by Cnut the Great (1018–35) collapsed on the death of his son Harthacnut (1040–42), and the reigns of Svein Estridsson (1047–74/76) and his son St Knut (1080–86) witnessed the final, fruitless Danish attempts to invade England.[1] From the death of Svein Estridsson onwards, Denmark was weakened by a series of disputes over the throne that lasted over a century, until Valdemar I the Great (1157–82) succeeded in defeating his rivals and established himself as sole ruler. From this time onwards the major ambitions of Danish kings were no longer directed to the west, as they had been during the Viking Age, but east

---

[*] General discussion of the historical background in this essay is largely based on the following works: Max von Domarus, *Die Beziehungen der deutschen Könige von Rudolf von Habsburg bis Ludwig dem Baiern zu Dänemark* (Halle an der Saale: G. Jalkowski, 1891); Geoffrey Barraclough, *The Origins of Modern Germany*, 2nd edn (Oxford: Blackwell, 1947); Ingvor Margareta Andersson, 'König Erich Menved und Lübeck', *Zeitschrift des Vereins für Lübeckische Geschichte und Altertumskunde*, 39 (1959), 69–116; Herbert Grundmann, *Wahlkönigtum, Territorialpolitik und Ostbewegung im 13. und 14. Jahrhundert*, Gebhart Handbuch der deutschen Geschichte, 5 (Stuttgart: Deutscher Taschenbuch, 1970); Erich Hoffmann, *Königserhebung und Thronfolgeordnung in Dänemark bis zum Ausgang des Mittelalters* (Berlin: Walter de Gruyter, 1976). I am grateful to Dr Kurt Villads Jensen (University of Southern Denmark) for commenting on an earlier draft. Unless indicated otherwise, English translations of passages in Middle High German are my own.

[1] Erich Hoffmann, 'Dänemark und England zur Zeit König Sven Estridsons', in *Aus Reichsgeschichte und Nordischer Geschichte*, ed. by Horst Fuhrmann, Hans Eberhard Mayer, and Klaus Wendt (Stuttgart: Klett, 1972), pp. 92–111.

and south along the land frontiers of Jutland and the shores of the Baltic Sea. Three areas in particular were targeted for expansion by the Danish kings and their supporters. Firstly, Nordalbingia, that is Schleswig and Holstein, with the important trading centre of Lübeck; this area was to remain a major bone of contention between Denmark and Germany right up to the war of 1864. Secondly, the southern shore of the Baltic, from eastern Holstein to Pomerania, inhabited in the earlier twelfth century by pagan, Slavic-speaking Wends; the Danish monarchy could present its ambitions in the context of mission and conversion, and thereby enlist the support of the papacy and the Danish Church. By the end of the twelfth century, Danish kings had conquered the island of Rügen and asserted their overlordship over Pomerania.[2] The third significant area of expansion was yet another theatre of crusade and mission: Estonia, on the eastern Baltic shore, which was conquered under Valdemar II (1202–41), remaining under Danish rule until 1346.[3]

In each case Danish ambitions came into conflict with the interests of German princes, institutions, and populations. The princes and nobles of Saxony had been just as keen as the Danes to colonize the Wendish territories, forcibly converting the Wends and bringing in settlers from Saxony, Holland, and Flanders. By 1200 the Wends, including the few surviving princely dynasties, had largely accepted Christianity and Germanization.[4] In the eastern Baltic lands, the Danes were rivalled by German clerics as well as by two military monastic orders, the Sword Brothers and the Teutonic Knights. Finally, there was the German monarchy itself, which was keen to uphold royal rights on the frontiers of the empire wherever possible. The history of these events is well known. Yet literary evidence has not always been fully exploited as a source for political or even cultural relations between Scandinavia and Germany. The purpose of this essay is to approach the issues of Danish-German conflict and coexistence by exploring what vernacular German literature reveals about the interests and ambitions of the Danish monarchy between the end of the twelfth and the early years of the fourteenth centuries.

---

[2] Tinna Damgaard-Sørensen, 'Danes and Wends: A Study of the Danish Attitude Towards the Wends', in *People and Places in Northern Europe, 500–1600: Essays in Honour of Peter Hayes Sawyer*, ed. by Ian Wood and Niels Lund (Woodbridge: Boydell, 1991), pp. 171–86; Stella Maria Szacherska, 'The Political Role of the Danish Monasteries in Pomerania, 1191–1223', *Mediaeval Scandinavia*, 10 (1977), 122–55.

[3] Tore Nyberg, 'The Danish Church and Mission in Estonia', *Nordeuropaforum*, 1 (1998), 49–70; Niels Skyum-Nielsen, 'Estonia under Danish Rule', in *Danish Medieval History: New Currents*, ed. by Niels Skyum-Nielsen and Niels Lund (Copenhagen: Museum Tusculanum Press, 1981), pp. 112–35; William Urban, *The Baltic Crusade*, 2nd edn (Chicago: Lithuanian Research and Studies Center, 1994), pp. 61–79; Torben K. Nielsen, 'The Missionary Man: Archbishop Anders Sunesen and the Baltic Crusade, 1206–21', in *Crusade and Conversion on the Baltic Frontier, 1150–1500*, ed. by Alan V. Murray (Aldershot: Ashgate, 2001), pp. 95–117.

[4] Barraclough, *The Origins of Modern Germany*, pp. 249–65; William Urban, 'The Wendish Princes and the *Drang nach Osten*', *Journal of Baltic Studies*, 9 (1978), 225–44.

I

Under Conrad III (1138–52) and Frederick I Barbarossa (1152–89), the first two rulers from the Hohenstaufen dynasty, the main interests of the German monarchy were focused on the southern parts of the German kingdom, Swabia, Franconia, and the Rhineland, where the bulk of the royal estates (*Reichsgut*) and the Hohenstaufen hereditary lands were concentrated, and on the wealthy urban landscape of Lombardy. The emperor rarely ventured to the north of Germany, but Barbarossa's power and prestige were sufficient for him to impose his overlordship on Denmark in 1152. The major rivals of the Hohenstaufen dynasty in Germany were the Welfs, who although originally from the south, had built up a major power base in northern Germany under Henry the Lion, duke of Saxony. For most of his life Henry had been the major rival to the Danish crown for control of Nordalbingia and the Wendish territories. However, in 1180 Frederick I overthrew Henry and deprived him of his duchy, which was broken up into smaller territorial units. The Lion retained only some of his allodial lands and went into exile in England where he remained until 1185.

The diminution of Welf power in northern Germany brought about a major change in the balance of power between Denmark and the Reich. On the death of Valdemar I in 1182, his son Knut VI (d. 1202) refused to recognize the suzerainty of the empire. He proceeded to impose Danish overlordship on Pomerania and Mecklenburg, and in 1187 refused to carry out a promise of marriage between Barbarossa's son Frederick of Swabia and a daughter of Valdemar I.[5] Under Barbarossa's successor, Henry VI (1189–97), the German monarchy was even more focused on Italian interests, particularly on the kingdom of Sicily, whose heiress Henry had married, but when he died unexpectedly in 1197 at an early age, the empire was thrown into crisis. His son, Frederick II, was at that time still a minor, resident in Sicily. The Hohenstaufen party therefore put forward as candidate for the throne the late emperor's younger brother, Philip, duke of Swabia. Opposition forces in Germany sought a rival and found a Welf candidate in Otto of Brunswick, count of Poitou, the second son of Henry the Lion. Since Otto had grown up at the Anglo-Norman court and was a favourite of his uncle, Richard the Lionheart, his candidature received strong political and financial backing from England and Cologne, England's major trading partner in Germany.[6]

The establishment of two rival German kings in the persons of Otto IV and Philip of Swabia, and the consequent formation of pro-Welf or pro-Hohenstaufen parties among the German territorial princes, now offered the Danish monarchy a major

---

[5] Hans-Joachim Freytag, 'Der Nordosten des Reiches nach dem Sturz Heinrichs des Löwen', *Deutsches Archiv für Erforschung des Mittelalters*, 25 (1969), 471–530.

[6] On the position of Otto within the Anglo-Norman realm, see Alan V. Murray, 'Richard the Lionheart, Otto of Brunswick and the Earldom of York: Northern England and the Angevin Succession, 1190–91', *Medieval Yorkshire*, 23 (1994), 5–12.

opportunity to extend its power across its southern frontier. In the course of the year 1201 a Danish army under Knut VI's brother Valdemar, duke of Schleswig, overran Nordalbingia and drove out Adolf III, count of Holstein. Since Adolf and many of the other German nobles who had opposed the Danes were supporters of Philip of Swabia, Denmark became particularly attractive to Otto IV as a potential ally.[7] At the end of the year Otto met Valdemar at Hamburg and agreed on two new marriages between members of their respective families. Helena, the sister of Knut VI and Valdemar, was to marry Otto's younger brother William of Winchester, lord of Lüneburg, while Valdemar himself was engaged to Richza, daughter of Otto's elder brother, the Count Palatine Henry.[8]

It is possible that this Danish-Saxon alliance was reflected in one of the most famous poetic works of the German Middle Ages. The *Nibelungenlied*, the orally transmitted epic poem which tells of the death of the hero Siegfried and the destruction of the Burgundians, drew on legendary and historical material dating from the Migration Period. By the time it came to be written down in its surviving form around the year 1200, the material had undergone numerous changes, and had introduced or elaborated themes with a more contemporary resonance. One of these was the nature of kingship, which in the Germany of the Hohenstaufen-Welf struggle from 1197 onwards was of great topicality.[9] One of the rather puzzling episodes in terms of its relevance to the overall storyline occurs in *Aventiure* 4, which begins by telling how messengers arrive at the court of Gunther, king of the Burgundians:

> Nu nâhten vremdiu mære in Guntheres lant
> von boten, die in verre wurden dar gesant
> von unkunden recken, die in truogen haz.
> dô si die rede vernâmen, leit was in wærlîche daz.
>
> Die wil ich iu nennen: ez was Liudegêr,
> ûzer Sahsen lande ein rîcher fürste hêr,

---

[7] Hans-Joachim Freytag, 'Die Eroberung Nordelbingens durch den dänischen König im Jahre 1201', in *Aus Reichsgeschichte und Nordischer Geschichte*, ed. by Fuhrmann, Mayer, and Wendt, pp. 222–43.

[8] Bernd Ulrich Hucker, *Kaiser Otto IV.* (Hanover: Hahn, 1990), pp. 372, 379–80.

[9] See, for example, Dietz-Rüdeger Moser, 'Zeit des Unheils im Nibelungenlied', in *Rhythmus und Saisonalität: Kongreßakten des 5. Symposions des Mediävistenverbandes in Göttingen, 1993*, ed. by Peter Dilg, Gundolf Keil, and Dietz-Rüdiger Moser (Sigmaringen: Thorbecke, 1995), pp. 161 70, Dieter Breuer and Jürgen Breuer, *Mit spaeher rede: Politische Geschichte im Nibelungenlied* (Munich: Fink, 1995); Alan V. Murray, 'Rumolt's Counsel and the Concept of Royal Responsibility in the *Nibelungenlied* and the *Klage*', *Forum for Modern Language Studies*, 33 (1997), 142–55; Dietz-Rüdeger Moser, 'Vom Untergang der Nibelungen: Augustinisches Denken im *Nibelungenlied*', in *Nibelungenlied und Klage: Ursprung – Funktion – Bedeutung. Symposium Kloster Andechs 1995*, ed. by Dietz-Rüdeger Moser and Marianne Sammer (Munich: Institut für Bayerische Literaturgeschichte der Ludwig-Maximilians-Universität, 1998), pp. 77–130.

> und ouch von Tenemarke der künec Liudegast.
> die brâhten in ir reise vil manegen hêrlîchen gast.[10]

The messengers proclaim the intention of the two rulers (who are revealed to be brothers) to invade the Burgundian kingdom. The response of Gunther is to send an army to Saxony to meet the invasion. The most important part in this campaign is played by Siegfried, a warrior newly arrived at the Burgundian court. Thanks to Siegfried's superhuman powers, the combined Saxon-Danish army is defeated. Liudegast and Liudeger are both captured by Siegfried and are obliged to make a humiliating peace:

> Die sigelôsen recken ze Tenemarke riten.
> done heten ouch die Sahsen sô hôhe niht gestriten,
> daz man in lobes jæhe; daz was den helden leit.
> dô wurden ouch die veigen von vriwenden sêre gekleit.[11]

This episode seems to have two main functions in terms of the overall story of the work. Firstly, it demonstrates Siegfried's great military prowess and the increasing dependence of the Burgundian kingdom on him. Secondly, it serves to establish Siegfried's reputation for knightly virtue with Gunther's sister Kriemhilt, whom he wishes to marry. It is the murder of Siegfried at the instigation of Gunther and his brothers that will many years later provoke the destruction of the Burgundians by Kriemhilt in revenge, an event which forms the climax of the epic. Nevertheless, it is unclear precisely why the Liudeger-Liudegast episode should be described at such great length, or why related rulers of Denmark and Saxony should figure as the aggressors.

Heinz Thomas has suggested that these political constellations would have had significant associations for a contemporary audience. The literary kingdom of the Burgundians with its capital at Worms on the Rhine could have been identified with the kingship of the Hohenstaufen dynasty, whose landed power lay in Franconia, Swabia, and the Rhineland, while a campaign directed against the Burgundians by related rulers of Saxony and Denmark was a reflection of the Danish-Welf alliance in the period of disputes over the German throne after 1198. It is thus possible that

---

[10] *Das Nibelungenlied*, 20th edn, ed. by Helmut de Boor (Wiesbaden: Brockhaus, 1972), strophes 139–40: 'Strange tidings were on their way to Gunther's country, borne by envoys that had been sent to the Burgundians from afar by unknown warriors who nevertheless were their enemies; hearing which, Gunther and his men were greatly vexed. I shall name those warriors for you. They were Liudeger, the proud and mighty sovereign of Saxony, and Liudegast, King of Denmark, and they were bringing a host of lordly intruders with them on their campaign.' Translation taken from *The Nibelungenlied*, trans. by Arthur T. Hatto (Harmondsworth: Penguin, 1969), p. 33.

[11] *Das Nibelungenlied*, ed. by De Boor, strophe 220: 'The Danes rode back defeated to Denmark, nor to their shame had the Saxons fought so marvellously as to earn themselves any glory. The fallen were deeply mourned by their kinsmen' (trans. by Hatto, p. 41).

the ambitions of the Danish monarchy had a direct influence on the content of the most important German heroic epic of the thirteenth century.[12]

The Hohenstaufen cause in Germany was thrown into disarray when Philip of Swabia was murdered in 1208. However, Otto IV's policies soon aroused opposition both in Germany and with the papacy, and Philip's nephew Frederick II (king of Sicily) emerged as the new Hohenstaufen candidate. For the Danish monarchy the continuing division of political power in Germany offered an opportunity to exploit, and as king in succession to his brother, Valdemar II extracted from Frederick the formal acknowledgement of Danish overlordship over Nordalbingia in 1214. The reign of Valdemar II proved to be something of a high-water mark for Danish expansion for at least a century. Despite his gains in Nordalbingia and the conquest of Estonia, Valdemar's ambition was checked by two events. In 1223, while on the small island of Lyø, both the king and his heir were captured in an audacious naval raid by Henry, count of Schwerin, who kept them captive until the end of 1225. On his release Valdemar acted energetically to make up for lost time, but at the battle of Bornhöved in 1227 he and his nephew, Otto 'the Child' of Brunswick-Lüneburg, suffered a great defeat at the hands of a coalition of German princes including Henry of Schwerin and Adolf of Holstein. In the following years the Danish realm was further weakened by the policy of successive kings of granting large portions of the kingdom as appanages to junior members of the royal house, often border areas such as Schleswig, Halland, Blekinge, or — on occasion — Estonia, or islands such as Lolland. The main result of such dispositions was to provide discontented princes with the means to try to gain the throne for themselves, and the rest of the century was marked by civil wars and the violent deaths of several kings.

II

The Liudeger and Liudegast episode in the *Nibelungenlied* represents something of a veiled allusion to contemporary political events around the year 1200. By contrast, in the course of the next 120 years a number of quite explicit references to kings of Denmark can be found in a quite different Middle High German literary genre. The works in question all belong to the genre known as *Spruchdichtung*, that is, strophic poems with a religious, ethical, or political content; most of them are panegyric in character. Fortunately there is enough information within the texts themselves or ascertainable from the rough chronology of the poets' activities to identify the Danish subjects in question. The corpus comprises the following works: a strophe in praise of Erik IV Plovpenning (1241–50), by Reinmar von Zweter; two poems (of one and three strophes respectively) on the murderers of Erik V Klipping (1259–86),

---

[12] Heinz Thomas, 'Die Staufer im Nibelungenlied', *Zeitschrift für deutsche Philologie*, 109 (1990), 321–54.

as well as a single strophe in praise of Erik VI Menved (1286–1319), by Rumelant; and a poem of two strophes, also in praise of Erik Menved, by Heinrich von Meißen, known by the artistic name of Frauenlob.[13]

Although the modern scholarly designation *Spruchdichtung* implies something spoken, the strophic form, as well as iconographic and other evidence, suggests that they may just as well have been sung, with or without musical accompaniment.[14] The fact that certain metrical patterns are used for numerous different strophes by the same poet means that it is difficult to know whether we should think in terms of longer works consisting of several different strophes, or of units of single strophes, with no other connection beyond a shared melody. The sometimes insuperable difficulties of producing coherent interpretations of metrically identical strophes have led to a tendency of literary historians to prefer interpretations based on generally small units. While the identification of the subjects is relatively easy, the circumstances of the commissioning and performance of the poems are much more problematic.

There is very little independent documentation about the lives and careers of the poets concerned beyond what can be deduced from the works recorded under their names, and some rather fleeting or exiguous references in the works of other poets. About Heinrich von Meißen rather more is known, including the date of his death; the one piece of surviving documentary evidence about him places him in the entourage of a southern prince, Henry, duke of Carinthia, who gave him money to purchase a horse.[15] For Reinmar von Zweter we are wholly reliant on the corpus of his work. This means that the discussions of lives and chronologies can be tentative in the extreme, resting on fragile assumptions or chains of assumptions deriving from matters of content whose dating or geographical location can rarely be established with absolute certainty.

The manuscript tradition suggests that monarchs and nobles were prepared to turn their hand and voice to *Minnesang*, that is, as composers and performers of love lyric, but they were not prepared to indulge in *Spruchdichtung*; when it came to poetry with a political message, rulers made use of professionals. We should therefore assume that the poets under discussion were dependent on patronage for a living, and that the content of their political poetry essentially reflected the interests of their paymasters.[16] It has often been assumed that a series of poems praising different

---

[13] For a literary analysis of these works, see Kurt Erich Schöndorf, 'Dänische Herrschergestalten in der politischen Lyrik des deutschen Mittelalters und der frühen Neuzeit', *Collegium Medievale*, 6 (1993), 36–79.

[14] One piece of internal evidence in favour of sung performance can be found in the final line of Rumelant's strophe *Alle künege, vürsten, herren, ritter, knaben, knehte*, cited below.

[15] Karl Stackmann, 'Frauenlob', in *Die deutsche Literatur des Mittelalters: Verfasserlexikon*, ed. by Kurt Ruh and others, 2nd edn, 10 vols (Berlin: Walter de Gruyter, 1978–99), II (1980), 865–77.

[16] Joachim Bumke, *Höfische Kultur: Literatur und Gesellschaft im hohen Mittelalter*, 2 vols (Munich: Deutscher Taschenbuch, 1986), II, 685–700.

rulers must necessarily reflect a series of different patrons, with changes of location and employment, and on the basis of the subjects of panegyric poetry some scholars have constructed complete biographies and itineraries for poets. Yet equally, if we have a series of poems in praise of different subjects, we could just as well assume that the poet spent the whole period represented in the service of one prince, acting as his mouthpiece to justify his political about-turns in supporting different allies or candidates for the German throne.

A further problem in establishing the context for political poetry is that courts were by no means fixed geographical institutions. Even when monarchs resided in one place for longer periods of time, one must question whether the number of people in permanent or near-permanent attendance would have been sufficient to make performances of political poetry worthwhile at all times. If we want to identify the most likely occasions for poetic performances, then we need to look to large gatherings such as the great liturgical feasts of Christmas, Whitsun, and Easter, when monarchs often took part in solemn crown-wearing ceremonies, and secular festivals such as weddings, peace-treaties, knighting ceremonies, and tournaments, especially since such gatherings would attract a public from beyond the immediate retinue of the poet's patron.[17]

It would be mistaken, therefore, to assume that the poetic works under discussion were performed 'at the Danish court' in terms of an institution with a fixed physical location. However, there is a possibly even greater problem than this one, which might be referred to as the socio-linguistic status of the poems. The language of the poems is — as in the case of the *Nibelungenlied* — a literary form of Middle High German, the language, or perhaps more accurately the group of dialects spoken in central and southern Germany, including Austria and parts of Bohemia. At this time, the language of most of northern Germany, including some areas under the domination of the Danish crown, was Middle *Low* German, with Frisian spoken along the north-eastern coast and some surviving pockets of Slavic in Wendish areas. Unlike the situation in recent times, Low German still had a relatively high status; for example, it was the language of urban records in towns such as Hamburg and Lübeck well into the early modern period. It was extensively used for trading purposes in the Scandinavian countries and, certainly after the conquest of Livonia at the beginning of the thirteenth century and its subsequent colonization by settlers from northern Germany, had acquired a status as a lingua franca of the entire Baltic region.[18] Low German was understood and used in governing circles in Denmark, both by those

---

[17] Bumke, *Höfische Kultur*, I, 276–341.

[18] *Handbuch der niederdeutschen Sprach- und Literaturwissenschaft*, ed. by Gerhard Cordes and Dieter Möhn (Berlin: Schmidt, 1983), pp. 98–153; Vibeke Winge, 'Zum Gebrauch des Niederdeutschen in Dänemark im Mittelalter', in *Niederdeutsch in Skandinavien II: Akten des 2. Nordischen Symposions 'Niederdeutsch in Skandinavien' in Kopenhagen, 18–20. Mai 1987*, ed. by Karl Hyldgaard-Jensen, Vibeke Winge, and Birgit Christensen (Berlin: Schmidt, 1989), pp. 106–15.

originating in Germany and by a number of native Danes. In the fourteenth century the language used for documents by the Danish royal chancery was still predominantly Latin (with a far smaller number of documents in Danish), while Middle Low German was used in correspondence with German rulers and the Hanseatic towns (a higher proportion of documents than Danish).[19] It is likely that at the end of the thirteenth century, familiarity with Middle *High* German in Denmark was minimal.

Although it was not the vernacular tongue in North Germany, Middle High German was in use there for some literary genres, notably chronicles and *Minnesang*, and the significant number of northern German princes recorded in the song manuscripts as composers of love lyrics indicates a familiarity with literary High German in court circles. By contrast, it is difficult to see whether there would have been a sufficient audience within Denmark for songs with a political content composed in High German. We must remember that *Spruchdichtung* was not mere entertainment, but literature with a purpose, whether it was to convince political neighbours and potential enemies to lend support to a ruler, or served simply as a piece of image polishing. We can more readily understand a political purpose for the poems in question if we try to see them in the context of gatherings that included not only the Danish king and his own subjects, but large occasions involving allies, enemies, and the uncommitted, particularly if these involved political players from Germany who were likely to have been familiar with political discourse in High German.

Let us look in more detail at some of the poems themselves to see what they might tell us about the interests of the Danish monarchy. The first in chronological terms is a single strophe by Reinmar von Zweter:

> Ein künec, der wol gecroenet gat,
> unde daz sin crone verre baz geküneget stat,
> da ziert der künec die crone baz, dan in diu crone gezieren müge.
> Ein wol geküneget cronetrage
> tuot dannoch mere, er stillet witwen unde weise clage,
> er süenet unde vridet unt ist bi liuten wol in eren hüge.
> Sin herze unt auch sin muot sint selten müezec,
> sin munt ist zallen ziten erengrüezec,
> im schimelt niht in siner arken.
> daz beziug ich mit dem besten wol:
> mit urloube ich in nennen sol:
> ez ist der künec Erich von Tenemarken.[20]

---

[19] Vibeke Winge, *Dänische Deutsche – deutsche Dänen: Geschichte der deutschen Sprache in Dänemark 1300–1800 mit einem Ausblick auf das 19. Jahrhundert* (Heidelberg: Winter, 1992), pp. 40–61.

[20] *Die Gedichte Reinmars von Zweter*, ed. by Gustav Roethe (Leipzig: Hirzel, 1887), p. 485, no. 148: 'A king who goes well crowned and whose crown makes him more royal: the king is a greater adornment to the crown than the crown is to him. Yet a royal crown-bearer does more: he redresses the grievances of widows and orphans, he brings reconciliation and

This strophe utilizes a rhetorical technique in which the subject's reputation is gradually built up through enumeration of his virtues and qualities, but with his name only being revealed in the last line. To what extent this element of suspense could have been maintained in a performance situation is, of course, questionable. Some of the qualities enumerated are the standard coinage of panegyric: honour (*ere*) and generosity, the latter a quality — as in the reference to the king's ever-open treasure-chest — which was of course of great importance for the professional poet. Nevertheless there is a quite clear message to this strophe. The word *crone* ('crown') is mentioned four times, but the essential point is that its bearer is more than worthy of the crown. The protection of widows and orphans had long been an important component of royal coronation promises and liturgies, particularly the coronation *ordines* used in connection with the German throne. This poem then, tells us that the king has kingly attributes; does this signify anything more than formulaic praise of a royal subject?

The oeuvre of Reinmar von Zweter constitutes one of the largest surviving corpora of political lyric in Middle High German. He seems to have been active during the second quarter of the thirteenth century, a particularly turbulent period in German history. During the 1230s Emperor Frederick II met with a rising tide of opposition in Germany, stoked by the papacy. Frederick had had his eldest son, Henry (VII) (d. 1242), elected King of Germany, but when Henry rebelled against him, Frederick had his son deposed and imprisoned. In March 1239 Gregory IX excommunicated Frederick, and the pro-papal party in Germany began making plans to elect a king in opposition to him. A letter of the papal legate, Albert Behaim (dated June 1239), reveals the intention of the pro-papal party to elect the young king of Denmark as king of the Romans (*regem Dacie juniorem in regem Romanorum*).[21] The *Gesta abbatum Horti Sanctae Mariae*, a chronicle from the abbey of Mariengaard in Friesland, records information under the year 1240 to the effect that Gregory IX had offered the crown in turn to the son of King Valdemar of Denmark and to Otto 'the Child' of Brunswick (nephew of Emperor Otto IV), but that both had declined the offer.[22] What has confused some modern historians is that in the MGH edition of this text, the son of Valdemar is unnamed, and recorded only as *filio Waldemari regis*, but is glossed as Abel (later King of Denmark) by the editor. The reason for this is probably that another source, one of various texts interpolated in the chronicle of Alberic of Troisfontaines, mentions in connection with the death of Valdemar of Denmark the fact that the pope had wanted one of his three sons, Abel, to become

---

peace, and is held in honour. His heart and his spirit are seldom idle. He gives honourable greetings at all times; no mould grows on his treasure chest. This I can testify, and with your leave I will name him: it is King Erik of Denmark.'

[21] *Die Gedichte Reinmars von Zweter*, ed. by Roethe, pp. 63–64.

[22] *Gesta abbatum Horti Sanctae Mariae*, ed. by G. H. Pertz, MGH, SS, 23 (Hanover: Hahn, 1874), p. 595.

King of Germany in opposition to Frederick.[23] We cannot exclude the possibility that both Danish princes were canvassed by the pope, but it is much more likely that the Alberic text is wrong, having simply confused the two brothers.

Erik IV Plovpenning was crowned as successor during his father's lifetime, in 1232.[24] This explains the description of him as 'junior king' in the Behaim letter, written at the time when his father was still alive; Abel at this time had only the title of Duke of Schleswig. In 1239 Erik married a German princess, Jutta, the daughter of Albrecht I, duke of Saxony from the Ascanian dynasty. The period before Erik succeeded to the Danish throne in 1241 was therefore one in which he was in his early twenties, old enough to play on the political stage, and was entering into a dynastic alliance with one of the most important north German families. If we look at the history of Germany in the thirteenth and early fourteenth centuries, it will be seen that the election of kings was very problematic. The question of which princes had the rights of election was in flux, as the idea of unanimity was giving way to the idea that certain of the princes were indispensable to a successful election, although there was as yet no agreement on which princes these should be. It was not until the fourteenth century that the number of electors was fixed at seven: three archbishops and four secular princes.[25] The period between the death of Henry VI in 1197 and the proclamation of the Golden Bull of 1356 by Charles IV saw a great number of disputed elections, often with two candidates being elected by different parties of princes, or by alliances electing an anti-king in opposition to a reigning monarch.

In this connection, it is perhaps significant that there are two other strophes by Reinmar which fit the same tune as the panegyric for Erik IV, which respectively praise the kingly qualities of the king of Bohemia and discuss the rights and responsibilities of some of the German electoral princes.[26] All indications are that these three related strophes were connected with the attempt to elect a king in opposition to Frederick II, and that the strophe devoted to Erik was intended to build him up as a potential candidate for the German throne. This would explain the repeated references to the crown, and royal duties of protecting orphans and widows. Who better could the German princes choose as king than someone who was a crowned king already? It is difficult to establish the reasons why Erik did not go through with this candidature. In the climate of shifting alliances it may have been perceived as too risky. Another reason may have been that Erik needed to concentrate fully on Danish affairs; he probably foresaw problems in the ambitions of Abel, who eventually was to bring about his murder. If we try to establish the literary context for this poem then we need to think not so much of Denmark, but of Germany. The prime movers

---

[23] Alberic of Troisfontaines, *Chronica*, ed. by Pertz, MGH, SS, 23, p. 949.

[24] Hoffmann, *Königserhebung und Thronfolgeordnung*, pp. 122–23.

[25] Charles C. Bayley, *The Formation of the German College of Electors in the Mid-Thirteenth Century* (Toronto: University of Toronto Press, 1949).

[26] *Die Gedichte Reinmars von Zweter*, ed. by Roethe, pp. 484–86, nos 146, 149.

in the pro-papal coalition were the King of Bohemia, Wenceslas I, and the Duke of Bavaria, Otto II. Since the political players whom it would be most crucial to impress would be those German princes who would be needed to elect Erik, it is most likely that this poem was originally performed not in Denmark, but at some gathering much further south.

III

The next known Middle High German panegyric on a Danish monarch is a strophe by a poet with the name of Rumelant (or Rumzlant). It praises the qualities of a king called Erik, who is referred to as son of another King Erik. It is this information which allows us to identify the subject as Erik VI Menved and the likely time of composition as between 1286, when his father, Erik V, was murdered, and 1319, when he himself died:

> Got in vil hohen vröuden saz,
> do er so lank, so breit, so groz, so riche maz
> daz lop, daz an dem edelen künige erschinet;
> Daz im in siner kindes jugent
> gebrichet niht ein har an voller mannes tugent.
> nu schouwet, wie er sich nach eren pinet,
> Ja er mak Erich heizen wol:
> sin lip, sin muot, sin herze ist eren riche.
> nie vuor mit eren vart so vol
> bi maniger zit, daz sprich' ich sicherliche,
> so der von Tenemarkenlant,
> der junge künik, der nach dem alten ist genant,
> ein Erich nach dem andern künik Eriche.[27]

The king's name is in fact the key to the poem, which is largely constructed around a pun on the German form *Erich(e)* as being equivalent to *eren riche*, that is, 'rich in honour'. This pun is not based on a true linguistic etymology, but it is one which poets evidently relished, as it offered the opportunity to discourse on the courtly virtues. There are no explicit clues to the circumstances of composition or performance of this work, but its themes may allow us to establish its most likely context. The essential message of Rumelant's poem is that its subject possesses all

---

[27] Ulrich Müller, *Politische Lyrik des Deutschen Mittelalters*, 2 vols (Göppingen: Kümmerle, 1972), I, 81: 'God was in a state of great joy when he set out the praiseworthiness that can be seen in the noble king — so tall, so wide, so great, and so rich. He does not lack a single hair of manly virtue. Now see how he strives after honour — his name should indeed be Erik: his body, his spirit, his heart are rich in honour. Never has anyone carried himself with honour for so long — this I assure you — as the one from Denmark, the young king, who is named after the old one: an Erik in succession to the first Erik.'

the necessary virtues and attributes of a king, despite his youth. The implication is that the young Erik not only has the same name but the same kingly qualities as his father and is thus eminently suited for the succession.

Erik VI Menved succeeded to the throne in precarious circumstances. His father, Erik V Klipping, was murdered in his bed at Finderup in northern Jutland by a group of traitors led by one Arvid Bengtsen. Erik Menved was still a minor, and he was opposed by a faction within the nobility as well as by Jens Grand, the future Archbishop of Lund. The queen mother, Agnes of Brandenburg, was obliged to accept Valdemar IV, duke of Schleswig and a rival to Erik V, as *tutor regni*, a concession which allowed him huge political influence in the kingdom, but ensured the succession for her son.[28] The actual murder itself was treated in condemnatory fashion in two further poems (of one and three strophes respectively) by Rumelant.[29] The most likely time for the composition and performance of all of these works would have been the period between the murder of Erik V on 22 November 1286 and the court held at Nyborg at Whitsun 1287, which brought about the formal condemnation of the murderers.

The longer of the two poems begins by describing the murderers and their deed, but finishes in the third strophe by addressing them directly:

> Die Tenschen morder haben den pris,
> ze morde nie man ist so wis,
> da man sol künige morden;
> Sie mordent gerne unt künnen'z wol:
> den hoehsten mort man prisen sol
> ze Jütlande in dem norden;
> Dar ist begangen mortlich mort; sie kunden
> iren künik unsanfte wekken
> Uf einem bette, da er slief,
> sehs unde vünfzik wunden tief
> durchstachen im die rekken
>
> Sie mügen wol kuene rekken sin,
> daz ist an irme lebene schin,
> die ez mit den handen taten.
> Ir varwe und ir gelaz ist hin,
> sich hat verwandelt al ir sin,
> die'z mit in haben geraten;
> Diene wizzen niht neheinen rat, sie gernt dem
> jungen künige bi ze stande,
> sie wellen sin unschuldik noch,
> unt bieten vür ir Tenisch loch:
> nein, an ez wirt anders gande.

---

[28] Hoffmann, *Königserhebung und Thronfolgeordnung*, pp. 137–38.

[29] Schöndorf, 'Dänische Herrschergestalten in der politischen Lyrik', pp. 44–47, 64–65.

Ir morder pruebet iuwern mort,
wie groz ein mortlich sünden hort
in iuwern kameren hordet;
seht, iuwer künik was iuwer kneht,
der iu gewalt gab unde reht;
den habet ir gemordet.
Des sit ir immer me versmat, von allen gnaden
vröudelos geschieden;
der mort ist iuwer heilvertrip:
man git daz kriuze uf iuwern lip,
unt slæt iuch sam die heiden.[30]

Some of the phraseology is difficult to translate precisely; however, certain salient points emerge. The narrator starts with ironic praise of the murderers, telling how they stabbed the king with fifty-six wounds as he lay sleeping in his bed. He goes on to say they now claim to be innocent and express their desire to support the young king. However, he makes it clear that the murder has deprived them of salvation, and they will also suffer earthly punishment, 'slain like the heathens'. These details, and the suggestion that the murderers hope to come to terms with the new regime, would seem to indicate that this poem was being performed *before* the judicial condemnation at the Whitsun court. The shorter of the two poems dealing with the murder is rather different in tone:

Alle künige, vürsten, herren, ritter, knaben, knehte,
in zwein unt sibenzik sprachen, Juden, heiden, Kristen, elle,
pfaffen unde leien, lantgebur, al menschen diet,
Nu helfet rechen uns den mort, durch Got unt durch daz rehte,

---

[30] Cited in Schöndorf, 'Dänische Herrschergestalten in der politischen Lyrik', p. 46: 'The Danish murderers are renowned that no one is so skilful as they are in the murder of kings; they murder willingly and well. Now the greatest murder is to be praised, in Jutland in the north. A deadly murder was committed there; they rudely woke their king on the bed where he was sleeping, and then the warriors stabbed him with fifty-six deep wounds. They may be brave warriors, and this is evident in the deeds they committed with their own hands. Changed is the appearance and demeanour of those who put them up to this. They have changed their tune: now they do not know what they should do. They ask that they might support the young king, they claim to be innocent still, and plead their Danish law. No, it will turn out differently. You murderers, consider your murderous deed, how great a hoard of mortal sins you are gathering in your chambers. See, your king was your servant, who gave you power and justice: it is he whom you have murdered. For this you shall forever be despised, and cut off from all mercy. The murder is the end of your salvation: you shall be marked with the cross, and slain like heathens.' For the interpretation of this poem I follow Reinhold Schröder, 'Dâvon sing ich u diz liet: Rumelands strofer i anledning af Erik Klippings død', in *Marsken rider igen: Om mordet på Erik Klipping, Rumelands sange og marsk Stig-viserne*, ed. by Jens E. Olesen and others (Odense: Laboratorium for folkesproglig Middelalderlitteratur, Odense Universitet, 1990), pp. 35–58.

vil me wan durch des küniges tot, daz reht geriht erschelle
dem künige, dem sin selbes volk mortlichen tot geriet.
Getriuwen Tensche liute, rechet
iuwern künik, des habet ir lob und ere,
die morder meldet, unde sprechet
an ir lip, daz sich ir heil verkere.
swelich Tenscher wil unschuldik sin, dar tuo, daz ich in lere,
der sol die morder helfen tilgen vientlichen sere,
daz ir laster mere:
davon sing' ich iu diz liet.[31]

The tone of this strophe is simple, urging the Danish people to unite to pronounce condemnation of the murderers. The most appropriate venue for performance would therefore have been the Whitsun court of 1287. This important gathering did much more than simply make judicial decisions. It was important to bolster public and foreign confidence in the new regime. To this end the young Erik Menved was knighted by Otto IV, margrave of Brandenburg (1282–1308). This was a particularly significant choice; in knighting ceremonies of this kind it was usual for a relatively young nobleman to be dubbed by a more senior and distinguished figure. The margrave, nicknamed Otto *mit dem Pfeil* ('with the arrow'), was the brother of the queen mother, and thus maternal uncle to the young king, a relationship which in the central Middle Ages was traditionally regarded as guaranteeing disinterested support and protection to the nephew. Otto was also known as a patron of literature in Middle High German and as a performer of *Minnesang*, although as a territorial prince he did not deign to perform *Spruchdichtung*.[32] Otto was thus an ideal choice from the points of view of both chivalry and kinship.

The presence of the margrave of Brandenburg and his German retinue would have made the performance of poetry in High German both likely and worthwhile. It is therefore probable that the two single strophes were composed by Rumelant in the service of Otto of Brandenburg, as a public relations exercise on the part of the new

---

[31] Cited in Schöndorf, 'Dänische Herrschergestalten in der politischen Lyrik', p. 44: 'All kings, princes, knights, squires, servants in seventy-two languages, Jews, heathens, Christians all — clerics and laymen, country people, and all humanity — help us to avenge the murder, for God and the law rather than (in vengeance) for the king's death, so that justice will be done for the king who suffered death at the hands of his own people. Faithful Danes, avenge your king, and gain praise and honour in doing so; announce the names of the murderers and judge them that their salvation will be lost. Whichever Dane wishes to be regarded as innocent, he will do what I instruct him: he will help to extirpate the murderers and increase their dishonour. Of these things I sing you this song.'

[32] In the so-called Manesse Song Manuscript (Heidelberg, Universitätsbibliothek, pal. germ. 848), seven love lyrics are ascribed to *Otto mit dem Pfeil*. The nickname, which was current in the margrave's lifetime, derived from an incident in which an arrow penetrated his helmet and left an arrowhead lodged in his head for several years. See Eberhard Schmidt, *Die Mark Brandenburg unter den Askaniern (1134–1320)* (Cologne: Böhlau, 1973), pp. 178–90.

regime, stressing the royal qualities and legitimacy of the young king. The same may well be true of the three-strophe poem. It is striking that some phrases stress Denmark as the scene of events described; 'Danish murderers' (*Tenschen morder*) and 'Jutland in the north' (*ze Jütlande in dem norden*) would seem unnecessary for a purely Danish audience. This raises the possibility that this work of Rumelant was meant for a mixed Danish-German audience in Denmark, or even that it was composed at the behest of Erik and Agnes's allies, the Margraves of Brandenburg, for performance in Germany as a means of influencing German political opinion to deny refuge to the fugitive murderers.[33]

IV

Once Erik Menved was established on the throne, his reign saw a resurgence of Danish political ambitions along the southern Baltic shore. During this time the German monarchs were preoccupied with building their own territorial power bases and fighting against rival candidates.[34] The punning praise on the name Erik which had already been utilized by Rumelant evidently offered a welcome opening for poetic composition. This may be the key to the two-strophe poem by Heinrich von Meißen (Frauenlob), some lines of which have not survived:

> Ich will des sinnes lie florieren
> mit roselohten worten schon probieren,
> mit redebluomen sunder vrist
> hie violvar volzieren
> ein lop daz hat sich also wit gebreitet.
> So hoch mit sunnen do genumen
> er tar sich erenricher werke rüemen:
> er darf durchgrunthaftiger list,
> swer ez sol spaehe blüemen,
> wan ez in biunde hat gar schon geleitet
> Min triuwer muot in triuwen ganz.
> sin rede ist alse ein blüender kranz,
> sin lop belibet sicher glanz,
> sin manlich tugent ie sunder schranz
> in küneclichen eren spranz.
> von Tenemarken ie ich bin
> prisaer des küneges: also kunst volsprich,
> [. . .]

---

[33] On 5 June 1287 Otto IV and his brother Conrad I jointly proscribed the murderers of Erik V. See *Diplomatarium Danicum*, ed. by Adam Afzelius and others, 2nd series, 12 vols (Copenhagen: Munksgaard, 1938–60), III (1939), 210–11, no. 252.

[34] Ingvor Margareta Andersson, *Erik Menved och Venden: Studier i dansk utrikespolitik 1300–1319* (Lund: Gleerupska universitetsbokhandeln, 1954).

Ein lustlich herze mit vollen sinnen,
durchspaehet mit der wunne uze und innen,
ein stolzer lip gar wunnesam
ze dienst der zarten minnen:
der kan sin ritterlicher muot sich neigen.
Rein alse ein rubin, luter, klar,
schein wunneclichen lustgevar
sin lop bi künigen, vürsten zwar;
hoch swebt ez sam ein adelar,
wan vrouwen zart gar offenbar
wisliche gert der vürste an mein:
sin reiniu art unt des et do begert.[35]

As we see, the poem does not name its subject directly; however, the narrator claims to be the 'praiser of the king of Denmark' (*von Tenemarken ie ich bin prisaer des küneges*). This, and the punning references to *erenricher werke* 'honourable deeds' and *küneclichen eren* 'kingly honour' have led most commentators to identify this subject, too, as Erik VI Menved. If we seek an event that would link the reign with the known chronology of Heinrich von Meißen, the most appropriate circumstances for the performance of this poem would undoubtedly be the great chivalric festival celebrated by Erik and his German allies outside Rostock in June 1311, which was celebrated in another poem by Heinrich von Meißen which he explicitly dates to this event.[36]

This festival was conceived not only as a celebration, but also as a political demonstration of Danish power and wealth, and was particularly intended to impress or intimidate the north German cities. Erik's household spent a year preparing for these events, which lasted five days, included a tournament, and had musicians, actors, and other entertainers in attendance.[37] The events and participants were described in some detail by Ernst von Kirchberg, whose Middle High German rhymed chronicle names among the participants several territorial princes from northern Germany: the Dukes of Saxony and Brunswick, Margrave Woldemar of Brandenburg, the Counts of Holstein, Wittenburg, and Schwerin, and Henry, count of Mecklenburg.[38] Additionally

---

[35] Müller, *Politische Lyrik des Deutschen Mittelalters*, I, 139.

[36] Frauenlob [Heinrich von Meißen], *Leichs, Sangsprüche, Lieder*, ed. Karl Stackmann and Karl Bertau, 2 vols (Göttingen: Vandenhoeck & Ruprecht, 1981), I, 13–17 (no. 5); Schöndorf, 'Dänische Herrschergestalten in der politischen Lyrik', pp. 57–58; Andersson, *Erik Menved och Venden*, pp. 140–51.

[37] Werner Paravicini, 'Rittertum im Norden des Reiches', in *Nord und Süd in der deutschen Geschichte des Mittelalters*, ed. by Werner Paravicini (Sigmaringen: Thorbecke, 1990), pp. 147–91.

[38] *Mecklenburgische Reimchronik des Ernst von Kirchberg*, ed. by Christa Cordshagen and Roderich Schmidt (Cologne: Böhlau, 1997), p. 344: 'Dar quam konig Erich / vor alle fursten lobelich. / Dy herczogin quamen ouch sundir krig / von Sassin vnd von Brunswig. / Ouch quam ubir kostlich dar / von Brandenborg marcgreue Woldemar. / Dy greuen quamen ouch

— although he is less specific on individual identities — Kirchberg mentions those from further afield: 'The Dukes of Poland also came, and the Wendish lords also made the journey to the court — it is true. Many came from Meißen, and the nobles of Thuringia were able to bring a great number of knights; from Westphalia, Swabia, and the Rhine came many of worthy appearance.'[39] Meißen, Thuringia, Swabia, and the Rhineland were of course High German–speaking areas. Another chronicler, Johann von Viktring, records that the King of Denmark held court 'with two dukes (his brothers), and an immense multitude of people of his land, with dukes, counts, and innumerable barons of Saxony and the Margraves of Schleswig, Stettin, Rügen as well as magnates from beyond these parts'.[40]

Since the news of the festival reached this chronicler writing in Carinthia, on the very southern border of the Reich, it is likely that the gathering included many political players whose everyday language was High German, or who were at least conversant with its literary and political vocabulary. Certainly the large numbers present, especially the fact that many youths were knighted, would have made this gathering an ideal forum for the performance of panegyric poetry. At the centre of proceedings was a ceremony in which Woldemar of Brandenburg was knighted by King Erik.[41] This constellation was thus an almost exact parallel to the case of Erik Menved and Otto of Brandenburg in 1287.

---

sundir pyn / von Holtzten, Wittenborg, Swerin. / Ouch quam der wyse wirdiglich / von Mekilnborg Lewe Hinrich.' See also Werner Knoch, 'Wismar, Rostock und Heinrich II. von Mecklenburg 1310/4 nach der Reimchronik Ernst von Kirchbergs (1378)', *Hansische Geschichtsblätter*, 110 (1992), 43–56.

[39] *Mecklenburgische Reimchronik des Ernst von Kirchberg*, ed. by Cordshagen and Schmidt, p. 344: 'Der Polenen herczogin ouch dar quamen, / dy vart ouch zu dem houe namen / dy wendischin herren, daz ist war, / vil Myssener ouch quamen dar. / Dy edeln von Doringen / vil rittirschaft kunden bringen. / Von Westphalen, Swoben vnd vom Ryne / quamen yn wirdiglichem schyne vil edeler zu dem gebrechte vnd ouch vil rittir vnd knechte.'

[40] Johann von Viktring, *Iohannis abbatis Victoriensis Liber certarum historiarum*, ed. by F. Schneider, MGH, SS rer. Ger., 36, 2 vols (Hanover: Hahn, 1909–10), II (1910), 44–45: 'Hac in curia fuit rex Daciae cum duobus ducibus, fratribus suis, et immensa multitudine populi terre sue, duces, comites, liberi barones innumerabiles de Saxonia et marchiones Sleswicensis, Stetinensis, Rugiensis, Magnipolensis et magnates tam de illis quam de exteris partibus, quorum numerus vix poterat estimari. Marchio manibus regis Dacie miles cum magna decencia insignitur, mille septingenti tyrones in tyrocinio hoc nove milicie cingulo per marchionem cum pompa maxima decorantur.'

[41] *Annales Lubicenses*, ed. by G. H. Pertz, MGH, SS, 16 (Hanover: Hahn, 1859), p. 422: '[. . .] Ericus Danorum rex, Woldemarus marchio Brandenburgensis et multi principes et nobiles, Rotstoke congregati, celeberrimam curiam celebrarunt. Et dictus Woldemarus ibidem factus est miles a dicto rege cum 20 principibus et comitatibus et aliis 80 personiis, per regem ob favorem eiusdem marchionis honoratis gloria militari, exceptis aliis militibus ab ipse rege et a singulis principibus et magnatibus ibidem factis, quorum numerus servari non potuit propter eorum multitudinem.'

The Middle High German panegyric poems in favour of Danish monarchs first seem to be found at the end of a period in which the Danish monarchy had gradually succeeded in divesting itself of the character of older Scandinavian kingship and taking on attributes which were common to the western European monarchies, and which were intended to strengthen its ideological and juridical foundations. These new features included the rites of coronation and unction of the king himself, the coronation of a successor during his father's lifetime, and the establishment of cults of royal saints.[42] The patronage of poets producing panegyric works may therefore have been part and parcel of a general process of westernization of the monarchy. Yet even if this was the case, it is unclear why the kings should have favoured poets performing in Middle High German rather than Danish. It may be that the definitive factor in the appearance of these poems in a Danish connection was simply the existence of a well-developed tradition of Middle High German *Spruchdichtung* by the mid-thirteenth century which could be tapped into. Nevertheless, the foregoing survey points to more positive reasons for the employment of Middle High German literature in the Danish interest. The cases and contexts discussed, which range from knighting ceremonies to a possible candidature for the German throne, suggest that we should perhaps move away from an interpretation that sees these poems as having necessarily been commissioned and performed at the Danish court for primarily Danish audiences, but rather that they may have been intended for mixed German and Danish, or even predominantly German, audiences. This argument is not meant to devalue the importance of Middle High German literature in connection with Denmark. In fact, it suggests that we regard this particular corpus of literature not as an indication of a place on a cultural periphery, but rather as a reflection of the political interests and weight of Denmark throughout the north of the German Reich in the thirteenth and earlier fourteenth centuries.

---

[42] On these features, see especially Hoffmann, *Königserhebung und Thronfolgeordnung*, pp. 56–125.

The Politics of Genealogies in *Sturlunga saga*

ÚLFAR BRAGASON*

T he theme of this volume is *Scandinavia and Europe 800–1350: Contact, Conflict, and Coexistence*. I do not intend to make heavy weather of the fact that Icelanders may take umbrage at being called Scandinavians. But I want to point out that there has been a tendency in research into the Icelandic Middle Ages, or 'ancient times' as we Icelanders often call this period, to emphasize the differences between Iceland and developments elsewhere in the Nordic countries. During the Romantic revival, Iceland was commonly known in northern Europe as the 'Saga Isle'. Although the persistence of this appellation has been an irritation to many Icelanders, they have in fact done their bit to prolong its life. The so-called Icelandic school of saga research in the early part of this century, coloured by nationalist leanings, emphasized the uniquely Icelandic nature of the sagas, although scholars also stressed that the sagas were authorial works and not simply products of oral tradition. This nationalist tendency also came to be predominant in the study of history, and this influence is still felt today (highlighting conflicting cultures). In the latter half of the twentieth century, some researchers, mostly in other countries, aimed to establish links between social and literary developments in Iceland in the Middle Ages and developments elsewhere in Europe (evidence of cultural contact). This research may be said to have suffered a setback when anthropology made its appearance in saga research and the study of medieval Icelandic society. Iceland now became to foreign scholars the 'Anthropology Isle', as backward as it had been before the works of the Icelandic school.[1]

---

* Translated from the Icelandic by Anna H. Yates.

[1] For the development of research in the field of saga study, see, for example, Thomas Bredsdorff, *Kaos og kærlighed: En studie i islændingesagaers livsbillede* ([Copenhagen]: Gyldendal, 1971), pp. 148–64; Jesse L. Byock, 'Modern Nationalism and the Medieval Sagas', in *Northern Antiquity: The Post-Medieval Reception of Edda and Saga*, ed. by Andrew Wawn (Middlesex: Hisarlik, 1994), pp. 163–87; George W. Rich, 'Problems and Prospects in the Study of Icelandic Kinship', in *The Anthropology of Iceland*, ed. by E. Paul Durrenberger and Gísli Pálsson (Iowa City: University of Iowa Press, 1989), pp. 53–79.

It is not my intention at this point to examine developments in the history of research into medieval Iceland on the basis of postcolonial criticism. The aim of this essay is to discuss genealogies in Old Icelandic literature, with particular reference to the *Sturlunga* compilation (dated *c.* 1300), and to show that the genealogies of *Sturlunga* bear witness to the changes which were taking place in the power structure of Icelandic society in the twelfth and thirteenth centuries. Everything goes to indicate that developments were similar to those in continental Europe (cultural coexistence), that in Iceland the 'conceptual reflex of [. . .] aristocratic appropriation of time, land, and name' was genealogy as in Britain and on the continent.[2] We should, however, bear in mind that genealogical literature indicates that history writing was utilized for political ends in the Middle Ages.[3]

Genealogies (*áttvísi, áttartal*) occupy, as is well known, considerable space in the sagas. Usually, they are recounted at the beginning of the saga, before the action proper begins, and at the end, thus 'framing' the actual narrative.[4] The sagas are often criticized for their 'weakness for genealogy and personal history'.[5] Scholars recognize, nonetheless, that genealogies are a part of the structure of the works, not simply an exposition of characters, and that they are linked to the works' origins and nature. In a paper I gave in Iceland in 1991, I stressed this fact.[6] Independently of me, Margaret Clunies Ross developed the idea of genealogy as a principle of literary organization in early Iceland.[7] One may therefore conclude that the designations 'Family Saga' and 'ættesaga' reflect more accurately what Icelandic scholars have chosen to call *Íslendingasögur* (Sagas of Icelanders) than the Icelandic term. Some of the sagas, admittedly, deal with a single generation, and some deal with more than one family, but the genealogical accounts are nonetheless an indication of the correlation of the status of the individual in saga-age society to relationships of family.[8]

---

[2] See Francis Ingledew, 'The Book of Troy and the Genealogical Construction of History: The Case of Geoffrey of Monmouth's *Historia regum Britanniae*', *Speculum*, 69 (1994), 665–704 (p. 675).

[3] See Gabrielle M. Spiegel, *The Past as Text: The Theory and Practice of Medieval Historiography* (Baltimore: Hopkins, 1997), pp. 83–98.

[4] Theodore M. Andersson, *The Icelandic Family Saga: An Analytic Reading*, Harvard Studies in Comparative Literature, 28 (Cambridge, MA: Harvard University Press, 1967), pp. 6–11, 26–29; Kathryn Hume, 'Beginnings and Endings in the Icelandic Family Sagas', *Modern Language Review*, 68 (1973), 593–606.

[5] Stefán Einarsson, *A History of Icelandic Literature* (New York: Hopkins, 1957), p. 134.

[6] Úlfar Bragason, 'Um ættartölur í *Sturlungu*', *Tímarit Máls og menningar*, 54 (1993), 27–35.

[7] Margaret Clunies Ross, 'The Development of Old Norse Textual Worlds: Genealogical Structure as a Principle of Literary Organisation in Early Iceland', *Journal of English and Germanic Philology*, 92 (1993), 372–85.

[8] Cf. Preben Meulengracht Sørensen, *Fortælling og ære: Studier i islændingesagaerne* (Århus: Aarhus Universitetsforlag, 1993), p. 171.

However, the concepts of 'Family Saga' and 'ættesaga' do not distinguish the sagas of Icelanders either from the *konungasögur* (Kings' Sagas) or from the *veraldlegar samtíðarsögur* (Secular Contemporary Sagas). Björn M. Ólsen maintained that Sturla Þórðarson's *Íslendinga saga*, the story of contemporary events in thirteenth-century Iceland, written in the second part of the century, could be interpreted as a collection of biographies.[9] This is correct, as far as it goes. The same applies to *Sturlunga*, the voluminous compilation of contemporary sagas, as a whole. The compilation is dated to the beginning of the fourteenth century. Although in comparison with the Sagas of Icelanders, genealogies do not occupy much space in this extensive compilation of contemporary sagas, and although the choice and handling of subject matter is only intermittently linked to family, concepts of biography and genealogy undeniably define the limits of the sagas and their overall structure to a considerable extent.

Genealogy is the perceptual grid and narrative frame into which the authors fit their material. Within this grid, the life stories of the principal participants in the events of the saga are recounted in chronological order, regardless of how many families and generations are involved. One may therefore assume, as Gabrielle M. Spiegel does with respect to medieval French history writing, that:

> genealogies were expressions of social memory and, as such, could be expected to have a particular affinity with historical thought, and, at least to a certain extent, to impose their consciousness of social reality upon those whose task it was to preserve for future generations images of society in the record of history.[10]

R. Howard Bloch has become a spokesman for so-called literary anthropology. In his view, medieval writing 'both reflects its cultural moment, thus enabling anthropological description, and is a prime vehicle for the change of that which it reflects'; medieval text is a '"generator of public consciousness", which can be said to exist *through* it just as society can be said to exist through language'.[11] Taking into consideration the narrative rules of the contemporary sagas, their delimitation of material, exposition, narrative method, style, and structure, the limitations of *Sturlunga* as a historical source are clear.[12] Bearing this in mind, the compilation can, nevertheless, give information on the era which made it, even more so than other sagas.

---

[9] Björn M. Ólsen, *Um Sturlungu*, Safn til sögu Íslands og íslenzkra bókmennta, 3 (Copenhagen: Hið Íslenzka Bókmenntafélag, 1902), p. 394.

[10] Spiegel, *The Past as Text*, p. 104.

[11] R. Howard Bloch, *Etymologies and Genealogies: A Literary Anthropology of the French Middle Ages* (Chicago: University of Chicago Press, 1983), pp. 15–16.

[12] Úlfar Bragason, 'On the Poetics of *Sturlunga*' (unpublished doctoral thesis, University of California at Berkeley, 1986), pp. 182–95.

Family and Lineage

Anthropology distinguishes principally between two forms of kinship system: lineages and kindreds. Lineage systems may be cognatic, including all descendants of a specified forefather and foremother, but tend to become agnatic, tracing descent only in the male line (*langfeðgatal*). In the Middle Ages, the word *ætt* seems to signify both the patrilineal kin group and cognatic kindred.[13]

The Icelandic kinship system was, however, mainly based upon kindreds. This can be deduced from regulations on vengeance, compensation, inheritance, marriage, and custody of children. The laws recognized kinship in the male and female lines for five generations (*þriðja bræðra*). This necessitated familiarity with one's descent for five generations, or from one's great-great-great-grandfather. The genealogies in *Landnámabók* (*Book of Settlement*) are undoubtedly attributable in some part to this requirement. They are also probably linked to the right to make a claim to property which has been sold in defiance of the rights of owners or heirs.[14]

Some genealogies, in fact, look further back in time than legal requirements made necessary; they trace descent back to famous settlers or ancient kings and heroes. This could indicate that both kindred and lineage systems applied in Iceland in ancient times — a possibility which has been rejected by Preben Meulengracht Sørensen. He does, however, point out that during the Sturlung Age there were several dominant families which were identified with certain properties and were known under a definite family name, such as Haukdælir, Oddaverjar, and Sturlungar. But, he says, these groups were not clearly defined, and the family name did not generally last more than two or three generations. The Sturlung family, for instance,

---

[13] Sigurður Líndal, 'Ætt', in *Kulturhistorisk leksikon for nordisk middelalder*, 22 vols (Copenhagen: Rosenkilde & Bagger, 1956–78), XX (1976), cols 591–94; Preben Meulengracht Sørensen, *Saga og samfund: En indføring i oldislandsk litteratur* (Copenhagen: Berlingske, 1977), pp. 30–36; Kirsten Hastrup, *Culture and History in Medieval Iceland: An Anthropological Analysis of Structure and Change* (Oxford: Clarendon Press, 1985), pp. 70–104; Kirsten Hastrup, *Island of Anthropology: Studies in Past and Present Iceland* (Odense: Odense University Press, 1990), pp. 44–58; William Ian Miller, *Bloodtaking and Peacemaking: Feud, Law, and Society in Saga Iceland* (Chicago: University of Chicago Press, 1990), pp. 139–78.

[14] Guðni Jónsson, 'Genealogier', in *Kulturhistorisk leksikon for nordisk middelalder*, V (1960), cols 247–49; Gunnar Karlsson, 'Nafngreindar höfðingjaættir í Sturlungu', in *Sagnaþing helgað Jónasi Kristjánssyni sjötugum*, ed. by Gísli Sigurðsson and others (Reykjavik: Hið Íslenska Bókmenntafélag, 1994), pp. 307–15; Jakob Benediktsson, 'Introduction', in *Íslendingabók. Landnámabók*, ed. by Jakob Benediktsson, Íslenzk Fornrit, 1 (Reykjavik: Hið Íslenzka Fornritafélag, 1968), pp. cxviii–cxx; Sveinbjörn Rafnsson, *Studier i Landnámabók: Kritiska bidrag till den isländska fristadstidens historia*, Bibliotheca historica Lundensis, 31 (Lund: Gleerup, 1974), pp. 142–51, 181–88; Sørensen, *Saga og samfund*, pp. 30–36; Sørensen, *Fortælling og ære*, pp. 165–70; cf. Georges Duby, 'French Genealogical Literature', in *The Chivalrous Society*, trans. by Cynthia Postan (Berkeley: University of California Press, 1980), pp. 149–57.

drew their name from Sturla Þórðarson of Hvammr, and they were only known by this name for two or three generations. Nor did they act as kinsmen, but as individuals, who often fought among themselves.[15]

This may not, however, be a particularly well-chosen example.[16] Families like the Ásbirningar, Svínfellingar, Seldælir, Vatnsfirðingar, Oddaverjar, and Haukdælir had a long history on which they based their claims to power. The Sturlungar could admittedly trace their lineage to Snorri goði (d. 1031), but the Snorrungar chieftaincy had only been in the family since about 1100, when Þórðr Gilsson, great-grandfather of Sturla Þórðarson the historian, took it over. The Sturlungar, then, were a new arrival on the power scene, whose aggression was a cause of disorder. There are strong indications that their efforts, whether armed with the sword or the pen, may be traced to their lack of a respectable lineage. In Sturla Þórðarson's *Íslendinga saga*, one may easily discern his disappointment at his family's lack of solidarity (see, for example, the descriptions of the way Sturla Sighvatsson rode roughshod over his uncle Snorri Sturluson in *Íslendinga saga*).[17] Furthermore, the saga says that his close relatives often invoke family ties when they seek his support, or in order to support their claims against his, and he swallows the bait.[18]

Genealogies did not only serve as a tool with regard to legal duties and rights. Victor Turner has, for example, pointed out that 'politics, or better politicking, rather than kinship duties alone' played a major role in the vengeance system.[19] Concomitantly, the genealogies were linked with family ambition and claims to political power, which became the domain of fewer and fewer individuals during the period of the Commonwealth. The Sagas of Icelanders, which can be interpreted as a continuation of the genealogies of *Landnámabók*, are also undoubtedly to some extent the result of this family ambition.[20]

---

[15] Sørensen, *Saga og samfund*, pp. 34–36, 80–86. See also Sørensen, *Fortælling og ære*, p. 175.

[16] Cf. Agnes Arnórsdóttir, *Konur og vígamenn: Staða kynjanna á Íslandi á 12. og 13. öld*, Studia Historica, 12 (Reykjavik: Sagnfræðistofnun, 1995), p. 72.

[17] *Sturlunga saga*, ed. by Jón Jóhannesson, Magnús Finnbogason, and Kristján Eldjárn, 2 vols (Reykjavik: Sturlunguútgáfan, 1946), I, 389–92. For a translation of the compilation, see *Sturlunga saga*, trans. by Julia H. McGrew and R. George Thomas, 2 vols, The Library of Scandinavian Literature, 9–10 (New York: Twayne, 1970–74).

[18] See, for example, Þórðr kakali Sighvatsson's call for help to his cousin Sturla in *Þórðar saga kakala* (*Sturlunga saga*, ed. by Jón Jóhannesson, Magnús Finnbogason, and Eldjárn, II, 7–8); and the exchange between Ólafr hvítaskáld and his brother Sturla in *Þorgils saga skarða* (*Sturlunga saga*, ed. by Jón Jóhannesson, Magnús Finnbogason, and Eldjárn, II, 130–31).

[19] Victor Turner, 'An Anthropological Approach to the Icelandic Saga', in *The Translation of Culture: Essays to E. E. Evans-Pritchard*, ed. by T. O. Beidelman (London: Tavistock, 1971), p. 165; compare Jón Viðar Sigurðsson, *Chieftains and Power in the Icelandic Commonwealth*, The Viking Collection, 12 (Odense: Odense University Press, 1999), pp. 151–85.

[20] Sørensen, *Saga og samfund*, pp. 82, 109; Sørensen, *Fortælling og ære*, pp. 173–76.

As early as the twelfth century, the Icelanders were showing interest in their language and its origins. The author of *Fyrsta málfræðiritgerðin* (*The First Grammatical Treatise*) believes that all the languages had developed from a common source, and in *Veraldar saga* (*The World's History*) all languages are said to spring from Hebrew. In the agnate pedigrees of the kings of Norway and Denmark, it had become customary to trace the genealogies to ancient gods, thus containing an assumption of euhemerism, as early as the twelfth century. In the thirteenth-century introduction to *Snorra Edda*, the origin of the Norse gods is discussed, and they are said to have come from Troy.[21] As Francis Ingledew points out, a 'symptom of genealogy as an appropriative instrument for princes and noble landowners, Troy was the conceptual product of a structure of power'.[22] The interest in tracing the family origin to Asia suggests, therefore, interest in power.

Similar interest in origin or in the family tree emerges in the Icelanders' genealogies. The genealogies in the genealogical section of *Sturlunga* start from the beginning of the twelfth century, and, as stated below, these generations were probably within the extent of human memory. However, *Landnámabók*, the first version of which is estimated to have been made in the early twelfth century, provides evidence of familiarity with genealogies as far back as the Settlement. Both are examples of genealogies constructed on a relatively reliable basis.[23] The fact that people wanted to know more and more, tracing their descent back further and further, is evidenced by the *fornaldarsögur* (Sagas of Ancient Times). In *Þorgils saga ok Hafliða*, for example, people are said to be able to trace their descent from Hrómundr Gripsson, when the saga recounts that Hrólfr of Skálmarnes told a story of him at the Reykjahólar wedding in 1119.[24] For this reason, the genealogies were constantly being extended, and more and more suppositious generations were added. Similar linking between interest in origin and storytelling is to be found in the popularity of the history of Troy and *Historia regum Britanniae* in Iceland.[25] As Anthony Faulkes has shown, genealogies of British kings and later Welsh lists provide the closest parallels to the Icelandic *langfeðgatöl*, though he does not believe 'that there is any direct link between these and Icelandic tradition'.[26]

---

[21] Eyvind Fjeld Halvorsen, 'Langfeðgatal', in *Kulturhistorisk leksikon for nordisk middelalder*, X (1965), cols 311–13; Anthony Faulkes, 'Descent from the Gods', *Mediaeval Scandinavia*, 11 (1978–79), 92–106.

[22] Ingledew, 'The Book of Troy and the Genealogical Construction of History', p. 674.

[23] Cf. Donnchadh Ó Corráin, 'Irish Origin Legends and Genealogy: Recurrent Aetiologies', in *History and Heroic Tale: A Symposium*, ed. by Tore Nyberg and others (Odense: Odense University Press, 1985), pp. 51–96 (pp. 83–84).

[24] *Sturlunga saga*, ed. by Jón Jóhannesson, Magnús Finnbogason, and Eldjárn, I, 27.

[25] See, for example, Randi Eldevik's essay in this volume.

[26] Faulkes, 'Descent from the Gods', p. 106.

Ari Þorgilsson traced his descent from Yngvi, king of the Turks, in *Íslendingabók* (*Book of the Icelanders*), which is believed to have been written *c.* 1130.[27] From a similar period come the Oddaverjar genealogies, traced from the Kings of Denmark. Admittedly, the Oddaverjar were particularly interested in genealogy due to their links with the kings of Norway in the twelfth century. This is clearly illustrated by the *Noregs konungatal*, composed in honour of Jón Loftsson, whose maternal grandfather was King Magnus Bare-Legs (Magnús berfœttr).[28] This example also demonstrates that the maternal line of descent was sometimes emphasized if the mother was of superior lineage to the father.[29] However, Sturla Þórðarson opts to forget his mother's family (or lack of it). By about 1300, genealogical fervour had reached a point where people, including the Sturlungar, could trace their descent from Adam.[30]

The Mass of Genealogies in Sturlunga

Scholars agree that the lawman and knight, Sturla Þórðarson, wrote his *Íslendinga saga* (dated *c.* 1280) as a continuation of *Sturlu saga*, and as a supplement to the contemporary sagas with which he was familiar.[31] The compiler of *Sturlunga*, who was probably Sturla's protégé, the lawman Þórðr Narfason of Skarð,[32] was simply continuing the work which his mentor had initiated. The genealogical section, which in *Sturlunga* is placed between *Þorgils saga ok Hafliða* and *Sturlu saga*, is therefore seen as Sturla's work also, although the compiler of *Sturlunga* is believed to have made some alterations: inserting, for example, information on his own family, and omitting the Haukdælir genealogy, which he then used in compiling *Haukdœla þáttr*.[33]

This genealogical section traces the families of Oddaverjar, Sturlungar, Ásbirningar, Svínfellingar, Seldælir, Vatnsfirðingar, and Grund in Eyjafjörður. None of these families are, however, given a proper name there. The names Oddaverjar, Sturlungar, Svínfellingar, and Vatnsfirðingar are all used elsewhere in the *Sturlunga* compilation. Ásbirningar, together with Sturlungar and Vatnsfirðingar, are used as the names of these families in *Eyrbyggja saga*, which scholars think was written in

---

[27] Jón Jóhannesson, 'Ólafur konungur Goðröðarson', *Skírnir*, 130 (1956), 61–63.

[28] Einar Ól. Sveinsson, *Sagnaritun Oddaverja: Nokkrar athuganir*, Studia Islandica, 1 (Reykjavik: Ísafold, 1937), pp. 11–16.

[29] See Sørensen, *Fortælling og ære*, p. 175.

[30] Faulkes, 'Descent from the Gods', p. 105.

[31] Ólsen, *Um Sturlungu*, pp. 391–93; Jón Jóhannesson, 'Um Sturlunga sögu', in *Sturlunga saga*, ed. by Jón Jóhannesson, Magnús Finnbogason, and Eldjárn, II, pp. vii–lvi (pp. xxxiv–xli).

[32] Guðbrandur Vigfússon, 'Prolegomena', in *Sturlunga saga*, ed. by Guðbrandur Vigfússon, 2 vols (Oxford: Clarendon Press, 1878), I, pp. xv–ccxiv (pp. civ–cv).

[33] Ólsen, *Um Sturlungu*, pp. 383–85; Jón Jóhannesson, 'Um Sturlunga sögu', p. xxv.

the power sphere of the Sturlungar in Snæfellsnes.[34] The proper nouns Seldælir and Grundarmenn are not used as names of families in *Sturlunga*. However, in the genealogies the families are linked to the estates at Selárdalur and Grund, like the Oddaverjar to the farm at Oddi and Vatnsfirðingar to Vatnsfjörður. The families have been traced from the time of Bishop Gizurr of Skálholt around 1100. They take the form of the lines of descent from Sæmundr fróði (the Wise), Þórðr Gilsson, Ásbjörn Arnórsson, Sigmundr Þorgilsson, Bárðr svarti (the Black), Þórðr of Vatnsfjörður, and Þorsteinn ranglátr. Jón Jóhannesson says: 'Allir ættfeðurnir voru uppi um svipað leyti, þótt þeir væru ekki alveg samtíðarmenn, og hlýtur eitthvað sérstakt að hafa vakað fyrir höfundinum, úr því að hann rakti einmitt ættir frá þeim, en ekki öðrum eldri eða yngri.'[35] He does not, however, pursue this idea any further. A possible explanation is that Sturla knew *Þorgils saga ok Hafliða* and wished to trace the genealogies back to the contemporaries of the protagonists of that saga. It may also be pointed out that the chieftaincy of the Sturlungar was rooted in the events of this period. Furthermore, the genealogies are approximately as extensive as Sturla's contemporaries were required to know for legal purposes.

Perhaps it is not by chance that the descendants of Sæmundr fróði are named first. It was from this line that the tradition of scholarship entered the Sturlung family, when Snorri was brought up by Jón Loftsson, whose paternal grandfather was Sæmundr fróði of Oddi. One may ask whether the genealogies were originally quite independent of *Íslendinga saga*. The most probable explanation seems to be that they form part of Sturla's preparatory work for writing the saga, a form of introduction to the saga.[36] This would explain the sparsity of genealogies in the saga proper. Finnur Jónsson, however, pointed out correctly that '*således*, med en bunke genealogier af den art, begyndte aldrig nogen islandsk saga'.[37] Another question is whether or not the genealogies were adjusted to fit the subsequent action of the saga. This is difficult to assess now, as we cannot tell how much the compiler of *Sturlunga* revised the text. But, with the exception of the genealogy of Þorsteinn ranglátr (of Grund), the genealogies are largely consistent with the narrative of the saga. These

---

[34] Einar Ól. Sveinsson, 'Introduction', in *Eyrbyggja saga*, ed. by Einar Ól. Sveinsson, Íslensk Fornrit, 4 (Reykjavik: Hið Íslenzka Fornritafélag, 1935), pp. xliii–lvii; see also Gunnar Karlsson, 'Nafngreindar höfðingjaættir í Sturlungu'.

[35] Jón Jóhannesson, 'Um Sturlunga sögu', p. xxv: 'All the founding fathers lived at much the same time, although they were not exact contemporaries, and the author must have had some particular purpose in mind, since he traced the genealogies precisely from them, and not from others, older or younger.'

[36] See also Stefán Karlsson's theory on Sturla's encyclopedia: Stefán Karlsson, 'Alfræði Sturlu Þórðarsonar', in *Sturlustefna*, ed. by Guðrún Ása Grímsdóttir and Jónas Kristjánsson, Rit Stofnunar Árna Magnússonar, 32 (Reykjavik: Stofnun Árna Magnússonar, 1988), pp. 37–60.

[37] Finnur Jónsson, *Den oldnorske og oldislandske litteraturs historie*, 2nd rev. edn, 3 vols (Copenhagen: Gad, 1920–24), II (1923), 723: 'No Icelandic saga ever began with such a mass of genealogies.'

are, in fact, not complete family trees, but a selection of those who enjoyed the most power and played the most important roles, and show how these families were inter-related and affiliated. The two works therefore seem to be related, and both bear witness to the accumulation of power in the hands of a few families, which was taking place in society.[38]

As mentioned above, the Sturlungar were a relatively new family in the theatre of power in the late twelfth and early thirteenth centuries. When a Sturlung enumerates the descendants of Þórðr Gilsson among a series of genealogies of the greatest fami-lies of chieftains in the country, and points out that the forefather, who holds the chieftaincy of Snorri Þorgrímsson of Helgafell (Snorrungar chieftaincy), was related further back to both the Ásbirningar and Vatnsfirðingar, thus breaking the rule of only mentioning descendants, he does so in order to demonstrate the social status of his own family. The Church had imported the art of writing in order to promote the Christian faith, but the chieftains had soon learned to employ this knowledge for their own purposes, to judge by *Fyrsta málfræðiritgerðin*, which counts laws and genealogies among the first records written on parchment. The Oddaverjar and Haukdælir were famed for their book learning in the twelfth century, when their power was already long established. The Sturlungar, however, seem to have deliber-ately used the art of narrative and writing in order to reinforce their position. Guðrún Ása Grímsdóttir's hypothesis, that Sturla Þórðarson was actually apprenticed to his uncle Snorri Sturluson in order to become the chronicler of the Sturlungar, is thus more than probable.[39]

Sturla the historian was illegitimate. Þóra, his mother, seems not to have been a woman of family, as he does not name her father.[40] His origins seem to have left their mark upon him, and some of his writings in *Íslendinga saga* seem intended to prove himself a true Sturlung, and to demonstrate that his father and other kinsmen recog-nized his true value. Not least of these features is the emphasis he places upon the fact that he was made his father's heir, and that he inherited his share of the Snorrungar chieftaincy. His wife's relatives of the Skarð and Staðarhóll families seem to have supported him in his rise to power, and contributed more than anyone else finan-cially. His seat was at their great estate of Staðarhóll in Saurbær.[41] Staðarhóll had been a residence of chieftains for centuries and was one of the largest manors in the

---

[38] See Jón Viðar Sigurðsson, *Chieftains and Power*, esp. pp. 17–83.

[39] Guðrún Ása Grímsdóttir, 'Sturla Þórðarson', in *Sturlustefna*, ed. by Guðrún Ása Gríms-dóttir and Jónas Kristjánsson, pp. 11–12.

[40] Marlene Ciklamini, 'Biographical Reflections in *Íslendinga saga*: A Mirror of Personal Values', *Scandinavian Studies*, 55 (1983), 207–08.

[41] Guðrún Ása Grímsdóttir, 'Sturla Þórðarson', pp. 12–14; Sveinbjörn Rafnsson, 'Um Staðarhólsmál Sturlu Þórðarsonar: Nokkrar athuganir á valdmennsku um hans daga', *Skírnir*, 159 (1985), 143–59.

country for centuries to come.[42] It has been suggested that Sturla's version of *Landnámabók* 'representerar godemaktens koncentration och dess tilltagande feodala karaktär. Man kan även skönja en tendentiös historieskrivning till Sturlungarnas förmån i S[*turlubók*]'.[43] Sturla wrote also of Norwegian kings who laid claim to power on the grounds of descent and inheritance, and he seems to have adopted their ideas to some extent. He chooses for his children respected names from his family and that of his wife, and attempts on the one hand to ensure his son, Snorri, will have a position of power after his time. Sturla gives him Staðarhóll as a residence, the estate where he had lived for much of his life and where he was buried. On the other hand, Sturla's other son, Þórðr, trained for the priesthood, presumably in order to assure him a living within the Church. Sturla married his daughters into powerful families in the North. He thus acquired new allies and the daughters were no longer a financial burden on his family.[44] His actions suggest that he was imitating the behaviour of the Kings of Norway and following the example of various leaders in this area of the world. In doing so, he was not alone among the Icelandic ruling class.

From the genealogies of *Sturlunga* we can deduce that the ruling families of the Sturlung Age felt that they had a claim to power, based upon the chieftaincies held by their ancestors for many generations, preferably as far back as the Settlement. In this sense, they wished to base their power on origins, just as the kings of Norway did. At the same time as the chieftains divided the country among themselves, and resided on choice estates, they also began to use specified names for their families and seemed to believe that they implied certain qualities. For example, Sturla Þórðarson says in *Íslendinga saga*: 'Hefir þat lengi kynríkt verit með Haukdælum ok Oddaverjum, at þeir hafa inar beztu veizlur haldit.'[45] And the luck of the family was believed to reside with certain names. Thus when Þorvaldr of Hruni names his son Gizurr he says: 'Mun ek son minn láta heita Gizur, því at lítt hafa þeir aukvisar verit í Haukdælaætt, er svá hafa heitit hér til.'[46] Also, links of friendship seem to embrace families as much as individuals, to judge by the reception described in *Sturlu þáttr* given to Sturla Þórðarson by Gautr of Mel, royal counsellor in Norway, on his first foreign journey.[47]

---

[42] See Magnús Már Lárusson, 'Á höfuðbólum landsins', *Saga*, 9 (1971), 41–50.

[43] Sveinbjörn Rafnsson, *Studier i Landnámabók*, p. 217: 'represents the concentration of the power of chieftains and its increasing feudal character. One may even observe a tendentious writing of history to the advantage of the Sturlungar in S[*turlubók*].'.

[44] Úlfar Bragason, '"Hart er í heimi, hórdómr mikill": Lesið í Sturlungu', *Skírnir*, 163 (1989), 54–71 (p. 62).

[45] *Sturlunga saga*, ed. by Jón Jóhannesson, Magnús Finnbogason, and Eldjárn, I, 483: 'It had long been the hallmark of the men of Haukadalur and of Oddi that they held splendid feasts.'

[46] *Sturlunga saga*, ed. by Jón Jóhannesson, Magnús Finnbogason, and Eldjárn, I, 250: 'I shall have my son named Gizurr, because up to now few who have been so named in the family of Haukadalur have been weaklings.'

[47] *Sturlunga saga*, ed. by Jón Jóhannesson, Magnús Finnbogason, and Eldjárn, II, 231–32.

The Compiler's Genealogical Knowledge

Þórðr Narfason of Skarð was no independent historian, but a collector of information, like many of his contemporaries. One of his interests was genealogy, not least his own, and in this he resembled his master Sturla. The additions which can be traced to him in the genealogical section refer to his own family, and indeed these interpolations, together with other evidence, provide the clues to his identity. Unlike the other genealogies in the section, these are traced backwards, rather than appearing in the form of a line of descent. They generally reach further back in time than the others, even to the time of the fall of St Edmund, king of the East Anglians, which Ari Þorgilsson calculated as being contemporary with the settlement of Iceland (*c.* 870). Þórðr may even have inserted the line of descent of Þorsteinn ranglátr, being one of Þorsteinn's descendants himself, although he is unlikely to be the author of this genealogy. The Grund family plays only a small part in *Íslendinga saga*, but an account of it is given in the compilation in *Guðmundar saga dýra*. At the beginning of this saga, there is also an interpolation on the genealogy of the Narfason family, and this also seems to be the case in *Sturlu saga*, where its origin is traced back to Sigurðr ormr-í-auga (Snake-Eyes), the son of Ragnarr loðbrók (Shaggy-Breeches). Thus their family origin is connected with the origin of the royal families of Norway and Denmark, the most honourable lineage in the North, and claims to power and glory at that time were tied to the legendary time of the *fornaldarsögur*.[48]

One reason for the inclusion of *Geirmundar þáttr heljarskinns* in the *Sturlunga* compilation is that its hero settled at Skarð. At the end of the *þáttr*, genealogies are traced, not, however, from Geirmundr, but from various settlers to the Skarð family. The compiler explains, for example, how he is connected with Sturla Þórðarson due to the relationship in the third generation between himself and Sturla's wife. He also shows how the Skarð family is related to good families like the Oddaverjar and Haukdælir. It is, however, clear from the genealogy of the family of Grund that the Narfasons were descendants of Geirmundr's twin brother, Hámundr heljarskinn.

Þórðr's relationship with the Haukdælir is certainly one of the reasons that prompted him to write a special section on the Haukdælir (*Haukdæla þáttr*) and insert it into *Íslendinga saga* in the compilation. Another factor is that *Haukdæla þáttr* emphasizes their role in the compilation, making them even worthier opponents of the Sturlungar than they were previously in *Íslendinga saga*. Various additions show that the compiler wished to add to the story of Jarl Gizurr, even emphasizing that the best solution after the domestic strife of the Sturlung Age was a jarldom under his rule.[49] In *Haukdæla þáttr*, the compiler traces the Haukdælir from the settler Ketilbjörn Ketilsson of Mosfell.

---

[48] See Bjarni Guðnason, 'Gerðir og ritþróun *Ragnars sögu loðbrókar*', in *Einarsbók: Afmæliskveðja til Einars Ól. Sveinssonar*, ed. by Bjarni Guðnason and others (Reykjavik: [Nokkrir vinir], 1969), pp. 28–37.

[49] Úlfar Bragason, 'On the Poetics of *Sturlunga*', pp. 170–78.

The efforts of the compiler of *Sturlunga* to trace his descent from the settlers, breaking the precedent set by Sturla in the genealogical section, bespeak Icelandic leaders' need to entrench themselves after the hostilities of the Sturlung Age. It also demonstrates, even more effectively than the case of Sturla, that the chieftains had learned from the ruling families of other countries, and knew how to tie their power to lineage. Þórðr Narfason linked his family so indissolubly with Skarð farm on Skarðströnd that they have lived there ever since.[50]

Conclusion

While the *Sturlunga* compilation does not prove that the thirteenth-century chieftains built their power on their lineages, the genealogical section shows a strong conscious movement in that direction. Genealogies of ruling families, preserved elsewhere, remove all doubt. The politics of genealogies are also demonstrated in the additions made by the compiler of *Sturlunga*. There was thus a clear contact between the ideas of Icelandic chieftains and the continental model, a move towards a lineage system of kinship. Ultimately, this facilitated the submission of Icelandic chieftains' power to the Norwegian Crown.[51]

The chieftains divided the country among themselves and resided on choice estates. Although on a smaller scale than many others, this was Sturla's pattern of behaviour. Staðarhóll became his chosen estate, and he sought power at the head of Breiða-fjörður and even as far south as Borgarfjörður. He was not born the heir to wealth, as he was illegitimate. But in word and in deed he became perhaps the ultimate Sturlung. With genealogy and chronology as his guides, he recorded on parchment the victories and defeats of his family, among other events, mourning the manner in which they used their power and how other families infringed on their rights. Although he perceived the power struggle in a similar way to the creators of the sagas of Icelanders, and fitted it into a similar framework,[52] it is nonetheless clear that the concept of family differs. Sturla felt unlimited respect for his father, from whom he inherited name, property, and social status.[53] He also wished to bring his son to a position of influence.

The chieftains had learned from their acquaintance with the Kings of Norway and their courtiers, and were beginning to see themselves as the heirs to power appertaining to family. Noble lineage was one of their main claims to power, which led ultimately to a desire to possess their agnate pedigrees stretching back to Adam. The

---

[50] See Einar G. Pétursson, 'Fróðleiksmolar um Skarðverja', *Breiðfirðingur*, 48 (1990), 71–72.

[51] Cf. Hastrup, *Island of Anthropology*, pp. 57–58.

[52] Úlfar Bragason 'On the Poetics of *Sturlunga*', pp. 37–83.

[53] Ciklamini, 'Biographical Reflections in *Íslendinga saga*', pp. 212–19.

patriarchal system thus sought justification in Christianity.[54] In the Sturlung Age, a small number of families had disputes over wealth, power, and influence. All were in the end compelled to submit to the power of the King of Norway. It was the new noble class of royal officials which gave the age its historical image. The family feeling of the *Sturlunga*, therefore, constitutes evidence of the mentality of the thirteenth-century chieftain. And this influence in the contemporary sagas must have reinforced that mentality.

---

[54] Cf. Spiegel, *The Past as Text*, p. 109.

Narrative, Contact, Conflict, and Coexistence: Norwegians in Thirteenth-Century Iceland

CHRIS CALLOW

O ne of the most frequently stated truisms about medieval Icelandic society is its dependence on Norway and Norwegian merchants for the supply of certain goods. Grain, wood, weapons, and other products not easily available in Iceland are frequently referred to in Sagas of Icelanders (Family Sagas or *Íslendingasögur*) and the importance of merchants in thirteenth-century political life is underlined by events in the narratives which make up *Sturlunga saga*.[1] Collectively Sagas of Icelanders also contain many episodes which detail the activities of Icelanders at the courts of Norwegian kings. These two aspects of Icelandic-Norwegian relations have often been commented upon in varying detail and they tell us a great deal about the economic position of Icelandic political leaders and some Icelanders' conceptions of what the Norwegian kings and the royal court were like.[2]

More interesting and often more entertaining, perhaps, are those episodes in Sagas of Icelanders and Contemporary Sagas (the *Sturlunga* compilation and Bishops' Sagas) which show Norwegians active in Iceland. Norwegians crop up in several guises in the saga literature about Iceland and we can often identify Norwegians even when their activities do not conform to the stereotypes into which saga literature often tries to fit them. The stereotyped and the unstereotyped Norwegians identifiable in saga narratives can tell us a great deal about Icelanders' attitudes towards Norwegians. In

---

[1] See Helgi Þorláksson, 'Kaupmenn í þjónustu konungs', *Mímir*, 13 (1968), 5–12, for the increasing political involvement of merchants and the Norwegian king in Icelandic affairs; Helgi Þorláksson, 'Social Ideals and the Concept of Profit in Thirteenth-Century Iceland', in *From Sagas to Society: Comparative Approaches to Early Iceland*, ed. by Gísli Pálsson (Enfield Lock: Hisarlik, 1992), pp. 231–45, for trade generally.

[2] See, for example, Theodore M. Andersson's study of attitudes to Norwegian kings in *Heimskringla* and *Egils saga Skallagrímssonar*, 'The Politics of Snorri Sturluson', *Journal of English and Germanic Philology*, 93 (1994), 55–78.

trying to analyse these images of Norwegians, however, the problem of how to deal
with sagas as historical sources inevitably arises. Whose attitudes do the sagas reflect?
How commonly were their attitudes felt? Do authors or writers show individual perceptions of Norwegians? Ultimately, there has to be a kind of play off between what
images of Norwegians in sagas actually tell us about Norwegians (and relations between Icelanders and Norwegians) and what the sagas say about Icelanders' common
perceptions of Norwegians. The pursuit of information about Norwegians in Icelandic narratives, a single aspect of sagas, necessarily suggests ways in which we can
use both Sagas of Icelanders and Contemporary Sagas as historical sources.

Certain problems instantly emerge in discussing the position of Norwegians in
medieval Icelandic society. The basic problem is in identifying Norwegians in the
first place. Medieval Icelanders and Norwegians had in common a practice of patro-
nymic naming, and at the same time their common language and culture meant they
had similar first names. The second potential problem in picking out Norwegians is
that the label which one might use to identify them is ambiguous. A merchant or
apparent 'outsider' of one sort or another is often called *austmaðr* (pl. *austmenn*),
literally 'east man', in saga narratives. While we have every reason to suspect that
this term is synonymous with terms for a trader (*kaupmaðr*) or a ship's captain
(*stýrimaðr*), *austmaðr* is a slightly ambiguous term. It does not necessarily mean 'a
Norwegian' in the more modern sense of the word.[3] Does *austmaðr* identify a person
supposed to have been of Norwegian origin or only a person who did things which
Norwegians (or merchants) typically did? This second difficulty is impossible to
resolve completely. The most that can be asserted is that *austmenn* usually appear in
sagas fulfilling the roles which we might otherwise expect Norwegians to occupy.[4]

Leaving these difficulties aside, it is possible to analyse the way in which *austmenn* are portrayed in Sagas of Icelanders and Contemporary Sagas. It makes sense
that both Sagas of Icelanders and many of the *Sturlunga saga* texts, as representations of an often distant past, should make use of stock Norwegian characters as they
do some other kinds of character. The majority of the images the sagas use can be
grouped together either according to the activities of the *austmenn* concerned or the

---

[3] Occasionally sagas use a precise term for a Norwegian: *Nóregsmaðr*, in ch. 8 of
Gunnlaugs saga ormstungu (published in *Borgfirðinga sögur*, ed. by Sigurður Nordal and
Guðni Jónsson, Íslenzk Fornrit, 3 (Reykjavik: Hið Íslenzka Fornritafélag, 1938), pp. 77, 78).
Another term, *Norðmaðr*, is usually used to mean 'northerner' or 'Scandinavian' (including
Icelanders). See, for example, *Gunnlaugs saga ormstungu*, p. 71, and *Heiðarvíga saga* (also
published in *Borgfirðinga sögur*, ed. by Nordal and Guðni Jónsson), p. 320. *Norrænir menn*
are also sometimes mentioned. See, for example, *Sturlunga saga*, ed. by Jón Jóhannesson,
Magnús Finnbogason, and Kristján Eldjárn, 2 vols (Reykjavik: Sturlunguútgáfan, 1946), I,
505. There seems to be no significance in writers' choice of either *austmaðr* or *Norégsmaðr*
when referring to Norwegians.

[4] Guðrún Kváran, 'Nöfn "austmanna" í íslendingasögum', in *Sagnaþing helgað Jónasi
Kristjánssyni sjötugum*, ed. by Gísli Sigurðsson and others (Reykjavik: Hið Íslenzka
Bókmenntafélag, 1994), pp. 269–76.

circumstances in which *austmenn* appear.[5] There is good reason to believe, as the examples below show, that *austmenn*, as non-Icelanders, are conceived of as distinct from Irish or Scottish characters. Many of these general ideas cut across any boundary which might exist between saga genres which is why it makes sense to organize the following discussion around the types of images rather than by saga genre.[6]

It is probably most useful to look at the most simplistic depictions of *austmenn* first. These are predominantly in Sagas of Icelanders, not least because Sagas of Icelanders, as narratives of the more distant past, tend towards less complex images generally than do those of the Contemporary Sagas which deal with events generally within living memory. In almost every Saga of Icelanders there is a reference to someone who is called *austmaðr*.[7]

In chapter 15 of *Droplaugarsona saga* somebody sells a half-share in a ship to some *austmenn*. Here, there appears to be no purpose in the narrative for talking about Norwegians.[8] In chapter 13 of the same saga, a chess-playing Norwegian casually kicks a child who then farts, which makes someone else compose a verse.[9] A third example of an inconsequential Norwegian appears in chapter 13 of *Vápnfirðinga saga*, when someone called Kollr Austmaðr is named as a member of a raiding party.[10] Nothing else is said of Kollr and, although we might suspect that the saga writer knew something else about him, this and the *Droplaugarsona saga* examples seem decorative. They tell us little about how the narrative works or about how Norwegians were perceived in Iceland.

More often, however, even brief references have a narrative purpose. *Sturlunga saga* provides a two-dimensional *austmaðr* in chapter 29 of *Íslendinga saga*. This man is given a speech in which he points out the presence of men fighting in another part of the valley (Eyjafjörður). His observations are dismissed by his Icelandic companion, Jón Eyjólfsson, who says that the men are only duelling or practising.[11]

---

[5] There is not space in this short article to comment in full on the many named individuals from *Sturlunga saga* who might be suspected to have been of Norwegian origin or ancestry. These are even less easy to categorize and it would require a detailed examination of the contemporary saga material to shed light on the portrayal of these individuals.

[6] Jónas Kristjánsson, 'Íslendingasögur og Sturlunga: Samanburður nokkurra einkenna og efnisatriða', in *Sturlustefna*, ed. by Guðrún Ása Grímsdóttir and Jónas Kristjánsson, Rit Stofnunar Árna Manússonar, 32 (Reykjavik: Stofnun Árna Magnússonar, 1988), pp. 94–111.

[7] For a fuller list of occurrences of the term in saga literature, see Sverrir Jakobsson, 'Strangers in Icelandic Society 1100–1400', forthcoming in an as yet untitled volume being edited by Orri Vésteinsson, Árni Daníel Júlíusson, and Chris Callow.

[8] *Austfirðinga sögur*, ed. by Jón Jóhannesson (Reykjavik: Hið Íslenzka Fornritafélag, 1950), p. 179.

[9] *Austfirðinga sögur*, ed. by Jón Jóhannesson, p. 172.

[10] *Austfirðinga sögur*, ed. by Jón Jóhannesson, p. 48.

[11] *Sturlunga saga*, ed. by Jón Jóhannesson, Magnús Finnbogason, and Eldjárn, I, 258.

It transpires that this had in fact been a real fight and the saga makes it clear that it had suited Jón Eyjólfsson to avoid this conflict. Jón was thought of as being complicit in the death of a man killed that day. In this account, then, the *austmaðr* is used in the story to highlight the saga's perspective on the events it describes. It seems quite clear that the *austmaðr* figure is only a cipher, but there seems no immediate reason, however, for the writer to choose an unnamed Norwegian in that role. Certainly the writer may not have known enough to name an individual who may have been with Jón Eyjólfsson at that particular time. But all the same, the writer has gone out of his way to choose an *austmaðr* as Jón's companion.

Slightly more complex, but almost as transparent, are the pairs of Norwegian characters who crop up in *Droplaugarsona saga* and *Bjarnar saga Hítdœlakappa*. The first of these cases really seems to revolve around one main Norwegian, whom the saga supplies with a companion when it comes to a fighting scene. The Norwegians are given names, Sigurðr skarfr and Önundr, and it is Sigurðr who kills a man with Önundr's assistance. The otherwise insignificant Önundr dies in the fight but Sigurðr skarfr goes on to make a speech in defence of his protector, Helgi Droplaugarson. In *Bjarnar saga Hítdœlakappa* two unnamed Norwegians appear as members of a group chasing the hero of the saga. One Norwegian throws a spear at Björn as he flees his enemies. The spear pierces Björn's leg only for Björn to pull the spear from his wound and throw it back. On its return, the spear kills an unspecified Norwegian and an important character, Kolbeinn Þórðarson, the son of Björn's enemy. This sort of role is one which Norwegians often fill in Sagas of Icelanders: a kind of social incompetent. In this narrative's terms, the Norwegian gets things wrong. He not only dares initiate violence with the saga's hero but also gets an Icelander killed. In this example it only becomes clear that there is a second Norwegian when Björn Hítdœlakappi's victims are listed. Within this list, it may well be significant that the brace of Norwegians is named next to a pair of outlaws.[12]

Austmenn appear in pairs in *Sturlunga saga* too, but apparently for different reasons. In *Sturlunga saga*, ships often arrive at Icelandic ports with two captains and those captains are frequently recorded as staying with two separate Icelandic leaders.[13] Take, for example, the arrival of a ship in Hrútafjörður in the 1220s when Þórðr Sturluson and Sturla Sighvatsson go to meet it. These chieftains are said to be on good terms and they take away a Norwegian each. The names of the captains are mentioned explicitly: Bárðr garðabrjótr and Bárðr trébót.[14] It is hard to believe that the description of this event has not been shaped by the writer's preconception that Þórðr and Sturla were (on this rare occasion) on amicable terms. Elsewhere two Norwegian brothers are said to have stayed with a certain Þórðr Þórarinsson who lived in Eyjafjörður. This

---

[12] *Borgfirðinga sögur*, ed. by Nordal and Guðni Jónsson, ch. 34 (p. 208).

[13] Sverrir Jakobsson, 'Strangers in Icelandic Society 1100–1400', p. 4.

[14] *Sturlunga saga*, ed. by Jón Jóhannesson, Magnús Finnbogason, and Eldjárn, I, 311 (*Íslendinga saga*, ch. 58)

Þórðr seems to be of some political significance locally although he was not well liked. The Norwegian brothers kill him. The event seems to be a kind of set-piece in which Þórðr's disappearance from the political scene is being rationalized by his humiliation by two relatively unknown characters.[15] There seems no reason to doubt that Þórðr was murdered but his death is deliberately not being blamed on an Icelander.

The *austmenn* mentioned above are not typical of all Norwegians in sagas. *Austmenn* can fulfil far more memorable roles in narratives. In *Flóamanna saga*, Helgi Austmaðr, for example, arrives in the south of Iceland and bumps into one of the saga's main characters, Þorgils, who is seventy years old. Helgi takes great amusement from the fact that the aged Þorgils nearly falls from his horse. Incidentally, we are told that the laughing *austmaðr* had an axe in his hand. Þorgils has a sword in his hand and he kills the Norwegian. The lesson from this seems quite obvious: an old, sword-wielding Icelander is better than an axe-wielding Norwegian.

Two years after this, however, the saga tells us that the brothers of the vanquished Norwegian turn up to take their revenge. They negotiate with Þorgils, whom they refuse to kill on the grounds that it would be wrong to kill an old man, and accept compensation. That compensation comprises five marks of silver and the sword that Þorgils used to kill Helgi. Richard Perkins has quite rightly pointed out that this story explains where Þorgils' fabled tenth-century weapon disappeared to,[16] but the story also does something else. It shows Norwegians losing out in a blood feud. Their acceptance of the weapon that killed their brother in compensation essentially serves to make them look stupid. This story is more detailed than that of the *austmaðr* whose spear hit Björn Hítdœlakappi, but at its core both show a similar set of values.

Austmenn can again be seen acting ineptly in a blood feud in *Hœnsa-Þóris saga*.[17] Here, there is a Norwegian who starts a feud which, the saga suggests, need never have happened. The *austmaðr*, Örn, is staying with Blund-Ketill. The Norwegian merchant kills the son of another chieftain with a bow and arrow and, by doing so, initiates a feud. Blund-Ketill had been on reasonable terms with this particular chieftain until the *austmaðr* intervened. Starting a feud by killing unnecessarily is a clear example of social incompetence with many parallels in saga literature.

One good example illustrates, however, how a partly similar image of a Norwegian is used in *Sturlunga saga* for a rather different purpose. It is worth describing

---

[15] *Sturlunga saga*, ed. by Jón Jóhannesson, Magnús Finnbogason, and Eldjárn, I, 209–10 (*Íslendinga saga*, ch. 24)

[16] Richard Perkins, 'Objects and Oral Tradition in Medieval Iceland', in *Úr Dölum til Dala: Guðbrandur Vigfússon Centenary Essays*, ed. by Rory McTurk and Andrew Wawn (Leeds: Leeds Studies in English, 1989), pp. 243–64 (pp. 252–54).

[17] This episode is frequently commented on in relation to Norwegian trading activity in Iceland. See most recently, Helgi Þorláksson, *Vaðmál og verðlag: Vaðmál í útanríkisviðskiptum og búskap Íslendinga á 13. og 14. öld* (Reykjavik: Fjölföldun Sigurjóns, 1991), pp. 165–68; Helgi Þorláksson, 'Social Ideals and the Concept of Profit in Thirteenth-Century Iceland'; Sverrir Jakobsson, 'Strangers in Icelandic Society 1100–1400', p. 1.

because it shows how common perceptions or story-telling motifs could be drawn on by saga writers. This event is recorded in chapters 84 and 85 of *Íslendinga saga* where Sturla Sighvatsson is seen to get revenge over two of his enemies, the brothers Þórðr and Snorri Þorvaldsson of Vatnsfjörður. There had been an uneasy peace between Sturla and these brothers ever since the brothers had ransacked Sturla's farm three years earlier. After some negotiations, a truce is brokered by Sturla's uncle, Snorri Sturluson, who then invites the Þorvaldssons to visit him in Reykholt. *Íslendinga saga* makes it clear, however, that no one expects Sturla Sighvatsson to keep his word.

The Þorvaldssons accept Snorri Sturluson's offer to visit him, but to get to Reykholt from their base in the West Fjords they have to travel through Sturla Sighvatsson's territory. They actually have to travel past Sturla's home, Sauðafell, the very farm they attacked three years earlier. It comes as no great surprise that Sturla is waiting for the Þorvaldssons. He gathers troops from surrounding valleys and traps the Þorvaldssons at a farm close to Sauðafell. The text has made it abundantly clear by this point that the Þorvaldssons are unlikely to come out of this alive: negotiations have failed to dissuade Sturla from attacking, and the Þorvaldssons and their small group of companions are said to have confessed, 'skriftast þeir', in anticipation of their deaths.[18]

It is at this point, while Sturla is organizing his attack on the Þorvaldssons in the defended farmstead, that we get told about a Norwegian. This is a Norwegian on his own with his bow, *handbogi*, who is with Sturla Sighvatsson. The crucial passage says:

Skagi hvíti Austmaðr var með Sturlu. Hann hafði handboga, ok bað Sturla hann skjóta at þeim í garðinn. Hann gerði svá, at hann skaut tveim örum eða þrimr í garðinn, ok geigaði þat allt. Hann var þó bogmaðr mikill. Sturla drap bogann ór hendi honum ok kvað eigi gagns ván at fýlu þeiri.[19]

The passage subsequently says that the attackers put all their efforts into throwing stones at the stronghold. As in many *Sturlunga saga* battles, this proves to be a successful way of fighting. We are told of a number of the Þorvaldssons' men who are hit by stones and weakened so that they can be set upon with swords and axes. We hear no more about Skagi hvíti Austmaðr and no more about bows. The two Þorvaldssons are summarily executed by Sturla's men as Sturla looks on.

Several conclusions can be drawn from this episode. First of all, we again have another rather simplistic or symbolic depiction of a Norwegian. But here it is not

---

[18] *Sturlunga saga*, ed. by Jón Jóhannesson, Magnús Finnbogason, and Eldjárn, I, 351 (*Íslendinga saga*, ch. 84).

[19] *Sturlunga saga*, ed. by Jón Jóhannesson, Magnús Finnbogason, and Eldjárn, I, 353 (*Íslendinga saga*, ch. 85). 'Skagi hvíti Austmaðr was with Sturla. He had a hand-bow, and Sturla asked him to shoot at those in the fortress. He did so, so that he shot two or three arrows into the fortress, and they all missed. He was nevertheless a great archer. Sturla knocked the bow out of his hands and said that nothing useful could be expected from this wretched man.' My translation.

simply the case that a Norwegian is ineffectual — it is significant that Sturla Sighvatsson is the person who is saying so. The standard 'Norwegians can't fight' topos is countered here by the saga claim that Skagi was actually a good bowman. In this respect, then, Sturla is portrayed as intolerant towards his own supporters and unable to appreciate their worth. Sturla's unreasonableness is the theme of the whole episode. The act of killing a small party of people whom he has sworn not to kill, through the use of excessive force, is being criticized. Sturla's victims were also young and the text points this out very carefully. This passage is one of many which Sturla Þórðarson, writing his narrative in the late thirteenth century, uses to depict Sturla Sighvatsson in a bad light. In this case Sturla's actions were not only cowardly but unheroic. His treatment of a Norwegian soldier forms a part of this general image.[20]

The appearance of Norwegians in saga narratives represents a conscious choice by the author to mention *austmenn*. The fact that Norwegians and Icelanders had similar names meant that a term like *austmaðr* could be used, or not, by the story-teller depending on whether a certain kind of narrative warranted it. And often the appearance of a Norwegian character tends to be used to explain how bad events could have taken place in Iceland or within a given locality. A good example is the appearance of Geirmundr in *Laxdœla saga*, the owner of the sword, *Fótbítr*, which Bolli uses to kill Kjartan.[21] The same is true of the incident mentioned above from *Hœnsa-Þóris saga*. In the case of the murder of Þórðr Þórarinsson an illegal killing is recorded by Sturla Þórðarson without him having to attribute it to a powerful Icelandic kin group.

The kinds of role for which Norwegians were used in sagas tells us a great deal about where they fitted into Icelanders' mental map. Norwegians were seen as essentially the same as Icelanders but often appear inferior when acting in Iceland. They did the same things as Icelanders but not always as well as Icelanders. At the same time they were not like other kinds of non-Icelanders who regularly appear in sagas. Norwegians were not generally conceived of as so alien that they could appear in Sagas of Icelanders as sorcerers or berserkers in the way that Hebrideans or Swedes could. Norwegians were similar to Icelanders but simply lesser, whatever their proclaimed social status in Norway. That is why we find Norwegians making mistakes in feuds or as in *Laxdœla saga*, to use the example of Geirmundr again, colluding with women in helping to bring about the deaths of men in a blood feud. The Icelandic audience of the sagas expected generic Norwegians to be marginal and weak like the old, the young, women, outlaws, and slaves.

Even in *Sturlunga saga* we find many depictions of *austmenn* which, although not entirely stereotypical, must reflect a popular view of Norwegians. For instance, most

---

[20] Marlene Ciklamini, 'Sturla Sighvatsson's Chieftaincy: A Moral Probe', in *Sturlustefna*, ed. by Guðrún Ása Grímsdóttir and Jónas Kristjánsson, pp. 222–41.

[21] *Laxdœla saga*, ed. by Einar Ól. Sveinsson, Íslensk Fornrit, 5 (Reykjavik: Hið Íslenzka Fornritafélag, 1934), pp. 151–56.

of the (few) references in *Sturlunga saga* to the use of a bow (*bogi* or *handbogi*) and arrows are in connection with *austmenn*. The association of *austmenn* with weapons is also common in Sagas of Icelanders.[22] It would seem to be such a well-known image that Sturla Þórðarson can turn it on its head in order to criticize his over-bearing cousin Sturla Sighvatsson. This association is a very strong one, to the extent that Icelanders virtually never get described as using bows.[23]

Ultimately, it is in glib and simple images that the term *austmaðr* seems to be most easily employed in both types of saga material. In *Sturlunga saga*, which has most of the more complex images, more often than not, when *austmenn* are identified, it is with little or no comment on their behaviour. In fact, the evidence of *Sturlunga saga* suggests, by the very rare reference to conflict between groups of Norwegians versus groups of Icelanders, that conflict between the two was actually rare in thirteenth-century Iceland. Most Norwegians, who must have been known to saga writers, are never identified as such and are referred to by their occupation as merchants or ships' captains.[24]

Just occasionally, Contemporary Sagas give glimpses of *austmenn* living in Ice-land and taking part in local politics, described in a seemingly straightforward way. This is the impression given by the appearance of an *austmaðr* called Þjóstarr,[25] who seems to cause a dispute in Dalir in western Iceland.[26] Þjóstarr is said to live at

---

[22] The Norwegian outlaw, Gunnarr þiðrandabani, for example, uses a bow in *Fljótsdæla saga* (ch. 17). Gunnar fits well into the mould of the Icelandic outlaw. The stories about him share strong similarities with those about the outlaws Gísli Súrsson and Grettir Ásmundarson. It is noticeable, however, that Gunnarr is different from these outlaws in using a bow. See *Austfirðinga sögur*, ed. by Jón Jóhannesson, pp. 193–211. See also *Borgfirðinga sögur*, ed. by Nordal and Guðni Jónsson, p. 179, *Eyrbyggja saga*, ed. by Einar Ól. Sveinsson, Íslensk Fornrit, 4 (Reykjavik: Hið Íslenzka Fornritafélag, 1935), pp. 125, 127; and *Sturlunga saga*, ed. by Jón Jóhannesson, Magnús Finnbogason, and Eldjárn, I, 349, 353, 405; II, 183.

[23] The farmer Árni Bassason, from Skarðsströnd in western Iceland, is a rare example of a bow-using Icelander in *Sturlunga saga*. Like Skagi hvíti Austmaðr, he has little success with the weapon. See *Sturlunga saga*, ed. by Jón Jóhannesson, Magnús Finnbogason, and Eldjárn, I, 92 (*Sturlu saga*, ch. 21). Hrafn Sveinbjarnarson, the subject of the contemporary *Hrafns saga Sveinbjarnar*, also uses a bow in one scene, *Sturlunga saga*, ed. by Jón Jóhannesson, Magnús Finnbogason, and Eldjárn, I, 219.

[24] Helgi Þorláksson, 'Kaupmenn í þjónustu konungs', pp. 8, 9. There has not been space in this essay to discuss the identities of those traders and ships' captains who appear in *Sturlunga saga* and might be suspected of being Norwegian on the basis of their occupations and (perhaps) names.

[25] Þjóstarr is actually accompanied by another *austmaðr*, Þorkell máni, but he is given an even less prominent role.

[26] *Sturlunga saga*, ed. by Jón Jóhannesson, Magnús Finnbogason, and Eldjárn, I, 312–14. It seems rather ironic that the one *austmaðr* depicted in a 'realistic' way in *Sturlunga saga* should have such an uncommon name, at least in an Icelandic context.

Ásgarðr, a farm of some local importance, and he clashes with a local man over payment of some goods. The dispute turns into a small-scale but violent clash between the men of Ásgarðr and the supporters of Þjóstarr's opponent. Here, Þjóstarr is still distinguished in this account by his military equipment (a spear and helmet); he is still undoubtedly a *kaupmaðr*, and in all probability in the employ of local aristocrats. Nevertheless, this account has an air of realism about it and it seems highly likely that Þjóstarr was a well-known local figure.[27] It must also be significant that one of the few *austmenn* who lived in the west of Iceland is depicted so neutrally by Sturla Þórðarson who himself was from the west. Sturla knew this story well and he had no obvious point to make about the dispute.

In spite of the existence of Norwegians like Þjóstarr, it was still the case that when Icelanders needed to find someone to be the butt of a joke or to make their history more palatable, then writers made use of a package of ideas of what an *austmaðr* exactly was. These popular images, even in the highly politicized contemporary narratives, arise from Icelanders' fairly loose sense of their own uniqueness and not clear-cut hostility to foreign oppression.[28]

---

[27] Þjóstarr is certainly still alive in Dalir five years later. See *Sturlunga saga*, ed. by Jón Jóhannesson, Magnús Finnbogason, and Eldjárn, I, 349.

[28] The same cannot be said, of course, of the portrayal of some Norwegian kings in Sagas of Icelanders.

Literacy and 'Runacy' in Medieval Scandinavia

TERJE SPURKLAND

The Material

If you ask Scandinavians the following question: 'When did writing come to Scandinavia?', the great majority would reply, 'I don't know'. Those who did know the answer would most probably answer in one of two ways. The most common answer would be that writing was introduced to Scandinavia together with Christianity, some time around the year 1000. A small minority would perhaps refer to runic inscriptions from pre-Christian times, but might doubt whether rune-carving could be described as 'writing'. At any rate, they would say that after the introduction of Christianity, and with it the Latin alphabet and its literary culture, rune-carving went out of use. Rune-carving in the Middle Ages is generally regarded as reflecting antiquarian interest, as regression to pre-Christian lore, or as graffiti — casual scribblings in hidden places like dark corners in churches. Indeed, this is in fact what most pupils learn at school today, at least in Norway.

However, nothing could be more wrong. The fact is that Scandinavia had its own script when the roman script was introduced at some time in the tenth or eleventh century. Moreover, the runic script was not immediately displaced by Latin literary culture. In Norway, people continued to use runes for another three hundred years. The major part of the medieval Scandinavian runic material consists of rune-sticks dug out of the medieval soil of cities like Oslo, Bergen, Trondheim, and Tønsberg in Norway, Old Lödöse, Skara, Nyköping, Söderköping, and Uppsala in Sweden, and Lund, Ribe, and Schleswig in Denmark.[1] These rune-sticks can in many cases not only be related to a relative chronology, but we are also able to provide an absolute date. This holds particularly true for the situation in Bergen. There, the rune-sticks were found below, in, or overlying layers of burnt detritus (fire-layers) which can be associated with historically dated fires.

---

[1] Although Lund and Schleswig were part of Denmark in the Viking Age, today Lund belongs to Sweden, and Schleswig to Germany.

In addition to the rune-sticks, there are runic inscriptions on grave monuments, in church buildings, on church artefacts and everyday utensils. Altogether there are around 2500 Scandinavian runic inscriptions dating from 1150 to the end of the fourteenth century. Some 1400 of them are from Norway. They range from religious and secular texts in Latin to Old Norse poetry and business correspondence; there are also everyday pieces of information, intimate confidences, pure obscenities, and incomprehensible hocus-pocus.

Alongside rune-carving, roman-script culture was expanding; canon laws, religious texts, historical works, and an increasing number of original charters were produced in Scandinavia. There are reasons to assume that, at the outset, the roman script had its catchment area in a very narrow social stratum that was associated with the Church and with secular power. We see a rather sharp social and functional divide between the roman and runic script. However, as the roman script was increasingly used for the vernacular, especially in Norway, and as those proficient in Latin also began to carve runes, the division between runes and the roman script was reduced in the sense that the same person mastered both writing systems. The scope of the runic material shows clearly that a good proportion of medieval runic carvers were literate in the sense that they were also masters of the roman script. Fifty runic inscriptions in Latin from Bryggen ('the Wharf') in Bergen and eighty Latin runic inscriptions from Sweden indicate that rune-carving was an activity with which literate people were also familiar.

It was, however, only under special circumstances that the two writing systems were used in the same context. Runes were made to be cut in wood; they are composed of vertical and sloping lines that go across the grain of the wood. Roman letters, however, were less appropriate for woodcarving because of their rounded curves and horizontal lines. The roman script was contingent upon parchment, pen, and ink. Therefore there was still a dichotomy between the two scripts, but it was not to the same degree dependent upon social conditions. The decisive factor may have been of a material nature; wooden sticks and a knife were more accessible than parchment, pen, and ink, especially in situations where there was an acute need for written communication.

The reason for the complementary distribution of the two scripts might also lie in the communicative context; something might be more appropriately expressed in wood than on parchment. For example, the announcement on a rune-stick from Bryggen (B390):[2] **inkibiørkunimerþaerikuarisþaf/akri**, 'Ingebjørg loved me when I was in Stavanger'. You did not kill a calf just to announce that you had succeeded in your advances towards Ingebjørg last time you visited the town of Stavanger.

Yet there are instances of overlapping, where the two writing systems operate side by side. We have epigraphic inscriptions — memorials — with the text in both runes

---

[2] B+number indicates preliminary registration in the Runic Archives in Oslo for runic inscriptions found in Bergen since 1955 and not yet published in *Norges Innskrifter med de yngre Runer*, ed. by Magnus Olsen, Aslak Liestøl, and James E. Knirk, 6 vols (Oslo: Norsk Historisk Kjeldeskrift-Institutt, 1941–).

and roman letters. In some cases exactly the same text is given in the two writing systems. From time to time runes occur as marginal notes in manuscripts, and runes may function as abbreviations or additional letters in otherwise literary manuscripts. There is one extant example of a manuscript written entirely in runes, the so-called Codex Runicus (AM 28, 8vo), dated to *c*. 1300, from Skåne in present-day Sweden.

Some Case Studies

The key question concerning the rise and fall of runes and runic inscriptions is therefore not why the runic script died out in the Middle Ages, but why it did not die out immediately after the introduction of the roman script to Scandinavia. And what role did the runic tradition play in a society where literacy was steadily increasing?

In the introduction to his translation of Snorri Sturluson's *Edda*, Anthony Faulkes characterizes thirteenth-century Scandinavian society as being marked by sets of socio-cultural dichotomies:[3]

1. The Church had become a powerful institution and was attacking the power of the chieftains.
2. The heroic world of the independent Vikings was giving way to the medieval world of feudalism and trade.
3. Oral poetry, which had been the principal means of expression and transmission, was being supplanted by written prose.
4. Sagas and poetry on native subjects were challenged by imported literary trends from the continent, such as chivalric romances and ballads.

To this list of binary oppositions, we could add runes and runic inscriptions versus roman script and manuscripts.

Scholars generally agree that Snorri, traditional and aristocratic as he was, regretted the loss of traditional culture. He wrote his *Edda* as a reaction to the superseding of skaldic poetry by both written prose and new kinds of poetry. Snorri's motivating force was to keep alive interest in traditional skaldic verse and to encourage young poets to continue to compose in the traditional Scandinavian oral style.

Could the persistence of the runic tradition in the Middle Ages be the result of the same reaction, often referred to as the Old Norse renaissance? To answer this question we have to take a closer look at some of the extant inscriptions from medieval Scandinavia. Inscription B380 from Bryggen in Bergen, located under the fire layer of 1198, certainly seems to be reminiscent of outdated lore:

---

[3] Snorri Sturluson, *Edda*, ed. and trans. by Anthony Faulkes (London: Dent, 1987), pp. viii–ix.

a) ᚼᛆᛁᛚ:ᛋᛂᚦᚢ:ᛆᚴ:ᛁᚼᚢᚼᚢᛘ:ᚵᛆᚦᚨᛘ
    hæil : seþu : ok: ihuhum : goþom

b) ᚦᛆᚱ:ᚦᛁᚴ:ᚦᛁᚴ:ᚵᛁ:ᛆᚦᛂᚾ:ᚦᛁᚴ:ᛆᛁᚼᛁ
    þor : þik : þig : gi : oþen : þik : æihi

'Hail to you and in good spirits! May Thor take you and Odin possess you!'

It appears to be an invocation of Odin and Thor. It is, however, not a curse or a malediction that is expressed in the text. On the contrary, line **a** conveys a friendly greeting and expresses good wishes for the spirits of the recipient. Line **b** should be interpreted in relation to line **a**, and so should also be understood as a wish of good fortune. During this period, invoking Odin and Thor would normally imply a malediction, but in this context it should instead be seen as a blessing. It is also possible that the whole inscription was made as a joke, aping old heathen beliefs. One thing is certain, however, the inscription is not evidence of seriously intended pre-Christian magic. Of the six hundred medieval runic inscriptions found at Bryggen in Bergen, this is the only one that mentions Odin and Thor or that otherwise refers to pre-Christian religion. The topic of this inscription is therefore not typical of the material.

Other inscriptions, however, contain undoubtedly religious texts. N617 is on a rune-stick, 271 mm long and 14 mm by 14 mm thick, also from Bryggen.[4]

a) ᛆᚢᛂᛘᛆᚱᛁᛆᚵᛈᚱᛆᛋᛁᛆᚴᚱᛁᛂᛐᛐᛆᛣᛁᛂᚾᛐᛁᛂᚴᛆᛘ
    aue maria gracia plena tominus tekom

b) ᛒᛂᚾᛂᛐᛁᚴᛐᛆᛐᚢᛁᚾᛘᚢᛚᛁᛂᚱᛁᛒᚾᛆᚦᛒᛂᚾᛂᛐᛁᚴᛐᚢᛋ
    benedikta t/u in mulieribus æþ benetikt/us

c) ᚠᚱᚢᚴᛐᚢᛋᛁᚢᛂᚾᛐᚱᛁᛋᛐᚢᛁᛆᛘᛂᚾ
    fruktus uentris tui amen

'Ave Maria, gratia plena, Dominus tecum. Benedicta tu in mulieribus, et benedictus fructus ventris tui. Amen.'

Thus we have a complete Hail Mary (Ave Maria) in the form the prayer had during most of the Middle Ages. There are several Our Father (paternoster) and Hail Mary inscriptions in runes from medieval Scandinavia, but in most cases it is only part of the prayer; the whole prayer is found on only a few of them. These inscriptions are usually found in ecclesiastical surroundings: on church buildings and on objects inside churches. However, the prayers, especially the Hail Mary, can also be found in more secular settings, like the example above, carved on a wooden stick that must have been deposited in the ground shortly before or after the fire of 1332. We also find just the first two words of the prayer, *Ave Maria*, on everyday objects like tankard bottoms and vessels for food and drink.

---

[4] N+number indicates inscription with publication number that has been published in *Norges Innskrifter med de yngre Runer*, ed. by Olsen, Liestøl, and Knirk.

This leads us to the question: Who were the carvers of Latin inscriptions such as this? The clergy, carving religious texts in runes on wooden sticks as a pastime? Or common people who had been taught just enough Latin to be able to spell it out in runes? Both alternatives are plausible. These texts could have been written by members of the clergy. However, religious education gave all adult members of the society oral knowledge of certain prayers in Latin. The carvers could therefore also be common people who knew the Christian prayers by heart and put them down into runic script, either because they were not acquainted with roman script or because parchment, pen, and ink were not available to them there and then, when they needed it.

What is remarkable is that the Latin in these inscriptions is, for the most part, grammatically correct. There are, however, certain systematic discrepancies in the spelling compared with contemporary Latin in roman script. This has been adduced as evidence for spelling in accordance with pronunciation ('orthophonic spelling'). If the inscriptions are the products of learned people, then the spelling discrepancies indicate that the carver deliberately deviated from classical orthography and adjusted his spelling to the way he pronounced the Latin. The other possibility is that we are dealing with common people who either knew a little Latin, or just remembered the prayers they heard so many times and spelt them accordingly. They could not have been directed exclusively by what they heard, however, as the variations between the different inscriptions would have been greater. They must have known a little Latin, and the deviations from manuscript Latin are so regular that it would be correct to talk about a special runic Latin tradition or a particular runic orthography for Latin. The same holds true for runic inscriptions in the vernacular. The deviations from the language found in Scandinavian manuscripts are very consistent, and the reason might be that the carvers felt free to adapt spelling to their pronunciation. Runic writing is therefore, to a certain extent, more orthophonic than manuscript writing.

It must be admitted, however, that there are also several inscriptions with religious texts where both the grammar and spelling are so corrupt that the carver could not have had any scholarly knowledge of the language in which he was carving. The only guide must have been what he had heard around him. In these cases there is no regularity in the deviations from the manuscript language.

The rune-carver of the following inscription (N604) knew his Latin. It is carved on a rune-stick that has been broken and the text is fragmentary. It probably dates from the last part of the thirteenth century.

a) ᛏᚢᚴᛁᛏᛂ:ᛁᛁᛰᚱᚴᛁᛏᛂ:ᚾᛁᛏᛆᛘ:ᚠᚾᛂ:[..ᛌᛁ.—
   d/ucite : diskrete : uita/m : ku/e : [..]n[.—

b) ᚢᛐᛁᛰᚱᛂ:ᛌᛁᚾᛌ᛬:ᛰᛁᛏᛂ:ᛁᛒ:ᚾᛆᛆᛁᛆ᛬:|—
   uæst/ra : salus : mete : siþ : næcia : |—

a) *ducite discrete vitam, que—*
b) *vestra salus mete sit nescia—*

'Conduct in a sensible way a life which...! May your health be unrestricted...'

This is a piece of secular or literary Latin, grammatically correct but with the usual deviations found in runic inscriptions.[5] It is impossible to say for certain how such a text may have found its way into the medieval soil of Bergen, but one possibility is that it was included in a collection of sayings used for teaching purposes. Someone liked it so much that it was learnt by heart and included in a repertory of literary gems that one could use should the occasion arise.

Another text takes us directly into the Norwegian war of succession in the late 1100s (N170):

+ᛁᛁᛈᚤᚱᚦᚱ:ᛁᛅᛁ''ᚤᚾᛁ:ᚱᛏᛁ'ᛏ:ᚱᚤᛘᛅᚱ:ᚦᛁ'ᛅᚱ:ᛁᚫᚤᛈᛅᚱ:ᛁᛅᛈᛁᚼ:ᛏᛈᛁᛁᚱ:ᛒᛅᛏᛅᚤᛈᛁ:
sigurþr : ialssun: ræist : runar : þesar : lo/uga/r : dagen : æftir : botolfs :

ᚤᛏᛁᛅ:ᛁᚱ:ᛁᚤ:ᚤᛈᛅᚦᛁ:ᚼᛁᛈᛏᛏ:ᛈᚤ:ᚾᛁᛘᛁ:ᛏᛁᛈᛁ:ᚤᛁᚤᛏ:ᛁᛁᚱ:'ᛏᛏᛅᚱ:ᚾᛁᛈ:
mæso : e/r : a/n : flyþi : higat :o/k: uildi : æigi : ga/ga : til : sæta/r : uiþ :

'ᚾᛏᚱᚱᛁ:ᚤᛅᛈᚤᚱ:ᛒᛅᛁᛁ:'ᛁᚼ:ᛁᚤ:ᛒᚱᛅᚦᚱᛅ:+
su/ærri : fo/þ/ur : bana : sin : o/k: brøþra

'Sigurðr Jarlsson carved these runes the Saturday after Botolf's mass when he had fled here and would not be reconciled with Sverrir, the killer of his father and brothers.'

The inscription was carved into the door frame of Vinje stave-church in Telemark. Although the church is no longer standing, the frame has been preserved. Sverrir Sigurðsson had made a claim to the Norwegian crown and confronted the ruling king, Magnús Erlingsson, and his father, Earl Erlingr skakki. During the ensuing war, Sverrir managed to kill the king, as well as the king's father and brother. The local legal assemblies, the things, reluctantly accepted him as the new king, but there was still strong resistance to his rule. The strongest opponent was the Church. This opposition was called *baglar* (from Old Norse *bagall*, meaning 'pastoral staff' or 'crozier'). One of the leaders of the *baglar* party was Sigurðr Jarlsson, half-brother of the slaughtered king and son of the slain earl. He continued the struggle against the usurper, and he is mentioned several times in *Sverris saga*. However, in this inscription, we meet him, so to speak, face-to-face in Vinje church, the Saturday after Botolf's mass, when he had been put to flight by his enemy, the king. By comparing the different literary sources, it has been inferred that this happened on Saturday 21 June 1197. So here we have a piece of first-hand information about medieval Norwegian history and a medieval linguistic record that can be dated to the very day of its origin.

This inscription is also a testimony to the fact that the aristocracy could be proficient in rune-carving when the situation demanded it. It is not necessary to ask why

---

[5] When Latin is written in roman letters, /e(:)/ is marked by <e> while the runic script alternates between ᛐ <e> and ᛐ <æ>, <uærsum> *versum*, <uæst/ra> *vestra*, <mete> *mete*. The roman letter <c> is carved ᚼ <c> preceding front vowels and ᛈ <k> in other positions: <d/ucite> *ducite*, <diskrete> *discrete*. In roman script unstressed /t/ is marked <t> while in runic script we often find ᚦ: <siþ> *sit*, <æþ> *et*.

Sigurðr resorted to runes given the situation he was in. This was not the first time he had carved runes either. He is a very experienced rune-carver: he dots his runes consistently;[6] he has very sophisticated bind-runes (ligatures); and he is one of the very few medieval rune-carvers who tries to distinguish between the vowels /ǫ/, /o/ and /ø/, using a very special character for the /ø/.

It is to be expected that Sigurðr Jarlsson would be literate, that is, that he knew how to read and write roman script. His runic inscription verifies such an expectation: the word division is consistent (every word is separated by a special character <:>), and some words are spelt with double consonants, which was not normal in runic tradition. However, the most significant trace of literate influence is what we see in connection with the word *flyþi* 'fled'. Here the carver has left out the l-rune. He realized this afterwards and tried to correct the error by putting the l-rune above the line on the spot where it should be, and inserting a referential sign, a sloping line between the f- and y-runes. This is a practice that is well known from manuscripts. The literate model is quite clear.

Whether Smith, who slept with Vigdís at Bryggen before the fire of 1332, was also literate is perhaps more questionable (B39):

a) ᛌᛘᛁᚦᚢᚱ:ᛌᛆ͡ᚱᚦ:ᚢᛁᚴᛏᛁᛌᛁ
smiþur : sa/rþ : uiktisi

b) ᛆᚠ:ᛌᚿᛅᛚᛏᚢ:ᛒᛂᚿᚢᛘ
af : snæltu : benum

'Smith had sexual intercourse with Vigdís of the Sneldubeins.'

The carver separates the words according to the literate tradition, although one possible exception is the last word, *Sneldubenum*, which he divides in two. There is otherwise nothing in the inscription that indicates that the carver did not know how to handle parchment, pen, and ink. Several different communicative contexts may underlie this inscription. Briefly, I would characterize it as a graffito, insofar as the concept of graffiti is relevant to medieval runic inscriptions.

The scope of the medieval runic finds shows clearly that like any other writing system, runes could be used for different purposes, not just one particular purpose. Every subject that it is possible to put into writing is represented in the material. One should therefore say that, in sum, the medieval runic script was a functional script. For that reason, I subscribe to the opinion that medieval runic inscriptions were not part of the so-called Old Norse renaissance and did not serve as a reaction against the new cultural trends that were affecting medieval Scandinavian society.

---

6 'Dotting' is the name given to the technique of adding a diacritic, in the shape of a dot, to otherwise ambiguous runes in order to disambiguate them.

Runes and Medieval Literacy

'Medieval literacy' has become a very common term among scholars whose field of
study is reading and writing in the Middle Ages. The concept is often connected to
the medieval meaning and connotations of *litteratus*. *Litteratus* implied a certain degree of knowledge of Latin. A person who did not know how to read and write Latin
was *illiteratus* or *laïcus*, even if he were proficient in reading and writing in the
vernacular.[7] Most scholars today, however, are inclined to extend the notion of being
literate to include anyone who could read and write any language. Or as Brian Stock
says in his book *The Implications of Literacy*:

> The literate, in short, was defined as someone who could read and write a language for
> which there in theory at least was a set of articulated rules, applicable to a written, and,
> by implication, to a spoken language.[8]

Anthropologists, who were among the first to make use of the notion of literacy
when they were studying the effects of learning to read and write on oral cultures,
understand *literate* as meaning more than just the ability to read and write. They
include an ideology of self-definition in the concept, where there is not only a chronological relationship between the oral and the written, but also a conceptual one.
When medievalists borrowed the term *literacy* and its derivatives *literate, literalize,
literarization* from anthropologists, they also to some extent adopted their understanding of the words.

As a consequence then, the term *literacy* has acquired a wide range of meanings
and connotations. Seth Lerer puts it this way in his study of *Literacy and Power in
Anglo-Saxon Literature*:

> 'Literacy' both as historical phenomenon and the subject of scholarly inquiry, con-
> notes a variety of cultural activities and practices. It can mean a practical skill, a
> pattern of individual behavior, and a set of ideologies and literary forms that arise in
> response to that behaviour. The word can be invoked to determine an individual's
> place in society and to assess the social norms against those distant in geography or
> time. The power of the literate, in these terms, is the power to include and exclude: to
> distinguish the self from the other, the civil from the savage, the mainstream from the
> subversive. But the power of the literate is also the ability to transform experience
> through writing.[9]

---

[7] Franz H. Bäuml, 'Varieties and Consequences of Medieval Literacy and Illiteracy', *Speculum*, 55 (1980), 237–65; M. T. Clanchy, *From Memory to Written Record: England 1066–
1307*, 2nd edn (Oxford: Blackwell, 1993), pp. 224–52.

[8] Brian Stock, *The Implications of Literacy: Written Language and Models of Interpretation in the Eleventh and Twelfth Centuries* (Princeton: Princeton University Press, 1983), p. 6.

[9] Seth Lerer, *Literacy and Power in Anglo-Saxon Literature* (Lincoln: University of
Nebraska Press, 1991), p. 22.

Based on these understandings of the concept of literacy, it has been the undertaking of many medievalists to focus on how the increasing use of writing influenced social structure and the administration of society, and to consider the effects of the written word superseding the spoken.

How then should we relate the medieval runic material to the concept of literacy? Are runic inscriptions part of Scandinavian medieval literacy, and is the carving and interpreting of runes a literate activity? If we follow Brian Stock's understanding of a literate as meaning anyone who could read and write a language for which there was a set of articulated rules, applicable to a written and to a spoken language, runic script must be said to represent literacy. It might perhaps be dependent on how strictly we emphasize 'the set of articulated rules'. I would suppose, though, that there would be a little reluctance to acknowledge that handling runes is a literate activity. And I find that the term literacy is so closely associated with Latin culture that I would restrict the use of this term primarily to the reading and writing of roman script. To meet these objections the term *runic literacy* has been suggested to designate literacy in runes. If, however, one feels the term *literacy* implies a degree of Latinity, then *runic literacy* would be a contradiction in terms.

In his discussion of the distinction between literacy in Latin and literacy in the vernacular, Brian Stock stresses the fact that in the Middle Ages *litteratus* referred almost invariably to literacy in Latin. Among the illiterates, he distinguishes between the lettered and the unlettered: those who could read and write the vernacular and those who could not read and write at all. In the Scandinavian case, then, we could say that a literate was a person who mastered the roman script, whether the language was Latin or the vernacular, while *the lettered* was a person proficient in the carving and reading of runes. A rune-carver might therefore be illiterate, but not unlettered.

There is one more aspect of the notion of literacy where medieval runic tradition does not fit in. That is the pragmatic and conceptual aspect of the notion. We arrived at the conclusion that the runic script was a functional script; it even had a pragmatic function in some sectors of social life such as trade and business transactions. It is, however, going too far to say that the use of runic inscriptions pervaded social institutions in the same way as the increasing use of roman-lettered documents.

However, not all manuscripts had a pragmatic function. There are at least two different modes of written text. One is manuscripts containing scholarly works, religious texts, and literary works. These texts were not called into service in the administration of society to the same extent as the other textual genre: for example, charters, law-codes, or any other document that contributed to the legal or administrative operation of society. One therefore often refers to two types of literacy, *cultural literacy* and *pragmatic literacy*.

Michael Clanchy, in his book *From Memory to Written Record*, illustrates how the increase in literacy led to an escalating use of documents in government administration in England after 1066. His subject matter is what we know as pragmatic literacy. This binary distinction between the *cultural* and *pragmatic* use of documents might also be applied to medieval runic inscriptions. The range of the material gives good reasons for introducing the concepts of *pragmatic runic literacy* and *cultural runic literacy*.

As I have already stated, however, I find the term *runic literacy* contradictory. Runic script and roman script have so many inbuilt idiosyncrasies separating them that I find it more reasonable to talk about two different script cultures. Scandinavia in the Middle Ages was a two-script community, where the two script systems mutually excluded each other, not completely, but to a great extent. Runic inscriptions and manuscripts were not produced in the same communicative contexts. The medium was different, parchment versus wood; roman manuscripts were primarily written in scriptoria, while rune-carving was an activity that took place far away from the scriptorium. This distance from any learned and literate setting was not only geographical but also conceptual. The literate mentality and everything that follows in its wake was more or less absent in the rune-carver's surroundings, where he sat handling his knife and incising his runes on a piece of wood.

It is commonly assumed that literacy was developed in response to the need for extending and materializing the collective memory. But the texts preserved for posterity, such as laws, religious texts, legends, historical narratives, charters, and even literary texts, were written in order to be delivered aloud on special occasions. Books and letters were intended for many people and were commonly read aloud and listened to. Runic script had a different purpose. What was carved in runes was primarily intended for silent reading. The addressee of most of the medieval runic inscriptions was not the collective but the individual. The text should not be broadcast but mediated from eye to eye.[10]

I am tempted to maintain that these two script cultures conveyed different mentalities and that the term *literacy* and its derivatives should be used for only one of them. I would therefore plead for a new term to refer to runic literacy, and my suggestion is — *runacy*. Runacy and literacy are what we are dealing with when we are studying the two-script culture of medieval Scandinavia. And if we accept this term runacy, we need a derivative covering the practitioners of that activity, that is the rune-carvers and the recipients of runic inscriptions, parallel to *literacy – literate*. May I take the liberty of suggesting *runatic* or perhaps *runate*? Is that stretching the parallel too far?

Scholarly studies of medieval literacy have generated one more term that could be relevant for the study of medieval runacy. My reference is still Brian Stock and his

---

[10] For reading as a process of listening, see M. B. Parkes, *Pause and Effect: An Introduction to the History of Punctuation in the West* (Aldershot: Scolar Press, 1992); and D. H. Green, *Medieval Listening and Reading: The Primary Reception of German Literature 800–1300* (Cambridge: Cambridge University Press, 1994). For the concept of reading in connection with runes and roman script, see T. Spurkland, 'Scandinavian Medieval Runic Inscriptions: An Interface Between Literacy and Orality?', in *Roman, Runes and Ogham: Medieval Inscriptions in the Insular World and on the Continent*, ed. by John Higgit, Katherine Forsyth, and David Parsons (Donington: Shaun Tyas, 2001), pp. 121–28.

voluminous work on the implications of literacy. The fundamental basis for Stock's analysis is the consequences of the progress of literacy on social organization or social relationships. In order to illustrate the thesis that literacy influenced group organization, he presents a series of case studies from the field of heretical or reformist religious groups. The use of texts is the characteristic connecting link between the members of these groups, which he designates 'textual communities':

> Eleventh-century dissenters may not have shared profound doctrinal principles or common social origins, but they demonstrated a parallel use of texts, both to structure the internal behaviour of the groups' members and to provide solidarity against the outside world. In this sense they were 'textual communities'.[11]

Thus the key question is whether Stock's concept of textual community is applicable to medieval rune-carvers, their inscriptions, and the recipients of the inscriptions. There is no doubt that the practitioners of runacy demonstrated a parallel use of texts, but the question is whether they can be said to use the texts, the runic inscriptions that is, as a group and to define themselves in opposition to the outside world. That is the pragmatic aspect of Stock's textual community concept:

> What was essential to a textual community was not a written version of a text, although that was sometimes present, but an individual, who, having mastered it, then utilized it for reforming a group's thought and action.[12]

He is thus thinking of a very special use of texts: how heretics and reformers used texts to justify their deviations from orthodoxy and the established church respectively.

If the prerequisite for a textual community is the common use of texts with identical intentions, then the carvers and readers of runic inscriptions did not represent a textual community. What was carved, to whom, and why, was far too diverse to meet that requirement. Nevertheless, runacy was so different from and independent of literacy that there are good reasons for saying that we are dealing with script communities of different kinds. If we remove Stock's concept of textual community from his heretics and reformers and modify the concept a little, it is also possible to say that practitioners of runacy constituted their own textual community.

Conclusion

A tentative conclusion might therefore be that medieval Scandinavian society distinguished itself not only by making use of two different languages, Latin and the vernacular, but also by the functional use of two script systems, roman script and vernacular script — the runes. These two scripts represented different ideologies of self-definition and manifested dissimilar conceptual relationships between the oral

---

[11] Stock, *The Implications of Literacy*, p. 90.

[12] Stock, *The Implications of Literacy*, p. 90.

and the written. Manuscripts and rune-sticks connoted divergent cultural activities and practices. It is therefore reasonable to say that the roman script culture was based on *literacy* while the runic tradition was characterized by *runacy*. Runacy and literacy found expression in different media and in different communicative contexts. They reflect different textual communities. Normally these communities did not intersect. There were, notwithstanding, instances where literacy and runacy met, indicating a mixture of textual communities. That, however, is a different story.

What's Hecuba to Them? Medieval Scandinavian Encounters with Classical Antiquity

RANDI ELDEVIK

Whenever the question of postclassical reception of the classics arises, the Renaissance is naturally the period that comes first to mind. But the importance of the classical tradition in the High Middle Ages is less only relatively, and in fact is quite considerable. Cultural historians often speak of a twelfth-century Renaissance.[1] In Scandinavia, the twelfth century was of course the time in which literary activity (that is, *literary* in the strict sense of the word — written texts as opposed to oral storytelling and poetry) was just getting well under way: not much time had yet passed since the initial Christianization of Scandinavia had brought with it the Roman alphabet and a tradition of Latin literature stretching back over more than a thousand years. Indeed, considering that some of these Latin texts, such as the *Ilias Latina*, were translations and reworkings of much earlier Greek texts, we can reckon it as a round two thousand years of European literary tradition that medieval Scandinavians began to absorb in the High Middle Ages. Of course the twelfth-century Renaissance carried over into the thirteenth century as well, and for Scandinavia it is in fact the thirteenth century that is most important. It is during the thirteenth century that literary activity of all kinds — both in Latin and in Old Norse — swells to a peak, and the thirteenth century will in fact be my main concern.

It must be noted that the Scandinavian literati of this time, even while they absorbed and assimilated the rich and varied literature of southern Europe, were by no means neglecting their own native cultural legacy: for many, the Roman alphabet became an opportunity for recording myths of the Æsir and legends of heroes such as Sigurd the Dragon-slayer (Sigurðr fáfnisbani). But in this process too, classical influences

---

[1] First and foremost, on this subject, see Charles Homer Haskins, *The Renaissance of the Twelfth Century* (Cambridge, MA: Harvard University Press, 1927); also, inter alia, Christopher Brooke, *The Twelfth Century Renaissance* (New York: Harcourt, Brace and World, 1969).

had a way of weaving themselves in. For example, Theodore Andersson has tentatively suggested that the portrayal of Brynhild in *Völsunga saga* owes something to
Virgil's characterization of Dido in the *Aeneid*.[2] That is debatable; a clearer and
more definite instance of classical influence upon the shaping of Scandinavian legendary narrative is Saxo's *Gesta Danorum*. Saxo Grammaticus was of course a learned
Dane who wrote in elegant Latin prose, and it has been conclusively shown that
Saxo included deliberate echoes of Virgil and other Roman authors in his narratives.[3]

The *Gesta Danorum* is in fact an excellent example for showing how Scandina-
vian/European literary relations could actually be a two-way interchange. Saxo may
have intended this text primarily for Danish readers, but since he was writing in the
international language of Europe rather than in his own vernacular, acquaintance
with the *Gesta Danorum* had the potential to become widespread far beyond Denmark. Hence one of Saxo's tales in particular, that of Amlethus, was destined to enrich the dramatic literature of England and the world when, hundreds of years later,
Shakespeare made Saxo's tale the basis of his tragedy *Hamlet Prince of Denmark*.
There is indebtedness on both sides, and credit to be claimed on both sides.

Though Shakespeare's *Hamlet* takes us beyond the Middle Ages, dwelling a bit
longer on this play will provide a useful avenue of approach to the main issue I
should like to raise: the issue of why classical myth and epic should matter to postclassical audiences. The fall of Troy, the death of the Trojan King Priam and the
ordeal faced by his surviving wife, Queen Hecuba, are events from the classical epic
tradition described in Act II of *Hamlet* by one of the travelling players whom Hamlet
encounters, and these events are all long ago and far away — from Hamlet's perspective, from Shakespeare's, and from ours. Not only that, they are also mythical,
imaginary, unreal — as Hamlet stresses when he calls the player's speech 'a fiction,
a dream of passion' (II. 2. 552).[4] Hamlet finds it astonishing that anyone could be
moved emotionally by mere words describing fictional events; hence his famous
question 'What's Hecuba to him [i.e., to the player delivering the speech], or he to
Hecuba, / That he should weep for her?' (II. 2. 559–60). Hamlet's question may

---

[2] See Theodore M. Andersson, *The Legend of Brynhild*, Islandica, 43 (Ithaca, NY: Cornell
University Press, 1980), p. 241.

[3] Commentary on this matter is extensive. See especially Karsten Friis-Jensen, *Saxo
Grammaticus as Latin Poet: Studies in the Verse Passages of the Gesta Danorum*, Analecta
Romana, Instituti Danici, Supplementum, 14 (Rome: Bretschneider, 1987); Karsten Friis-
Jensen, *Saxo og Vergil* (Copenhagen: Museum Tusculanum, 1975); *Saxo Grammaticus. The
History of the Danes Books I–IX*, ed. by Hilda R. Ellis Davidson and Peter Fisher, 2 vols
(Cambridge: D.S. Brewer, 1980); Giorgio Brugnoli, 'Gli auctores di Saxo', and Giovanni
Polara, 'Tra fantasmi e poeti: Coincidenze e reminiscenze classiche nelle parti in versi dei
Gesta Danorum', in *Saxo Grammaticus: Tra storiografia e letteratura*, ed. by Carlo Santini
(Rome: Il Calamo, 1992), pp. 27–45 and pp. 261–80 respectively.

[4] Shakespeare quotations are from *The Riverside Shakespeare*, ed. by G. Blakemore Evans
(Boston: Houghton Mifflin, 1974).

seem a very odd one. We tend to take it for granted that epic events like the Trojan War matter, and that the pathetic downfall of a character like Hecuba, a once mighty and proud queen, matters.

But it is always salutary to go back to the basics and to question the very things we tend most to take for granted. And in that respect, Hamlet's question stands as a crucial one for literary criticism and theory. It need not specifically involve Hecuba, of course; Hecuba should be taken as a synecdochic representation of any and all fictional characters, indeed of fiction as a whole. That is the larger importance of Hamlet's question. But now I would like to use Hecuba synecdochically in a more narrow and specific way. For my present purposes, 'Hecuba' is also a shorthand way of summing up the classical tradition as a whole — all the literature that we have inherited from ancient Greece and Rome. Granted, there is much more involved in our classical legacy than myths and legends alone, just as there is more to mythographic and heroic literature than the story of Hecuba alone. But mythic/heroic story material can offer an especially convenient focal point for exploring both the differences and the similarities between two cultures that have come into contact with one another.

Revival of the classics may have been one characteristic feature of literary activity in southern Europe from the twelfth century onwards, but Scandinavian readers and writers at that time had many calls on their attention and were obliged to set priorities. It can be highly instructive to look at what sorts of texts from elsewhere in Europe show up in medieval Scandinavia, for these will be the texts containing the things that medieval Scandinavians most desired to import from southern Europe. When we think of the vast array of written information available in the twelfth century and after, in French, German, English, and Latin texts — a thousand years' worth of Christian religious writings from the early Church Fathers all the way up to the latest exciting developments from, for instance, the school of St Victor,[5] and writings reflecting developments in secular society such as chivalric romance and troubadour lyrics of courtly love, to name only a few examples — it is remarkable, and a tribute to the vitality of classical mythology, that any of it should be included. Yet there were, indeed, Scandinavian retellings of the Trojan War story: the multiple redactions of *Trójumanna saga*[6] are my chief concern, but I might also mention in

---

[5] For Victorine theology in medieval Scandinavia, see Gunnar Harðarson, *Littérature et spiritualité en Scandinavie médiévale: La Traduction norroise du 'De arrha animae' de Hughes de Saint-Victor*, Bibliotheca Victorina, 5 (Turnhout: Brepols, 1995).

[6] All the known redactions have been edited by Jonna Louis-Jensen: *Trójumanna saga*, Editiones Arnamagnaeanae, Series A, 8 (Copenhagen: Munksgaard, 1963), and *Trójumanna saga: The Dares Phrygius Version*, Editiones Arnamagnaeanae, Series A, 9 (Copenhagen: Reitzels, 1981). The most important commentary on them is in the introductions to her editions; but see also the new study by Stefanie Würth, *Der 'Antikenroman' in der isländischen Literatur des Mittelalters* (Basel: Helbing & Lichtenhahn, 1998), which appeared too late for me to consult in writing this paper. My discussion of Hecuba focuses exclusively on the Alpha redaction of the saga.

passing Snorri Sturluson's use of the Troy story in his euhemerization of Thor and the other Æsir — which shows the prominence that Troy had in Snorri's world. Thus Hecuba, both as an individual character and as a synecdoche, becomes the subject of a question similar to that which Hamlet asked, but with a change of pronoun from singular *him* to plural *them*, so as to include all medieval Scandinavians, the writers and the audiences of Old Norse narratives based on classical myths and legends. It is all these to whom I refer when I ask 'What's Hecuba to them?'

Actually, this question is quite similar to one asked by Torfi Tulinius in his recent book *La 'matière du Nord'* — only Tulinius is concerned with the native Scandinavian legends about Sigurd and the rest, which are the subject-matter, the *matière*, of the *fornaldarsögur* ('sagas of ancient times').[7] If long-established conventional usage did not restrict the word *fornaldarsögur* to narratives set in ancient Scandinavia, then a work such as *Trójumanna saga* would have the right to be called a *fornaldarsaga* as well, for it certainly takes place in very ancient times. In either case, the situation involves archaic story materials and their handling by Icelanders of a later time, whose way of life differed from that of the characters in the ancient legends. But at least the narratives that are conventionally labelled *fornaldarsögur* (that is to say, *Völsunga saga* and the like) have a northern European setting and characters whom Icelanders regarded as their own distant ancestors. The gulf of separation between thirteenth-century Icelanders and Greek mythological characters was — one might think — absolute. In the same way, the English public today might be expected to feel a more visceral connection with a legendary English hero such as Robin Hood than with any ancient Greek hero.

But if ethnic identity were the only important thing, hero-tales would never spread from one ethnic community to another. And yet they do. Just as Robin Hood has attained popularity outside of England, so Greek heroes such as Hercules, Jason, and Odysseus have repeatedly done, in a series of ever-widening circles expanding outward from Greece itself. In doing so, these heroes have not remained unchanged from what they originally were. Hercules, for example, was depicted in medieval France as a suave and polished courtier who displayed his skill at jousting in tournaments[8] — a far cry from the savage and boisterous club-wielding Hercules of ancient tradition, but a model of aristocratic conduct and an exemplar of chivalric values much more pertinent to the concerns of medieval Frenchmen. This kind of transformation was the way in which the gulf could be crossed. Likewise, Tulinius has

[7] See Torfi H. Tulinius, *La matière du Nord': Sagas légendaires et fiction dans la littérature islandaise en prose* (Paris: Presses de l'Université de Paris-Sorbonne, 1995), passim. The question is so central to *La 'matière du Nord'*, so pervasive in Tulinius's inquiry, that it is impossible to point to specific pages. There is now an English translation available: Torfi H. Tulinius, *The Matter of the North: The Rise of Literary Fiction in Thirteenth-Century Iceland*, trans. by Randi C. Eldevik (Odense: Odense University Press, 2002).

[8] See Marc-René Jung, *Hercule dans la littérature française du XVIᵉ siècle: De l'Hercule courtois à l'Hercule baroque* (Geneva: Droz, 1966), passim.

shown how the *fornaldarsögur*, in spite of their ancient settings, express the concerns of Icelanders caught up in the social and cultural developments of the thirteenth century, when these texts were written.

Continental values of chivalry and aristocracy, of a hierarchical social organization with a king at the apex, were gaining more and more of a hold on Icelandic minds; lofty ideals of conduct, the ideals of honour and *drengskapr*,[9] were prominent in everyone's awareness; but in the scramble for power and position, those ideals were often violated in practice, and ethical questions concerning proper conduct took on a new acuteness and urgency. In short, it was the Age of the Sturlungs, an age of turmoil and contradictions. As Einar Ólafur Sveinsson puts it in his study of this period, 'I have tried to show that the Sturlung Age was anything but all of a piece. Vices and virtues existed side by side, and where the vices seemed about to prevail absolutely, words or incidents could crop up to show the opposite.'[10] We need only hark back momentarily to the plot of a *fornaldarsaga* such as *Völsunga saga*, with its many acts of treachery and the breakdown of bonds of kinship and friendship, to see how much resonance this text has with the concerns of the Sturlung Age. Almost every character in *Völsunga saga* displays such a mixture of right and wrong in his or her conduct that it is hard to apply the simplistic designations of 'hero' and 'villain', hard to sympathize with or to condemn any of the characters utterly. For an audience interested in complex moral and ethical dilemmas, *Völsunga saga* provides strong meat to chew on. And so too do many of the best-known Greek myths and heroic legends.

Granted a leap of the imagination to carry Icelanders across the ethnic gulf, it can easily be seen how the people of the Sturlung Age could find much that was pertinent, much that was recognizable, in the spotted careers of such Greek heroes as Jason, Theseus, and Hercules. All this is true, to an even greater degree, of the Trojan War legends. From the very first incident leading up to the war — the Judgment of Paris, in which that prince showed a lack of integrity in accepting a bribe to skew his decision and in defying the rules of hospitality to seduce Helen — to the very end of the war, in which Greek victory is brought about through unscrupulous trickery, we see situations that, for all the exoticism of their setting, must have struck thirteenth-century Icelanders as close parallels with the conflicts and the struggles of their own lives. And, of course, Icelandic writers could take existing similarities and enhance them through the transforming process mentioned above.

For a case in point, let us take an episode from the middle of the Trojan War. Prince Paris (as I shall call him here, though he is called by his alternative name Alexander in *Trójumanna saga* and in some Latin sources) is involved, along with

---

[9] The term *drengskapr* is difficult to translate precisely. Perhaps 'heroism' is best, but it has connotations of manliness, virtue, courage, and the like.

[10] Einar Ól. Sveinsson, *The Age of the Sturlungs: Icelandic Civilization in the Thirteenth Century*, Islandica, 36 (Ithaca: Cornell University Press, 1953), p. 75.

his mother Hecuba. At this point in the war, many of the most powerful Trojan champions — chief among them Hector — have been killed, and the Trojan situation is looking more and more desperate. But an opportunity unexpectedly comes for Queen Hecuba to snatch victory from the jaws of defeat. She is secretly contacted by the most powerful of all the Greek warriors, Achilles. During a truce, he had caught sight of Hecuba's daughter, Princess Polyxena, and fallen in love with her. Achilles is willing to do anything he must to obtain Polyxena — even make a separate peace with the Trojans and renege on his commitments to his fellow Greeks. With Achilles' secret negotiations, ethical issues have already been raised in the minds of Icelandic readers: in Achilles, *fin amour* (to use the medieval French term), a sentiment highly esteemed by anyone exposed to French ideas of courtliness, comes into conflict with the bonds of warrior brotherhood, which commanded equally high esteem. There is also the question of what is the right way for Queen Hecuba to respond to Achilles' offer. By gaining Achilles' fighting strength for the Trojans, she could save her entire people, whose lives are in great jeopardy as matters stand. But even so, should she accept salvation on Achilles' terms? Achilles is, after all, the killer of her favourite son, Hector, and other sons of hers as well. Could Hecuba honourably give her daughter in marriage to a husband whose hands were stained with the blood of the bride's brothers?

The pragmatic mentality — the mentality of realpolitik — might say yes, do what you must to survive. But both lofty ideals and earthy passions (the passions of a mother grieving for her slain sons) would say no, there can be no compromise, no accommodation with a foe who has done so much harm. The principle of kinship loyalty alone would make Hecuba duty-bound to seek vengeance on her sons' killer. Thus one might say that Hecuba, in rejecting the practical advantages of a marriage alliance with Achilles, is behaving very idealistically. But the way in which she then goes about fulfilling her duty of vengeance is far from idealistic. The honourable way to go about it would have been for Hecuba's surviving son Paris to challenge Achilles to single combat. After all, it was in honourable single combat that Achilles had killed each of the other Trojan princes. But Hecuba knows that Paris, of middling prowess as a warrior, stands no chance against the might of Achilles. If Paris is to be the instrument of her revenge upon Achilles, it will have to be in an underhanded way that violates the code of honour. And Hecuba accepts that necessity. To achieve vengeance, she is willing to do whatever it takes. Honour and dishonour are inextricably woven together in her actions.

The situation I have just outlined is that which exists in the Latin sources used by the anonymous Icelandic writer whom we shall designate the Alpha redactor of *Trójumanna saga*.[11] The basic idea of Achilles' death coming about through the

---

[11] As Louis-Jensen's title for her edition of the Alpha redaction (*Trójumanna saga: The Dares Phrygius Version*) suggests, the late classical prose text *Daretis Phrygii de excidio Troiae historia* is the main source used by this redactor — and in the incident involving Hecuba, Paris, and Achilles, probably the sole source.

treacherous dealings of Hecuba and Paris is a given of the classical tradition, however vaguely it is sketched in Latin. The Alpha redactor recognized the potential interest of the situation and enhanced it. His Hecuba becomes a fierce, passionate woman, hell-bent on achieving vengeance at any cost, and willing to manipulate her kinsmen however she must in pursuit of her goals. Unscrupulous, scheming, driven more by personal passions than by abstract ideals, she becomes comparable to many strong, ruthless female characters from Icelandic literature who, in their traditional Germanic role of *Hetzerin* (or female inciter to revenge),[12] are of cardinal importance to the outcomes of these sagas: for example, Njáll's wife Bergþora and Gunnarr's wife Hallgerðr (both from *Brennu-Njáls saga*), and Guðrún — both the Icelandic Guðrún of *Laxdæla saga* and the legendary continental Guðrún of *Völsunga saga* and the Eddic lays.

More than just plot function is involved, for in the Latin sources too Hecuba functions as the mastermind of the revenge scheme. Beyond this, what really places Hecuba in the company of the above-named Scandinavian characters is the specific details with which the Icelandic redactor fleshes out her characterization. The most striking detail is the sardonic comment he invents for her, 'þijki mier ei órvænt ad hann muni verda stilltur af ofurást þeirre hann hefur á henni'.[13] What Hecuba does not explicitly state, but what is clearly implied, is that the 'cure' she contemplates will entail the death of the patient. The dry wit, the understated humour, the gleeful morbidity of this comment are such as could be found nowhere but in an Icelandic saga. I can easily imagine Bergþora making the same quip in such a situation; I cannot imagine the Hecuba of Greek and Roman poets doing so.

In classical tradition overall, the Trojan War legends are vast and multifarious, consisting of a basic core with many accretions clustering around it. The episode of Achilles' love for Polyxena and Hecuba's plan for a treacherous ambush of the lovesick Achilles is one such accretion. Though available to the Alpha redactor of *Trójumanna saga*, and apt to his purposes, it is an episode located at the periphery of the overall tradition. Some Greek and Roman writers who deal with the Trojan War never mention it at all.[14] What, then, is Hecuba's primary role in the classical tradition? What is the core of her character in the core of the Troy-legends? The image of Hecuba that most often comes to mind is that which we get in the player's speech in *Hamlet*: Hecuba as victim of Greek brutality, Hecuba fluttering helplessly about the ransacked palace, trying in vain to escape being captured by the Greeks who have

---

[12] See Rolf Heller, *Die literarische Darstellung der Frau in den Isländersagas* (Halle: Niemeyer, 1958), pp. 98–122.

[13] Quoted from Louis-Jensen, *Trójumanna saga: The Dares Phrygius Version*, p. 56. Translation: 'And it seems to me not unlikely that he will be cured of the infatuation that he has for her.' (My translation, as are all the following translations from *Trójumanna saga*.)

[14] This incident plays no part in Virgil's account of the Trojan War and is likewise absent from Homer's.

just slaughtered her husband, Priam. This is an image that comes mainly from Virgil's *Aeneid*, a work of great importance for the classical tradition overall, though of less importance for the Alpha redactor of the saga, who incorporates only a few Virgilian details into his account. Those few details, however, are concerned specifically with the very end of the war, and the sack of Troy — an event which receives more lavish descriptive detail from Virgil than from any other ancient writer. The Alpha redactor seems to have been unable to resist including some of Virgil's more striking images, such as the fiendish, inhuman appearance of the Greek warrior Pyrrhus as he ruthlessly slaughters King Priam before Hecuba's very eyes. Pyrrhus is actually the son of Achilles, too young to have taken part in earlier stages of the war, but arriving in the final stage in response to his father's death because he feels a duty to pursue vengeance for it. The obligation of avenging slain kinsmen is a principle common to both classical and Scandinavian culture, and one of the features of classical narrative with which medieval Scandinavians could most easily sympathize. But in Virgil's *Aeneid*, as in the Shakespeare passage inspired by Virgil, Pyrrhus is not a sympathetic character but a brutal savage — for Virgil's proclivities are entirely anti-Greek and pro-Trojan. In the *Aeneid*, the Trojans are altogether noble and incapable of wrongdoing, defeated not by any fault of their own but by ruthless fate conspiring with Greek deceitfulness. And the image of the helpless, pathetic Queen Hecuba fluttering dishevelled about the palace communicates that view of Trojan innocence.

Trójumanna saga does not share Virgil's biased, one-sided view. In the saga, Pyrrhus does indeed behave vilely when he enters the action; but before that, the Trojan Prince Paris had behaved vilely toward Pyrrhus's father Achilles, lying in wait and taking him by surprise and at a disadvantage, with numbers of men and weapons heavily in Paris's favour. If Pyrrhus's massacre of the helpless King Priam at the end of the war seems vile and dishonourable, so too did Paris's massacre of the disadvantaged Achilles seem vile and dishonourable previously. The Alpha redactor makes this clear in several ways: by his moving narration of Achilles' death scene; by the words he puts in the mouth of Paris's brother Helenus, 'það öngva hefnd hans óvinum',[15] a comment not found in the Latin sources; and by the words the narrator himself uses, such as 'þjoflegu svikræði' and 'svivirdilegu tilstilli',[16] in a rare departure from the Icelandic norm of objective reporting of events by saga narrators. Outstanding because of their rarity, the Icelandic writer's explicitly stated opinions are highly effective in highlighting the moral and ethical concerns of this saga. They do, however, seem a bit out of place when directed at Paris, who really has always been a louche and unscrupulous character — something the narrator momentarily

---

[15] Louis-Jensen, *Trójumanna saga: The Dares Phrygius Version*, p. 58. Translation: 'That was no proper revenge against his enemies.'

[16] Louis-Jensen, *Trójumanna saga: The Dares Phrygius Version*, p. 56. Translation: 'furtive treachery' and 'disgraceful wiles'.

ignores for the sake of making his point more strongly. As the narrator would have it, much blame in this matter falls upon Hecuba. She is the real instigator, and Paris only her pawn. This image of Hecuba as a strong-willed ramrod of a woman is the most vivid that we get of her in *Trójumanna saga*. The Icelandic writer has judiciously chosen, from all the aspects of Hecuba available from his sources, the one aspect that is most meaningful in terms of his own culture and his own concerns, and he has stressed this aspect. That is what Hecuba is to him.

But what of the aspect of Hecuba made famous by Virgil and Shakespeare — the pathetic, fugitive Hecuba at the end of the war? Is it entirely omitted by the Alpha redactor of *Trójumanna saga*? No, not entirely, for we catch a glimpse of her fleeing the palace: 'marger leitudu filsna ad hiálpa sijnu lijfi, Hecuba mætti Æneæ er hun flijdi j burt ur hóllini, hun bad hann ad fela Polixstenam firer fiandmonnum sijnum, enn hann feck hana j hendur þeim manne er Archilaus het, og feck hann fordad henni umm stundar saker.'[17] The narrator follows her actions, but does not milk them for pathos as he could have done by a lavish use of descriptive details such as we see in Shakespeare's *Hamlet*. The Shakespearean/Virgilian Hecuba is utterly helpless and ineffectual; the Icelandic Hecuba is still active, trying to do what she can to salvage a disastrous situation. Just as her earlier actions in the saga were prompted by concern for her children (in that case, her sons), so now when all else has been lost her one concern is to preserve the life of her remaining daughter, Polyxena, who is a special target of Greek vengeance because she unwittingly had been made the means of Achilles' ruin. The bloodthirsty Greeks neither know nor care that the girl was totally unaware of Achilles' love for her and totally uninvolved in the assassination plot. The plot was Hecuba's, and at the last she tries to make amends for it by ensuring that punishment shall at least not fall upon her innocent daughter. Consistently, from first to last, the bond of kinship between mother and child has been Hecuba's top priority, and whether it leads her into honourable or dishonourable actions, she pursues it unflaggingly. It is an approach that the Guðrún of *Völsunga saga* might well appreciate, and its pointed development in *Trójumanna saga* is surely motivated by the same concerns that motivated the embellishment of Guðrún's plight by other Icelandic poets and prose writers.

The example of Hecuba is only one of many in *Trójumanna saga* that might fruitfully undergo analysis of this kind. To reiterate: there is much more in classical myths and legends than just Hecuba. And at this point it would also be well to remember that there is more to medieval Scandinavia than Iceland. The conditions prevalent in Iceland during the Sturlung Age differ, of course, from those in the other Scandinavian countries. But that is far too big a matter to encompass in the present study, aside from our brief glance at Saxo's *Gesta Danorum*. In conclusion,

[17] Louis-Jensen, *Trójumanna saga: The Dares Phrygius Version*, p. 282. Translation: 'Many sought hiding places to save their lives. Hecuba encountered Aeneas as she fled the palace. She asked him to hide Polyxena from their enemies, and he put her into the hands of a man called Archilaus, and he kept her safe for a while.'

it will be useful and illuminating for us to reconsider the Icelandic *Trójumanna saga* and the *Gesta Danorum* in juxtaposition, for they stand in marked contrast to one another as alternative ways in which medieval Scandinavian authors could use the classical tradition. In the *Gesta Danorum*, we have essentially Scandinavian subject-matter, but it is couched in elegant Latin redolent of Virgil, and has absorbed much of the feel, the atmosphere, of classical epic. In *Trójumanna saga*, however, the story material is classical and the action is still set in and around the Mediterranean — that has not changed — but the story of the Trojan War is suffused with the tone, the atmosphere, the outlook of Old Norse heroic literature.

The process of transformation was not massive or strenuous in this case; it was an easy stretch for the Icelandic writer, precisely because the archaic hero-tales that make up the Troy story had in themselves always contained much that was congruent with the native Scandinavian heroic tradition. For Scandinavians in the thirteenth century, finding narratives of honour, treachery, vengeance, and gallantry among the Latin texts to which they had fallen heir must have been a gratifying encounter that suggested the larger world was not so strange and different after all. For these Scandinavians, southern European culture would have been like a palimpsest, overwritten with scholastic philosophy, courtly urbanity, and the latest trends in Christian doctrine, but with underlying texts still legible — and among the earliest of these, the classical myths and legends which, in their congruity with Scandinavian traditions, gave encouragement and incentive to the literary and cultural fusion then taking place. 'Long ago and far away', yes — but one might also say, 'so far, and yet so near'.

On the Far Edge of Dry Land: Scandinavian and European Culture in the Middle Ages

SVERRE BAGGE

T he first part of *The King's Mirror*, a work written in Norway around the middle of the thirteenth century, contains a discussion about nature and geography in which the author suggests that Greenland is so far down on the globe that the reflection of the sun when underneath it may be seen from there.[1] Like other learned men of the time, the author of *The King's Mirror* believed that the earth was spherical but that all the land, divided into three continents, formed a circle on the top of the globe, with the area where the three continents met, that is Palestine or the Middle East, at the centre. It was generally believed that Jerusalem was at the very centre, on the top of the globe, where the North Pole is situated in our world picture. By contrast, the polar regions were situated near what to us is the equator, which explains the assumption that the light of the sun when under the globe can be seen from there.

Greenland was far away for contemporary Norwegians. However, so too was the centre of the world around Jerusalem. The great ocean, surrounding the earth, did not start at the far coast of Greenland but at the very coast of Norway. There could thus be no doubt of Scandinavia's position on the periphery of the inhabited world. By contrast, the old, pre-Christian picture of the world envisaged the gods living in the centre, surrounded by the area inhabited by human beings. The Scandinavians were people as close to the gods as anyone else, if not closer, as they were the gods' real worshippers. Thus, the learned, Christian world picture had established new distinctions between the various peoples on Earth and placed the Scandinavians on the periphery.

In another passage, the author of *The King's Mirror* opens his discussion of strange phenomena in the North by commenting on people's tendency to disbelieve the things they hear about distant places. He cites as an example the wonders of

---

[1] *Konungs skuggsiá*, ed. by Ludvig Holm-Olsen (Oslo: Dybwad, 1945), p. 33 (lines 4–6).

India told in a book which had recently been brought from this country to Norway. But, says the author, would not people in other parts of the world refuse to believe the strange things happening in our part of the world, such as people moving on skis swifter than the fastest animal, the sun shining the whole night in summer in the northern part of the country, or a swamp changing wood into stone?[2] Thus, the author is not only aware of living at a distance from the central parts of the world, but also in a country that may appear equally strange to people living in other parts of the world as the Far East was to himself and his fellow countrymen.

Scandinavia was not only geographically peripheral. During the pre-Christian period, learning was ancient wisdom, transmitted from ancestors, and the wisest person was the one who had lived longest and was most familiar with the local culture. Christianity turned these ideas upside-down: 'for it is clear that those who gain knowledge from books have keener wits than others'.[3] Knowledge from books was abstract, foreign knowledge. The book brought God's word to the Scandinavians and taught them to reject all that their ancestors had considered holy and venerable. The greatest heroes were not the ancestors or the legendary figures of old, but some men and women with strange names who had lived long ago in distant places and, instead of performing heroic deeds, had distinguished themselves by being tortured to death by their enemies.

Of course, things did not change completely. Books were rare in the Middle Ages, and we do not know exactly how much the ordinary population was affected by them. No doubt, local traditions survived; ideas and norms from the pre-Christian period continued to exist, and it was perfectly possible to be considered wise without having read books. Nevertheless, if we confine ourselves to the learned elite, as I shall in the following, the change is drastic. No part of Scandinavian literature from the Middle Ages is unaffected by European impulses, and a large part of it is directly imported, in the form of translations or adaptations.[4] The learned elite distinguished itself from the rest of the population by its contacts with the great cultural and literary centres of Christendom; its position as an elite depended on the definition of Scandinavia as peripheral.

In this situation, two strategies were possible: (1) try to become as similar as possible to what was understood as the 'common European culture', or (2) cultivate one's own originality and show that one's own traditions were equal to those of the rest of Europe. Both strategies are found all over Scandinavia, but generally the first

---

[2] *Konungs skuggsiá*, ed. by Holm-Olsen, pp. 13–14.

[3] *Konungs skuggsiá*, ed. by Holm-Olsen, pp. 4–5: 'þvi at þat er raunar at alra annara er vit minna en þeirra er af bokum taca monvit'. See also *The King's Mirror*, trans. by Laurence M. Larson (New York: Twayne, 1917), p. 81.

[4] For a general overview, regarding Old Norse literature, see Marianne Kalinke, 'Old Norse-Icelandic Literature, Foreign Influence on', in *Medieval Scandinavia: An Encyclopedia*, ed. by Philip Pulsiano and others (New York: Garland, 1993), pp. 451–54.

approach is more common in Denmark and Sweden, and the second in Iceland, with Norway in an intermediate position. In the following, I shall pay particular attention to this second strategy, not because it is more important than the first one but because it is more familiar to me.

Saxo Grammaticus opened the prologue to his Danish history by stating that the Danes are a great people whose deeds should be recorded and presented to a wider audience. He wrote that unfortunately, this had not yet been done properly because of the backwardness of the country: the Danes had only recently become Christian, and their knowledge of Latin was still poor. Consequently, Saxo himself had been charged by his patron, Archbishop Absalon, with carrying out this difficult task, despite his professed unworthiness.[5] Saxo is a Danish patriot in his preface as well as in the rest of his work, aiming at depicting the ancient glory of his people. He is clearly aware, however, that this can only be done properly in Latin and that, before the advent of Christianity, the Danes lacked not only the true religion but also the true literary language and rhetorical culture. Thus, in this case at least, Saxo's strategy clearly places him in the first category mentioned above, that is, that of the 'common European culture'.

Saxo's prologue indicates that Latin created a great divide. It was used all over Scandinavia, but there was a marked difference between Denmark and Sweden on the one hand and Norway and Iceland on the other, in administrative as well as literary use. The vernacular was the normal language for administrative purposes in Iceland and Norway. In Norway, the vernacular was used in the royal chancery from the beginning, whereas Latin was used in the royal chanceries of Denmark and Sweden until around 1400.[6] Most of the literature in Iceland and Norway was also in the vernacular. Admittedly, the vernacular was increasingly used as a literary language all over Europe from the twelfth and particularly the thirteenth centuries.[7] What was

---

[5] 'Danorum maximus pontifex Absalon patriam nostram, cuius illustrandæ maxima semper cupiditate flagrabat [. . .] mihi [. . .] res Danicas in historiam conferendi negotium intorsit [. . .] Quis enim res Daniæ gestas litteris prosequerertur? quæ nuper publicis initiata sacris, ut religionis, ita Latinæ quoque vocis aliena torpebat': Saxo Grammaticus, *Saxonis Gesta Danorum*, ed. by J. Olrik and H. Ræder, 2 vols (Copenhagen: Levin & Munksgaard, 1931–57), I (1937), 3.

[6] The earliest diploma in Danish is from 1371, and Danish did not become the normal administrative language until *c.* 1425. The corresponding dates in Sweden are 1343 and *c.* 1400. See Didrik Arup Seip, 'Diplomspråk', in *Kulturhistorisk leksikon for nordisk middelalder*, 22 vols (Copenhagen: Rosenkilde & Bagger, 1956–78), III (1958), cols 92–95. Actually, Denmark was one of the last countries of Europe to change from Latin to the vernacular as the language of administration; see Thorkild Damsgaard Olsen, 'Dansk som skriftsprog', in *Dansk litteraturhistorie*, ed. by Søren Kaspersen and others, 2nd edn, 9 vols (Copenhagen: Gyldendal, 1990), I, 392–403 (p. 403).

[7] Erich Auerbach, 'Das abendländische Publikum und seine Sprache', in *Literatursprache und Publikum in der lateinischen Spätantike und im Mittelalter*, ed. by Erich Auerbach (Bern: Francke, 1958), pp. 203–59.

characteristic of Norway and Iceland, however, was that it was used, not only for
poetry and heroic or romantic narrative, the normal genres in the rest of Europe, but
also for learned literature, such as *The King's Mirror*, the grammatical and astro-
nomical treatises, and the fairly heavy theology in the part of *Stjórn* dating from the
early fourteenth century, that is, Genesis and the first part of Exodus.[8] Furthermore,
there is a vast amount of religious literature, mostly saints' legends, translated into
Old Norse which, however, is less surprising against a European background; the
earliest vernacular literature is usually religious,[9] and with increasing emphasis on
the piety of the laity in the High and Later Middle Ages, it was natural for the
Church to provide devotional literature in the vernacular.

By contrast, hardly anything is preserved in Danish before 1300, except for the
laws, whereas the Latin literature is fairly extensive. There is more Danish-language
literature after 1300, but to judge from what is extant, the great breakthrough for
Danish as a literary language comes in the period after 1450.[10] Most of Sweden's
medieval literature dates from after 1300, but here the vernacular is comparatively
more important than in Denmark. It includes the original narrative work *Erikskrönikan*,
but also learned works like the translation and commentary of the Pentateuch from
the first half of the fourteenth century and an adaptation of Egidius Romanus's *De
regimine principum*.[11] In addition, both Denmark and Sweden have a fairly extensive
devotional literature in the vernacular, including a large number of sermons.[12] From
the late thirteenth and early fourteenth centuries onwards, the reception of scholasti-
cism creates another great divide within Scandinavia. In the late thirteenth century,
Boethius de Dacia, probably a Dane, was a leading representative of Averroism in
Paris;[13] the Swedish Dominican Petrus de Dacia was a theologian as well as a

---

[8] *Stjórn*, ed. by C. R. Unger (Christiania [Oslo]: Feilberg & Landmark, 1862), pp. 1–299;
see also Reidar Astås, *An Old Norse Biblical Compilation: Studies in 'Stjórn'*, American
University Series 7, Theology and Religion, 109 (New York: Lang, 1991).

[9] Auerbach, 'Das abendländische Publikum', pp. 214–15.

[10] Damsgaard Olsen, 'Dansk som skriftsprog', pp. 392–403.

[11] Sten Lindroth, *Svensk lärdomshistoria*, vol. I, *Medeltiden* (Stockholm: Norstedt, 1975),
pp. 81–86 and 94–102.

[12] Anne Riising, *Danmarks middelalderlige prædiken* (Copenhagen: Gad, 1969), pp. 48–68.
In addition, a number of saints' legends and other religious works must have existed, at least
from the thirteenth century onwards, but most of this material has been lost; see Damsgaard
Olsen, 'Dansk som skriftsprog', p. 395. In Sweden, the most important milieu for such
writings was the Birgittine monastery of Vadstena; see Lindroth, *Svensk lärdomshistoria*, pp.
173–81. See also Roger Andersson, *Postillor och predikan*, Sällskapet Runica et Mediævalia,
Scripta Minora, 1 (Stockholm: Sällskapet Runica et Mediævalia, 1993), pp. 24–25.

[13] Étienne Gilson, *History of Christian Philosophy in the Middle Ages* (London: Sheed &
Ward, 1955), pp. 399–402; Sten Ebbesen, 'Danske skolastikere i udlandet', in *Dansk litteraturhistorie*, ed. by Kasperson and others, I, 415–23.

devotional writer and a spokesman for the mystic Christina of Stommeln. In the fourteenth century, the Swedish Magister Mathias, St Birgitta's confessor, was an important theological as well as devotional writer.[14]

This difference corresponds to the differing number of students visiting European universities; there can be no doubt that the number of Danes and Swedes by far exceeded that of Norwegians and Icelanders from *c.* 1300.[15] However, we might have had a different picture if we had material from the twelfth and early thirteenth centuries; we know of a number of Norwegians and Icelanders studying abroad during this period.

The difference between Denmark and Sweden on the one hand and Norway and Iceland on the other can be explained partly by their relative proximity to the main centres of Christendom, partly by their integration into the common European culture, and partly by a greater economic surplus in Denmark and Sweden than in Norway and Iceland. Maybe this is even the main explanation of numbers of Nordic students at foreign universities. Nevertheless, it is possible to detect some kind of deliberate strategy in Norway and Iceland to stress the values of local culture and to try to be equal, not in the sense of being identical but in the sense of having a culture of equal value. This may of course be understood as an attempt to make a virtue out of necessity. Even so, it is interesting to have a closer look at the means used to achieve this aim.

Let us start with the language. Not only was the vernacular used for most literary purposes, it also became an object of study, which was highly unusual. There was a considerable interest in language and grammar in the learned circles of medieval Europe, but the object of such studies was normally Latin. The reason for this was partly practical, as Latin always had to be learnt as a foreign language, and partly the result of the prestige of this language and the tradition of grammatical studies going back to antiquity. The Icelanders, however, made a point of studying their own language theoretically. *The First Grammatical Treatise*, dating from the twelfth century, mainly deals with phonetics and orthography. In it the author states that languages are phonetically different and should therefore have their own alphabet, capable of

---

[14] Lindroth, *Svensk lärdomshistoria*, pp. 63–81.

[15] There is only scattered information on students before *c.* 1350. Notarial sources from Bologna 1285–1300 contain the names of nineteen Danish, eleven Swedish, and six Norwegian students, and we know of thirty-two Danes, eighty-five Swedes, and one Norwegian studying in Paris in 1333. For the period after 1350, the total number of students found in the *matricula* of various universities in Germany, the Low Countries, and Central Europe are 2146 Danes, 821 Swedes (including 97 Finns), and 219 Norwegians. Furthermore, thirty-one Danes, forty-nine Swedes (including eighteen Finns), and one Norwegian are known to have studied in Paris between 1350 and 1450. See Sverre Bagge, 'Nordic Students at Foreign Universities until 1660', *Scandinavian Journal of History*, 9 (1984), 1–29 (pp. 5 and 13 with references to earlier literature).

correctly rendering their specific sounds. He adds a number of examples of sounds that are specific to Icelandic and thus require other letters than those of the Latin alphabet.[16] In *The Third Grammatical Treatise*, which also includes stylistics and poetry, the author, Ólafr hvítaskáld (1216–59), a nephew of Snorri Sturluson, claims that skaldic poetry is essentially similar to that of ancient Greece, that is, classical and Old Norse poetry are derived from the same roots.[17] The survival of pagan mythology and its treatment in Snorri's *Edda* may be understood in a similar way. From a practical point of view, some knowledge of mythology was necessary to understand and practise the art of skaldic poetry, but the survival of this poetry as well as the mythology associated with it may also be understood as the preservation of a common, specifically northern, learning with which educated people were supposed to be familiar. From a religious point of view, this use of Old Norse mythology was no more a problem than the corresponding use of classical mythology in learned circles in contemporary Europe. From a cultural point of view, however, it is highly significant that Norse paganism and its poetry were preferred to classical equivalents, or at least used alongside them and considered equally important.

A similar attitude is also expressed in Snorri's account of the distant past. In his *Edda*, he links the history of the Nordic countries to the ancient world, by identifying the god Thor (Þórr) with the Trojan prince Trór,[18] a practice that had many parallels in contemporary Europe; Troy (Troja) of course was the most prestigious place of origin, as the Romans were believed to have come from this city. In *Heimskringla*, however, he is more original, or maybe he simply abbreviates his earlier story. Odin (Óðinn), who in the *Edda* was descended from Thor in the twelfth generation, has now become the original founding father. He is the prince of the city of Ásgarðr in Central Asia and a contemporary of the Roman conquerors. Having prophetic powers, Odin understands that the future of his descendants lies in another region of the world than that of the Romans and moves north to conquer this area.[19] Rather than letting the people of the North be descended from the Romans, Snorri here

---

[16] *The First Grammatical Treatise*, ed. by Hreinn Benediktsson, Publications in Linguistics, 1 (Reykjavik: Institute of Nordic Linguistics, 1972).

[17] 'Í þessi bók má gjörla skilja, at öll er ein listin, skáldskapr sá, er rómverskir spekingar námu í Aþenisborg á Griklandi ok sneru síðan í latínumál, ok sá ljóðaháttr eða skáldskapr, er Óðinn ok aðrir Asiemenn fluttu norðr híngat í norðrhálfu heimsins, ok kendu mönnum á sína túngu þesskonar list, svo sem þeir höfðu skipat ok numið í sjálfu Asíalandi, þar sem mest var fegrð ok ríkdóm ok fróðleikr veraldarinnar': 'Málskruðs-fræði af Ólafi hvítaskáld', in Snorri Sturluson, *Edda Snorra Sturlasonar*, ed. by Sveinbjörn Egilsson (Reykjavik: Helgi Helgason, 1848), p. 181.

[18] Snorri Sturluson, *Edda Snorra Sturlusonar*, ed. by Finnur Jónsson (Copenhagen: Gyldendal, 1931), pp. 3–5.

[19] Snorri Sturluson, *Heimskringla*, ed. by Finnur Jónsson, 4 vols (Copenhagen: Møller, 1893–1900), I (1893), 14.

imagines a kind of *divisio imperii* between the two peoples. Admittedly, Saxo is here even more patriotic, starting with Dan, the founder of both the Danish people and the kingdom of Denmark, which are not connected with any other civilization.[20] He explicitly rejects Dudo of Saint-Quentin's suggestion that the Danes are descended from the ancient Greeks, that is the Danai, and he omits any reference to the Roman Empire until the age of Charlemagne. Despite his veneration of the Latin language, from a purely historical point of view, Saxo represents the same attitude as Snorri, emphasizing that the Danes were a people equal to and not descended from the ancient Mediterranean peoples.[21] Thus, the desire for originality and specificity can be found outside Norway and Iceland, but it is more widespread and expressed in a greater variety of ways in these countries.

The examples of Nordic self-assertion given so far are all Icelandic, with the exception of Saxo. Skaldic poetry and ancient mythology must, however, have been common to Iceland and Norway, most probably also to the rest of Scandinavia. Icelandic skalds were frequent visitors to the Norwegian court, and most of the Kings' Sagas were known in Norway, some of them were even commissioned by Norwegian kings.

Moreover, a similar attitude is also to be found in a Norwegian work, *The King's Mirror*, which is at first sight a very European work, with its moralizing attitude, its numerous biblical examples, and its highly rhetorical, ornate style, very unlike the sagas. No doubt the author's aim is to introduce European learning, manners, and ideology to this country on the outskirts of Western Christendom. However, he also aims at applying these ideas to the specific conditions of his country. The discussion about natural phenomena in the first part of the work includes geographical descriptions of three countries, Ireland, Iceland, and Greenland, most probably picked because they were all situated on the edge of the inhabited world, near the great ocean.[22] Ireland was of course not unknown to other Europeans, nor has the author of *The King's Mirror* much to say about this country that cannot be found in other sources. Apart from the interest this information may have had for his Norwegian readers, the author's main reason for including Ireland must have been the fact that he considered it one of the best countries in the world and thus a contrast to the other two, in particular Iceland, where the volcanoes and hot springs formed evidence of the presence of the Devil, just as the miracles and saints in Ireland were evidence of the presence of God.

In contrast to the description of Ireland, those of Iceland and Greenland contain much information that even modern scholars have found highly interesting, mainly

---

[20] Saxo Grammaticus, *Saxonis Gesta Danorum*, I, 10.

[21] Lars Boje Mortensen, 'Saxo Grammaticus' View of the Origins of the Danes and his Historiographical Models', *Cahiers de l'Institut du moyen-âge grec et latin*, 55 (1987), 170–76.

[22] On this part of *The King's Mirror*, see Sverre Bagge, 'Nature and Society in *The King's Mirror*', *Arkiv för nordisk filologi*, 109 (1994), 5–42 (pp. 7–18).

about natural phenomena in these countries and the sea around them. Most of this account must be based on the author's own experience or information from people who
had visited these countries. The author, however, does not confine himself to pure
description; he tries to explain his observations in light of the learned world picture.
Thus, in his account of Greenland, he discusses the nature and cause of the northern
lights and suggests three possible explanations: (1) they form part of the great fire
surrounding the earth, (2) they are the reflection of the sun when it is under the globe,
and (3) they are caused by the ice which is so hard and cold that It gives off light,[23]
The first two explanations are, as we have seen, taken directly from the learned world
picture and explain northern phenomena from the position of these far-away countries
on the utmost edge of the world. The author thus does not confine himself to understanding his own region as peripheral but also tries to add to the learned description
of the world by including information from his particular area and explaining it by
the general 'laws' that were believed to govern the universe. In a similar way, he
uses the current doctrine of the king as God's representative on earth and responsible
for the social hierarchy and for justice in his realm in a very precise way to argue in
favour of social change in contemporary Norway.[24] His most important aim is to
replace the traditional system of justice, based on feuds or individual settlement
between people, with public justice, exercised by the king and his representatives.
Both the doctrine of nature in the first part of the work and a series of examples from
the Old Testament are exploited for this purpose,[25] as is also the current doctrine of
the 'three orders' or estates which the author adapts in a fairly original way to
emphasize the organic unity of society and the king's place within it.[26]

How original were the learned men of the medieval North? Did they succeed in
creating something specifically Scandinavian? The Icelandic Family Sagas (also
known as Sagas of Icelanders) are usually considered the most original product of
Scandinavian culture, but there has been considerable discussion as to whether they
represent a fundamentally novel achievement on the part of the Icelanders, or
whether they are adaptations of European models.[27] The same questions present

---

[23] *Konungs skuggsiá*, ed. by Holm-Olsen, p. 33 (lines 1–12).

[24] Sverre Bagge, *The Political Thought of 'The King's Mirror'* (Odense: Odense University
Press, 1987), pp. 71–85, 113–30, 153–54, 210–18, and passim.

[25] Bagge, 'Nature and Society', pp. 18–42; and Bagge, *The Political Thought*, pp. 53–71,
126–30.

[26] Sverre Bagge, 'Old Norse Theories of Society: From *Rígsþula* to *Konungs skuggsiá*', in
*Speculum regale: Der altnorwegische Königsspiegel (Konungs skuggsjá) in der europäischen
Tradition*, ed. by Jens Eike Schnall and Rudolf Simek (Vienna: Fassbaender, 2000), pp. 1–45.

[27] For an account of this and other discussions of saga literature, with an extensive bibliography, see Carol Clover, 'Icelandic Family Sagas', in *Old Norse-Icelandic Literature: A
Critical Guide*, ed. by Carol J. Clover and John Lindow (Ithaca: Cornell University Press,
1985), pp. 239–315. The recent discussion about the sagas as 'pure' literature or an expression

themselves regarding a related genre, the Kings' Sagas, with which I am more familiar, and which I shall use as my main example here.

The Kings' Sagas bear some resemblance to the classicizing historiography which is particularly prominent from the Carolingian renaissance until the renaissance of the twelfth century[28] — the sagas may even be said to be a late offspring of the latter.[29] The relationship between the Kings' Sagas and classical and medieval Latin historiography is still relatively unclear. There can be no doubt about the European origin of features like the speeches, the portraits, and the chronological arrangement; even the style may be influenced by some variety of Latin prose.[30] Nevertheless, there is in all likelihood also a considerable amount of originality, not necessarily in the sense of 'unpolluted' remains from an ancient Nordic past, but in the sense of adaptation of the Latin culture to contemporary Nordic conditions. I have dealt with Old Norse historiography from this point of view on several other occasions,[31] so I shall confine myself here to one particular aspect, the use of oratory and its connection to contemporary discourse and political rhetoric.[32]

In the summer of 1180, King Sverrir fought a battle with his adversary King Magnús Erlingsson outside Niðaróss, present-day Trondheim. Sverrir had the previous year defeated and killed Magnús's father Erlingr, who had until then been the

---

of society is of some relevance for this problem. See Preben Meulengracht Sørensen, *Fortælling og ære: Studier I islændingesagaerne* (Århus: Aarhus Universitetsforlag, 1993); Lars Lönnroth, 'Sagan som dikt och samhällsspegel: Aktuell forskning om isländsk litteratur', *Samlaren*, 115 (1994), 95–105.

[28] R. W. Southern, 'Aspects of the European Tradition of Historical Writing: 1. The Classical Tradition from Einhard to Geoffrey of Monmouth', *Transactions of the Royal Historical Society*, 5th series, 20 (1970), 173–96.

[29] Sverre Bagge, 'Icelandic Uniqueness or a Common European Culture? The Case of the Kings' Sagas', *Scandinavian Studies*, 69 (1997), 418–42.

[30] For some discussion of these questions, see for example Lars Lönnroth, 'Det litterära porträttet i latinsk historiografi och isländsk sagaskrivning: En komparativ studie', *Acta Philologica Scandinavica*, 27 (1965), 68–117; Frederic Amory, 'Saga Style in Some Kings' Sagas', *Acta Philologica Scandinavica*, 32 (1979), 67–86; Jonas Kristjánsson, 'Learned Style or Saga Style?', in *Speculum Norroenum: Norse Studies in Memory of Gabriel Turville-Petre*, ed. by Ursula Dronke and others (Odense: Odense University Press, 1981), pp. 260–92.

[31] Sverre Bagge, *Society and Politics in Snorri Sturluson's 'Heimskringla'* (Berkeley: The University of California Press, 1991), pp. 240–47 and passim; Sverre Bagge, *From Gang Leader to the Lord's Anointed: Kingship in 'Sverris saga' and 'Hákonar saga Hákonarsonar'* (Odense: Odense University Press, 1996); and Bagge, 'Icelandic Uniqueness'.

[32] See also Sverre Bagge, 'Oratory and Politics in the Sagas', in *L'Histoire et les nouveaux publics dans l'Europe médiévale (XIIIᵉ–XVᵉ siècles), Actes du colloque international organisé par la Fondation Européenne de la Science à la Casa de Vélasquez, Madrid, 23–24 avril 1993*, ed. by Jean-Philippe Genet (Paris: Publications de la Sorbonne, 1997), pp. 215–28.

real ruler of the country, and established himself in the Trøndelag region. Sverrir had now changed from a guerrilla leader to an established king, commanding a part of the country and able to meet his adversaries on equal terms. Nevertheless, the battle outside Trondheim, usually named the Battle of Ilevollene, was the first pitched battle Sverrir and his men fought against a prepared enemy and consequently represented a new stage in his career as a military leader.

In *Sverris saga*, Sverrir addresses a speech to his men before the battle.[33] He begins by describing the difficult situation facing them: King Magnús's men, with their gilt weapons and costly clothes, are filling the field, so that Sverrir's men have to fight against overwhelming odds. To illustrate their situation and what is to be done, Sverrir refers to a dialogue between a father and a son before the son goes to the battlefield. The father asks his son what he would do if he knew that he would be killed in the battle. The son answers that his only option would be to fight as bravely as possible. When asked what he would do if he knew he would not be killed, the son answered that he would do the same. Then the father draws the conclusion that there are two possible outcomes in a battle: either one is killed or one survives. Fate determines what will happen. Consequently, the only course of action is to fight as bravely as possible. The worst thing of all is to be killed while fleeing.

After these gloomy words, Sverrir strikes a lighter tone asking his men to try out their swords 'on the mead-paunches of those men from the Vík'.[34] He argues that the enemy will be unable to exploit their numerical superiority, and besides, they will have less to fight for because of their wealth: they are 'more at home at a wedding than a fight, and are more accustomed to mead-drinking than to warfare'.[35] As for the ordinary peasants they have mobilized, their attitude can be expressed in the words of the poet who says that he desires 'Ingunn with the rosy mouth' whatever happens in the encounter between Magnús and Sverrir.[36]

Speeches are a traditional element in historiography from classical antiquity onwards and are common in the Middle Ages as well as the Renaissance. And the typical situation for a speech to be delivered is before a battle. Battle speeches serve to enhance the importance of the battle in question, to characterize the situation as seen from the point of view of the commanders of the opposing armies, and to make known to the readers their tactical thinking, thus making the outcome of the battle intelligible. Finally, the speeches allow the author to show his rhetorical skill. Sverrir's speech on this occasion as well as numerous other speeches that occur in

---

[33] *Sverris saga*, ed. by Gustav Indrebø (Christiania [Oslo]: Dybwad, 1920), ch. 47, pp. 50–51.

[34] *Sverris saga*, ed. by Indrebø, p. 50: 'at reyna sverðin a miaðar-istrunai þeim Vicveria'.

[35] *Sverris saga*, ed. by Indrebø, p. 50: 'er betr vœri fallit til bruð-manna en hirðmanna. oc meir hefir vaniz mioð-dryckio en herscap'.

[36] *Sverris saga*, ed. by Indrebø, p. 50: 'Etla ec mer hina mæro / munnfagra Jngunni / hvegi er fundr með frægium / ferr Magnusi oc Sverri.'

the sagas belong to this tradition and may well be influenced by classical rhetoric. Nevertheless, they also have to be understood against the background of contemporary society.

Facing his men at Ilevollene, Sverrir was not a general in the classical sense. He was a leader of a group of men who had joined him because they believed in his ability to lead them to victory and thereby the wealth and glory that are the fruits of victory. The relationship between Sverrir and his men is based on an implicit contract: they will aid him in winning the throne in return for a share in the power and wealth he will then enjoy. Sverrir has neither a legal right to command them nor an ideological 'cause' binding him and his men together and obliging them to follow his will. They have a common purpose for which they will fight together as long as it is in their interest to do so. Consequently, Sverrir's rhetoric, as depicted in the saga, aims at convincing his men that it is still in their interest to serve him and to fight under his command to the best of their ability. Therefore, Sverrir's battle speeches, as recounted, or, more likely perhaps, constructed, in his saga, are closely connected to the situation. Thus, in the speech referred to above, Sverrir is concerned on the one hand with the difficulty of a pitched battle against a well-trained and numerically superior enemy, while on the other hand he encourages his men by pointing out the advantages of poverty in making men brave, tough, and motivated for fighting and danger, all the while hinting at what they can gain from victory. The two arguments come dangerously close to contradicting each other — is Sverrir trying to convince his men of the difficulty or the ease of their task? However, the point here is the emotional appeal and the effect of Sverrir's personality as expressed through his rhetorical skill, rather than strict logic. Rhetoric becomes the cement holding Sverrir's faction together.

Sverrir was of course a special case. His royal descent was not based on any firm evidence but was a matter of belief. And the motive for belief was probably what the believer could gain from his conviction. Apart from his alleged royal descent, Sverrir lacked the network of prominent relatives and friends a faction leader could normally muster. Nevertheless, even faction leaders, who were better established, depended on their own personality for their position, as they lacked the bureaucratic command structure of later ages as well as the ties of vassalage of contemporary feudal society. Admittedly, the strength of the links between lord and vassal in contemporary Europe should not be exaggerated; frequent shifts of allegiance were normal. The similarity between Norway and the rest of Europe was considerable among the upper classes, but less so lower down the social scale. The common people were more important militarily in Norway than in most other parts of Europe and had to be mobilized by faction leaders in internal struggles and by the king in struggles against other countries. Eloquence was one way to achieve this. Speeches are often fairly conventional in European historiography in the earlier part of the Middle Ages, and verbal exchanges normally take place in private. Open discussion is very rare; there was too much prestige attached to verbal expression for great men to risk being contradicted. The most important form of public encounter was through ritual and symbolic expression which was highly developed.[37] By contrast, the sagas are full of speeches and dialogues, in public as well as in private, and eloquence is a quality highly esteemed in a leader. A likely explanation of this difference is the greater political and military importance of the common people in Norway and even more so in Iceland.

The same difference serves to explain the greater emphasis on political manoeuvring in the sagas. Medieval historiography was, like that of classical antiquity and the Renaissance, exemplary, serving to show good deeds as a model and bad ones as a warning, as is expressed in numerous prologues of the period. This also applies to the sagas. Historiography can, however, be exemplary in many different ways, emphasizing for instance religious, chivalric, or patriotic ideals. Most of the sagas are not particularly concerned with religious or patriotic ideals; they are 'secular' or 'individualistic', being concerned with the individual's success or honour. They are therefore closer to the contemporary 'secular' or 'aristocratic' tradition than to the clerical one. However, they are not 'chivalric' to the same extent as their European counterparts. Honour is no doubt of great importance but is closely linked to success, rather than to adherence to strict rules of chivalry. And success is not so much the result of individual performance in battle as of tactical skills and, above all, the ability to create alliances and build up a following. Consequently, the sagas come closer to what we would consider as political history than the typical aristocratic chronicle of contemporary Europe. It must be emphasized, however, that European chronicles may also contain a considerable amount of political manoeuvring, and differ from the sagas in degree more than in kind.[38]

The kind of eloquence most commonly found in the sagas is of the same kind as in Sverrir's battle speeches, appealing to the interests of the audience, not to national solidarity, religious convictions, or the duty of loyalty to a king or leader. Ideology is thus of no importance, at least not in the sense that it serves as a line of division between factions. Nor do ideological differences seem very important in other European countries in the Early Middle Ages. The Investiture Contest changed this situation drastically. A flow of pamphlets appeared, and most historical writings in

---

[37] Gerd Althoff, *Spielregeln der Politik im Mittelalter* (Darmstadt: Wissenschaftliche Buchgesellschaft, 1997), pp. 157–84, 229–57.

[38] Bagge, *Society and Politics*, pp. 164–73, 224–31, and 240–47, where, however, I have somewhat exaggerated the difference, and 'Icelandic Uniqueness', pp. 422–35. For the understanding of politics in contemporary European historiography, there are many useful examples in Althoff, *Spielregeln*, e.g., pp. 21–56, although his concern is with political reality rather than its representation in historical writings. I have examined the latter in *Kings, Politics, and the Right Order of the World in German Historiography c. 950–1150* (Leiden: Brill, 2002), while Kristel Skorge is about to finish her dissertation under my supervision on political and military behaviour as represented in Froissart's chronicle from the second half of the fourteenth century.

Germany during the period (1075–1122) express the views of one of the two contending parties. A similar situation occurred in Norway around one hundred years later, in the age of Sverrir, who met resistance from prelates throughout his career, most seriously in the 1190s, when first the archbishop and then the rest of the bishops went into exile in Denmark. The last and most dangerous faction rising against Sverrir, the *Baglar*, had the support of the bishops.

This conflict is not very prominent in *Sverris saga* but plays a major part in other sources. Towards the end of his reign, Sverrir commissioned one of his adherents, trained in canon law, to write a pamphlet defending his cause, commonly referred to as *The Speech against the Bishops*.[39] By the middle of the thirteenth century, the anticlerical ideology of this work was adopted and in some respects developed further in *The King's Mirror*. In particular, *The King's Mirror* applied the doctrine of kingship by the grace of God not only to the Church, as *The Speech against the Bishops*, but also to society in general.[40] The saga of Sverrir's grandson, Hákon Hákonarson (r. 1217–63), which was written 1264–65, also contains considerably more royalist ideology than earlier sagas.[41] Characteristically, most of the numerous speeches in this saga appeal to ideological principles, rather than to the interests of the audience.[42]

The turn towards explicit ideology is no doubt an expression of a closer contact with the rest of Europe, even of a deliberate wish to introduce European royalist ideology to Norway. The rhetorical expression of this ideology is also influenced from abroad. Nevertheless, there seems to be a continuity from the earlier local tradition, not only in the use of the vernacular but also in the attempts to reach a non-learned audience through clear and explicit statements, striking expressions, and the use of stories and anecdotes. Propaganda and agitation, whether ideological or not, had to address the same non-learned and to some extent non-aristocratic audience in order to be effective.[43]

During the Later Middle Ages, the aristocratic and intellectual classes became more exclusive over most of Europe, including Scandinavia; international, Latin learning apparently became even more firmly established in Sweden and Denmark with the foundation of the universities of Uppsala (1477) and Copenhagen (1479).

---

[39] *En tale mot biskopene*, ed. by Anne Holtsmark, Skrifter utgitt av Det norske vitenskaps-akademi i Oslo, II Historisk-filosofisk klasse, 9 (Oslo: Dybwad, 1931). See Erik Gunnes, *Kongens ære* (Oslo: Gyldendal, 1971), and Sverre Bagge, 'Oratio contra clerum Norvegiae', in *Medieval Scandinavia*, ed. by Pulsiano and others, p. 455.

[40] Bagge, *The Political Thought*, pp. 22–26, 43–49, 87–97, 155–66, etc.

[41] Bagge, *From Gang Leader*, pp. 89–155.

[42] Bagge, *From Gang Leader*, pp. 104–06.

[43] For some reflections along these lines, see Bagge, *The Political Thought*, pp. 218–24, and *Society and Politics*, pp. 240–47.

However, other literate as well as politically influential groups emerged: a new middle class of burghers and minor officials in the royal or ecclesiastical administration or in the service of noblemen. Such people formed the social background to the surge of vernacular literature in Denmark in the period after 1450. They needed to be able to read and write and were interested in literature, but lacked the time and the resources to get a Latin education.[44] In the following century, they played a prominent role in the Reformation movement which had its main centres in the cities of Copenhagen and Malmö.

Similar developments were underway in Sweden. Although the towns were less important there, the political situation had similar effects. Opposition to the Union of Kalmar and the Danish king from 1434 onwards was expressed in a large propagandist literature, including several historical works. In terms of social organization, Sweden was in an intermediate position between Denmark and Norway. Parts of the country had a strong aristocracy of secular and ecclesiastical landowners and a subject peasant population, while in others, the peasants owned the land and formed a politically important class that could be mobilized for 'national' purposes. The successful Sture faction, which ruled Sweden during most of the period 1471–1520, was based on an alliance between parts of the landowning aristocracy and the free peasants, and developed a vernacular propaganda that can be regarded as a counterpart to the one we have already met in twelfth- and thirteenth-century Norway.[45]

The rise of the middle class in the Later Middle Ages is not specific to Denmark and Sweden, but is part of a common European trend. It may nevertheless throw some light on the earlier period in Norway and Iceland. The milieu of vernacular literature in Norway and Iceland was not the middle class; it was the ecclesiastical and particularly the secular aristocracy of these countries, which was usually less wealthy and above all less exclusive than in most other countries. The relative poverty of the elite and its greater dependence on the ordinary population, at least its higher levels, may have contributed to a somewhat different attitude to the international, learned culture of contemporary Europe in Norway and Iceland than in Denmark and Sweden.

No very extensive comparison between Scandinavia and the rest of Europe exists, and the preceding pages are only intended as glimpses of some fields that need to be explored further. If any general conclusion is to be drawn, it must be the following. The literate culture of Scandinavia was deeply influenced by that of the rest of Europe. The 'original' Scandinavian achievement consists less in unique traditions going back to the pre-Christian — and 'pre-European' — period, but rather in adapting the common European culture to suit particular Scandinavian purposes. The

---

[44] Damsgaard Olsen, 'Dansk som skriftsprog', pp. 386–91, 402–03.

[45] Lars-Olof Larsson, *Kalmarunionens tid* (Stockholm: Tiden Athena, 1997), pp. 318–432; Lindroth, *Svensk lärdomshistoria*, pp. 160–73.

greater emphasis on local traditions in Norway and Iceland compared to Denmark and Sweden is the result, not only of greater geographical distance but also of social differences, notably the relative strength and exclusivity of the ecclesiastical and secular aristocracy. The degree of 'uniqueness' in Scandinavia should also, however, be compared to other peripheries surrounding the feudal and scholastic centre in Northern France and its adjacent areas, for example Southern and Eastern Europe.

Lightning Source UK Ltd.
Milton Keynes UK
UKOW031457121212

203572UK00001B/48/P